G. I. TUNKIN

Selected Works

STUDIES IN RUSSIAN, EAST EUROPEAN, AND EURASIAN LAW

WILLIAM E. BUTLER (SERIES EDITOR)

1. Butler, W. E., Russian Law and Legal Institutions. 3d ed.; 2021. ISBN 978-854901449

2. Il'in, I. A., On the Essence of Legal Consciousness, ed., introduced, & transl. W. E. Butler, P. T. Grier, and Paul Robinson. 2d rev. ed.; 2023. ISBN-13 978-1-61619-679-03.

3. Butler, W. E., Russian-English Legal Dictionary. 2d rev. ed.; Clark, New Jersey, Talbot Publishing, 2023. ISBN 978-1-61619-682-0

4. Butler, W. E., Russian Inheritance Law. 2d rev. ed.; Clark, New Jersey, Talbot Publishing, 2025. ISBN 978-1-61619-692-9

5. Butler, W. E. (ed. and transl.), G. I. Tunkin Selected Works. Clark, New Jersey, Talbot Publishing, 2025. ISBN 978-1-61619-695-0

Studies in Russian, East European, and Eurasian Law

G. I. TUNKIN
Selected Works

Grigorii Ivanovich Tunkin

Translated and **Edited** by

William E. Butler

John Edward Fowler Distinguished Professor of Law,
Penn State Dickinson Law
Emeritus Professor of Comparative Law,
University College London
Foreign Member, Russian Academy of Natural Sciences,
National Academy of Sciences of Ukraine, and
National Academy of Legal Sciences of Ukraine

TALBOT
PUBLISHING
Clark, New Jersey
2025

ISBN 9781616196950

TALBOT PUBLISHING AN IMPRINT OF
The Lawbook Exchange, Ltd.
33 Terminal Avenue
Clark, New Jersey 07066-1321

Please see our website for a selection of our other publications and fine facsimile reprints of classic works of legal history www.lawbookexchange.com

Library of Congress Cataloging-in-Publication Data
Names: Tunkin, G. I. (Grigoriĭ Ivanovich), author. | Butler, William Elliott, 1939- translator, editor.
Title: G. I. Tunkin : selected works / Grigorii Ivanovich Tunkin ; translated and edited by William Elliott Butler.
Description: First edition. | Clark : Talbot Publishing, an Imprint of The Lawbook Exchange, Ltd., 2024. | Series: Studies in Russian, East European, and Eurasian law | Includes bibliographical references and index. | Summary: "A collection of selected works on international legal theory by Grigorii Tunkin in English translation"-- Provided by publisher.
Identifiers: LCCN 2024044203 | ISBN 9781616196950 (hardcover)
Subjects: LCSH: International law--Russia (Federation)--Philosophy. | International law--Europe, Eastern--Philosophy. | International law--Eurasia--Philosophy.
Classification: LCC KZ3405.T865 A2 2024 | DDC 341.01--dc23/eng/20240919
LC record available at https://lccn.loc.gov/2024044203

First published in 2025 by
Talbot Publishing Ltd

Printed in the United States of America on acid-free paper

CONTENTS

Introduction xvii

Translation Note xxxi

The Korean Question After the Second World War in the Light of International Law

[Introduction] 3

Part One

Korean Question in the Period 1945 to 1950

Chapter I. International Agreements Concerning Korea After the Second World War and the Principle of Self-Determination of Nations 7

Chapter II. The Liberation of Korea by the Soviet Army and the Sojourn of Soviet Forces in North Korea in the Light of International Law 11

Chapter III. The American Occupation Regime in South Korea – Flouting of International Law 17

Chapter IV. Struggle of the Soviet Union for Precise Fulfillment of the Moscow Agreement on Korea and Violation by the United States of this Agreement During the Period of Negotiations in the Joint Soviet-American Commission for Korea 21

Chapter V. Creation by American Occupation Authorities of Separate Puppet Government in South Korea in the Light of Principles of International Law 23

Chapter VI. The Formation of the Korean People's Democratic Republic and the International Legal Status Thereof 27

Chapter VII. The Korea Question at the Third and Fourth Sessions of the United Nations General Assembly 31

Part Two

Civil War in Korea and Aggression of the United States

Chapter VIII. The Preparation and Unleashing by the United States and the Puppet Clique of Syngman Rhee of Civil War in Korea 34

Chapter IX. Civil War and United States Aggression in Korea 36

Chapter X. Violation of the Laws and Customs of War by United States Armed Forces in Korea 43

Chapter XI. United States Aggression Against China 45

Chapter XII. The Struggle of the USSR, Chinese People's Republic, Korean People's Democratic Republic, and Progressive Forces of the Entire World for the Prevention of War in Korea and Peaceful Settlement of the Korea Questions 48

Fundamental Principles of Contemporary International Law

Chapter One. Concept of International Law and Sources Thereof 56

1. Concept and Types of Subjects of International Law 56
2. Coexistence of Two Systems and International Law 60
3. International Law and Municipal Law 63
4. Sources of International Law 66

Chapter Two. Subjects of International Law 72

1. Concept and Types of Subjects of International Law 72
2. International Recognition of States and Governments 79
3. International Legal Responsibility of State 83

Chapter Three. Basic International Legal Principles of Peaceful Coexistence of States 87

1. Principle of Mutual Respect for Territorial Integrity and Sovereignty 87

2. Principle of Nonaggression 88

3. Principle of Noninterference in Internal Affairs of States 91

4. Principle of Equality and Mutual Advantage 93

5. Principle of Peaceful Coexistence and Economic Cooperation 94

Chapter Four. International Organizations 98

1. General Characteristics of Contemporary International Organizations 98

2. United Nations 101

3. International Regional Organizations for General Questions 108

A. Organization of American States (OAS) and League of Arab States 110

B. Creation by Imperialist States After Second World War of Military Blocs Under Name of Regional Organizations 111

C. Warsaw Treaty of 14 May 1955 114

4. Specialized Agencies of the United Nations and Other Specialized International Organizations 116

Theory of International Law

Part I: The Development of International Law After the Great October Socialist Revolution

Chapter I. The International Legal Ideas of the October Revolution and the Making of Contemporary International Law 127

1. The Principles of Socialist Internationalism 128

2. The Principles of Equality and of Self-Determination of Nations 132

3. The Principles of Peaceful Coexistence 140

Chapter II. Peaceful Coexistence and General International Law. The Influence of the Breakup of the Colonial System 148

1. The Unfoundedness of the Theory that the Developmental Base of International Law is Contracting 149

2. Peaceful Coexistence of States with Different Social Systems and General International Law 166

Chapter III. Modification of the Fundamental Principles of International Law During the Period of Coexistence of the Two Systems 179

1. The Emergence of New Principles of International Law 180

(a) The principle of nonaggression 180

(b) The principle of peaceful settlement of disputes 190

(c) The principle of self-determination of peoples 194

(d) The principle of peaceful coexistence 205

(e) The principle of disarmament 211

(f) The principle of respect for human rights 216

(g) The prohibition of war propaganda 221

2. The Development and Strengthening of the Old Democratic Principles of International Law 225

Part II: The Process of Forming Norms of Contemporary General International Law

Chapter IV. The Basic Processes of Forming Norms of International Law 231

1. International Treaties 231

(a) Treaties between States 231

(b) Treaties between States concluded within the framework of international organizations 245

(c) Regulations adopted by specialized international organizations 247

(d) Treaties of international organizations 251

2. International Custom 260

3. Treaty and Custom in Contemporary International Law 285

(a) The dominant role of the treaty in the development of international law 285

(b) The international treaty and general international law 289

(c) The interaction of treaty and custom 295

4. The Principles of *Jus Cogens* 301

Chapter V. Subsidiary Processes of Forming Norms of International Law 319

1. Resolutions of the United Nations General Assembly 320

2. Recommendations of Specialized International Organizations 338

3. Decisions of the International Court and of International Arbitration Tribunals 342

4. National Legislation and Decisions of National Judicial Instances 348

Chapter VI. Doctrine and the Opinions of Social Organizations 350

1. International Legal Doctrine 350

2. Opinions and Resolutions of Social and Scientific Organizations 352

Chapter VII. The Problem of "General Principles of Law" 354

Part III: The Legal Nature and Essence of Contemporary General International Law

Chapter VIII. The Legal Nature of Agreement as the Mode of Creating Norms of International Law 375

1. The Bourgeois Doctrine of "Agreement" 375

2. Agreement as the Result and the Embodiment of the Concordance of the Wills of States 380

3. The International Legal Positions of States and Concordant Wills Reflected in Norms of International Law 386

4. The Unfoundedness of the Concept of the "Fundamental Norm" 389

Chapter IX. The Character and Essence of Contemporary General International Law 397

1. Bourgeois Science on the Social Nature of International Law 397

2. The Societal Laws of the Development of International Law 405

(a) The laws of the development of society and international law 405

(b) The unfoundedness of the bourgeois concept of *ubi societas ibi jus* 411

(c) International law and international organization 414

3. Modification of the Character and Essence of General International Law During the Past Half-Century 419

(a) Fundamental changes in general international law after the Great October Socialist Revolution 419

(b) The position of bourgeois practice and doctrine on the question of changes in international law 435

4. The Question of an "Intermediate Status" Between War and Peace 447

Part IV: International Law, Foreign Policy, and Diplomacy

Chapter X. The Influence of Foreign Policy and Diplomacy Upon the Development of International Law 457

Chapter XI. The Influence of International Law on Foreign Policy and Diplomacy 463

Chapter XII. International Law as a Support for Foreign Policy 480

Part V: The Legal Nature of Contemporary General International Organizations

Chapter XIII. The Laws of Societal Development and International Organizations 495

1. The Internationalization of Economic Life and International Organizations 498

2. Coexistence of the Two Opposed Social Systems and International Organizations 503

3. The Breakup of the Colonial System and International Organizations 508

4. The Existence of Sovereign States and International Organizations 513

Chapter XIV. The Basic Features of the Legal Nature of General International Organizations. The Charter as the Basis of an Organization's Activity 516

1. Charters of International Organizations: Treaties or Constitutions? 516

2. The Jurisdiction of International Organizations 521

(a) The concept of "inherent jurisdiction" 522

(b) The concept of "implied powers" 527

3. Change of the Charters of International Organizations 534

Chapter XV. The Basic Features of the Legal Nature of Contemporary General International Organizations (continued) 544

1. The Interstate Character of General International Organizations 544

(a) The principle of the equality of States in international organizations 544

(b) The right to withdraw from an international organization 550

2. International Organizations as Organs of Peaceful Coexistence 552

3. The International Legal Personality of International Organizations 561

(a) The legal basis and extent of the legal personality of international organizations 563

(b) The legal personality of international organizations and third States 569

Chapter XVI. The Problem of a World State and Prospects for the Development of International Organizations 572

1. Bourgeois Concepts of a World State 572

2. Marxism and the Problem of a World State 579

3. Ways of Strengthening the United Nations 586

Part VI: The General Character and Forms of State Responsibility Under International Law

Chapter XVII. The Character of State Responsibility Under International Law Before the Great October Socialist Revolution 595

Chapter XVIII. State Responsibility Under Contemporary International Law 610

1. The Concept of the International Legal Criminal Responsibility of a State 610

2. Some New Aspects of State Responsibility 621

(a) Prohibition of the use of force and State Responsibility 621

(b) Subjects of legal relations in instances of international legal State responsibility 635

(c) Types and forms of State responsibility in contemporary international law 642

Annex : Several Reflections in Connection with the Draft "Charter of the International Tribunal for the Consideration of Cases Concerning Crimes Committed on the Territory of Former Yugoslavia" 651

- G. I. Tunkin

Bibliography of Works by G. I. Tunkin 653

Index of Names 698

INTRODUCTION

William E. Butler

When these works first appeared between 1954 and 1970, it was commonplace to speak of "international law in a divided world" or of an "international law of peaceful coexistence and cooperation". Those times are past, at least in the sense in which those expressions were used. Although the law of peaceful coexistence remains embedded in international legal documentation of the era, it has passed beyond the horizons of the rising generation, which in both East and West has no memory of what the discussion was all about. As for a "divided world", the division along these lines is confined principally to China, North Korea, and Cuba and, since February 2022, Russia again. Even in those countries the subject matter of this book, while pertinent, has receded into the background.

As it happens, the Korean People's Democratic Republic played a significant role in the diplomatic and intellectual career of Grigorii Ivanovich Tunkin (1906-1993). He was assigned to be on site as a diplomatic and legal advisor, years during which he produced works on North Korean legal development, some under the pseudonym of G. Tavrov (see Bibliography herein). He produced the only known doctoral dissertation in the Russian language on the Korean Question. It was never published and the text has not been accessible. The abstract of the dissertation, circulated in 60 copies prior to the defense and dated 19 April 1954, does exist however, and I am grateful to a colleague for making it available to me.

Tunkin's "Fundamental Principles" is widely considered to be the first elaborated published version of his formulation of "agreement between States" constituting the foundation of contemporary international law. In its day the work was certainly the most influential among the major Russian works outlining the legal foundations of peaceful coexistence, associated with the Khrushchev era of Soviet leadership. It was subsequently expanded into a monograph (1962) and the full-fledged Theory of International Law, published in Russian (1970, 2000, and 2006) and, with revisions by the author, in English (1974, 2003, and now 2025).

Although published in a print-run of 20,000 copies, the "Fundamental Principles" is uncommon today and difficult to find. Few western libraries acquired a copy at the time. Vsevolod Nikolaevich Durdenevskii (1889-1963) acted as editor of the work for the Higher Party School. The actual printing was completed at the Printing House of the Higher Party School attached to the Central Committee of the Communist Party of the Soviet Union, then located at ul. Fridrikha Engelsa, 46. The publication was signed to press of 13 December 1956, which suggests almost certainly that it did not appear before sometime in January 1957 notwithstanding the year designated on the title page. In this translation minor misprints have been corrected.

We then turn to the fully-fledged Theory in its final and mature form. The foundations of international law set out in that volume, stripped of their ideological dress, continue to inform Russian approaches to the theory of international law. Three decades on since Professor Tunkin passed away, there is no "substitute" or "replacement" theory, as yet, to supersede the insights into international behavior identified by Academician G. I. Tunkin. And as and when there is a replacement, the probabilities are high that the substitute will best be comprehended against that which preceded. In short, Tunkin's theory proved to be the dominant contribution of the Soviet era to public international law, and its legacy remains a vital part of the Russian efforts to readjust to the new situation in the international community.

No doubt it was partly for this reason that the ultimate version of Tunkin's mature views, translated here, was published for Russian law students in 2000, with a reprint in 2006, under the editorship of Tunkin's successor in the Chair of International Law, the late Lev Nikitich Shestakov (1937-2009).

As I look back on my Introduction to my English translation of 1974, I am struck by the attention given to terminology. For good reason. Terminology was the key to Soviet attempts to "capture" international law, to reformulate its principles in ways congenial to Marxist-Leninist ideology; it also offered insight, through another prism, into certain of the divergences between continental European and Anglo-American approaches to international law. I felt then, and still do, that the translation will have achieved some purpose if the reader comes away with a little feeling for the various strands of Marxist-Leninist, continental, international, and Russian elements in the mental background in which the exposition originates.

The appearance of Tunkin's Теория международного права [Theory of International Law], published in 1970 and reissued in a revised and final edition in the year 2000, reprinted in 2006, was and remains a signal event in several respects. Within the former Soviet Union it was the first book to merit the unqualified appellation "theory of international law". In the past, Soviet jurists had produced "outlines", "fundamental principles", "basic principles", "questions of theory", "courses", "manuals", and so forth treating certain aspects of theory or written with certain presumptions about theory in mind. The writings of Evgenii Aleksandrovich Korovin (1892-1964), Petr Ivanovich Stuchka (1865-1932), Evgenii Bronislavovich Pashukanis (1891-1937), Sergei Borisovich Krylov (1888-1958), Fedor Ivanovich Kozhevnikov (1903-1998), David Bentsionovich Levin (1903-1990), Nikolai Mikhailovich Minasian (1911-1978), Roman L'vovich Bobrov (1910-1979), Igor Ivanovich Lukashuk (1926-2007), and other names more or less well-known to Anglo-American international lawyers belonged to that genre. The celebrated definition of international law advanced by Andrei Ianuar'evich Vyshinskii (1883-1954) is another example; his formulation dominated Soviet legal thought for nearly two decades, but it was not in and of itself a theory, despite its incontestably enormous influence on Soviet writing about the nature of international law.

Tunkin's treatise was therefore the most profound and comprehensive study of international legal theory produced by a Soviet jurist. Effectively blending the author's broad experience in diplomacy and academic pursuits, it was a masterfully conceived and executed application of Marxist-Leninist concepts and principles to the advancement of Soviet interests in the era of peaceful coexistence. It remained also for many years, rather surprisingly, the sole major work of a Soviet or prerevolutionary Russian international lawyer to be translated into the principal language of the common law.[1]

Neither the 1970 nor the 2000 editions of Tunkin's Теория contained a preface. In the prefatory remarks to his Вопросы теории международного права [Questions of the Theory of International Law] (1962), of which the 1970 version was a revised, much enlarged, and significantly retitled version and the 2000 version a more polished and slightly abbreviated edition, Tunkin related his inquiry to two domestic happenings. The first was the "profound analysis" of the international situation and long-term prospects for its development reflected in the decisions of the XXII Congress of the Communist Party of the Soviet Union held in 1961; that is, during the Khrushchev era. The second was the rejection by the XX Party Congress in 1956 of the "cult of personality of Stalin, alien to Marxism-Leninism and the bases of our social system" and the embarking on a course "to liquidate its harmful consequences" and open a "broad road for the development of the social sciences, including international law".

In the absence of an express statement in either the 1970 or 2000 editions, it falls to me to divine and describe the changes introduced by the author.[2] We commence with the 1970 version.

The 1970 publication retained intact the theory of international law which ran throughout the author's earlier

[1] For the prerevolutionary period, see the monumental F. F. Martens, *Contemporary International Law of Civilized Peoples*, transl. W. E. Butler (2021-2022). 2 vols.

[2] Changes made for the 1974 English translation by the author are described in the Translation Note.

writings and also preserved the essential structure of the 1962 volume, itself reflective of Tunkin's approach. The author did, of course, update the materials, especially with references to recent multilateral conventions, developments in international organizations, and doctrinal literature published after 1962. Many sections were rewritten, deleted, or augmented. Copious references to Nikita Sergeevich Khrushchev (1894-1971) in the 1962 edition were replaced by quotations of the Brezhnev leadership. Of greatest importance was the addition of new chapters treating the influence of the 1917 October Revolution on the development of international law and the legal nature of contemporary general international organizations. Substantial modifications also were introduced into the discussion of norm-formation and socialist internationalism. In all, those changes added 180 pages to the 330 in the 1962 edition.

The principal changes in the 1970 Russian edition were as follows. In Part I the first chapter treating the international legal ideas of the October Revolution and the making of contemporary international law was a new addition. Chapter 2 on peaceful coexistence and international law and on the breakup of the colonial system was enlarged and rewritten to take account of recent events and of comments made by western jurists on the author's earlier views. The third chapter expanded the discussion of the principles of nonaggression and of peaceful settlement of disputes to include the relevant deliberations of United Nations organs in the intervening period. The principle of self- determination of peoples was relegated from "the most important" to "one of the most important" generally-recognized principles of contemporary international law. Subsection 3(A)(4) on the principle of peaceful coexistence was reworked and abbreviated, leaving the impression that the principle was a shade less important than formerly. The principles of disarmament and of human rights were new to the 1970 edition.

Parts II and III of the 1970 edition were recast from Part II of the 1962 version. The effect was to delineate sharply the discussion of the norm-formation process from the necessarily more abstract consideration of the legal nature and essence of contemporary international law. As part of his expanded treatment of international organizations in the 1970 edition, the author introduced into Chapter 4, subsections A(2) and (3) on treaties between States concluded within the framework of international organizations and on regulations adopted by specialized international organizations; similarly, Chapter 4(A) (4) on treaties of international organizations was updated and expanded, reflecting the author's perception of their enhanced role in creating rules that were becoming part of the international legal system. Opinio juris was treated in greater detail in Chapter 4(B), as was the interrelationship between treaty and custom in 4(C). Section 4(D) on jus cogens was new. The materials on subsidiary processes of norm- formation were kept distinct in the 1970 edition from the role of international legal doctrine and from the problem of "general principles of international law". Distinctions also were drawn clearly in the 1970 edition between United Nations General Assembly resolutions and those of other specialized international organizations; both are discussed at greater length. Chapters 5(C) and (D) and Chapter 6 contained only very minor modifications. However, the discussion of "general principles of law" in Chapter 7 was substantially augmented.

In Part III of the 1970 version, the treatment of the legal nature of agreement in Chapter 8 was expanded to take account of recent writings, particularly those of Paul Guggenheim. Chapter 9(A) contained an enlargement of the author's previous criticism of the natural law school and solidarism, the latter with special reference to Professor George Scelle. The remainder of Chapter 9 was substantially rewritten; some materials on the concept of a world State that appeared in Chapter 6(2) of the 1962 volume were transferred to a new Chapter 16 in the 1970 version. Chapter 6(3) of the 1962 volume on the "cold war and international law" appeared here as Chapter 9(D), "the question of an `intermediate status' between war and peace".

In Part V of the 1970 edition, Chapter 10 was basically unchanged; Chapter 11 reformulated certain aspects of the influence of international law on foreign policy and diplomacy;

and Chapter 12 expanded upon the author's critique of Professor M. S. McDougal's views.

Part V was new; Part VI was virtually unchanged from the 1962 edition.

Part VII contained substantial changes which reflected an expanded program of economic integration within Eastern Europe and reformulations of the doctrine of socialist internationalism following the Czechoslovak events of 1968.

With respect to the 2000 version, the following should be pointed out. Professor Tunkin had revised the book at the time of his passing in 1993 and discussed at length the adjustments made with his colleague, pupil, protegé, and eventual successor in his Chair, Professor Lev Nikitich Shestakov (1937-2009). The changes are fundamentally three in nature. First, certain references to Party documents timely in the 1970s but not in the 1990s were deleted. Second, Part VII on International Law in Relations Between the Countries of the World System of Socialism, was excluded. This was done, Professor Shestakov observed in his Foreword to the Russian edition of 2000, because the propositions contained therein had "lost their political significance", but not because Tunkin's views had proved to be "theoretically waning". While he noted that the conclusions and proposals "contained in that Part of the work cannot be used in practice ... in this world there is nothing unalterable, and it is not precluded that in a subsequent republication this Part would be included in the book". Third, the author made minor adjustments to his formulations of bringing the wills of States into concordance, especially with respect to State responsibility, with a view to clarifying his position in response to criticisms and observations made in Soviet and Russian doctrinal writings after the appearance of the book in 1970. While these criticisms and observations were welcomed and valued by Tunkin, some of them, Shestakov observed, were made not to clarify the theory, but rather to alter it. Tunkin did not share such alterations. In particular, the view that bringing the wills of States into concordance amounted to bringing the interests of States into concordance was specifically rejected by Shestakov as a distortion of the Tunkin approach. The will of a State, Shestakov observed, is a "norm-forming category", whereas the "interests of States" are not such a category. "State interests together with other phenomena form State will and directly tell on the process of creating norms of international law".

Shestakov also observed that Tunkin's rejection of attempts to treat concepts of general international law as customary law has proved to be prescient. "In the 30 years which have elapsed from the time of publication of his book, nothing has occurred either in the theory of international law or in international practice which would refute the thesis uttered by Tunkin, not to mention even give rise to doubts about it. Moreover, the process of the codification and progressive development of international law affirm Tunkin's conclusion that the general international treaty occupies the largest place in general international law as a source".[3]

Tunkin's long experience in day-to-day diplomacy strongly influenced his conception of international law, for, as he was fond of pointing out to his students, it is at international meetings and conferences or within international organizations that one can observe most readily the process of State wills being brought into concordance. The range of that experience was evident in accounts of Tunkin's personal achievements and his publications.

Grigorii Ivanovich Tunkin was born in the Arkhangel'sk Province of the Russian Empire on 13 October 1906. Of peasant stock, he graduated from a forestry technical school in 1928 and enrolled in the Moscow Juridical Institute in 1932. Upon completion of his undergraduate law studies in 1935, he was invited to proceed immediately on to postgraduate research. His кандидат, or candidate thesis, defended in 1938, was entitled "The Parliamentary Reform of 1832 in England". He then served briefly as head of a department in the People's

[3] See L. N. Shestakov, "Слово об авторе" [A Word on the Author], in G. I. Tunkin, Теория международного права [Theory of International Law] (2000), pp. xiv-xv.

Commissariat of the Navy of the USSR. From 1 January 1939 Tunkin was a Senior Scientific Associate at the Department of the Theory and History of State and Law of the All-Union Legal Academy, leaving in October 1939 to enter the diplomatic service. In the Ministry of Foreign Affairs of the USSR he served first as assistant to the head of the legal section and then as the Soviet consul in Gorgan (Iran).

From 1942 to 1944 he was posted in Canada as counsellor of the Soviet Embassy. Returning to Moscow, Tunkin was appointed deputy head of the Ministry's Second European Section (1944-45) and then head of the First Far Eastern Section (1946-48). The latter posting evidently commenced a period, several years in duration, of sustained concentration of Asian affairs. Tunkin published extensively on Korea, including under a pseudonym, editing a collection of North Korean legal documents in the Russian language and devoting considerable attention to the international legal aspects of the Korean conflict. From 1948 to 1951 he was Minister-Counsellor of the Soviet Embassy in the Korean People's Democratic Republic, returning briefly in 1951-52 again as head of the First Far Eastern Section.

In 1954 he submitted and defended a massive doctoral dissertation on "The Korean Problem After the Second World War in the Light of International Law"; the degree доктор юридических наук (doctor of juridical sciences) was conferred in 1955. A translation of the abstract of that dissertation is published herein, raising and leaving open the question of whether at that stage in his intellectual development Tunkin had begun to address the concepts more evident in his 1956 Fundamental Principles – a landmark in the early formulations of the legal dimensions of peaceful coexistence and a clear harbinger of what ultimately became his Theory. I have been unsuccessful in locating the full dissertation.

In May 1952 Tunkin became head of the legal section of the Ministry of Foreign Affairs, a position he occupied until August 1965. While legal adviser, he also held adjunct academic appointments as head of the Department of International Law of the Moscow Juridical Institute (1949-54), as docent and then professor of international law at Moscow State University, as head of the Department of Legal Disciplines of the Higher Diplomatic School of the Ministry of Foreign Affairs, and as professor at the Moscow State Institute of International Relations (1954-63).

In his dual role of diplomat and scholar, Tunkin played a prominent role in shaping the orientation of international law in the Soviet Union. Shortly after assuming the post of legal adviser in 1952, he registered strong disagreement with Korovin's concept of two international laws: bourgeois and socialist. Setting forth what continued to be the dominant theme in his conception of international law, Tunkin insisted that "agreement between States lies at the base of international legal norms". Such agreement, he argued, "is incompatible with the concept of two international laws ... which is contrary to Soviet international legal theory and the diplomatic practice of the Soviet State".[4]

Tunkin elaborated his thesis in a small but highly influential supplemental text published by the Higher Party School attached to the Central Committee of the Communist Party of the Soviet Union, also included in the present volume.[5] His view came to be accepted, and continues to be so, by the great majority of Russian international lawyers and can be said without exaggeration to have comprised one of the principal legal pillars on which East-West cooperation was constructed following the XX Party Congress of the Communist Party of the Soviet Union in 1956, up to and including the ultimate demise of the Soviet Union in 1991 and subsequently.

As a member of the United Nations International Law Commission from 1957 to 1966 (Chairman in 1961; Second Vice-

[4] See the report of a discussion organized by the Department of International Law of the Academy of Social Sciences attached to the Central Committee of the All-Russian Communist Party (bolshevik) and by the Sector of International Law of the Institute of Law of the USSR Academy of Sciences, in Советское государство и право [Soviet State and Law], no. 7 (1952), p. 69.

[5] Tunkin, Основы современного международного права [Fundamental Principles of Contemporary International Law] (1956).

Chairman in 1958 and 1964), Tunkin had ample opportunity both to expound his approach to international legal theory and to observe the process of international law creation. During his tenure on the ILC, he worked on draft articles relating to the law of the sea, diplomatic and consular relations, the law of treaties, and special diplomatic missions. At the 1958 and 1960 Geneva Conferences on the Law of the Sea and the 1961 Vienna Conference on Diplomatic Intercourse and Immunities, he was head of the Soviet delegation. He also was in attendance at the conclusion of the Soviet-Polish treaty on the legal status of Soviet forces in Poland (1956), signed the 1957 Soviet-Norwegian sea frontier agreement on behalf of the USSR, was acting head of the Soviet delegation at the 1959 conference to draft the treaty on the Antarctica, served as the USSR delegate at the XVI Session of the Sixth (Legal) Committee of the United Nations General Assembly in 1961, and was a member of or adviser to other Soviet delegations at international conferences.

In autumn 1965 Tunkin assumed a full-time professorship in and chairmanship of the Department of International Law in the Law Faculty of Moscow University, a post in which he remained until his death in 1993. A Corresponding Member of the USSR (later Russian) Academy of Sciences, he was awarded a State Prize (1987) for his contributions to legal scholarship and a prize by the Encyclopedia Britannica (1990).

Professor Tunkin was the President of the Soviet (later Russian) Association of International Law from its establishment in 1957 until his death. He was a member of the editorial board of the Soviet Yearbook of International Law for 1958 and editor-in-chief for the 1959-62 issues. From 1956 to mid-1969 he served on the editorial board of the central law journal in the USSR, Советское государство и право. In the diplomatic service he held the career rank of Minister Extraordinary and Plenipotentiary, Second Class.

Tunkin lectured at the Hague Academy of International Law on several occasions (1958, 1966, 1975, 1989) and became a member of the Curatorium of that Academy, was an Associé of the Institute of International Law (1959), and a member of the Hague Permanent Court of Arbitration (1960). In November 1972 he was awarded a doctorate honoris causa by the University of Paris (Sorbonne), and another by the University of Budapest. The title Honoured Scientist of the RSFSR was conferred upon Professor Tunkin by Edict of the Presidium of the Supreme Soviet of the RSFSR on 16 November 1972 "for services in developing legal science and fruitful pedagogical activity".

Tunkin's colleagues in Russia paid tribute to his immense energy, his erudition and expertise, and his ability to link "science with practice". The majority of his nearly 200 published works were prepared while he was engaged in diplomatic service. In his day he was noteworthy both for his command of numerous foreign languages and his ability and willingness to use foreign materials extensively. He drew upon not merely the principal classical and modern writings of continental and Anglo-American jurists, but also upon those by Latin American, African, and Asian colleagues. As Professor Lukashuk wrote in his tribute to Tunkin, "The merit of Grigorii Ivanovich was that he did much to create a theory of international law taking into account the realities of the world in which he lived".[6]

More than fifty-five years ago the translation of Tunkin's Theory, it was hoped, would cast a flicker of illumination to assist those who sought to comprehend and come to terms with the positions of an opposite party. Today it is the heritage and continued impact of this theory which requires understanding, and the translations herein are offered in the same spirit as previously.

One may argue about what constitutes a "new edition" and what does not. This is not presented as a "new edition"; neither is it a mere republication of the previous version. It is, if you will, the "ultimate edition" which reflects those changes that the author in a free Russia was at liberty to make as he chose without concern for Party policies. He chose to excise in some

[6] See I. I. Lukashuk, "Светлой памяти Григория Ивановича Тункина" Российский ежегодник международного права 1993-1994 [Russian Yearbook of International Law 1993-1994] (1995), p. 10.

places and to tweak formulations in others. "Updating" was not his aim, for so far as he was concerned, he had identified and elaborated the essential components of his theory in the age during which he lived; nothing had happened thereafter to require more adjustments than those he decided to introduce. Readers should bear in mind, however, that Tunkin, as a legal diplomat, was accustomed to slight changes of verb tense constituting, in that world, a momentous change that made agreement possible.

The present volume therefore constitutes the "definitive" text of the Theory as he wished to see it and the two available major works which preceded it. Those who have the 1974 edition will be wise to retain it, for the differences between that version and this will deservedly be the subject of careful analysis by those who investigate the elements of continuity and difference in the Soviet and post-Soviet eras in the development of international legal doctrine. To those who believe that Tunkin should have "updated" his book to take account of events between 1974 and his death, Tunkin's response seems clear enough. Not only did he believe this was not called for, but he removed some passages which updated his work between 1970 and 1974 (that is, between the Russian and English language versions). In his view those additions merely piled up what he saw as the evidence of the correctness of his theory rather than advanced the argument (also see the Translation Note, below). His "testament" in this respect is evident, however much one may have enjoyed (or not) what his perceptions of international relations during those years may have been. For those perceptions we have two vital contributions preceding his Theory and his other writings set out in the Bibliography below, which now have to be read against this ultimate version of his Theory.

TRANSLATION NOTE

Translators arrogate to themselves a near insuperable task in attempting to transfer an intellectual product from one linguistic medium to another. Styles vary, equivalents of terminology or of colloquialisms may be nonexistent, expressions of great precision in one language may appear nonsensical or ambiguous in another, phrases deliberately vague in the original may be "improved" in the course of translation, and so forth. These are familiar problems, and every effort was made in the first edition of the English translation and has been made in this revised version to deal with them as conscientiously as possible.

The present volume contains two landmark works preceding Tunkin's Theory, both produced during the decade of major change in the Soviet perception of its own place in the world community. Although both have been available to Soviet and post-Soviet international lawyers, neither, to the best of my knowledge, has been addressed by them in discussing the formation of Tunkin's theoretical legacy, including the observations of Shestakov. Both first appeared in *Sudebnik*, XI (2006); I have made further editorial emendations.

With respect to Tunkin's Theory, the present volume differs in certain key respects from the original Russian version that appeared in 1970 and, to a much lesser extent, from the 2000 version. To avoid any misunderstanding, and to assist those who may wish to consult the original 1970 or 2000 versions, or the 1974 English version, I outline the editorial practices followed and changes introduced in preparing this English text, incorporating those observations still relevant to the 1974 English version.

The substance of the book is identical to the 2000 Russian edition in toto, except insofar as Professor Tunkin himself requested additions or deletions reflected in the 1974 English translation which did not always find themselves in the 2000 version. The reason would appear to be lapse of memory and the fact that I hold the originals of those changes, whereas Professor Tunkin did not. By agreement with Professor Shestakov, it has been decided that this was an accidental omission duly repaired in this translation.

It will be noted immediately by the Reader that Tunkin did not attempt to update his sources nor take into account new Russian or foreign literature except insofar as he responded to criticisms and observations in his subsequent adjustments. These are made without attribution to any particular outside source of inspiration. In Tunkin's view his central thesis remained intact and reflects the era in which and basis on which it was formulated.

The translator has reworked the footnotes completely, modifying the form of citation to correspond to general western practices and, in this edition, using the original Cyrillic in titles of articles and books. Numerous corrections were made, including errors in spelling, pagination, volume number, and so forth. Full citations to the relevant works of Marx, Engels, and Lenin have been provided, sometimes followed by a bracketed reference to the time and place of original publication. Quotations were checked against the original in virtually every instance. Words or phrases deleted from material quoted in the original Russian version but not so stipulated by punctuation were appropriately indicated here. For the 2025 edition, I have translated in square brackets the titles of Russian-language books, journals, and articles.

The List of published writings by Professor Tunkin is the most comprehensive in existence, and more so than in any of the Russian editions of this book.

The translator benefitted immensely from several discussions with the author before and after the preparation of the first English translation about problems of terminology that arose during the preparation of the English text. The considerations entering into the choice of English equivalents for several key terms may be of interest to the Reader, even more so in the twenty-first century than the last. One of the most vexsome terms was закономерность, or закон развития общества, rendered herein as "law of societal development". Russian international lawyers, as Professor Tunkin pointed out in the text, themselves sometimes failed to distinguish between rules of international law and the laws of societal development; hence the importance of delineating sharply between the two concepts here. Terms such as "natural law", "natural imperative", or "law of evolution", favoured by others who translated Tunkin's works, were discarded on the ground they were likely to mislead those to whom such expressions have meaning outside a Marxist framework.

Central to the author's concept of the norm-formation process in international law is the phrase согласованные воли государств, translated as "concordant wills of States", and согласование воль, expressed rather awkwardly as "bringing wills into concordance". The author's preference for this terminology is intended to stress two points. First, norm-formation in his view is a process, dynamic in nature and not mechanical. He wishes the reader to visualize States interacting, struggling, to bring their separate wills into agreement with respect to a particular rule of international law. Second, "concordance" as a term is meant to connote something different from theories of "common" or "coincident" wills that have been advanced by other jurists. The extent to which the author succeeds in establishing his view on this point is for the reader to judge.

The term сближение is given here with considerable misgivings as "rapprochement". It arises in connection with the "rapprochement" or, more literally, the "coming together" of peoples. It implies something more than rapprochement as that term is commonly used in international relations. Peoples are contemplated as "coming together" virtually to the point of amalgamation, and the term is especially used in connection with the various peoples inhabiting the former Soviet Union.

While Tunkin was generous in responding to various queries I raised and prepared the revisions for the 1974 English edition, in no sense did he endorse or approve the final text (although I can say today, he professed himself to have been extremely pleased with the English edition); errors of omission or commission in translation and editing rest squarely with me.

I am grateful to Professor Tunkin's son, Vladimir Grigorevich Tunkin, for authorizing the translation of the 2000 edition and in a different but related project for collaborating in the English edition of the Tunkin diaries, a volume which contains major contributions to Professor Tunkin's post-Theory elaborations.

WEB

Newville, Pennsylvania

Kandidat of Legal Sciences,
Docent G. I. TUNKIN

THE KOREAN QUESTION AFTER THE SECOND WORLD WAR IN THE LIGHT OF INTERNATIONAL LAW

Abstract of Dissertation for Conferral of the
Learned Degree of Doctor of Legal Sciences

City of Moscow, 1954

60 copies printed
19 April 1954

CONTENTS

[Introduction]

Part One

Korean Question in the Period 1945 to 1950

Chapter I. International Agreements Concerning Korea After the Second World War and the Principle of Self-Determination of Nations

Chapter II. The Liberation of Korea by the Soviet Army and the Sojourn of Soviet Forces in North Korea in the Light of International Law

Chapter III. The American Occupation Regime in South Korea – Flouting of International Law

Chapter IV. Struggle of the Soviet Union for Precise Fulfillment of the Moscow Agreement on Korea and Violation by the United States of this Agreement During the Period of Negotiations in the Joint Soviet-American Commission for Korea

Chapter V. Creation by American Occupation Authorities of Separate Puppet Government in South Korea in the Light of Principles of International Law

Chapter VI. The Formation of the Korean People's Democratic Republic and the International Legal Status Thereof

Chapter VII. The Korea Question at the Third and Fourth Sessions of the United Nations General Assembly

Part Two

Civil War in Korea and Aggression of the United States

Chapter VIII. The Preparation and Unleashing by the United States and the Puppet Clique of Syngman Rhee of Civil War in Korea

Chapter IX. Civil War and United States Aggression in Korea

Chapter X. Violation of the Laws and Customs of War by United States Armed Forces in Korea

Chapter XI. United States Aggression Against China

Chapter XII. The Struggle of the USSR, Chinese People's Republic, Korean People's Democratic Republic, and Progressive Forces of the Entire World for the Prevention of War in Korea and Peaceful Settlement of the Korea Questions

[Introduction]

In recent years the question concerning the war in Korea and the peaceful settlement of the Korea problem has unavoidably been among the major international issues on which the attention of the international public has been concentrated since the preservation and strengthening of peace, in which all peoples are interested, depends upon the proper resolution of such questions.

The Soviet Union, being in the vanguard of all progressive forces, consistently is carrying out a policy of peace while adhering to the aim that there are no disputed issues in international relations which can not be resolved by peaceful means, by means of mutually acceptable agreements between interested States.

In carrying out its peace policy the Soviet Union finds itself in unanimity with other countries of the democratic camp. This policy corresponds to the vital interests of all peaceloving peoples.

The peace policy of the Soviet Union and other countries of the democratic camp is encountering resistance from international aggressive circles, above all the aggressive circles of the United States, who are putting together aggressive blocks directed against the USSR and the countries of people's democracy and continuing an arms race which brings enormous profits to capitalist monopolies.

The collapse of the American military adventure in Korea did not bring the aggressive circles of the United States to reason. Not wishing to renounce their delirious plans of world domination, the American imperialists are seeking to maintain and intensify international tension, endeavoring to obstruct the resolution of international problems which have arisen, and cynically flout international law.

The countries of the democratic camp headed by the Soviet Union with the support of all peaceloving peoples tirelessly struggle for the strengthening of peace and international cooperation and fight for democratic principles of international law while striving for a peaceful settlement of the Korea question and the resolution of other urgent international problems.

The struggle of the two orientations in international politics determines the character and development of contemporary international law.

This is natural because the problems of international law can not be considered as divorced from the struggle and cooperation of States in the international arena which unfold at each determined historical stage, especially around the most important international questions.

Among such important and acute international questions is undoubtedly the Korea question. An investigation of the international-legal aspect of this question is of practical and political interest and of great scholarly interest since the Korea question in its development affects a vast ambit of urgent international legal problems.

A number of articles, a pamphlet by E. A. Korovin, and a book by P. S. Romashkin concerning the war crimes of the United States in Korea are devoted to the Korea question in Soviet international legal doctrine, and also several unpublished kandidat dissertations. In the said works, a list of which is given in the list of literature appended to the dissertation, a number of international-legal problems are touched upon to some degree that relate to the Korea question. The author has used these works in his study, having noted when considering respective problems both those basic provisions contained in the said works with which he concurs and those propositions which, in the author's view, are mistaken.

However, a significant part of the international legal problems connected with the Korea question remains to this day insufficiently worked out or not touched at all in Soviet international legal doctrine. Among these are, for example, such general and particular international legal problems as the problem of aggression in connection with civil war and, in particular, with the war in Korea; the principle of self-determination of nations as a principle of contemporary international law and the struggle around this principle in the Korea question; the question of the international legal status of Korea after the Second World War; the legal nature of the sojourn of forces of the territory of a friendly country liberated from enemy occupation; the character of the sojourn of Soviet forces in North Korea; the character and mechanism of American occupation of South Korea; the concept of indirect aggression and its application to determined actions of the United States in Korea; the question of the "threat to peace" and the possible application of this concept to civil war; the question of the principle of the unanimity of the great powers in the Security Council in connection with the abstention of a permanent member when voting and the absence thereof at a session of the Security Council; the problem of an armistice in the light of the provisions of the United Nations Charter, in particular, the significance of the armistice in Korea, and others.

In addition, there is no general study in Soviet international-legal doctrine devoted to the Korea question in which the basic international legal problems connected with this question are illuminated in connection with one another and in correlation with general problems of international law.

The present work is an attempt to fill this gap.

During the postwar period it is doubtful that there are other questions of international relations and other international-legal problems around which such fantastic lies, hypocrisy, and deliberate distortions have been knocked together as the Korea question and the international-legal problems connected with the Korea question.

Bourgeois politicians, journalists, international lawyers, and others seek to represent the aggressive policy of the United States on the Korea question, which abounds in flagrant violations of generally-recognized principles and norms of international law, as an example of a policy corresponding to the "new principles" of international relations and the "new grounds" of international law.

The "United Nations action in Korea" and resolutions of organs of the United Nations connected with this, flouting the basic provisions of the United Nations Charter, are extolled as a "turning point" in international law, as the first step in the development of a "new international law" which should supposedly replace prevailing international law.

Upon close examination these "new principles" of international relations, that is, principles of a policy "from a position of strength", turn out to be the principles of the old "power politics" compromised in the eyes of the peoples of the world. As regards the "new grounds" of international law and the "new international law" of which these bourgeois international lawyers speak, they are based on the same "power politics", that is, represent a denial of international law, the homily of an unbridled international imperialist assault with violence.

In unmasking the critical constructions advanced by bourgeois international lawyers whose purpose is to conceal in the name of international law the most flagrant lawlessness created by the Anglo-American bloc in various parts of the globe and, in particular, in Korea, the author emphasized the progressive role of Soviet international legal science in the struggle for peace and democratic principles of international law.

The work consists of an introduction, twelve chapters, and a conclusion. It is divided into two parts: the first part is devoted to international legal problems connected with the formation of a unified independent democratic Korean State during the period 1945 to 1950; in Part Two of the work international legal problems are investigated that are connected with the war and armistice in Korea and the peaceful settlement of the Korean question.

Part One

Korean Question in the Period 1945 to 1950

Chapter I

International Agreements Concerning Korea After the Second World War and the Principle of Self-Determination of Nations

1. From the standpoint of international law one speaks on the Korea question first and foremost about the application to Korea of the principle of self-determination of nations.

Two lines are visible throughout the entire history of the Korea question during and after the Second World War: for and against the principle of self-determination of nations.

In a situation of the constant rise of the national-liberation movement in colonial and dependent countries the struggle for the affirmation, concretization, and practical application of the principle of self-determination of nations is one of the central points of the struggle for democratic principles of international law. The creative working out of the problem of self-determination of peoples, illumination of the struggle of the two camps on this question, and unmasking of attempts of imperialists to "kill" this principle or reduce it to nil in the event of practical application therefore constitutes one of the major tasks of the Soviet science of international law.

After recognition of the principle of self-determination of peoples in the United Nations Charter the struggle around this principle became even more dogged and acute. The work illuminates the consideration of the question concerning self-determination of nations in United Nations organs in recent years, unmasks the maneuvers of imperialists and efforts of the imperialist doctrine of international law to deny the existence of the principle of self-determination of nations in contemporary international law or reduce the content thereof to a political declaration (Kelsen, Eagleton, Lauterpacht, Sibert, and others) and on the basis of an analysis of the provisions of the United Nations Charter shows that the principle of self-determination of peoples is a principle of contemporary international law.

Many other forces also now favor the principle of self-determination of nations together with the mighty camp of democratic States headed by the Soviet Union: the movement of proponents of peace, the growing national-liberation movement in colonial and dependent countries headed by the working class of these countries; and a certain part of the bourgeoisie of the colonial and dependent countries.

One of the brightest pages of the national-liberation struggle of the peoples of the East is the heroic struggle of the Korean people for their freedom and independence.

An investigation of the Korea question in connection with the problem of self-determination of nations discloses the sharp struggle of two camps for and against the principle of self-determination of nations, demonstrates the grandeur of the international-legal position of the Soviet Union, makes it possible to elicit the forms and methods of struggle of imperialists against the effectuation of the principle of self-determination of nations and the means of "international legal" disguising used by imperialists in order to conceal their actual rejection of the principle of self-determination of nations.

2. At the initiative and insistence of the Soviet Union the principle of self-determination of nations underlies the Moscow Agreement on Korea of December 1945.

The Moscow Agreement provides for ensuring the Korean people with the possibility to use their right to self-determination, and also to render to the Korean people assistance in the cause of creating an independent democratic State and restoring the national economy and culture.

The attempts of American representatives and Syngman Rhee-ites to construe the Moscow Agreement on Korea so as to reduce the content thereof to the funding of a trusteeship over Korea had the aim of distorting the essence of this Agreement.

Trusteeship with respect to Korea, which should never be identified with an ordinary trusteeship under the United Nations Charter, was not the main aspect of the Moscow Agreement on Korea.

3. A trusteeship with respect to Korea in that form as provided by the Moscow Agreement materially differed from the institution of trusteeship under the United Nations Charter.

(a) the object of the trusteeship under the Moscow Agreement is not a "territory" (in the sense of this word as used in Chapter XII of the United Nations Charter), but a State, since in accordance with the Moscow Agreement even before the effectuation of measures named in the Agreement as a trusteeship the Korean State should have been restored and a Korean Government created.

Other major peculiarities of the trusteeship provided by the Moscow Agreement also are determined by this, in comparison with the trusteeship under the United Nations Charter;

(b) the trusteeship under the Moscow Agreement was established not "for the administration" (Article 75, United Nations Charter) of Korea since at the moment of establishing the trusteeship the existence of a Korean Government was assumed which "administers" Korea, but in order to effectuate certain measures of aid and assistance to the new Korean State;

(c) under the United Nations Charter a major purpose of a trusteeship is to further the "progressive development" of the population of trustee territories "in the direction towards self-government or independence". The Moscow Agreement on Korea in the part concerning trusteeship proceeded from the fact that the Korean State already exists. Therefore the Moscow Agreement spoke not about the achievement of independence, but about measures for rendering aid and assistance to the "establishment of State independence of Korea" in the sense of strengthening the independence of a Korean State already in existence;

(d) since the agreement on trusteeship should have been worked out after the formation of the Provisional Korean Democratic Government, the Moscow Agreement provided for the participation of this government, and also the involvement of Korean democratic organizations, in working out measures called a trusteeship, which is an important peculiarity of the provision of the Moscow Agreement on trusteeship;

(e) the subjects of the agreement on trusteeship under the Moscow Agreement on Korea should have been the USSR, United States, Great Britain, and China. At the same time, in the meaning of the Moscow Agreement the conclusion of an agreement on trusteeship among the four powers assumed the consent of the Provisional Korean Democratic Government with the conditions of this agreement.

A trusteeship under the Moscow Agreement materially differed from a trusteeship within the framework of the United Nations and also from the American proposal on trusteeship over Korea advanced at the 1945 Moscow Conference.

Having signed the Moscow Agreement on Korea but not having the intention to fulfill it, the American imperialists attempted to falsify the provisions contained in the Moscow Agreement relative to the trusteeship, to represent this trusteeship as "foreign administration", and thereby to facilitate its struggle against the Moscow Agreement. The struggle of Korean reactionary groups against the Moscow Agreement was organized in South Korea under the guidance of the American command under the banner of the struggle against a trusteeship.

Chapter II

The Liberation of Korea by the Soviet Army and the Sojourn of Soviet Forces in North Korea in the Light of International Law

1. The task fell to the Soviet Army to liberate Korea from the Japanese yoke. Having routed the Japanese Kwantung Army, the Soviet forces after the surrender of Japan in accordance with the agreement among the allies remained on the territory of Korea northward of the 38th parallel.

The entry of the Soviet Union into the war against Japan and the initial reports concerning the headlong advance of the Soviet Army in Manchuria and Korea caused a mighty growth in the national-liberation movement in Korea. The struggle of the Korean people against the Japanese yoke merged with the liberation war of the Soviet Union against Japanese imperialism.

After the liberation of Korea from the Japanese yoke both in the northern part of the country, where Soviet forces were situated, and in the south before the arrival there of American forces, a situation was created that was exceedingly favorable for the unleashing of the activity of the democratic forces of the Korean people.

On the basis of documentary and literary sources it is shown in the work that people's committees arose after the liberation of Korea and took power into their own hands not only in the northern part of the country, where Soviet forces were situated, but also in South Korea.

The people's committees arose on the base of a wide coalition of anti-Japanese democratic forces, the basis of which was an alliance of the working class and peasantry under the leading role of the working class. Naturally, the Communist Party of Korea played a leading role in the people's committees, consistently having struggled for the liberation and independence of the motherland against the Japanese enslavers.

2. When analyzing the legal nature of the sojourn of Soviet and American forces in Korea the question arises of the international-legal status of Korea after its liberation by the Soviet Army.

This question, which has great significance for an international legal assessment of the policies of the Soviet Union and the United States with respect to Korea during the sojourn in Korea of the forces of these States, has not received so far illumination in Soviet international legal doctrine.

As regards bourgeois international lawyers, they in the majority of instances assiduously avoid this question, not being in a position to give an answer to it which would justify the actions of the American occupation authorities in South Korea.

The international legal status of Korea after the liberation was determined by general provisions of international law and provisions of the Cairo Declaration, the Act on the Surrender of Japan, and the Moscow Agreement on Korea.

The Cairo Declaration and the Moscow Agreement proceeded from recognition of the unlawfulness of the forcible accession of Korea to Japan and declared this act to be invalid.

Relying on the works of Soviet international legal scholars (S. B. Krylov, E. A. Korovin, F. I. Kozhevnikov), the author shows that recognition of the unlawfulness of the seizure of Korea by Japan corresponds to the principles of contemporary international law and that the annexation of Korea also was unlawful under the international law which prevailed at the moment of the seizure of Korea by Japan.

The "principle of effectiveness" propagated by the most reactionary bourgeois jurists (Kelsen, Guggenheim, Verdross), according to which the annexation of Korea by Japan should be regarded as legal since it was effective, is not a principle of contemporary international law. The "principle of effectiveness", putting force in the place of law in international relations, is a direct rejection of international law.

Since the accession of Korea to Japan was unlawful and the treaty concerning the annexation of Korea by Japan was invalid, the power of Japan in Korea should be considered to be a temporary de facto power, and the territory of Korea should be regarded as foreign territory unlawfully occupied.

However, Korea could not be regarded as an ally of Japan. The Korean people did not actually take part in the war against the Allies and its resistance to the Japanese colonizers, expressing an unwavering aspiration of the Korean people for independence, rendered certain assistance to the Allies.

It follows from these propositions that the territory of Korea should be regarded not as the territory of a hostile State, but as the territory of a friendly country liberated from enemy occupation.

3. The bourgeois science of international law does not differentiate the sojourn of foreign forces on the territory of a friendly or allied country liberated from enemy occupation from other institutions of occupation. Bourgeois international lawyers usually distinguish between two types of occupation: military occupation (occupation de guerre) and peaceful occupation (occupation pacifique).

As regards the sojourn of foreign forces on the territory of a friendly country liberated from enemy occupation, the bourgeois science of international law either evades this question in silence or equates this type of sojourn of forces on foreign territory to military occupation (Travers, Hyde).

The theoretical unfoundedness and imperialist essence of such conceptions, especially manifest during the Second World War when the imperialist States shamelessly used for their predatory purposes not only the occupation of enemy territories but also the sojourn of their forces on the territories of friendly or allied countries, are unmasked in the work.

In pointing out that the character of relations between States whose forces are situated on foreign territory and the State or country on whose territory these forces are situated should underlie the distinction between institutions of occupation, the author substantiates the position that the sojourn of foreign forces on the territory of a friendly or allied country liberated by these forces from enemy occupation should be regarded as an autonomous institution of international law, having in view that norms of international law relating to the occupation of enemy territory are not applicable in this event.

The Soviet Union during the Second World War made a significant contribution to the forming of this institution of international law.

The position of the Soviet Union on the question of the conditions of sojourn of foreign forces on the territory of a friendly or allied country liberated from enemy occupation was precisely formulated by the Soviet Government during the war against Hitlerite Germany, and the specific conditions of such sojourn were fixed in agreements concluded by the Soviet Government with the governments of Czechoslovakia, Poland, China, and Norway.

The said agreements proceeded from the fact that unlike the occupation of enemy territory during wartime the de facto power does not pass to the forces situated on the territory of a friendly country liberated by these forces from enemy occupation, except for military operations zones. Here, in the author's view, lies the principal peculiarity of the institution of the sojourn of foreign forces on the territory of a friendly country liberated from enemy occupation from the institution of occupation of enemy territory during wartime.

The sojourn of foreign forces on the territory of a friendly country after the end of the War, as a rule, is not permitted and may be justified only by special circumstances.

As regards Korea, the sojourn there of Soviet forces which entered the territory of Korea in the course of combat operations against the Japanese army, and also the sojourn of American forces which arrived in South Korea after the surrender of Japan in order to accept the surrender of Japanese forces, was linked with the fulfillment of the Cairo Declaration and Moscow Agreement on Korea and should have a short-term character.

4. In addition to the afore-cited provisions of international law relative to the sojourn of foreign forces on the territory of a friendly country liberated from enemy occupation important conclusions arose from the Cairo Declaration and the Moscow Agreement on Korea concerning the sojourn of Soviet and American forces on the territory of Korea.

It followed from the Cairo Declaration that the territory of Korea should be regarded by parties to the Declaration not as enemy territory but as the territory of a friendly country with respect to which the parties to this Agreement assumed the obligation to take necessary measures to ensure the independence thereof.

From these provisions the conclusion is suggested that the sojourn on the territory of Korea of foreign forces should not be used for the purpose of creating obstacles to the taking by the Korean people of steps directed towards restoring Korean statehood but, on the contrary, in accordance with the general sense of the Cairo Declaration, such initiative of the Korean people should find support on the part of the military authorities.

This conclusion arose with the special clarity from the Moscow Agreement on Korea, underlying which was the unreserved recognition of the right of the Korean people to form their own national State.

In addition under the Moscow Agreement on Korea the parties thereto not only should not cause obstacles but should render assistance to democratic forces of the Korean people in their struggle for liquidation of the consequences of Japanese domination in all spheres of life of the country.

5. The provisions of international law set out above concerning the sojourn of foreign forces on the territory of a friendly country liberated from enemy occupation, and also the provisions of the Cairo Declaration and Moscow Agreement on Korea, were strictly complied with by Soviet forces in North Korea.

Acting in the spirit of friendship of peoples and respect for their sovereign rights, the Soviet Army on the territory of North Korea ensured complete freedom of activity to democratic parties and social organizations and the unobstructed unfolding of the initiative of the Korean people in the creation of new democratic agencies of power and the effectuation of democratic transformations.

The Soviet command considered the people's committees created by the Korean people to be legal agencies of power in North Korea.

People's committees in North Korea with the active participation of the broad people's masses effectuated historical democratic transformations embodying the centuries of expectations of the Korean people. These transformations, primarily of an anti-imperialist and anti-feudal character, created however conditions facilitating the transition thereafter to the path of the construction of socialism in Korea.

The liberation of Korea by the Soviet Army and the presence of Soviet forces on the territory of North Korea exerted enormous influence on the development of the country.

The rout of the Japanese army and liberation of Korea by the Soviet Army from the Japanese yoke inflicted a decisive blow on Korean reaction which had been the support of Japanese dominance in Korea. The elimination of the Japanese into whose hands fell not only the State apparatus in Korea but also the basic economic positions significantly facilitated the Korean people in their struggle against Korean reaction – the large Korean bourgeoisie and landowners.

However, the very fact of the liberation of Korea by the Army of the Soviet socialist State and also the sojourn in Korea of units of the Soviet Army implanted in the democratic forces an assurance of the victorious outcome of their struggle for liberation and independence of the motherland and, on the other hand, caused dismay and panic in the ranks of reaction who were deprived of support on the part of the Japanese imperialists.

The presence in North Korea of the Soviet Army deprived Korean reaction of the possibility to unleash with the assistance of their American patrons a civil war in Korea and averted foreign military intervention.

As already noted in Soviet international legal doctrine (A. Ia. Vyshinskii, F. I. Kozhevnikov, S. B. Krylov), the special quality of the Soviet socialist State as a subject of international law told on all the actions of the Soviet Union in the international arena. The Soviet Union, acting in accordance with generally-recognized principles and norms of international law, applies them consistently and profoundly. The Soviet Union is introducing a fresh spirit in these democratic principles and norms of international law. The application by the Soviet Union in Korea of the institution of the sojourn of foreign forces on the territory of a friendly country liberated from enemy occupation and strict respect for the principle of self-determination of nations are clear examples of this progressive role of the Soviet Union.

Chapter III

The American Occupation Regime in South Korea – Flouting of International Law

1. American imperialism, which for a long time aspired to seize Korea, used the sojourn of American forces in South Korea for political and economic subordination of this part of the country to the United States of America. The methods and means which have been used by the United States for these purposes, as well as the means of "international legal" camouflage of this imperialist policy, are unmasked in the dissertation.

In analyzing the mechanism of American occupation of South Korea, the author considers the structure, functions, and activity of the apparatus of the American military administration in the center and in the provinces. This apparatus, augmented by pro-Japanese elements which have now entered the service of the new masters, was a powerful instrument of the American imperialists in the cause of the effectuation of their predatory plans with respect to Korea.

The American military administration: (a) restored the operation of Japanese legislation hated by the Korean people, which at the moment of the arrival of the American forces in South Korea was not applied in significant part; (b) restored and improved the police apparatus left over after the Japanese, having created terrorist youth organizations to assist this apparatus, these having become a genuine scourge of the population; (c) retained the Japanese judicial system, which facilitated it in effectuating the purposes of American imperialism in Korea.

In order to disguise the imperialist essence of the policies of the United States in Korea, to create the appearance of the participation of Koreans in the administration of South Korea, and also in order to gradually impose Korean reactionaries on the Korean people as rulers who were imported from American or who had recommended themselves as enemies of the Korean people in the service of the Japanese, the American command created fictitious representative agencies attached to the American military administration in South Korea: "Consultative Committee" (1945), "Constitutive Assembly", "Democratic Chamber" (February 1946); "Provisional Korean Legislative Assembly" (December 1946). These agencies, composed basically of American servitors, were powerless appendages of the American military administration.

The Japanese imperialists relied in Korea on landowners and a certain part of the Korean bourgeoisie which was closely linked with Japanese capital and the Japanese colonial apparatus in Korea. American imperialism when effectuating its predatory plans with respect to Korea could find support only in these social strata.

Pushing back against the resistance on the part of democratic forces of the Korean people struggling for independence of the country and democratic transformation, the ruling circles of the United States saw in the rout of the democratic movement the principal condition for the realization of its predatory plans with respect to Korea.

The dissertation considers the principal measures of the American military authorities in South Korea whose purpose was to smother the democratic movement, a description is given of the major regulations and orders of the American command which were the "legal" basis of the occupation regime of lawlessness and arbitrariness, and the courageous struggle is illuminated which the Korean people waged in South Korea under the guidance of the Communist Party against the occupiers for liberation and independence of the motherland.

The occupation of South Korea by the American forces was shamelessly used by the American monopolies to extort the wealth of the Korean people and subordinate the economy of South Korea to American capital. The dissertation identifies those levers and methods which the United States used to achieve this aim.

South Korea, economically drained by the American occupation, could not do without American "assistance", the receipt of which led to the increasing economic and political independence of South Korea on the United States.

3. In order to take advantage of the occupation of South Korea for its imperialist purposes, the United States proceeded to a flagrant violation of the provisions of international law, and also the provisions of the Cairo Declaration and the Moscow Agreement on Korea. These violations were expressed in the following:

(a) the sojourn of American forces in South Korea was regarded as the occupation of enemy territory, if not as the occupation of a conquered country in that significance of this concept which is alien to contemporary international law;

(b) the refusal of the American command to recognize the national agencies of power created by the Korean people and the dissolution of the people's committees which were the sole legal agencies of power in Korea after the liberation;

(c) the attempts to restore the activity of agencies of the Japanese colonial administration in Korea at a time when by virtue of the recognition of the unlawfulness of the seizure of Korea by Japan the Japanese agencies of administration in Korea could not be regarded as legal agencies of power;

(d) the seizure by the American command of power in South Korea at a time when in the event of the sojourn of foreign forces on the territory of a friendly country de facto power, unlike the occupation of enemy territory, does not pass to these forces, except for the zone of military operations. In addition, this act of the American military authorities was incompatible with the obligation arising from the Cairo Declaration and Moscow Agreement on Korea to respect the authority of national agencies of power of the Korean people;

(e) the attempt to smother the democratic movement, support of reaction, not allowing democratic transformations, and the elimination of democratic freedoms already achieved by the Korean people after liberation were a violation of the principle of self-determination of nations, and also of the Moscow Agreement on Korea;

(f) the unlawfulness of the American occupation regime in South Korea was determined also by the unlawfulness of its purposes, which were the enslavement of the Korean people and conversion of Korea into a colony and military platform of the United States.

The flouting by the American military authorities in South Korea of international law and agreements on Korea transformed the sojourn of American forces in South Korea into an unlawful occupation of foreign territory.

Chapter IV

Struggle of the Soviet Union for Precise Fulfillment of the Moscow Agreement on Korea and Violation by the United States of this Agreement During the Period of Negotiations in the Joint Soviet-American Commission for Korea

1. The principle of the good-faith fulfillment of international treaties based on the principle of the equality of States and respect for State sovereignty is related to the group of major generally-recognized principles of contemporary international law. Under conditions of coexistence of States of two opposed socio-economic systems this principle acquires special significance since in the contemporary international situation international cooperation is possible only on the basis of arrangement and coordination of the measures of an international-legal order.[1]

However, the history of the foreign policies of the capitalist States is replete with examples of violations of international treaties. During the period of imperialism and, especially, of the general crisis of capitalism, violations of international agreements by imperialist States became more frequent and serious in scale. The most aggressive imperialist States are especially noteworthy in this respect.

The shameless violation of international agreements was a characteristic feature of the foreign policy of Hitlerite Germany. At present the United States is acting as the leader and organizer of the undermining of international agreements. A violation of international agreements is one aspect of the American policy "from a position of strength".

The attitude of the Soviet Union and the United States of American to the Cairo Declaration and the Moscow Agreement on Korea is a clear example of two trends in contemporary international politics in the fulfillment of international agreements: the good-faith fulfillment of its obligations under international agreements on the part of the Soviet Union and

[1] See Academician A. Ia. Vyshinskii, Вопросы международного права и международной политики [Questions of International Law and International Politics] (Gosiurizdat, 1949), p. 479.

other countries of the democratic camp and flagrant violation of international agreements by the United States of America and other imperialist States.

2. An analysis of the work of the Joint Soviet-American Commission for Korea shows that during the entire work of this Commission the aspiration of the Government of the United States to not permit the realization of the Moscow Agreement on Korea appeared as a red thread. Having signed the Moscow Agreement on Korea under conditions of the postwar situation which did not correspond to the predatory plans of American imperialism, the Government of the United States carefully but undeviatingly proceeded along the path of the final undermining of the fulfillment of the Moscow Agreement, using for these purposes also the Joint Soviet-American Commission for Korea.

The tactical methods used by the American side to undermine the fulfillment of the Moscow Agreement and the methods of "international legal" disguise of the de facto refusal to fulfill this Agreement are unmasked in the work. These means and methods included, in particular: the "interpretation" of the Moscow Agreement for the purpose of distorting the meaning of this Agreement; disinformation for the purpose of creating an incorrect impression of the position of the Soviet Union both during the period of the conclusion of the Moscow Agreement on Korea and during the negotiations relative to its fulfillment; the organization of the struggle of reactionary groups on the territory of South Korea occupied by the United States against the Moscow Agreement under the false flag of the struggle against trusteeship; use of the occupation of South Korea for the purposes of creating a situation excluding the possibility of fulfilling the Moscow Agreement (arrests of representatives singled out for consultations with the Joint Commission, terror against democratic elements, and so on); attempts to deflect the Joint Commission for Korea from its principal task – rendering assistance to the Korean people in forming a provisional democratic government – and to supplant the plan of measures contemplated in the Moscow Agreement with a plan for the "economic unification of Korea" which actually provided for the transfer of the economy of all of Korea into the hand of the American command so achieve by this means the subordination to American monopolies of the economy of both North and South Korea; the organization and support of reactionary groups and attempts to represent these groups which had no support in the Korean people as representatives of the people of South Korea; preparation for the creation from these groups of a puppet South Korean government; the creation of artificial complications in the course of negotiations in order to obstruct the reaching of an agreement; demagogic statements and gestures having the purpose to show the "impossibility" of an agreement with the Soviet Union and placing on the Soviet Union fault for the failure to fulfill the Moscow Agreement on Korea.

Chapter V

Creation by American Occupation Authorities of Separate Puppet Government in South Korea in the Light of Principles of International Law

1. In order to justify its refusal to fulfill the Moscow Agreement on Korea and camouflage future imperialist measures with respect to Korea, the United States used an international organization.

The American proposal at the Second Session of the United Nations General Assembly in 1947 to include the Korea question on the agenda of the Session put to the forefront the question concerning the interpretation of Article 107 of the United Nations Charter. Analyzing the provisions of the United Nations Charter, the author concludes that the sole correct interpretation of Article 107 conforming to the spirit and letter of the United Nations Charter is that according to which issues of post-war reconstruction are not within the competence of the United Nations. The work discloses the complete bankruptcy of Kelsen's interpretation, according to which Article 107 of the United Nations Charter only limits but does not exclude the competence of the United Nations on issues of postwar reconstruction.

The Korea question is relegated to questions of postwar reconstruction since it was linked with measures relating to Japan and therefore is not subject to the competence of the United Nations. Two international agreements exist on this question and the organs of the United Nations were not empowered to review the conditions of these agreements. Therefore, the inclusion of the Korea question on the agenda of the Second Session of the General Assembly was contrary to the United Nations Charter.

2. The proposals put forward by the Soviet delegation at the Second Session of the United Nations General Assembly on inviting representatives of the Korean people to the Session and the withdrawal of foreign forces from Korea had important political and international-legal significance. From the international-legal aspect these proposals proceeded from the spirit of the United Nations Charter and principle of self-determination of nations and were directed towards the realization of this principle in the Korea question.

Since the principle of self-determination of nations means the right of nations autonomously to resolve their own affairs, it follows that any decree of an international organization affecting the fate of a particular nation can not be legally adopted without the participation of representatives of this nation, without taking account of its opinion and wish. The rejection of the proposal of the Soviet Union to invite representatives of the Korean people to participate in the discussion of the Korea question at the Session of the General Assembly violated the spirit of the United Nations Charter and was a violation of the principle of the self-determination of nations.

The proposal of the Soviet Union concerning the simultaneous withdrawal of Soviet and American forces from Korea was directed towards achieving the purposes of the Moscow Agreement on Korea and restoration of the flouted rights of the Korean people. The cessation of the American occupation of South Korea was used by the United States to effectuate its predatory plans with respect to Korea and became a principal obstacle on the path towards the effectuation by the Korean people of the right to self-determination, would have ensured the resolution of the Korea question in accordance with the expectations of the Korean people and the interests of strengthening international peace and security.

3. The dissertation discloses the unlawful character of the General Assembly Resolution on the Korea Question of 14 December 1947, which was adopted in violation of Article 107 of the United Nations Charter in the absence of a representative of the Korean people and sanctioned in advance the flagrant interference of the American occupation authorities in South Korea in the affairs of the Korean people and was to serve as a camouflage for the effectuation of an American plan for the creation of a separate puppet government in South Korea.

Under the cover of this resolution and decrees of the Temporary United Nations Commission for Korea formed in accordance with it (the first United Nations Commission for Korea), the American occupation authorities, cruelly putting down resistance of the Korean people, held separate falsified elections in South Korea and created a puppet government.

An analysis of events in South Korea during the period of preparing and holding separate elections enables the following conclusions to be drawn:

(1) the elections in South Korea of 10 May 1948 to the so-called national assembly were held on territory occupied by foreign forces which effectuated de facto power completely on this territory;

(2) the organization of the elections was in the hands of American occupation authorities;

(3) the preparation and holding of elections occurred under the most unceremonious interference of American occupation forces and the Korean police under their control and leadership, Korean terrorist organizations, and so on;

(4) the separate elections in South Korea were imposed on the people of South Korea, who opposed these elections;

(5) the separate elections were held under conditions of a terrorist occupation regime and police persecution of democratic elements and other opponents of these elections;

(6) besides the general conditions which precluded the possibility of a free expression of will of the Korean people (situation of terror, interference of occupation forces, and so on) in the course of the preparation and holding of elections there occurred everywhere flagrant violations of elementary requirements of a democratic procedure for elections.

The international-legal conclusions arising from the said de facto aspect of the matter can not give rise to doubt. The actions of the United States in South Korea, linked with the organization and holding of separate elections in May 1948, was a flagrant violation of the principle of self-determination of nations and the provisions of international law relating to the sojourn of foreign forces on the territory of a friendly country liberated from enemy occupation.

4. The question is considered in the work of the status of the South Korean "Government" from the standpoint of international law. The Syngman Rhee "Government" created by the American occupation authorities was a typical puppet government.

The formation and replacement of governments and States is relegated to the internal affairs of a State and in accordance with the principle of noninterference is not regulated by international law. As regards nations, then according to the principle of self-determination a nation in the event of its forming its own autonomous State itself decides questions connected with the formation of this State and no coercive interference in the affairs of a nation is permitted. But in the event of the creation of a puppet government such a government is created not as a result of the struggle of internal forces in the country, but as the result of the actions of a foreign State. Such actions of a foreign State are subject to international-legal assessment and should be undoubtedly deemed to be unlawful as violating the principle of noninterference in the internal affairs of a State, and when we speak of a nation – the principle of self-determination of nations.

The South Korean "Government", just as any puppet government imposed by a foreign State which acted in violation of the principles of international law, can not be regarded as a legal government.

Having recognized the Syngman Rhee "Government" and having forced a number of States dependent on the United States to do the same, the Government of the United States used this institution of international recognition, as in many other instances, in violation of the principles of international law.

The work unmasks the unlawful cabalistic character of agreements imposed by the United States on South Korea with the assistance of the Syngman Rhee "Government". These agreements had the purpose to remove the traces of anti-people's activity and the plundering of national wealth of the Korean people during the period of rule by the American military administration and to fence off the dominance of American imperialism in South Korea from any incidents.

Chapter VI

The Formation of the Korean People's Democratic Republic and the International Legal Status Thereof

1. The holding of separate elections, the creation of the so-called national assembly and forming of a puppet government in South Korea, the unbridled terror against democratic elements and cynical flouting of the rights of the people, the unconcealed lording about of the American military authorities in South Korea visually demonstrated the falsity and hypocrisy of the United Nations General Assembly Resolution on the Korea Question of 14 November 1947 and the disgraceful role of the United Nations Commission for Korea, which concealed the effectuation of the American plan for the split of the country and the transformation of South Korea into a colony and military platform of the United States.

Against the experience of the severe reality of South Korea, the Korean people learned to recognize the maneuvers of the new claimants to dominance in Korea. The authority of the labor party was raised yet higher and the alliance of the working class and the peasantry strengthened under the banner of the national-liberation struggle headed by the working class, and the ranks of true patriots of Korea were more closely forged.

An expression of this solidarity of forces of the Korean people was the second united meeting of representatives of political parties and social organizations of the North and South (June-July 1948), at which the historical decision was adopted to hold elections throughout the entire territory of Korea to the Supreme National Assembly of Korea. This meeting marked the rise of the national-liberation movement of the Korean people to a new higher level.

2. The author considers the formation of the Korean People's Democratic Republic in the light of the use by the Korean people of the right to self-determination.

Elections in North Korea were held in accordance with a Statute worked out on the basis of a draft of an all-Korean constitution, which was prepared by the National Assembly of North Korea and temporarily until the unification of the country introduced into operation on the territory of North Korea.

As regards elections in South Korea, having regard to the aspiration of the American occupation authorities to obstruct the effectuation thereof, these elections were held secretly. The distinctiveness of the elections on the territory of South Korea caused by the extraordinary conditions of foreign occupation does not make these elections less significant.

International law does not contain norms regulating the character of decisions and the procedure for their adoption by a nation on the basis of its use of the right to self-determination. The right to self-determination means that a nation itself decides its fate, itself decides the question concerning the creation of its own autonomous State – and itself may establish the procedure for the adoption of such a decision, and also the procedure for resolving all other questions connected with the effectuation of the right to self-determination.

Therefore the Korean people had the undoubted right to hold elections in South Korea by that means which it considered possible to use under the conditions existing in South Korea.

The right to self-determination also means that no State may coercively interfere in the affairs of a nation and in the resolution by it of questions connected with self-determination.

It follows that foreign forces situated at the time on Korean territory had no legal grounds to interfere in the effectuation by the Korean people of this right, the more so since the obligation not to interfere arose also from the Cairo Declaration and the Moscow Agreement on Korea, parties to which were the Soviet Union, and also the United States, whose forces were situated in Korea.

Soviet forces, respecting the principle of self-determination of nations and in accordance with obligations assumed by the Soviet Union under the Agreement on Korea, did not interfere in the holding of elections.

The obstacles which were caused to the holding of elections in South Korea by the American authorities were a new violation of the principle of self-determination of nations, and also the provisions of the Cairo Declaration and Moscow Agreement on Korea.

3. The formation of the Korea People's Democratic Republic signified the emergence of a new subject of international law.

In considering the question of the legal personality of the Korean People Democratic Republic, the author concludes that the Korean People's Democratic Republic from the standpoint of international legal personality represents all of Korea.

The Korean People's Democratic Republic was created as a result of the effectuation of the right to self-determination of the entire Korean nation; elections to the Supreme National Assembly of Korea occurred both on the territory of the North and on the territory of South Korea; the Supreme National Assembly represented the will of the overwhelming majority of the population of North and South Korea.

It is considered to be generally-recognized in international law that in the event of internal struggle in a State, the territorial limits of the power of a particular government are determined by the de facto situation and the representative of the State in international relations is that government which de facto effectuates power on the territory of States.

But this position relates only to an internal struggle occurring without the interference of foreign States. In this instance the impossibility of the effectuation by the Government of the Korean People's Democratic Republic of power on the territory of South Korea was not the result of internal struggle, but a result of the unlawful foreign occupation.

Therefore, the sovereignty of the new Korean State legally extended to the entire territory of Korea, although its de facto effectuation as a consequence of foreign occupation of South Korea was confined to the territory of North Korea.

4. In considering the question of the international-legal recognition of the Korean People's Democratic Republic, the author expresses the notion that in connection with the recognition of the principle of self-determination of nations as a principle of international law the problem of the recognition of States arising as a result of the effectuation by peoples of the right to self-determination should be now raised anew.

The right of nations to self-determination includes the right to form an autonomous State. Therefore, refusal to recognize a State which arose as a result of the effectuation by a nation of the right to self-determination should be regarded as a refusal to recognize the right to self-determination for this nation, which would be a violation of international law.

As regards Korea, the obligation to grant international recognition anew to the Korean State arose for States-parties to the Moscow Agreement on Korea also from the provisions of this Agreement, as Kim Din Tai has correctly noted in his dissertation.[2]

Recognition of the Korean People's Democratic Republic by the Soviet Union and the evacuation of Soviet forces from North Korea in accordance with the request of the Supreme National Assembly of the Korean People's Democratic Republic was testimony to the respect of the Soviet Union for the principle of self-determination of nations and sovereignty of the new Korean State.

The failure of the Government of the United States to recognize the Korean People's Democratic Republic, and also the refusal to withdraw its forces from Korea despite the demand of the supreme agency of power of the Korean State, was a violation of international law and the Moscow Agreement on Korea.

Chapter VII

The Korea Question at the Third and Fourth Sessions of the United Nations General Assembly

1. The ruling circles of the United States intended to use the discussion of the Korea question at the III Session of the General Assembly especially in order to "legalize" the separate government of South Korea created by means of falsified elections.

The Soviet delegation unmasked the imperialist plans of the United States with respect to Korea and in accordance with the principle of self-determination of nations insisted on granting to the Korean people the possibility to autonomously decide their own internal affairs. The Soviet delegation again put forward

[2] Kim Din Tai, Корейская Народно-Демократическая Республика как субъект международного права [Korean People's Democratic Republic as a Subject of International Law] (kandidat dissertation) (Leningrad State University, 1951), pp. 267-268.

a proposal concerning the withdrawal of foreign forces from Korea, and also suggested the United Nations Commission for Korea be abolished.

The work identifies the maneuvers of the ruling circles of the United States and their Syngman-Rhee acolytes in Korea who had the purpose to assist the American delegation at the III Section of the General Assembly in extricating themselves from the difficult situation in which they were as a result of the decision of the Soviet Government concerning the evacuation of Soviet forces from Korea.

The work shows that the resolution adopted by the General Assembly under the pressure of the United States on 12 December 1948 was contrary to principles of international law and the provisions of the United Nations Charter. This Resolution meant that American imperialism used in the Korean question an international organization not only for the "international legal" camouflage of the creation of a puppet government in South Korea, but also to accelerate international recognition of this "government", and also in order to counteract the recognition by States of the legal representative created by the Korean people. This is a new moment in the practice of the creation and recognition by imperialist States of puppet government.

2. The second United Nations Commission for Korea, just as the first Commission, was an instrument of the aggressive policy of the United States and a means of interference in the internal affairs of Korea. An analysis of the activity of the Commission and report submitted by it to the IV Session of the General Assembly shows that the Commission not only did nothing to unify Korea but, in accordance with United States policy, obstructed the effectuation of proposals concerning the peaceful unification of the country. At the same time, the Commission attempted in its Report to vindicate the reactionary regime in South Korea.

The work gives a characterization of the terrorist regime and wild outburst of police terror in South Korea, which intensified even more after the formation of the separate government, and the heroic struggle is illuminated of the Korean people against foreign occupation and the Syngman Rhee clique and the growing partisan movement in South Korea.

Forced to take into account the growth of the movement against continuing American occupation of South Korea, seeking to strengthen the position of the Syngman Rhee "government", and having in mind to wash its hands in the future of civil war in Korea, the aggressive circles of the United States considered it advisable to withdraw American forces from South Korea in the summer of 1949. But the American militarists did everything so that American forces might at any time within several hours be thrown back into South Korea. All necessary armaments were left behind, aerodromes and ports were left in combat readiness, and a group of American military advisors, numbering according to official figures 500 persons, remained in South Korea in order to engage in the further training of the Syngman Rhee army.

3. At the IV Session of the United Nations General Assembly in 1949 the Soviet delegation together with the delegations of other democratic countries again opposed the desecration of the rights of the Korean people and insisted on the provision to the Korean people of the possibility to themselves decide questions of unification and the creation of a single democratic State, and also the liquidation of the United Nations Commission for Korea, which obstructed the peaceful unification of the country, and was an instrument of American interference in the affairs of the Korean people.

Seeking not to allow the unfolding discussion of the Korean question at the IV Section, the Anglo-American bloc dragged out the resolution concerning approval of the activity of the second United Nations Commission for Korea and the creation of a new commission for Korea which would cover the preparation of the American imperialists and the Syngman Rhee-ites for civil war in Korea.

Part Two

Civil War in Korea and Aggression of the United States

Chapter VIII

The Preparation and Unleashing by the United States and the Puppet Clique of Syngman Rhee of Civil War in Korea

1. The triumph of the people's revolution in China was a powerful blow to the entire system of imperialism. This was the greatest defeat of the policies of American imperialism in Asia, which intended to transform China into a gigantic appendage of the world American empire and use it as the principal base for its dominance in Asia and as one of the decisive links in the encirclement of the Soviet Union.

Aggressive circles of the United States, distraught by their lack of success in Asia and especially by the collapse of their predatory plans with respect to China, feverishly prepared for a new onslaught against the national-liberation movement in Asia, intending to use Korea for these purposes. The historical experience of the Japanese imperialists pointed out to the new claimants for dominance in Asia that Korea might serve as a convenient platform for aggressive actions against China.

2. On the basis of an analysis of events which preceded the commencement of civil war in Korea, secret documents of the Syngman-Rhee Government, materials of the United States Congress, testimony of eminent representatives of the Syngman-Rhee clique, and other evidence relating to the preparation of civil war in Korea, the work establishes the following:

(1) the Syngman Rhee "Government", in unleashing the civil war in Korea, operated under the instructions and guidance of official representatives of the United States and with the material assistance on the part of the United States;

(2) the United States both before and after the official withdrawal of American forces from South Korea (June 1949) through the numerous military mission fully held in its hands the army of the puppet Syngman-Rhee "Government" and

effectuated the training of this army for a "campaign in the North";

(3) the United States intensified supplying the Syngman-Rhee army with armaments;

(4) the United States provided the Syngman-Rhee "Government" with monetary means necessary to prepare for civil war;

(5) the official representatives of the United States directly led the suppression of the people's movement, in particular, partisan movement in South Korea, which was regarded as a necessary step in preparing the rear for the contemplated civil war;

(6) under the direct guidance and instructions of American official persons spies and saboteurs were sent to North Korea for the purpose of organizing murders of leading political figures of the Korean People's Democratic Republic, destroying important industrial objects and disseminating epidemic illnesses by means of the use of bacteriological means;

(7) at the instruction of the Government of the United States the reactionary Syngman-Rhee clique rejected all proposals for peaceful unification of the country made by the Unified Democratic Fatherland Front and the Supreme National Assembly of the Korean People's Democratic Republic;

(8) American military advisors led directly the military actions of the South Korean Army which were commenced by the Syngman Rhee-ites on 25 June 1950;

(9) the civil war in Korea was regarded by ruling circles of the United States as the prelude and pretext for armed intervention of the United States in Korea, China, and other countries of Asia.

Thus, the United States, which acted through the puppet clique of Syngman Rhee, and also through its official representatives, flagrantly interfered in the internal affairs of Korea, having prepared and unleashed a civil war in the country. Such actions of the United States should be classified as camouflaged intervention of the United States in Korea.

3. Intervention is an unlawful act since it is a violation of a major principle of international law – the principle of noninterference in the internal affairs of a State.

In considering the arising of the principle of noninterference, the sharp struggle which occurs around this principle at present, and the ever more shameless violation of this principle by the imperialist States, the author reveals the complete bankruptcy of attempts of bourgeois international lawyers to justify these violations by means of substantiating the "right to intervention" and, in particular, the "right to collective intervention".

The preparation and unleashing by the United States of a civil war in Korea was camouflaged intervention, but this does not make it less unlawful and criminal; intervention remains intervention also when it is camouflaged.

A new feature of camouflaged intervention of imperialist States in the postwar period is a feature which is plainly manifest in the United States intervention in Korea, being the use of United Nations organs, in this instance the United Nations Commission for Korea, to cover the intervention.

As regards the concept of indirect aggression, formulated for the first time in the 1953 Soviet definition of aggression, the author considers the camouflaged intervention of the United States in Korea as one of the examples of indirect aggression.

The author suggests that the concept of indirect aggression to a certain extent is interlaced with the concept of intervention and that certain forms of intervention fall under the concept of indirect aggression. However, indirect aggression may be manifested as happened in Korea, as a preparatory stage for armed aggression.

Chapter IX

Civil War and United States Aggression in Korea

1. The armed intervention of the United States in Korea signified the transition of the Anglo-American bloc from a policy of preparing a new war to direct acts of aggression.

In transforming the United Nations into an instrument of its aggressive policies, the ruling circles of the United States forced on the international organization of a number of decisions contrary to the United Nations Charter and international law on the Korea question in order to use these decisions for the "international-legal" camouflage of its armed intervention in Korea and to involve other countries to participate in this intervention.

This new "international-legal" camouflage distinguishes the armed intervention in Korea from those armed interventions of imperialist States which occurred earlier, without changing, however, the essence of armed intervention.

2. The resolutions of the Security Council of 25 and 27 June and 7 July 1950 by which American armed intervention in Korea was concealed, put with new sharpness such international legal problems as problems of aggression, "threat to the peace", noninterference in civil war, and significance of the absence of a permanent member of the Security Council in connection with the principle of unanimity of the great powers in the Security Council.

In considering the problem of an international legal definition of the concept of aggression, the author illuminates the struggle around the Soviet definition of aggression in the 1930s and at present and shows the leading role of the Soviet Union in working out the definition of aggression and in the struggle for the introduction of this definition in international law.

An analysis of international agreements – multilateral and bilateral – and especially the United Nations Charter which speaks of aggression and gives a definition of aggression and the Soviet definitions of aggression of 1933 and 1953, and also an analysis of the utterances of eminent specialists on international law of various countries on the question of aggression, shows that although at present there is no generally-recognized definition of aggression, it is firmly established that aggression is determined actions of one State or group of States against another State or group of States.

The concept of aggression under contemporary international law is applicable only to inter-State relations. The concept of aggression is inapplicable to civil war, which is an internal conflict.

One may speak about aggression in connection with civil war only with regard to relations of a State in which a civil war is happening with other States, that is, for example, in the event of an armed intervention of a foreign State in a civil war, or in the event of an attack of a State in which a civil war is happening against another State. However, in these instances we have an outside element distinct from the civil war which is not a necessary element of a civil war, being a struggle of internal forces in the State.

3. The collapse of attempts to justify the use of the concept of aggression to the civil war in Korea led to the emergence of a new legal construction (Kelsen) based on the assertion that if one may not speak about aggression or a breach of the peace with respect to a civil war since a civil war is not a violation of international law, one may speak about a "threat" to the peace and on this basis apply Chapter VII of the United Nations Charter to a civil war.

In considering the question of a "threat to the peace", the author concludes that just as in the case of a "breach" of international peace the Charter speaks about a "threat" to the peace only with regard to international peace, that is, to relations between States. A "threat to peace" in the meaning of United Nations Charter provisions is that state of international relations between States which is fraught with a breach of international peace.

The Charter speaks of disputes and situations in connection with a "threat to peace".

The provisions of the United Nations Charter leave no doubt that in all instances when the Charter speaks of a dispute and the parties to a dispute it has in view disputes between States and assumes States to be parties.

Disputes between States may lead to a threat to international peace arising. But a civil war is an internal dispute and therefore the concept of "dispute" used in the United Nations Charter is not applicable to a civil war.

As regards situations, since the Charter speaks about a threat to "international peace" it is evident that such a threat may represent merely an international situation or an international aspect of a particular situation.

The question of a "threat to peace" in connection with a civil war may, just as a question concerning aggression, also arise not with respect to a civil war as such, but to an external concomitant element, if there is such. Such an external element relating to relations between States may be, for example, interference of a foreign State in a civil war or the behavior of the State itself in which the civil war occurs.

It is evident that no actions of Korea represented a threat to peace.

In connection with the civil war in Korea one may speak about a threat to peace only with respect to actions of the United States before the commencement of open armed intervention; the last represented a breach of the peace.

4. In order to drag out the illegal resolutions with regard to the Korea question essential to cover the American armed intervention in Korea the Anglo-American bloc proceeded to violate major provisions of the United Nations Charter concerning the procedure for the adoption of Security Council decisions, namely:

(a) established for the adoption by the Security Council of decisions by a qualified majority of votes;

(b) the principle of unanimity of the great powers in the Security Council.

The dissertation considers the question concerning the representation of China in the United Nations since both the first and the second violation of the Charter affects this question.

The question of the representation of China in the United Nations belongs to the group of those questions in which international lawlessness is most clear, being created by the ruling circles of the United States when effectuating their aggressive policies.

It is considered to be generally-recognized in international law that in the event of changes in a State which happened as a result of the operation of internal forces a government is the representative of a State in international relations which de facto effectuates power on the territory of a State.

The Central People's Government of the Chinese People's Republic received powers from the people and effectuates power on the territory of China, being the actual government of China. The Government of the Chinese People's Republic is the sole legal government of China having the right to represent China in international relations and only representatives appointed by this government may represent China in United Nations organs.

Since the vote of the Kuomintang representative is by virtue of the above reasons invalid, only six valid votes were cast for the resolution on the Korea question from 27 June to 7 July 1950. This means that the said resolutions did not receive the necessary number of votes for the adoption of decisions by the Security Council.

5. The adoption by the Security Council of resolutions on the Korea question in the absence of a representative of the USSR, and also the legal representative of China, was a violation of the principle of unanimity of the great powers in the Security Council, which is the foundation of the United Nations.

The work reveals the complete bankruptcy of the thesis advanced by the Department of State that the absence of a permanent member at Security Council sessions is analogous to the abstention of a permanent member when voting and therefore cannot be regarded as a veto.

In analyzing the practice of the use of abstention of permanent members in the Security Council and the character of rules established on this question, the author concludes that there are no grounds to legally equate the absence of a permanent member at a session of the Security Council to the abstention thereof during voting. Without the consent of a permanent member the absence thereof may not be regarded as the equivalent of an abstention.

In this event two permanent members of the Security Council – the Soviet Union and the Chinese People's Republic – declared that their absence cannot be construed as an abstention and objected to the decisions adopted by the Security Council.

The lack of substantiation also is shown in the work for the other thesis advanced by the Department of State, according to which the absence of a permanent member of the Security Council supposedly has not significance for the adoption of decisions by the Council.

Thus, the illegality of resolutions of the Security Council on the Korea question of 25 and 27 June and 7 July 1950 arises from the following basic propositions:

(1) these resolutions are based on the application to the civil war in Korea of the concept of aggression, which is contrary to the principles of contemporary international law;

(2) during the voting on the said resolutions the representatives of two permanent members of the Security Council were absent, which by virtue of the principle of unanimity of the permanent members deprived the Council of the right to adopt decisions on nonprocedural questions;

(3) six votes were cast for the resolution of 27 June and 7 July 1950 since the seventh vote – the vote of the Kuomintang representative, not having the right to represent China, was invalid, whereas not less than seven votes are necessary to adopt decisions;

(4) being a cover for American aggression in Korea, the said resolutions were contrary in their purpose to the United Nations Charter;

(5) deprived of its "international-legal" cover, the action of the United States in Korea was ordinary armed intervention of one State into a civil war occurring on the territory of another State.

The work analyzes the question of noninterference in a civil war and is a completely bankrupt attempt of bourgeois international lawyers to use international law in order to legalize armed intervention (Strupp, Sibert, Kelsen, Potter).

In accordance with the principle of noninterference it is essential, in the author's view, to proceed from the fact that armed intervention is inadmissible also when it is effectuated at the request of one of the combatant parties. Allowing the legality of armed intervention in a civil war at the request of one of the combatant parties would completely undermine the significance of the principle of noninterference with respect to a civil war.

But armed intervention of one State in a civil war occurring in another State is not simply interference in internal affairs. This is a special type of interference – interference with the use of armed force; this is armed aggression.

The actions of the United States in Korea have all the indicia of armed aggression. These actions were undertaken by the United States against the Korean People's Democratic Republic, although the last did not attack the United States and in general attacked no one. Thus, here one can not speak of the use by the United States of America of the right to self-defense in accordance with Article 51 of the United Nations Charter (Frankenstein).

Consequently, the armed intervention of the United States in Korea was aggression, an aggressive war, which is the gravest crime under contemporary international law.

Chapter X

Violation of the Laws and Customs of War by United States Armed Forces in Korea

1. The heroic resistance of the Korean people defending the freedom and independence of their motherland destroyed the plan for an easy victory on which the interveners had counted.

Enraged by the stubborn resistance and endeavoring to break the will of the Korean people to resist, the American aggressors passed on to more cruel means and methods of waging war, not taking norms of international law into account.

The evil deeds of the American interveners in Korea are a clear manifestation of the trends of imperialism in the domain of the laws and customs of war.

War is a continuation of the policy of the ruling classes by means of force. The aspiration of the bourgeoisie in the period of imperialism "to rescue it from the legality created by it and which has become unbearable for it",[3] both within the country and in the international arena, is expressed in the domain of waging war by flagrant violations of the laws and customs of war.

Flouting the rules for waging war acquires gigantic dimensions in aggressive wars of imperialism. In this is found the link between the character of war and means and methods of waging it. The aggressive, predatory character of war is predetermined by the violation by a party waging such a war of the laws and customs of war, as Professor P. S. Romashkin has correctly noted.

Clear affirmation of this proposition is the crimes of the German fascists and Japanese militarists during the Second World War and the barbaric actions of the American interveners in Korea.

A reflection of these trends in the bourgeois theory of international law is the attempts to justify the violation by

[3] Lenin, Сочинения [Works], XVI, p. 284.

imperialist States of the laws and customs of war b means of advancing the fascist theory of "total war" into a norm of international law.

In the author's view, the attempts at an international legal legalization of total war are being undertaken at present along three orientations:

(a) denial of the distinction between combatants and noncombatants;

(b) denial of the distinction between military and nonmilitary objects;

(c) propaganda of the doctrine of free choice of the means and methods of waging war.

These cannibalistic conceptions, which find no confirmation in contemporary international law, are unmasked in the work.

During the postwar period the mighty camp of democratic States headed by the Soviet Union and the powerful movement of proponents of peace – all the forces of fighters for peace against a new war – favor at the same time the humanization of war, in particular, the prohibition of atomic weapons and other means of the mass destruction of people and oppose the inhumane theories of "total war".

Under the influence of these forces the charters of the Nuremberg and Tokyo tribunals once more confirmed the significance of norms of international law concerning the waging of war, declaring the violation thereof to be criminal, and the 1949 Geneva Conventions on the protection of victims of war have made a further, although insufficiently decisive, step along the path of the humanization of the rules for the waging of war.

2. Waging in Korea a war that is unjust, predatory, having the purpose to enslave the Korean people and transformation of the territory of Korea into a platform for the further aggression of the United States, the American imperialists cynically are flouting the laws and customs of war.

The dissertation considers individual types of violations by the armed forces of the United States of the laws and customs of war: barbaric bombings of peaceful cities and villages of Korea, violations of the immunity of sanitary formations, crimes on the occupied territory, the use of chemical and bacteriological weapons, and violations of the regime for a prisoner of war.

The barbaric actions of American interveners not only did not break the will of the Korean people to resist American aggression, but on the contrary reinforced and strengthened the resolve of the Korean people in the struggle for freedom and independence and more closely drawing the Korean people around the labor party – the organizer of the struggle of the Korean people against foreign invasion.

In waging war against foreign predators, the Korean People's Army and the Chinese people's volunteers strictly have complied with the laws and customs of war. This attitude of the Korean-Chinese side to the laws and customs of war was determined by the liberation purposes of the war which it waged and the peculiarities of the Korean-Chinese armed forces.

Chapter XI

United States Aggression Against China

1. The war in Korea was used by aggressive circles of the United States as an occasion for open aggression against China.

American imperialism actually having effectuated for a number of years camouflaged armed intervention in China, using the war in Korea, moved on to open acts of aggression against the Chinese People's Republic.

The first open act of aggression of the United States against China was the actions of the United States on Taiwan and the Taiwan Strait in June 1950, expressed in the de facto occupation of Taiwan and transformation thereof into an American military base.

The dissertation considers the international-legal status of Taiwan after the Second World War, the aggressive actions of the United States against China connected with Taiwan, and concludes that the aggression of the United States on Taiwan consisted of the following elements:

(a) intrusion of the armed forces of the United States into the islands of Taiwan, which are part of the territory of China;

(b) blockade of part of the coast of China by the armed forces of the United States so as not to permit the occupation of Taiwan by the armed forces of the legal Chinese government – the Government of the Chinese People's Republic. Blockade in the meaning of the United Nations Charter undertaken not on the basis of a decision of the Security Council and not on the basis of Article 51 of the Charter is an unlawful act and aggression. The Soviet definition of aggression relegates blockade to the group of acts of aggression;

(c) armed interference in the internal affairs of China in order to save the Kuomintang clique expelled by the Chinese people and inhabiting Taiwan.

In addition to the occupation of Taiwan, the United States systematically violated the air boundaries of the Chinese People's Republic in areas adjacent to Korea.

The United Nations under the pressure of the Anglo-American bloc refused to condemn the aggression of the United States against China and to take effective measures to terminate this aggression.

2. The dissertation shows the complete legal and moral unfoundedness of the accusation of aggression which was advanced by the Government of the United States against the Chinese People's Republic in connection with the participation of Chinese volunteers in the war in Korea.

Analyzing the General Assembly Resolution of 1 February 1951 relative to the declaration of the Chinese People's Republic as an aggressor and the question of the correlation of the competence of the Security Council and the General Assembly, the author concludes that this resolution was illegal for the following reasons:

(a) it was unsubstantiated in essence and contrary to international law since there were no grounds to declare the Chinese People's Republic an aggressor;

(b) the resolution established the existence of aggression and declared the People's Republic of China to be an aggressor, However, under the United Nations Charter only one organ of the United nations, namely the Security Council, is empowered to establish the existence of a threat to peace, breach of the peace, or act of aggression and determine which State is the aggressor;

(c) the resolution contained a recommendation concerning enforcement measures when according to the United Nations Charter the General Assembly is not empowered to make such recommendations. This obviously arises from an analysis of Articles 10, 11, and 12 of the United Nations Charter;

(d) being called upon to serve as camouflage and a means for the further aggressive actions of the United States against the Chinese People's Republic, this resolution was by its purpose in crying contradiction with the United Nations Charter.

These propositions relate entirely to the resolution of the General Assembly of 18 May 1951 in which all States are recommended to introduce an embargo on deliveries of arms and strategic materials to the Chinese People's Republic and the Korean People's Democratic Republic.

3. During the entire period of war in Korea and thereafter the United States did not cease its aggressive actions against the Chinese People's Republic. The work examines the violations of air boundaries of China by the American Air Force, the use of bacteriological weapons on the territory of north-eastern China, attempts of the United States to organize an economic boycott of the Chinese People's Republic, support of the Chiang Kai-Shek clique for the purpose of using it for new provocations against the Chinese People's Republic, and piratical actions of the Kuomintang banks of the coasts of China.

Aggressive acts of the American imperialists did not frighten the Chinese people. In reply to American provocations in China a powerful people's movement of struggle against American aggression unfolded to render assistance to China. The aggression of the American imperialists led to a closer solidarity of the Chinese people around the glorious Communist Party of China and the Central People's Government of the Chinese People's Republic.

Chapter XII

The Struggle of the USSR, Chinese People's Republic, Korean People's Democratic Republic, and Progressive Forces of the Entire World for the Prevention of War in Korea and Peaceful Settlement of the Korea Questions

1. As the armed intervention of the United States in Korea commenced, a broad movement in defense of the Korean people unfolded in all countries against the American aggression and for a peaceful settlement of the Korea problem. The end of the war in Korea, which concealed the threat of the most serious international complications, was regarded by peaceloving peoples as a major task in the struggle for peace.

The Soviet Union, whose interests are inseparable from the cause of peace throughout the world, consistently strove for the cessation of bloodshed in Korea and the peaceful settlement of the Korean question, repeatedly making peace proposals and supporting all proposals of other countries moving in this direction. The work analyzes the peace proposals made by the Soviet Union, Chinese People's Republic, and Korean People's Democratic Republic, and also the peace steps of certain Asian countries, in particular India, and unmasks the maneuvers of aggressive circles of the United States who aspired not to permit the adoption of any proposals which might facilitate the settlement of the Korean conflict.

Under the pressure of the forces of peace, the ruling circles of the United States, who did not seek to cease the war in Korea, were forced to sign an armistice agreement, although they dragged out the negotiations on this question for more than two years.

2. As the main pretext for dragging out the armistice negotiations the American delegation used the question of the repatriation of prisoners of war, advancing the principle of so-called voluntary repatriation. The work in this connection illuminates the question of the repatriation of prisoners of war in contemporary international law and draws the conclusion that the principle of repatriation of all prisoners of war fixed in international conventions, affirmed by State practice, and also by the doctrine of international law, is a principle of international law.

The principle advanced by the American side of "voluntary repatriation" of prisoners of war was therefore in contradiction with international law. In fact this principle is merely a chimera which should cover the effectuation of the American plan for the forcible detention of prisoners of war.

Thanks to the insistent struggle of all forces of the world, the aggressive circles of the United States did not succeed in breaking off the conclusion of an armistice and the United States was forced ultimately to sign the armistice agreement. The work analyzes the basic provisions of the Korean armistice agreement signed 27 July 1953. The author shows the peculiarities of this armistice arising chiefly from the peculiarities of the war in Korea which, being primarily an international war, at the same time contained elements of a civil war.

3. In connection with the armistice in Korea and the threat of a violation of this armistice by the American side, the question of the legal nature of the institution of armistice in contemporary international law acquires special actuality.

International legal doctrine treats the problem of armistice by proceeding from the IV Hague Convention on the Laws and Customs of Warfare. The author expresses disagreement with this treatment of the problem, pointing out that in the light of provisions of the United Nations Charter certain provisions of the said Hague Convention concerning armistice should be deemed to have lost force.

The conclusions of the author on this question come down to the following: under contemporary international law a general armistice does not "suspend", but "terminates" military actions; in this respect it is equivalent to a peace treaty. No, however "material" a violation of the armistice, except for the renewal of military actions, gives the other side the right to renew military actions. The side which first renews military actions commits an act of aggression.

Thus, if the American command renewed military actions in Korea, this would be a new act of aggression on the part of the United States. If the Syngman Rhee-ites, having violates the armistice agreement on Korea, renewed military actions, this would be an act of aggression committed by one party to the armistice agreement, for the actions of which the American command and the United States as a State of which this command is an agency would bear responsibility.

* * *

The conclusion of the armistice in Korea was an important event in international relations which facilitated a reduction of international tension. The armistice in Korea served as a point of departure for peaceloving forces of new conditions in the struggle for the peaceful resolution of unregulated international problems.

The Korea question continues to remain among such unresolved problems. Undoubtedly, the peaceful settlement of the Korea question would be a major contribution to the cause of lessening tension in international relations and strengthening peace and security in the Far East and throughout the entire world.

The agreement on the armistice in Korea is the first step along the path towards a peaceful settlement of the Korea problem, and the precise fulfillment by the parties of the conditions of the armistice agreement would facilitate the final settlement of the Korea question.

The Korean-Chinese side, displaying a sincere aspiration for peace, is strictly fulfilling the conditions of the armistice.

Seeking to create new obstacles on the path towards a peaceful settlement of the Korea question, the American side has flagrantly violated and is violating the armistice agreement, in particular, the provisions on prisoners of war, on not allowing the bringing in of reinforcements to Korea, the inviolability of the demilitarized zone and territory under the control of the other party, a political conference on the Korea question, and so on.

The question of convoking a political conference on Korea came to a standstill at the Berlin Conference of Ministers of Foreign Affairs of the Four Powers, where as a result of the efforts of the Soviet Union an agreement was reached to convoke in Geneva on 26 April 1954 a meeting for the peaceful settlement of the Korea question with the participation of representatives of the five great powers, the two parties fighting in Korea – the Korean People's Democratic Republic and South Korea, and also other States who took part in the military actions in Korea. The Chinese People's Republic for the first time took its legal place at the meeting with other great powers, which in and of itself has great international significance.

During the postwar period a struggle is proceeding on the Korea questions around two possible means of resolving this question. Countries of the camp of socialism and people's democracy headed by the Soviet Union and all peaceloving peoples favor a democratic means of resolving the Korea question on the basis of the principle of self-determination of nations in accordance with the centuries-old expectations of the Korean people and in the interests of strengthening peace and security. The forces of imperialism headed by the United States favor the imperialist path of resolving the Korea question – the path of new enslavement of the Korean people and subordination thereof to foreign dominance and the transformation of Korea into a camouflaged colony and platform for the effectuation of the predatory plans of aggressive States.

After the triumph of the people's revolution in China, which inflicted a crushing blow on the plans of American imperialism in Asia, the United States has attempted by military means to resolve the Korea issue, having unleashed with the assistance of the Syngman Rhee clique a civil war and having undertaken open armed intervention in China. Of course, this military adventure American imperialism pursued the purpose far exceeding the limits of the Korea question.

The American plan for an imperialist resolution of the Korea question by military means completely collapsed. The Korean people, having showed the greatest courage, steadfastness, and heroism, with the assistance of their Chinese friends repulsed the invasion of interventionists. The bankruptcy of the American plan for a "military resolution" of the Korea question was a new major defeat for American imperialism in Asia and once again demonstrated the bankruptcy of the policy "from a position of strength".

The plans for an imperialist resolution of the Korea question were doomed to fail. Under the contemporary correlation of forces in the international arena the democratic path towards resolving the Korea question is the sole real means of resolving this problem. Only this path corresponds to the hopes of the Korean people and the interests of ensuring peace and security in the Far East and throughout the entire world.

HIGHER PARTY SCHOOL
attached to the CENTRAL COMMITTEE OF THE
COMMUNIST PARTY
OF THE SOVIET UNION

Chair of State Law and
Soviet Construction

G. I. Tunkin
doctor of legal sciences

FUNDAMENTAL PRINCIPLES OF CONTEMPORARY INTERNATIONAL LAW

Instructional Manual

Moscow 1956

CONTENTS

Chapter One. **Concept of International Law and Sources Thereof**

1. Concept and Basic Peculiarities of International Law
2. Coexistence of Two Systems and International Law
3. International Law and Municipal Law
4. Sources of International Law

Chapter Two. **Subjects of International Law**

1. Concept and Types of Subjects of International Law
2. International Recognition of States and Governments
3. International Legal Responsibility of State

Chapter Three. **Basic International Legal Principles of Peaceful Coexistence of States**

1. Principle of Mutual Respect for Territorial Integrity and Sovereignty
2. Principle of Nonaggression
3. Principle of Noninterference in Internal Affairs of States
4. Principle of Equality and Mutual Advantage
5. Principle of Peaceful Coexistence and Economic Cooperation

Chapter Four. **International Organizations**

1. General Characteristics of Contemporary International Organizations
2. United Nations

3. International Regional Organizations for General Questions

A. Organization of American States (OAS) and League of Arab States

B. Creation by Imperialist States After Second World War of Military Blocs Under Name of Regional Organizations

C. Warsaw Treaty of 14 May 1955

4. Specialized Agencies of the United Nations and Other Specialized International Organizations

Chapter One

Concept of International Law and Sources Thereof

1. Concept and Types of Subjects of International Law

International law is the aggregate of norms created by means of agreement between States and regulating relations between them in the process of struggle and cooperation, expressing the will of the ruling classes of these States and ensured, when necessary, by coercion effectuated by States individually or collectively.

International public law is simply called – international law. Hereinafter we shall speak only about this law.[1]

This definition of international law encompasses the general features peculiar to any branch of law. For example, international law represents the aggregate of norms which regulate determined social relations, express the will of the ruling classes, and are ensured by State coercion. This definition notes also the basic peculiarities of international law concerning the subjects thereof, the creation of norms, the class essence thereof, and the forms of coercion in international law.

Natural persons, institutions, and organizations, and also the State itself, may be subjects of law – the participants of legal relations, the bearers of powers, and also of legal duties, in municipal (national) law. International organizations created by States are subjects of international law only within a rather limited domain. Natural persons are not subjects of international law at all.

The fact that international law regulates relations between sovereign States-participants in international relations is the basic peculiarity thereof. All other peculiarities of international law to some extent are linked with this chief peculiarity thereof.

[1] On the question of international private law, see S. B. Krylov and I. S. Pereterskii, Международное частное право [Private International Law] (1940); L. A. Lunts, Международное частное право [Private International Law] (1949).

States-subjects of international law act in international relations as independent formations over which there is no power capable of dictating norms of law; international law knows no legislative organ creating international legal norms. Therefore, the sole possible path of creating norms of international law is the path of agreement between States, which may be either clearly expressed (treaty) or tacit (international custom). It follows from this that norms of international law created as a result of agreement between States express not the will of the ruling class of one State, but the will of the ruling classes of different States. Formed in the process of struggle and cooperation of States, norms of international law are the result of the conflict and bringing of wills into concordance of the ruling classes of different States.

When creating norms of international law sovereign States act. The wills of the ruling classes of different States conflicting in the process of forming these norms are legally of equal significance, and therefore one may not speak about the will of the ruling class of one State being imposed on another State. But, of course, the true influence of these wills when forming norms of international law is not identical. It depends upon that role which a particular State plays in international relations, on the character of propositions which it advances, and so on.

Norms of international law, just as norms of any law, are ensured by coercion. However, coercion in international law has a different form than in municipal (national) law since in international relations there is no apparatus standing above States that has the power capable of compelling subjects of law to fulfill norms of law. As a consequence, coercion in international law is effectuated by the subjects of international law themselves – States acting individually or collectively. Although coercion in international law is not so effective as coercion in municipal law, it undoubtedly exists.

It is essential to strictly distinguish compulsory measures adopted by States individually or collectively and compulsory measures adopted by the United Nations.

The existence of a violation of international law in the first instance, by virtue of the peculiarities of international law, is established by the interested State itself or by several interested States. A State may autonomously, at its discretion, take in the event of a violation of international legal norms affecting the interests of that State, measures against the violator-State permitted by international law.

Before the First World War international law permitted in this event the use against a violator-State, besides other measures, also armed force. The victim State or the State considering itself to be such might resort to satisfying its claims by war against another State. In the period between the First and Second World Wars a prohibition stably entered international law against resort to war as a means of settling international disputes.

Measures permitted by international law which individual States may take against a State which has violated a norm of international law are rather diverse (limitation of trade, limitation of entry of citizens to their territory, limitation on ships putting into ports, recall of diplomatic representation, rupture of diplomatic relations, and so on), but they may not include the use or threat of force against the territorial integrity or political independence of the other State (Article 2(4), United Nations Charter).

Contemporary international law recognizes the right of States to individual or collective self-defense. According to Article 51 of the United Nations Charter, the provisions thereof do not affect the "inherent right of individual or collective self-defense if an armed attack occurs against a Member of the United Nations, until the Security Council has taken measures necessary to maintain international peace and security". This means that in the event of an armed attack against a State, the State may at its discretion take various measures against the attacking State up to and including the use of armed force.

It must be emphasized that the United Nations Charter, in authorizing the use of armed force by way of self-defense, at the same time limits the use of force by way of using the right to self-defense, precisely establishing that it may occur only in the event of an "armed attack".

This provision of the United Nations Charter is a significant step forward in comparison with the Covenant of the League of Nations (1919) and the Kellogg-Briand Pact (1928). As is well-known, neither the Covenant of the League of Nations nor the Kellogg-Briand Pact mentioned the right to self-defense. The Covenant of the League of Nations prohibited resort to war "as an instrument of national policy", saying nothing about the right of States to self-defense, although this right, naturally, was in mind. The absence of any definition of the framework for the use of force by way of exercising the right to self-defense was a loophole which an aggressor could use. Even the Hitlerites, having unleashed an aggressive war, referred in justification of their actions to self-defense, although not only did no one attack Germany, no one threatened her.

The United Nations Charter, being the principal document of contemporary international law, allows the use of force by way of the exercise of the right to self-defense only in the event of an armed attack and until the Security Council has taken necessary measures to maintain international peace and security.

As regards enforcement measures which might be undertaken by the United Nations, according to the United Nations Charter such measures may be effectuated by the United Nations not in all instances of a violation by a State of international law. In accordance with the character of the United Nations, which has the purpose of maintaining international peace and security, the Charter provides for the application of enforcement measures against a State only in the event of a threat to the peace, disturbance of the peace, or act of aggression. In these instances collective measures may be applied by decision of the Security Council adopted in accordance with the procedure specified in the Charter.

2. Coexistence of Two Systems and International Law

At the present time two opposed socio-economic systems exist which are developing according to different laws in different directions. After the Second World War socialism was transformed into a world system and, consequently, the coexistence is now occurring of two world social systems. The coexistence of the two social systems is a law of societal development for a determined historical period.

Is an international law possible which regulates relations between States of two such opposed social systems? This question is often raised in bourgeois international-legal literature, some jurists answering it negatively.[2]

The possibility of the existence of such a general international law determines the possibility of the peaceful coexistence of States of opposed social systems.

Since agreement between States lies at the basis of norms of international law, the possibility of agreement States of the two systems is a necessary condition of the existence of international law.

The peaceful coexistence of States with different socio-economic systems includes cooperation between them. Contemporary States are not isolated from one another. Each State is situated in a system of States, it coexists with other States. Coexistence inevitably gives rise to various international problems for the resolution of which the cooperation of interested States is essential. If this cooperation is lacking, the problems arising will lead to a sharpening of the contradictions between States, which is fraught with the danger of war. But cooperation between States of the two opposed social systems presupposes a determined degree of the possibility of agreement between them, that is, that which is essential for the existence of international law. Therefore, the possibility of

[2] See, for example, G. Leibholz, "Zur gegenwärtige Lage des Völkerrechts", *Archiv des Völkerrechts*, I (1948-49), p. 421.

peaceful coexistence of States of two opposed systems also is the possibility of the existence of general international law.

Peaceful coexistence of States of the two systems – this is a bilateral process in which the conflict occurs of opposed social laws and social forces acting for and against peaceful coexistence.

On the part of the socialist States peaceful coexistence is stably secured. The aspiration for international peace is a law of societal development of the foreign policy of States of the socialist camp. The lack of private ownership of the instruments and means of production and replacement thereof with social ownership, the elimination of the exploitation of man by man, the transition of power into the hands of the working people creates a reliable basis for the peace policies of these States.

As regards the capitalist world, then, on one hand, under imperialism the economic foundation of wars is preserved and, on the other, imperialism itself gives rise to forces acting against imperialist wars and against imperialism in general. "So long as capitalism remains on earth, reactionary forces representing the interests of capitalist monopolies will continue to aspire to military adventures and aggression and may attempt to unleash war".[3]

However, in contemporary conditions the fatal inevitability of war does not exist since there are powerful objective and subjective factors operating in the direction of peaceful coexistence.

Among such factors are relegated the danger of a new war for capitalism since a new world war, if it were unleashed, inevitably would lead to the perishing of the capitalist system.

The necessity for peaceful coexistence is dictated, moreover, by the development of productive forces of society. At the contemporary level of development of productive forces

[3] N. S. Khrushchev, Отчетный доклад Центрального Комитета КПСС XX съезду партии [Report of the Central Committee of the Communist Party of the Soviet Union to the XX Congress of the Party] (1956), p. 33.

no country can normally develop without economic and cultural links with other countries. The laying of international economic links is an objective economic necessity conditioned by the requirements of the development of production. But the development of economic links is the development of peaceful relations.

After the Second World War the single all-encompassing world market broke up, and two world markets were formed. However, this does not mean that economic links between States with different social systems can not successfully be developed. Experience shows that when there is a wish to cooperate and a renunciation of any kind of discriminatory measures these relations may successfully develop to the mutual advantage of the parties.

The growth of the forces of peace has especially great significance for ensuring peaceful coexistence of States of different social systems. The increase of the might of the camp of socialism, consistently implementing a policy of peace, and the emergence of an ever greater number of States who have thrown off the yoke of colonialism and oppose war, the powerful workers' movement in capitalist countries, and the mighty movement of advocates of peace – all these factors are operating in the direction of peaceful coexistence. Under contemporary conditions there are real possibilities for ensure a prolonged and stable peace.

Thus, the peaceful coexistence of States of two opposed systems is fully possible and the significance of real factors operating in the direction of ensuring peaceful coexistence in the years after the Second World War has significantly grown.

Generally-recognized principles and norms of contemporary international law developing under conditions of two different economic systems can not be socialist since agreement between socialist States and capitalist States is impossible on this basis. These principles and norms can not go further than the democratic purposes of regulating relations between

States in the interests of ensuring international peace and the development of relations on mutually-advantageous bases.

International law, just as any law, is an instrument of policy. The foreign policy of socialist States and the foreign policy of capitalist States differ sharply in their social essence, in their orientation. Nonetheless, both socialist and capitalist States use international law in the effectuation of their foreign policies to some extent.

What has been said does not mean that international law can be an instrument of any policy. Generally-recognized principles and norms of international law are in their essence democratic and may be used as an instrument of foreign policy of States only within those limits which are determined by the content of these norms.

3. International Law and Municipal Law

When considering the correlation of international law and municipal (national) law of States one must not, as is usually done, reduce the matter to the issue of the preferential force of norms of international law over norms of national law, or *vice versa*. The correct resolution of the problem of the correlation of international and national law may be given only by way of eliciting the real links between them in the process of forming norms of international law, on one hand, and in the process of applying norms of international and national law – on the other.

As already noted, norms of international law are formed in the process of the struggle and cooperation of States by means of clearly expressed or tacit agreement between them. In so doing each State participating in the formation or in a change of norms of international law exerts a certain influence, makes its contribution in the cause of the development of international law.

The foundations of foreign policy of a State and, consequently, its position with regard to major issues of international relations are determined ultimately by the economic system of a society, the basis thereof. The foreign policy of a State, just as its law, is a category of the superstructure, the general character of which is determined by the particular basis thereof.

In addition, a certain link exists between national law and the foreign policy of a particular State. The law of each State contains provisions concerning foreign policy. Of course, law also in the domain of foreign policy acts as an instrument of policy, legislatively consolidating at the same time the foundations thereof.

The link between national law and foreign policy of a State is manifest not only in the aforesaid propositions. The legal system of a State as a whole exerts an influence on foreign policy. As regards the creation of new or a change of prevailing norms of international law, then naturally the principles of the policy of each State proceeds in these questions above all from the foundations of its national law. Since norms of international law are created and change as a result of agreement between States, each State acting from its legal positions, national law exerts influence on the development of international law. This influence is basic. States create international law, and not *vice versa*.

In the domain of international law, just as everywhere in life, the struggle of the new against the old is occurring. The forces standing for the strengthening and development of democratic principles of international law are struggling against all that is obsolete and is holding back social development, against all that is reactionary, young and old, and they grow day to day. Among such forces are States of the growing and strengthening world socialist system, consistently supporting democratic principles of international law and striving for the introduction of new progressive principles in international law. Among these are many other States who favor the strengthening of peace and compliance with the basic principles of international law, all the forces struggling for peaceful coexistence of States irrespective of their social system. Under these conditions the impact can not fail to intensify on international law of the progressive systems of national law whose principles reflect the legal consciousness of peoples.

The second aspect of the problem of the correlation of international and municipal (national law) comprises the legal correlation of the norms of these systems of law. In Soviet literature the opinion is expressed that generally-recognized norms of international law are simultaneously also norms of municipal law.[4] One can not agree with this view because it inevitably leads to one of two identically incorrect conclusions: either there is in the system of Soviet law supposedly a "branch" of law consisting of norms which are not socialist; or that generally-recognized norms of contemporary international law are socialist.

International law – is the aggregate of legal norms binding upon States; it fixes the rights and duties of States as sovereign subjects of international relations. Norms of international law must be complied with by States irrespective of whether these norms are an integral part of national law of a particular State or not.

A State must ensure the fulfillment of its obligations under international law by means convenient above all for the particular State. If in order to fulfill international obligations it is required to implement respective legislative measures, they should be effectuated; such measures are implemented, of course, by taking into account the peculiarities of the social and State system of each State. This situation is especially important under conditions of the coexistence of States of the two opposed social systems. Therefore, international law does not and can not contain generally-recognized norms binding State automatically to include norms of international law within their national law.

A specific State may establish that generally-recognized norms of international law are also internal norms of law thereof, but it may also proceed from the fact that norms of international law become prevailing law in a particular country

[4] See E. A. Korovin, «Некоторые основные вопросы современной теории международного права» [Certain Basic Questions of the Contemporary Theory of International Law], Советское государство и право [Soviet State and Law], no. 6 (1954), p. 35.

by virtue of a special legislative act in each individual instance. Whereas in either instance the fulfillment of obligations of a particular State is ensured, no one may assert that the State violated norms of international law. The practice of States proceeds from this position. The constitutions of some States adhere to the first of the said two systems, establishing that generally-recognized norms of international law are by virtue of this also norms of internal law, whereas other States adheres to the second system.

In the event of an inconsistency between norms of municipal law and norms of international law (or conflict between them) the State must fulfill its international obligations, for reference to internal legislation can not relieve it from the fulfillment of these obligations. Difficulties in the domain of the failure of norms of national law and norms of international law to conform and the elimination of the consequences thereof are resolved by way of the internal competence of each State. The requirement of international law is that irrespective of which way out is found, the obligations of a State under international law must be fulfilled.

4. Sources of International Law

The question of sources of international law, that is, the forms in which norms of international law are identified or fixed, has not only theoretical but also great practical significance. For those who study international law, and especially those who encounter this in practice, it is vital to know where, in what documents, one should seek norms of international law, to what extent one may refer to an international treaty, an international custom, a resolution of the United Nations and other international agencies, to awards of international arbitral tribunals and decisions of courts, national legislation of States, and decisions of national courts and the utterances of specialists on international law.

The peculiarities of international law find their reflection also in the system of sources thereof. Since norms of international law are created in the struggle and cooperation of States, as a result of clearly expressed or tacit agreement between them, it is evident that sources of international law will be those forms in which this agreement is fixed, in which the bringing of wills of the ruling classes of different States into concordance finds its expression and the recognition of such agreement as a legal norm.

Hence follows the conclusion that there are two basic sources of international law (on auxiliary sources, see below): international treaty and international custom.

An international treaty is an agreement between two or more States relative to their mutual rights and duties. Treaties to be concluded by international organizations between themselves and with States also are considered to be international treaties, although these treaties differ materially from treaties between States.

According to a view generally-recognized in Soviet international legal literature, an international treaty concluded on the basis of voluntariness and not contrary to generally-recognized principles of international law is the chief source of international law.[5] A treaty represents a clearly expressed agreement between States in which the result of bringing the wills of States into concordance of the ruling classes of different States is fixed definitely and in the overwhelming majority of instances in written form. Since agreement underlies the binding force of norms of international law for sovereign States, the precise fixation or consolidation of the moment of agreement has great significance for establishing the fact of recognizing a particular provision as a norm of international law. An international treaty precisely fixed and consolidated the achieved bringing of wills into concordance – agreement.

In addition, by their weight treaty norms occupy in contemporary international law the chief and ever more

[5] See V. N. Durdenevskii and S. B. Krylov (eds.), *Международное право* [International Law] (1947), p. 21; E. A. Korovin (ed.), *Международное право* [International Law] (1951), p. 16; F. I. Kozhevnikov, *Советское государство и международное право* [The Soviet State and International Law] (1948), p. 220; V. I. Lisovskii, *Международное право* [International Law] (Kiev, 1955), p. 28.

important place in connection with the enormous increase in the number of international treaties with regard to political, economic, cultural, and other questions of relations between States.

Among all international treaties the United Nations Charter[6] occupies the most important place as the fundamental international treaty. The participants of this treaty are the majority of States, and the principles of the United Nations Charter are recognized now by all States. The United Nations Charter consolidates and develops existing and establishes new generally-recognized principles and norms of international law. This treaty stands higher than all international treaties. Any regional agreements (that is, agreements encompassing a group of States of a determined geographic region) must be compatible with the purposes and principles of the United Nations Charter (Article 52, United Nations Charter). According to Article 103 of the United Nations Charter, when obligations of a member of the United Nations under the Charter "prove to be in contradiction with the obligations thereof under any other international agreement, the obligations under the present Charter have preferential force".

International custom as a source of international law encompasses the principles and norms formed in international practice as a result of their extended application by States and recognition as a legal norm. Article 38 of the Statute of the International Court of Justice relegates to sources of international law "international custom as evidence of general practice recognized as a legal norm".

A peculiarity of a customary norm of international law is that the arising and practical application thereof precedes legal classification. Not every repetition creates a customary norm of law. Repeated actions may be consolidated in the form of norms of behavior or crystallized in the form of norms of international morality or international comity. Only recognition of "general practice" as a "legal norm" has decisive significance, is the

[6] See Chapter IV below on this organization.

completion of the process of the formation of a customary norm of international law.

Auxiliary sources of international law, unlike basic sources, although not a form in which an agreement between States relative to norms of international law is fixed, nonetheless represent an important moment in the process of forming such agreement or assist in establishing the fact of the existence of a particular norm of international law. Among such auxiliary sources of international law are: resolutions of international organizations, decisions of international courts, national legislation of States and decisions of national judicial instances, and utterances of specialists on international law.

Resolutions of international organizations, especially of the General Assembly and the Security Council adopted in accordance with the provisions of the United Nations Charter, play an important role in the process of forming new principles and norms of international law, and also in the process of confirming, consolidating, developing, and interpreting existing principles and norms. Resolutions of the General Assembly are not in and of themselves sources of international law since, according to the United Nations Charter, these resolutions with regard to various types of issues concerning relations between States can not go beyond recommendations. At the same time, resolutions for which States of different social systems have voted, including the Great Powers, undoubtedly possess great moral authority.

The Security Council may issue decisions binding upon members of the United Nations and in accordance with Article 25 of the United Nations Charter members of the Organization are obliged to comply with these decisions adopted in accordance with the Charter and to fulfill them. However, decisions of the Security Council by their character are acts concerning certain one-off instances; the Security Council can not create new norms of international law. However, decisions as precedents may have a certain international-legal significance.

Decisions of international courts (judicial precedents) play the role of a subsidiary means for the determination of the existence or absence of particular principles and norms of international law, and also the interpretation thereof (see Article 38, Statute of the International Court of Justice). Thus, for example, the International Court of Justice in its decision of 1949 in the case concerning the incident in the Strait of Corfu affirmed the principle of the sovereignty of the State over its territorial waters. On the contrary, in its decision in the Anglo-Norwegian dispute of 1951 the International Court of Justice favored the so-called ten-mile rule, according to which the waters of bays and gulfs may be considered internal waters of the coastal State only if the breadth of the entrance to these bays and gulfs does not exceed ten miles is not a generally-recognized norm of international law.

National legislation and decisions of national judicial instances of different States also may be an auxiliary means for the establishment of legal norms since in legislation just as in the decisions of authoritative judicial instances of States the position of a particular State may be expressed on particular issues of international law. As an example one may cite the provision of the 1935 Air Code of the USSR establishing that "full and exclusive sovereignty over the airspace of the USSR shall belong to the USSR" (Article 1, Air Code of the USSR), and also the United States "Air Commerce Act" of 1926 in which it was said that "The United States of America is hereby declared to possess and exercise complete and exclusive national sovereignty in the airspace above the United States ..." [sec. 6].[7]

The said provisions of national legislation of the Soviet Union and the United States show that both the Soviet Union and the United States recognize the principle of international law according to which the sovereignty of the State extends to airspace located above the land and water territories thereof.

Studies by specialists on international law (doctrine of international law) also may be a subsidiary source for

[7] H. G. Hotchkiss, *A Treatise on Aviation Law* (2d ed.; 1938), pp. 171, 180.

determining norms of international law, especially if the difficulty of contrasting and interpreting sources of international law is taken into account. Therefore references often are made in the official statements of States to well-known cours and monographs on international law.

As regards general principles of law, which are mentioned in Article 38 of the Statute of the International Court of Justice, according to the view in Soviet international-legal literature these general principles are not a special source of international law. But if these general principles are applied in international law, they find their recognition either in international treaties or in international customs.[8]

[8] See Korovin (ed.), Международное право [International Law] (1951), p. 17.

Chapter Two

Subjects of International Law

1. Concept and Types of Subjects of International Law

By virtue of the peculiarities of international law sovereign States – subjects of international-legal relations – are at the same time the creators of norms of international law; they effectuate in necessary instances coercion individually or collectively.

The chief characteristic feature of the basic subjects of international law – States – is their sovereignness. By State sovereignty is understood the supremacy inherent in a State over its territory and independence in international relations.

The essence of State sovereignty of a particular State is determined by the class character of this State; the sovereignty of a socialist State differs profoundly from the sovereignty of a capitalist State. However, this question relates to the internal affairs of a State and in no way concerns international law.

The question of the correlation of State sovereignty and international law is one of the most complex and important questions of the theory and practice of international law. A formal-dogmatic approach can not give the correct resolution of this issue. For example, one eminent bourgeois jurist who is a representative of the normativist school of law – Hans Kelsen – attempts to juxtapose State sovereignty with international law. Sovereignty, in Kelsen's view, "everywhere stands in the path" of the development of international law. So long as the sovereignty of States is recognized, international law, Kelsen asserts, can not escape from its "primitive state" in which it supposedly finds itself at the present time,[9] and even the recognition of international law itself as law would mean that States are not sovereign.[10]

[9] H. Kelsen, *Problem der Souveränität und die Theorie des Völkerrechts* (Berlin, 1928), p. 320.

[10] Kelsen, *Principles of International Law* (1952), pp. 108-110.

Proponents of such conceptions endeavor to approach international law through the standards of national law, forgetting that international law is a law of a special type.

Contemporary international law emanates from the fact of the existence of sovereign States as an objective law of societal development for our era. The sovereignty of a State exists not on the basis of international law; a State acts in international relations as a sovereign formation; its sovereignty is not the result of participation in international relations. On the contrary, the creation of norms of international law is the result of the actions of sovereign States.

The international aspect of the sovereignty of a State, expressed in its independence in international relations, just as supremacy within, does not mean an unlimited freedom of actions, as certain opponents of State sovereignty attempt to demonstrate, representing it in the form of some sort of "absolute sovereignty". In addition to the fact that the actions of the State in international relations have been determined by the entire aggregate of internal and external circumstances, the freedom of action of the State in international relations also has legal limitations. When we speak about the sovereignty of the State in the international aspect, we understand by this not some sort of "absolute sovereignty" or "unlimited freedom of action". The sovereignty of the State in international relations is an independence of the State that really exists and is not unlimited.

International law protects the sovereignty of States. The basic principles of contemporary international law are principles of respect for State sovereignty, nonaggression, noninterference, equality, and so on. These principles, being the foundation of international legality, have important significance for the protection of the sovereignty of States.

One major principle of contemporary international law is the principle of self-determination of nations. As is well-known, the birth of this principle is relegated to the period of bourgeois revolutions. Under the banner of the "principle of nationality" the bourgeoisie, seeing to establish their dominance, struggled in the nineteenth century for the creation of autonomous national States. But even on the European scale this principle was not generally-recognized.

The Soviet State, having effectuated the principle of self-determination of nations in its internal State construction, also advanced it as a major principle of international relations directed against any sort of national oppression, including the right of nations to self-determination up to and including separation and the formation of an autonomous State and in equal measure applicable to all peoples, and not only to "civilized", as previously.

Supported by peoples, the principle of self-determination of nations (or the principle of self-determination of peoples) was consolidated in the United Nations Charter (Articles 1, 55, and 76, United Nations Charter), affirmed in a number of General Assembly Resolutions (in particular, in General Assembly resolutions of 5 February 1952 and 16 December 1952) and at present may be considered to be a generally-recognized principle of international law.

In the resolution of 16 December 1952 the General Assembly recommended that all States "uphold the principle of self-determination of all peoples and nations" and that they "recognize and promote the realization of the right of self-determination of the peoples of Non-Self-Governing and Trust Territories".

From the principle of self-determination of nations it logically follows that the sovereignty of a State at present can not be based on suppression of the right to self-determination, but must be based on respect for this right, for the realization thereof.

The principle of self-determination of nations does not pre-decide the international legal status of a particular nation. A nation has the right to freely combine with another nation(s), and in this event depending on the character of the association the respective national formation will or will not act in international relations as a subject of international law (in the USSR the union republics act as subjects of international law, whereas the autonomous republics and other national formations do not act autonomously in international relations). A nation may also choose the path of creating its own separate State which, of course, will act in international relations as a subject of international law.

Thus, the creation of a State formation which is a subject of international law must depend upon the free decision of the nation itself. The resistance of a colonial power to the effectuation of the aspirations of the people of a colonial or dependent country for independence is a violation of international law. Therefore, a nation struggling for independence and the creation of its own State should be considered to be a subject of international law, although it as a consequence of the resistance of the colonizers could not yet form an autonomous State and is merely on the path to the creation thereof.[11] However, in this event not the nation as such but the incipient State whose formation in violation of international law is caused obstacles are regarded as the subject of international law.

International organizations act in the international arena. In this event we have in view inter-State organizations and do not touch upon the issue of numerous international nongovernmental organizations. Inter-State (or intergovernmental) organizations, which we hereinafter will call simply international organizations, are created on the basis of treaties between States. The sphere of operation of an international organization and the functions and powers thereof are determined by an international treaty, in accordance with which such organization is created.

Generally-recognized norms do not exist which would determine the legal status of all international organizations. Whereas in conformity with generally-recognized norms each

[11] S. B. Krylov, in Korovin (ed.), Международное право [International Law] (1951), p. 158; F. I. Kozhevnikov, Учебное пособие по международному публичному праву [Instructional Manual of Public International Law] (1947), p. 52.

State is a subject of international law, with respect to international organizations, although they also act in international relations, there is no such generally-recognized norm.

However, international law does not contain norms obstructing the endowing of a particular international organization with certain features of international legal personality. The extent of such legal personality is determined with respect to each international organization by that international treaty on the basis of which it is created. Of course, in and of itself one may speak about the legal personality only of those international organizations whose purposes and activity are compatible with the purposes and principles of the United Nations Charter.

Many international organizations have been endowed in accordance with treaties on the basis of which they were created with certain features of international legal personality, in particular, the right to maintain relations with other international organizations and States and to conclude agreements with them. For example, the United Nations[12] in the person of the Security Council is empowered by the United Nations Charter to conclude agreements with individual States or groups of States who are members of the Organization relating to placing at the disposition of the Security Council, at the request thereof, armed forces, assistance, and facilities (Article 43, United Nations Charter). The United Nations may conclude agreements with various intergovernmental international organizations engaging in special questions relative to conditions on which these organizations are brought into relationship with the United Nations (Articles 57 and 63, United Nations Charter). The United Nations in the person of the Economic and Social Council may conclude agreements with members of the Organization and with specialized agencies relative to receiving reports from them on the steps taken to give effect to recommendations of the Economic and Social Council and recommendations of the General Assembly on questions within the competence of ECOSOC (Article 64,

[12] See Chapter IV below.

United Nations Charter). The United Nations in accordance with the Charter shall effectuate relations both with individual States and with international organizations. Representations of States exist attached thereto. The United Nations shall enjoy in the territory of each Member of the Organization the privileges and immunities as necessary in order to attain the purposes of the Organization (Article 105, United Nations Charter).

Undoubtedly, thus, the United Nations possesses certain features of international legal personality. Certain other international organizations possess the features of legal personality to a lesser degree, for example: UNESCO, International Labor Organization (ILO), World Health Organization (WHO), and others.

The general participation of States in a particular international organization possessing legal personality or the recognition of the legal personality of such an organization not only by the members thereof but also by other States, make such an international organization a generally-recognized subject of international law. One may consider, for example, the United Nations, Universal Postal Union, International Telecommunications Union, and a number of other organizations with universal or near universal membership to be generally-recognized subjects of international law within the framework determined by treaties and conventions relative to the creation of such organizations.

The recognition of international legal personality for particular international organizations does not mean that these organizations thereby are equated to the principal subjects of international law – States. In any legal system there are various subjects of law. This also happens in municipal law, where together with natural persons we see other subjects of law. We observe in international law, where together with the basic, chief subjects of law – States – there are other subjects of law – international organizations materially different from States as subjects of international law.

The international legal personality of international organizations in those instances when it exists is confined to a very narrow domain of relations determined by the Charter or other international agreement concerning the creation of a particular international organization. International organizations do not possess sovereignty and territorial supremacy and do not have their own population.

This is sufficient to conclude that the efforts to placed international organizations and States into a single block as subjects of international law are unfounded. International law remains an inter-State law since agreement between States, whose relations it is called upon to regulate, underlies it.

The Soviet science of international law is unanimous in acknowledging that individuals are not subjects of international law.[13] The legal status of individuals is determined by municipal, and not by international, law.

The majority of contemporary major specialists on international law also adhere to the view that despite certain exceptions the legal status of individuals as a whole is determined by the internal law of States and thus individuals are not subjects of international law. Professor Verdross, of the Law Faculty of the University of Vienna, wrote: "According to the prevailing view, individuals in principle are not subjects of international law ...".[14]

However, there is a conception rather widespread in contemporary bourgeois international-legal literature that individuals are subjects of international law together with States.[15]

[13] See Durdenevskii and Krylov (eds.), Международное право [International Law] (1947), pp. 109-110; Korovin (ed.), Международное право [International Law] (1951), p. 157; L. A. Modzhorian, О субъекте международного права [On the Subject of International Law] (1948), pp. 5-7.

[14] A. Verdross, *Völkerrecht* (Vienna, 1955), p. 112; also see Ch. Rousseau, *Droit international public* (Paris, 1953), p. 215; C. de Visscher, "Les tendances internationals des constitutions modernes", *Recueil des cours*, LXXX (1952), 559-560; L. Cavaré, *Le droit international public positif* (Paris, 1951), I, p. 6; Ch. Hyde, Международное право [International Law], transl. from English (1950), I, pp. 87-90.

[15] C. Fenwick, *International Law* (1948), p. 134; M. Sibert, *Traité de droit international*

These conceptions are based on an incorrect interpretation of the United Nations Charter and other international agreements.

Conceptions of international legal personality of individuals are theoretically unfounded and politically dangerous. These conceptions are objectively directed against State sovereignty and are used by aggressive circles in order to justify interference in the internal affairs of other States.

2. International Recognition of States and Governments

Recognition of State. The question of the recognition of the State arises when a new State emerges.

Recognition of a new State on the part of existing States consists of the fact that the last declares or otherwise shows that it considers the new State formation to be a sovereign State, a full-fledged participant of international relations.

On the question of the significance of recognition in bourgeois international-legal literature there are two principal theories: declarative and constitutive.

According to the declarative theory (Anzilotti, Bustamante, Verdross, Sibert, Lauterpacht, and others) a State becomes a subject of international law from the moment of emergence into the international arena as a sovereign State; recognition of the State is merely an announcement, a declaration, concerning the existence of this fact.

Proponents of the constitutive theory of recognition (Oppenheim, Kelsen, and others) assert, on the contrary, that a State becomes a subject of international law only by virtue of its recognition by existing States and that, thus, recognition creates (constitutes) a subject of international law. According to the constitutive theory, a newly arisen State is from the standpoint of international law supposedly non-existent so long as it is unrecognized by other States. The international community

---

public (Paris, 1951), I, p. 1; L. Oppenheim, *International Law,* ed. H. Lauterpacht (1955), I, p. 639.

is similar, thus, to a closed union of States, access to which is possible for new States only by special authorization.

The constitutive theory reflects at present the tendencies of reactionary groups who aspire to use the institution of international recognition against new States, especially against States which are formed as a result of the victory of a socialist revolution or victory of a national-liberation movement in various countries.

In accordance with the basic provisions of contemporary international law, each State is a subject of international law; it is becoming such by virtue of its sovereignty, which enables it to act in international relations as an autonomous entity capable of having international rights and fulfilling international obligations. It has been said above that international law does not make a State sovereign, but international law proceeds from the fact of the existence of sovereign States. A State becomes a subject of international law not as a result of any actions of other States, but as a result of the fact of the emergence thereof. This fact entails legal consequences – a State becomes a subject of international law.

International law recognizes for any sovereign State basic generally-recognized rights and duties such as the right to respect for territorial integrity and sovereignty and the duty corresponding thereto to refrain from a violation of territorial integrity and sovereignty of other States; the right to individual and collective self-defense; the right to effectuate international intercourse; in particular, to exchange diplomatic representations, conclude international treaties, be a participant in various international organizations. Such rights and duties are inherent in any State irrespective of by how many States it is recognized, that is, irrespective of recognition. The non-recognition by any State of a State newly arisen does not mean that it can not be considered to have the rights by a State which does not recognize it. Recognition of a State comes down to a statement that a new State has emerged and that it is a sovereign State.

This conception found reflection in a number of foreign policy actions of the Soviet State. For example, in a message of the Chairman of the USSR Council of Ministers, N. A. Bulganin, to the Prime Minster of Sudan on the occasion of the proclamation of the independence of Sudan it was said:

> "Being guided by the great principle of self-determination of peoples and respecting the just national aspirations of Sudan, the Soviet Government solemnly declares the recognition of Sudan by it as an independent and sovereign State and expresses readiness to establish with Sudan diplomatic, consular, and trade relations and to exchange diplomatic representations".[16]

However, taking into account the peculiarities of relations between States as sovereign formations, as a result of which there is no apparatus or instance in international relations which could render decisions biding upon subjects of international law relative to the personality of a new State formation, recognition of a State has legal significance together with political.

The political significance of recognition is completely obvious. Recognition is an important factor of the normalization of relations between States, which is a necessary condition of ensuring international peace and development of international cooperation.

But recognition also has legal significance, which consists, however, not in the fact that it constitutes a new subject of international law, but in the fact that it creates a stable normal legal foundation for relations between two States.

Recognition of a new State may be expressed in various forms, namely: in the form of an express statement (recognition by the Soviet Union of Sudan in 1956; Indonesia – in 1956; Israel – in 1948) or other actions which testify to recognition or include recognition. Thus, for example, the establishment of diplomatic relations with a new State undoubtedly includes the recognition

[16] Правда [Pravda], 4 January 1956. Also see relative to Tunisia and Morocco, Правда [Pravda], 16 June 1956.

thereof (established of diplomatic relations between the Soviet Union and the United States in 1933, between the Soviet Union and, respectively, the Korean People's Democratic Republic in 1948, Chinese People's Republic in 1949, and Federal Republic of Germany in 1955).

Recognition of Government. The question of the recognition of a government occurs when in a State there is a formation of a government as a result of a State coup d'état, or a change of the form of government; in other words – in instances of the formation of new governments not as a result of an ordinary, constitutional change of government.

When considering the question of recognition of a government it is necessary to have in view that the struggle of internal forces in a State and a change of governments which are the result of this struggle is relegated to the internal affairs of a State and not regulated by international law.

Moreover, since international law does not regulate internal struggle in a State, as a consequence of which a State coup d'état has occurred which changed the form of government and led to the arising of a new government, it considers to be the representative of the State in international relations that government which actually and autonomously exercises power on the territory of the State.

In these instances recognition of a new government is merely recognition of the fact that this government actually effectuates power on the territory of the State and that the events which occurred are the result of the operation of internal forces in a State. Unless other circumstances cause doubt, the question of recognition does not arise. Thus, for example, when in 1955 a new government was created in Argentina as a result of a State coup d'état which turned to foreign States with a request for recognition, the Soviet Government in a Note of the Embassy of the USSR in Argentina of 27 September 1955 addressed to the Ministry of Foreign Affairs and Cult of the Argentine Republic communicated that the Soviet Union, while regarding the political events which had happened in the Argentine Republic as the internal affair of Argentina, would continue existing diplomatic relations between the Argentine Republic and the Union of Soviet Socialist Republics.

In those instances when a State or States consider that the emergence of a new government was the result of interference of a foreign State the question arises of nonrecognition of the new government in accordance with the provision on nonrecognition of the consequences of unlawful actions of a foreign State expressed in interference in the internal affairs of another State.

Recognition de jure and de facto. Recognition *de jure* and *de facto* relate both to recognition of a State and to recognition of a government. Recognition *de jure* is final, complete, unreserved recognition of a State or government; recognition *de facto* is temporary, incomplete recognition.

Both recognition de jure and recognition de facto are legal recognition but if recognition *de jure* creates a normal legal foundation for relations of two States, recognition *de facto* has much less significance in this respect.

3. International Legal Responsibility of State

A violation by a State of its obligations under international law (international delict) entails international-legal responsibility.

States are primarily and chiefly the subjects of responsibility under international law. The responsibility of international organizations is not excluded, however; for example, in the event of the failure of an international organization to fulfill a treaty concluded by it with a State or with another international organization. In individual instances the responsibility of natural persons occurs. In contemporary international law the principle of individual responsibility is recognized (side by side with the responsibility of a State) for crimes against peace, war crimes, and crimes against humanity.[17]

[17] See the charters and judgments of the Nuremberg and Tokyo international military tribunals and the United Nations General Assembly Resolution of 11 December 1946 on confirmation of the principles of international law recognized

The responsibility of a State may arise as a result of unlawful actions of the State itself (for example, a violation by the authorities of the inviolability of a foreign diplomatic representative) or as a result of an unlawful failure to act, that is, the failure of a State to take measures which it should have effectuated in order to fulfill its obligations under international law (for example, the failure to take legislative measures necessary to fulfill an international treaty, a participant of which the particular State is).

Since the actions of a State in practice are reflected in the actions of its agencies, international-legal responsibility of a State arises from the actions of agencies of a State. Hence both the actions of agencies of State administration and the actions of legislative and judicial agencies are so relegated. If the legislative agency of the State issued a law violating obligations of this State under international law, or did not issue a law necessary for the fulfillment by this State of its obligations, the international-legal responsibility of the State arises.

International-legal responsibility also arises if an agency of State administration violates by its acts the obligations of a State under international law or does not take measures necessary in order to fulfill such obligations by the State. References to the fact that in a particular instance agencies of State administration acted in accordance with internal legislation of the State do not relieved the State from responsibility under international law.

Responsibility of a State may arise also from the actions of its judicial instances since the court also is an agency of the State.

A State does not bear responsibility for the actions of individual persons as such. However, in certain instances international-legal responsibility of the State may be linked with activity of private persons. For example, in the event of an attempt against a foreign ambassador international-legal responsibility arises for the State if necessary measures were not taken on the part of agencies of the State to protect this

---

by the Statute of the Nuremberg Tribunal.

diplomatic representative. The grounds of responsibility of the State are its failure to fulfill its obligations under international law.

Political and material responsibility are the chief forms of responsibility of the State under international law.

The political responsibility of a State varies within very broad limits – from moral satisfaction up to occupation of State territory, depending on the character of the delict and the damage inflicted. Thus, after the Second World War the political responsibility of Germany was expressed in the limitation of its sovereignty and occupation of territory. In accordance with the Declaration Regarding the Defeat of Germany and the Assumption of Supreme Authority by the Allied Powers of 5 June 1945 and other international agreements the allies took supreme authority into their hands in Germany and established the postwar occupation regime on its territory.

To the political form of responsibility one must also relegate so-called moral satisfaction since it also is expressed in certain actions of a political character. If, for example, a tactless offense with respect to a foreign diplomatic representative has occurred on the part of the authorities of a State violation a diplomatic privilege, then this State should express regret to the diplomatic representative through its Ministry of Foreign Affairs, and in more serious instances – take other measures, for example, punish the guilty officials.

Material responsibility may be expressed in restitution, that is, in the return in kind of particular articles or in compensation for damage caused (reparations). Thus, the peace treaties of 1947 with Italy, Finland, Hungary, Romania, and Bulgaria contain provisions concerning compensation (partial) of losses caused to the Allied Powers by military actions and occupation of their territory, and also provisions concerning restitution of ownership on the territory of all the said former allies of Germany which was taken out by the Axis powers from the territory of any of the members countries of the United Nations.

A State may bear simultaneously both political and material responsibility for a single violation. The combining of political and material responsibility we have, for example, in the 1947 peace treaties.

The procedural aspect of the establishment of international legal responsibility of a State has material peculiarities in comparison with that which we observe in municipal law. Since in international relations there is no judicial instance which might consider disputes between States and established the responsibility of a State independently of the consent of the disputing parties (the absence of a norm on compulsory jurisdiction), an important role in establishing the international-legal responsibility of a State, and also the forms and amounts of satisfaction, is played by negotiations between the interested parties.

The principle of peaceful settlement of disputes fixed in Article 2(3) of the United Nations Charter is a generally-recognized principle of international law. In accordance with this principle each State is obliged to use only peaceful means for the settlement of its international disputes.

Therefore, for the purpose of establishing the fact of unlawful actions and international-legal responsibility States may resort to any means of peaceful settlement of a dispute; for example, direct negotiations, creation of mixed commissions, or an arbitration tribunal, recourse to the International Court of Justice, and so on.

Chapter Three

Basic International Legal Principles of Peaceful Coexistence of States

Contemporary international law plays an important role in ensuring the peaceful coexistence of States. The basic international-legal principles of peaceful coexistence are in essence basic principles of international law, that is, its chief generally-recognized principles having especially great significance for the regulation of relations between States.

The five principles of peaceful coexistence which were formulated in the Joint Indian-Chinese Communiqué of 28 June 1954 are widely known, and then confirmed in a number of other international and national documents: mutual respect for territorial integrity and sovereignty, nonaggression, noninterference in internal affairs of one another, equality and mutual advantage, peaceful coexistence, and economic cooperation.

1. Principle of Mutual Respect for Territorial Integrity and Sovereignty

The principle of respect for the sovereignty of States is a major and generally-recognized principle of international law. In accordance with this principle States are obliged to respect the sovereignty of other States and the supreme power thereof irrespective of State and social system. This is a basic condition and expression of the peaceful coexistence of States of two opposed social systems.

The principle of respect for State sovereignty includes respect for the integrity of State territory.

A State possesses territorial supremacy, that is, effectuates supreme power on its territory. By the territory of a State is understood the part of the earth with its subsoil, waters, and also airspace over this part of the earthy and waters which are under the sovereignty of the particular State. Territorial supremacy is an inalienable part of State sovereignty; it includes the power of the State over territory and over people situated on this territory.

The principle of respect for territorial integrity and sovereignty has received reflection and consolidation in the United Nations Charter (in particular, Article 2(1) and (4), United Nations Charter).

This principle has important significance for the development of peaceful relations between States. The aspiration to seize another's territories and to retain illegally captured territories inevitably gives rise to conflicts between States fraught with the outbreak of war. The same consequences entail disrespect for State sovereignty. The aspiration of a particular State to subordinate another State to itself actually and juridically does not promote the strengthening of international peace and security. The colonial system, which rests on the suppression of sovereignty and seizure of another's territories, is a disgrace to contemporary mankind and incompatible with the principles of the United Nations.[18]

2. Principle of Nonaggression

The principle of nonaggression means in the most general form a prohibition against attack and, consequently, the obligation of a State to refrain from attacking other States.

International law, as is well-known, before the First World War recognized the so-called "right of a State to wage war", in accordance with which each State had the right at its discretion to resort to warfare in order to settle its disputes with other States.

The principle of the prohibition of aggressive war entered international law during the period between the First and Second World Wars.[19] The Soviet State was the first to officially raise this question, favoring the prohibition of

[18] See N. A. Bulganin, О поездке в Индию, Бирму и Афганистан [On the Trip to India, Burma, and Afghanistan] (1955), p. 30.

[19] For details, see K. A. Baginian, Агрессия – тягчайшее международное преступление [Aggression – Gravest International Crime] (1955).

aggressive war. In the Dekret on Peace which was adopted by the II All-Russian Congress of Soviets on 8 November 1917, the Soviet Government declared an aggressive, predatory war to be the "greatest crime against mankind".[20]

The opposition of the Soviet State to aggression and its policy of peace played an important role in establishing the international-legal prohibition of aggressive war.

The Covenant of the League of Nations did not contain a prohibition against aggressive war, but limited the right of States-members of the League of Nations to resort to war in order to settle international disputes. Only the 1928 Kellogg-Briand Pact, despite the imperfection of the content thereof, established a prohibition against aggressive war. Article 1 of this Pact provided: "The High Contracting Parties solemnly declare in the names of their respective peoples that they condemn recourse to war for the resolution of international controversies and renounce it as an instrument of national policy in their relations with one another".[21]

The principle of nonaggression was consolidated in the United Nations Charter and is now a generally-recognized principle of international law.

One cannot agree with the opinion of some bourgeois legal scholars that the prohibition of aggressive war so far is not a generally-recognized principle of international law since it has supposedly been established by local international treaties, to which the relegate the United Nations Charter. Nor can one agree that general international law supposedly at before considers war as one of the legal means of settling international disputes.[22] Such a conception theoretically is unfounded especially because the principles of international law fixed in

[20] СУ РСФСР (1917), no. 1, item 2.

[21] Сборник действующих договоров, соглашений и конвенций [Collection of Treaties, Agreements, and Conventions in Force], V, p. 6.

[22] See Kelsen, *Principles of International Law* (1952), p. 36; P. Guggenheim, *Traité de droit international public* (1954), II, p. 93.

the United Nations Charter are generally-recognized principles (see Chapter 1). From the political aspect the said conception is not directed towards strengthening the cause of peace and international cooperation but, on the contrary, unleashes the hands of a possible aggressor.

The content of the principle of nonaggression at present is determined by provisions of the United Nations Charter. The last prohibits the use in international relations of the "threat or use of force against the territorial integrity or political independence of any State, or in any other manner inconsistent with the Purposes of the United Nations" (Article 2(4), United Nations Charter). The armed aggression of England, France, and Israel against Egypt, sharply condemned by the majority of members of the United Nations, is a flagrant violation of the principle of nonaggression and the said Article of the United Nation Charter.

It must be emphasized that the United Nations Charter prohibits not only the use of force, but also the threat of force.

The Charter provides the possibility of the use of force in international relations by way of collective measures for the maintenance of international peace and security by decision of the Security Council legally adopted in accordance with the provisions of the United Nations Charter.

As regards the use of force by individual States against other States, the United Nations Charter (if we do not consider provisions of a temporary character contained in Articles 106, 107, and 53 concerning former enemy States in the Second World War) provides only one exception from the provisions relating to the prohibition of the use of force in international relations. This exception is fixed in Article 51 of the United Nations Charter, according to which States by virtue of the right to individual or collective self-defense in the event of an armed attack against a State, but only in this event, are not bound by the provisions on the prohibition of the use of force.

Thus, the principle of nonaggression, which includes the obligation of States not to attack other States, that is, not to use force first against other States, is one of the basic generally-recognized principles of contemporary international law.

The principle of nonaggression in indissolubly linked with the principle of respect for territorial integrity and sovereignty. An attack against a State is the most flagrant violation of sovereignty, and consequently the principle of respect for it. However, an attack does not only come down to a violation of sovereignty; such excessive juridicization would ignore the specific features of this most grave international violation.

The principle of nonaggression is directed towards the maintenance of international peace and applicable only to international relations.

3. Principle of Noninterference in Internal Affairs of States

The principle of noninterference means that no State may arbitrarily interfere in affairs within the internal competence of another State.

Recognition by States of this principle as an immutable principle of international law finds confirmation in numerous bilateral and multilateral international treaties.[23] This principle is consolidated in Article 2(7) of the United Nations Charter, which provides: "Nothing contained in the present Charter shall authorize the United Nations to intervene in matters which are essentially within the domestic jurisdiction of any State or shall require the Members to submit such matters to settlement under the present Charter; but this principle shall not prejudice the application to enforcement measures under Chapter VII". The said principle is generally-recognized; however, there is no uniform view as to what is included in the concept "matters which are essentially within the domestic jurisdiction of any State".

Undoubtedly, the concept of "domestic matters" or "matters which are essentially within the domestic jurisdiction", is a

[23] For details, see Baginian, Нарушение империалиситческими государствами принеципа невмешательства [Violation of Principle of Non-Interference by Imperialist States] (1954).

concept that changes with the development of international law. It encompasses all questions and actions of the internal life of a State, except those which have been placed by States under international-legal regulation.

The concept of "domestic matters" is not a territorial concept. The actions of a State on its territory also may be a violation of norms of international law (for example, a violation by the authorities of a State of the diplomatic immunity of a foreign diplomatic representative on the territory of the particular State); in this event to the extent such actions are a violation of norms of international law, they may not be regarded as within the internal affair of a State.

The formula "domestic matters" requires when applying it a consideration of the circumstances of the matter in each specific instance. However, the relative ambiguity of this formula does not shake the principle of noninterference in the internal affairs of a State by which, for example, questions of the social and State system of a particular State are without doubt.

The Soviet Union in its foreign policy steadfastly adheres to the principle of noninterference in internal affairs of other States. V. I. Lenin repeatedly laughed at the statements of bourgeois public figures with regard to the so-called export of revolution from the Soviet State and its interference in the internal affairs of capitalist States. "Of course", Lenin said, "there are people who think that a revolution may be born in another country by order, by agreement. These people either are mindless or provocateurs. We have survived two revolutions during the past twelve years. We know that they can not be made by order nor by agreement, that they grow when tens of millions of people come to the conclusion that they can no longer live so".[24]

The principle of noninterference has been consolidated in treaties of the USSR with foreign States. The foreign policy of the Soviet State is a shining example of respect for this major principle of contemporary international law. "We always have

[24] V. I. Lenin, Сочинения [Works], XXVII, p. 441.

affirmed and affirm", said the Report of the Central Committee of the Communist Party of the Soviet Union to the XX Party Congress, "that the establishment of a new social system in a particular country is the internal affair of the peoples of these countries".[25]

4. Principle of Equality and Mutual Advantage

The principle of equality, or equality of States, just as the principle of respect for State sovereignty, was advanced in the period of bourgeois revolutions in the struggle against feudal inequality and was confirmed as a generally-recognized principle of international law.

This principle found confirmation and consolidation in the Charter of the United Nations, in accordance with which States are obliged "to develop friendly relations among nations based on respect for the principle of equal rights and self-determination of peoples ..." (Article 1(2), Charter) and which establishes that the "Organization is based on the principle of the sovereign equality of all its Members" (Article 2(1), Charter).

The principle of equality means that States are equal with one another as sovereign, independent participants of international relations, as subjects of international law. This is legal equality. Economically and politically States are not, of course, equal in their role in international relations.

It follows from the principle of equality that relations between States should be built on the basis of recognition of that position that no State may attempt to dictate its will to other States. In relations with other States each State should regard its partners as equal subjects and seek to achieve a resolution of a particular issue by means of an arrangement. The policy of diktat, thus, is contrary to this principle.

As a result of the application of the principle of equality of States at international conferences each State has one vote. An

[25] N. S. Khrushchev, Отчетный доклад Центрального Комитета КПСС XX съезду партии [Report of Central Committee of Communist Party of the Soviet Union to the XX Congress of the Party] (1956), p. 32.

important consequence of the principle of the equality of States is that a State is not subject to the jurisdiction of the courts of another State (*par in parem non habet imperium* – an equal has not power over an equal).

The principle of equality, not permitting as already noted the use of diktat in international relations and obliging States to relate to their partners as to equal subjects of international relations, consequently means that relations between States should be built by taking into account the legal interests of each State, that is, on the basis of mutual advantage.

The Soviet Union, consistently adhering to the principle of equality in its relations with other States, always opposed and opposes the imperialist policy of diktat and the imposition by the capitalist State of cabalistic conditions on weaker partners. A clear example of this policy of the socialist State is: renunciation of unequal treaties imposed by Tsarist Russia on oriental States and the establishment with these States of relations on the basis of complete equality, support of dependent countries in their struggle for an equal place in international relations, and so on.

5. Principle of Peaceful Coexistence and Economic Cooperation

The principle of peaceful coexistence of States irrespective of their social system is among the major principles of contemporary international law.

Although the expression "peaceful coexistence" is not expressly used in the United Nations Charter, the principle of peaceful coexistence in essence underlies the United Nations. The Preamble of the United Nations Charter speaks about resolve "of future generations to avoid the calamities of war" and appeals to States to "display tolerance and to live with one another in peace as good neighbors". Article 1 of the Charter obliges States to "maintain international peace and security", to "develop friendly relations between nations", and so on.

The principle of peaceful coexistence is the most general principle of the five basic principles of international relations;

it embraces all the preceding four principles. However, in its content it is broader than the total of these four principles.

The principle of peaceful coexistence imposes on States the obligation to adhere in their relations with other States to peaceful means and methods, to develop peaceful relations with other States, to conduct that policy which would promote the peaceful coexistence of States, and not to permit actions which might prejudice or threaten peaceful relations between States.

The policy "from a position of strength", the arms race, the "cold war", and the policy bringing a State to the "edge of war" is contrary to the principle of peaceful coexistence since they lead to an exacerbation of international tension, intensification of mistrust between States, and thereby do not promote the strengthening of peaceful relations but, on the contrary, intensify the danger of the violation thereof.

Compliance with the principle of peaceful coexistence of States means a renunciation not only of the methods of the use of force against another State, a renunciation of war, but also a renunciation of a policy which may lead to war, the obligation to carry out a policy capable of strengthening international peace and security. The principle of peaceful coexistence is directed towards the maintenance and strengthening of peaceful relations between States under peaceful competition of the two systems in the economic, scientific, technical, cultural, and other domains of peaceful construction.

Peaceful coexistence does not mean the preservation of the existing position. Soviet people are convinced that the socialist system will triumph in peaceful competition with capitalism since the socialist means of production has decisive advantages over capitalism. Between the position of the inevitability of the triumph of communism throughout the entire world and the principle of peaceful coexistence, despite the assertions of bourgeois ideologues, there is no contradiction. The principle of peaceful coexistence has in view relations between States. It, just as all of international law, does not touch internal relations within States nor the revolutionary struggle for the restructuring of society.

The principle of peaceful coexistence does not mean compromise in ideological questions. One can never reconcile a capitalist and a socialist world outlook, nor does peaceful coexistence require this. Each may maintain his own positions on ideological issues, but should not serve as an obstacle to cooperation on economic questions, questions of the maintenance of international peace and security, and so on.

The development of economic cooperation between States, especially the development of trade, is an important basis of peaceful coexistence. "It is our firm opinion", said A. I. Mikoyan at the XX Congress of the Communist Party of the Soviet Union, that "*stable peaceful coexistence is inconceivable* without trade, being good for this as a base and after the formation of two world markets".[26]

The principle of peaceful coexistence is a basic principle of the foreign policy of the USSR. The "general line of foreign policy of the Soviet Union", it was said in a Resolution of the XX Congress of the Party with regard to the Report of the Central Committee of the Communist Party of the Soviet Union, "was and remains the Leninist principle of peaceful coexistence of "States with a different social system".[27]

The Soviet Union with unwavering energy is striving for a reduction of international tension and is taking practical measures to improve relations between States, to resolve by means of arrangements such major international problems as the problem of the reduction of armaments, prohibition of atomic and hydrogen weapons, problem of ensuring security in Europe, and others.

[26] A. I. Mikoyan, Речь на XX съезде КПСС [Speech at the XX Congress of the Communist Party of the Soviet Union] (1956), p. 17.

[27] Резолюция XX съезда Коммунистической партии Советского Союза [Resolution of XX Congress of the Communist Party of the Soviet Union] (1956), pp. 8-9.

The five principles considered above are thus major generally-recognized principles of contemporary international law. "These principles represent the best formula under present conditions for mutual relations of States with a different social system and may serve as the basis for stable peaceful relations between States of the entire planet".[28]

[28] Ibid., p. 7.

Chapter Four

International Organizations

1. General Characteristics of Contemporary International Organizations

Contemporary international organizations are exceedingly diverse with regard to objects of activity (questions of peace and security, economic questions, questions of culture, public health, railway, maritime, and air transport, and so on), by character of participants (intergovernmental and nongovernmental organizations), extent of powers, and so on.

It is necessary to distinguish intergovernmental and nongovernmental international organizations. By intergovernmental international organizations are understood international organizations whose participants are States; the participants of nongovernmental international organizations are social organizations of various countries (trade union, cooperative, scientific, sport, and so on), and also individual persons.

In this Chapter we speak of intergovernmental international organizations: the United Nations, regional organizations, specialized agencies of the United Nations, and other specialized international organizations.

What are the basic characteristic features of contemporary intergovernmental international organizations?

Above all, the participants of these international organizations are States – sovereign participants of international relations. International organizations are created on the basis of treaties between States. A treaty concerning the creation of an international organization, just as any international treaty, must satisfy those requirements which there are for international treaties in accordance with the United Nations Charter and other provisions of international law.

Contemporary international organizations are inter-State and not supranational. The participants of these organizations continue to remain sovereign States; limitations of sovereignty connected with membership in an international organization is, as a rule, insignificant. International organizations are organizations of international cooperation and the struggle of sovereign States, and not agencies of power over these States.

Undoubtedly, during the period after the First and especially after the Second World War a trend is evident towards expanding the powers of various international organizations. This relates both to international organizations with regard to general questions and to international organizations for special questions. Thus, the United Nations has significantly greater powers than the former League of Nations.

The enlargement of the powers of international organizations is a societal process. The expansion and intensification of international links which are the result of the growth of productive forces of contemporary society inevitably leads to an increase of the number of questions connected with relations between States in various domains. This finds reflection in international treaties and agreements, on the basis of which international organizations are created. However, the existence within many international organizations of a large number of States and the need to ensure the efficient resolution of issues leads to an expansion of the rights and powers of international organs in resolving these questions, to be sure, within the boundaries determined in each individual instance by the Statute of the organization. The expansion of functions of international organizations occurs, thus, both along the line of expanding the group of questions over which they have jurisdiction and the line of expanding the powers of international organs in resolving these issues.

The laws of societal development which condition the trend towards an expansion of the functions and powers of international organizations determine at the same time the boundaries of such expansion. These boundaries are placed above all and chiefly by the existence of two opposed systems, and also the contradictions within the capitalist system.

Under conditions of coexistence of two opposed world social systems the possibility is excluded of creating international organizations with the participation of States of both systems and with any significant supranational powers.

On the other hand, contradictions in the camp of capitalism are leading to attempts to create international organizations with extensive supranational powers, participation in which is limited only to capitalist countries, and these also do not enjoy success. Under conditions of sharp struggle for markets and sources of raw material such attempts, as the experience of history shows, always are linked with the aspiration of a particular large imperialist power or group of imperialist powers to use such an international organization for the purpose of ensuring its hegemony and subordinating weaker partners. The clearest example of such an attempt at founding a supranational organization with extensive powers is the effort to create the so-called European Defense Community. The Treaty on the Creation of the European Defense Community of 27 May 1952, the principal inspirers of which were the United States, having misrepresented the path of legalization of the renaissance of militarism in West Germany, provided for the transfer of armed forces of States-parties to the Treaty to the supranational command and deprivation of these States of important attributes of sovereignty. As is well-known, despite strong pressure on the part of the United States, the Treaty on the creation of the European Defense Community was not ratified by France and did not enter into force. Thus, as a result of contradictions between capitalist States this attempt to create an international organization with far-reaching supranational powers ended with collapse.

Many works have been published during recent decades in capitalist countries, the authors of which appeal for the creation of a world State, a world government. They attempt to prove that supposedly the renunciation by States of their sovereignty and the creation of an international organization with extensive supranational powers would be the best resolution of international problems, including problems of ensuring peace, and that without the creation of such a world State international law will "have an illusory existence, as a consequence of which the very notion of it as a system of law will be unstable and controversial".[29]

Plans for the creation of a world State or world government under contemporary conditions are unrealistic since they do not correspond to the laws of societal development in our era. These concepts are not only utopian, but also reactionary since, in diminishing the significance in international relations of the principles of respect for State sovereignty and noninterference in internal affairs, they facilitate the large imperialist powers in conducting a policy of diktat and interference in the internal affairs of other States.

Therefore, the inter-State and not the supranational character of international organizations is under contemporary conditions a reflection of objective laws of societal development and from the standpoint of the interests of strengthening international peace and security international organizations of the inter-State type represent the best form of international organization of our days.

2. United Nations

A universal international organization for the maintenance of international peace and security[30] was created in the flames of the great battle against fascism. The draft United Nations Charter was prepared at a conference of representatives of the three powers – the USSR, the United States, and Great Britain – at Dumbarton Oaks (August-October 1944). At the San Francisco Conference (April-June 1945) the United Nations Charter was finally worked out and signed by fifty States on 26 June 1945. The Charter entered into force on 24 October 1945.[31] From the

[29] L. Oppenheim, Международное право [International Law] (1948), I, p. 340; Oppenheim, *International Law*, ed. H. Lauterpacht (1955), I, p. 370.

[30] See «Московскую декларацию СССР, США и Великобритании от 30 октября 1944 года» [Moscow Declaration of the USSR, USA, and Great Britain of 30 October 1944], Внешняя политика Советского Союза [Foreign Policy of the Soviet Union], I, pp. 360-361.

[31] See on this question S. B. Krylov, Материалы к истории Организации Обьединенных Наций [Materials on the History of the United Nations] (1949).

time of the San Francisco Conference until 15 November 1956 the number of United Nations members has grown to 79 States.

The fact that the United Nations Charter was drafted during a period of liberation struggle, when millions of people with weapon in hand struggled against fascist aggressors, anticipating from governments the taking of effective measures for the prevention of wars in the future, and that the Soviet Union, steadfastly upholding progressive principles of international relations, took an active part in the preparation of the Charter and exerted enormous influence on the content of the United Nations Charter.

The United Nations Charter takes into account the lamentable experience of the League of Nations, which did nothing to prevent aggressors from effectuating their predatory plans. The contradictions between the great capitalist powers, and chiefly the aspiration of these powers to direct the aggressive aspirations of the aggressors against the first socialist State in the world, were the principal reasons for this situation. The severe experience of the Second World War, just as the experience of the League of Nations, convincingly showed that only the amity and unity of actions of the great powers in the cause of the maintenance of peace and in the struggle against possible aggression might make a new international organization a true instrument in ensuring peace.

As already pointed out, the United Nations Charter proceeds from the principle of peaceful coexistence of States irrespective of the social systems thereof.

The principal purpose of the United Nations is the maintenance of international peace and security and the development of friendly relations between States.

The United Nations is based on the principle of sovereign equality of States (Article 2[1]). Members of the United Nations are sovereign and equal States. The United Nations does not interfere in matters that are in essence within the domestic jurisdiction of any State (Article 2(7), United Nations Charter).

The United Nations Charter contains the obligation to peacefully settle international disputes (Article 2[3]). It prohibits the threat and use of force in international relations both against the territorial integrity or political independence of any State or in any other manner inconsistent with the Purposes of the United Nations (Article 2[4]).

All members of the United Nations should give every assistance in any action undertaken by it in accordance with the Charter and refrain from giving assistance to any State against which the United Nations is taking preventive or enforcement action (Article 2[5]).

The principal organs of the United Nations are the General Assembly, Security Council, Economic and Social Council, Trusteeship Council, International Court of Justice, and the Secretariat (Article 7).

General Assembly. The General Assembly consists of representatives of all members of the Organization. Regular sessions of the General Assembly are convoked once a year.

The General Assembly is empowered to discuss any questions within the competence of the United Nations and to adopt respective recommendations, except for instances when a particular question is on the agenda of the Security Council (Articles 10 and 12). But, being empowered to discuss any questions, the General Assembly should if with regard to any question it is necessary to undertake actions transfer this question to the Security Council before or after the discussion (Article 11). Therefore, the General Assembly can not, for example, adopt recommendations relative to the use of enforcement measures against a particular State.

Each member of the Organization has one vote in the General Assembly. Decisions of the Assembly with regard to important questions are adopted by a two-thirds majority of the members of the Assembly present and participating in the voting. Decisions with regard to other questions are adopted by a simple majority of votes (Article 18). Upon the recommendations of the Security Council (see below) the United Nations General Assembly admits new members to the United Nations and may exclude a member or suspend the effectuation of the rights thereof by a member.

The General Assembly has a number of auxiliary organs (committees, commissions, and so on). The United Nations Economic and Social Council and the Trusteeship Council work under the guidance of the General Assembly.

Security Council. The Security Council consists of 11 members of the Organization, 5 of which (China,[32] France, USSR, Great Britain, United States) are permanent members of the Council. Six other members of the Council are elected by the General Assembly for a two-year period, with renewal of one-third. Each member of the Security Council has one representative. The Security Council is a permanently operating organ.

The United Nations Charter places on the Security Council chief responsibility for the maintenance of international peace and security. The Security Council is the sole organ of the United Nations which may render decisions binding upon all members of the Organization. When performing its duties the Security Council acts on behalf of members of the United Nations, and members of the Organization, it says in Article 25 of the Charter, agree in accordance with the Charter to accept and carry out decisions of the Security Council. In so doing, to be sure, the Council must act in accordance with the provisions of the United Nations Charter (Article 24).

Since chief responsibility for the maintenance of international peace and security is placed on the Security Council, this organ establishes the existence of any threat to the peace, any disturbance of the peace or act of aggression. The Security Council also determines what measures should be taken to maintain or restore international peace and security (Article 39).

[32] In violation of the principles of the United Nations Charter and other principles of international law the Kuomintangites still act as the representative of China in the United Nations, although only the plenipotentiary representative of the Chinese People's Republic has the right to represent China in the United Nations.

Taking into account the special role of the Security Council in questions of maintenance of international peace and security, the United Nations Charter provides for the application of the principle of unanimity of the great powers when deciding important questions in the Security Council; decisions of the Security Council with regard to all matters except procedural are considered to be adopted only when the votes of seven members of the Council, including the concurring votes of all permanent members of the Council, have been cast for them (Article 27).

The said principle has exceptional significance for the activity of the United Nations, being in essence the foundation of this organization.[33] It is directed towards ensuring the coordination of the actions of the great powers in the maintenance of international peace and security, without which the actions of the international organization can not be effective. On the other hand, it has the purpose of preventing the possibility of converting the United Nations into the instrument of a particular group of States and more reliably ensures the rights and interests of all the great and small members of the United Nations.

The Security Council is a continuously operating organ. In addition to period sessions, the sessions of the Security Council are convoked at the discretion of the chairman thereof or at the request of any member of the Council.

A member of the United Nations which is not a member of the Security Council or a State which is not a member of the United Nations, if it is a party to a dispute under consideration by the Security Council, shall be invited to participate, without vote, in the discussion relating to the dispute (Article 32). In those instances when a United Nations member is not a party to a dispute but its interests are specially affected by the question which is brought before the Security Council, it has the right

[33] V. M. Molotov, Вопросы внешней политики [Questions of Foreign Policy] (1948), p. 259.

to participate without vote in the discussion of this question (Article 31).

The Security Council submits to annual reports to the General Assembly and, when necessary, special reports (Article 24[3]).

Economic and Social Council. Eighteen members of the Organization, elected by the General Assembly for three years with renewal of one-third comprise the Economic and Social Council. The Economic and Social Council is concerned with questions of international cooperation in the domain of the economy, society, culture, education, public health, and so on. It may effectuated necessary studies with regard to these questions and prepare recommendations, draft conventions, and so on. Decisions of the Council are adopted by a majority vote.

Trusteeship Council. The Trusteeship Council at present consists of 14 members. The total number of members of the Trusteeship Council is distributed equally between States administering and not administering trust territories (Article 86). The permanent members of the Security Council and trustee States must be on the Trusteeship Council; the other members are selected by the General Assembly for three years.

The Trusteeship Council acting under the direction of the General Assembly must observe over compliance by States which have a trusteeship over particular territories[34] with the principles of the international system of trusteeship. The Trusteeship Council may consider reports submitted by the administering authority (that is, the States having trust territories), accept petitions and examine them, arrange periodic visits to the trust territories, and so on (Article 87). Decisions of the Trusteeship Council are adopted by a majority vote.

[34] At present there are under trusteeship: Great Britain – Togo, Cameroon, Tanganyika; France – Togo, Cameroon; Australia – New Guinea; Belgium – Rwanda-Urundi; New Zealand – Western Samoa; Italy – Somalia; United States – Marshall Islands, Marianne and Carolina Islands (before the Second World War under the mandate of Japan); and under the joint trusteeship of Great Britain, Australia, and New Zealand – Nauru.

The activity of the Trusteeship Council is encountering serious obstacles on the part of colonial powers who strive to establish the usual colonial regime in trust territories and to use these territories for tests of nuclear weapons, and so on.

International Court of Justice. The International Court of Justice is the chief judicial organ of the United Nations. It acts in accordance with a special Statute which is an integral part of the United Nations Charter.[35]

All members of the United Nations are parties to the Statute of the International Court. States which are not members of the United Nations also may be parties to the Statute of the International Court on conditions which are determined in each individual instance by the General Assembly upon the recommendation of the Security Council. On 1 April 1956 in addition to members of the United Nations Switzerland, Liechtenstein, San Marino, and Japan were parties to the Statute of the International Court.

In accordance with the Statute of the International Court only States may be parties to cases heard under the Statute (Article 34, Statute of ICJ). The jurisdiction of the International Court of Justice is optional; for the International Court to accept a case for consideration the consent of all States which are parties to the dispute is necessary. This consent, however, with respect to determined categories of cases may be given by a State beforehand.

Besides judicial decisions the International Court may give advisory opinions on legal questions put by the General Assembly, any three members of the United Nations Security Council, and other organs and agencies authorized by the General Assembly.

[35] See for details N. N. Polianskii, Международный суд [International Court] (1953).

3. International Regional Organizations for General Questions

The existence of the United Nations does not obstruct the existence of regional (or local) organizations for general questions, including questions of international peace and security. However, the United Nations Charter contains certain requirements which such organizations must satisfy so as not to be used at odds with the purposes of the maintenance and strengthening of universal peace and security.[36]

In accordance with the United Nations Charter agreements on regional organizations and the activity of these organizations must be consistent with the Purposes and Principles of the United Nations (Article 52). Since the maintenance of international peace and security and the development of friendly relations between States are the basic purposes of the United Nations, any regional organization which is an aggressive grouping directed against other States does not correspond to the said requirements of the United Nations Charter.

The United Nations Charter provides that States which are participants in regional organizations must make every effort to achieve pacific settlement of their disputes with the assistance of these regional organizations before referring these disputes to the Security Council (Article 52).

The Security Council may, if it finds this advisable, use regional organizations to effectuate enforcement actions. However, no enforcement actions may be undertaken by regional organizations without the authorization of the Security Council. This provision does not relate to actions undertaken as a result of the Second World War with respect to States who fought against the Allies. The said provision does not also affect provisions of regional agreements directed against the renewal

[36] See on this question M. Lachs, «Система коллективной безопасности к вопросы обеспечения безопасности» [System of Collective Security on Questions of Ensuring Security], and Cz. Berezowski, «Договоры о взаимной помощи и система коллективной безопасности» [Treaties in Mutual Assistance and the System of Collective Security], in Проблема коллективной безопасности в Европе [Problems of Collective Security in Europe] (Warsaw, 1955).

of an aggressive policy on the part of the former enemy States so long as responsibility may be placed on the United Nations at the request of interested governments for the prevention of further aggression on the part of such States (Article 53).

The principal exception from this general rule established by Article 53 of the United Nations Charter, which says that no enforcement actions shall be undertaken by regional organizations without the authorization of the Security Council, is contained in Article 51 of the Charter. This Article provides that nothing in the Charter impairs the right of States to individual or collective self-defense if an armed attack occurs against a Member of the United Nations. In accordance with this Article of the United Nations Charter a regional organization may in the event of an armed attack use armed force also without the authorization of the Security Council since this is provided for by a respective regional agreement. But the application by States-participants of a regional organization of armed force in this event at their discretion may occur only so long as the Security Council does not take measures necessary for the maintenance of international peace and security. In addition, measures undertaken by the regional organization in the effectuation of the right to self-defense should not affect the powers and responsibility of the Security Council determined by the United Nations Charter with respect to the taking of such actions which it considers to be necessary for the maintenance or restoration of international peace and security.

Any international regional organization must satisfy such basic requirements. To what extent a particular regional organization in reality meets these requirements is determined, of course, not only by the provisions of the respective international agreement on the creation of such organization, but above all and chiefly by the character of activity of this organization.

At the moment of signature of the United Nations Charter only two regional organizations existed for general questions: the Organization of American States and the League of Arab States.

A. Organization of American States (OAS) and League of Arab States

Organization of American States. The origins of the Organization of American States were laid in 1890 when a decision was adopted at the First International Conference on the creation of the "International Union of American Republics" and the founding of the "Commercial Bureau of the American Republics" as a permanent organ of this organization. The functions of this organization were gradually enlarged, and it accumulated numerous agreements, conventions, and institutions.

In 1948 the Charter of the Organization of American States was adopted. Twenty-one American States are members of this organization (all States of America except Canada).

The highest organ of the organization is the Inter-American Conference, convoked once every five years (except for extraordinary conferences). In the interval between conferences the highest organ is the council, in which there are representatives of all members of the organization. The Council of Ministers of Foreign Affairs is an advisory organ convoked by decision of the council. The working apparatus of the organization (secretariat) is situated in Washington and bears the name "Pan American Union".

Under the guidance of the council of the organization such organs work as the Inter-American Economic and Social Council, Inter-American Juridical Committee, Inter-American Council for Culture, and so on.

The Organization of American States is used by the United States as an effective means of effectuating its influence on the countries of Latin America. Under the pressure of the United States, the Organization of American States has acquired to a significant degree the character of a military alliance. Many provisions of the 1947 Inter-American Treaty on Reciprocal Assistance and other inter-American military treaties connected with this organization are contrary to the provisions of the United Nations Charter.

League of Arab States. The League of Arab States was created on the basis of a pact between the Arab States signed on 22 March 1945.

The participants of the League on 1 January 1956 were eight States: Egypt, Syria, Lebanon, Saudi Arabia, Yemen, Jordan, Iran, and Libya. On 19 January 1956 Sudan acceded to the League.

The League has as its purpose the defense of the integrity and independence of its members and the effectuation of cooperation with regard to economic, financial, and customs questions, questions of culture, communications, transport, public health, and others. The pact also provides for taking measures against aggression.

The highest organ of the League – the council – consists of representatives of all States participating in the League. The council, as well as the secretariat of the League, is situated in Cairo. Committees exist attached to the council for political, legal, economic, cultural, and social questions and questions of communications.

The creation and activity of the League of Arab States reflects the development of the national-liberation struggle of the Arab peoples for independence and liberation from the yoke of colonialism.

Aggressive circles of the colonial powers have undertaken many efforts to use the League of Arab States in the interests of weakening the anti-imperialist struggle of the Arab peoples. Since such attempts have experienced failure, these aggressive circles, especially aggressive circles of the United States, are attempting in recent years to disrupt and to pull down the League of Arab States acting as the organizer of the struggle of the Arab peoples for freedom and independence.

B. Creation by Imperialist States After Second World War of Military Blocs Under Name of Regional Organizations

North Atlantic Treaty Organization (NATO). After the Second World War a number of aggressive blocs and alliances contrary to the United Nations Charter were created under the name of regional international organizations. The creation of these aggressive blocs was a direct result and manifestation of the policy "from a position of strength". The North Atlantic Treaty Organization is the principal such bloc.

The North Atlantic Treaty was signed on 4 April 1949 by twelve States (United States, Great Britain, France, Canada, Italy, Belgium, Netherlands, Luxembourg, Norway, Denmark, Spain, Portugal). In 1952 Greece and Turkey were admitted to NATO, and in 1955, in accordance with the Paris Agreements, West Germany also became a member of NATO.

The Atlantic Council is the executive organ of NATO, composed of the ministers of foreign affairs, ministers of defense, and ministers of finances of the member States of the organization. The permanent organ is the council of representatives of member States of NATO. The military committee, secretariat, and other organs function under the guidance of the council.[37]

The United States plays the leading role in NATO, under whose influence this organization and its members carry on intensive military measures, in particular, for the preparation of atomic warfare. By decision of NATO a command of the unified armed forces in Europe has been created, both in the zone of the English Channel and in the Mediterranean Sea.

Western European Union. The Western European Union was formed by the 1954 Paris Agreements as a result of the reorganization of the Western Alliance based on the 1948 Brussels Treaty (Great Britain, France, Belgium, Netherlands, Luxembourg). The Paris Agreements provided for a change of the Brussels Treaty, renaming of the Western Alliance to the

[37] For details on the organization of NATO, see V. Demidov, «Структура агрессивного Атлантического блока» [Structure of the Aggressive Atlantic Bloc], Международная жизнь [International Life], no. 3 (1955). Also see M. P. Tolchenov, Военные блоки империалистических государств – угроза миру и безопасности народов [Military Blocs of Imperialist States – Threat to Peace and Security of Peoples] (1956).

Western European Union, and entry of Italy and the Federal Republic of Germany into the composition thereof.

The Western European Union is, in essence, a branch of NATO. In accordance with the Paris Agreements, the military committee and defense headquarters which existed under the 1948 Brussels Treaty were liquidated. The Paris Agreements provided that, recognizing the undesirability of duplication of work of military establishments of NATO, the council of the Western European Union and its organs would be based on the respective military authorities of NATO with respect to information and consultations on military questions. Thus,, the Western European Union does not have its own executive military organs.

SEATO. In September 1954 at a meeting in Manila (Philippines) a new military aggressive bloc was created at the initiative of the United States in southeast Asia (South East Asia Treaty Organization, abbreviated – SEATO.

The participants of SEATO are the United States, England, France, Australia, New Zealand, Thailand, Philippines, and Pakistan. The principal States of Asia refused to participate in this aggressive bloc.

The highest organ of SEATO is the council of representatives of all participants of the organization.

The provisions of the Manila Treaty on the creation of SEATO are to a significant degree analogous to the provisions of the North Atlantic Treaty, but they go farther along the line of interference in internal affairs, creating under the guide of struggle against "subversive activity" broad possibilities for interference in the internal affairs of the countries of Asia.

SEATO is an aggressive bloc of colonial powers aimed against the peaceloving States of Asia. With this assistance of this bloc the colonial powers are endeavoring to strengthen their reeling position in Southeast Asia.

Baghdad Pact Organization. After the plans of the United States and England relative to the creation in the Near and

Middle East of an aggressive bloc under the name of the Middle Eastern Command collapsed as a result of resistance from the Arab States, attempts were undertaken to break up the Arab States in order to attract them into a newly knocked-together aggressive bloc one after another.

On 24 February 1955 the Baghdad Pact was concluded between Turkey and Iraq. In that same year England, Pakistan, and Iran acceded to this Pact.

The trend characteristic of the postwar period to make treaties on the creation of aggressive blocs as sweeping as possible was plainly manifested in the Baghdad Treaty. The treaty did not contain any specific provisions relative to the activity of the future organization. It provided only for cooperation (Article 1). As regards the forms of this cooperation, it was pointed out in the treaty that necessary measures would be worked out later by competent agencies of the parties (Article 2).

The sweeping character of the aggressive treaties had the purpose to conceal or in any event not to disclose to the public the true purposes of this type of treaties and thereby facilitate the conclusion and effectuation thereof.

The permanent council at the level of ministers is the highest organ of the Baghdad Pact Organization.

SEATO and the Baghdad Pact Organization are not only aggressive military and political groupings, but also a new form of colonial subordination, a means of enslaving the countries of Asia and Africa, which are combining common interests of struggle to strengthen national independence against colonialism in any form.

C. Warsaw Treaty of 14 May 1955

Warsaw Treaty Organization. The conclusion of the Paris Agreements and creation of a new aggressive military grouping in Europe and the revival of militarism in West Germany and failure of the United States, England, and France to wish to accept the proposal of the USSR concerning the creation of an all-European regional organization for questions of peace and security forced peaceloving States of Europe to create their own regional organization in order to ensure own security and to best cooperate to ensure peace in Europe.

On 14 May 1955 a Treaty was signed in Warsaw on friendship, cooperation, and mutual assistance. The parties to the Treaty were: People's Republic of Albania, People's Republic of Bulgaria, Hungarian People's Republic, German Democratic Republic, Polish People's Republic, Romanian People's Republic, Union of Soviet Socialist Republics, and Czechoslovak Republic.

The Warsaw Treaty provides for the rendering of mutual assistance in the event of armed attack in Europe against any of the parties of the treaty, consultation on all important international questions affecting common interests of the participants thereof, and the further development of economic and cultural links between them.

In accordance with the Warsaw Treaty the following organs were created: Political Consultative Committee, in which each State-party to the Treaty is represented by a member of the government or other specially appointed representative; Unified Command of the Armed Forces, which were singled out to the jurisdiction of this command.

The Political Consultative Committee may, according to the treaty, create auxiliary organs which prove to be necessary (Articles 5 and 6). A decision was adopted at a session of the Political Consultative Committee in Prague in January 1956 to create a Permanent Commission with the task of working out recommendations for political questions and a Unified Secretariat.

The Warsaw Treaty Organization in its purposes and by the character of its activity fully meets the requirements of the United Nations Charter. Obliged to create their own organization, the parties to the Warsaw Treaty did not renounce the struggle for the creation of a system of collective security in Europe. In concluding the Treaty, they affirmed their "aspiration to create a system of collective security in Europe based on the participation therein of all European States irrespective of their social and State system which would enable them to combine their efforts in the interests of ensuring peace in Europe" (Preamble, Warsaw Treaty).

The Warsaw Treaty contains a special condition, according to which in the event of the creation of an all-European system of collective security and the conclusion for this purpose of an all-European treaty on collective security, it will lose force from the day of entry into operation of the all-European treaty (Article 11).

4. Specialized Agencies of the United Nations and Other Specialized International Organizations

In the period after the First World War and especially after the Second World War a significant increase is observed in the number of international organizations for special questions (specialized international organizations). The increase in the number of such international organizations is a result of the expansion and intensification of international economic, cultural, scientific, and other links. The expansion of these links caused by the growth of productive forces and the international division of labor creates the need to regulate relations between States in these domains, conclude agreements, and create permanent international agencies.

The United Nations Charter provides that the basic international organizations for special questions created by intergovernmental agreements will be linked with the United Nations (Article 57). This link is established by means of the conclusion of agreements between the said international organizations for special questions and the United Nations. In the name of the United Nations such agreements are concluded by the Economic and Social Council and are subject to confirmation by the General Assembly (Article 63). International specialized organizations thus linked with the United Nations are called specialized agencies of the United Nations.

On 1 January 1956 the following specialized agencies of the United Nations existed: Universal Postal Union, International

Telecommunications Union, International Labor Organization, United Nations Educational, Scientific, and Cultural Organization (UNESCO), World Meteorological Organization, World Health Organization, Food and Agricultural Organization (FAO), International Monetary Fund, International Bank for Reconstruction and Development, and International Civil Aviation Organization. The USSR is a participant in the first five of the said organizations.

The agreements concluded by the United Nations with international organizations for special questions are in general of one type; they provide for mutual representation at sessions of the respective organs of the United Nations and in specialized agencies (without the right to participate in voting), the possibility of raising questions for discussion at these agencies, the right of the United Nations to make recommendations and to coordinate the activity of specialized agencies, coordination of the programs of activity of specialized agencies and of respective United Nations organs, and so on.[38]

In addition to the specialized agencies of the United Nations there are a large number of other specialized international intergovernmental organizations. Some of such organizations by the character of their activity are universal, that is, their activity encompasses various areas of the world (International Office of Epizootics, International Cold Institute, International Sugar Organization, International Union for the Publication of Customs Tariffs, and others); the activity of others is of a regional character (Danube Commission, Inter-American Institute of Agricultural Sciences, Council for Questions of Technical Cooperation in South and Southeast Asia, European Forestry Commission, and others).

A characteristic of international organizations given at the outset of this Chapter relates fully also to specialized organizations. These are intergovernmental, inter-State

[38] For details, see Labeiri-Menachem, Специализированные учреждения Организации Объединенных Наций [Specialized Agencies of the United Nations] (1955).

organizations. It follows that one should note that by virtue of the technical character of questions with which specialized organizations are engaged (this, of course, does not mean that such questions do not have political significance) the participants of these organizations, side by side with States, are often non-self-governing territories, which makes it possible for organs of international organizations to maintain direct contact with the respective departments of the non-self-governing territories.

THEORY OF INTERNATIONAL LAW

G. I. Tunkin

Professor and Head of Chair of International Law
Moscow Lomonosov State University

Third Revised English Edition

Moscow
1970

FOREWORD TO THE 2000 RUSSIAN EDITION

Lev N. Shestakov

The past twentieth century was a period of significant development for the science of international law facilitated by circumstances of an objective and subjective order. To the first, in particular, may be relegated the significant increase in various types of linkages between States, the emergence of new subjects of the international community and an increase of their number which led to the activization of the process of norm-formation, to the numerical growth of the norms of international law, and thereby enlarged the "field of research" of international lawyers.

To subjective circumstances may be relegated the fact that in the last century many talented scholars laboured. Of them one may single out five to seven who made the largest contribution to the development of the science of international law – among them one of the most prominent undoubtedly was G. I. Tunkin.

Nature endowed him with an analytical turn of mind and staggering capacity to work. Continuous work in the Ministry of Foreign Affairs of the USSR gave him an excellent knowledge of international practice and illuminated the requirements for legal regulation of the foreign policy activities of States.

Time has reduced the group of persons who knew Tunkin, who communed with him, and therefore it is instructive here to set out certain information about his life.

Grigorii Ivanovich Tunkin was born in 1906 in the Archangel Province into a peasant family. Upon completing school he studied in a forestry polytechnic. Then he worked in the system of the forestry department. In 1932 he enrolled in the Moscow Juridical Institute, upon completing which he was accepted for postgraduate study in that Institute. He defended a кандидат dissertation in 1938 on the subject of the 1832 parliamentary reform in England.

After completing his postgraduate studies, he worked briefly as the head of a section in the People's Commissariat of the Navy of the USSR, and in January 1939 took up work as a senior scientific associate in the Institute of State and Law of the USSR Academy of Sciences.

From October 1939 he began work at the People's Commissariat of Foreign Affairs of the USSR, which continued until 1965. While working in the Ministry of Foreign Affairs he held various posts in the central apparatus and abroad, and from 1952-1965 headed the Treaty Law Section of the USSR Ministry of Foreign Affairs. He was a participant in many international conferences, heading Soviet delegations to many of them. From 1957-1966 he was a member of the International Law Commission.

From 1965 until his death in 1993 he headed the chair of international law at the Law Faculty of Lomonosov Moscow State University. These years were the most fruitful for his scholarly and pedagogical activities. His principal works appeared during that period, namely: Идеологическая борьба и международное право [Ideological Struggle and International Law] (1967); Теория международного права [Theory of International Law] (1970); Право и сила в международной системе [Law and Force in the International System] (1983). In 1975 and 1989 he lectured at the Hague Academy of International Law, of whose Curatorium he was a member. Tunkin was a Corresponding Member of the USSR Academy of Sciences, Meritorious Figure of Science of the Russian Federation, laureate of a State Prize (1987), and awarded a medal by the *Encyclopedia Britannica*. He was awarded honorary doctorates by the University of Paris (Sorbonne) and University of Budapest.

Tunkin's principal contribution to the science of international law was advancing and substantiating the concept of the bringing of the wills of States into concordance. The basis of this conception was the theory of agreement worked out in the nineteenth century. In accordance with that theory, agreement was regarded as the sole means for creating norms of international law, but it did not disclose the essence of agreement, leaving outside its framework an investigation of the processes which occur when creating norms of international law. These questions were the subject of investigation by Tunkin. The results of the study might be expressed in the following concise formula: agreement – is the result and embodiment of bringing the wills of States into concordance.

In a recent work on the theory of international law the view was expressed that a "will" is a "thing in itself" and therefore only the external manifestation of a will can be brought into concordance, that is, the expression of will. This is a very complex issue requiring serious investigation, and therefore one should not hasten to concur with that view, nor to reject it. Now it is vital to stress that this view of a very serious writer does not reject the concept of the bringing of wills into concordance as such. The author attempts to clarify and develop certain elements of this conception, which may be regarded as confirmation of its being true.

In Russian doctrine there have been utterances made also apparently for the purpose of clarifying Tunkin's conception but in fact have nothing in common with it. It has been suggested that instead of bringing wills into concordance one should speak of bringing the interests of States into concordance. But the fact is that the will of a State is a norm-forming category, which the interests of a State as such are not. State interests together with other phenomena form State will and directly influence the process of creating norms of international law.

During the last decade enormous changes have occurred in the world, and this has, of course, told on positive international law and on the science of international law. Naturally certain propositions advanced in this book require clarification. But these are secondary issues; the basic propositions and conclusions made by Tunkin in 1970 are reliable also in our troubled times. On this plane we dwell on attempts to form the notion that general international law is customary law. Tunkin rather well-foundedly criticized that understanding of general international law. In the thirty years that have elapsed since this publication of his book nothing has happened either in the theory of international law or in international practice which would refute Tunkin's thesis nor even give rise to doubt as to its reliability. Moreover, the process of codification and progressive development of international law confirms the conclusion of Tunkin that as a source the general international treaty occupies an ever larger place in general international law.

In the process of preparing the book for republication a certain abridgement of the text has been made. This abridgement affects those propositions which under modern conditions have lost their political significance and do not affect the legal positions of the author. Part VII on international law in relations between countries of the world system of socialism has been omitted. This was done not because Tunkin's ideas expressed in that part were theoretically waning. The profound theoretical thinking which existed at the time in the practice of international life also was present in that part of the book. At the same time, the conclusions and proposals contained in that part of the work could not be used in practice. But in this world there is nothing immutable, and it is not precluded that in the event of a future republication this part would be included in the book.

In the present edition the fullest list of works by Tunkin is given based on a list drawn up by the author himself not long before his death.

As an annex is given Tunkin's opinion on the draft charter of an international tribunal for the consideration of cases concerning crimes committed on the territory of the former Yugoslavia. This opinion (or as the author called it – "reflections") was the last written work by Tunkin.

In preparing the work for republication, re-reading again and again familiar pages, one comes to the view that the theoretical ideas of this great and talented scholar have undergone the most difficult test – the test of time. They have become the most significant contribution of the Russian science of international law to world science. Sad to say, the biblical saying is appropriate here with respect to my Teacher, that one is not a prophet in one's own land. Indeed, there is an impression that Tunkin's works are better known and more appreciated abroad than in his Motherland.

I hope that the republication of his work will make it possible for the young generation of international lawyers to know and assess that which has been done for the science of international law by G. I. Tunkin. As work with his students shows, they have a desire to go beyond the syllabus and learn more about Tunkin's works, but regrettably the majority of them have become a bibliographic rarity. The republication of this his principal work will ease access for them to the ideas of this great scholar.

PART I.
THE DEVELOPMENT OF INTERNATIONAL LAW AFTER THE GREAT OCTOBER SOCIALIST REVOLUTION

CHAPTER I. THE INTERNATIONAL LEGAL IDEAS OF THE OCTOBER REVOLUTION AND THE MAKING OF CONTEMPORARY INTERNATIONAL LAW

The Great October Socialist Revolution, from which commenced the creation of a new socio-economic formation, affected all aspects of social relations. It also laid the beginning for profound changes in international relations and in international law.

The socialist State created by the revolution, fundamentally different in its class nature from all States which has existed theretofore, put forward a number of new guiding principles for relations among peoples and States. Symbolically, the first dekret of the socialist State was the Dekret on Peace.

The political and international legal ideas and principles of the October Revolution infused a qualitatively new spirit into international relations and international law. These principles reflected the class nature of the Soviet State; the fundamental principles of the new socialist social system were linked inextricably with the basic tenets of the ideology of the working class. But inasmuch as the working class is the leading fighter for the liberation of all working people, the international legal ideas of the October Revolution reflected the basic expectations and interests of the broad masses of the people. The humanism of those ideas and principles, their internationalism, also is determined by this.[1]

On the level of their influence upon international law and international relations, the international legal ideas of the October Revolution can be divided into three basic, closely intertwined groups:

(a) principles of socialist internationalism in relations between socialist States;

[1] On the humanism of socialist ideas, see A. F. Shishkin and K. A. Shvartsman, XX век и моральные ценности человечества [The Twentieth Century and Moral Values of Mankind] (1968).

(b) principles of equality and self-determination of nations and peoples, whose spearhead is aimed against the system of colonialism, as well as against any national oppression and inequality;

(c) principles of peaceful coexistence, aimed first and foremost at relations between States with different social systems.

These ideas and principles of the October Revolution have operated in the direction of creating new international relations and a new international law.

1. The Principles of Socialist Internationalism

The principles of socialist internationalism corresponded to the new type of international relations – to relations between socialist States. The bases of these principles were formed by the theory of Marxism-Leninism and by the practice of the workers' movement. These were the principles of the international workers' movement and the principles of relations between nations and peoples.

The guiding principle of the international workers' movement was the principle of proletarian internationalism, which signified the fraternal friendship, close cooperation, and mutual assistance of the working class of various countries in the struggle for their liberation.

The principle of proletarian internationalism emerged as the principle of the workers' movement when the development of capitalism and of the workers' movement itself attained a sufficiently high level. The internationalization of production and exchange, the internationalization of the domination of capital, the intensification of ties among the workers of individual countries, the growth of the consciousness of the unity of purpose and the need for unified efforts of the proletariat of various nations in the struggle for their liberation and for the creation of a new society not knowing exploitation – these are the basic reasons for the emergence of the principle of socialist internationalism.

The objective laws of societal development of capitalism, the experience of the workers' movement, find reflection in the class consciousness of the proletariat; proletarian internationalism is becoming an inseparable part of the ideology of the working class. The slogan "Proletarians of all countries, unite!" put forward in the Communist Manifesto proclaimed the international character of the struggle of the working class and since has become the immutable motto of every true proletarian movement.

Proletarian internationalism – is part of the ideology of the working class. It is an ideology of the fraternity and friendship of workers of all countries and, at the same time, an ideology of the friendship of peoples. Proletarian internationalism reflects not only the interests of the working class, but also the interests of all the working people. The working class, as the vanguard class of contemporary society waging a struggle for the overthrow of capitalism and the creation of a socialist society, acts in the interests of all working people and, together with them, as their allies.

Other principles applied both in the relations of the working class of various countries and its parties and in relations between nations or, depending upon the character of the principles, only to relations between nations, also have been formed together with the principle of proletarian in the developmental process of the workers' movement.

The principles of proletarian internationalism were embodied in the mutual relations of the Soviet republics which were formed on the territory of the former Russian Empire after the October Revolution. Under the leadership of the Bolshevist party, the class- conscious workers and peasants and the Soviet governments created in the individual republics strove for unification in order to build socialism together and to defend the gains of the socialist revolution together against the swoops of imperialists. Relations of the new type between the Soviet republics, crowned by the formation of the Union of

Soviet Socialist Republics, were formed precisely on the basis of the principles of proletarian internationalism.2[2]

The principles of socialist internationalism influenced the entire foreign policy of the proletarian State and its international legal position. In any event the Soviet State acted in the international arena by taking into account the principles of proletarian internationalism. It always took into account its duties with regard to the working class and the oppressed peoples of other countries, at the same time counting upon their support.

Revolutions occurred in a number of western European countries under the influence of the October Revolution: revolutions in Germany and in Hungary. And although the periods during which the revolutionary governments existed in these countries were brief – these revolutions were repressed by imperialism – those principles on which the Soviet State intended to build its relations with them were manifest at once; these were the principles of proletarian internationalism.

Notification of the revolution in Germany was received at the beginning of November 1918. The Soviet Government hailed the revolution, and the very next day the All-Russian Central Executive Committee adopted a decree on sending grain to revolutionary Germany despite the gravely serious grain shortage in Russia itself. In the Decree of the All-Russian Central Executive Committee of 13 November 1918 on the annulment of the Treaty of Brest-Litovsk, the Soviet State, pursuant to the principles of proletarian internationalism, proposed to the peoples of Germany and Austro-Hungary to establish not only peaceful relations but an "... alliance of the toiling masses of all nations in their struggle to create and strengthen the socialist system...".[3] V. I. Lenin's greeting to the

[2] For more detail, see O. I. Chistiakov, Взаимоотношения советских республик до образования СССР [Mutual Relations of Soviet Republics Before the Formation of the USSR] (1955); D. L. Zlatopol'skii, СССР -- федеративное государство [USSR – Federative State] (1967).

[3] Ministerstvo inostrannykh del SSSR, Документы внешней политики СССР [Documents of Foreign Policy of the USSR] (1957-), I, 566.

Bavarian Soviet Republic, formed in April 1919, was imbued with cordiality and fraternal solidarity.[4]

A revolution took place in Hungary in 1919, and the Hungarian Soviet Republic was formed. The Eighth Congress of the Russian Communist Party of Bolsheviks, convened in March 1919, adopted a warm greeting to the Hungarian Soviet Republic drawn up by V. I. Lenin with an assurance that the working class of Russia would assist it with all of its strength and together with the workers of all countries "shall not permit the imperialists to raise their hands against the new socialist republic".[5]

"Relations between Soviet Russia and Soviet Hungary," wrote Academician I. I. Mints – "based upon friendship and mutual assistance, were a prototype of the fraternal relations which have been formed now among countries of the socialist commonwealth".[6]

Relations with Mongolia, which began several years after the October Revolution, are a shining example of relations based upon the principles of proletarian internationalism. The people's revolution triumphed in Mongolia with the fraternal assistance of the Soviet Union. The Mongolian People's Republic has achieved great economic and cultural successes and, bypassing the capitalist stage of development, has proceeded to the construction of socialism.

The principles of socialist internationalism were developed further in relations among the countries of the world socialist system. While remaining political principles, at the same time they also are becoming international legal principles, their

[4] V. I. Lenin, "Приветствие Баварской советской республике" [Greetings to Bavarian Soviet Republic], Полное собрание сочинений [Complete Collection of Works] (5th ed.; 1962), XXXVIII, 321.

[5] Lenin, "Приветственная радиотелеграмма от имени съезда правительства Венгерской советской республики" [Radio-Telegram of Greetings in Name of Congress of Government of Hungarian Soviet Republic], ibid., p. 186.

[6] V. A. Zorin and others (eds.), История дипломатии [History of Diplomacy] (2d ed.; 1959-65), III, 195.

content is being enriched, and a number of new socialist principles and norms are being formed.

2. The Principles of Equality and of Self-Determination of Nations

The principles of equality, self-determination, and sovereignty of nations advanced by the October Revolution possessed enormous potential force. They correctly reflected one of the most important laws of societal development in the new epoch opened by the October Socialist Revolution: the downfall of the colonial system.

Worked out by the classics of Marxism-Leninism and by the practice of the workers' movement, these principles were not merely a revival of principles which had been advanced by bourgeois revolutions of the seventeenth and eighteenth centuries. Nor were they a reproduction of the "nationality principle", which never was generally recognized even within the framework of European international law and did not interfere with the annexationist policy pursued by European States.

The principle of self-determination in its new formulation meant the right of a nation to determine its own foreign policy status, the right to decide its own affairs, and the inadmissibility of coercion upon the will of nations.

A nation has the right to self-determination. But a nation in a capitalist society has been divided into antagonistic classes waging a bitter struggle among themselves. The effectuation of the self- determination of nations is not only an all-national, but also a class problem. Which class will stand at the head of the struggle for the self-determination of nations is of decisive significance. The content and the results of that struggle are dependent on this.

The Bolshevist party naturally strove so that the leading role in effectuating the self-determination of nations belonged to the working class and so that the self-determination of nations was part of the socialist revolution. And in this instance, as the experience of the self-determination of the nations that had been part of the former Russian Empire confirmed, self-determination can be effectuated most completely and profoundly when one finds expressed therein the interests and the will of the working people, the overwhelming majority of a nation.

The principles of equality and of self-determination of nations resounded in the Dekret on Peace, which proposed "to all belligerent peoples and their governments to commence immediate negotiations for a just and democratic peace".[7] It was explained in the Dekret that "by such a peace the Government considers an immediate peace, without annexations (that is, without the seizure of foreign lands; without forcibly annexing foreign peoples), and without in- demnities".[8]

The Dekret contains the celebrated Leninist definition of annexation, which stressed that annexation is contrary to the principle of the self-determination of nations. Annexation was defined as "any addition of a small or weak people to a large or powerful State without the definitely, clearly, and voluntarily expressed consent and desire of this people irrespective of when this coerced addition occurred and also irrespective of how developed or backward the nation forcibly annexed or forcibly retained within the frontiers of the State concerned. Irrespective, finally, of the fact that this nation lives in Europe or in lands far beyond the seas". The Dekret went on to say: "If any nation whatsoever is retained within the boundaries of a given State by coercion, if despite its expressed desire it is not granted the right by a free vote, ... with the complete withdrawal of the forces of the annexing or generally more powerful nation, to decide without the slightest coercion the question of the form of State existence of this nation, then its accession is an annexation; that is, by seizure and coercion".[9]

[7] Документы внешней политики СССР [Documents of Foreign Policy of the USSR], I, 11.

[8] Ibid., p. 12.

[9] It is asserted in Western international legal doctrine that the principle of the self-determination of nations supposedly was put forward as a universal principle of international law for the first time by President Woodrow Wilson in his well-

In the Appeal to the Toiling Masses of All Countries in the name of the All-Russian Central Committee of Workers', Soldiers', and Peasants' Deputies, of the All-Russian Peasants' Congress, of the Petrograd Soviet of Workers' and Soldiers' Deputies, of the Headquarters of the Red Guard, and of Trade Union representatives of 22 December 1917, the workers of all countries were called upon "to struggle for a general armistice, for universal peace without annexations and indemnities on the basis of self-determination of peoples".[10]

The Appeal of the People's Commissariat of Foreign Affairs of the Russian Republic to the peoples and governments of the allied countries in December 1917 contained a call "... to build peace upon the basis of the complete and unconditional recognition of the principle of self-determination for all peoples ...".[11]

The People's Commissar for Foreign Affairs, G. V. Chicherin, wrote V. I. Lenin on 10 March 1922: "Our international program must bring all oppressed colonial peoples into the international scheme. The right to secession or to home rule must be recognized for all peoples ... The novelty of our international scheme must be in the fact that Negroes, as well as other colonial peoples, have participated on an equal footing with European peoples in conferences and committees and have had the right not to permit interference in their domestic life".[12] On this letter Lenin underlines the words "and other

---

known Fourteen Points, set forth in a Message to Congress on 8 January 1918. See, for example, A. Verdross, *Völkerrecht*, ed. S. Verosta and K. Zemanek (5th ed.; Vienna, 1964), p. 84. The unfoundedness of this assertion already has been pointed out in the literature of the socialist countries. See, for example, Zorin and others (eds.), История дипломатии [History of Diplomacy], III, 112-115; S. Iu. Vygodskii, У истоков советской дипломатии [At the Sources of Soviet Diplomacy] (1965), pp. 14-15; R. Arzinger, *Das Selbstbestimmungsrecht im allgemeinen Völkerrecht* (Berlin, 1966), pp. 70-71.

[10] Документы внешней политики СССР [Documents of Foreign Policy of the USSR], I, 59.

[11] Ibid., I, 69.

[12] Lenin, "Письмо Г. В. Чичерину" [Letter to G. V. Chicherin], Полное собрание сочинений [Complete Collection of Works], XLV, 36.

colonial peoples have participated on an equal footing", "not to permit interference", and on the margin makes the notation: "Right!"[13]

The Soviet State gave the world a shining example of resolving the national question on the basis of the principle of self-determination. The Soviet State made the principles of equality and of self-determination of nations its own constitutional principles. The equality and sovereignty of the peoples of Russia already had been announced in the Declaration of Rights of the Peoples of Russia, of 15 December 1917: the right to self-determination up to and including secession and the formation of an independent State; the abolition of all national privileges and limitations; freedom of national minorities to develop.[14] These principles were consolidated in the first Soviet constitution – the RSFSR Constitution of 1918.

The Russian Communist Party struggle for the unification of all nations of Russia because the interests of the proletarian revolution required this; struggled for unification on a voluntary basis, so that individual nations in effectuating their right to self-determination have expressed themselves freely for unification with the other socialist soviet republics. The Union of Soviet Socialist Republics was created on this basis.

The Soviet State broke completely and immediately with the colonial policy of tsarism and repudiated all treaties of Tsarist Russia having a colonial, annexationist, unequal character.[15] It steadfastly has pursued the principles of equality and of self-determination of nations, being a consistent fighter against colonialism and racial discrimination.

13 Ibid.

14 Документы внешней политики СССР [Documents of Foreign Policy of the USSR], I, 15.

15 For greater detail, see N. V. Zakharova, "Отказ Советского государства от договоров царской России, нарушавших права народов восточных стран" [Renunciation by Soviet State of Treaties of Tsarist Russia Which Violated Rights of Peoples of Eastern Countries], Советский ежегодник международного права 1962 [Soviet Yearbook of International Law 1962] (1963), pp. 126-134.

As treaty norms, these principles were fixed for the first time in treaties of the Soviet State with countries of the East. These treaties signified the establishment of new relations with such countries, which the imperialist countries had considered to be objects of their colonial expansion.

First and foremost should be mentioned the treaty with Persia of 26 February 1921, the treaty with Afghanistan of 28 February 1921, and the treaty with Turkey of 16 March 1921.

In the treaty between the RSFSR and Persia the Soviet Government condemned the policy of the government of Tsarist Russia as "not only having violated the sovereignty of the States of Asia, but also as having led to organized brute violence of the European plunderers upon the living body of the peoples of the East".[16] The parties recognized in Article 4 of the treaty "the right of each people to the free and unimpeded resolution of its own political fate".[17]

The treaty between Russia and Turkey of 16 March 1921 proclaimed "the principles of the fraternity of nations and the right of peoples to self-determination", noted "the solidarity in the struggle against imperialism" existing between the RSFSR and Turkey, and declared "the contiguity between the national and liberation movement of the peoples of the East and the struggle of the working people of Russia for a new social system".[18] When the Soviet ambassador presented his credentials in July 1921, the leader of the new Turkish Government, Ataturk, said in his speech: "We are highly appreciative that Soviet Russia has repudiated the former treaties and put forward the principle of self-determination".[19]

[16] Документы внешней политики СССР [Documents of Foreign Policy of the USSR], III, 537.

[17] Ibid., III, p. 538.

[18] Ibid., III, pp. 597, 599.

[19] See "Зарубежная печать о революции в России и событиях в Советской республике" [Foreign Press on the Revolution in Russia and Events in the Soviet Republic], Международная жизнь [International Life], no. 4 (1967), p. 63 [citing

The revolutionizing influence of the great principles of equality and of self-determination of nations and peoples upon international law truly was enormous. As a result of the struggle of the Soviet Union, of the working class of the capitalist countries, of the peoples of colonies and dependent countries, and of all progressive forces, these ideas took hold in international law, being transformed into international legal principles and norms and supplanting old institutions in international law that had sanctified national oppression and colonial domination.

The idea of the invalidity of unequal treaties, advanced in the Dekret on Peace, played and continues to play a large role in the development of international law.[20] The Soviet State announced in this Dekret that it would commence immediately to publish Russian secret treaties. "The entire content of these secret treaties", said the Dekret on Peace, "insofar as it was aimed, as in the majority of instances it was, at giving advantages and privileges to Russian landowners and capitalists, at maintaining and increasing annexations of the Great Russians, the Government announces their unconditional and immediate abrogation".[21]

Among the treaties published and repudiated by the Soviet State were, in particular, the 1915 Russo-Japanese agreement relating to joint colonialist operations in China, the 1916 agreement among Russia, Great Britain, and France concerning the partition of Turkey, the 1907 Anglo-Russian secret treaty and convention relating to spheres of influence in Iran and others.

Бюллетень НКИД [Bulletin of People's Commissariat of Foreign Affairs], no. 91 (10 September 1921), pp. 61-62].

20 See A. N. Talalaev and V. G. Boiarshinov, "Неравноправные договоры как форма удержания в колониальной зависимости новых государств Азии и Африки" [Unequal Treaties as Form of Holding New States of Asia and Africa in Colonial Dependence], Советский ежегодник международного права 1961 [Soviet Yearbook of International Law] (1962), pp. 156-169.

21 Документы внешней политики СССР [Documents of Foreign Policy of the USSR], I, 13.

For the first time in history, a great power voluntarily repudiated treaties granting it rights and privileges in other countries. In place of the cabalistic treaties of Tsarist Russia, the Soviet State began to conclude treaties with countries of the east on the basis of full equality and respect for sovereignty. In the treaty between the RSFSR and Persia of 26 February 1921, the Soviet Government once again solemnly declared "the irrevocable repudiation by Russia of the rapacious policy, with regard to Persia, of the imperialist Russian governments overthrown by the will of its workers and peasants"[22]

"In conformity therewith, and in wishing to see the Persian people independent, prosperous, and freely disposing of their own weal", the treaty went on to say, "the Russian Soviet Government declares all treaties, conventions, and agreements concluded by the former Tsarist Government with Persia and resulting in derogation of the rights of the Persian people to be abrogated and to have lost any force".[23] The Soviet Government also declared "its refusal to take part in any measures whatsoever tending to weaken or violate the sovereignty of Persia," and announced as "abrogated and having lost any force, all conventions and agreements concluded by the former Government of Russia with third powers to the detriment of Persia or relating thereto".[24]

In the treaty between the RSFSR and Turkey of 16 March 1921, the contracting parties agreed to recognize "as abrogated and not having force" all treaties concluded between Russia and Turkey, as the parties had recognized that they "did not correspond to their mutual interests".[25]

Renunciation of consular jurisdiction, one of the important instruments of colonial domination, was a major element of the Soviet State's policy toward the countries of the

[22] Ibid., III, 536.

[23] Ibid., III, pp. 536-537.

[24] Ibid., III, p. 537.

[25] Ibid., III, p. 599.

East. Thus, the treaty with Turkey said: "The Government of the Russian Federation, recognizing the regime of capitulations to be incompatible with the free national development of any country, as well as with the full exercise of its sovereign rights, shall consider as having lost force and as abrogated any kind of activities or rights having any relation whatsoever to this regime".[26] The treaty with Persia, wherein the Soviet Government affirmed a declaration renouncing consular jurisdiction made previously, said that "Russian citizens residing in Persia, and likewise Persian citizens residing in Russia, from the moment the present treaty is signed shall enjoy the rights and shall be subordinate to the laws of the country of their sojourn equally with local citizens".[27]

In the agreement between the USSR and the Republic of China of 31 May 1924, the parties agreed to annul "all conventions, treaties, agreements, protocols, contracts, and so forth, concluded between the Government of China and the Tsarist Government and to replace them with new treaties, agreements, and so forth on the basis of equality, mutuality, and justice ...".[28] The Soviet Government confirmed once again in this agreement the declaration previously made abrogating all treaties and agreements concluded by Tsarist Russia with third countries which affect the "sovereign rights and interests of China".[29] The Soviet Government renounced special rights and privileges relating to concessions in China acquired by the Tsarist Government, as well as rights of extraterritoriality and consular jurisdiction.[30]

The idea of the invalidity of unequal treaties set forth in the Dekret on Peace, the abrogation by the Soviet State of all unequal treaties contracted by Tsarist Russia, and the conclusion

26 Ibid., III, pp. 599-600.

27 Ibid., III, p. 542.

28 Ibid., VII, 332.

29 Ibid., VII, p. 332.

30 Ibid., VII, p. 335.

of treaties with all countries, large and small, on the basis of equality were an inspiring example for the dependent countries. It has become much more difficult for imperialist States to impose unequal treaties, although, taking advantage of the weakness of some States, especially the new States, they also frequently compel them to sign such treaties at the present time.

3. The Principles of Peaceful Coexistence

The third group of ideas and principles put forward by the October Revolution was aimed at ensuring international peace and the peaceful cooperation of States with different social systems.

To the question of how relations should be built between States of opposed social systems when the first socialist State in the world comes into existence, Lenin and the Communist Party, in working out the theory of the proletarian revolution, gave an answer even before October 1917. After the revolution, these propositions were developed further and were transformed into reality.

In rejecting the "absurd leftist" trotskyist "permanent revolution", V. I. Lenin resolutely opposed the concept of extending the socialist revolution to other countries by force of arms. In an article, "Strange and Monstrous", published in *Pravda* on 28 February and 1 March 1918, Lenin wrote, appealing to the authors of a resolution adopted by the Moscow Regional Party Bureau: "Perhaps the authors suppose that the interests of the international revolution require that it be given a push, and such a push can be given only by war, never by peace, which might give the masses the impression that imperialism was being "legitimated". Such a 'theory' would break completely with the growing acuteness of the class antagonisms that give birth to revolutions".[31]

[31] Lenin, "Странное и чудовищное" [Strange and Monstrous], Полное собрание сочинений [Complete Collected Works], XXXV, 403 [Published in Правда [Pravda], 28 February-1 March 1918].

A resolution of a conference of the foreign sections of the Russian Social-Democratic Workers' Party, convened in Bern from 27 February to 4 March 1915, pointed out that the future state of the dictatorship of the proletariat will resort to war only "to protect the gains won in the proletariat's struggle against the bourgeoisie".[32] A resolution of the Seventh (April) All-Russian Conference of the RSDRP(b) of 1917 indicated that in the event the proletariat took power in Russia it "immediately and openly would propose a democratic peace to all peoples on the basis of a complete renunciation of any annexations or indemnities whatsoever".[33]

In conformity with these propositions the newly emergent Soviet State proposed to lay down the principle of peaceful coexistence as the basis for the peaceful regulation of future international relations. In the Dekret on Peace of 8 November 1917, the socialist State declared that annexationist, aggressive wars it "considers the greatest crime against humanity ..." and called upon all belligerent States to cease the sanguinary war and to commence immediate negotiations for a just and democratic peace.[34]

At the same time, basing his remarks on the experience of history, particularly the experience of bourgeois revolutions and especially the eighteenth century French bourgeois revolution, Lenin cautioned the Party, the working class, and the working people of Russia that the ruling classes of capitalist States would not leave the newly emergent socialist State in peace, that they are using every means, including military, to attempt to destroy the new social system just emerging based upon the liquidation of private ownership of the instruments and means of production and signifying the end of domination of the capitalist class in Russia.

32 КПСС в резолюциях и решениях съездов, конференций и пленумов ЦК [CPSU in Resolutions and Decisions of Congresses, Conferences, and Plenums of the Central Committee] (1954), I, 329.

33 Ibid., I, p. 337.

34 Документы внешней политики СССР [Documents of Foreign Policy of the USSR], I, 11-12.

In the Report of the Central Committee to the Eighth Congress of the RKP(b) on 18 March 1919, Lenin said: "We live not only in a State, *but in a system of States,* and the existence of the Soviet Republic side by side with imperialist States for a prolonged period is inconceivable. Ultimately either one or the other shall be victorious. And when this end comes, a number of terrible conflicts between the Soviet Republic and bourgeois States are inevitable".[35]

This utterance of Lenin's, as well as a number of his other remarks on this question, are cited repeatedly by opponents of peaceful coexistence in justification of their fabrications that Lenin supposedly regarded peaceful coexistence between States of two systems as impossible and that, in Lenin's view, the new socialist State must go to war against capitalist States in order to spread socialism with the aid of arms.[36]

Lenin pointed out that the attempts of imperialists to suppress the young Soviet State could and would lead inevitably to military conflicts between States of the two systems despite the peace policy of the socialist State. Lenin spoke of the "self-defense" of the proletarian State in calling for it to create its own military organization. Lenin warned the Party and the people of the need for vigilance and for strengthening the defense capability of the socialist State.

V. I. Lenin and the Party did not consider the policy of peaceful coexistence of a socialist State with capitalist countries which the Soviet State pursued as a temporary policy, dictated by the then

[35] Lenin, "Отчет центрального комитета 18 марта" [Report of Central Committee of 18 March], Полное собрание сочинений [Complete Collection of Works], XXXVIII, 139.

[36] See, for example, the speech of the Uruguayan representative, Dominguez-Campora, at the 465th plenary session of the United Nations General Assembly on 2 December 1953. United Nations General Assembly (VIII), *Official Records*, p. 391; also see the speech of the French representative, Georges-Picot, at the Twelfth Session of the General Assembly. United Nations General Assembly (XII), *Official Records*, p. 273; G. Kennan, "Peaceful Coexistence: A Western View", *Foreign Affairs*, XXXVIII (1960), 173; B. Meissner, "Zwölf Gebote der Koexistenz: Moskaus neue Völkerrecht", *Der Spiegel*, XVIII (1964), no. 3, pp. 62-63.

existing military-industrial supremacy of capitalism over socialism, but as the policy most responsive to the interests of the working people and to the requirements of proletarian internationalism. The Soviet State has struggled persistently for peace. A resolution of the Seventh All-Russian Congress of Soviets in December 1919 said: "The Russian Socialist Federated Soviet Republic wishes to live in peace with all peoples".[37]

The Soviet Government has emphasized repeatedly that a socialist State is prepared to establish not only normal, but also friendly relations, and it is not its purpose to extend the socialist system and communist ideology by force of arms.

Thus, a Note of the People's Commissar of Foreign Affairs to the German Consul General of 18 September 1918 stated: "The Workers-Peasants' Government desires with full resolve the observance of good-neighbourly relations and peaceful cohabitation with Germany despite all the differences in the system of both States, and it is convinced that the German Government also wishes to live together peacefully with it; while living together, it shall survive by itself, as also the German Government, and it expects that the latter, as itself, will consider these differences with all of the consequences, which, however, have not obstructed the establishment now taking place between both States of good-neighbourly relations cor- responding to the true and deeply rooted interests of both sides".[38]

In his Statement to the newspaper correspondents of the *Observer* and the *Manchester Guardian* in 1922 Lenin pointed out: "We believe that completely friendly relations with both powers [having in mind France and England – *G.T.*] are wholly possible and constitute our purpose".[39]

[37] Документы внешней политики СССР [Documents of Foreign Policy of the USSR], II, 298.

[38] Ibid., I, 488.

[39] Lenin, "Интервью корреспондента "Observer" и "Manchester Guardian" М. Фарбману" [Interview of Correspondent of the "Observer" and "Manchester Guardian", M. Farbman], Полное собрание сочинений [Complete Collection of Works], XLV, 237.

V. I. Lenin and the Party proceeded from the fact that after the failure of the armed intervention against Soviet Russia, economic competition had become the decisive sphere of struggle for the States of the two systems. In 1921 Lenin indicated: "Now we are exerting a major influence upon the international revolution by our economic policy ... But this field of struggle has been transferred to a world- wide scale. We solve this task – and we have won once and for all on an international scale. Therefore, questions of economic construction acquire very exceptional significance for us. On this front we must gain victory slowly, gradually – never quickly – but by a steady rise and movement forward".[40]

In a draft decree on the tasks of the Soviet delegation at the 1922 Genoa Conference, Lenin pointed out that peaceful coexistence necessarily includes mutually advantageous agreements of the Soviet State with capitalist countries not only upon economic, but also political questions.[41] Lenin derided proponents of the concept of "no compromises with capitalist States", showing the absurdity and harmfulness of this concept from the standpoint of the proletarian revolution. At the same time, Lenin stressed that the Soviet State, in making compromises, would not depart from positions of principle.

Would capitalist countries establish economic and other relations with the Soviet State? V. I. Lenin answered this question as follows: "There is a force greater than the desire, will, and decision of any of the hostile governments or classes; this force is general world-wide economic relations, which compel them to embark upon the path of intercourse with us".[42]

[40] Lenin, "Речь при закрытии конференции 28 мая" [Address at Closed Conference of 28 May], Полное собрание сочинений [Complete Collection of Works], XLIII, 341.

[41] Lenin, "Проект постановления ЦК РКП(б) о задачах советской делегации в генуе" [Draft Decree of Central Committee of Russian Communist Party (Bolshevik) on the Tasks of the Soviet Delegation in Genoa], ibid., XLIV, 407.

[42] Lenin, "О внутренней и внешней политики республике: отчет ВЦИК и СНК 23

On a broad historical plane, Lenin understood peaceful coexistence of States of opposed social systems, socialist and capitalist, to be a form of struggle of these systems in the course of which a new system triumphs over the old; such a struggle precludes armed struggle between States of these systems and includes cooperation between them on various questions of mutual interest.

The Soviet State strove so that the principle of peaceful coexistence entered into international law and became a generally- recognized principle.

This principle received international legal expression for the first time in treaties with countries of the East: Persia, Afghanistan, and Turkey.

The leading capitalist countries refused to accept the peaceful coexistence of States of the two systems, expecting to destroy the new system. "There is one category of people", said the herald of anticommunism, Winston Churchill, at this time, "with whom it is useless, in my view, to seek agreements. I speak of the Bolsheviks ...".[43] The imperialists organized armed intervention, a blockade, and other aggressive actions against Soviet Russia. But life compelled capitalist States to recognize the Soviet State, to conclude treaties with it, to create an anti-Hitlerite coalition, as well as to accept the United Nations Charter, where this principle received wide, and then universal recognition (see Chapter III).

On the plane of developing the principles of peaceful coexistence, the young Soviet State advanced two exceedingly important and fruitful ideas in the Dekret on Peace: the ideas of the prohibition of and the criminality of

---

декабря" [On the Internal and Foreign Policy of the Republic: Report of the All-Russian Central Executive Committee and Council of People's Commissars of 23 December], ibid., XLIV, 304-305.

[43] See "Зарубежная печать о революции в России и событиях в Советской республике" []Foreign Press on Revolution in Russia and Events in the Soviet Republic], Международная жизнь [International Life], no. 3 (1967), p. 86 [citing Бюллетень НКИД [Bulletin of People's Commissariat of Foreign Affairs], no. 2 (10 March 1920), p. 1].

aggressive war. "The Government considers it the greatest crime against humanity to continue this war so that the strong and weak nations can divide among themselves the weak peoples they have seized", said the Dekret.[44] The Fourth Extraordinary All-Russian Congress of Soviets condemned "all predatory wars" in the decree ratifying the Brest Peace Treaty in 1918.[45]

The principle of prohibiting aggressive war already had been laid down in general form in the treaties of Soviet Russia with Persia, Afghanistan, and Turkey concluded at the beginning of 1921. It received more concrete expression in treaties of the USSR on nonaggression and neutrality with Turkey of 17 December 1925, and with Persia of 1 October 1927. The treaty with Turkey, for example, said that "each Contracting Party shall be bound to refrain from any attack upon each other ..., not to participate in any hostile act by one or several third powers directed against the other Contracting Party".[46]

The idea of the criminality of aggressive war expressed in the Dekret on Peace later was reflected in a number of international documents and was transformed into a prevailing principle of international law (see Chapter III).

* * *

During the past half century, international law has developed under the beneficial influence of the ideas of the Great October Socialist Revolution. The international legal ideas of the October Revolution injected into international law as a result of the struggle of the Soviet Union and other progressive forces have led to its fundamental change.

The creative role of the international legal ideas of the October Revolution is far from exhausted. The change of the co-relation of forces to the advantage of socialism and peace

[44] Документы внешней политики СССР [Documents of Foreign Policy of the USSR], I, 12.

[45] Ibid., I, 213.

[46] Ibid., VIII, 740.

ensures a further enhancement of the role of the international legal ideas of the October Revolution in the development of contemporary international law.

CHAPTER II. PEACEFUL COEXISTENCE AND GENERAL INTERNATIONAL LAW. THE INFLUENCE OF THE BREAKUP OF THE COLONIAL SYSTEM

The problem of the co-relation of peaceful coexistence and international law has three aspects.

The coexistence of States with different social systems means their simultaneous existence. Peaceful coexistence is a type of such coexistence. If the coexistence and struggle of the two systems are a law of societal development of the transition period from capitalism to socialism, then peaceful coexistence is a necessity and a possibility which grow and to an ever greater degree are realized. But, as the experience of more than half a century of the coexistence of States with opposed social systems shows, it was not always peaceful. Academician Fedoseev is completely correct in writing: "Having proclaimed the principle of peaceful coexistence of States with different social systems, Lenin at the same time repeatedly cautioned that one must be constantly on the alert, be prepared to repulse imperialist aggression. He understood the principle of peaceful coexistence as a real necessity and possibility, but not as an already achieved result guaranteed by the immutable laws of history. He firmly explained that the entire world situation is determined by the struggle between the Soviet republics and the imperialist States standing against them".[1] Therefore, the first aspect of the problem being considered is what influence is exerted on international law by the very fact of the coexistence and struggle of the two opposed social systems.

A second and more important aspect is the influence which peaceful coexistence exerts on international law. This influence is so multifaceted that it is dealt with in many chapters of this work. In the present Chapter it is considered very generally.

[1] P. N. Fedoseev, "В. И. Ленин – великий теоретик коммунизма" [V. I. Lenin – Great Theoretician of Communism], Коммунист [Communist], no. 1 (1969), p. 17.

And finally, the third aspect of the problem of the co-relation of peaceful coexistence and international law is what influence inter- national law exerts on the peaceful coexistence of States with different social systems; that is to say, what is the role of contemporary inter- national law in securing peace in general and the peaceful coexistence of States of opposed social systems in particular. The answer to this question can be given only after an analysis of those fundamental changes which have taken place in international law during the past half-century, and in connection with a consideration of the problem of the essence of contemporary international law (see Chapter IX).

1. The Unfoundedness of the Theory that the Developmental Base of International Law is Contracting

Is general international law, that is, a law recognized by all States and regulating among them, possible in a period of the existence of States of two opposed world social systems? If such a law is possible and exists, is its developmental base expanding or contracting? What significance does the breakup of the colonial system and the formation of a large number of new States have for international law?

At the present time, these questions are not only of theoretical interest, but are vital questions of international relations. Two international legal positions corresponding to two trends in international politics have emerged: one position, a component part of the policy "from a position of strength", amounts to an actual denial of the possibility of the existence of general international law and to a justification of power politics in international relations; the second position, the position of the socialist and other peaceloving States, proceeds from the fact that general international law exists and the possibilities of its progressive development are not diminishing, but are growing.

The concept that during the past fifty years the developmental base of general international law has contracted in consequence of the existence of States of two opposed social systems and opposed ideologies, as well as the emergence of a large number of new States whose cultural heritage is substantially different from Western civilization, it is widely disseminated in the bourgeois doctrine of international law. Politically, this concept reflects first and foremost the influence of the policy of anticommunism, which rejects peaceful coexistence of States with opposed social systems and the possibility of agreement between them. Bourgeois legal doctrine is its theoretical base.

Among the followers of this concept we find writers of very different political orientations, from blatant anticommunism to actual proponents of peaceful coexistence.

Proceeding from the idealistic concept, according to which law, including international law, is a reflection of common ideology, and stipulating that there is no such common ideology now between the States of the two systems, some bourgeois international lawyers maintain that general international law is impossible in the presence of two opposed social systems or they believe that it only is functioning temporarily, insofar as the heritage of the past has remained with us, and gradually is breaking up into separate regional systems. Other bourgeois jurists express apprehension for the fate of general international law or assert that the developmental base of general international law has contracted with the emergence of socialist States and the new States of Asia and Africa.

Thus, a West German jurist, Kordt, attempts to ascribe to the Soviet State and to Soviet international legal theory the thesis that general international law is rejected in order to justify his own personal arguments that there is no place for general international law in relations between socialist and capitalist States since there is no common ideology. "Since," he writes, "the minimum community of views is absent, of course, this assumption [relating to the existence of general international law – *G. T.*] falls".[2]

[2] E. Kordt, "Weltherrschaftsstreben und Völkerrecht", *Jahrbuch für Internationales Recht*, XI (1962), 199 [*Festschrift für Rudolf Laun zu seinam achtzigsten Geburtstag*].

Another West German jurist, Professor G. Leibholz, asserts that in order to speak of an "international legal community" there must be a "minimum community world outlook", which at present there is not.[3]

A Dutch professor, F. Asbeck, writes "... nations are divided by a high wall – a conflict of fundamental convictions ... As long as the antagonism in fundamental convictions continues to divide the world, the road to an international legal order for the world as a whole lies barred ...".[4]

An English professor, H. A. Smith, wrote in 1947 that within the last thirty years the "... common cultural unity upon which the law was originally founded" has been destroyed.[5] In his view, there is no basis for international law since there is "no common agreement upon a Divine or `natural' law to which all human law and all political power, event the mightiest, is bound to conform".[6]

An American professor, J. Kunz, in his 1955 lectures at the Hague Academy entitled "La crise et les transformations du droit des gens" raises the question: "Could not global ideological conflict lead to the disintegration of the existing universality of international law? In essence, the author answers this question affirmatively, referring to the "crisis of contemporary international law" and considering this crisis to be the result of a "moral, philosophical, and religious crisis".[7]

Doubt about the possibility of developing general international law is expressed by Q. Wright, an American professor, in whose opinion "... international law tends to split

[3] G. Leibholz, "Zur gegenwärtigen Lage des Völkerrechts", *Archiv des Völkerrechts*, I (1948-49), 415-423.

[4] F. M. Asbeck, "Growth and Movement of International Law", *International and Comparative Law Quarterly*, XI (1962), 1071.

[5] H. A. Smith, *The Crisis of the Law of Nations* (London, 1947), p. 18.

[6] Ibid., p. 101.

[7] J. Kunz, "La crise et les transformations du droit des gens", *Recueil des cours*, LXXXVIII (1955), 18, 25.

into opposing ideologies of Western and Soviet international law".[8]

In an extensive article on "International Law and Global Ideological Conflict", an American professor, K. Wilk, reaches very pessimistic conclusions regarding the future development of general international law. He begins with the customary thesis of bourgeois legal scholars that for law to exist within any group there must be a common understanding of the values within it.[9]

The acceptance of obligations necessary for the existence of international law, says Wilk, "depends upon a minimum of human relationships across national frontiers that admit of and call for international regulation, and upon a minimum of values that are understood or understandable across national frontiers and that may serve as standards for such regulations. On this assumption, the area of the dominion of international law extends as far as such relationships and commonly understood or understandable values extend".[10] In Wilk's view, the said relationships across national frontiers do exist. But he is doubtful that there exist some "shared standards", since there are differing points of view as to whether there are "legal standards" in general.

Wilk correctly notes that a common ideology is by no means necessary to the existence of international law. As evidence of this he cites the fact that "national societies live under law without achieving comprehensive or fundamental unity of belief in values, or even agreement as to wha values are the fundamental ones". As regards international law, he points out that "there is no reason to consider wider or more basic agreement internationally the prerequisite of

[8] Q. Wright, "International Law and Ideologies", *American Journal of International Law*, XLVIII (1954), 617.

[9] See K. Wilk, "International Law and Global Ideological Conflict", *American Journal of International Law*, XLV (1951), 657.

[10] Ibid., p. 658.

international law. To expect it of global law, international or supra-national, is utopian".[11]

Yet Wilk comes to the conclusion that the deep division between the major States on fundamentals encourages trends away from general international law, to its breaking-up, and toward the development of local agreements and the growth of regional systems of international law. He points out that the development of international law in this direction could lead to the fact that "universal agreement would no longer survive on matters that used to be governed by universal international law. Carried to its extreme, such a development could break up the universal system of international law, as it has come down to us, into regional or other partial systems, with no international legal rules to govern the actions of States across the frontiers of the various systems. This would involve, he says, "a state, if not of virtual isolation, then of extreme hostility ...".[12]

We dwell in detail on Professor Wilk's article only because he set forth in greater detail than other bourgeois specialists in international affairs the concept of the breakup of general international law.

This point of view, widely propagated in the United States, is shared by many leading bourgeois international lawyers in other countries. Another more widespread and more moderate concept, tending in the same direction, is that in consequence of the emergence of the socialist countries and the new States of Africa and Asia, the developmental base of contemporary general international law has contracted.

In Professor C. de Visscher's view, the enormous and sudden expansion in international relations form the standpoint of the participation "of human communities which enter into international relations, as from the standpoint of the interests

[11] Ibid., p. 667.

[12] Ibid., pp. 668-670.

which these relations embrace ... diminishes the homogeneity of the traditional community of law ...".[13]

An American professor, A. Freeman, believes that the emergence of new independent States "has impeded, not advanced, the emergence of a mature code of conduct",[14] for example, international law as a whole.

An Indonesian writer, J. J. G. Syatauw, suggests that "the growing interdependence ... may have a favourable influence on the development of world prescriptions, but this interdependence being principally of material rather than of ideological nature, will certainly not lead to the strengthening of the Christian principles of international law". The author calls this a "weakening development".[15]

Professor A. Verdross previously also regarded the October Revolution and the gaining of independence by colonial peoples as a manifestation of a trend toward a contracted base of general international law. He pointed out in this connection that the Soviet Union "does not recognize all previously existing international law in its entirety, but only individual customary law norms and the international treaties which it has concluded".[16]

As regards the emergence of new States in consequence of the liberation of colonies, in Verdross's view this also represents a certain danger to international law, since "new states have entered the community of states which never have

13 C. de Visscher, *Théories et réalites en droit international public* (2d ed; Paris, 1955), p. 198. One can only welcome the fact that in the latest edition of this book the author refers not to a "weakening of the unity of the traditional legal community" but to a "weakening of the traditional unity of the international community". *Théories et réalites en droit international public* (4th ed.; Paris, 1970), p. 178. This, of course, corresponds to reality.

14 A. V. Freeman, "Professor McDougal's *Law and Minimum World Public Order*", *American Journal of International Law*, LVIII (1964), 712.

15 J. J. G. Syatauw, *Some Newly Established Asian States and the Development of International Law* (The Hague, 1961), p. 21.

16 A. Verdross, Международное право [International Law], transl. from 3d ed. by F. A. Kublitskii and R. L. Naryshkina; ed. G. I. Tunkin (1959), p. 67.

belonged to Christian-European culture and which therefore represent legal attitudes that diverge from the western concept of law".[17]

Verdross nonetheless refrained from accepting the concept of the "breakup" and "degradation" of international law. He said that all States recognize international law and, since it "derives from universally human values in the ethical nature of man, we may hope that these values will be generally accepted in the near future".[18]

In the last edition of his treatise on international law, Verdross still expresses no doubts and emphasizes the importance of the cooperation of all States for the progressive development of international law.[19]

The concept that the basis of law is community, particularly a common ideology, is completely unfounded. Proponents of this concept frequently point out that in the absence of a specific community between people, the existence of law in general and of international law in particular is impossible. Of course, in the absence of a specific community between people, the existence of human society, and consequently of law, is inconceivable, but it still does not follow that the community is the reason for the formation of law or is reflected in law. The history of human society shows completely the opposite: in a pre-class society, where this community between people was more significant, there was no law: only with the emergence of class contradictions, with the destruction of the tribal community, does law emerge.

Law, including international law, emerged not as a result of an increase in community among people, but as a result of the division of society into classes and the formation of new class

[17] Ibid.; on the unfoundedness of analogous views of Western jurists, see N. Singh, *India and International Law* (New Delhi, 1969).

[18] Verdross, ibid., pp. 67-68.

[19] A. Verdross, *Völkerrecht* (5th ed.; Vienna, 1964), pp. 83-94.

contradictions unknown to tribal society. International law, just as municipal law, is a phenomenon peculiar to a class society.

The theoretical unfoundedness of the concept of a common ideology as a necessary condition for the existence and development of international law does not make this concept less dangerous.

Of course, as has already been noted, among the proponents of this concept are people of various political orientations. The most reactionary of these (Dulles, Smith, Kordt, Asbeck, and others) assert that the Soviet Union and socialist ideology, whose content they distort beyond all recognition, are guilty of everything. The majority of those who accept this concept simply state the fact of a deep ideological conflict and draw, proceeding from the thesis that a common ideology is the basis of law, the corresponding theoretical, and sometimes practical, conclusions.

What are these practical conclusions?

Professor P. Jessup sees a withdrawal toward creating a "selective community", by which he means the so-called "free world", and he appeals for the creation and development of a regional international law of the "free world".[20]

Professor J. Kunz believes that "profound ideological differences are leading to the concluding of regional alliances".[21]

Professor F. Asbeck, in asserting that ideological differences preclude the creation of a common world legal order, writes: "Let us then work all the more strenuously to achieve a real regional legal order".[22]

The danger of this concept consists in the fact that the practical conclusions which are derived therefrom correspond to the political credo of the most reactionary circles of the imperialist powers. In reality, even putting to one side the aspersions relating

[20] P. Jessup, *The Use of International Law* (Ann Arbor, 1959), pp. 29, 153.

[21] Kunz, "La crise et les transformations du droit des gens", p. 15.

[22] Asbeck, "Growth and Movement of International Law", p. 1071.

to the foreign policy of the Soviet Union disseminated by the most reactionary adherents of this concept, the conclusion itself of the impossibility of agreement between capitalist and socialist States by virtue of the ideological differences existing between them plays into the hands of advocates of the policy "from a position of strength". As is well- known, the champions of this policy attempt to justify their assertions that agreements among capitalist and socialist States are impossible, that such agreements are of little value, and that in relations with the socialist countries one supposedly can only rely upon force. The former United States Secretary of State, John Foster Dulles, declared, for example, at a news conference on 16 October 1957: "An agreement is a meeting of the minds, and so far I do not know of any agreement that the Soviet Union has made which has reflected a real meeting of the minds. We may have agreed on the same form of words, but there has not been a meeting of the minds".[23]

The aforesaid by no means signifies that ideological differences have no importance for the development of international law. But everything depends upon how concretely the question of ideology is raised.

Many international lawyers approach the question formalistically as to whether the emergence of socialist States, as well as of new States created in consequence of the liberation of the colonies, has led to a limitation of the developmental base of general international law. They frequently point out that the Soviet Union did not recognize all norms of general international law prevailing at the time it emerged. However, in this connection the most important fact is lost sight of – that the Soviet Union refused to accept only reactionary norms of international law.

The Soviet State collided with the international law existing at the time of its formation, which, together with democratic principles and norms aimed at ensuring friendly relations among States (the principle of respect for State sovereignty, the principle of equality, the principle of noninterference,

[23] *The Department of State Bulletin*, XXXVII (1957), 711-712.

and others), contained reactionary principles and norms that reflected and strengthened the system of national oppression, colonial plundering, and imperialist robbery (colonies, protectorates, unequal treaties, spheres of influence, consular jurisdiction, and so forth).

The international legal position of the Soviet State had already been formulated by V. I. Lenin on the day after the Revolution. In concluding the Report on Peace of 8 November 1917, Lenin said: "The secret treaties must be published. The provisions concerning annexations and contributions must be abrogated. There are various provisions, comrades – why the predatory governments not only agreed about the plunderings, but amidst such agreements they also accommodated economic agreements and various other provisions concerning good-neighborly relations ... We reject all provisions regarding plunder and coercion but all provisions where good- neighborly terms and economic agreements have been concluded we heartily welcome, we can not reject these".[24]

The statement of the Soviet State opposing reactionary institutes of international law commenced its being cleared of harmful weeds which "justified" oppression and inequality in international relations. At the same time, the Soviet country accepted all generally- recognized democratic principles of the then-existing international law (and, above all, such principles as respect for State sovereignty, equality, noninterference in internal affairs) and was strictly guided by these in its relations with other States. Moreover, it promoted in every possible way the deepening and the development of the content of these principles.

It should be mentioned that previously the said principles and norms of international law were operative essentially only in relations among "civilized" or "Christian" countries. Almost all of Africa and a significant portion of Asia had colonial status.

[24] V. I. Lenin, "Заключительное слово по докладу о мире 26 октября (8 ноября)" [Concluding Word on Report Concerning Peace of 26 October (8 November)], Полное собрание сочинений [Complete Collection of Works] (5th ed.; 1962), XXXV, 20.

But even in relations with independent States of Asia and Africa, the colonial powers did not consider themselves bound by the principles and norms of international law, flagrantly flouting the sovereignty of these States, brazenly interfering in their internal affairs, rejecting with disdain the idea of complete equality of the eastern and western countries as subjects of international law.

The young Soviet State was then the only country which favored the complete application of the democratic principles of international law to all States, true equality. In the Dekret of the Council of People's Commissars of the RSFSR of 4 June 1918, for example, it was said: "The Russian Socialist Federated Soviet Republic proceeds in its international relations from recognizing the full equality of large and small nations". It is further pointed out in the Dekret that "in conformity with the basic idea of international law – as a community of equal States – to consider as identical plenipotentiary representatives all diplomatic agents of foreign States accredited to the Russian Socialist Federated Soviet Republic, irrespective of their rank".[25]

It is correct that with the emergence of the Soviet State certain norms of the then existing norms of general international law rejected by the Soviet State ceased to be norms of general international law. But it is very important to add in this connection that the contraction of general international law occurred at the expense of reactionary norms.

There is, however, another aspect to this problem, which bourgeois international lawyers usually lose sight of. The Soviet Union, and now the other socialist States as well, tirelessly struggle for the introduction of new progressive principles and norms into international law so that it becomes a more effective means of strengthening international peace and developing friendly relations among States on the basis of equality and self-determination of peoples.

[25] Ministerstvo inostrannykh del SSSR, Документы внешней политики СССР [Documents of Foreign Policy of the USSR] (Moscow, 1957-), I, 345-346.

Proceeding therefrom, the Soviet Union and the other socialist countries favor the progressive development of international law and its strict observance by all States.[26] At the initiative of the socialist States, for example, as well as a number of Asian and African States, despite the opposition of Western powers, important resolutions defining the basic orientation of United Nations activity in the progressive development and codification of international law were adopted at sessions of the United Nations General Assembly.

It has been pointed out in a resolution of the Fifteenth Session of the United Nations General Assembly[27] that work on the codification and progressive development of international law should promote "the establishment of friendly relations and cooperation among States". A resolution of the Sixteenth Session of the United Nations General Assembly emphasized even more distinctly the "important role of codification and progressive development of international law with a view to making international law a more effective means of furthering the purposes and principles set forth in Articles 1 and 2 of the Charter of the United Nations".[28] This same resolution provided that the Sixth Committee of the General Assembly be called upon to work out the fundamental principles of con- temporary international law.

The position of the Soviet Union and the other socialist States on questions of the progressive development and codification of international law in the United Nations General Assembly, in the International Law Commission, the Commission on Human Rights, and at international conferences convincingly shows that the Soviet Union and the other socialist countries are striving tirelessly to perfect international law as an instrument of peace and international cooperation.

[26] See A. P. Movchan, Кодификация и прогрессивное развитие международного права [Codification and Progressive Development of International Law] (1972).

[27] G.A. Res. 1505 (XV), 12 December 1960.

[28] G.A. Res. 1686(XVI), 18 December 1961.

New States which have arisen in consequence of liberation of the colonies now represent a great force in developing international law. It suffices to point out that they comprise more than half the members of the United Nations and specialized agencies and the majority of participants in general diplomatic conferences concerning the codification and development of international law. It is completely natural that the international legal position of these States attracts great attention.

From the concept that the basis of law, including international law, is a common ideology, it follows that the emergence of a large number of new States in the international arena whose cultural heritage undoubtedly is distinct from "Western civilization" leads to a contraction of the developmental base of contemporary general international law. This conclusion is rarely expressed openly and expressly, but it inevitably arises out of the said concept.

In this case, however, this conclusion is groundless. The attitude of new States toward international law is defined first and foremost by the fact that they did not participate directly in its creation and that the principles and norms of international law were in their time frequently a means of enslaving and exploiting peoples of these countries. Their position, which coincides a great deal with the position of the Soviet State and which consists in the fact that they do not consider themselves automatically bound by principles and norms of international law only because such principles have been accepted as generally binding by existing States, is, therefore, wholly justified and, as we have seen above, a lawful one.

As the Indian member of the International Law Commission, R. Pal, correctly stated: "International law is no longer the almost exclusive preserve of peoples of European blood, 'by whose consent it exists and for the settlement of whose differences it is applied or at least invoked'. Now that international law must be regarded as embracing other peoples, it clearly required their consent no less ...".[29]

[29] United Nations, *Yearbook of the International Law Commission 1957* (New York,

The new States declare that they reject all provisions relating to colonial seizures, colonial domination, and racial inequality, the doctrine of acquired rights, unequal treaties, the Western doctrine of succession to international treaties, provisions concerning responsibility for harm caused to aliens, protection of foreign citizens, and others.

Since the time of its formation, the Soviet State has consistently opposed these and other reactionary provisions of the old international law. As Abi-Saab correctly notes: "one should not underestimate the impact of this position of the Soviet State upon the attitude toward international law of States which have emerged as a result of colonial liberation".[30]

Before a large group of new States had come into being, these and other reactionary principles and norms of international law had, as a result of the struggle of the Soviet Union and later of the other socialist countries, as well as of emergent new States of all progressive forces, already ceased to exist if they were principles and norms of general international law binding upon all States.

While frequently opposing the said provisions, official and unofficial representatives of the new States take them almost for norms of prevailing international law, not taking into account the fact that everything already had been done to liquidate these provisions of international law before their emergence into the international arena. The representatives of new States thereby unwittingly assume the position of Western jurists, who all are still attempting to claim these provisions are prevailing international law, and weaken the position

---

1958), I, 158; also see R. P. Anand, "Attitude of the Asian-African States Toward Certain Problems of International Law", *International and Comparative Law Quarterly*, XV (1966), 63; H. Bokor-Szegó, "The New States and International Law", *Questions of International Law* (Budapest, 1968), p. 22.

[30] See G. M. Abi-Saab, "The Newly Independent States and the Rules of International Law", *Howard Law Journal*, VIII (1962), 101 [The editor is unable to locate a phrase in this publication which corresponds to that cited by Professor Tunkin. However, Abi-Saab does remark in this connection on p. 101 that: "The influence of the earlier example of the Soviet Union cannot be minimized" – *WEB*].

of all those who are struggling to completely purge international law of reactionary survivals.

Just as the young Soviet State, the new States do not reject international law as a whole. In nothing the prudent position of the new States, the Indian author R. P. Anand correctly emphasizes: "This does not, however, mean that the `new' Asian-African countries are not prepared to accept the whole body of present international law. International law has in fact come to be accepted by these countries except where it is still found to support past colonial rights or is clearly inequitable by the present standards of civilization".[31]

In the majority of instances the new States favor, together with the socialist countries, the progressive development of international law, manifesting an interest, naturally, in the development first and foremost of those areas of international law which in their view are especially important for economic, technological, and cultural development and protecting their newly gained independence. Thus, the new States display great activity in questions of international law connected with the struggle against colonialism and neocolonialism, the elimination of racial discrimination, sovereignty over natural resources, economic development, international trade, and others.[32]

At the same time, they also are very active in questions of international law relating to problems of maintaining international peace and security, disarmament, the prohibition of nuclear weapons, the creation of nuclear free zones, and so forth. They resolutely supported the proposal of the socialist countries concerning the codification of the basic

[31] R. P. Anand, "Role of the 'New' Asian-African Countries in the Present International Legal Order", *American Journal of International Law*, LVI (1962), 388; also see Abi-Saab, "The Newly Independent States and the Rules of International Law", p. 106; M. Sahovic, "Influence des états nouveau sur la conception du droit international", *Annuaire français de droit international*, XII (1966), 30-49; Bokor-Szegó, "The New States and International Law", pp. 7-35.

[32] See M. A. D'Estefano, *Subdesarollo y derecho internacional publico* (Havana, 1973).

principles of contemporary international law, which grants to new States a highly exceptional opportunity to participate in the general work of reviewing and developing the basic provisions of contemporary general international law. Thus, for example, the 1964 Declaration of the Cairo Conference of Heads of States and Governments of Non-Aligned Countries points out that "The Conference recommends that the United Nations General Assembly adopt in connection with its twentieth anniversary, a declaration on the principles of peaceful coexistence. Such a declaration would be an important step on the path toward preparing a code of such principles".

These States, which previously not only had no opportunity to take part in creating norms of international law but with regard to whom international law was an instrument of suppression, now are making a valuable contribution to the cause of the progressive development of international law.

Thus, the emergence of the socialist States and the formation of the world system of socialism and the appearance in the international arena of new Asian and African States are by no means leading either to a split of general international law or to a contraction of its developmental base. On the contrary, the growth of the forces of peace supporting international law as a means of ensuring peace signifies that the developmental base of general international law is expanding and growing in strength.

The Soviet doctrine of international law has proceeded and does proceed from the fact that general international law, whose norms regulate relations among all States irrespective of their social systems, exists and the possibilities of its further development are increasing with the growth of the forces of peace.

International lawyers in other countries of the socialist camp also support the development and strengthening of general international law.

The attempts of some bourgeois international lawyers to ascribe to the Soviet State or to Soviet international legal science the concept of the rejection of general international law[33] is explainable in the majority of instances by an insufficient knowledge of the facts, and sometimes by their deliberate distortion.[34]

This does not mean, of course, that there are no serious obstacles in the path of developing contemporary general international law. Such obstacles exist, but they derive not from the socialist States or other States adhering to the principles of peaceful coexistence. They are created by those States and those social forces which pursue the policy "from a position of strength", the policy of an arms race and the preparation of a new war.

[33] See, for example, H. Kelsen, *The Communist Theory of Law* (New York, 1955), p. 156; W. W. Kulski, "Les tendances contemporaines dans le droit international soviétique", *Revue de droit international de sciences dip- lomatiques et politiques,* XXXI (1953), 272; A. Ulloa, *Derecho internacional publico* (4th ed.; Madrid, 1957), I, 18-19; W. L. Gould, *An Introduction to International Law* (New York, [1957]), p. 92.

[34] A Canadian professor, E. McWhinney, maintains in a recent article, for example, that some time ago Soviet jurists, and especially Professor E. A. Korovin, "evidently were disposed to cast aside all norms of international law ... which existed before 1917". The author goes on to assert that changes have occurred in the Soviet doctrine of international law since Tunkin "publicly recognizes" the "old democratic principles of international law". E. McWhinney, "Le 'nouveau' droit international et la 'nouvelle' communauté mondiale", *Revue générale de droit international public,* LXXII (1968), 326. The fact is, as I noted in 1956, the Soviet State, as well as the Soviet doctrine of international law, despite individual unfortunate utterances of some Soviet international lawyers, always has recognized the existence of general international law and the presence therein of customary norms. See G. I. Tunkin, "Мирное сосуществование и международное право" [Peacevful Coexistence and International Law], Советское государство и право, no. 7 (1956), pp. 5-6; see also Tunkin, "Coexistence and International Law", *Recueil des cours,* XCV (1958), 59-60; Tunkin, Идеологическая борьба и международное право [Ideological Struggle and International Law] (Moscow, 1967). In 1925- 26 E. Pashukanis defined international law in the "technical-juridical" sense as the "aggregate of norms regulating relations between States". E. B. Pashukanis, "Международное право" [International Law], Энциклопедия государства и права [Encyclopedia of State and Law] (Moscow, 1925-26), II, col. 857. With respect to sources of international law, Pashukanis wrote: "Since States have no higher authority above them which would establish norms of conduct for them, the sources of international law in the technical juridical sense of the word are custom and treaty". Ibid., col. 873.

2. *Peaceful Coexistence of States with Different Social Systems and General International Law*

Peaceful coexistence is not some sort of idealistic concept, divorced from reality; it reflects the laws of relations among socialist and capitalist States.

Relations among States always have been characterized by a struggle among them. The roots of this struggle, which had a varying degree of intensity, are found in the class contradictions of society.

Earlier in history, relations took place among States with different social systems, but these always were relations among States based on private ownership and the exploitation of man by man (for example, relations among bourgeois and feudal States of the eighteenth century). With the emergence of the Soviet socialist State, and thereafter the entire system of socialist States, relations arose among States not only with different but with diametrically opposed social systems: with the old capitalist States, whose social system is characterized by the existence of private ownership of the means of production and the exploitation of man by man, and new socialist States, whose social system is based upon social ownership and the elimination of exploitation of man by man. There had never been such international relations in the history of mankind.

If earlier, when non-opposed class States existed, the struggle among them was a law of international relations, this law was all the more peculiar to our epoch, when class-opposed States exist. In the contemporary world system of international relations, relations among States with opposed economic and social systems are the most acute and dangerous for mankind.

Of course, States, not classes, enter into international relations; international relations are relations among States. But the foreign policy of States is determined by the predominant classes in these States; this is class policy. Therefore the struggle of the two systems, socialist and capitalist, affects relations among socialist and capitalist States.

Thus, the specific feature of this "class struggle" consists, first and foremost, in the fact that this struggle manifests itself in relations among States, and not directly between classes.

At the same time, the concept of peaceful coexistence does not allow every means of struggle among States; it precludes armed struggle and permits only peaceful competition among them. Consequently, reflecting the true inevitability of struggle among States of the two systems, the concept of peaceful cooperation includes this struggle. But struggle does not preclude cooperation. In reality, struggle and cooperation exist simultaneously in relations among States of the two systems and in international relations in general; cooperation has been permeated by struggle. The intensity of struggle and the degree of cooperation differ in relations among various and betwen one and the same States on various questions and at various times.

The experience of history has shown the correctness of the Leninist thesis that economic competition is the decisive domain of struggle of States of the two systems during peaceful coexistence. In ensuring a higher tempo of economic development, a steady rise in the material prosperity of the people, the socialist States in fact are proving the correctness of Marx's theory, according to which the transformation of private ownership, the liquidation of the power of monopolies, the elimination of the exploitation of man by man, and the creation of a socialist society is dictated not only by the requirements of social justice, but also by the need to ensure the future progress of human society. At the same time, side by side with economic cooperation of the two systems, there occurs economic cooperation of socialist and capitalist States on the basis of mutual advantage.

The concept of peaceful coexistence includes political struggle between States of the two opposed social systems. This struggle is not only inevitable and natural, but without it the concept of peaceful coexistence itself would be a wish that is out of touch with reality. A struggle of all the forces of peace against the forces of aggression and war is necessary to prevent war and to ensure peaceful coexistence in contemporary conditions.

Side by side with this there is a wide field for cooperation of States of the two systems not only on economic, but also on political questions. The principal examples of such cooperation are the creation of the United Nations, the 1947 peace treaties, the 1954 Geneva agreements on Indochina, the 1962 agreement on the neutrality of Laos, the 1963 Moscow treaty on the prohibition of nuclear tests in three spheres, the 1967 treaty on the principles of activities of States in outer space, the 1968 treaty on the nonproliferation of nuclear weapons, and others.

Peaceful coexistence of socialist and capitalist States does not and can not mean cessation of the ideological struggle between them. A special feature of this form of struggle is the fact that compromises and agreements here are impossible.

Peaceful coexistence is applicable only to relations among States. It does not mean class struggle in individual countries or the struggle of colonial peoples for their independence. Class struggle within a State is an internal affair and can not be regulated by international law. As regards the national liberation movements in colonies, contemporary international law, the most important principles of which are the principles of equality and self- determination of peoples, affirms the right of these peoples to use any means, including military, in the struggle for independence which is being denied to them.

The primary element of peaceful coexistence consists in the fact that, despite the very sharp struggle between States with opposed social systems, it precludes armed conflicts and ensures peace and the development of cooperation among them in the interests of strengthening world peace. The question is whether in the epoch of transition from capitalism to socialism, the greatest and, as all great upheavals, very painful upheaval underway in society will proceed without international armed conflicts (internal conflicts are in- evitable).

An understanding of peaceful coexistence as a specific form of class struggle between socialism and capitalism reflects the immutable laws of society development in the contemporary stage, which can not be changed or repealed by people.

Excluding armed forms of such struggle – and this is most important – is not yet a reflection of such laws. This part of peaceful coexistence is a necessity and a possibility for whose realization one must struggle. This element of the concept of peaceful coexistence also is not a mere wish or appeal, but is based on specific trends and laws of societal development.[35]

War no longer is a means of settling international disputes, both by its nature and because it has been prohibited by international law. The emergence of terrible means of mass destruction makes the question of the inadmissibility of a thermonuclear world war a question of the existence of human civilization.

The most important element of this objective necessity of peaceful coexistence is the internationalization of economic life. The internationalization of economic life and other aspects of contemporary society is a law of development which decisively influences the expansion and development of international cooperation in various areas, the most convincing evidence of which is the development of international organizations.

Peaceful coexistence also is a real possibility based not only on the said objective factors but also on the growth of social forces which oppose war.

The mightiest power of the modern world, the Soviet Union, is a great factor for peace and peaceful coexistence. The policy of peaceful coexistence arises out of the very essence of the socialist system and is a law of societal development thereof.

[35] For greater detail, see R. L. Bobrov, Основные проблемы теории международного права [Basic Problems of the Theory of International Law] (Moscow, 1968), pp. 89-121.

This law of societal development is peculiar to the policy of other States of the socialist system which, together with the Soviet Union, favor peaceful coexistence. The absence of private ownership of the instruments and means of production and its replacement by social ownership, the elimination of exploitation of man by man, the transfer of power to the hands of the working people create the necessary basis for the peaceful policy of these States. In the socialist States there are no forces which would have an interest in war. Peoples who always have suffered from war are therefore opposed to war. The aspiration for peace is peculiar to the very nature of socialist States as States which reflect the interests and expectations of peoples.

The breakup of the colonial system and the formation of independent States which, as a rule, are for peace, oppose imperialism, and uphold the policy of peaceful coexistence have the greatest significance for developing and strengthening peaceful coexistence. Relations of sincere friendship, reflecting a coincidence of the vital interests of the peoples of these two groups of States, have been formed and are developing among the socialist countries and these new States.

A broad zone of peace has been created in which, side by side with socialist States, there are a significant number of nonsocialist States which are not interested, for various reasons, in an unleashing of war.

The popular masses, whose opportunities actively to intervene in deciding international questions have grown immeasurably, are becoming an ever more powerful force of peaceful coexistence.[36] The international working class – the most consistent fighter against imperialist wars – is the great organizing force of the all-people's struggle for peace, against war. The all-people's movement for peace is the greatest factor for peaceful coexistence.[37]

[36] Professor R. L. Bobrov is wholly correct in emphasizing that there exists an "interest in preserving peace unreservedly common to the working people of both socio-economic systems ...". Ibid., p. 166.

[37] For greater detail, see V. M. Chkhikvadze, Борьба за мир – неодолимое

Together with the unprecedented growth of the forces of peace there has occurred a sharp, comprehensive weakening of capitalism and an aggravation of its general crisis. The essence of imperialism, its aggressive nature, of course, has not changed. Therefore, while imperialism remains, the danger of aggressive wars will remain, but a world war would be the ruin of imperialism. At the same time, the possibilities of imperialism have contracted sharply, as the aggressive war of American imperialists in Vietnam testifies in particular. For several years the greatest imperialist power has not been in a position to subdue the opposition of the Vietnamese people fighting for their independence, whose just cause enjoys the support of the socialist countries and progressive mankind as a whole.

Peaceful coexistence of socialist and capitalist States is the only reasonable policy and state of relations between them, since it creates the greatest possibilities in contemporary conditions for guaranteeing the prevention of a world war and the best means of promoting the progress of human society. Such progress in our epoch is bound up with the transition of society to socialism and communism. This transition, dictated by the laws of societal development, is a most profound social revolution on a world scale, being formed from social upheavals in individual countries. Peaceful coexistence is directed first and foremost toward the fact that the transition from capitalism to socialism should not give rise to international armed conflicts. Communists openly declare that they do not renounce the struggle to restructure society, that peaceful coexistence, in promoting progress, promotes the victory of socialism, but they see in peaceful coexistence one of the possibilities of ensuring the most painless transition of society from capitalism to socialism.

Opponents of peaceful coexistence are distorting the views of our Party, asserting that the doctrine of Marxism-Leninism has nothing in common with peaceful coexistence, that

---

движение современности [Struggle for Peace – Invincible Movement of Modern Times] (Moscow, 1969).

the slogan "peaceful coexistence" is a temporary tactical maneuver of communists, and such. An American senator, William Knowland, declared in the United States Senate: "It is my belief that the Soviet Union is advancing the Trojan horse of coexistence only for the purpose of gaining sufficient time to accomplish ... atomic stalemate".[38] The West German Chancellor, Konrad Adenauer, speaking in 1956 at Yale University, declared that for the Soviet Union peaceful coexistence is "only a new tactical phase in weakening the bonds of the free world". The Deputy Permanent Representative of the United States at the United Nations asserted that "communist doctrine" precludes "countries with different social systems from living in peace with one another" and does not correspond to peaceful coexistence.[39]

The opponents of peaceful coexistence most often attempt to represent the concept of peaceful coexistence advanced by the Soviet Union as consisting of the absence of war, as being the parallel existence of States of two opposed social systems excluding cooperation between them.

Thus, a committee of the American Branch of the International Law Association states that it opposes "peaceful coexistence" because this term signifies "a struggle for power rather than cooperation".[40] The Chief Legal Advisor of the English Foreign Office, F. Vallat, in his lecture at the University of London in January 1962, declared that, according to the Soviet point of view, "... peaceful coexistence is not the same as anything expressed in the Charter of the United Nations and does not mean friendly cooperation and mutual respect between the Soviet Socialist and other systems of government".[41] Professor John Hazard,

[38] *United States News and World Report*, 26 November 1954, p. 74.

[39] Plimpton, in the Sixth Committee, United Nations General Assembly (XVI), *Official Records*, p. 161 (1 December 1961).

[40] *Proceedings and Committee Reports of the American Branch of the International Law Association 1961-1962* (New York, 1962), p. 72.

[41] F. Vallat, "International Law – A Forward Look", *Yearbook of World Affairs*, XVIII (1964), 251.

of Columbia University, alleges that the Marxist concept of peaceful coexistence presupposes only the "maintenance of peace between the two opposed systems" and therefore non-Marxists prefer the term "cooperation".[42]

As already has been pointed out, peaceful coexistence means both cooperation and struggle. The assertion that peaceful coexistence supposedly does not include the cooperation of States has nothing in common with reality.

Peaceful coexistence is understood by the Soviet State as something more than peace and the absence of war, although peace and refraining from settling questions in dispute with the aid of war are the primary elements in the concept of peaceful coexistence.

In this connection one must note the completely unfounded and artificial contrast of "peaceful coexistence" and "active peaceful coexistence" which certain Yugoslav international lawyers allow. They assert that "active peaceful coexistence" should be distinguished from "peaceful coexistence", which includes cooperation between States and therefore a higher level of "peaceful coexistence".

In a report on the topic "The Juridical Aspects of Active Peaceful Coexistence Among States" submitted in 1956 to a conference of the International Law Association, a Yugoslav professor,

M. Bartos, asserted that two types of peaceful coexistence exist: passive coexistence and active coexistence.[43] In his view, "passive peaceful coexistence" is reflected in the fact that a State is bound not to violate the rights of another, not to resort to force nor to the threat of force in its relations with other States. "Such coexistence", Bartos says, "is peaceful because the use of force is

[42] J. N. Hazard, "Codifying Peaceful Coexistence", *American Journal of International Law*, LV (1961), 111-112; see also the speeches in the Sixth Committee of the U. N. General Assembly of the Belgian (8 November 1963) and the Canadian (20 November 1963) representatives.

[43] M. Bartos, "Aspect juridique de la coexistence pacifique active entre états", *Report of the Forty-Seventh Conference of the International Law Association* (London, 1957), p. 33.

prohibited; it is passive because it is reflected in refraining from actions prohibited by the U.N. Charter which could harm other States".[44]

In Bartos's opinion, "active peaceful coexistence" consists in the fact that "each state should develop its own activity in the international community, participate in the organization and improvement of this community, develop its activity with the guarantee that it will not be the object of aggression, that its activity will not give rise to obstacles, and that means which could breach the peace or create a threat to peace will not be used against it".[45]

Bartos says, in concluding, that "Coexistence is an ancient institute. Peaceful coexistence is a comparatively new institution and depends basically upon the prohibition of resort to war. Active coexistence is an institute which has emerged very recently and depends upon a democratic order in international relations, the principle of equality and of sovereign equality of states, and the right to participate in the affairs of an international organization".[46]

Another Yugoslav jurist, Professor M. Radoikovich, also expresses the same thought when in his memorandum submitted to the Committee on Juridical Aspects of Coexistence of the International Law Association he wrote: "A very long path has been traversed from 'coexistence' to 'peaceful coexistence' and 'active peaceful coexistence' ...".[47] In Radoikovich's view, "active peaceful coexistence" presupposes, in comparison with "peaceful co- existence", a "significantly more developed life of international society; that is to say, a significantly greater degree of economic integration of the community of states, organized from both the political

[44] Ibid.

[45] Ibid., p. 34.

[46] Ibid., p. 36.

[47] *Report of the Forty-Ninth Conference of the International Law Association* (London, 1961), p. 371.

and juridical point of view to realize common purposes and especially to maintain peace".[48]

Of course, as a condition of relations among States peaceful coexistence is not something fixed once and for all. Peaceful coexistence in one period may significantly differ from peaceful coexistence in another developmental period of international relations, both from the viewpoint of the breadth and depth of cooperation and also with regard to the reliability of peaceful coexistence, and so forth. Peaceful coexistence of the two opposed social systems in our days differs significantly from peaceful coexistence before the Second World War.

Peaceful coexistence between different States also is characterized by a differing degree of cooperation which, as has just been pointed out, in its turn is dynamic. Thus, relations between the Soviet Union and India at the present time are characterized by a much higher degree of cooperation than relations between the Soviet Union and the United States.

In principle, however, it is untrue to assert that peaceful coexistence can be "passive" and that it signifies only refraining from violation the rights of another State and from using force against other States. This assertion coincides with the views of bourgeois jurists and politicians previously set forth. In reality, there never has been "passive peaceful coexistence". Peaceful coexistence as passive coexistence characterized only by refraining from actions is inconceivable.

The attempt to create a distinction between "peaceful coexistence" and "active peaceful coexistence" and to contrast one to another distorts the content of the concept "peaceful coexistence" which has been widely recognized both on the part of States and of peoples. Such a contrast brings confusion, by representing "peaceful coexistence" as supposedly inadequate and in contrasting it to the so-called "active peaceful

48 Ibid.

coexistence" which in fact adds nothing new to the concept of peaceful coexistence.[49]

What is the influence of the peaceful coexistence of States of opposed social systems on international law? In considering this problem, one must keep in mind that the question is not one of "interbloc" law,[50] which is nonexistent (of course, there are norms of local international treaties concluded between individual socialist and capitalist States), but of general international law.

Norms of international law are created and are modified in the course of international relations. It is therefore natural that the state of international relations exerts a decisive influence upon the development of international law. The cooperation and agreement of States – above all, the States with different social systems – is required to create norms of general international law. Moreover, cooperation and agreement among States are the most important elements of the peaceful coexistence of States with different social systems.

The co-relation of international relations and of international law is characterized by the fact that, even though international law influences the development of international relations, the latter exert a basic and decisive influence on the development of international law. Therefore, the influence which peaceful coexistence exerts as a state of international relations upon the development of international law is basic and decisive in the co-relation of peaceful coexistence and international law. The more developed is peaceful coexistence of States with different social

[49] In the report of the Committee on Juridical Aspects of Coexistence of the International Law Association, after a lengthy discussion at the Geneva session of this committee in June 1960, the word "active" was deleted at the insistence of the author of the present work. In a note to the Committee's Report it was pointed out that some members of the committee favored the term "peaceful coexistence" and others suggested the epithet "active" be added, but "all were agreed that the concept of peaceful coexistence includes active cooperation among states". *Ibid.*, p. 365.

[50] See E. McWhinney, *"Peaceful Coexistence" and Soviet-Western International Law* (1964).

systems, the more durable and favorable are the conditions for the progressive development of international law.

Since general international law is now universal, the struggle and cooperation of States on a world-wide scale influences its development. In this world-wide system relations are a reflection of the contradictions which presently exist among economic systems, State structures, legal systems, ideologies, and so forth, of various countries. Obviously, since international relations are not the total amount of relations among States of the two opposed social systems, the contradictions which are present in international relations are not the sum total of the contradictions among socialist and capitalist States.

On the plane of world-wide international relations one often speaks of the peaceful coexistence of States "irrespective of their social system".

The development of contemporary international law must be regarded, consequently, not only on the plane of peaceful coexistence of socialist and capitalist States, but also in the wider aspect of relations among all States. But at the same time, one must stress again that peaceful coexistence of States of the two opposed social systems is determinative.

The degree of development of peaceful coexistence has significance first and foremost in the sense of improving the international climate, of promoting the progressive development of international law.

Peaceful coexistence of States with different social systems is, as already has been pointed out, that state of relations between them which is characterized by a more or less significant degree of cooperation and agreement between them on international questions. But the possibility of agreement of States, above all the possibility of agreement of States of two opposed social systems, which does not preclude struggle between them but is born in such struggle, also is the basic condition that is essential for general international law to exist, since its principles and norms are created by agreement between States (see Chapters VIII and IX). Consequently, the possibility of peaceful coexistence of States with different social systems includes the possibility of the existence of general international law. The social forces which act in pursuance of ensuring peaceful coexistence are at the same time forces which promote the development and strengthening of general international law.

The contrast of ideologies and uncompromising ideological struggle are not as insuperable obstacle to creating norms of international law. When States of the two systems reach an agreement relating to recognizing a particular rule as a norm of international law, the question is not one of agreement on ideological problems.[51] There is no need for States to have reached agreement on the nature of international law, its social essence, and so forth. It is important that they can agree with regard to specific principles and norms of international law.

For thousands of years jurists have debated about definitions of law, but notwithstanding this law has existed. States, politicians, and jurists of different countries can hold various theories relating to the nature of international law, but this difference of opinion does not create insuperable obstacles to achieving agreements relating to the acceptance of specific rules of conduct as international legal norms.

The development of international cooperation in the interest of peace, characteristic of peaceful coexistence, promotes the creation of new norms of international law, which is strengthened by the level of international cooperation achieved as well as of norms aimed at further developing and strengthening peaceful coexistence.

The history of international relations after the Great October Socialist Revolution confirms this thesis. The progressive develop- ment of international law in general has reflected the development of peaceful coexistence of States of the two opposed social systems.

[51] G. I. Tunkin, Идеологическая борьба и международное право [Ideological Struggle and International Law] (1967).

CHAPTER III. MODIFICATION OF THE FUNDAMENTAL PRINCIPLES OF INTERNATIONAL LAW DURING THE PERIOD OF COEXISTENCE OF THE TWO SYSTEMS

If one retraces the development of international law during the period of coexistence of the two opposed social systems, one can not help but note the substantive changes which have occurred in international law. Many reactionary institutes have gone out of fashion; new principles and norms having important significance for ensuring peace and the independence of peoples have emerged; and the old democratic principles and institutes of international law have been developed and strengthened.

These changes, being the result of the struggle of progressive forces against reaction, have affected all branches of international law in varying degrees. They are reflected not only in the changes in principles and norms as such, but also in the changes in the character and essence of international law (see the following Chapters).

We limit ourselves in the present Chapter to examining the changes in the fundamental principles of contemporary international law, without claiming to treat the question exhaustively.[1]

[1] On the question of the concept of fundamental principles of international law see V. Outrata, "K pojmu obecných a základnich zásad mezinárodniho práva", *Časopis pro mezinárodni právo*, no. 3 (1961), pp. 177-191; V. M. Chkhikvadze and others (eds.), Курс международного права в шести томах [Course of International Law in Six Volumes] (1967), II, 5-15; P. A. Steiniger, ed., *Die sieben Prinzipien der friedlichen Koexistenz* (Berlin, 1964); B. Graefrath, *Zur Stellung der Prinzipien im gegenwärtigen Völkerrecht* (Berlin, 1968); G. Geamanu, *Principiile fundamentale ale dreptului international contemporan* (Bucharest, 1967), pp. 7-35; R. Bierzanek, "Legal Principles of Peaceful Coexistence and Their Codification", *Polish Yearbook of International Law 1966/67* (1968), I, 17-44.

1. The Emergence of New Principles of International Law

(a) The principle of nonaggression. One of the most important changes in international law during the period of coexistence of the two systems was the emergence of the principle of nonaggression.

Before the Great October Socialist Revolution, international law had recognized the right of States to go to war (*jus ad bellum*), pursuant to which one State could resort to war against another whenever it considered this advisable. Of course, a particular claim always was found against the State that was attacked in order to justify the aggression, the claims being well-grounded or unfounded.

The principle of the prohibition of aggressive war entered international law in the period between the First and Second World Wars. Immediately after its emergence, the Soviet State raised the question of prohibiting aggressive war. The Dekret on Peace of 26 October (8 November) 1917 – the first decret of the Soviet State – solemnly declared that an annexationist war is "the greatest crime against humanity".[2] This idea met with a warm response in the hearts of not only the peoples of Soviet Russia, but also those far beyond its frontiers.

The consistent struggle of the Soviet Union for peace and the demand of progressive forces to have done with war, which brings enormous casualties and deprivations to peoples, were the principal reasons that led to the prohibition of aggressive war by international law.[3]

[2] Ministerstvo inostrannykh del SSSR, Документы внешней политики СССР [Documents of Foreign Policy of the USSR] (1957-), I, 12.

[3] On this question see G. Sharmazanashvili, Принцип ненападения в международном праве [Princiiple of Non-Aggression in International Law] (1958); Sharmazanashvili, От права войны к праву мира [From the Law of War to the Law of Peace] (1967); K. A. Baginian, Борьба Советского Союза против агрессии [Struggle of the Soviet Union Against Aggression] (1959); V. Romanov, Исключение войны из жизни общества [Exclusion of War from the Life of Society] (1961); Chkhikvadze, Курс международного права [Course of International Law], II, 111-145.

The Covenant of the League of Nations did not prohibit aggressive war, although it limited the right of member States of the League to resort to war and provided for sanctions with regard to members who waged war in breach of the provisions of the Covenant.

In this respect, the Covenant of the League of Nations was a noteworthy step forward in comparison with the Hague conventions of 1899 and 1907 on the peaceful settlement of international disputes, which in fact merely contained an appeal "before recourse to arms" to have recourse "as far as circumstances allow" to good offices or mediation.[4]

The draft Treaty on Mutual Assistance adopted by the League of Nations Assembly in 1923 (but which did not move farther) echoed still distinctly the reasons for the Soviet Dekret on Peace. "The High Contracting Parties", said the draft, "solemnly declare that aggressive war is an international crime and severally undertake that no one of them will be guilty of its commission".[5]

Aggressive war also was classified as an "international crime" in the Declaration on Aggressive Wars adopted by the League of Nations Assembly in 1927.

Finally, the Pact of Paris of 27 August 1928, despite certain imperfections in its provisions, contained a prohibition of aggressive war. Article 1 of the Pact provided: "The High Contracting Parties solemnly declare in the names of their respective peoples that they condemn recourse to war for the solution of international controversies, and renounce it as an instrument of national policy in their relations with one another". Article 2 of the Pact stipulated the obligation of the parties to settle their disputes by pacific means.[6]

[4] L. A. Modzhorian and V. K. Sobakin (comps.), Международное право в избранных документах [International Law in Selected Documents], ed. V. N. Durdenevskii (1957), II, 248.

[5] League of Nations, *Official Journal*, Records of the Fourth Assembly, Plenary Meetings, Special Supplement No. 13 (Geneva, 1923), p. 403.

[6] See Modzhorian and Sobakin (comps.), Международное право в избранных

H. Kelsen attempts to construe the provisions of the Pact of Paris in such a way that it does not prohibit a war in defense of violated rights. In referring to the provisions of the Pact on renunciation of war "as an instrument of national policy", Kelsen considers it possible to interpret the Pact so that a war which is a reaction against a violation of international law – that is, a war undertaken in support of international law – also is considered to be an instrument of international policy.[7]

In criticizing Kelsen's view, Verdross correctly points out that if the matter stood as Kelsen represents it, this would mean that the Pact of Paris had introduced nothing new in comparison with the classical doctrine, according to which a State could resort to war whenever its rights had been violated by other States.[8]

If one examines the interdependence of its provisions, the 1928 Pact of Paris undoubtedly introduced a new, exceptionally important principle into international law. Renunciation of war "as an instrument of national policy", reinforced by the obligation to settle disputes only by peaceful means, signified a renunciation of aggressive war – that is, a war which a State commences first. Kelsen's construction is farfetched and unfounded. War "as an instrument of national policy" is understood in the Pact as a war which a State commences itself, in contrast to actions undertaken pursuant to the resolution of a competent international organ.

The Soviet Union did not participate in working out the said international documents. It is undisputable, however, that the Soviet State, the very fact of whose emergence caused the powerful growth of the forces of peace and progress and which put forward and steadfastly propagandized the idea

---

документах [International Law in Selected Documents], III, 4.

[7] H. Kelsen, *Principles of International Law*, ed. R. W. Tucker (2d ed.; 1967), p. 38.

[8] See A. Verdross, Международное право [International Law], transl. from 3d ed. by F. A. Kublitskii and R. L. Naryshkina; ed. G. I. Tunkin (1959), p. 426.

of prohibiting aggressive war, played a decisive role in the birth of this principle.

The principle of nonaggression was developed further in the charters of the Nuremberg and Tokyo international tribunals, which proceed form the fact that not only aggressive war, but also its preparation, have been prohibited by international law.[9]

The United Nations Charter was an important new stage in the development of the principle of nonaggression. The United Nations Charter does not limit itself to prohibiting aggressive war, but prohibits as well as the threat or use of force "against the territorial integrity or political independence of any state, or in any other manner inconsistent with the purposes of the United Nations" (Article 2[4]). At the same time, the Charter contains an obligation to settle international disputes "by peaceful means in such a manner that international peace and security and justice are not endangered" (Article 2[3]).

According to the Charter, only the United Nations has the right to use armed force against a State only in two instances (if one does not take into account Article 106 of the United Nations Charter, which provides for a third instance of the possible use of force). Above all these are collective measures applied by decision of the Security Council in order to prevent or eliminate a threat to peace and suppress acts of aggression or other breaches of the peace. These are measures of the United Nations. As regards the use of force by one State against another outside the framework of the United Nations, this may occur only in the event of individual or collective self-defense, "if in response to an armed attack", and only insofar as the Security Council does not take measures necessary for the maintenance of international peace and security (Article 51, United Nations Charter).

[9] See P. S. Romashkin, Военные преступления импераилизма [War Crimes of Imperialism] (1953); Romashkin, Преступления против мира и человечества [Crimes Against Peace and Mankind] (1967); A. N. Trainin, Зашита мира и борьба с преступлениями против человечества [Defense of Peace and Struggle Against Crimes Against Mankind] (1956); A. I. Poltorak, Нюрнбергский процесс [Nuremberg Trials] (1966).

The content of this principle at the present time consists of the prohibition of the use of force by a State against the peoples of colonies and dependent countries for the purposes of obstructing the effectuation by them of their right to self-determination. Such use of force is a violation of Article 2(4) of the United Nations Charter. As

G. Sharmazanashvili correctly notes, the use of armed force by a metropolitan against colonies is contrary to the purposes of the United Nations.[10] On the other hand, the armed struggle of colonial peoples for their liberation as a retaliatory action against the use of armed force by the metropolitan is lawful self-defense under contemporary international law. This proposition arises from the United Nations Charter and found reflection, for example, in such international documents as the 1954 Geneva agreements concerning Indo-China,[11] and in numerous United Nations General Assembly resolutions, particularly in the Declaration on Granting Independence to Colonial Countries and Peoples, of 14 December 1960; resolution 2107 (XX) of 21 December 1965, resolution 2184 (XXI) of 12 December 1966, and resolution 2270 (XXII) of 17 November 1967.[12]

The principle of the prohibition of the use of force in international relations was discussed commencing from 1964 at sessions of the Special Committee of the United Nations on Principles of International Law Concerning Friendly Relations and Co-operation of States. The Committee could not, however, adopt an agreed text defining the content of that principle. Despite this, it would have been incorrect to draw

[10] Sharmazanashvili, От права войны к праву мира [From Law of War to Law of Peace], p. 135.

[11] M. Lachs, Женевские соглашения 1954 г. об Индо-Китае [Geneva Agreements of 1954 on Indo-China] (1956), pp. 189-193.

[12] Also see the Declaration of the Cairo Conference of Heads of States and Governments of 10 October 1964; the Declaration of the Conference of Jurists of the Afro-Asian Countries adopted at a Conference in Conakry, October 1962. *Revue de droit contemporain*, IX (1962), no. 2, p. 174; and M. Sahovic, "Influence des états nouveaux sur la conception du droit international", *Annuaire français de droit international*, XII (1966), 42-43.

pessimistic conclusions relative to the existence of this principle in general or the content thereof.[13]

The question has various aspects. The work of the Special Committee testifies above all to the agreement of States as regards a common understanding of the principle of the prohibition of the use of force as set out in the United Nations Charter and its significance in contemporary international relations. Thus, the Report of the session of the Special Committee stressed in 1967: "Again general agreement was reached that the said principle is the cornerstone of the contemporary international legal order and of the cooperation, friendly relations, and peaceful coexistence of States".[14]

All proposals concerning this principle which were submitted for consideration of the Special Committee on Principles of International Law reproduced without change the provision of Article 2(4) of the United Nations Charter.

The content of the principle of nonaggression in contemporary international law consists of two parts: the prohibition of aggressive war and the prohibition of the use or threat of force as this has been defined in the United Nations Charter. As regards the prohibition of aggressive war, which constitutes the core of the principle of nonaggression, there were no substantive disagreements unless, of course, one considers the closely related question of the definition of aggression, which is at a standstill as a result of the resistance of the western powers.[15]

The points agreed in the Special Committee on Principles of International Law concerning the content of the principle of

[13] Declaration on the Principles of International Law Concerning Friendly Relations and Cooperation among States in accordance with the United Nations Charter, adopted 24 October 1970 [G. A. Res. 2625 (XXV) – *L. N. S.*].

[14] Report of the Special Committee on Principles of International Law Concerning Friendly Relations and Co-operation among States, Doc. No. A/6799, para. 29 [hereinafter: Report of the Special Committee on Principles of International Law].

[15] For the new Soviet draft definition of aggression see Doc. No. A/AC.134/L.12 (XXIV), 25 February 1969.

the prohibition of the use or threat of force in international relations include, in particular, the following provision: "An aggressive war is a crime against peace, and the guilty persons shall bear responsibility according to international law".[16]

In the Special Committee, however, a significant difference emerged in the position of States with regard to the second part of the content of the principle of nonaggression: the prohibition of the use or threat of force. Two lines emerged: the line of the imperialist powers and their allies, having the purpose to narrow the concept of the prohibition of the use of force, and the line of the socialist and developing countries, having the purpose to make the prohibition of the use of force in international relations as broad as possible.

Agreement in principle was reached in the Special Committee concerning the fact that the content of the principle of the prohibition of the use or threat of force in international relations includes: prohibition of the "use or threat of force for the purpose of violating existing boundaries of another State or solving international disputes, including territorial disputes and problems concerning frontiers of States"; prohibition of reprisals "involving the use of force"; prohibition of the "organizing or encouraging the organization of irregular forces or armed bands, including mercenaries, for incursion into the territory of another State"; prohibition of "participation in civil strife or terrorist acts in another State". Agreement was not reached, in particular, on whether this principle includes "the duty to refrain from the use of economic and political coercion or any other forms of coercion aimed against the political independence or territorial integrity of States"; with regard to the definition of the concept of "force"; concerning the prohibition of the "use of force against the peoples of dependent territories"; and concerning the right

[16] The definition of aggression was adopted by the United Nations General Assembly on 14 December 1974. G. A. Res. 3314 (XXIX) – *L. N. S.*].

of peoples of dependent territories to use force "against colonial domination".[17]

The position of the Western powers undoubtedly was the principal reason for difficulties in the work of the Special Committee on this question, who from the outset opposed codification of the basic principles of international law. At the same time, there are also a number of objective difficulties linked with the very complexity of the issue and affecting very diverse and numerous aspects of relations between States concerning the specific formulation of provisions regarding the prohibition of the use or threat of force in international relations.

In the form in which it was defined by the provisions of the United Nations Charter, the principle of nonaggression is a principle of general international law. More than 120 States are presently members of the United Nations.[18] Other States which have not yet been admitted to the United Nations repeatedly have declared in one form or another that they recognize the principles of the United Nations Charter as binding in relations among all States. Therefore, the said principles, including the principle of nonaggression, undoubtedly must be considered to be generally recognized principles of international law.

One can not, therefore, agree with those bourgeois jurists who suggest that the provisions of the United Nations Charter are merely principles of a "particular international law" in contrast to general international law. Proceeding from this premise, they frequently draw the conclusion that norms prohibiting the use of force in international relations are lacking in contemporary general international law. Professor Kelsen, for example, regarding the previously cited provisions of the Charter concerning the prohibition

[17] Report of the Special Committee on Principles of International Law, para. 111. On the question of the concept of force, see D. B. Levin, "Понятие силы по Уставу ООН" [Concept of Force under the United Nations Charter], Советское государство и право [Soviet State and Law], no. 8 (1968), pp. 68-74.

[18] At the end of 2024, 193 States – [*W. E. B.*].

of force as relating to the "law of the United Nations", declares that "general international law does not prohibit the use of force or war and that, consequently, any state may resort to force in conformity with general international law if it supposes that its rights were violated by other States". "General international law", Kelsen says, "authorizes the state, the individual member of the international community, to resort, in case of a violation of its rights, to reprisals or war against that state which is responsible for the violation".[19]

Kelsen maintains in another work: "If reprisals and war – typical measures of self-help – are not considered as legal sanctions because a minimum of centralization is considered to be an essential element of the law, the social order we call general international law can not be regarded as law in the true sense of the term".[20]

And so according to Kelsen, international can not exist without war. The conclusion follows inevitably from this that if it prohibits war, it thereby undermines its own basis. One can reach this absurd conclusion only by carrying formalism to an extreme.

One also can not agree with those bourgeois writers who underestimate the significance of this most important principle of contemporary international law. Thus, although one Argentine professor, Moreno Quintana, refers in his treatise on international law to the 1928 Pact of Paris, recapitulating its provisions, not one word is said in the work about the fact that the Pact of Paris represented an important stage in the formation of a generally recognized principle of international law prohibiting aggressive war. Moreno Quintana only remarks pessimistically

[19] H. Kelsen, "Collective Security and Collective Self-Defence Under the Charter of the United Nations", *American Journal of International Law*, XLII (1948), 783.

[20] Kelsen, Principles of International Law, p. 31; see also P. Guggenheim, "Les principes de droit international public", *Recueil des cours*, LXXX (1952), 169; Guggenheim, *Traité de droit international* (1954), II, 93-94; R. Quadri, *Diritto internazionale publico* (2d ed.; 1956), p. 23; R. Monaco, *Manuale di diritto internazionale publico* (1960), pp. 421-425.

that "the absence of sanctions for those who violate this Pact deprived the said document of any ef- fectiveness".[21]

One can note the same tendency in Professor de Visscher's work. He speaks of this principle among others, thereupon declaring: "... to bring about an effective renunciation of a prerogative so closely bound up with the individualist conception of sovereignty as is the right of war will certainly require something more than the signature of conventions, however solemn they may be, between states".[22] Of course, to prohibit the use of force still does not mean cessation of the use of force, just as to prohibit the killing of persons in municipal law does not signify the elimination of murders. But the great significance of this principle of international law is incontestable.

Contemporary international law prohibits States from resorting to war against other States. But this does not mean, of course, that with the emergence of the principle of nonaggression international law as a system of norms regulating specific social relations has become weaker. The international legal prohibition of aggressive war undoubtedly was a step forward on the path of transforming international law into a more effective means of securing peace, of developing the peaceful coexistence of States. And if with the prohibition of aggressive war international law turned its face toward peace for the first time in history, then its role in securing effective peaceful coexistence of States has grown and it consequently has become more effective.

The new generally recognized principle which has emerged as a result of the activity of progressive forces, the principle of nonaggression, has enormous significance for securing peaceful coexistence, since peaceful coexistence means above all, although not only, the renunciation of war, joint existence in conditions of peace.

[21] L. M. Moreno Quintana, *Tratado de derecho internacional* (1963), II, 401.

[22] C. de Visscher, *Théories et réalites en droit international public* (2d ed.; 1955), p. 359.

(b) The principle of peaceful settlement of disputes. The principle of peaceful settlement of disputes, that all States are bound to settle their disagreements solely by pacific means, is linked closely to the principle of nonaggression. Both these principles are, in a sense, two sides of the same coin. If States are prohibited from resorting to force in their relations with other States and, consequently, in settling disputes with such States, this means that only peaceful methods of settling disputes are available. On the other hand, the principle of peaceful settlement of disputes means that force can never be used to settle them.

But, as is seen from the above comparison, the principle of nonaggression is broader in the sense that it prohibits resort to war and the use of force in relations among States in all instances in accordance with Article 2(4) of the United Nations Charter. Of course, resorting to force first is prohibited, just as the use of force in response to an attack would be self-defense.

The principle of peaceful settlement of disputes developed in parallel with the principle of nonaggression. It did not exist in international law prior to the Great October Socialist Revolution. The 1899 and 1907 Hague conventions on the pacific settlement of international disputes only contain the desire, "when possible", to refrain from using force and to have recourse to peaceful means of settling disputes. "With a view to obviating as far as possible recourse to force in the relations between states", says Article 1 of the 1907 Hague Convention, "the Contracting Powers agree to use their efforts to ensure the pacific settlement of international differences".[23] Article 2 of this Convention provided an obligation "in case of serious disagreement or dispute, before an appeal to arms, ... to have recourse as far as circumstances allow to the good offices or mediation of one or more friendly Powers".[24]

Thus, according to the Hague conventions, peaceful means of settling disputes were not even a compulsory stage in settling

[23] Modzhorian and Sobakin (comps.), Международное право в избранных документах [International Law in Selected Documents], II, 247-248.

[24] Ibid., p. 248.

disputes. The obligation contained in the convention "before an appeal to arms", to have recourse to peaceful means of settling disputes in essence amounted to nothing and was transformed into a simple desire by the stipulation "as far as circumstances allow".

The Covenant of the League of Nations went significantly farther in this respect. It contained specific elements of the principle of peaceful settlement of international disputes, but this principle still was not completely embodied therein.

According to the League Covenant, the use of peaceful means of settling disputes "likely to lead to a rupture" was obligatory, but the use of peaceful means did not preclude resort to force.

Article 12 of the League Covenant provided that members of the League will submit disputes arising between them "likely to lead to a rupture" either to arbitration or judicial settlement, or to enquiry by the League Council. "They further agree", it goes on to say, "in no case to resort to war until three months after the award by the arbitration, or the judicial decision, or the report by the Council".

If a dispute between League members "likely to lead to a rupture" were not submitted to arbitration or judicial settlement, it could be submitted for consideration of the League upon the notice of one of the disputant parties. If, in considering the dispute, the Council and the majority of all other members (exclusive in each case of the representatives of the parties to the dispute), the members of the League were free "to take such action as they shall consider necessary for the maintenance of right and justice" (Article 15, League Covenant).

In this instance, consequently, peaceful means were directly transformed into the first stage of the settlement of a dispute.

If the Council adopted the report unanimously or the Assembly adopted the report with the concurrence of representatives of all League members represented on the Council and the majority of the other members (exclusive in each case of the representatives of the parties to the dispute), the members of the League were bound "not to resort to war against any Party which conforms to the findings of the report" (Article 15, League Covenant). The latter provision also in this instance legally and in fact opened the possibility of having recourse to force and transformed the peaceful procedure of settling disputes merely into the initial stage of settling them.

With regard to certain disputes the League Covenant seemed to provide the principle of their compulsory peaceful settlement, but again this obligation was not carried through to the end. Article 13 of the League Covenant said: "Disputes as to the interpretation of a treaty, as to any question of international law, as to the existence of any fact which if established would constitute a breach of any international obligation, or as to the extent and nature of the reparation to be made for any such breach, are declared to be among those which are generally suitable for submission to arbitration". However, the very same article opened the way to nonpeaceful means of settling disputes. It said that League members will not resort to war against States complying with an arbitral or judicial decision and that in the event of the failure to carry out the decision, the League Council shall propose steps which should ensure its execution. Consequently, it speaks here again of the possibility of resort to war in the event of the failure to carry out an arbitral or judicial decision, and the procedure for consideration of the question by the League Council, as already has been pointed out, did not preclude this.

Thus, the complex provisions of the League Covenant concerning the settlement of disputes did not embrace all possible disagreements between States and did not preclude nonpeaceful means of settling the disputes to which they extended.

The 1928 Pact of Paris, having established the principle of nonaggression as a principle of the prohibition of aggressive war, also established the principle of peaceful settlement of disputes. Article 2 of this Pact stated: "The High Contracting

Parties agree that the settlement or solution of all disputes or conflicts of whatever nature or of whatever origin they may be, which may arise among them, shall never be sought except by pacific means".[25]

In proclaiming that any disputes between States must be resolved by peaceful means, the Pact of Paris formulated the principle of the peaceful settlement of disputes which, just as the principle of nonaggression, gradually was transformed into a generally recognized principle of international law.

The General Act for the Pacific Settlement of International Disputes, adopted by the Assembly of the League of Nations on 26 September 1928, provided for the compulsory submission of disputes between parties to the Act, which have not been settled by negotiations or a conciliation procedure, for decision of the Permanent Court of International Justice or an arbitration tribunal; that is to say, the General Act provided for the compulsory jurisdiction of the Permanent Court of International Justice. Only twenty States ratified the General Act, and it did not play a notable role. With certain formal changes arising out of the fact of the creation of the United Nations, the liquidation of the Permanent Court of International Justice, and the formation of the International Court of Justice of the United Nations, this Act was adopted by the General Assembly on 28 April 1949, and has been ratified by six States (Belgium, Sweden, Norway, Denmark, Luxembourg, and Upper Volta) on 1 January 1969.

Thus, at the time the United Nations Charter was adopted, the principle of peaceful settlement of disputes already existed in international law and remained only to be fixed in precise form. This was done in Article 2(3) of the United Nations Charter, where it said that: "All Members shall settle their international disputes by peaceful means in such a manner that international peace and security, and justice, are not endangered".

[25] Ibid., III, 4.

The content of the principle of peaceful settlement of disputes consists of States being bound to settle all disputed questions arising between them by peaceful means. The principle of peaceful settlement of disputes leaves the selection of such means to the discretion of the States concerned. According to Article 33 of the United Nations Charter, "parties participating in any dispute, the continuation of which could threaten the maintenance of international peace and security" must first attempt to settle the dispute by negotiation, enquiry, mediation, conciliation, arbitration, judicial settlement, recourse to regional organs or agreements, or other peaceful means of their choice. It is important that States should settle their disputes solely by peaceful means. As regards the use of a particular peaceful means, the States concerned may choose any one of them, taking into account the circumstances of the specific dispute. The right of "free choice" of peaceful means of settling international disputes by the parties is emphasized in the 1970 Declaration on the Principles of International Law. The Declaration provides: "International disputes shall be settled on the basis of the sovereign equality of States and in accordance with the principle of free choice of means". At the same time, the Declaration emphasizes that the "parties to a dispute have the duty, in the event of failure to reach a solution by any one of ... the peaceful means, to continue to seek a settlement of the dispute by other peaceful means agreed upon by them".

(c) The principle of self-determination of peoples. One of the most important generally recognized principles of contemporary international law is the principle of self-determination, which has received recognition as a result of the persistent struggle of the Soviet Union and other progressive forces.[26]

[26] For greater detail on this question, see G. B. Starushenko, Принцип самоопределения народов и наций во внешней политике Советского государства [Principle of Self-Determination of Peoples and Nations in Foreign Policy of Soviet State] (1960); Starushenko, Нация и государство в освобождающихся странах [Nation and State in Countries Being Liberated]

As is well-known, the origin of the said principle dates back to the period of the bourgeois revolutions. Under the banner of the "principle of nationality", the bourgeoisie, striving to establish its predominance, struggled in the nineteenth century for the creation of independent national States in Europe. The "principle of nationality", however, was not generally recognized even within the framework of European International Law.[27]

A new period of struggle to introduce the principle of self-determination of nations into international law began with the emergence of the Soviet State.

Having placed the right of nations to self-determination at the base of its policy on the nationality question, the Soviet Government pressed for the recognition of the principle of self-determination of nations as a principle of international law.

In the Dekret of Peace the Soviet Government had proposed the adoption of the principle of self-determination of nations as the basis of a peaceful settlement after the First World War. As

---

(1967); D. I. Baratashvili, За свободу и независимость народов [For Freedom and Independence of Peoples] (1960); Baratashvili, Новые государства Азии и Африки и международное право [New States of Asia and Africa and International Law] (1968); L. V. Speranskaia, Принцип самоопределения в международном праве [Principle of Self-Determination and International Law] (1961); D. B. Levin, "Принцип самоопределения наций в международном праве" [Principle of Self-Determination of Nations in International Law], Советский ежегодник международного права 1962 [Soviet Yearbook of International Law 1962] (1963), pp. 25-45; R. A. Tuzmukhamedov, Национальный суверенитет [National Sovereignty] (1963); N. V. Chernogolovkin, Крушение колониализма и международное право [Collapse of Colonialism and International Law] (1963); G. V. Ignatenko, От колониального режима к национальной государственности [From Colonial Regime to National Statehood] (1966); V. M. Chkhikvadze and others (eds.), Курс международного права в шести томах [Course of International Law in Six Volumes] (1967-73), II, 202-234; L. Antonowicz, *Likwidacja kolonializmu ze stanowiska prawa miedzynarodowego* (1964); R. Arzinger, *Das Selbstbestimmungsrecht im allgemeinen Völkerrecht der Gegenwart* (1966); H. Bokor-Szegó, *New States and International Law* (1970); Geamanu, *Principiile fundamentale ale dreptului international contemporan*, pp. 110- 166; G. Dumitrescu, "Neocolonialismul – incalcare a principiilor dreptului international contemporan", *Principii de drept international public* (1968), pp. 162-190.

[27] See V. P. Danevskii, Системы политического равновесия и легитимизма и начало национальности в их взаимной связи [Systems of Political Equilibrium and Legitimacy and Principle of Nationality in Mutual Linkage Thereof] (1882), p. 267.

already has been pointed out, on the initiative of the Soviet Union the principle of self-determination of nations was reflected in a number of bilateral treaties concluded by the USSR with eastern countries.

At the height of a difficult war against fascism, in an interallied conference at London in September 1941, the Soviet Government, striving to strengthen the anti-Hitler coalition, declared its agreement with the basic principles of the Atlantic Charter. In doing so, the Soviet Government contrasted the vague and diffuse formulas of the Atlantic Charter on respect for the right of all peoples "to choose the form of government under which they will live" and on the aspiration "to see sovereign rights and self-government restored to those who have been forcibly deprived of them" to a precise and clear position on the question of the right of nations to self-determination.

In a declaration at this conference, the Government of the USSR stated: "The Soviet Union has implemented and is im- plementing in its foreign policy the high principle of respect for the sovereign rights of peoples. In its foreign policy the Soviet Union has been and is being guided by the principle of self-determination of nations ... Being guided in all of its policies and in all of its relations with other peoples by these principles, the Soviet Union unfailingly has opposed with consistency and resolve all violations of the sovereign rights of peoples, aggression and aggressors, and all and any attempts of aggressive countries to impose their will upon peoples and to plunge them into war".[28]

Proceeding from the basic principles of the nationality policy of our State, the Soviet delegation, when the United Nations Charter was being worked out, strove to include therein appropriate provisions which would strengthen the principle of self-determination of nations as a principle of contemporary international law.

[28] Внешняя политика Советского Союза в период Отечественной войны [Foreign Policy of Soviet Union in Period of Fatherland War] (1944), I, 146.

The USSR delegation proposed to supplement Article 1 of the Charter by stipulating that one of the purposes of the Organization is the development of friendly relations among nations "based on respect for the principle of equal rights and self-determination of peoples".[29] This proposal of the Soviet delegation was included among the four-power amendments which were submitted to the San Francisco Conference on 5 May 1945, and adopted by it.

During the discussion of the American draft chapter of the United Nations Charter relating to international trusteeship, the Soviet delegation, coming to the defense of the rights of dependent peoples, proposed to stipulate in the Charter that an objective of trusteeship is the development of trust territories not only in the direction of self-government but also in the direction of self-determination "having the aim to expedite the achievementby them of the full national independence".[30]

The delegations of the imperialist powers – the United States, England, and France – attempted by every means to prevent the inclusion of this Soviet amendment in the Charter. Taking advantage of their majority at the conference, they succeeded in changing the Soviet amendment, striking out the words concerning the speedy achievement of full State independence. They were, however, compelled to include a reference to independence in the Charter as one of the purposes of trusteeship together with "self-government". But a reference to independence was not included in the Declaration Regarding Non-Self Governing Territories (Chapter XI of the Charter), as a result of which Article 73 of the Charter speaks only of the obligation of members of the organization

[29] *Documents of the United Nations Conference on International Organization* (1945), III, 622; see also S. B. Krylov, История создания ООН [History of the Creation of the United Nations], ed. G. I. Tunkin (1960), p. 94.

[30] *Documents of the United Nations Conference on International Organization*, III, 618; Krylov, История создания ООН [History of the Creation of the United Nations], p. 161.

within whose jurisdiction these territories are situated "to develop self- government".[31]

Notwithstanding the imperfections of the provisions contained in the Charter on this question (the formula "self-determination of peoples" was not developed), they represent an exceedingly important step in the development of contemporary international law, signifying the confirmation of the principle of self-determination of peoples as a most important principle of international law being now generally recognized.

The history of the origin of the principle of self-determination of nations is an example of the bitter struggle which frequently takes place during the formation of international legal principles. Recognition of the principle of self-determination of peoples in the United Nations Charter by no means brought an end to the struggle over this principle; it quickly became even more sharp and bitter. Representatives of the colonial powers, while recognizing the words of the principle of self-determination of peoples, in fact strove to transform it into an empty shell, to emasculate and reduce its liberation orientation to nothing, and sometimes even to deny the existence of this principle of international law.

The sharp struggle over the principle of self-determination of peoples developed in connection with the preparation of draft declarations and covenants on human rights. The proposal put forward by the Soviet delegation in the course of the discussion at the Third Session of the United Nations General Assembly in 1948 of the Universal Declaration of Human Rights to include in the draft declaration an article on the right of nations to self-determination served as the point of departure for the subsequent consideration of this question in the organs of the United Nations.

Representatives of the colonial powers prevented the inclusion of the article on the right of peoples to self-determination proposed by the Soviet Union in the draft Declaration on

[31] Krylov, История создания ООН [History of the Creation of the United Nations], p. 161.

Human Rights. They also strove to prevent the inclusion of an analogous article in the draft covenants on human rights. Hypocritically stating that they recognize the principle of self-determination of nations, the representatives of the colonial powers pointed out the danger of applying this principle, the possibility of a "violation of the public order and of the rights and interests of other states", urged one should not be precipitous, and occupied themselves primarily with a theoretical working out of the concept of a "people" and "nation", and so forth. Frightened by the growth of the national liberation movement, they even opposed those proposals which in essence only repeated the provisions of the United Nations Charter. Thus, at the Eighth Session of the Commission on Human Rights in 1952 the United States representative voted alone against a point contained in a draft resolution prepared by the Indian delegate in which it was recommended "that Member States of the United Nations should uphold the principle of self-determination of peoples and nations and respect their independence".[32]

Some western jurists attempted and still are attempting to dispute the existence of the principle of self-determination of peoples in contemporary international law. Such attempts have been undertaken, in particular, in the Commission on Human Rights. Through an arbitrary interpretation of United Nations Charter provisions, some representatives of western powers in the Commission attempted to maintain that Articles 1 and 55 of the United Nations Charter, where it speaks of the self-determination of peoples, do not mean the right of peoples to self- determination at all, but respect for State sovereignty.[33]

Professor C. de Visscher resolutely denies the existence of the principle of self-determination of peoples. He says that this principle "in its present total lack of precision, in no way represents a principle of law".[34]

32 Doc.No. E/CN.4/L.26, Rev. 1 (ECOSOC, 8th session, Commission on Human Rights).

33 See the Report of the Commission on Human Rights (8th session), Doc. No. E/2256.

34 Visscher, *Théories et réalites en droit international public*, p. 166.

An American professor, C. Eagleton, in passing over the question of self-determination of peoples as a principle of international law, attempted to reduce it to a moral principle. He called the principle of self-determination of peoples a "laudable ideal", but at the same time he classified the discussion in the United Nations on extending this principle to all peoples and nations as "wild talk". Cautioning against a "rash" application of the principle of self- determination of peoples, Eagleton urged in essence that one should wait to realize this principle in practice until the United Nations works out appropriate "criteria and methods".[35]

A French professor, M. Sibert, calls the principle of self- determination of nations "hypothetical and fallacious", asserting that this principle contains within it the "embryo of struggle and destruction" of a State and nation. Sibert confines the application of the principle of self-determination of peoples within very narrow limits, requiring compliance with a number of conditions which must be stated in advance by the United Nations, in essence urging the establishment of some "permissive system" for peoples to take advantage of the right to self-determination.[36]

In a monograph devoted to the self-determination of nations, an English jurist, A. Cobban, proceeding from the concept of the international legal personality of the individual, comes to doubt even the possibility of the existence of the right of nations to self- determination.[37]

The attempts to dispute the existence of the principle of self-determination of peoples as an international legal principle are completely unfounded; they contravene sufficiently definite provisions of the United Nations Charter.

[35] C. Eagleton, "Self-Determination in the United Nations", *American Journal of International Law*, XLVII (1953), 91-93.

[36] M. Sibert, *Traité de droit international public* (1951), I, 304-305.

[37] A. Cobban, *National Self-Determination* (1945), p. 47.

The principle of self-determination of peoples fixed in the United Nations Charter found authoritative confirmation and concretization in resolutions adopted by the United Nations General Assembly on 5 February and 16 December 1952; in the Declaration of the United Nations General Assembly on the Granting of Independence to Colonial Countries and Peoples, adopted 14 December 1960, upon the initiative of the Soviet Union (Resolution 1514 (XV) of 14 December 1960), in the Declaration on Principles of International Law of 24 October 1970, in the covenants on human rights, and in many other international documents.

Eighty-nine States voted for the 1960 Declaration, the text of which was proposed by a group of forty-three Asian and African States; nine States abstained (the United States, England, France, Australia, Belgium, Portugal, Spain, the Union of South Africa, the Dominican Republic), and not one State voted against.

The Declaration of the General Assembly "solemnly proclaims the necessity of bringing to a speedy and unconditional end colonialism in all of its forms and manifestations". "All peoples", the Declaration says, "have the right to self-determination; by virtue of that right they freely determine their political status and freely pursue their economic, social, and cultural development". The Declaration stresses that no reference to inadequate political, economic, social, or cultural preparedness may serve as a pretext for delaying the granting of independence.

The Declaration classified colonialism as an unlawful phenomenon, pointing out that the "subjection of peoples to alien subjugation, domination, and exploitation constitutes a denial of fundamental human rights, is contrary to the Charter of the United Nations and is an impediment to the promotion of world peace and cooperation". Opposition to the national liberation movement is a violation of international law, and references to the inadequacy of the development of a particular people can not be a justification for such violations.

The provisions of the Declaration not only confirm and interpret but they also develop the respective provisions of the United Nations Charter which, as the Soviet delegation pointed out at the San Francisco Conference, did not go far enough. As a resolution of the United Nations General Assembly, the Declaration does not have direct legally binding force. Its great significance, however, both on the factual and legal planes, consists primarily in the fact that it draws specific conclusions from the general provisions of the Charter. On the basis of the experience of the struggle of peoples for the liberation of colonies and dependent countries, the Declaration formulates the basic elements of the content of the principle of self-determination of peoples, representing an authoritative expression of the position of the overwhelming majority of States, including States of different social systems. This fact has very important significance in the process of creating norms of international law by means of custom (see Chapter IV).

Finally, the covenants on human rights adopted on 16 December 1966 by the United Nations General Assembly contain a detailed formulation of the right to self-determination, which was absent in the 1948 Universal Declaration of Human Rights. Article 1 of both covenants states:

1. All peoples have the right to self-determination. By virtue of that right they freely determine their political status and freely pursue their economic, social, and cultural development.

2. All peoples may, for their own ends, freely dispose of their natural wealth and resources without prejudice to any obligations arising out of international economic cooperation, based upon the principle of mutual benefit, and international law. In no case may a people be deprived of its own means of subsistence.

3. All States Parties to the present Covenant, including those having responsibility for the administration of Non-Self- Governing and Trust Territories, shall promote the realization of the right of self-determination, and shall

> respect that right, in conformity with the provisions of the Charter of the United Nations.[38]

Thus, as has been pointed out repeatedly in Soviet literature and in the literature of other socialist countries, the right of peoples to self-determination is defined in these documents not merely as the right of a people or nation to create its own State. It includes the right of a people independently to decide the question of its own economic, social, and cultural development and to dispose of its own natural wealth".[39]

The question of "the principle of equality and self-determination of peoples" was discussed at sessions of the United Nations General Assembly Special Committee on the Principles of International Law Relating to Friendly Relations and Cooperation Among States in 1966, 1967, and 1968. The colonial powers, having attempted in general to prevent progress on this question, especially objected to the adoption of provisions on the illegality of colonialism, the prohibition of colonial wars, and the right of colonial peoples to resort to means of armed struggle in the struggle for independence.[40] In the 1970 Declaration on the Principles of International Law it says: "By virtue of the principle of equal rights and self-determination of peoples enshrined in the Charter, all peoples have the right freely to determine, without external interference, their political status and to pursue their economic, social and cultural development, and every State has the duty to respect this right in accordance with the provisions of the Charter".

The Declaration goes on to point out that every State has the duty to promote the realization of this principle, refraining from any forcible actions which deprive peoples of their

[38] G. A. Res. 2200 (XXI), 16 December 1966.

[39] For greater detail on the legal content of the right to self-determination, see Bokor-Szegó, *New States and International Law*, pp. 30-51.

[40] See the proposal of Czechoslovakia (Doc. No. A/C.125/L.16, part VI); the proposal of Algeria, Ghana, India, Cameroon, Kenya, Madagascar, Nigeria, United Arab Republic, Syria, and Yugoslavia (Doc. No. A/AC.125/L.48).

right to self- determination, and in their actions against such measures peoples struggling for independence are entitled to seek and receive support.

The principle of self-determination of nations does not predetermine the international legal status of a particular nation. A nation has the right freely to unite itself with another nation or nations, and depending upon the nature of the unification in this event, the corresponding national entity will or will not enter into international relations as a subject of international law (in the USSR, the union republics are subjects of international law, whereas the autonomous republics and other national entities do not act independently in international relations). A nation may elect the course of creating its own individual State which, of course, will enter into international relations as a subject of international law.

Thus, the creation of a State formation – a subject of international law – depends upon the free decision of the nation or people itself.

The opposition of a colonial power to the effectuation of the aspiration of a people of a colonial or dependent country for independence is a most flagrant violation of international law. A nation struggling for independence and the creation of its own State must, therefore, under contemporary international law be considered to be a subject of international law, even though as a result of the opposition of the colonizers it could not form an independent State yet but is only on the path of creating it.[41]

[41] See, for example, V. N. Durdenevskii and S. B. Krylov (eds.), Международное право [International Law] (1947), p. 111; G. I. Tunkin, Основы международного права [Fundamental Principles of International Law] (1956), p. 17; E. A. Korovin (ed.), Международное право [International Law] (1951), p. 158 (the part written by S. B. Krylov); L. A. Modzhorian, Субъекты международного права [Subjects of International Law] (1958), p. 14. N. A. Ushakov is of the opinion that every nation "as a bearer of the right to self-determination is a subject of international law irrespective of whether it has achieved independent statehood or not". N. A. Ushakov, "Субъекты современного международного права" [Subjects of International Law], Советский ежегодник международного права 1964-1965 [Soviet Yearbook of International Law 1964-1965] (1966), p. 64.

The principle of self-determination of nations by no means signifies, however, that a nation is obliged to want to create a State unifying the entire nation. The right of nations to self-determination is a right, not a duty. There are several historical examples where individual parts of a nation populating a defined territory have created an independent State which began to develop along several or completely different economic or political paths.

(d) The principle of peaceful coexistence. The emergence of the principle of peaceful coexistence opens a new page in the development of international law.

The Soviet State also has played a leading role in the making of this principle of international law.

Being guided by the interests of peoples, for whom war always entails death and deprivation, the Soviet State steadfastly has pursued a policy of peaceful coexistence, striving that the principle of peaceful coexistence be recognized by all States as a principle of international law.

Having already proclaimed the idea of peaceful coexistence in the Dekret on Peace, the Soviet State consolidated this principle in treaties with eastern countries concluded in the initial years of the existence of Soviet power. Although the expression "peaceful coexistence" is not used in these treaties, the idea of peaceful coexistence permeates them from beginning to end (see Chapter I).

The leading capitalist countries at that time refused to recognize the principle of peaceful coexistence of socialist and capitalist States, believing that they would succeed in destroying the first socialist country in the world. But in the end they had to begin normalizing relations with Soviet Russia.

Recognition of the Soviet State by the major capitalist countries was in important stage in forming the principle of peaceful coexistence in contemporary international law. First, it signified official recognition of the fact that relations between capitalist States and socialist States are regulated by generally recognized norms of international law, which at that time already contained specific elements of the principle of peaceful coexistence (for example, the principle of respect for sovereignty, the principle of equality of States and of noninterference in internal affairs); second, recognition, as a constituent part of the normalization of relations between States of the two systems, facilitated the further development of these relations.

At the same time, the chief prerequisite for the emergence of the principle of peaceful coexistence in general international law was lacking at that time, the principles of nonaggression and of peaceful settlement of disputes still being in the formative stage. The emergence of the principle of the prohibition of aggressive war and of the principle of peaceful settlement of disputes, and the broader recognition of these principles by States, were an important step in the course of forming the principle of peaceful coexistence.

The tireless struggle of the Soviet Union and the struggle of all progressive forces for peace, disarmament, the prohibition of aggressive war, the liberation of peoples of colonies and dependent countries, and the organization of a collective rebuff to mounting fascist aggression have played a decisive role in forming the principle of peaceful coexistence.

From the standpoint of the process of forming the principle of peaceful coexistence, the Second World War had two aspects. On the part of the fascist aggressors, this was a war against peaceful coexistence. On the part of the anti-Hitler coalition, despite anti- soviet currents within it, objectively this as a whole was a war against aggression, for the liquidation of the consequences of aggression, and for peaceful coexistence. Cooperation of States of the anti-Hitler coalition was an important experiment in the cooperation of States of the two systems, clearly demonstrating that it might develop significantly further than perhaps both sides had previously believed.

The experience of peaceful coexistence of the States of the two systems and especially the cooperation of these States during the Second World War led to the principle of peaceful coexistence being placed at the base of the United Nations Organization, whose Charter was being drawn up even as the bloody world battle was being fought. Tens of millions of people who fought against fascism with weapon in hand, many of whom gave up their life in this struggle, demanded their governments take such measures as would be a sufficient guarantee against a rebirth of aggression and as would ensure peaceful coexistence. Such was the urgent demand of all freedom-loving peoples.

This demand of peoples found reflection in the provisions of the United Nations Charter. Although the term "peaceful coexistence" is not used in the Charter, the principle of peaceful coexistence runs throughout the Charter of this international organization. The preamble of the Charter speaks of the determination "to save succeeding generations from the scourge of war", "to establish conditions under which justice and respect for the obligations arising from treaties and other sources of international law can be maintained". States are called upon "to practice tolerance and live together in peace with one another as good neighbours". Article 1 of the United Nations Charter obliges States "to maintain international law and peace and security, and to that end: to take effective collective measures for the prevention and removal of threats to the peace, and for the suppression of acts of aggression or other breaches of the peace, and to bring about by peaceful means, and in conformity with the principles of justice and international law, the adjustment or settlement of international disputes or situations which might lead to a breach of the peace", "to develop friendly relations among nations", to take "other appropriate measures to strengthen universal peace", "to achieve international cooperation in solving international problems of an economic, social, cultural, or humanitarian character, and in promoting and encouraging respect for human rights and for fundamental freedoms for all without distinction as to race, sex, language, or religion". Finally, the United Nations Charter says that this international organization must "be a centre for harmonizing the actions of nations in the attainment of these common ends", having in view, naturally, the harmonized actions of States of different social systems.

The inclusion of the principle of peaceful coexistence in the United Nations Charter was a decisive stage in the process of transforming this principle into a generally recognized principle of international law.

After this, the principle of peaceful coexistence found reflection in many multilateral and bilateral international statements and treaties, and also in resolutions of the United Nations General Assembly.

The principle of peaceful coexistence presupposes the existence of other important principles of international law, such as nonaggression, respect for sovereignty, noninterference in internal affairs, equality of States and peoples, and others. It reflects their content in a generalized form, although it does not constitute the simple sum of these principles.

The principle of peaceful coexistence as a principle of general international law has the character of universality; it is a principle of ensuring peace and security and of the development of cooperation between States "irrespective of the social system".[42] Professor M. Virally is completely correct in calling attention to the importance of this formulation.[43] R. L. Bobrov writes that the principle of peaceful coexistence as a principle of general international law signifies "the obligatoriness of maintaining good-neighbourly relations among States irrespective of their social system on the basis of the democratic principles consolidated by the United Nations Charter".[44]

[42] See Tunkin, Основы современного международного права [Fundamental Principles of Contemporary International Law], p. 31.

[43] M. Virally, "Jusqu'au la coexistence pacifique", *Revue de droit contemporain,* XIII (1966), no. 1, p. 19.

[44] R. L. Bobrov, Основные проблемы теории международного права [Basic Problems of the Theory of International Law] (1968), p. 204 [The last two words

At the same time, it is exceedingly important to emphasize that the peaceful coexistence of States of the two opposed social systems is the principal element in the content of this principle. Professor Bobrov is wholly correct in noting that "the decisive socio- political trend of the principle of peaceful coexistence of contemporary States consisted of the demand to ensure the peaceful coexistence of *States with different social systems*. This demand is the general trend of the general international legal principle of peaceful coexistence ...".[45]

As a principle of general international law, the principle of peaceful coexistence includes the obligation of States to recognize the social systems existing in various States, not to attempt to impose its own system on another State with the aid of force, economic pressure, and so forth. One must agree with Professor Suzanne Bastid of the University of Paris, who says that "to effectuate peaceful coexistence means to cast aside the idea that one system must prevail over another and, if necessary, put an end to the crusade with the aid of force. This means a particular system should be considered as a different form of political organization; this means it should be recognized that political disagreements can arise between States without necessarily raising the question of the legality of one or another political, economic, or social system. One should not expect that States might live in complete harmony, without problems or disputes arising among them, but one can expect that they will not mutually dispute the legality of their political, economic, and social systems ...".[46]

---

of Bobrov's original text in the quotation above are "обще-демократических основах", or "general-democratic bases" – *WEB*].

[45] Bobrov, Современное международное право [Contemporary International Law] (1962), p. 80; Bobrov, Основные проблемы теории международного права [Basic Problems of the Theory of International Law], p. 199.

[46] S. Bastid, "Les conditions juridiques de la 'coexistence'," *Politique étrangere*, XX (1955), 10; see also M. Bartos, "Aspect juridique de la coexistence pacifique active entre états", International Law Association, *Report of the Forty-Seventh Conference of the International Law Association* (1957), p. 32; C. Chaumont, "Les rôles respectifs de l'Assemblée et du Conseil de Securité", *Revue de droit contemporain*, XII (1965), no. 2, pp. 24-25.

An important aspect of the principle of peaceful coexistence is the idea of the equality of the two systems side by side with the equality of States, irrespective of their social system.[47]

In international organizations and at international conferences it is finally being realized that any attempts to decide international questions on a plane unacceptable to the socialist States, who for the time being are in the minority, are harmful to the cause of peace and international cooperation, and that the single correct means of deciding such questions is agreement among the States of the two systems. In the United Nations this idea has been reflected first and foremost in the principle of unanimity of the permanent members of the Security Council (see Chapters XIII and XIV), and in recent years also in the structure of a number of subsidiary organs (for example, the Committee on Disarmament and the Committee on the Peaceful Uses of Outer Space).

The principle of peaceful coexistence requires not only renouncing methods of the use or threat of force against other States, renunciation of war, but also renunciation of policies which could lead to war, and includes the obligation to pursue policies which promote the strengthening of international peace and security. The 1970 Declaration on Principles of International Law points out that all States shall "strive to adopt appropriate measures to reduce international tension and strengthen confidence among states".

Since in contemporary conditions peace is indivisible, the obligation to maintain international peace and security naturally also includes the duty of States to strengthen mutual understanding, trust, and cooperation with other countries in questions of maintaining and consolidating international peace.

[47] See R. L. Bobrov, "Принцип равноправия двух систем в современном международном праве" [Principle of Equality of Two Systems in Contemporary International Law], Советское государство и право [Soviet State and Law], no. 11 (1960), pp. 42-50; M. Lachs, "The United Nations and Peaceful Coexistence", *Polish Perspectives*, III (1960), no. 4, p. 9.

The principle of peaceful coexistence includes the obligation to develop economic and cultural cooperation between States on the basis of complete equality and mutual advantage irrespective of their social systems and, consequently, includes renunciation of a policy of boycott against individual States on the ground that their social system does not please the ruling circles of a given State.

As is said in the Declaration on Principles of International Law, "States have the duty to cooperate with one another, irrespective of the difference in their political, economic, and social systems, in the various spheres of international relations, in order to maintain international peace and security and to promote international economic stability and progress, the general welfare of nations and international co-operation free from discrimination based on such differences".

The principle of peaceful coexistence is aimed at maintaining and strengthening peaceful relations between States, primarily between States of the two opposed social systems in their peaceful competition in the economic, scientific, technical, cultural, and other spheres of peaceful construction.

In reflecting and legally strengthening the practice of cooperation of States of different social systems, the principle of peaceful coexistence contains in the most general form the basic requirements of peaceful coexistence.

From the principles of peaceful coexistence and nonaggression arises the right of States to peace, which in a political sense can be called the right of peoples to peace, since ensuring the right of States to peace is, in fact, ensuring peace for peoples.

(e) The principle of disarmament. The process of forming new progressive principles and norms of international law is continuing. The formation of the principle of general and complete disarmament has special significance.

Under the pressure of peace-loving forces, certain provisions relating to the limitation of armaments were included in the League of Nations Covenant. Article 8 of the Covenant recognized "that the preservation of peace requires limiting national armaments to the minimum obligations imposed by common action". The League Council was charged with preparing plans for the limitation of armaments to be submitted subsequently to the governments for consideration. In the same spirit, the League Assembly repeatedly adopted resolutions on questions of reducing armaments.[48]

However, the Preparatory Commission for a Disarmament Conference, which commenced its work in 1925, and the Dis- armament Conference itself, which opened in 1932, distinctly showed the reluctance of imperialist circles to limit armaments. Proposals of the Soviet Government concerning complete disarmament, as well as proposals concerning partial disarmament, were rejected. The capitalist monopolies saw in the arms race not merely a source of enormous profits, but also a means of ensuring their domination both within their own countries and also in the colonies.

The United Nations Charter, prepared with the active participation of the Soviet Union, reflects a different international situation, characterized by a significant growth of democratic forces. The United Nations Charter contains with regard to the disarmament question provisions which are more specific and far-reaching than those in the League of Nations Covenant. Article 11 of the Charter empowers the General Assembly "to consider the general principles of cooperation in the maintenance of international peace and security, including the principle governing disarmament and the regulation of armaments, and to make recommendations with regard to such principles to the Members or to the Security

[48] See E. A. Korovin and V. V. Egor'ev, Разоружение [Disarmament] (1930); V. M. Khaitsman, СССР и проблема разоружения (между первой и второй мировыми войнами) [USSR and Problem of Disarmament (Between First and Second World Wars] (1959); O. V. Bogdanov, "Разоружение в свете международного права" [Disarmament in Light of International Law], Советский ежегодник международного права 1958 [Soviet Yearbook of International Law 1958] (1959), pp. 93-123.

Council or to both". Article 26 entrusts to the Security Council "responsibility for formulating, with the assistance of the Military Staff Committee referred to in Article 47, plans to be submitted to the Members of the United Nations for the establishment of a system for the regulation of armaments".

A General Assembly resolution of 14 December 1946 (41/I) said that in pursuance of Article 11 of the Charter and with a view to strengthening international peace and security, the General Assembly "recognizes the necessity of an early general regulation and reduction of armaments and armed forces".

The same motives are echoed in numerous subsequent resolutions of the General Assembly. In particular, a General Assembly resolution of 4 November 1954 (808/IX) relating to the extent of disarmament measures said that an international convention on disarmament should provide for "the regulation, limitation, and significant reduction of all armed forces and all conventional armaments", as well as "the complete prohibition of the use and manufacture of nuclear weapons and any type of weapon of mass destruction, as well as the conversion of existing stocks of nuclear weapons to peaceful purposes".

Despite a certain vagueness of the Charter provisions regarding disarmament questions which resulted from the positions of a number of capitalist States who did not want disarmament, important progressive principles are contained in it. The United Nations Charter opposes the arms race, stressing the need to reduce armaments in order to ensure peace. The principle of disarmament and the regulation of armaments, according to Article 11, relates to "general principles of cooperation in the maintenance of international peace and security".

The United Nations Charter imposes upon members of the Organization the obligation to cooperate for the purpose of reducing and regulating armaments.

It should be added that the arms race, inevitably leading to an aggravation of the international situation, contravenes the principle of peaceful coexistence of States which is laid down in the United Nations Charter and is a generally recognized principle of international law. Consequently, the obligation to refrain from an arms race also arises out of this principle.

However, a reduction of armaments under contemporary conditions already is inadequate. The international situation urgently requires a more cardinal statement of the disarmament question.

The General Assembly Resolution "On General and Complete Disarmament" of 20 November 1959 (1378/XIV), adopted at the initiative of the Soviet Union, emphasizes the need for general and complete disarmament under effective international control in order to be delivered from the danger of a new destructive war. The General Assembly recognized "that the question of general and complete disarmament is the most important one facing the world today".

Effectuation of general and complete disarmament would have decisive significance for increasing the effectiveness of international law. From the standpoint of the progressive development of international law, the Soviet proposal was linked closely with the principle of nonaggression.

The principle of nonaggression, as already has been pointed out, includes the prohibition of aggressive war and the use or threat of force in international relations against the territorial integrity and political independence of any State.

Even though establishing a legal norm which prohibits war does not mean that war is eliminated, a real diverse influence of the norm upon the conduct of subjects of international law is possible. The actual guarantees of the effectiveness of an international legal norm may be legal or nonlegal.

The next logical stage of the development of international law in this sphere should be the international legal prohibition of the means of aggression; that is to say, general and complete disarmament.

The conclusion of a treaty on general and complete disarmament and the elimination of weapons of war would create effective legal and material guarantees for compliance with the principle of nonaggression and consequently also with the principle of peaceful coexistence.

The said proposal of the Soviet Union signifies an advancement of the principle of general and complete disarmament, which is a development of the principle of disarmament established in the United Nations Charter. This position was reflected in the Declaration on Principles of International Law, where it is said: "All States shall pursue in good faith negotiations for the early conclusion of a universal treaty on general and complete disarmament under effective international control ...".

The formation of the principle of disarmament is taking place in contemporary international law. It therefore would not be incorrect to assert that contemporary international law does not contain any State obligations with regard to disarmament. At the same time, it is doubtful whether one can assert that a generally-recognized principle of disarmament already has been completely formulated.

In order to correctly determine the formative stage of this principle and its content at the present time, one must proceed from the fact that the principle of disarmament could emerge in international law and could develop and be filled with broader content only on the basis of the agreement of States. The logical conclusions from the other principles of international law may carry weight and make an impact upon the formation of the principle, but these in themselves are not sufficient to prove the existence or define the content of any principle or norm of international law.

The question is, consequently, what is the content of the already existing agreement between States relating to disarmament, which is still in the process of being negotiated? To assert, for example, that at the present time the entire matter consists of States fulfilling their obligations arising out of the principle of disarmament is to put the cart before the horse and to present a wish is a reality.

In substance, however, virtually all Soviet jurists who have analyzed this question, despite various views and general assertions, come in essence to one conclusion concerning the specific content of the principle of disarmament at the contemporary stage of its development, namely: the content of the principle of disarmament in contemporary international law comes down to the obligation of States to strive for disarmament by means of concluding an international agreement.[49] This is all the same not an obligation of a State to disarm. But the legal obligation to strive for disarmament (partial or complete) by concluding an international agreement – is an important obligation which did not exist in the old international law. The conduct of States testifies to the fact that they recognize this obligation, and it has been confirmed in a number of international treaties, particularly the 1963 Moscow treaty prohibiting nuclear tests in three spheres and in the 1968 treaty on the nonproliferation of nuclear weapons. The international community attaches very great significance to this obligation and insists that it be complied with, demanding the conclusion of agreements both on partial and more cardinal disarmament measures.

(f) The principle of respect for human rights. The emergence in international law of principles and norms affecting human rights was part of the process of progressive change in international law. Here the influence of the ideas of the Great October Socialist Revolution and of socialist democracy as a new, higher type of democracy has had a very distinct effect. It is sufficient to point out that whereas the provisions of the

[49] See, for example, O. V. Bogdanov, Всеобщее и полное разоружение [General and Complete Disarmament] (1964), p. 130; V. A. Zorin and G. I. Morozov (eds.), ООН и актуальные международные проблемы [United Nations and Urgent International Problems] (1965), p. 113; S. A. Malinin, Правовые основы разоружения [Legal Foundations of Disarmament] (1966), p. 27; see also G. Hajdu, "Co-operation and Disarmament", *Questions of International Law* (Budapest, 1962), p. 28; J. Schulz, *Völkerrecht* (Berlin, 1967), pp. 123-124.

Covenant on Civil and Political Rights basically reflect similar legislative norms of capitalist and socialist States, the provisions of the Covenant on Social, Economic, and Cultural Rights reflect norms of Soviet legislation concerning the right to labor, the right to social security, the right to education, and so forth.[50]

The most material changes in the international protection of human rights occurred after the Second World War. The upsurge of the struggle of peoples against fascism, with its appalling flouting of human rights, led to the principle of respect for the basic human rights and freedoms, although this had been fixed in a general form in the United Nations Charter. The Charter urges: "to reaffirm faith in fundamental human rights, in the dignity and worth of the human person, in the equal rights of men and women of nations large and small" (Preamble). The Charter stipulates that with a view to the creation of conditions which are necessary for peaceful and friendly relations among States, the United Nations shall promote "universal respect for, and observance of, human rights and fundamental freedoms for all without distinction as to race, language, or religion" (Article 55).

While not giving a list of "fundamental human rights and freedoms", the United Nations Charter nonetheless introduced the principle of respect for basic human rights into international law, imposing corresponding obligations on States.

The bitter struggle between States of the two systems unfolded in the United Nations during the process of drafting the Universal Declaration of Human Rights in 1947-48. The Soviet Union and other socialist countries sought to work out a document which could be used in the struggle for the rights of the working people. They insisted upon including in the Declaration provisions concerning economic and social rights,

[50] See A. P. Movchan, Международная защита прав человека [International Defense of Human Rights] (1958); N. V. Mironov, Советское законодательство и международное право [Soviet Legislation and International Law] (1968), pp. 119-133; Ia. A. Ostrovskii, ООН и права человека [United Nations and Human Rights] (1968).

provisions aimed against colonialism, social discrimination, fascist propaganda, social and religious enmity, and so forth. This struggle of the socialist States was not without result; it positively affected the content of the Universal Declaration of Human Rights adopted by the United Nations General Assembly on 10 December 1948. The Western powers, however, taking advantage of the "mechanical majority" they then had in the United Nations General Assembly, rejected many proposals of the Soviet Union and other socialist countries.[51] Because of this, the socialist States abstained in the voting on the Declaration.

An even more bitter and prolonged struggle between the States of the different socio-economic systems unfolded as the covenants on human rights were being worked out.[52] The crux of this struggle remained generally the same as in working out the Universal Declaration of Human Rights. However, the negative attitude of the capitalist States toward including obligations with regard to socio- economic rights in an international convention was manifested even more clearly. As a result, at the insistence of the Western powers the single draft covenant on human rights was divided into two covenants, one for civil and political, and another for the social, economic, and cultural rights. The covenant on economic, social, and cultural rights was so formulated that it does not impose strict obligations on its parties to grant such rights to citizens.[53]

During the preparation of the covenants on human rights which the General Assembly adopted in 1966, such important

[51] For greater detail, see Ostrovskii, ООН и права человека [United Nations and Human Rights] , pp. 46-61; I. Szabo, "La portée juridique de la Déclaration", *Revue de droit contemporain*, XV (1968), no. 1, pp. 39-52.

[52] See A. Movchan, "Советский Союз и утверждение принципа всеобщего уважения основных прав и свобод" [Soviet Union and Affirmation of Principle of Universal Respect for Basic Rights and Freedoms], in F. I. Kozhevnikov (ed.), Советское государство и международное право [Soviet State and International Law] (1967), pp. 289-312; Ostrovskii, ООН и права человека [United Nations and Human Rights], pp. 78-122.

[53] See Article 2 of the Covenant on Economic, Social, and Cultural Rights. G. A. Res. 2200 (XXI), 16 December 1966.

international conventions on human rights as the Convention on the Prevention of the Crime of Genocide (1948), the Convention on the Political Rights of Women (1953), the Convention on the Nationality of Married Women (1957), and the Convention on the Elimination of All Forms of Racial Discrimination (1965) also were adopted within the framework of the United Nations.

Many conventions aimed at ensuring human rights were adopted by specialized agencies, especially by the International Labor Organization and UNESCO. Nor should one forget the four 1949 Geneva conventions on the protection of victims of war.

The principle of respect for basic human rights has become one of the most important principles of international law. A new branch of international law is emerging which defines the duties of States to ensure the basic rights and freedoms to all peoples, irrespective of race, language, religion, or sex.

Contemporary international law proceeds from the fact, and this is exceedingly important, that a close link exists between a State's ensuring basic human rights and freedoms and the maintenance of international peace and security. This link is stressed in many international conventions (particularly the Convention on the Elimination of All Forms of Racial Discrimination and the covenants on human rights) and in United Nations General Assembly resolutions.

International law has intruded into an area which was considered to relate to the domestic jurisdiction of States and in which specific features of the different social systems are manifested very prominently and strongly. However, this "intrusion" of the regulatory influence of international law into the domain of human rights does not mean that human rights are directly regulated by international law nor that they have ceased basically to be the domestic affair of a State.

At the same time, the emergence in international law of norms relating to human rights raises a number of theoretical problems, especially as regards the content of such norms.

The extent and character of human rights within a specific State (they do not exist outside a State) are defined in the final analysis by the nature of the State, and this nature is itself a product of the economic system of a given society.[54] And both the extent of rights and the substance thereof are different in States with different social systems.

The differences in the content of socialist democracy and bourgeois democracy frequently raise doubts about the possibility of concluding agreements on human rights among socialist and capitalist States. Life has shown that such assertions are unfounded.

As regards the content of norms concerning the international protection of human rights, just as the content of international legal norms in general, is determined in each specific instance by the content of the agreement between States relating to the creation of such norms. In the present instance, two circumstances have decisive significance. The first is that, notwithstanding the completely different essence of socialist and bourgeois democracy, there is a general concept of democracy and a general democratic concept of human rights.[55]

One should bear in mind in this connection, of course, that "pure" democracy and "pure" human rights do not really exist. There are, in fact, various historical types and forms of democracy. But fascism, for example, was a negation of democracy and of human rights in general and representatives of both the capitalist and socialist States agreed to this (see for example, the provisions of the 1945 Potsdam Agreements on Germany).

[54] For greater detail, see V. M. Chkhikvadze, Государство, демократия, социализм [State, Democracy, Socialism] (1967).

[55] For greater detail, see G. I. Tunkin, Идеологическая борьба и международное право [Ideological Struggle and International Law] (1967), pp. 27-32.

Second, it is also of great importance that international norms concerning human rights are expected to be implemented through the municipal law of individual States, taking into account the special features of their socio-economic system. Conventions on human rights do not grant rights directly to individuals, but establish mutual obligations of States to grant such rights to individuals.

That which exists in contemporary international law pertaining to human rights is far from perfected, but it also is not the end of an ongoing evolution. There are many untapped possibilities for the further development of international law in this field, especially with regard to social and economic rights, as well as the improvement of methods for international control over the implementation of conventions on human rights. The further development of the international protection of human rights depends upon many circumstances, primarily upon improving the international situation, terminating the aggressive activities of imperialist powers, the arms race they have engendered, and the aggravation of international relations.

One proposition of cardinal importance should not be forgotten: securing human rights remains and will remain basically the domestic affair of States. Therefore, the principal field of struggle for human rights is the internal system of a State, and especially its socio- economic system. The international protection of human rights, effectuated primarily by international legal means, is, although important, merely an auxiliary means of securing such rights.

(g) The prohibition of war propaganda. The principle of the prohibition of war propaganda essentially arises out of the principle of the prohibition of aggressive war. If aggressive war has been prohibited, then the preparation of such an especially dangerous criminal act also is unlawful.

The said principle also arises out of the principle of peaceful coexistence, inasmuch as war propaganda aimed at stirring up hatred among peoples, at worsening relations among States, contravenes the principle of peaceful coexistence.

The Second World War showed with full clarity how important an instrument war propaganda is for the preparation of war; fascist Germany and imperialist Japan, intending to unleash an aggressive war, extensively developed ideological preparation for war. As the Chief Prosecutor for the USSR, R. A. Rudenko, pointed out at the Nuremberg trials, the propaganda machine of fascism worked at full capacity, for the purpose of preparing an aggressive war, instilling in the German people the absurd idea of racial supremacy, stirring up savage instincts, appealing openly or covertly for the destruction of other peoples.[56]

Basing itself on the principle of the prohibition of aggressive war, the International Military Tribunal, as the court for the major German war criminals, recognized that the planning and preparation of war were a crime against peace.[57] The same principles are found in the Charter of the Tokyo Military Tribunal.

Although the Charters of the International Military Tribunals as a court for the major war criminals are concerned with the responsibility of natural persons, this responsibility, especially as it relates to crimes against peace, is linked closely with State responsibility arising out of their breaches of norms of international law.

Since the ideological preparation of war and, consequently, war propaganda are recognized as an international crime in the charters and judgments of the international military tribunals, State responsibility for war propaganda and, consequently, the principle of international law as a result of

[56] See K. P. Gorshenin and others (eds.), Нюрнбергский процесс: сборник материалов [Nuremberg Trials: Collection of Materials] (1952), I, 248-250.

[57] See the Statute of the International Military Tribunal, ibid., p. 16; the Judgment of the Nuremberg International Military Tribunal, ibid., II, pp. 452, 456.

whose violation such responsibility arises, also is recognized thereby.

In a resolution adopted 11 December 1946, the General Assembly affirmed the principles of international law recognized by the Charter and the judgment of the Nuremberg tribunal. In a draft Code of Offenses against the Peace and Security of Mankind drawn up by the International Law Commission in conformity with the said United Nations General Assembly resolution, the preparation by the authorities of any State for the employment of armed force against another State is considered to be a crime against the peace and security of mankind. According to this draft, conspiracy to commit the crimes specified in the draft code, the direct complicity in their commission, also are considered to be crimes against the peace and security of mankind.[58]

Moreover, it is possible to regard the principle of war propaganda arising out of the principles of nonaggression and peaceful coexistence as having been consolidated in the said documents as an independent principle of international law.

Soon after the Second World War, however, the imperialist powers seemingly forgot about the existence of this principle. The licentious campaign against the Soviet Union in a number of capitalist countries was accompanied by an exaggerated war psychosis and an extensive propaganda war against the Soviet Union and the other socialist States. Under such conditions the Soviet Union, steadfastly aspiring to strengthen peace among peoples, submitted a draft resolution concerning measures which should be adopted against the propaganda and the instigators of a new war to the 1947 session of the General Assembly. On the international legal plane, the purpose of this proposal was to confirm the principle of the prohibition of war propaganda and to formulate precisely the State obligations arising therefrom.[59]

[58] See United Nations, *Yearbook of the Internatinal Law Commission 1951* (1962), II, 135.

[59] Doc. No. A/BUR/86, 18 September 1947.

As a result of this step of the Soviet Union, the session of the General Assembly adopted a resolution concerning measures which should be taken against propaganda and the inciters of war.[60] In this resolution the General Assembly condemned "all forms of propaganda in whatsoever country conducted, which is either designed or likely to provoke or encourage any threat to the peace, breach of the peace, or act of aggression". The purport of this resolution is that war propaganda is considered to be contrary to the principles of the United Nations Charter, and this also means of principles of international law in general. The resolution, therefore, confirmed and strengthened the principle of the prohibition of war propaganda. In recent years the principle of the prohibition of war propaganda has received new confirmation in Article 20 of the International Covenant on Civil and Political Rights and in the 1970 Declaration on the Principles of International Law, which provides: "In accordance with the purposes and principles of the United Nations, States have the duty to refrain from propaganda of wars of aggression".

It follows from the principle of the prohibition of war propaganda that States are bound not only to prevent the conducting of war propaganda by their own agencies, but also to take measures so that war propaganda is not carried on by private persons, organizations, and so forth on their territory".[61]

The principle of the prohibition of war propaganda was confirmed in numerous resolutions of such authoritative international social organizations as the congresses of advocates of peace, the Congress of Democratic Lawyers, and others. An Appeal of the Second World Congress of the Advocates of Peace to the United Nations said: "We believe

[60] G. A. Res. 110 (II), 3 November 1947.

[61] For greater detail on this question, see A. N. Trainin, Защита мира и борьба с преступлениями против человечества [Defense of Peace and Struggle with Crimes Against Mankind] (1956), pp. 161-177; G. I. Morozov, "К вопросу об ответственности за пропаганду войны" [On the Question of Responsibility for War Propaganda], Советский ежегодник международного права 1959 [Soviet Yearbook of International Law] (1960), pp. 312-323.

that the propaganda of a new war creates the greatest threat to the peaceful cooperation of peoples and is one of the greatest crimes against humanity".

Expressing the will of the Soviet people, the Supreme Soviet of the USSR adopted the Law on the Defence of Peace on 12 March 1951, which says:

1. War propaganda shall be regarded in whatever form it is carried out as undermining the cause of peace, creating the threat of a new war, and is by virtue thereof the gravest crime against humanity.
2. Persons guilty of war propaganda shall be bound over to a court and tried as very grave criminals.

The Law of the USSR on Criminal Responsibility for Crimes against the State of 25 December 1958 provides punishment in the form of deprivation of freedom for a term of from three to eight years for the conducting of war propaganda in any form.[62]

Legislative provisions provided for the prohibition of war propaganda also have been adopted in other socialist countries.[63]

Despite the fact that the principle of the prohibition of war propaganda constantly is violated in imperialist States, there is every reason to suppose that it will develop and grow stronger; it has a firm base in international law, since its principles are generally recognized and it enjoys the powerful support of the socialist States and the peoples of the world.

2. *The Development and Strengthening of the Old Democratic Principles of International Law*

Side by side with the formation of important new principles aimed at ensuring peace and the development of

[62] Ведомости Верховного Совета СССР [Gazette of Supreme Soviet of USSR] (1959), no. 1, item 8.

[63] See Законы о защите мира [Laws on Defense of Peace] (1953); P. S. Romashkin, Преступления против мира и человечества [Crimes Against Peace and Mankind] (1967), pp. 40-49.

friendly relations among States, the further development and strengthening of the old democratic principles of international law, such as the principles of respect for State sovereignty, noninterference in internal affairs, equality of States, good-neighborly fulfillment of international obligations (*pacta sunt servanda*), and so forth, has taken place during the period of coexistence of the two systems.

The struggle of the Soviet Union, and later also of other socialist countries, the developing countries, and all progressive forces, to strengthen and to develop these democratic principles of international law further has produced results.[64]

In the old international law these principles were obliged to get along with such institutions as spheres of influence, the regime of capitulations, consular jurisdiction, unequal treaties, intervention, and so forth, which consecrated the predatory policy of imperialism. This could not but limit the content of these democratic principles of international law.

As the reactionary institutions, principles, and norms were rooted out, the path was cleared for the fuller development of the democratic content of the said democratic principles.

[64] On this question, see E. A. Korovin, "Борьба СССР за суверенитет" [Struggle of USSR for Sovereignty], Ученые записки Академии общественных наук при ЦК ВКП (б) [Learned Papers of Academy of Social Sciences Attached to Central Committee of All-Russian Communist Party (Bolshevik)] (1947), I, 3-46; F. I. Kozhevnikov, Советское государство и международное право [Soviet State and International Law] (1948); S. B. Krylov, "Борьба СССР за основные принципы международного права" [Struggle of USSR for Basic Principles of International Law], Ученые записки Академии общественных наук при ЦК ВКП (б) [Learned Papers of Academy of Social Sciences Attached to Central Committee of All-Russian Communist Party (Bolshevik)] (1949), III, 19-32; Baginian, Борьба Советского Союза против агрессии [Struggle of USSR Against Aggression; N. A. Ushakov, Суверенитет в современном международном праве [Sovereignty in Contemporary International Law](1963); L. A. Modzhorian, Основные права и обязанности государств [Basic Rights and Duties of States] (1965); D. I. Fel'dman, Признание государств в современном международном праве [Recognition of States in Contemporary International Law] (1965); Kozhevnikov (ed.), Советское государство и международное право [Soviet State and International Law]; Chkhikvadze and others (eds.), Курс международного права [Course of International Law], I-III.

The emergence of important new progressive principles has exerted great influence upon the further development of the old generally-recognized democratic principles of international law. Thus, the emergence of the principle of nonaggression in that form in which it exists in contemporary international law also affects the content of such principles as respect for sovereignty and noninterference in the internal affairs of States. Aggressive wars, armed interventions, armed reprisals, and the threat of force were the most flagrant forms of violating the sovereignty and interfering in the internal affairs of States. Their prohibition in conformity with the principle of nonaggression led, naturally, to an expanded and more profound democratic content of the principles of respect for State sovereignty and noninterference in the internal affairs of States.

* * *

Thus, the development of international law during the period of the existence of States of the two systems is characterized by the emergence of new and the strengthening and development of old principles aimed at ensuring the peaceful coexistence of States, irrespective of their social system, and ensuring the equality and self- determination of peoples.

PART II.
THE PROCESS OF FORMING NORMS OF CONTEMPORARY GENERAL INTERNATIONAL LAW

In approaching the question of the essence of international law, the investigation must begin with the process of the formation of its norms.

Those social forces which determine the normative content and the essence of international law as a whole also operate in the process of norm-formation; that is, in the course of creating, of developing, and of changing norms of international law.

Norms of international law are formed in the process of relations among States. There is no organ in international relations similar to the legislative organ of a State that can promulgate legal norms binding upon States as the basic objects of international law.

One of the important peculiarities of international law is that its norms are created by the subjects of this legal system themselves. This peculiarity makes the process of norm-formation in international law much more complex in comparison with the process of norm- formation in the municipal law of individual States.

The process of forming norms of general international law includes basic processes, which include those methods of forming norms as a result of whose completion an international legal norm emerges, and also subsidiary processes, which are specific stages of the process of making an international legal norm but which, however, do not complete this process.

CHAPTER IV.
THE BASIC PROCESSES OF FORMING NORMS OF INTERNATIONAL LAW

1. International Treaties

(a) *Treaties between States.* We encounter most of all in contemporary international law an enormous number of norms created by treaties between States. An interstate treaty as a method of creating norms of international law is a clearly expressed agreement between States relating to the recognition of a particular rule as a norm of international law or to the change or liquidation of existing norms of international law.

Taking into consideration that, with rare exceptions, treaties are concluded in written form, the draft articles on the law of treaties adopted by the International Law Commission in 1966 and the 1969 Vienna Convention on the Law of Treaties define a treaty as "an international agreement concluded between states in written form" (Article 2 of the Convention). Article 3 of the Convention, however, stipulates that this does not affect the legal force of agreements which were not concluded in written form, nor "the application to them of any of the rules set forth in the present Convention to which they would be subject under international law, independently of the Convention".

A conventional norm of international law is the result of an agreement expressed in a specific form, in the form of treaties between States. The name of a treaty (treaty, convention, agreement, declaration, exchange of notes, and so on), and whether a treaty consists of one or several documents, of course, has no influence upon its law-making role.

In the second half of the nineteenth century, especially in the works of C. Bergbohm and H. Triepel, the theory that only a certain group of international treaties plays a role in norm-formation was worked out. According to Bergbohm, two categories of treaty exist between States. Some treaties contain provisions which do not go beyond the possible limits already granted to States under prevailing international law; these were contractual treaties.[1] Such treaties never or very rarely are sources of international law. Treaties creating abstract norms which are recognized or established by States as norms of conduct for the future comprise another group of treaties. These are law-making treaties. In Bergbohm's view, not just treaties with a large number of parties, but also bilateral treaties, may come within the group of law-making treaties.

The difference between the said two groups of international treaties, according to Bergbohm, is defined by the difference of purpose which the contracting parties set for themselves. If the purpose of the treaty were to establish a general abstract norm, this is a law-making treaty, a source of international law. If the parties did not assume the task of establishing a norm of conduct for a long period of time, this is a contractual treaty, which is not a source of international law.

The Russian scholar Korkunov similarly divided international treaties into "constitutive" and "regulatory" treaties. Constitutive treaties, according to Korkunov, regulate "an individual concrete relationship"; they "do not establish a legal norm as the general rule". Regulatory treaties have the purpose of "standardizing a whole series of uniform relationships" and establish "general norms for all uniform relationships".[2] As will be shown below, however, he believed that this division was not significant from the viewpoint of the norm- forming role of treaties.

Another Russian scholar, F. Martens, divided treaties into "those formulating legal norms binding upon States which are respected in practice as principles of international law", and into contractual treaties "concerning private interests". Noting the similarity of provisions of international treaties pertaining to private questions, however, Martens says: "Considered

[1] C. Bergbohm, *Staatsverträge und Gesetze als Quellen des Völkerrechts* (1876), pp. 79-81.

[2] N. M. Korkunov, Международное право [International Law] (1886), pp. 121-122.

from this viewpoint, private agreements undoubtedly must be recognized to be a substantive source of positive international law".[3]

Triepel, concurring with the division of international treaties into those which are norm-establishing and those which do not create norms of international law, believes the basis of Bergbohm's division is inad- equate. He attempts to find a more profound distinction between these two categories of international treaties. In Triepel's view, there is a divergence of wills of the contracting parties in a treaty which does not create norms of international law (*Vertrag*), whereas there is a coincidence of wills and their amalgamation into a common will (*Gemeinwille*) in a treaty which creates norms of international law (*Vereinbarung*).[4]

Great attention has been devoted subsequently in international legal literature to the problem of dividing treaties into law-making treaties and contractual treaties. The theory of Bergbohm, Korkunov, and Triepel was adopted by the majority of scholars and jurists of the second half of the nineteenth and the beginning of the twentieth century.

Many contemporary writers also adhere to a point of view very close to that said theory. In his voluminous treatise on international law, a Peruvian jurist, A. Ulloa, expressed the view that the majority of international treaties are not a source of international law and do not influence its development. Such treaties, in Ulloa's opinion, simply arise out of prevailing international law.[5]

An Austrian, Professor A. Verdross, divides international treaties into law-making treaties (*Vereinbarungen*) and contracts (*Rechtsgeschðfte*). To the first category he relegates multilateral

[3] F. F. Martens, Современное международное право цивилизованных народов [Contemporary International Law of Civilized Peoples] (2d ed.; 1887), I, 189.

[4] H. Triepel, *Völkerrecht und Landesrecht* (1899), pp. 26-81.

[5] A. Ulloa, *Derecho internacional publico* (4th ed.; 1957), I, 51-52.

and bilateral treaties which establish general abstract norms, and to the second, treaties pertaining to specific questions.[6]

Rousseau expresses himself in the same spirit, asserting that since the time of Bergbohm and Triepel, only "law-making treaties" (traitйs-lois) are recognized as sources of international law.[7]

A Uruguyan professor, Jimenez de Arechaga, believes that although both law-making and contractual treaties create legal norms, only those treaties which form general norms are a source of international law. "Consequently", he writes, "a contractual treaty establishing particular legal norms is not a source of international law, as is, on the contrary, a law-making treaty, which creates general legal norms".[8]

The elaboration of this problem, especially in the initial period, was characterized by the transference of categories of municipal law into international law, which naturally could not lead to correct conclusions.

At the present time, many bourgeois writers reject the division of international treaties into law-making and contractual treaties or recognize the conditional nature and theoretical unfoundedness of such a division. Thus, Rousseau says that the said division of international treaties is of interest only from the viewpoint of description and classification. "In effect", he continues, "a contractual treaty and a law-making treaty have the same force in positive international law and no hierarchy exists between them as exists, for example, between contract and law in municipal law".[9]

6 A. Verdross, *Völkerrecht* (5th ed.; 1964), pp. 143-144. The Russian translation made from the third edition gives a division of treaties into law-making and bilateral transactions. A. Verdross, *Международное право*, transl. F. A. Kublitskii and R. L. Naryshkina; ed. G. I. Tunkin (1959), pp. 156-157. The issue is treated differently in the last edition.

7 C. Rousseau, *Principes généraux du droit international public* (1944), I, 135; Rousseau, *Droit international public* (1953), pp. 19-20; see also G. Dahm, *Völkerrecht* (1958), I, 21.

8 E. Jimenez de Arechaga, *Curso de derecho internacional publico* (1959), I, 102.

9 Rousseau, *Principes généraux du droit international public*, I, 137.

The Oppenheim-Lauterpacht treatise on international law points out that, although the division of treaties into "law-making treaties" and "contractual treaties" in a certain sense is of practical importance, it is "theoretically faulty" and "in principle, all treaties are law-making inasmuch as they lay down rules of conduct which the parties are bound to observe as law".[10]

C. de Visscher remarks that although law-making treaties and contractual treaties play an unequal role in the development of international law, both are law for the contracting parties, "creating in the relations between the parties an objective law of a local character".[11] He sees a difference between the first and second only in that "contractual treaties" (*traitüs-contrats*) are concluded with regard to private questions, are short-term, and after being fulfilled terminate their operation, whereas "law-making treaties" (*traitüs- lois*) relate to a wider sphere of relations and are concluded for a prolonged period.

Kelsen completely rejects a similar division of treaties, since "the essential function of the treaty is to make law, that is to say, to create a legal norm, whether a general or an individual norm".[12] "The so-called law-making treaties", Kelsen says, "are treaties creating general norms, whereas the others are law-making treaties creating individual norms".[13]

Professor P. Guggenheim notes that the difference between law-making treaties and contractual treaties "has no importance". "The difference", he says, "affects only the

10 L. Oppenheim, *International Law*, ed. H. Lauterpacht (8th ed.; 1955), I, 878-879.

11 C. de Visscher, "Coutume et traité en droit international public", *Revue générale de droit international public*, LIX (1955), 360; see also M. Sibert, *Traité de droit international public* (1951), I, 34-35.

12 H. Kelsen, *Principles of International Law*, ed. R. W. Tucker (2d ed.; 1967), p. 457.

13 Ibid.

content and, essentially, the interpretation, but not the legal nature of international conventions".[14]

The view has been expressed in Soviet international legal literature that any international treaty has law-making significance. Pointing to the controversial division of treaties into normative treaties (law-making treaties) and contractual treaties, F. I. Kozhevnikov wrote: "All treaties in principle have a norm-formative character in one degree or another, since they establish rules of conduct which their parties are bound to observe". In Kozhevnikov's view, treaties may be divided into those establishing rules "for the whole sphere of relations among States" and into "those devoted to a definite concrete question".[15] V. M. Shurshalov adheres to Kozhevnikov's view.[16]

In the opinion of E. A. Korovin, the division of treaties into law-making and contractual treaties is "unfounded, since any treaty, as an act originating with States-subjects of international law, has a particular law-making significance".[17]

A Polish professor, M. Lachs, referring to the thesis expressed by some jurists that only a multilateral treaty may be norm-formative, and a bilateral treaty, being essentially a contract, does not have such a character, writes: "In reality, however, an international treaty, either bilateral or multilateral, is a source of

[14] P. Guggenheim, *Traité de droit international public* (2d ed.; 1967), I, 130: see also A. Sereni, *Diritto internazionale* (1956), I, 136; I. Shihata, "The Treaty as a Law-Declaring and Custom-Making Instrument", *Revue Egyptienne de droit international,* XXII (1966), 56-57.

[15] See F. I. Kozhevnikov (ed.), Международное право [International Law] (1957), pp. 244-245; see also his section of V. N. Durdenevskii and S. B. Krylov (eds.), Международное право [International Law] (1947), p. 396; Kozhevnikov, Учебное пособие по международному праву [Instructional Manual on International Law] (1947), p. 117.

[16] See V. M. Shurshalov, Основные вопросы теории международного договора [Basic Questions of the Theory of the International Treaty] (1959), p. 118; E. B. Pashukanis only mentions a similar division of international treaties, but does not express a definite attitude toward this division. See E. B. Pashukanis, Очерки по международному праву [Essays on International Law] (1935), pp. 153-154

[17] E. A. Korovin (ed.), Международное право [International Law] (1951), p. 16.

rights and duties, even when it regulates very commonplace questions of everyday life".[18]

In Lach's view, the more correct method is to compare a new treaty with already binding treaty law principles, with norms arising out of treaties, and with other sources of law. On this basis, he proposes the following division of treaties:

(1) Treaties affirming or formulating certain already existing binding principles and norms of law for the purpose of greater clarity;

(2) Treaties creating new principles and norms;

(3) Treaties applying existing principles or norms of law *ad casum*.[19]

The significance of this problem, in our view, is much exaggerated in bourgeois international legal literature. It essentially never arises in practice. Even Korkunov, in referring to the division of treaties into law-making treaties and contractual treaties, wrote: "In accepting this classification, however, we must mention that its significance is exclusively theoretical. It has no practical significance, since all agreements without distinction have identical force and importance".[20]

Any valid international treaty has legally binding force for its parties and in this sense is law-making. However, the different significance in the international legal system of general treaties, in which all or nearly all States participate, of multilateral agreements with a limited number of parties, and of bilateral treaties; of treaties establishing norms of a general character, concluded for a long period, and of treaties containing provisions relating to narrow and less- important questions and of short-term validity, should be taken into account.

18 M. Lachs, *Многосторонние договоры*, transl. from Polish by G. F. Kalinkin; ed. V. N. Durdenevskii (1960), p. 263.

19 Ibid., p. 264.

20 Korkunov, Международное право [International Law], p. 122.

If, further, one approaches treaties from the viewpoint of introducing new elements into international law, then as Professor Lachs correctly suggests, one must compare their content with prevailing principles and norms of international law and appraise each treaty individually.

A treaty may reproduce and, consequently, affirm norms of prevailing international law, render them more concrete, develop them, or create new or liquidate old norms.

The United Nations Charter is an example of an international treaty which has all of these elements. It affirms the principle of sovereign equality of States (Article 2[1]) and the principle of peaceful settlement of disputes between States (Article 2[3]). The Charter affirms and develops the principle of the prohibition of aggressive war (principle of nonaggression), establishing the prohibition of the use or threat of force against the territorial integrity or political independence of any State or in any other manner inconsistent with the purposes of the United Nations (Article 2[4]). The Charter affirms the principle of self-determination of peoples, proclaimed earlier in certain local international treaties and agreements, develops it, and raises it to the level of a generally-recognized principle of international law.

The experience of the United Nations International Law Commission and of various international conferences in codifying international law also testifies that, as a rule, a new general international treaty includes both elements of a declarative order and elements of the progressive development of international law. The preamble of the 1958 Convention on the High Seas indicates specially that its provisions are generally declaratory of existing principles and norms of international law. In contrast, the 1958 Convention on the Continental Shelf contains basically new norms. The 1958 Convention on the Territorial Sea and Contiguous Zone includes provisions reproducing, often more precisely, prevailing norms of international law as well as new provisions.

The conclusion of an international treaty is a process embracing several stages: negotiations, initialling, adoption by the international conference or organ of the international organization, signature, confirmation, ratification, exchange or deposit of instruments, entry into force.

It is not obligatory that the conclusion of a specific treaty pass through all of these stages. Depending upon the arrangements of the parties, individual stages may be omitted. Until recently, signing a treaty was an obligatory stage in the process of concluding it. During recent decades, however, there have been instances when even the original partners to the treaty do not sign it. In the International Labor Organization, for example, conventions adopted by the ILO General Conference are not signed by States. These conventions are ratified by States without a signature beforehand.[21]

The process of concluding an international treaty is the process of bringing the wills of States into concordance, the result of which is an agreement that is embodied in the norms of the treaty. When does this process commence, and when does it end?

The rapporteur of the International Law Commission for the law of treaties, an English jurist, G. Fitzmaurice, a former member of the United Nations International Court, divorcing the text of a treaty form the content of agreement between States, regarded the drafting of a text of a treaty as a technical process irrelevant to the process of bringing wills into concordance and the forming of an agreement.

[21] See Article 19, Constitution of the International Labor Organization. Ministerstvo inostrannykh del SSSR, Сборник действующих договоров, соглашений и конвенций, заключенных СССР с иностранными государствами [Collection of Treaties, Agreements, and Conventions in Force Concluded by the USSR with Foreign States] (1925-), XVI, 360-361. An Israeli professor, Rosenne, has noted that the trend toward simplifying the process of concluding treaties in the United Nations is essentially characteristic of all international organizations wherein international treaties are concluded. See S. Rosenne, "United Nations Treaty Practice", *Recueil des cours*, LXXXVI (1954), 431-432.

In fact, however, Fitzmaurice himself was obliged tacitly to recognize the incorrectness of this judgment, since he considers the signature of a treaty to be the final establishment of the text and, moreover, as consent to the text. But the question is one of consent to the content of a treaty – that is, of agreement among the plenipotentiary representatives of States with respect to the treaty text. This agreement still may not be final, but is only one stage in the formation of the final agreement; it can not be considered to be simple consent to the text, as with a collection of formulations not connected with agreement. In this instance one has in view the negotiating process among representatives of States as distinct from the preparation of a draft treaty by experts who are not plenipotentiary representatives of States. The process of concluding a treaty commences with negotiations among official State representatives irrespective of the form or at what level those negotiations take place.

Fitzmaurice goes on to say in his reports that establishing and authenticating the text of a treaty strikes him as a formality.[22] This assertion of the author is not in accord with his basic premise, which is to consider a text from the technical legal viewpoint, in isolation from agreement; one can not speak of the validity of a text unless one regards it as the text of a treaty and, consequently, as a text fixing agreement or a specific stage in the process of forming agreement.

The construction proposed by Fitzmaurice is artificial; it does not reflect reality because it isolates the form of a treaty from its content.[23] The International Law Commission did not follow this path.

The working out of the text of a treaty by plenipotentiary representatives of States is the process of forming agreement. The content of agreement is formed in the course of working out

[22] United Nations, *Yearbook of the International Law Commission 1956* (1957), II, 111.

[23] For a discussion of this question, see ibid., 1959, 1; see also A. N. Talalaev, Юридическая природа международного договора [Legal Nature of International Treaty] (1963), pp. 77-79.

a treaty text during the process of negotiations between States, at international conferences, and in organs of international organizations, and is fixed in this text. The final establishment of a treaty text occurs by initialling, signature, or enactments of international conferences or international organizations. Completion of this stage of concluding a treaty signifies that the text has been established, and no participant in the negotiations or conferences can insist upon its being changed. This in principle completes the forming of the content of agreement with regard to a particular treaty norm.

There is, however, an exception to the general rule: the institution of reservations. Reservations may introduce a new element into the content of an agreement even after the stage of working out the treaty text is completed.[24]

Under contemporary international law any State participating in the process of concluding a treaty or acceding to a treaty has the right to make reservations unless the particular treaty contains provisions prohibiting reservations thereto. At the same time, each party to the treaty has the right to agree or not to agree with reservations put forward by other parties to the treaty. If not a single party to the treaty expresses objections against the declared reservation, it introduces changes into the content of the treaty in its application between the State which has declared the reservation and all other parties to the treaty. If some States-parties to the treaty object to

[24] On the question of reservations, see S. Borisov, "Суверенное право государств-участников многосторонных договоров заявлять оговорки" [Sovereign Right of States-Parties of International Treaties to Declare Reservations], Советское государство и право [Soviet State and Law], no. 4 (1952), pp. 64-69; V. N. Durdenevskii, "К вопросу об оговорках в международных договорах" [On the Question of Reservations to International Treaties], Советское государство и право [Soviet State and Law], no. 4 (1956), pp. 97-100; Kozhevnikov (ed.), Международное право [International Law], who wrote chapter 6 treating this question; S. V. Filippov, Оговорки в теории и практике международного договора [Reservations in the Theory and Practice of the International Treary] (1958); V. F. Gubin, "Советский союз и оговорки к многосторонним договорам" [Soviet Union and Reservations to a Multilateral Treaty], Советский ежегодник международного права 1959 [Soviet Yearbook of International Law 1959] (1960), pp. 126-141; Gubin, "Возникновение и развитие института оговорок к многосторонним договорам" [Origin and Development of Institution of Reservations to Multilateral Treaties], ibid., 1960, pp. 232-240.

the declared reservation, it is operative only between the State which has declared the reservation and those States-parties which have not objected to it. As regards States which have objected to reservations, the legal consequences depend upon the nature of the objection.[25] Objections to reservations may take the character of declarations which do not have any legal consequences in view. A state objecting to a reservation may consider itself not bound by the terms of a treaty with the state which has made the reservation.[26]

A norm of international law is, as a rule, the result of the completion of the process of concluding an international treaty. Such a concluding stage may be the exchange of instruments of ratification, depositing them, ratification, confirmation by governments, signature – depending upon the conditions of the specific treaty.

One must distinguish the entry of a treaty into force, which may not coincide with any of the aforesaid acts. A treaty may provide that it enters into force at a specified time after signature, exchange of instruments of ratification, or deposit; the treaty may provide that it enters into force only when a specified

[25] Article 25 of the 1969 Vienna Convention on the Law of Treaties says with regard to this question: "An objection by another contracting state to a reservation does not preclude the entry into force of the treaty as between the objecting and reserving state unless a contrary intention is definitely expressed by the objecting state". In the International Law Commission the author of the present work proposed to indicate that the nonacceptance of a reservation did not preclude the entry into force of a treaty between the respective states unless the objecting state declared a contrary intention, but this proposal was not adopted then.

[26] In the Comments on the draft Single Convention on Narcotic Drugs sent by the Ministry of Foreign Affairs of the USSR to the United Nations Secretary- General in 1960, the right of States to enter reservations to the treaty was noted, and it was pointed out further: "The legal consequences of such reservations is that the treaty is operative between the State which has entered the reservation and all other parties to the treaty, with the exception of that part of the treaty to which the reservation relates. Each State may also notify the Secretary-General of the United Nations that it does not agree to consider itself bound by the Convention with the State which entered the reservation, and in this event the Convention will not be considered to be operative between this State and the State which entered the reservation".

number of instruments of ratification have been deposited or upon the expiry of a certain period thereafter, and so forth.[27]

The process of concluding a treaty is completed by the last act or acts of States which have been provided for in the particular treaty. If a treaty enters into force at a certain time after completion of the process of concluding it, a norm of international law emerges in this instance with the completion of the process of concluding the treaty, but during this time it still is not a prevailing norm.

Sometimes the co-relation is reversed, as when a treaty enters into force before the process of concluding it is complete; for example, from the moment of signature, but subject to later ratification.[28]

In these instances a legal norm exists and commences to operate even before the process of concluding the treaty is completed. The operation of such a norm is provisional, however, since a refusal to ratify is possible.

[27] Thus, the 1958 Geneva conventions on the law of the sea have the following article: "1. This Convention shall come into force on the thirtieth day following the date of deposit of the twenty-second instrument of ratification or accession with the Secretary General of the United Nations.
2. For each state ratifying or acceding to the Convention after the deposit of the twenty-second instrument of ratification or accession, the Convention shall enter into force on the thirtieth day after deposit by such State of its instrument of ratification or accession". United Nations Conference on the Law of the Sea, Geneva, 1958, *Official Records* (1958), II, 132-143.

[28] A provision on the entry of a treaty into force from the moment of its signature and on subsequent ratification is found, for example, in the Treaty on Friendship, Mutual Assistance, and Postwar Cooperation between the USSR and Czechoslovakia of 12 December 1943; the Treaty on Friendship, Mutual Assistance, and Postwar Cooperation between the USSR and Poland of 21 April 1945; the Treaty on Friendship, Cooperation, and Mutual Assistance between the USSR and Romania of 4 February 1948; the Treaty on Friendship, Cooperation, and Mutual Assistance between the USSR and Bulgaria of 18 March 1948; the Agreement on Cultural Cooperation between the USSR and the Republic of Guinea of 26 November 1959. The Treaty on Trade and Navigation between the USSR and Iran of 25 March 1940 says that the Treaty is to be ratified, but enters provisionally into effect on the day of its signature. The Trade Agreement between the USSR and Canada of 29 February 1956 says that the Agreement will be ratified and enter formally into force on the day of the exchange of instruments of ratification; however, the Agreement will enter into force provisionally on the day of its signature. An analogous formulation is found in the Agreement on Navigation between the USSR and the United Arab Republic of 18 September 1958.

Until a treaty norm of international law has entered into force, no legal obligations whatever arise for the parties to the negotiations on the basis of it. This does not affect the question of obligations which may arise from the agreement itself concerning negotiations. The consent of States to enter into negotiations does not in itself impose obligations to conclude a treaty. The process of concluding a treaty may be interrupted at any stage, particularly if a State refuses to continue negotiations, or if, when agreement concerning the text is achieved, a State refuses to initial or sign the treaty, or if, after signing a treaty, a State sometimes does not ratify it. Instances also are possible when a State has ratified a treaty, but has not deposited its instruments of ratification.

Completion of the process of concluding an international treaty is completion of the process of forming a norm of international law.

Modification or liquidation of a treaty norm may occur by treaty, and in certain instances, also by means of custom. Modification of a norm by treaty occurs by concluding a supplemental or a new treaty. Inasmuch as all parties to a treaty are equal and no one party or group of parties to a treaty may modify treaty provisions without the consent of the other parties, any modification of a treaty requires the consent of all parties unless the treaty itself provides otherwise.[29]

In a number of instances, however, individual parties to a multilateral treaty may have created or create norms which are different from the norm of this treaty but which concern the same questions. Norms of such a narrow treaty bind only its parties; norms of the first treaty continue to be

[29] See Lachs, Многосторонние договоры [Multilateral lTreaties], p. 222; Arechaga, *Curso de derecho internacional publico*, I, 175. In a Note of the USSR *chargé d'affaires* in France to the Minister of Foreign Affairs of 2 September 1926 in connection with a Spanish proposal to convene a conference to review the Act of Algericas of 7 April 1906, it was said in particular: "I am authorized by my Government to remind you that my country, having taken part in the Algericas Conference, has the same right as other members of this Conference to participate in the proposed revision in order to set forth its own views, based on the principles of its foreign policy, on the questions being put forward".

operative in relations between the States which concluded the narrow treaty and all other parties to the broader treaty.

Modification of international legal treaty norms sometimes may be accomplished by means of custom. The liquidation of an international legal treaty norm occurs, as a rule, by means of the treaty (expiry of the term of the treaty, agreement of the parties, denunciation, abrogation, and so on) and, exceptionally, by means of custom (see Section 3 of the present Chapter).

(b) *Treaties between States concluded within the framework of international organizations.* International intergovernmental organizations increasingly are concentrating in their hands the organizing of the conclusion of multilateral treaties among States concerning questions which relate to the domain of their activities. In this connection certain new forms of the process of concluding international treaties, in comparison with the traditional procedure, are being formed.[30]

Within the framework of the United Nations the process of concluding international treaties is, in general, close to the traditional. The text of an international treaty is adopted by the United Nations General Assembly or by a special conference convened by decision of the General Assembly. It is subject to signature by the plenipotentiary representatives of States, whereafter follows ratification and the depositing of instruments of ratification.

In contract, in specialized international organizations the texts of international treaties are adopted in the majority of instances by organs of the international organizations. There is an obvious trend toward simplifying the procedure of concluding international treaties.

Thus, for example, according to the Constitution of the International Labor Organization a convention adopted by

[30] Tunkin, "Remarks on the Normative Function of Specialized Agencies", *Estudios de Derecho Internacional Homenaje a D. Antonio de Luna* (1968), pp. 282-291.

the General Conference of the ILO is signed by the conference chairman and the director-general of the ILO, after which certified copies of the convention are sent to the member States. Each State, having ratified a convention, notifies the director-general of the ILO about this ratification (Article 19, ILO) Constitution). The said procedure does not provide, therefore, for signature of the treaty by representatives of States, nor for deposit of instruments of ratification. An analogous simplified procedure for concluding international treaties is provided for by the UNESCO Constitution (see Article 4). In addition, the UNESCO Constitution (as also the constitutions of certain other specialized agencies) provides for the possibility of convening, by decision of the General Conference of UNESCO, international conferences to discuss and adopt corresponding international conventions (see Article 4).

The role of international organizations in concluding treaties among States consists of preparing and adopting the final text of an international treaty or of preparing the preliminary text of a treaty (if a special international conference is convened).

What place does such activity of international organizations occupy in the process of creating treaty norms of international law?

The process of forming both customary and treaty norms of international law has two aspects: bringing into concordance the wills of States with respect to the content of rules of conduct and with respect to recognition of this rule as a norm of international law. These two aspects may coincide chronologically, but most often they do not (see Chapter VIII).

In concluding multilateral international treaties among States within the framework of international organizations, these two aspects of bringing the wills of States into concordance never coincide. The adoption of a treaty text as final by an organ of an international organization or by a conference of plenipotentiaries of States created by decision of this organization represents completion of the process of bringing into concordance the wills of States with regard to the content of the norms of an international treaty.[31] When a treaty text is adopted by an organ of an international organization, this portion of bringing the wills of States into concordance is completed within the framework of the international organization. In the event a special international conference is convened to work out and adopt a treaty text, only part of this process proceeds within the international organization itself.

There remains the second part of the whole process of norm-formation: bringing the wills of States into concordance with regard to recognition of treaty norms as norms of international law. This part is formed from the individual actions of States (signature of the treaty, ratification, deposit of instruments of ratification or notification of ratification, and so forth), without which the treaties adopted by an international organization could not become legally binding upon States.

(c) Regulations adopted by specialized international organizations. Many specialized international organizations (the Universal Postal Union, International Telecommunications Union, World Health Organization, World Meteorological Organization, International Civil Aviation Organization, and others) adopt normative regulations (having various names). The emergence of such regulations has been caused by the increase in the number of primarily technical questions with which the corresponding international organizations have had to occupy themselves. Since technology moves forward rapidly, norms relating to technical and organizational questions must change frequently. Making them outside the framework of the basic convention (or charter, statute, or such) permits these changes to be effectuated by way of a simplified procedure).

Regulations are adopted by plenary organs of international organizations (the International Telecommunications Union, Universal Postal Union, World Health Or-

31 The institute of reservations to multilateral treaties is an exception to this general rule.

ganization, World Meteorological Organization) or by lesser organs (for example, the Council of the International Civil Aviation Organization).

The charters of modern international organizations provide two types of procedure for the entry of a regulation into force: express or tacit adoption by States. Thus, Universal Postal Union regulations are subject to ratification, and International Telecommunications Union regulations require the approval of States.

Tacit approval of regulations by States is a comparatively new practice, but already is widely used. The procedure of tacit recognition consists of a State's not objecting or not refusing to accept a particular regulation within a prescribed period, the regulation then being regarded as accepted. Thus, for example, sanitary regulations adopted by the World Health Organization become binding upon all member- States within a prescribed period (usually from three to nine months) which have not declared their refusal to recognize a particular regulation or have not notified their reservations thereto. The question of the acceptability of reservations is decided by the World Health Organization Assembly, which may reject a reservation if it contravenes the character or purpose of the corresponding regulation. In this instance the corresponding regulation does not apply to the State which made the reservation. The International Civil Aviation Organization and the World Meteorological Organization also apply tacit recognition to the entry of regulations into force.[32]

What is the legal nature of regulations promulgated by specialized United Nations agencies? Some writers suggest that such regulations are international legislation. Professor P. Guggenheim, referring to the sanitary rules adopted by the World Health Organization, says "they are an expression of a new technique of creating norms of international law which

[32] On ICAO's very flexible practice, see T. Buergenthal, *Law-Making in the International Civil Aviation Organization* (1969).

approximates the legislative and regulatory procedure of municipal law".[33]

Professor W. Friedmann, referring to those same sanitary rules, writes that "those powers, which have been exercised through the issue of nomenclature and sanitary regulations, are in effect legislative".[34]

Professor P. Vellas, of the University of Toulouse, writes: "Here one speaks of true legislative power: regulations promulgated by an international organization are adopted in execution of its constitution just as State laws are adopted in execution of the domestic constitutions of States".[35]

Professor Ingrid Detter, of the University of Stockholm, in suggesting that although regulations have noting in common with simplified agreements, decisively repudiates the theory according to which regulations are "if not identical, yet equivalent to treaties between states". "Regulations", she continues, "are more acts of the organization than agreements between the Member-States".[36]

The legal adviser of UNESCO, H. Saba, pointing to the regulations, conventions, and recommendations adopted by United Nations specialized agencies, writes: "These examples show that international conventions, the character of concluding which has changed considerably, are not the sole means of creating international norms. The community of nations now has at its disposal those forms which depart more and more from the concept of a contract freely concluded by

[33] Guggenheim, *Traité de droit international public,* I, 284; see also E. Giraud, "Modification et terminaison des traités collectifs", *Annuaire de l'Institut de droit international,* XLIX(I) (1961), 151.

[34] W. Friedmann, *The Changing Structure of International Law* (1964), p. 280.

[35] P. Vellas, *Droit international public; institutions internationales* (1967), p. 210.

[36] I. Detter, Law-Making by International Organizations (1965), pp. 321-322. See also K. Skubiszewski, "A New Source of the Law of Nations: Resolutions of International Organizations", *Recueil d' études de droit international en hommage a Paul Guggenheim* (1968), pp. 508-520.

States and are coming to resemble unilateral legislative acts enacted by a parliament and having binding force".[37]

In order to define the legal nature of regulations correctly, they must be considered in the context of the processes of creating norms of international law.

In confirmation of the viewpoint that regulations are a form of international legislation, it is usually pointed out that they have binding force after their promulgation upon all States which have not objected.

And although such a reference is factually correct, the interpretation of this factual aspect is incorrect. Indeed, any regulation becomes binding upon member States of a respective international organization only if this State accepted it. In one case this "acceptance" is, as we have seen, clearly expressed; in the other case, tacitly. But when, in conformity with the charter of an organization, a regulating becomes binding unless a State objects within a prescribed period, the State has a choice – to accept the regulation or not. If the State accepts, it makes no statement at all; if it does not accept, then it declares its objections and the regulation does not become binding upon it. Consequently, when a State makes no statement whatever, it thereby expresses its will and accepts this regulation.[38]

From the viewpoint of the process of creating norms of international law, a regulation adopted by an international organization is in the same position as the text of an international treaty adopted by an international organization. The content of the norms already has been finally determined. But for the norms to become binding upon States, an expression of its will is necessary (express or tacit) to recognize such norms as

[37] H. Saba, "L'Activité quasi-législative des institutions spécialisées des Nations Unies", *Recueil des cours*, CXI (1964), 615-616.

[38] See H. Waldock, "General Course on Public International Law", *Recueil des cours*, CVI (1962), 99; H. Blix, Review of I. Detter, *Law-Making by International Organizations*, in *Cooperation and Conflict*, I (1966), no. 2, p. 111.

international legal norms. The conclusion is that regulations are, in essence, international treaties.[39]

The process of concluding such treaties differs significantly from the ordinary. This is a new phenomenon, linked to the development of international organizations and having the purpose of accelerating and simplifying the process of concluding or modifying this kind of international treaty. But the binding force of norms of regulations is based upon agreement (that is, upon bringing the wills of States into concordance), and not upon the legislative power of international organizations.

(d) Treaties of international organizations. Treaties of international (intergovernmental) organizations between themselves and with States, which appeared essentially only after the First World War, have become exceedingly numerous since the Second World War.

The existence of such agreements is a result of the development of international organizations that are subjects of international law.

There are, at present, two categories of treaties of international organizations: treaties concluded by international organizations with each other, and treaties concluded by international organizations with States.

Virtually all treaties concluded by international organizations are bilateral, although several international organizations frequently are a party. Thus, the United Nations, International Labor Organization, United Nations Food and Agricultural Organization, UNICEF, International Civil Aviation Organization, World Health Organization, International Telecommunications Union, World Meteorological Organization, International Atomic Energy Agency, Universal Postal Union, and Intergovernmental Maritime Consultative Organi-

[39] E. A. Shibaeva, Специализированные учреждения ООН [Specialized Agencies of the United Nations] (1966), p. 105.

zation participate as a party in the Standard Agreement on Mutual Assistance to Jordan.[40]

In the majority of instances the treaties of international organizations take the form of an ordinary international treaty with all of its attributes. In rare instances, just as treaties between States, they take the form of an exchange of notes. Frequently an exchange of notes constitutes the last act of concluding such treaties. There also are exceedingly rare instances of the conclusion of agreements between international organizations through the adoption of parallel resolutions.[41]

Treaties of international organizations relate, by object, to a significantly narrower sphere of relations than treaties between States. Thus, under agreements between the United Nations and specialized international organizations, the latter acquire the status of specialized agencies of the United Nations. The agreements basically provide for mutual representation at conferences and in committees, the exchange of information, granting to specialized agencies the right to request advisory opinions from the International Court, and cooperation in questions of administration and statistics.[42]

Agreements between specialized agencies provide for cooperation and consultation in questions of common interest to such organizations, mutual representation at conferences and in committees, the exchange of information and documents, cooperation in statistical questions, and so forth.[43]

[40] See the *Statement of Treaties and International Agreements Registered or Filed and Recorded with the Secretariat* (1968), p. 5. [The Intergovernmental Maritime Consultative Organization has been renamed the International Maritime Organization – *L.N.S.*].

[41] See H. Chiu, *The Capacity of International Organizations to Conclude Treaties and the Special Legal Aspects of the Treaties so Concluded* (1966), pp. 51-63.

[42] See, for example, the Agreement between the United Nations Organization and the International Labor Organization of 1946, 1 U.N.T.S. 186; the Agreement between the United Nations Organization and UNESCO of 1946, 1 U.N.T.S. 233; the Agreement between the United Nations Organization and the Universal Postal Union of 1948, 19 U.N.T.S. 219; the Agreement between the United Nations Organization and the International Telecommunications Union of 1949, 30 U.N.T.S. 316.

[43] See, for example, the Agreement of the International Labor Organization

Agreements of international organizations with States relate primarily to the location of the organizations and their organs, the holding of conferences and meetings, privileges and immunities, as well as the rendering of technical assistance to States by international organizations or by other States through the medium of international organizations. The latter group of treaties is very numerous. Treaties of mutual assistance usually provide for obligations of an international organization relating to the granting of assistance, the amount and types of such assistance, the procedure of granting it, cooperation with the government, as well as the obligation of the State to whom assistance is rendered to cooperate with the organization, to submit necessary data, to render other cooperation, and to grant the organization and its employees privileges and immunities on its territory.[44]

What is the legal nature of treaties concluded by international organizations? Are such treaties international treaties, and if so, how do they differ from treaties between States?

The view has been expressed in Soviet international legal literature that treaties of international organizations are treaties between States or are a special category of treaties between States. Naturally this view arose out of a denial of the legal personality of international organizations. It was

with UNESCO, concluded in 1948, 18 U.N.T.S. 345; the 1948 Agreement between the ILO and FAO, 18 U.N.T.S. 335; the 1948 Agreement between the World Health Organization and FAO, 76 U.N.T.S. 171; the 1959 Agreement between the International Labor Organization and the Intergovernmental Maritime Consultative Organization, 327 U.N.T.S. 309.

44 See, for example, the Basic Agreement between the World Health Organization and the Government of Ghana for the Provision of Technical Advisory Assistance, concluded in 1958, 307 U.N.T.S. 3; the Basic Agreement between WHO and the Government of Indonesia of 1958 for the Provision of Technical Advisory Assistance, 307 U.N.T.S. 15; the Agreement between the United Nations, the International Labor Organization, FAO, UNESCO, the International Civil Aviation Organization, WHO, the International Telecommunications Union, and the World Meteorological Organization, on one side, and Saudi Arabia, on the other, of 17 February 1957, 271 U.N.T.S. 2. Of the treaties providing for aid by one State to other States through the medium of an international organization, one can mention the Agreement of the International Atomic Agency and the Soviet Union of 11 May 1959, on the Making Available of Fissionable Materials to the Agency, 339 U.N.T.S. 341.

expressed in general form by L. A. Modzhorian in 1948[45] and in a more definite and developed form in 1958. In Professor Modzhorian's view, agreements concluded by the United Nations "give rise to obligations and rights not for the United Nations as such, but for member States of the U.N.".[46] However, Modzhorian went on to write, "the activity of both the United Nations and of specialized agencies, strictly defined by member-States, gives rise to rights and duties only for their member- States ...".[47]

Professor F. I. Kozhevnikov wrote rather more cautiously but in the same spirit: "States are subjects of a treaty. Treaties concluded by international organizations reflect in the final analysis a delegation of rights by the States themselves as subjects of international law".[48] He repeated this formulation in 1966 with a modification: "However, in the final analysis these treaties reflect a delegation of rights by the States themselves as the principal subjects of international law".[49]

Professor Modzhorian later also softened her position somewhat, indicating that agreements of international organizations "give rise to rights and duties in the final analysis for their member- States ...".[50]

With the confirmation in Soviet international legal doctrine of the thesis that international organizations have legal personality, the view that treaties of international organizations are in fact "treaties of international organizations" and not

45 L. A. Modzhorian, О субъекте международного права [On the Subject of International Law] (1948), pp. 13-14.

46 Modzhorian, Субъекты международного права [Subjects of International Law] (1958), p. 33.

47 Ibid., pp. 33-34.

48 Kozhevnikov (ed.), Международное право [International Law], p. 242.

49 F. I. Kozhevnikov (ed.), Курс международного права [Course of International Law] (1966), p. 327.

50 L. A. Modzhorian, Основные права и обязанности государств [Basic Rights and Duties of States] (1965), p. 24.

simply a variant form of treaties between States also has been confirmed.[51]

In international practice the treaties of international organizations have occupied a definite place as treaties under which international organizations acquire rights or assume specific obligations. International organizations are created by States, but they are organizations distinct from States; they are brought into operation by States, but the actions of international organizations are not the same as actions of States, either in fact or in law (see Chapter XIII).

It is characteristic that in discussions of the draft articles on the law of treaties in the International Law Commission, in the Sixth Committee of the General Assembly, as well as in the Vienna Conference on the Law of Treaties in 1968-69, neither the international character of treaties of international organizations nor their distinctiveness from treaties between States were the subject of doubt.

The International Law Commission initially proposed to include treaties of international organizations within the scope of the draft articles on the law of treaties.

In the report of Professor J. Brierly, the first special rapporteur on the law of treaties, the article defining the operative sphere of the articles was formulated as follows: "A `treaty' is an agreement in writing between two or more States

[51] See G. I. Tunkin, Основы современного международного права [Fundamental Principles of Contemporary International Law] (1956), p. 11; Tunkin, Вопросы теории международного права [Questions of the Theory of International Law] (1962), pp. 80-84; I. I. Lukashuk, "Международная организация как сторона в международных договорах" [International Organization as a Party to International Treaties], Советский ежегодник международного права 1960 [Soviet Yearbook of International Law 1960] (1962), pp. 144-154; Lukashuk, Стороны в международных договорах [Parties to International Treaties] (1966), pp. 133-141; Talalaev, Юридическая природа международного договора [Legal Nature of International Treaty], pp. 30-35; Shibaeva, Специализированные учреждения ООН [Specialized Agencies of United Nations], p. 109; V. M. Chkhikvadze and others (eds.), Курс международного права в шести томах [Course of International Law in Six Volumes] (1967-73), V, 128-129.

or international organizations which establishes a relation under international law between the parties thereto".[52]

Brierly pointed out in his commentary that now "it is impossible to ignore this class of agreements, or to regard its existence as an abnormal feature of international relations".[53]

After discussing Brierly's report, the Commission recorded in its own report that "a majority of the Commission were also in favour of including in its study agreements to which international organizations are parties".[54]

At the following session in 1951, however, the Commission decided, without changing in principle its decision also to occupy itself with treaties of international organizations, that it was necessary first to work out articles having in view only treaties between States in order to study later what modifications are required to be introduced in these articles to make them applicable to treaties of international organizations. At the suggestion of the American member, Professor Manley Hudson, the Commission decided "to leave aside, for the moment, the question of the capacity of international organizations to make treaties, that it should draft the articles with reference to States only and that it should examine later whether they could be applied to international organizations as they stood or whether they required modification".[55]

The Commission's second rapporteur on this question, Professor H. Lauterpacht, defined the operative sphere of the articles on the law of treaties in his report as follows: "Treaties are agreements between States, including organizations of States, intended to create legal rights and obligations of the parties".[56]

[52] United Nations, *Yearbook of the International Law Commission 1950*, II, 223.

[53] Ibid., p. 228.

[54] Ibid., p. 381.

[55] Ibid., 1951, I, 136.

[56] Ibid., 1953, II, p. 93.

Pointing out that agreements of international organizations "have now become a prominent feature of international relations",[57] Lauterpacht insisted that the Commission prepare draft articles on the law of treaties which also would apply to treaties of international organizations. Lauterpacht submitted in this connection that treaties of international organizations are very close to treaties between States. "An analysis of any of these treaties", he wrote, "will show how closely they approach the traditional type of treaty".[58]

The Commission's third rapporteur on the law of treaties, Gerald Fitzmaurice, also proceeded from the fact that the draft articles on the law of treaties should extend to treaties of international organizations.[59]

Professor H. Waldock, the Commission's fourth rapporteur on the law of treaties, wrote in his first report: "In fact the number of international agreements concluded by international organizations in their own names, both with States and with each other, and registered as such with the Secretariat of the United Nations is now very large, so that inclusion in the general definition of 'international agreements' for the purposes of the present Article seem really to be essential".[60]

The Commission, however, affirmed its previous decision to work out at the beginning draft articles relating only to treaties between States. At the same time, as was pointed out in the Commission's report, it "recognized that international organizations may possess a certain capacity to enter into international agreements and that these agreements fall within the scope of the law of treaties".[61]

57 Ibid., p. 100.

58 Ibid., p. 99.

59 Ibid., 1956, II, 107.

60 Ibid., 1962, p. 32.

61 Ibid., p. 161.

In discussing the final draft articles on the law of nations in 1965, the Commission excluded from the definition of a treaty, at the suggestion of the author of the present work, any mention of "other subjects of international law"[62] in order to bring this definition into conformity with the scope of the articles. The new definition stated: "The present articles relate to treaties concluded between States".[63] But in its own report the Commission again emphasized that treaties of international organizations "fall within the scope of the law of treaties".[64] The Commission's report also pointed out the following: "If a ... convention covering treaties concluded between States were concluded, then it would ... remain possible, if found desirable, to supplement it by a further convention dealing specially with treaties concluded by international organizations".[65]

Thus, the International Law Commission held consistently to the view that agreements concluded by international organizations are international treaties.

The sentiment was the same in the Sixth Committee of the United Nations General Assembly, where the overwhelming majority of delegates concurred with the Commission's position. At the same time, some delegates of developing countries stressed the significance of these treaties for developing countries and expressed regret that the draft submitted by the Commission does not embrace them.[66]

The international character of treaties concluded by international organizations is determined by the international legal personality of international organizations. If an

[62] See ibid., 1965, I, p. 11.

[63] Ibid., II, 159.

[64] Ibid., p. 158.

[65] Ibid.

[66] See, for example, the observations of the representatives of Ceylon, Cyprus, Dahomey, and Liberia. United Nations Conference on the Law of Treaties, *Analytical Compilation of Comments and Observations Made in 1966 and 1967 with respect to the Final Draft Articles on the Law of Treaties: Working Paper Prepared by the Secretariat*, I, pp. 53-58. Doc. No. A/CONF.39/5.

international organization has been delegated the powers to conclude treaties with other subjects of international law, those treaties within the scope of the international organization *qua* subject will be international treaties.[67]

However, even writers who consider treaties between subjects of international law as not necessarily being international treaties or who do not have a definite position on this question also come to the conclusion that the overwhelming majority of treaties of international organizations have an international character.[68]

The validity of treaties of international organizations is determined on the basis of international law, primarily on the basis of the charters of these organizations, which are international treaties. Questions arising in connection with the operation of the said treaties do not fall within the scope of the municipal law of States unless the treaty itself provides otherwise, but are resolved in an international procedure by means of negotiations, arbitration, and so forth.

Recognizing agreements of international organizations as international treaties in no way signifies that such treaties can be equated to treaties between States. The specific feature of international organizations as subjects of international law affects the treaties which they conclude.

Norms of treaties concluded by international organizations between themselves, just as norms of treaties concluded by international organizations with States,

[67] In his report on the law of treaties, Lauterpacht correctly noted that "it is not the subjection of an agreement to international law which makes of it a treaty. It is its quality as a treaty which causes it to be regulated by international law". One may suppose in this connection that the international character of a treaty, in Lauterpacht's view, is determined by the fact that it was concluded by subjects of international law. United Nations, *Yearbook of the International Law Commission 1953*, II, 100.

[68] See J. Brierly, "Report on the Law of Treaties", *ibid., 1950*, II, p. 228; K. Zemanek, *Das Vertragsrecht der internationalen Organisationen* (1957), pp. 54ff; B. Kasme, *Le capacité de l'Organisation des Nations Unies de conclure des traités*, preface by P. Reuter (1960), pp. 111-115; Chiu, *The Capacity of International Organizations to Conclude Treaties*, p. 209.

always are of a secondary nature.[69] Their basis always is the charter of an international organization, which contains norms of a primary order. Therefore, treaties of international organizations, in contrast to treaties between States, contain, at the present time at least, only local norms.

As regards the application to agreements of international organizations of norms of the law of treaties which relate to treaties between States, it would be just as untrue to deny this as to insist upon their unconditional and complete application. The International Law Commission therefore acted completely correctly, having decided to work out at the beginning articles applicable to treaties between States in order to study later to what extent and with what changes these norms may be applied to treaties of international organizations.

Thus, the general conclusion is that treaties of international organizations may create and in fact do create norms that enter into the system of contemporary international law which are binding upon parties to such treaties.

2. *International Custom*

Customary norms play a significant role in international law. States constantly are referring to them in their mutual relations.

The problem of customary norms of international law is one of the most important and, at the same time, one of the most complex theoretical problems of international law. It is therefore natural that the question of customary norms of international law has been the object of the constant attention of specialists for a century.

Customary norms of international law are being formed in international practice, as a rule, gradually. What are the basic elements of international practice which lead to the creation of customary norms of international law?

[69] See Zemanek, *Das Vertragrecht der internationalen Organisationen*, pp. 60-61; I. I. Lukashuk, *Источники международного права* (Kiev, 1966), p. 55.

It should be pointed out that the process of forming a customary norm of international law, just as a treaty norm, is the process of the struggle and cooperation of States. The formulation of a customary rule occurs as a result of the intercourse of States, in which each State strives to consolidate as norms of conduct those rules which would correspond to its interests.

A customary norm of international law arises in consequence of the repeated actions of States. The element of repetition is basic to the formation of a rule of conduct. In the majority of instances the repetition of specific actions in analogous situations can lead to the consolidation of such practice as a rule of conduct.

The element of repetition in individual instances also may not take place, but a rule of conduct arises as a result of only one precedent.[70] Such instances are, however, a rare exception.

Continuity, that is to say, the element of time, also usually plays an important role in the process of forming a customary norm of international law. The element of time, however, does not in itself create a presumption in favor of the existence of a customary norm of international law. There is even less basis to believe that it is legally necessary for a customary rule to be "old" or of significant antiquity.[71]

Indeed, characterizing a particular rule as "old" can have two aspects. On one hand, it could mean that a given rule observed in international practice for a long period has passed the test of time. This very characteristic at the same time raises the question to what extent is this "old" rule responsive to contemporary circumstances?

[70] See Rousseau, *Principes généraux du droit international public,* I, 825; A. Klafkowski, *Prawo miedzynarodowe publiczne* (1964), p. 33; B. Cheng, "United Nations Resolutions on Outer Space: 'Instant' International Customary Law?" *Indian Journal of International Law,* V (1965), 23-48.

[71] See J. Basdevant, "Règles générales du droit de la paix", *Recueil des cours,* LVIII (1936), 513, 518; J. Kunz, "The Nature of Customary International Law", *American Journal of International Law,* XLVII (1953), 666.

Although time in fact plays a significant role in the process of forming a customary norm of international law, legally the element of time has in and of itself no significance. Depending upon the circumstances, a customary norm may be formed over a long period or it may be formed quickly.[72] Therefore, one can agree completely with Professor R. R. Baxter, who says that "the time factor as a separate element in the proof of custom now seems irrelevant".[73]

It has been pointed out repeatedly in international legal literature that not every repetition creates a customary norm of international law. Repetition of one and the same action also may not lead to the creation of a norm of conduct, and if such a norm of conduct emerges, it is not necessarily a legal norm: it may be a usage (a custom which is not legally binding), a norm of international morality, or a norm of international comity. In international relations, especially in the area of diplomatic relations and maritime navigation, there are many norms that have existed for a long period which, however, are not norms of international law. Thus, exempting diplomats' baggage from customs inspection and a number of diplomats' privileges on the territory of third States ordinarily are granted by all States. Before the entry into force of the 1961 Vienna Convention on Diplomatic Relations, the respective norms were not regarded as international legal norms, but were considered to be norms of international comity.

Some writers express the view that only uninterrupted international practice can lead to the creation of a customary norm of international law.[74] This assertion does not correspond to reality. It would be more correct to say that very likely not a

[72] See Verdross, Международное право [International Law], p. 154.

[73] R. R. Baxter, "Treaties and Custom", *Recueil des cours*, CXXIX (1970), 67.

[74] See, for example, A. Cavaglieri, "Règles générales du droit de la paix", *Recueil des cours*, XXVI (1929), 336-337; G. Morelli, *Nozioni di diritto internazionale* (3d ed.; 1951), p. 29; Kunz, "The Nature of Customary International Law", p. 666; Sereni, *Diritto internazionale*, I, 121.

single customary norm of international law has come to light as a consequence of uninterrupted international practice.

Take, for example, the principle of noninterference, one of the generally-recognized principles of international law. This principle was advanced for the first time during the bourgeois revolutions of the eighteenth century. Its introduction into international law took a significant period of time and was far from uniform. It earned ever greater recognition, although in the formative process it sometimes retreated before the pressure of reactionary forces. After the French Revo- lution of the eighteenth century, when the policy of intervention was proclaimed to be the official policy of the European powers (Napoleonic wars, policy of the Holy Alliance, and so forth), the process of forming the principle of noninterference in essence ceased. But then this process began again, and gradually the principle of noninterference was transformed into a generally-recognized principle of international law.

It would be at the same time incorrect to assert that an interruption of international practice exerts no influence upon the formation of a customary norm of international law. Interruption may destroy a customary rule of conduct which is still in the formative process or may lead to no rule of conduct being formed in general; everything depends upon the character of the interruption. At the same time, and this is the main point, noninterruption, just as the element of time, does not play a decisive role in the formative process of a norm of international law.

The question of whether a customary norm of international law only arises out of positive actions or whether abstaining from actions also can lead to the formation of a customary norm of international law has produced many arguments. Professor J. Basdevant, representing France in the *Lotus* Case before the Permanent Court of International Justice in 1927, expressed an opinion on this question which still is cited frequently. He stated: "The custom observed by states to refrain from prosecuting foreign nationals accused of causing a collision of vessels on the high seas is a customary norm of international law".[75]

A contrary view was expressed by the Turkish representative and by Judges Nyholm and Altamira, who asserted that acts of abstaining from actions do not create a customary norm of in- ternational law.[76]

A customary norm of international law grows out of international practice. State practice may consist of their undertaking specific actions in certain circumstances or, on the contrary, of refraining from taking actions. As a rule, it is much easier to ascertain the existence of a customary norm of international law when States take positive actions; however, there is no basis for rejecting the possibility of creating a customary norm by the practice of abstaining from actions. The custom not to undertake actions under specific circumstances in a number of instances undoubtedly leads to the creation of a norm of conduct which may be a legal norm.

Everything said previously with regard to the elements of repetition, time, and noninterruption also applies to the practice of abstention.

It should be noted that many principles and norms of international law contain to some extent the obligation of States to abstain from specific actions in their relations with other States. Thus, the principle of respect for sovereignty obliges States to abstain from any actions which represent interference in the internal affairs of another State. How could such customary principles of international law arise unless the practice of abstention also is regarded as leading to the creation of a customary norm of international law?

[75] Permanent Court of International Justice, Series C, Acts and Documents Relating to Judgments and Advisory Opinions Given by the Court, No. 13-II- Twelfth (Ordinary) Session (1927), Documents Relating to Judgment No. 9 (September 7th 1927), *The "Lotus" Case* (1927), p. 69.

[76] Ibid., p. 112. Permanent Court of International Justice, Collection of Judgments, Series A. No. 9, *The Case of the S. S. "Lotus"* (1927), pp. 59, 96; an analogous view is expressed by G. Gianni, *La coutume en droit international* (1931), p. 126; K. Strupp, "Règles générales du droit de la paix", *Recueil des cours*, XLVII (1934), 307.

Thus, not only positive actions of States, but also the abstention from actions in specific situations, may lead to the creation of a customary norm of international law.[77]

All the aforesaid elements of a customary norm of international law in aggregate still do not create a customary norm of international law. They testify only to the existence of a usage. The term "usage" has not taken root in Soviet international legal literature and practice. The 1947 textbook on international law gave a very confused and imprecise demarcation between a usage and a custom.[78] Usage is not mentioned at all in the 1957 textbook.[79]

As we use it, the term "custom" has two meanings: in the sense of a customary rule which is not a legal norm, and in the sense of a customary norm of international law. To avoid confusing different concepts, it would be advisable in the first instance to speak of an international custom, and in the second, of an international legal custom or, better still, of a customary norm of international law.

Consequently, the statement that an international custom (or usage) exists is not the same as a statement that a customary norm of international law exists, for a custom, or a customary rule of conduct, is not necessarily a legal norm.

The establishment of a custom is a specific stage in the formative process of customary norm of international law. This process is completed when States recognize a custom as legally binding; that is to say, recognize a customary rule of conduct as a norm of international law. The process of forming a customary norm of international law is completed and an

[77] Ulloa, *Derecho internacional publico*, I, 48-49; P. Guggenheim, "Les deux éléments de la coutume en droit international", *La technique et les principes du droit public; études en l'honneur de G. Scelle* (1950), I, 280; Y. Gouet, *La coutume en droit constitutionnel interne et en droit constitutionnel international* (1932), p. 73; M. Sørenson, *Les sources du droit international* (1946), pp. 90-101.

[78] See Durdenevskii and Krylov (eds.), Международное право [International Law], p. 24.

[79] See Korovin (ed.), Международное право [International Law], p. 8.

international custom (or usage) becomes an international legal custom or, that is to say, a customary norm of international law, only as a result of such recognition.[80]

It is in this sense, in our view, that Article 38(b) of the Statute of the International Court of Justice (the imperfection of its formulation is pointed out constantly in international legal literature), according to which "international custom, as evidence of a general practice accepted as law", is one of the sources of international law, should be understood. A customary norm of general international law presupposes, above all, general practice. However, general practice is not sufficient to declare that a customary norm of international law exists. A rule of conduct which is the result of general practice, as already indicated, becomes a customary norm of international law only when it is accepted or recognized by States as legally binding, as a norm of law.

The necessity of "recognition as an international legal norm" for a rule of conduct being formed in practice to become a norm of international law is a generally-recognized proposition.

In Soviet legal literature it was formulated carelessly in V. N. Durdenevskii's and S. B. Krylov's textbook, where it was said that "custom has more norm-establishing character, whereas usage contains a mixture of a legal source and a certain technical norm, and therefore has a dispositive, and not an imperative, character".[81]

V. I. Lisovskii speaks only of practice repeated over a long period.[82]

[80] Professor de Visscher correctly points out: "In a given instance, fact precedes juridical classification; but the latter remains decisive, and uniformity and external repetition never in themselves give a basis for conclusions regarding its normative significance". Visscher, "Coutume et traité en droit international public", p. 357.

[81] Durdenevskii and Krylov (eds.), Международное право [International Law], p. 24.

[82] V. I. Lisovskii, Международное право [International Law] (1961), p. 9.

In all other recent Soviet international legal literature, however, this proposition is considered to be a necessary element of a customary norm of international law.[83]

The absolute necessity of "recognition" or *opinio juris* for the creation of a customary norm of international law also is emphasized in the literature of other socialist countries.[84]

International legal doctrine of other countries, with rare exceptions, considers "recognition", or *opinio juris*, a necessary and decisive element for the creation of a customary norm of international law.[85]

[83] Korovin (ed.), Международное право, p. 16; Tunkin, Основы современного международного права [Fundamental Principles of Contemporary International Law], p. 13; D. B. Levin, Основные проблемы современного международного права [Basic Problems of Contemporary International Law] (1958), p. 100; N. M. Minasian, Источники современного международного права [Sources of Contemporary International Law] (1960), p. 98; P. I. Lukin, Источники международного права [Sources of International Law] (1960), p. 80; Lukashuk, Источники международного права [Sources of International Law], p. 58; Kozhevnikov (ed.), Курс международного права [Course of International Law], p. 40; Chkhikvadze and others (eds.), Курс международного права [Course of International Law], I, 181.

[84] See, for example, M. Genovski, Основи на международното право [Fundamental Principles of International Law] (2d ed.; 1966), p. 22; Klafkowski, *Prawo miedzynarodowe publiczne*, pp. 32-33; L. Gelberg, *Zarys prawa miedzynarodnowego* (1967), p. 74; S. Nahlik, *Wstep do nauki prawa miedzynarodowego* (1967), pp. 351-371; S. Avramov, *Medjunarodno javno pravo* (1963), pp. 47-48; A. Magarasevic, *Osnovi medjunarodnog prava* (1965), pp. 85-86; M. A. D'Estefano, a Cuban professor, believes in contrast to this that a customary norm of international law is a norm observed by States repeatedly and without interruption; a second necessary element, in M. A. D'Estefano's view, is the conformity of this norm "to the idea of justice and humanity". M. A. D'Estefano, *Derecho internacional publico* (1965), p. 12.

[85] See, for example, Oppenheim, *International Law*, I, 26; C. de Visscher, *Théories et réalites en droit international public* (2d ed.; 1955), p. 188; Verdross, *Völkerrecht*, p. 138; Morelli, *Nozioni de diritto internazionale*, p. 25; Rousseau, *Droit international public*, p. 63; M. Sørenson, "Principes de droit international public", *Recueil des cours*, CI (1960), 47; F. Berber, *Lehrbuch des Völkerrechts* (1960), I, 43; P. Reuter, "Principes de droit international public", *Recueil des cours*, CIII (1961), 464; Arechaga, *Curso de derecho internacional publico*, I, 56; Waldock, "General Course of Public International Law", pp. 47-48; Friedmann, *The Changing Structure of International Law*, p. 121; D. O'Connell, *International Law* (1965), I, 16; A. K. Pavithran, *Substance of Public International Law Western and Eastern* (1965), pp. 62-63; I. Brownlie, *Principles of Public International Law* (1966), pp. 6-7; Sereni, *Diritto internazionale*, I, 121; J. G. Starke, *Introduction to International Law* (6th ed.; 1967), p. 37; G. Schwarzenberger, *A Manual of International Law* (5th ed.; 1967), p. 32; M. Virally, "The Sources of International Law", in M. Sørenson, ed., *The Manual of Public International Law* (1968), p. 130.

Very few bourgeois international lawyers adhere to the normativist concept that the international practice of States in and of itself is a norm of international law without the necessity of its being recognized by States as a legal norm.

H. Kelsen writes: "The basis of customary law is the general principle that we ought to behave in the way our fellow men usually behave and during a certain time used to behave. If this principle assumes the character of a norm, custom becomes a law-creating fact. This is the case in the relations between states. Here custom, a long-established practice of states, creates law".[86]

At the same time, however, Kelsen says: "If the conduct of the states is not accompanied by the opinion that this conduct is obligatory or right, a so-called `usage,' but not a law-creating custom, is established".[87] Moreover, the new edition of *Principles of Inter- national Law* prepared by R. Tucker even speaks about the consent of States. "Indeed", it says in this edition, "it is redundant to stress the importance of consent in the development of custom since it is obviously implicit in the constituent elements of custom".[88] This inconsistency is actually the result of the fact that previously Kelsen had rejected the necessity of this second element.[89]

An analogous evolution, which can only be welcomed, has taken place in Professor P. Guggenheim's works.

Previously Guggenheim had resolutely opposed *opinio juris*. He asserted that usage (*consuetudo*) without any *opinio juris*, without any "recognition by states as a legal norm", is a customary norm of international law. Acceptance of the concept of *opinio juris*, or recognition of a customary rule

[86] Kelsen, *Principles of International Law*, p. 441.

[87] Ibid., p. 440.

[88] Ibid., pp. 453-454.

[89] Verdross, for example, points to this, citing Kelsen's article in *Revue internationale de la théorie du droit* (1939). See A. Verdross, "Das völkerrechtliche Gewohnheitsrecht", *Japanese Annual of International Law*, VII (1963), 1.

as a norm of international law, he wrote, makes custom superfluous as an independent source of international law. He believed it necessary to eliminate this "subjective element".[90]

Ultimately, however, Guggenheim in fact arrived at "re- cognition". He wrote: "The existence of custom should be considered as proved when repeated positive or negative acts become an expression of conduct which organs competent to apply the corresponding rule classify as custom".[91]

But what does "classify" mean? Classify means recognizing as norms of international law. According to Guggenheim though, recognition proceeds not from States, but from international organs. These organs, in the author's view, must be guided by defined criteria, by continuity, and by constant and effective application. In addition, breach of a rule should be linked with a sanction.[92] Guggenheim went on to say: "... an organ attributes the quality of a customary norm to universal acts, basing itself upon its own discretionary power. It confers upon the material element of a rule the character of a legal norm ...".[93]

Thus, Guggenheim in fact has allowed for the necessity of recognizing a customary rule as a legal norm. But in believing that such recognition should follow from an international organ, he has led his discussion up a blind alley, since no international organ exists which would attach to its authority the legal character of customary rules of conduct.

In the second edition of his *Traitŭ de droit international,* the first volume of which appeared in 1967, Guggenheim already specifically refers to two elements of a customary norm of international law. Citing Article 38 of the Statute of

[90] Guggenheim, "Les deux élements de la coutume en droit international", pp. 275-280.

[91] Ibid., p. 280.

[92] Ibid., p. 281.

[93] Ibid., p. 284.

the International Court of Justice, Guggenheim writes: "Under these conditions, an organ which considers itself bound by a usage (*usage*) should be convinced not only that its repeated actions conform to an actual usage, but also that it acts in conformity with a norm of positive law ...".[94]

Among those few writers who now reject the necessity of State recognition of a usage as a norm of international law, is, for example, an Italian professor, R. Quadri. "Custom", he wrote, "represents in social reality nothing other than a tradition, a series of uniform actions, generalized and prolonged for an indefinite period".[95] "Tradition" becomes a norm of law not because it has been recognized by a State as such, but because the "will of a social organism attaches such capacity to it".[96] The sociological explanation of this phenomenon given by Quadri is that tradition creates an "expectation" that actions will be repeated, which is important for "social equilibrium".[97]

An American professor, O. Lissitzyn, also decisively rejects the second element of a customary norm of international law, calling this construction "artificial".[98] The author, following McDougal, mixes the legal and other elements or, rather, simply casts the legal elements aside. In rejecting the need for a usage to be recognized as a norm of international law, the author inevitably comes to proclaim practice as a norm of international law. "... Custom, or `general practice'," Lissitzyn writes, "creates legally binding norms".[99]

The writers who deny the second element of an international legal norm lose sight of the specific features of legal norms.

[94] Guggenheim, *Traité de droit international public*, I, 104 ["... non seulement de se conformer d'une manière constante et uniforme à un usage utile et opportun ..." – *WEB*].

[95] R. Quadri, *Diritto internazionale publico* (4th ed.; 1963), p. 95.

[96] Ibid., p. 96.

[97] Ibid., p. 95.

[98] O. J. Lissitzyn, *International Law Today and Tomorrow* (1965), p. 34.

[99] Ibid., p. 35.

"Universal practice" creates not merely legal, but also moral international norms and norms of international comity. But of the general mass of such international norms, only those become norms of international law which acquire the said element – recognition by States as international legal norms.

It seems to us that it was this view which was held by the International Law Commission when the question arose of whether a particular customary norm of international law exists. Thus, in considering the question of diplomatic privileges and immunities of admi-nistrative and technical personnel, as well as of the service personnel of diplomatic representations, the Commission ascertained that certain States (the United States, Great Britain, the Soviet Union, and others) grant diplomatic privileges and immunities to ad- ministrative-technical personnel, and some even to service personnel of foreign diplomatic representations, although there are significant differences in the extent of their privileges and immunities, on the basis of reciprocity. Taking into account the absence of universal practice on this question, the Commission came to the conclusion that "in these circumstances it cannot be claimed that there is a rule of international law on the subject ...".[100]

With regard to exempting diplomats from customs duties upon articles imported for personal use, the Commission stated: "In general, customs duties are likewise not levied on articles intended for the personal use of the diplomatic agent or members of his family belonging to his household (including articles intended for his establishment)". Thus, the Commission came to the conclusion that in this case the practice of exemption from customs duties is, in essence, universal. But it was noted at the same time that the said exemption from customs duties "... has been regarded as based on international comity", and, consequently, although universal practice does exist in the present instance, it still has not been

[100] See the Report of the International Law Commission on the Work of Its X Session. United Nations, *Yearbook of the International Law Commission 1958*, II, 101.

recognized as a legal norm. On its part, the Commission proposed, inasmuch as this practice was widespread, to recognize it as a norm of international law. A corresponding provision was included in the draft Convention on Diplomatic Relations and Immunities.[101] The 1961 Vienna Conference incorporated this norm in the Convention on Diplomatic Relations (Article 36).

The unanimous or virtually unanimous recognition by representatives of different social systems and ideologies, as well as by international practice, of the position that two elements – the emergence of a rule of conduct and its recognition by States as a legal norm – are necessary for a customary norm of international law to arise is exceedingly important for the practice of international law. This does not mean that disagreements over customary norms of international law have no practical significance. But the said unanimity of opinion is sufficient for customary norms of international law, which still comprise an important part of contemporary general international law, to function and develop.

What is recognition by States of a specific rule as a norm of international law? What is the essence of such recognition? Recognition or acceptance by a State of a particular customary rule as a norm of law signifies an expression of a State's will, the consent of a State, to consider this customary rule to be a norm of international law. It must be emphasized that one is speaking of recognition "as a norm of international law" and not "as a legal norm" in general. States, for example, also recognize "as a legal norm" the norms of national legal systems of other States. Moreover, courts of States frequently apply norms of foreign law.

But the Statute of the International Court refers to recognition of a particular rule as an international legal norm or, more precisely, of a norm of general international law. The Statute speaks of "general practice", "accepted as law"; that is, local

[101] Ibid., II, p. 26.

customary international legal norms are pushed to the side. Such norms exist, although they do not play a large role in the general system of international law.

It would be more accurate to say "recognized as an international legal norm" in Article 38(b) of the Statute instead of "accepted as law". Taking into account, however, that the words "is to decide in accordance with international law such disputes as are submitted to it" were included in the preamble of Article 38 of the Statute upon the proposal of the Chilean delegation at the San Francisco Conference,[102] the prevailing text of the Statute indicates sufficiently clearly that the question is one just of recognition "as an international legal norm".

This fact is of material importance. In recognizing a norm of international law, a State takes upon itself before other States the obligation to comply with a rule of conduct as binding upon itself, from which it may not arbitrarily free itself. At the same time, it acquires the right to demand that this norm be complied with by other States.

Thus, the bonds between a State accepting a customary norm of international law and the other States who already have recognized this norm are basically identical with those bonds established among States with the aid of an international treaty.[103]

Consequently, the essence of the process of creating a norm of international law by means of custom consists of agreement between States, which in this case is tacit, and not clearly expressed, as in a treaty (on the legal nature of agreement, see Chapter VIII).

If a customary norm of international law is the result of agreement between States, the operative sphere of this norm is limited to relations between States who have recognized

[102] See S. B. Krylov, История создания ООН [History of Creation of the United Nations], ed. G. I. Tunkin (1960), p. 228.

[103] See Tunkin, Основы современного международного права [Fundamental Principles of Contemporary International Law], p. 11.

it as a norm of international law, that is to say, to relations between those States who are parties to the corresponding tacit agreement.

The operative sphere of a principle or customary norm of international law may gradually expand, and it is by this means, as a rule, that customary norms of international law become generally recognized. There are frequent instances when the declaration of a single State is a formative moment. Many principles of international law were proclaimed, for example, by revolutionary France in the eighteenth century. Among them are the principles of respect for State sovereignty, noninterference, equality of States, and the principle that military operations must be directed only against military objects and not against the civilian population, and others. In the Dekret on Peace and other State documents, the Soviet State advanced the principles of the prohibition and criminality of aggressive war, the principle of self-determination of nations, the principle of peaceful coexistence, and a number of other principles of international law.

In all the aforesaid instances the principles initially proclaimed by one State gradually were recognized by other States and were transformed partially by custom and partially by treaty into generally- recognized principles of contemporary international law.

The question frequently is raised: how can the origin of a norm of international law be explained on the basis of the concept of agreement if another customary norm of international law already exists on the given question? Professor Basdevant says, for example, that the doctrine pursuant to which the essence of the process of creating a customary norm of international law consists of tacit agreement is in contradiction with the changed character of customary norms. He declares that it is impossible, without resorting to a fiction, to assert that "we have here the case of a tacit agreement consecrating this change, an agreement to which all states who previously were bound by the corresponding customary norm are participants".[104]

One should not forget, however, the specific feature of international law that subjects of international law are themselves the creators of norms of international law. The fact that States are bound by prevailing norms of international law does not preclude the possibility of their creating new norms of international law by treaty or custom that may differ from prevailing norms. With regard to norms of international law which are not of an imperative character, the question is resolved relatively simply.

A new norm deviating from a prevailing norm (and, consequently, recognized by the respective powers) will, of course, be binding only upon States which have recognized it, and this new norm replaces the respective old norm in relations among these countries. The latter, however, will be operative among States which still have not recognized the new norm, as well as in relations between these States, on one side, and the powers who already have recognized the new norm, on the other. The operative sphere of this new norm gradually may be expanded at the expense of reducing the operative sphere of the old norm, and ultimately the new norm may completely supplant the old norm.

The principle of the prohibition of aggressive war, for example, entered international law as a conventional principle of the 1928 Pact of Paris. In the relations among parties to this treaty the said principle replaced the previously prevailing principle of general international law under which each State had the right to go to war. The new principle was recognized by other States by accession to the Pact of Paris or by custom, so that for some countries this was a conventional principle whereas for others, a customary principle of international law. By such means the principle of the prohibition of aggressive war gradually was transformed into a generally-recognized principle of international law, having replaced "the right of

104 Basdevant, "Règles générales du droit de la paix", pp. 515-516.

states to go to war". This principle was developed further in the United Nations Charter.

One of the principal arguments advanced against the concept that the essence of custom as a specific method of creating a norm of international law consists of agreement between States is the assertion that this concept contradicts the situation supposedly existing wherein a customary norm legally binds States irrespective of its being "recognized" or "accepted" by these States. This kind of objection is advanced both by proponents and opponents of the concept of *opinio juris*.

H. Kelsen, calling the notion that a customary norm is a tacit agreement a fiction, asserts that "international customary law could be interpreted as created by a consent of the states only if it were

possible to prove that the custom which evidence the existence of a norm of international law is constituted by the acts of all the states which are bound by the norms of customary law, or that a norm of customary law is binding upon a state only if this state by its own acts participated in establishing the custom in question".[105] In developing this thought, Kelsen points out that since customary norms of international law are binding upon all States, it would be necessary to prove that all States have agreed to the recognition of all customary norms of international law by their actual conduct, by participating in creating the respective custom which testifies to the existence of a customary norm. Such evidence, Kelsen says, is not needed under international law. Customary norms of international law, he asserts, are created not by the "common consent of members of the international community", but by the "long-established practice of a great number of states, including the states which with respect to their power, their culture, and so on, are of certain importance...".[106]

[105] Kelsen, *Principles of International Law*, p. 444.

[106] Ibid., p. 445.

Kelsen maintains in addition that it supposedly should follow from the concept of agreement that all States must participate in creating each norm of international law. It is wholly obvious that this is not so. It is not obligatory in the least that a respective practice leading to the creation of a customary norm of international law be "universal".

A customary rule may be created by the practice of a limited number of States. In being recognized as a legal norm, it sometimes is initially a customary norm having a limited sphere of application which, as this norm is recognized by other States, gradually expands, bringing the respective norm closer to a generally-recognized norm of international law.

Expansion of the operative sphere of a customary norm is to some extent analogous to that which takes place with regard to conventional norms of international law. In reality, norms of a particular international treaty very frequently are created by only a few of the countries which become parties to this treaty. Those States which subsequently accede to the treaty have not participated in creating the norms of this treaty.

Many other writers, together with Kelsen, insist that the position – which in their view is the existing position – that customary norms of international law recognized by a large number of States become binding in virtue thereof upon all States makes the concept of the customary norm as a tacit agreement unacceptable and contrary to reality. "Tacit agreements", writes A. Sereni, "bind only States which are parties to these agreements; a customary norm, on the contrary, binds States as soon as it is formed irrespective of their consent or participation in its formation".[107]

It is difficult to avoid noticing that the argumentation of these writers pretends to have proved just what is to be proved; to

[107] Sereni, *Diritto internazionale*, I, 123; see also Arechaga, *Curso de derecho internacional publico*, I, 59-60; Quadri, *Diritto internazionale publico*, p. 94; Guggenheim, *Traité de droit international public*, I, 107-108.

wit, the binding character of customary norms upon all States which have been recognized by the majority of States.

The thesis that a customary norm of international law recognized by a significant number of States is binding upon all other countries enjoys wide support in contemporary bourgeois international legal literature.

Professor Verdross makes an interesting reservation: "Despite the fact that the formation of a general customary norm does not presuppose its application by all States, a universal customary rule may not arise which would contravene the legal convictions of any civilized people".[108] But if recognition of a new customary norm of international law as such is necessary on the part of a respective State, why should a newly-formed State be in a worse position? Why may this State not object to any customary norm of international law with which it does not agree? This was at one time the position of the Soviet State and is now the position of new States formed in consequence of the liberation of colonies.[109]

The concept that customary norms of international law recognized as such by a significant number of States must be considered to be binding upon all States is actually based upon the presupposition that a majority of States may dictate norms of international law binding upon all other States in international relations.

This position is carried on to its logical conclusion by R. Quadri, an Italian professor. In developing his theory of a "collective or social will" (*volontà collettiva o sociale*), Quadri maintains that will, the decision of a group of States, may create legal norms in international relations binding upon all States; that

108 Verdross, Международное право [International Law], p. 155.

109 See G. M. Abi-Saab, "The Newly Independent States and the Rules of International Law", *Howard Law Journal*, VIII (1962), 106; R. P. Anand, "Attitude of the Asian-African States Toward Certain Problems of International Law", *International and Comparative Law Quarterly*, XV (1966), 64-67; H. Bokor-Szegó, "The New States and International Law", *Questions of International Law* (1968), pp. 7-35; M. Sahovic, "Influence des états nouveaux sur la conception du droit international", *Annuaire français de droit international*, XII (1966), 34-35.

is to say, create norms of general international law. According to Quadri, international law is based upon a decision of the predominant force in the international community.[110] In another work, published in the *Recueil des cours* of the Hague Academy of International Law, Quadri explains what he means by the expression "predominant force". He writes: "It is sufficient that there exist a will, decision, and action common to a specific group which is in a position, if necessary, to impose its authority".[111]

The concept is in blatant contradiction to the fundamental principles of international law, especially the principle of equality of States.

Indisputably, this principle signifies only legal equality, which does not correspond to the real inequality of States in international relations. There is no doubt that the position of the majority of States, including States of the two systems, and above all the position of the great powers, has decisive significance in the process of creating generally-recognized norms of international law. Such is the actual situation. Legally, however, the wills of different States are of equal significance in the process of creating a norm of international law. This legal equality is of great importance. It follows from this that the majority of States in international relations can not create norms binding upon other States and do not have the right to attempt to impose given norms of other States. This proposition is especially important for contemporary international law, which regulates relations of States belonging to different and even opposed social systems.

The wills of States, reflected in their recognition of a customary norm of international law, is determinative. Force of circumstances compels individual States in the majority of instances to consider as binding those norms which the overwhelming majority of States already have recognized,

[110] Quadri, *Diritto internazionale publico*, p. 28.

[111] Quadri, "Le fondement du caractère obligatoire du droit international public", *Recueil des cours*, LXXX (1952), 625.

including the States of the two systems and the great powers. But this actual situation never should be confused with the legal situation.

As regards newly emergent States, legally they have the right not to recognize a particular customary norm of general international law. If, however, a new State enters without reservations into official relations with other countries, this signifies that it accepts the specific complex of principles and norms of prevailing international law as being the basic principles of relations among States.

In practice, in all instances when it is necessary to ascertain the existence of a particular generally-recognized norm of international law, the normal procedure is to investigate whether there is a "general practice" and, if such a practice exists, whether it has been recognized as a legal norm and by how many States.

When establishing whether a State has recognized a particular rule as a norm of international law, the issue of the "silence" of a State presents significant difficulties. As I. Brownlie points out, "silence may signify either tacit consent or the absence of interest in the particular matter".[112]

Assuredly, not every silence can be regarded as consent. Particularly in those instances when the respective forming of a customary norm does not affect a State's interests at the given time, its silence cannot be considered to be tacit recognition of this norm. But in those instances when an emerging rule affects the interests of a particular State, the absence of objections after a sufficient time can, as a rule, be regarded as tacit recognition of this norm.

Recognition of a particular rule as an international norm by a large number of States may be a basis for presupposing that this norm has been generally-recognized, but only as a presupposition, and not a final conclusion.[113]

[112] I. Brownlie, *Principles of Public International Law* (2d ed.; 1973), p. 7.

[113] Strupp, for example, believes that if a customary norm is applied by

Undoubtedly it is not always possible and perhaps even impossible in the majority of instances to determine with mathematical precision that a particular customary norm of international law has been recognized by all States without exception. However, a similar situation is created in social phenomena rather frequently, and the difficulties which may arise in the process of similar calculations never have been regarded as undermining the rule itself.

The misgivings expressed by writers who criticize the concept of tacit agreement, that acceptance of this viewpoint would lead in practice to the necessity of proving in each individual instance whether a given State had recognized the corresponding customary norm or not, are greatly exaggerated. In the overwhelming majority of instances in disputes between States which relate to this question, the issue is not whether a particular State has recognized a specific customary norm of general international law, but rather a matter of the content of this norm and of its application in a concrete situation.[114]

There have been instances, however, when a dispute involved precisely whether a norm recognized by a majority of States was binding upon other States who had not recognized this norm. The question of the three-mile breadth of territorial waters may serve as an example. As is well-known, at the 1958 and 1960 Geneva Conferences on the Law of the Sea, the western States, relying upon the bourgeois doctrine adduced above, attempted to maintain that the three-mile limit of territorial waters had existed for a long time, and had been recognized as a norm of international law by the majority of States, and therefore is a norm of general international law binding upon all States. These claims of the Western powers, however, did not obtain even two-thirds of the votes at the said conferences, the socialist States and a significant number of

a significant number of States "here already is a normal presumption, a *presumptio juris* which, however, can be rebutted, a presumption in favor of the validity of this norm for all states". Strupp, Règles générales du droit de la paix", pp. 310-311.

114 See, for example. Waldock, "General Course on Public International Law", p. 52.

Asian and African States opposing the assertions of the Western powers. Two conclusions follow from this. First, the three-mile rule is not a norm of general international law. Second, and more generally, an international legal norm recognized by a majority of States is not recognized by States as being binding upon all other States.

The doctrine that customary norms of international law recognized as such by a significant number of States are binding upon all States not only has no basis in contemporary international law but also conceals a very great danger. This doctrine in essence justifies the attempts of a specific group of States to impose upon new States, socialist or newly emergent States of Asia and Africa, for example, certain customary norms which never have been accepted by the new States and which may be partially or wholly unacceptable to them. Of course, this tendency on the part of the large imperialist powers to dictate norms of international law to other States in contemporary conditions is doomed to failure, but at the same time such attempts undoubtedly may lead to serious international complications.

Many bourgeois specialists in international affairs who reject the concept of "tacit agreement" at the same time adhere to the view that "recognition", "acceptance", or "consent" to consider a particular rule as legally binding is a decisive element in the process of creating a customary norm of international law.

Thus, Basdevant, in considering the concept of agreement with regard to customary norms of international law to be unfounded, writes that custom "is the result of precedents which indicate recognition of such a rule as law (*opinio juris*)".[115] In another place Basdevant points out that customary norms "born spontaneously, from the exigencies of international life, acquire a positive character, as a result of which they become recognized by those who are in a position to ensure their application in international life".[116]

[115] Basdevant, "Règles générales du droit de la paix", p. 513.

[116] Ibid., p. 316.

Professor C. de Visscher writes in several nebulous passages:

> "... In international relations a customary norm forms when a practice is, through simultaneous application, sufficiently stabilized so that in it can be perceived an expression of an equilibrium of only a temporary stabilization of existing interests, and in consequence thereof an element of order legally accepted by the majority of states".[117]

In rejecting the concept of tacit agreement, these writers at the same time speak of *opinio juris* as a necessary element of a customary norm of international law. In Professor Basdevant's view, *opinio juris* signifies that "a corresponding rule has been recognized as a legal norm".[118] Professor C. de Visscher writes: "From the assimilation of custom to tacit convention, which in our judgment is quite fictitious, must be distinguished the requirement of *opinio juris sive necessitatis,* regarded here as reflecting the attitude of power in relation to a given practice".[119]

It must be noted that this understanding of *opinio juris* has virtually the same significance as the concept of recognition of a particular rule as a norm of international law and leads, consequently, to the concept of tacit agreement.

Frequently, however, the term *opinio juris* has a completely different meaning. Professor Kunz, for example, defines *opinio juris* as follows: "The practice must have been applied in the conviction that it is legally binding".[120] At the same time, Kunz is obliged

[117] Visscher, "Coutume et traité en droit international public", p. 356.

[118] Basdevant, "Règles générales du droit de la paix", p. 513.

[119] Visscher, *Théories et réalites en droit international public,* p. 188; see also Morelli, *Nozioni di diritto internazionale,* pp. 25-29; Arechaga, *Curso de derecho internacional publico,* I, 56-70; Sereni, *Diritto internazionale,* I, 123-128. M. Virally says that a customary norm is "based on consent". See Sørenson, ed., *Manual of Public International Law,* p. 135.

[120] Kunz, "The Nature of Customary International Law", p. 667; see also L. Kopelmanas, "Custom as a Means of the Creation of International Law", *British Year Book of International Law,* XVIII (1937), 129. G. Scelle, in accordance with his general conception, sees the criteria of obligatoriness in the conformity of a customary rule to "the general welfare and social goals". He says: "Custom is born as the result of the

to acknowledge the difficulties to which this concept of *opinio juris* leads. On one hand, he says, it is asserted that practice plus *opinio juris* creates a customary norm of international law, but, on the other hand, for such a norm to be formed States must act in the conviction that they are acting in conformity with a legal duty. However, insofar as a customary norm of international law still has not been formed, this conviction has no legal basis in and of itself. Kunz adds in this connection: "Hence, the very coming into existence of such a norm would presuppose that the states acted in legal error".[121]

In reality, the term "*opinio juris*", understood in this sense, signifies that States must act in the conviction that the respective norm of international law already exists, and it follows form this that such a norm can not appear in consequence of State practice but must be assumed to exist irrespective of such practice. This reasoning inevitably leads to the conclusion that a customary norm as postulated by the said concept of *opinio juris* is not a customary norm at all, growing out of the international practice of States, but rather represents a certain norm of "natural law".

The difficulties arise in connection with the nondialectical approaches to the question of "recognizing practice as a norm of law" or to *opinio juris*. The creation of a customary norm of international law is a process; the elements of a legal norm build up gradually.

Opinio juris signifies that a State regards a particular customary rule as a norm of international law, as a rule legally binding on the international plane. This is an expression of the will of a State, in its way a proposal to other States. When other States also express their will in the same direction, a tacit agreement

---

recurrence of identical conduct, individual or collective. It is affirmed by the conviction ... that such conduct conforms to the general welfare and social goals". G. Scelle, *Manuel de droit international public* ((1948), p. 10.

[121] Kunz, "The Nature of Customary International Law", p. 667; see also Quadri, *Diritto internazionale publico*, p. 94; Gianni, *La coutume en droit international*, p. 157.

is formed with regard to recognizing a customary rule as an international legal norm.

From what has been said, it follows that a customary norm of international law is the result of agreement, that is, of the concordance of the wills of States. Professor C. Chaumont rightly emphasized in his lecture at the Hague Academy that with regard to customary norms "one can not escape the logic of agreement".[122]

Modification or abolition of a customary norm of international law may be accomplished by treaty or by custom. In either case a new agreement among States is formed. Modification by custom consists of a modification of "general practice", which is accompanied by recognition as an international legal norm.[123] Such recognition is implied in those instances when a new practice which departs from a prevailing norm of international law is not objected to by other States.[124]

3. *Treaty and Custom in Contemporary International Law*

(a) The dominant role of the treaty in the development of international law. Proportionately, treaty norms presently occupy the principal place in international law as a result of the large growth in the number of international agreements.

An international treaty possesses specific features which make it a highly suitable and important means of creating norms of international law in our day. It is an agreement of States clearly expressed. This fact is of great significance

[122] C. Chaumont, "Cours général de droit international public", *Recueil des cours,* CXXIX (1970), 440.

[123] Professor Verdross, proceeding from the concept of law-consciousness as the basic of international law, writes: "... A norm of international law can not be abolished by means of recurrent practice and the general diffusion of the violation which has occurred unless some new legal conception is reflected therein". Verdross, Международное право [International Law], p. 156; also see Morelli, *Nozioni di diritto internazionale,* pp. 25-26.

[124] See D. B. Levin, Дипломатический иммунитет [Diplomatic Immunity] (1949), p. 153.

for ascertaining the existence and content of a particular norm of international law.

Moreover, in the contemporary period of rapid change in all spheres of international life the treaty is an especially suitable means of concretizing, developing, modifying, or creating new norms of international law.[125]

The predominant role of the international treaty in the de- velopment of international law is a comparatively new phenomenon. It is true that even now custom still plays an important role in international law. A significant portion of the norms and principles consolidated in international treaties continue to remain, to a certain extent, customary principles and norms. Among these are, for example, the principle of respect for State sovereignty, noninterference in internal affairs, nonaggression, and equality. These principles have been fixed in the United Nations Charter. But above all they remain basically customary principles of international law for States who are not members of the United Nations. We say "basically" because some of those States have obligations under local treaties to comply with the principles of the United Nations Charter. Moreover, the provisions of the Charter which fix the said principles also may not exhaust the content of these principles as customary principles of international law. It is doubtful, for example, whether the provisions of the Charter relating to equality of States fully embody the content of this principle as it exists in contemporary international law.

Treaty formalization also occurs in connection with the further development of entire branches of international law. On the basis of a draft prepared by the International Law Commission, the 1958 Geneva Conference worked out four conventions relating to basic questions of the international law of the sea which entered into force between September 1962 and March 1966.

[125] For greater detail, see Lukashuk, Источники международного права [Sources of International Law], pp. 47-49.

A second important branch of international customary law – ambassadorial law – also has been subjected to being formulated in a treaty. At the 1961 Vienna Conference, a Convention on Diplomatic Relations was adopted which entered into force in April 1964.

At the 1963 Vienna Conference, a Convention on Consular Relations was adopted which entered into force in March 1967. Since the draft of this Convention prepared by the International Law Commission deteriorated significantly at the conference, many countries (including the Soviet Union) abstained from signing it.[126]

As a result of the International Law Commission's long and difficult work, a draft convention embracing a major branch of international law – the law of treaties – was prepared. On the basis of this draft, the 1968-1969 Vienna Conference adopted the Convention on the Law of Treaties.

The norms of these conventions, to the extent they have entered into force for individual States, replace or will replace customary norms of international law in relations among their parties.

However, this does not preclude customary norms of international law continuing to be operative even among parties to the convention if for some reason individual questions remain unregulated by these conventions. At the suggestion of the Swiss delegation at the Vienna Conference, this obvious proposition was stated in the preamble of the Convention on Diplomatic Relations of 18 April 1961, where it says that "norms of international customary law will continue to regulate questions not expressly for by the provisions of the present Convention". Analogous provisions are contained in the preambles of the 1963 Convention on Consular Relations and the 1969 Convention on the Law of Treaties.

Moreover, new customary norms of international law may be formed in the future in these branches.

126 The USSR ratified the Convention on 16 February 1989 – [*L.N.S.*]

As regards the predominant role of the international treaty in creating norms of international law in areas which up to now have not been affected or have been slightly affected by international legal regulation, this is obvious. It suffices to mention a number of the more important international treaties which have appeared in recent years: the 1963 Moscow treaty on the prohibition of nuclear testing in three spheres; the 1967 treaty on the principles of activities of States in exploring and exploiting outer space, including the moon; the 1968 treaty on the nonproliferation of nuclear weapons; the 1965 convention on the elimination of all forms of racial discrimination adopted by the United Nations General Assembly; and the two covenants on human rights adopted by the United Nations General Assembly in 1966.

Taking these circumstances into account, the Soviet doctrine of international law, while by no means denying the important role of custom, regards the international treaty as the basic source of international law.[127]

The predominant role of the international treaty in the development of contemporary international law also is emphasized in the international legal literature of other socialist countries.[128]

[127] See, for example, Durdenevskii and Krylov (eds.), Международное право [International Law], p. 20; Korovin, Международное право [International Law], p. 16; F. I. Kozhevnikov, Советское государство и международное право [Soviet State and International Law] (1948), p. 220; V. I. Lisovskii, Международное право [International Law] (Kiev, 1955), p. 28; Tunkin, Основы современного международного права [Fundamental Principles of Contemporary International Law], p. 12; Shurshalov, Основные вопросы теории международного договора [Basic Questions of the Theory of the International Treaty], p. 8; Minasian, Источники современного международного права [Sources of Contemporary International Law], p. 47; Lukin, Источники современного международного права [Sources of Contemporary International Law], p. 56; Talalaev, Юридическая природа международного договора [Legal Nature of the International Treaty], pp. 164ff; Kozhevnikov (ed.), Курс международного права [Course of International Law], p. 40; Lukashuk, Источники международного права [Sources of International Law], pp. 42ff; Chkhikvadze and others (eds.), Курс международного права [Course of International Law], I, 170; L. A. Modzhorian and N. T. Blatova (eds.), Международное право [International Law] (1970), p. 57.

[128] See, for example, V. Outrata, *Mezinárodni prбvo veřejnü* (1960), p. 26; Avramov, *Medunarodno javno pravo* (2d ed.; 1973), p. 36; V. Pěchota, *Mnohostrannü mezinárodnн smlouvy a přistup k nim* (1965), p. 7; Nahlik, *Wstep do nauki prawa miedzynarodowego*, p.

Bourgeois international legal doctrine still basically adheres to the old concept of the predominant role of custom. With the aid of this concept, capitalist States frequently attempt to uphold old, in the majority of cases customary, norms of international law advantageous to them which were created by these States when the capitalist system was dominant in the world.

An ever greater number of international lawyers in the bourgeois countries, however, are moving away from this concept, realizing that it is hopelessly obsolete and does not reflect contemporary international reality. Thus, C. de Visscher, pointing out that in the modern era of rapid changes there is no "degree of passivity", which was important for the formation of custom, believes that the international treaty now plays the principal role in the development of international law, "leaving only a subordinate role to custom".[129]

Professor W. Friedmann writes: "It is obvious that, in the fast- moving articulate and complex international society of today, the international treaty increasingly replaces custom as the principal source of international law".[130]

The new edition of Kelsen's *Principles of International Law* also refers to the diminishing role of custom in comparison with the treaty. In an addition to the paragraph on custom it is pointed out that there is presently occurring an "erosion, if not the disappearance, of the conditions, which have favoured the development of law through custom ...".[131]

(b) The international treaty and general international law. Since treaty and customary norms of international law are the result of agreement between States, their operative sphere is defined by the participation of States in a clearly expressed (international treaty) or tacit (custom) agreement.

170; G. Haraszti, *Some Fundamental Problems of the Law of Treaties* (1973), p. 57.

129 Visscher, "Coutume et traité en droit international public", p. 359.

130 Friedmann, *The Changing Structure of International Law*, pp. 123-124.

131 Kelsen, *Principles of International Law*, p. 452.

The concept that an international treaty is not a source of general international law still is significantly widespread in bourgeois international legal literature. The proponents of this concept assert that general international law is exclusively customary law. "General international law", D. Anzilotti wrote, "is exclusively customary law".[132]

H. Kelsen points out: "General ... international law is customary law valid for all states belonging to the international community (customary law is law created by the habitual practice of the states). Particular international law is valid form some states only and comprises, for the most part, norms created by treaties valid only for the contracting parties".[133]

Kunz is of the same mind. He asserts that "... general international law is created only by custom", and "treaty-created norms always constitute particular international law only ...".[134]

This concept has been well-known for a long time. Even Vattel wrote: "Since it is obvious that a treaty binds only the contracting parties, the conventional law of nations is not universal, but special law".[135]

O'Connell, proceeding from the concept that international law is only general international law, writes that "traditionally international law is customary law ...".[136] He generally does not regard international treaties as sources of international law. "It is quite incorrect", he writes, "to speak of treaties as `sources' of international law. They are no more than contracts between the parties ...".[137]

[132] D. Anzilotti, *Курс международного права*, transl. from 4th ed. by A. Sakketti and E. M. Fabrikova, ed. D. B. Levin (1961), p. 97.

[133] Kelsen, *Principles of International Law*, p. 17.

[134] Kunz, "General International Law and the Law of International Organizations", *American Journal of International Law*, XLVII (1953), 457.

[135] E. de Vattel, Право народов [Law of Nations], ed. V. N. Durdenevskii (1960), p. 33.

[136] O'Connell, *International Law*, I, 4.

[137] Ibid., p. 22.

The concept that general international law is exclusively customary law was correct during Vattel's time and even in the nineteenth century. Now, however, this concept is obsolete and does not reflect contemporary international reality.

The existence of a large number of multilateral international treaties in which all or nearly all States participate, as well as important activity in the codification of international law, create a situation whereby international treaties are becoming a means of directly creating, modifying, and developing norms of general international law.[138] It is true that in the majority of instances this take place with some assistance of custom (see subsection (c) of this Chapter).

This already is being noticed also by many authoritative bourgeois specialists in international affairs. In the latest edition of Oppenheim's *International Law*, Professor Lauterpacht wrote: "*Universal* international law is created when all or practically all the members of the *Family* of *Nations* are parties to these treaties ... many law-making treaties have been concluded which contain *general* International Law because the majority of States, including the leading Powers, are parties to them ...".[139]

"International customary law", writes Verdross, "is the oldest source of general international law. Only recently, in connection with the growing codification of international law, has it been relegated somewhat to the second plane".[140]

General treaties now play a special role in the development of general international law. These are treaties relating to questions of interest to all States and having the purpose of creating norms binding on all States – that is, norms of general international law. The question of such treaties was raised in the

138 See G. I. Tunkin, "40 лет сосуществования и международное право" [40 Years of Coexistence and International Law], Советский ежегодник международного права 1958 [Soviet Yearbook of International Law 1958] (1959), p. 19.

139 Oppenheim, *International Law*, I, 28; see also Dahm, *Völkerrecht*, I, 21.

140 Verdross, *Völkerrecht*, pp. 137-138.

International Law Commission, which in 1962 included in its draft articles on the law of treaties the following definition of a general international treaty: "`General multilateral treaty' means a multilateral treaty which concerns general norms of international law or deals with matters of general interest to the States as a whole".[141]

The question of general international treaties is linked closely to the question of the participation of all States in such treaties. It would be an obvious contradiction to work out a treaty for the purpose of creating norms binding upon all States and at the same time to include therein a provision closing this treaty to certain States. As a French professor, E. Giraud, has wholly correctly pointed out, general international treaties "are open treaties in the sense that all states of the world in principle may become parties".[142] The right of any State to participate in general international treaties derives from basic principles of international law and, in particular, from principles of respect for sovereignty and equality of States. It follows from these principles that, on one hand, States are free to select their partners in concluding an international treaty and, on the other, all States have the right to participate in general international treaties since they are intended to regulate relations of interest to all States.

In conformity therewith, a Soviet jurist introduced the following proposal in the International Law Commission: "In the case of a general multilateral treaty, every State may become a party to the treaty".[143]

In the comments of competent authorities of the USSR upon the draft articles prepared by the International Law Commission it was pointed out: "... in codifying the law of treaties, it is necessary to proceed from the assumption that general international agreements should be open to participation by all

[141] United Nations, *Yearbook of the International Law Commission 1962*, II, 161.

[142] Giraud, "Modification et terminaison des traités collectifs", p. 17.

[143] United Nations, *Yearbook of the International Law Commission 1965*, I, 117.

States. This is required by the principle of the equality of States. Moreover, as such treaties usually regulate matters of interest to each and every State and are intended to establish or develop universally recognized principles and rules of contemporary international law which are binding on all States, to deny certain States the possibility of becoming parties to such treaties is contrary to their very spirit and purpose and is harmful to in- ternational co-operation".[144]

It is well-known that capitalist States, in violation of fun- damental principles of contemporary international law, persistently strive to insert formulas in general international treaties limiting the circle of parties to such treaties to United Nations members, to members of the United Nations specialized agencies and the Statute of the International Court, as well as to States specially invited to participate by the United Nations General Assembly. This formula presently precludes the possibility of some socialist States participating in such treaties: the German Democratic Republic, the Korean People's Democratic Republic, and the Democratic Republic of Vietnam.[145]

From the very beginning, Western jurists in the International Law Commission opposed the inclusion of provisions on general international treaties in the draft articles. As already has been pointed out, however, during the first discussion of the draft article in 1962 the Commission inserted a definition of a "general multilateral treaty", as well as a provision on participation in such treaties which provided: "In the case of a general multilateral treaty, every State may become a party to the treaty unless it is otherwise provided by the terms of the treaty itself or by the established rules of an international organization".[146]

144 Reports of the International Law Commission on the second part of its seventeenth session 3-28 January 1966 and on its eighteenth session 4 May- 19 July 1966. GAOR (XXI), Supp. No. 9 (1966), p. 288. Doc. No. A/6309/ Rev. 1.

145 For greater detail, see G. Schirmer, *Universalität völkerrechtlicher Vertrage und internationaler Organisationen* (1966).

146 United Nations, *Yearbook of the International Law Commission 1962*, II, 167-168.

This formulation was a compromise and inadequate, but it nonetheless embodied the principle of universal participation in general treaties.

In their comments upon the Commission's draft, the governments of the United States and England expressed disagreement with the principle set forth in this article.[147]

When the Commission discussed this provision a second time, agreement was not reached on these questions, and this was noted in the Commission's report.[148] As a result thereof, the final draft articles did not contain either provisions relating to general multilateral treaties or articles on the participation of States in multilateral treaties in general.

The question of general international treaties was raised anew at the Vienna Conference on the Law of Treaties. The delegations of Hungary, the Congo (Democratic Republic), the United Arab Republic, the United Republic of Tanzania, Poland, Romania, the Ukrainian Soviet Socialist Republic, and Czechoslovakia introduced the following amendment to draft Article 2 (definition of terms): "'General multilateral treaty' means a multilateral treaty which is connected with questions of general interest to the international community of states".[149] At the same time, the delegations of Hungary, India, Mongolia, the United Arab Republic, Romania, Syria, the Ukrainian SSR, Ceylon, Yugoslavia, Algeria, and Mali introduced a proposal to add to the draft convention the following article: "All states possess the right to participate in general multilateral treaties in accordance with the principle of sovereign equality".[150]

[147] See *Law of Treaties: Comments by Governments on parts I and II of the draft articles on the law of treaties drawn up by the Commission at its fourteenth and fifteenth sessions*, pp. 163, 151. Doc. No. A/CN.4/175, 23 February 1965.

[148] See United Nations, *Yearbook of the International Law Commission 1966*, II, 189, 200.

[149] United Nations Conference on the Law of Treaties, Doc. No. A/CONF.39/C.1L.19/Rev. 1, 29 March 1968.

[150] Ibid., Doc. No. A/CONF.39/C.1/L.74, 1 April 1968.

Under the pressure of the Western powers, however, these amendments were not accepted by the conference. Thus, the problem of general multilateral treaties remained unresolved in the conference on the law of treaties.[151]

Multilateral treaties with a limited number of participants, as well as bilateral treaties, also influence the development of general international law. They sometimes lead to the conclusion of general international treaties, an example being the 1963 Vienna Convention on consular questions, on which bilateral consular conventions exerted great influence. Norms of such treaties may obtain general recognition by treaty or custom and become norms of general international law.

(c) The interaction of treaty and custom. International treaty and international custom are the two methods of creating norms of general international law. The essence of these methods lies in agreement between States as regards recognition of a specific rule as a norm of international law. The binding legal force of conventional and customary norms of international law is identical, as the practice of States testifies. The United Nations Charter speaks of respect "for the obligations arising from treaties and other sources of international law" (Preamble).

In principle it is possible to change a customary norm by means of treaty and a treaty by norm by means of custom.[152] This is completely applicable, however, only in those instances when the question concerns one and the same group of States-parties both in the first case (when a treaty norm replaces or modifies a customary norm) and in the second (when a customary norm replaces or modifies a treaty norm). Here, in essence, arise new

151 At the Conference a Declaration was adopted concerning universal participation in the Vienna Convention on the Law of Treaties which contained this definition of general treaties: treaties "which deal with the codification and progressive development of international law, or the object and purpose of which are of interest to the international community as a whole" – [*L. N. S.*]

152 See T. Perassi, "Teoria dommatica delle fonti di norme guiridiche in diritto internazionale", *Rivista di diritto internazionale*, XI (1917), 303; Guggenheim, *Traité de droit international public*, I, 113; Rousseau, *Principes généraux du droit international public*, I, 859; Rousseau, *Droit international public* (1970), I, para. 283.

agreements, clearly or tacitly expressed, which supersede the previous agreements relating to recognition of the respective norms of international law.

But when the group of parties to the agreement (express or tacit) is not identical, modification of a customary norm by way of treaty and of a treaty norm by means of custom is not precluded, as well be demonstrated below, unless the modified or superseded norm is of an imperative character.

Instances of modifying customary norms of international law by means of treaty are quite frequent, especially at present with the broad scope of work relating to the codification of international law. As the experience of the International Law Commission shows, the codification of "old" branches of international law inevitably involves not only the supplementation of new norms, but also the clarification and modification of prevailing customary norms of international law.[153]

In the beginning a new treaty norm usually embraces a narrower group of States than the old customary norm. Expansion of the sphere of the recognition and operation of a new norm frequently takes place by means of both treaty and custom, in consequence of which for others which have recognized it by means of custom.[154] It is as though they were mixed customary-treaty norms.

The International Law Commission provided for this possibility in Article 34 of the final draft on the law of treaties, which stated: "Nothing in Articles 30 to 33 precludes a rule set forth in a treaty from becoming binding upon a third state as a customary rule of international law".[155] At the Vienna

[153] R. Ago, "La codification du droit international et les problèmes de sa réalization", *Mélanges Guggenheim,* pp. 93-131.

[154] See G. Fitzmaurice, "Report on the Law of Treaties", in United Nations, *Yearbook of the International Law Commission 1960,* II, 72-107; Waldock, "Third Report on the Law of Treaties", *ibid., 1964,* II, 27; Verdross, *Völkerrecht,* p. 145; Virally, "The Sources of International Law", p. 129.

[155] United Nations, *Yearbook of the International Law Commission 1966,* II, 182.

Conference, the words "recognized as such" were added to this formulation (Article 38).

It is necessary to bear in mind, however, that in this case the question is not the binding character of a treaty upon States not parties thereto, but whether a treaty norm is binding upon them not as a treaty but as a customary norm. Therefor, Professor Ulloa's assertion that treaties to which nearly all States are parties also are binding upon States who are not parties to such treaties is incorrect. The author actually has in mind the case when a State which is not party to a treaty has recognized a treaty norm as a customary norm of international law.[156]

The 1928 Pact of Paris, which established the principle of the prohibition of aggressive war, is an example of a customary norm being replaced by means of treaty. In the relations among the parties to the treaty this new principle superseded an old norm which had approved "the right of a State to resort to war" and gradually acquired, through treaty and custom, the character of a generally-recognized principle of international law.

The principle of the prohibition of aggressive war underwent further development in the United Nations Charter, which goes farther than the Pact of Paris in providing for the prohibition of the use or threat of force against the territorial integrity or political independence of any State. The new content of this principle has been recognized, but again partly by treaty and partly by custom.

As another example, one could cite the numerous local agreements concerning the regulation of fishing on the high seas which provide certain restrictions upon the freedom of their parties to fish and hunt on the high seas. There is every basis to assert that at present, primarily as a result of the conclusion of these numerous local agreements concerning the regulation of fishing, a new principle of international law is being formed,

[156] See Ulloa, *Derecho internacional publico*, I, 52.

the principle of conserving the living resources of the high seas, which is modifying the prevailing principle of the freedom to fish and hunt.

Instances of modifying a treaty norm by means of custom are less common, since treaties as a rule provide a procedure for amendment or denunciation. Legally, however, such changes are possible with the general consent of all parties to the treaty. More often in such instances the question is one of the development, supplementation, or interpretation of treaty norms.

The question of modification of a treaty by subsequent practice was raised in the Third Report of the International Law Commission's rapporteur, H. Waldock.[157] Waldock cited two judicial precedents in this connection. The first was the Judgment of the International Court of 15 June 1962 concerning the dispute between Cambodia and Thailand over the boundary in the area of the Preah Vihear Temple, in which the Court concluded that since both parties actually had recognized a boundary line other than that stipulated in the treaty over a long period of time, the result of this practice was a modification of the treaty.[158]

Thus, the International Court regarded the practice of Cambodia and Thailand in the question of fulfilling a boundary treaty, a practice which diverged from the treaty provisions, as being evidence of a supplemental tacit agreement modifying certain provisions of the treaty.

The second case cited in Waldock's report was the arbitral award of 22 December 1963 (R. Ago (President), P. Reuter, and H. P. de Vries) in the dispute between the United States and France over the interpretation of a 1946 agreement on air transport services between these countries.

[157] United Nations, *Yearbook of the International Law Commission 1964*, II, 198.

[158] International Court of Justice, Reports of Judgments, Advisory Opinions and Orders, *Case Concerning the Temple of Preah Vihear (Cambodia v. Thailand), Merits, Judgment of 15 June 1962* (1962), p. 33.

It is indicated clearly in the award that a specific practice of the parties was considered by the arbitrators as evidence of a "tacitly concluded agreement", which is an "independent agreement supplementing the agreement of 27 March 1946 and reflecting the same general principles".[159]

As a result of the discussion of this question, the International Law Commission included in the draft articles on the law of treaties Article 38 as follows: "A treaty may be modified by subsequent practice in the application of the treaty establishing the agreement of the parties to modify its provisions".[160]

Bourgeois international legal doctrine usually considers this problem to be a question of interpreting an international treaty, which is completely untrue. It is possible to interpret only that which is in the treaty.[161] Moreover, some bourgeois writers even attempt to pass the "Uniting for Peace" resolution of the United Nations General Assembly of 3 November 1950 as treaty interpretation,[162] although it is generally recognized that the resolution was in sharp contradiction with the provisions of the United Nations Charter.[163]

Having included in its draft an article concerning modification of a treaty by subsequent practice, the Commission made an attempt, although not wholly successfully, to formulate a norm which arises logically from the character of customary and treaty norms and which, evidently, already is being formed

159 "Sentence arbitrale du 22 decembre 1963", *Revue générale de droit international public*, XXXVI (1965), 258.

160 United Nations, *Yearbook of the International Law Commission 1966*, II, 236.

161 "The task of interpreting an international treaty", wrote Pereterskii, "is to make out the will of the parties, that is, the content of the rules established by them in the treaty which define their rights and duties and the purpose for which the given treaty was concluded". I. S. Pereterskii, Толкование международных договоров [Interpretation of International Treaties] (1959), p. 22.

162 Professor L. Goodrich maintains that this resolution was a "liberal interpretation" of the United Nations Charter. L. Goodrich, *The United Nations* (1959), p. 168.

163 For greater detail, see G. I. Tunkin, "The Legal Nature of the United Nations", *Recueil des cours*, CXIX (1966), 1-68.

as a customary norm of international law. The adoption of a treaty norm on this question undoubtedly would facilitate the elimination of disputes which arise frequently in corresponding instances.

The Commission was far from thinking that any practice might modify the provisions of a treaty. The Commission's draft contains two essential elements. Practice must testify to an agreement of the parties to modify a provision of the treaty. As the Commission points out in the commentary to this article, "in formulating the rule in this way the Commission intended to indicate that the subsequent practice, even if every party might not itself have actively participated in the practice, must be such as to establish the agreement of the parties as a whole to the modification in question".[164]

Consequently, the first condition is that only such practice as shows an agreement of the parties may introduce a change in a treaty[165] – that is, the concordance of their wills relating to such changes. Individual digressions from treaty provisions, even though they have taken place with the common consent of the parties, but do not testify to their intention to change a treaty provision, do not modify the treaty.

The second condition is that an agreement testified to by such practice must embrace all (or almost all) parties to the treaty. This question was the subject of lively discussion in the Commission. It was recognized that, in principle, such agreement must embrace "all" parties to the treaty. For practical considerations, however, the word "all" was not inserted in the article so as not to carry its content to an extreme, when even

164 United Nations, *Yearbook of the International Law Commission 1966*, II, 236.

165 See Oriol Casanovas la Rosa, "La Modification de los Acuerdos Internacionales por la Practica Posterior", *Revista Española de derecho internacional*, XXI (1968), 328-345. Professor Cahier suggests, on the contrary, that international judicial and arbitral practice on this question, "although theoretically proceeding from the wills of States, in fact does not take it into account". P. Cahier, "Le comportement des états comme source de droits et d'obligation", *Mélanges Guggenheim*, p. 265.

the objection of a single State (for example, of one hundred or more parties to the treaty) could block such an agreement.

The Commission's proposal on this question objectively was aimed against attempts to pass as treaty modification (or an interpretation modifying the treaty) a practice which does not testify to an agreement relating to modification of a treaty provision, as well as the practice of a majority but not all (or almost all) parties.

At the same time, the discussion of this question in the Commission showed how little it had been studied, in particular that very little is known about State practice with regard to this question. The formulation of the article proposed by the Commission was imperfect. It is doubtful that there are grounds for considering that there exists a customary norm of international law in conformity with which any treaty provisions may be modified by means of custom, or that such a norm is advisable *de lege feranda*. Such an extreme would be dangerous for the stability of international treaties.

These dangers, reinforced by the imperfections of the formulation proposed by the Commission, led to this question being generally excluded from the draft convention at the Vienna Conference on the Law of Treaties, which can only be regretted.

4. *The Principles of* Jus Cogens

With the International Law Commission's raising the question of the invalidity of international treaties which contravene imperative principles of international law (principles of *jus cogens*), the question of the character of these principles acquired great contemporary interest.[166]

The essence of the question lies in ascertaining whether there are in contemporary general international law imperative

166 For a bibliography on this question, see Professor E. Suy's report "The Concept of Jus Cogens in International Public Law" which he submitted to a conference at Lagonissi, Greece, in 1966. Carnegie Endowment for International Peace, *The Concept of Jus Cogens in International Law* (1967), pp. 17-77.

principles and norms, the operation of which States may not suspend by agreement in their mutual relations.

For followers of the natural law school, as well as for proponents of contemporary natural law concepts, this question is easily resolved: natural law exists independently of the will of States and is binding upon them; States must follow the prescriptions of this law. Grotius declares that natural law is so immutable that even God himself can not change it.[167]

Vattel wrote, having in mind natural law or, as he called it, "the necessary law of nature": "As this law is immutable and imposes necessary and inevitable duties, nations may not introduce any changes in these by their own agreements and may not exempt themselves therefrom by a unilateral renunciation nor mutually exempt each other.

It is this principle, in being guided by which one may distinguish lawful agreements and treaties from unlawful, and reasonable and good customs from unjust or proper censure".[168]

We find that the majority of nineteenth century writers were of the same viewpoint. Bluntschli wrote: "Treaties whose content violates generally-recognized human laws or imperative norms of international law are invalid".[169] F. Martens, adhering to Bluntschli's view, pointed out that an international treaty is not binding if it restricts or destroys the basic rights of States.[170]

Proponents of normativist concepts favor the view that international law does not contain imperative norms (*jus*

[167] H. Grotius, О праве войны и мира [On the Law of War and Peace], transl. A. L. Sakketti; ed. S. B. Krylov (1956), p. 1, chaps. 1, 5, 10.

[168] Vattel, Право народов [Law of Nations], p. 27.

[169] J. C. Bluntschli, *Das moderne Völkerrecht der civiliserten Staten* (2d ed.; 1872), p. 236.

[170] See F. F. Martens, Современное международное право цивилизованных народов [Contemporary International Law of Civilized Peoples] (3d ed.; 1895), I, 406; see also A. N. Stoianov, Очерки истории и догматики международного права [Survey of the History and Dogmatics of International Law] (Kharkov, 1875), p. 494.

cogens), and States may establish any international legal norms in their mutual relations by way of treaties.

The principal representative of the "pure" theory of law, Kelsen, declares that the "... content of the treaty must not conflict with a norm of general international law which has the character *jus cogens*, and not that of *jus dispositivum*".[171] However, in considering the question of whether norms of general international law have the character of *jus cogens*, Kelsen says that a clear answer can never be found in the traditional theory of international law. Some writers, he continues, maintain that there exists complete, or almost complete, freedom to conclude treaties; others, to the contrary, adhere to the view that treaties which are at variance with universally-recognized principles of international law are null and void. To this he makes a characteristic addition: "But they do not and can not precisely designate the norms of general international law which have the character of *jus cogens*, that is to say, the application of which can not be excluded by treaty". At the same time, he is forced to acknowledge that a treaty by which two or more States release one another from the obligations imposed upon them by the norm of general international law prohibiting occupation of part of the high seas very likely would be declared null and void by an international tribunal competent to deal with the case.[172]

Thus, Kelsen does not give a clear answer to the question being raised, but he favors the view that all norms of general international law are of a dispositive character and that imperative norms, which can not contravene the norms of a treaty concluded by two States or a group, are only of a local character. This point of view has been expressed more concretely in the new edition of *Principles of International Law*.

171 Kelsen, *Principles of International Law* (1952), pp. 322-323; the paragraph quoted is absent in the new edition. See *Principles of International Law* (1967), p. 460.

172 Kelsen, *Principles of International Law* (1967), p. 483.

This viewpoint was set forth by Guggenheim more resolutely. He wrote: "Norms of international public law are not of an imperative character. Consequently, in conformity with international law, a treaty may have any content without any limitation whatever ...".[173] In the second edition of this treatise, however, Guggenheim expresses his opposition to the existence of the principles of *jus cogens* in contemporary international law must more cautiously. He writes: "Although there are no logical grounds not to assume the existence of principles of *jus cogens,* there are certain difficulties in assuming their existence within the limits of the actual procedure for creating international law. The principal difficulty springs from the fact that contemporary international law does not contain general rules which automatically invalidate ... conventional norms that contravene them".[174]

The arguments of opponents of *jus cogens* can be reduced to the fact that such principles are possible only in a well-organized and effective legal system, and since international law is not such a system, the existence of principles of general international law having the character of *jus cogens* is impossible. This argument is set forth especially clearly by Professor G. Schwarzenberger. "Unlike muni- cipal law", he writes, "international customary law (in Schwarzenberger's view general international law is customary law) lacks rules of *jus cogens* or international public policy, that is, rules which, by consent, individual subjects of international law may not modify. In fact, *jus cogens,* as distinct from *jus dispositivum,* presupposes the existence of an effective *de jure* order, which has at its disposal legislative and judicial machinery, able to formulate rules of public policy and, in the last resort, can rely on overwhelming physical force".[175]

173 P. Guggenheim, *Traité de droit international public* (1953), I, 57.

174 Guggenheim, *Traité de droit international public* (2d ed.), I, 128.

175 G. Schwarzenberger, *A Manual of International Law* (5th ed.; 1967), pp. 29-30; Schwarzenberger, "International Jus Cogens", *Texas Law Review,* XLIII (1965), 455-478. J. Nisot rejects the concept of *jus cogens* because it supposedly does not define "what these principles are". J. Nisot, "Le concept du *jus cogens* envisagé par

An Italian professor, A. Sereni, decisively rejects the existence of imperative principles in international law.[176] At the same time, just as many other Italian authors,[177] Sereni speaks of the existence of "constitutional principles which reflect the specific constitutional features of the international community and order", but which do not coincide with "principles of international law".[178] G. Morelli admits the existence of imperative norms in international law but interprets them completely differently. In Morelli's view, a treaty which contravenes an imperative norm of international law is not invalid; the treaty "is valid between the parties, but unlawful with regard to other addresses of an imperative norm".[179] But this still is tantamount to a denial of imperative norms, since a specific feature of an imperative norm is that it does not permit a digression from such a norm by agreement between two or several States, and an agreement contravening an imperative norm is invalid.

According to the concept most prevalent in contemporary bourgeois international legal literature, there are, as a rule, no imperative norms in contemporary international law, and therefore treaties concluded by States may digress from generally-recognized norms. Nonetheless, it admits that general international law contains some norms of an imperative character which may not be contravened by treaties.

As regards the character of imperative norms, the majority of bourgeois writers carry categories of municipal law over to international law, suggesting that imperative principles are

---

rapport au droit international public", *Revue belge de droit international,* IV (1968), 7.

176 Sereni, *Diritto internazionale,* I, 166-170.

177 See, for example, S. Romano, *Corso di diritto internazionale* (4th ed.; 1939), p. 31; R. Monaco, *Manuale di diritto internazionale publico* (1960), pp. 42-46.

178 Sereni, *Diritto internazionale,* I, 112-113.

179 G. Morelli, "A proposito di norme internazionali cogenti", *Rivista de diritto internazionale,* LI (1968), 116.

principles of "public order" which do not depend upon the will and consent of States.

Professor Verdross wrote: "In principle, a State freely concludes treaties with other States on any questions; however, such agreements must remain within the limits of general international law".[180] Speaking of instances of the invalidity of an international treaty, Verdross points out: "This occurs, however, only when an international treaty violates a compulsory norm of international law. But in view of the fact that general international law, as a rule, is dispositive law (*jus dispositivum*), comparatively few instances exist of a violation of general international law by an international treaty".[181]

It should be noted that in the fourth and fifth editions of this work Verdross lays great stress upon imperative norms of international law. The reminder that general international law, as a rule, is dispositive law is omitted here and instead the following is said: "In addition, however, there are norms which may not be modified by States even as regards their mutual relations".[182]

In his report submitted to the International Law Commission Professor H. Lauterpacht proposed the adoption of an article providing for the invalidity of a treaty or its individual provisions "if its perform- ance involves an act which is illegal under international law ...".[183]

In the commentary to this draft article he pointed out that the question is one of "the inconsistency with such overriding principles of international law which may be regarded as constituting ... international public policy".[184] In so doing,

[180] Verdross, Международное право [International Law], p. 185.

[181] Ibid., p. 186.

[182] Verdross, *Völkerrecht* (4th ed.; 1959), p. 79; ibid. (5th ed.; 1964), p. 130. See also Verdross, "Jus Dispositivum and Jus Cogens in International Law", *American Journal of International Law*, LX (1966), 55-63.

[183] United Nations, *Yearbook of the International Law Commission 1953*, II, 154.

[184] Ibid., p. 155.

Lauterpacht, just as the majority of bourgeois writers, identified these principles to a significant extent with moral principles.[185]

In the Third Report to the International Law Commission, G. Fitzmaurice expresses approximately the same point of view. He writes: "It is essential to the validity of a treaty that it should be in conformity with or not contravene, or that its execution should not involve an infraction of, those principles and rules of international law which are in the nature of *jus cogens*".[186]

Lord McNair suggests that imperative principles of inter- national law exist, but that such principles are peculiar to any legal system. "It is difficult to imagine any society", he writes, "whether of individuals or of States, whose law sets no limit whatever to freedom of contract".[187]

Professor Dahm believes that imperative principles exist in international law, although they also are an exception.[188]

Professor U. Scheuner, of the University of Bonn, suggests that imperative principles of international law exist and that these are "norms of international law creating obligations upon States independent of their agreement".[189]

Professor C. Rousseau very cautiously acknowledges the existence of imperative principles, pointing out that the principle of public policy "is almost nonexistent" in international law.[190]

185 Ibid.

186 Ibid., 1958, II, 26.

187 A. McNair, *The Law of Treaties* (1961), pp. 213-214; see also G. Geamanu, "'Jus Cogens' en droit international contemporain", *Revue roumaine d'études internationales*, nos. 1-2 (1967), p. 90; K. Marek, "Contribution à l'étude du *jus cogens* en droit international", *Mélanges Guggenheim*, p. 456.

188 G. Dahm, *Völkerrecht*, I, 6.

189 U. Scheuner, "Conflict of Treaty Provisions with a Peremptory Norm of General International Law and Its Consequences", *Zeitschrift für auslandisches öffentliches Recht und Völkerrecht*, XXVII (1967), 531.

190 Rousseau, *Principes généraux du droit international public*, I, 340-341.

Professor P. Reuter also does not deny the existence of imperative principles in international law but rather favors the view that there is only a "trend" toward forming them.[191]

Professor R. Quadri suggests that "there are no obstacles to speaking of the existence of international public policy in international law; that is, the aggregate of imperative norms (*jus cogens*) which annuls any norm in contravention thereof, either customary or conventional".[192] Quadri says that the force of such imperative norms "is nothing other than the power of the international social organism, whose will is the highest instance".[193]

"In any event," writes a Uruguyan professor, E. Jimenez de Arechaga, "the international law prevailing at the present time rests upon `*jus cogens*'; that is, upon specific principles and norms from which the parties to a treaty may not digress in their discretion".[194]

The discussion of this question in the International Law Commission commenced in 1963. The Commission's rapporteur, Professor H. Waldock, following the example of the previous rapporteurs (Lauterpacht and Fitzmaurice), proposed the inclusion of a draft article providing for the invalidity of treaties which contravene principles of *jus cogens*.[195]

The rapporteur's proposal to include the said article met with the unanimous approval of Commission members. "The most surprising feature of the Commission's debates is the

[191] P. Reuter, "Principes de droit international public", *Recueil des cours,* CIII (1961), 467.

[192] R. Quadri, "Cours general de droit international public", *Recueil des cours,* CXIII (1964), 335.

[193] Ibid.

[194] Arechaga, *Curso de derecho internacional publico,* I, 120.

[195] United Nations, *Yearbook of the International Law Commission 1966,* II, 52.

unanimity with which members of the Commission approved the idea of *jus cogens*", writes E. Suy, a Belgian professor.[196]

This article was discussed a second time after receiving the comments of governments and the discussion of the Commission's Draft in the Sixth Committee of the United Nations General Assembly. In the Commission's final draft the article on imperative principles (Article 50) was formulated as follows: "A treaty is void if it conflicts with a peremptory norm of general international law, from which no derogation is permitted and which can be modified only by a subsequent norm of general international law having the same character".[197]

As regards the nature of imperative principles, of course, the views of the members of the Commission were different. Naturally, the Commission also did not set itself the task of working out a unified conception of the nature of these principles. As the Hungarian delegate, E. Ustor, correctly noted in the Sixth Committee at the Eighteenth Session of the United Nations General Assembly, "... although the members of the Commission disagreed on the origin of the peremptory rules of international law, they had nevertheless agreed to recognize their existence, and their ideological differences had not prevented them from reaching a solution that met the needs of practice".[198]

The Commission refrained from attempts to work out a list of imperative principles, pointing out that this question did not relate to the law of treaties. The author of the present work pointed out in the Commission that unequal treaties undoubtedly fall within the effect of the article prepared by the Commission.[199]

196 Carnegie Endowment for International Peace, *Concept of Jus Cogens in International Law*, p. 50.

197 United Nations, *Yearbook of the International Law Commission 1966*, II, 247.

198 Sixth Committee, United Nations General Assembly (XX), *Official Records*, p. 40.

199 United Nations, *Yearbook of the International Law Commission 1963*, I, 69.

In the course of discussing the draft articles on the law of treaties in the Sixth Committee of the General Assembly in 1963, 1966, and 1967, the article on imperative principles of international law received wide support, especially from delegates of socialist and developing countries. This also applies to the comments of governments upon the Commission's draft.

It became clearer, however, both from the comments of governments and from the remarks of delegates in the Sixth Committee that the United States, England, and France, as well as a number of other countries linked to them by military alliances (in particular, Canada, Belgium, Turkey), were opposing this article under various pretexts (chiefly, the pretext of the ambiguity of the article or the absence of compulsory international jurisdiction to apply it). In its comments on the Commission's draft in 1965, the United States Government recommended that the Commission "reconsider the provisions of that article and all aspects of the manner in which it might be applied, particularly the question as to who will decide when the facts justify application of the rule".[200]

This was said even more decisively in a Note of the Permanent Representative of the United States to the United Nations of 2 October 1967: "If such careful and meticulous delineation of existing peremptory norms is not carried out, article 50 might have a most disastrous effect upon international co-operation and harmony because it could radically weaken the treaty structure upon which that harmony and co-operation depends so heavily".[201]

The English representative in the Sixth Committee of the United Nations General Assembly, Darwin, declared in 1967 that "... the concept of *jus cogens* was still so little developed

[200] Law of Treaties: Comments by Governments, p. 186. Doc. No. A/CN.4/ 175, 23 February 1965.

[201] Doc. No. A/6827/Add. 2 (XX).

that it still was not ripe for inclusion in the codification of the law of treaties".[202]

The same tendencies manifested themselves at the Vienna Conference on the Law of Treaties. The delegations of the socialist States and of the majority of Asian-African States resolutely supported the article relating to imperative principles of international law. The representative of Mali, Maiga, declared in his speech at the Conference on 7 May 1968 that norms of *jus cogens* are the cornerstone of the progressive development of contemporary international law. They are, he pointed out, essential to the stability of international relations and one of the most effective instruments for ensuring peaceful coexistence of States with different economic and social systems.[203]

The delegations of the principal capitalist powers and of States linked with them attempted to prevent the adoption of this article. The United States delegation proposed to replace the text of the article submitted by the International Law Commission with the following: "A treaty is void if, at the time of its conclusion, it conflicts with a peremptory rule of general international law which is recognized in common by the national and regional legal systems of the world and from which no derogation is permitted".[204]

With the obvious purpose of confusing the issue, the English delegation at the Vienna Conference proposed to define which rules are peremptory,[205] and the English representative, Vallat, declared that the delegation of Great Britain would probably

[202] Sixth Committee, United Nations General Assembly (XXII), *Official Records*, p. 55 (11 October 1967).

[203] United Nations Conference on the Law of Treaties, *Official Records, Vienna, First Session, 1968-1969* (1969), p. 327. Doc. No. A/CONF.39/C.I/SR.56.

[204] Ibid., Documents of the Conference (1971), p. 174. Doc. No. A/CONF.39/C.I/L.312.

[205] Ibid., p. 174. Doc. No. A/CONF.39/C.I/L.312.

vote against the convention as a whole if the article on imperative norms were left in the convention.[206]

The United States amendment had a strong flavor of the nineteenth German concept which represented international law as external State law. The Cuban representative, Alvares Tabio, noted quite justly with regard to this question that the United States' proposal would allow a State, by invoking its domestic legislation, to thwart any imperative norm of international law.[207] Professor C. de Visscher called this article "the most significant innovation of the Vienna Convention".[208]

Despite the negative position of the said countries and a number of others, the article on the invalidity of treaties contravening an imperative norm of international law was adopted by the Vienna Conference on the Law of Treaties by eighty-seven votes, with eight opposed and twelve abstentions, without material changes. "A treaty is void", says Article 53, "if at the moment of conclusion it contravenes an imperative norm of general international law. Under the present Convention, an imperative norm of general international law is a norm accepted and recognized by the international community of states as a whole as a norm, the departure from which is inadmissible and which may be modified only by a subsequent norm of general international law of the same character".

The position has been taken in Soviet international legal doctrine that an international treaty must conform to the basic principles of international law.[209] However, until

[206] Ibid., *Official Records*, p. 330. Doc. No. A/CONF.39/C.I/SR.57.

[207] Ibid., p. 297. Doc. No. A/CONF.39/C.I/SR.52; see also the statement of the Tanzanian representative, Bishota, of 7 May 1968. Ibid., p. 322. Doc. No. A/ CONF.39/C.I/SR.56.

[208] C. de Visscher, "Stages in the Codification of International Law", in W. Friedmann, L. Henkin, and O. J. Lissitzyn, eds., *Transnational Law in a Changing Society: Essays in Honor of Philip C. Jessup* (1972), p. 29.

[209] See, for example, Korovin (ed.), Международное право [International Law], p. 16; Tunkin, Основы современного международного права [Fundamental Principles of Contemporary International Law], p. 12; Kozhevnikov (ed.), Международное право [International Law], pp. 242-243; Minasian, Источники современного международного права [Sources of Contemporary International

comparatively recently the problem had not been worked out theoretically by Soviet scholars.[210]

V. M. Shurshalov attempts a theoretical analysis of this question in his work *Основные вопросы теории международного договора*. The author upholds the generally recognized thesis that only treaties whose provisions conform to basic principles of international law have legal force and makes a number of correct observations, particularly on the question of the effectiveness of international treaties and their role in the development of international law.[211] One can not agree, however, with his opinions on the co-relation of the international treaty and of generally-recognized principles of international law.

In our view, Shurshalov's opinions are based upon a confusion of the laws of societal development with juridical laws, with principles of international law. This leads him to regard the actual laws of societal development as the criterion of the legal validity of an international treaty. These laws of societal development are considered to be juridical principles with which the norms of a treaty are to be compared. If the treaty norms conform to such laws of societal development, they are deemed by the author to be valid; if they contradict them, to be invalid.[212]

Law], p. 48; Lukin, Источники международного права [Sources of International Law], p. 75; Bobrov, Современное международное право [Contemporary International Law], p. 77; Talalaev, Юридическая природа международного договора [Legal Nature of the International Treaty], p. 220; Lukashuk, Источники международного права [Sources of International Law], p. 50; Chikhikvadze and others (eds.), Курс международного права [Course of International Law], I, 172-173.

210 Professor L. A. Aleksidze's report to the XII Annual Meeting of the Soviet Association of International Law in January 1969 is evidence of the growing interest in this problem in Soviet international legal doctrine. See also Tunkin, "Jus Cogens in Contemporary International Law", *University of Toledo Law Review* (1971), 107-118.

211 Shurshalov, Основные вопросы теории международного договора [Basic Questions of the Theory of the International Treaty], pp. 231-244.

212 Ibid., pp. 237-239.

The development of international law, just as other categories of the superstructure, ultimately is determined by the laws of societal development. Those principles and norms of international law, including those established by treaty, which conform to the laws of societal development are as a consequence are progressive, may be expected to be consolidated in international law. Principles and norms which are in contradiction to the laws of societal development and which inhibit the progressive development of society inevitably are swept away and cast aside.

The question can be raised, of course, as to the co-relation of the legal validity of a treaty and its conformity to the laws of societal development, on one hand, and the legal invalidity of a treaty and its nonconformity to the laws of societal development, on the other. There undoubtedly is a definite link here, since in the final analysis the laws of societal development define the general features of the development of international law. It is, however, incorrect to assert that the juridical lawfulness or validity of an international treaty is determined by its conformity to the laws of societal development, or the legal invalidity of an international treaty by the fact that it is in contradiction to these laws.

The validity of a treaty is determined on the basis of legal criteria provided for by international law. If a local treaty contravenes generally-recognized principles of international law of an imperative character, it is legally invalid.

The content of generally-recognized principles of international law also is determined in the final analysis by the general laws of societal development. These laws, however, are not themselves principles of international law or a part thereof. Identifying the laws of societal development (we are not concerned here with the meaning of the laws) with juridical norms, as is well-known, is peculiar to the solidarists (see Chapter VI).

The conformity or nonconformity of a particular norm of international law to the laws of societal development defines its true effectiveness or efficacy. But the legal validity of a norm and its efficacy or effectiveness are not one and the same thing, although it would be incorrect to assert that the inefficacy or ineffectiveness of a norm can not influence its legal validity. The legal validity of a norm, however, can by virtue of a number of circumstances be made ineffective or less effective, since with a change of situation the degree of effectiveness of the norm may change.

V. M. Shurshalov in essence repeats the error of F. F. Martens, who wrote: "On this basis it is possible to make it a rule that the degree to which international treaties are binding or are to be performed is to be determined by the extent to which they conform to the truly reasonable requirements of States in their mutual relations".[213]

The general conclusion is that the existence of imperative principles and norms in contemporary international law is almost generally-recognized.

The basic reason for the formation of such principles and norms is the growing internationalization of various aspects of the life of society, especially of economic life and the expansion and in- tensification of international ties. As a result thereof, the number of questions whose free regulation on a local multilateral or bilateral basis may harm the interests of other States is increasing. The growth of the forces of socialism and progress, their increasing influence, and the increase in this connection of the importance of moral principles in international relations also promote the creation of imperative principles and norms of international law. Therefore, the quantity of imperative principles and norms in contemporary international law is growing.

To imperative principles should be relegated essentially all fundamental generally-recognized principles of contemporary international law, although in this connection the problem arises of the incomplete imperative nature of

[213] Martens, Современное международное право [Contemporary International Law] (3d ed.), I, 392.

certain of them. Could, for example, States establish by a bilateral agreement that they will not be bound in their mutual relations by the principle of nonaggression? Obviously, there can be only one answer to this question – a negative one. Peace is indivisible, and an armed attack by one State upon another, irrespective of whether large or small States are concerned, is a breach of the general peace, in whose maintenance all States are interested.

The question of the legal nature of imperative principles of international law is a complex one. As regards the methods of their creation, they do not differ in this respect from other principles of international law. Norms of general international law, including imperative principles, are created by the agreement of States. One must agree with McNair that imperative principles are "rules which have been accepted, either expressly by treaty or tacitly by custom ...".[214]

Among the principles and norms of general international law created by agreement of States are those to which special importance is attached by these agreements.[215] This special importance is that individual States in their mutual relations and on the basis of agreement can not deviate therefrom or act otherwise than these principles and norms prescribe.

Of course, such norms have a special binding force.[216] But at the same time the question does not reduce itself to binding force in general. All norms of international law are binding upon

[214] McNair, *The Law of Treaties*, p. 215. M. Virally notes that the sources of imperative principles are the same as the sources of other norms of international law. M. Virally, "Réflexions sur le 'jus cogens'," *Annuaire français de droit international*, XII (1966), 16.

[215] See L. Aleksidze, "Проблема *jus cogens* в современном международном праве" [Problem of Jus Cogens in Contemporary International Law], Советский ежегодник международного права 1969 [Soviet Yearbook of International Law 1969] (1970), p. 142; Geamanu, "'Jus Cogens' en droit international contemporain", p. 94.

[216] As Professor M. Yasseen, the Iraqi representative at the Vienna Conference on the Law of Treaties, stated: "it could be said that some rules of international law were more binding than others ...". United Nations Conference on the Law of Treaties, *Official Records*, p. 296.

the respective subjects of international law. Their violation entails international legal responsibility. But in the majority of cases, and therein is one of the distinctive features of international law, States may, by concluding local agreements, establish that they will apply in their mutual relations norms other than the norms of general international law pertaining to this question. Such deviation is inadmissible with regard to imperative principles and norms. This relates both to treaty and to customary norms.

Imperative principles obviously are not immutable. As all other principles and norms of general international law, they may be modified by the agreement of States, by means of treaty or custom. In this way certain existing principles and norms of international law may acquire the character of imperative norms; new imperative principles and norms may be formed from the moment they come into existence. Certain moral norms may become imperative norms or existing imperative norms may, while remaining norms of international law, also become generally-accepted normal norms simultaneously.[217]

The Nuremberg principles relating to crimes against humanity, for example, which in our view are included among imperative principles, represent to a certain extent all three of the aforesaid instances. The norms relating to war crimes originated long ago, but comparatively recently they have acquired an imperative character. The norms regarding crimes against peace are relatively new imperative norms. The norms relating to crimes against humanity were until recently to some extent moral norms which now are imperative norms of international law.

Since a treaty may be a means of establishing or modifying generally-recognized principles and norms or, that is to say, principles and norms of general international law, this problem

[217] For greater detail on moral norms in relations between peoples, see A. F. Shishkin and K. A. Shvartsman, XX век и моральные ценности человечества [XX Century and Moral Values of Mankind] (1968), pp. 224-270.

does not arise with regard to general treaties in which all or almost all States participate, including, consequently, States of the two systems, among them the great powers. Such treaties may modify or abolish principles and norms of general international law, including imperative norms.

The problem of the co-relation of treaty norms and of generally-recognized norms of international law arises, therefore, only with regard to local treaty norms; that is, norms of bilateral and of multilateral treaties to which a limited number of States are parties. This problem also arises equally with regard to local customary norms of international law.

The existence of imperative norms by no means inhibits the progressive development of international law; they do not obstruct the creation of new norms which go farther than old norms in the direction of ensuring peace and friendly relations among States.

CHAPTER V.
SUBSIDIARY PROCESSES OF FORMING NORMS OF INTERNATIONAL LAW

Treaty and custom are the two methods of forming and changing norms of general international law, the two direct means of establishing its norms. These means, as we have seen, sometimes are parallel, sometimes cross, sometimes merge. The completion of any of them signifies the completion of the process of forming a norm of international law, as a result of which a new norm emerges or a previously existing norm changes.

It can be said that general agreement exists with regard to recognizing treaty and custom as a means or method of forming principles and norms of general international law. But are there other methods of creating norms of international law? Very different opinions are expressed with regard to this matter not only in bourgeois but also in Soviet legal literature.

Confusion results to a significant extent from the fact that the term "sources", even when used in a so-called formal sense (a very unfortunate expression), is, as H. Kelsen points out, highly ambiguous.[1] The category of sources usually includes not just the process of forming norms of international law and its results, but also the various factors influencing the process.

In order to gain an understanding of the complex process of norm-formation, one must separate from it everything that does not enter into the process yet still influences it. That is to say, one must separate the process of forming agreement relating to recognizing a particular rule as a norm of international law from the numerous phenomena which influence the course of this process and its content.

Norm-formation is international law is not limited to treaty and custom; several other processes enter into it. These processes do not lead directly to the formation of a norm of

1 H. Kelsen, *Principles of International Law* (1952), p. 304.

general international law, that is, do not lead to completion of the making of a norm, but represent specific stages in making, developing, changing, and abrogating norms of international law – that is to say, stages in the forming of agreement of States with regard to these questions.[2]

1. Resolutions of the United Nations General Assembly

International organizations (intergovernmental) are created by States on the basis of treaties which define the structure of the given organization, the jurisdiction of its organs, the effect of resolutions of these organs, and so forth.

Of course, the decisions of any international organization may have a certain legal force just for members of this organization. The numerous interpretations of Article 2(6) as supposedly establishing legal obligations for States which are not members of the United Nations have no basis thereunder.

Paragraph 6 says the Organization shall ensure that nonmember States act in accordance with the principles of the United Nations so far as may be necessary for the maintenance of international peace and security. As A. Verdross correctly remarks, the provision of the Charter does not establish "direct obligations for third States".[3] It establishes a norm which the Organization and its members must follow.

As regards the resolutions of international organizations, the resolutions of the United Nations General Assembly are of greatest interest in this respect. They are mentioned most frequently in legal literature as sources of international law.

The view repeatedly has been expressed in Soviet international legal literature that resolutions of international organizations are a source of international law. S. B. Krylov wrote that

[2] See G. I. Tunkin, "Сорок лет сосуществования и международное право" [Forty Years of Coexistence and International Law], Советский ежегодник международного права 1958 [Soviet Yearbook of International Law 1958] (1959), p. 20.

[3] A. Verdross, Международное право [International Law], transl. from 3d ed. by F. A. Kublitskii and R. L. Naryshkina, ed. G. I. Tunkin (1959), p. 529.

"sufficient attention is not always devoted to this source of international law, whereas the role and significance of this source are great".[4] In developing this thought, he went on to point out that resolutions such as the resolutions of the Assembly of the League of Nations, as well as its organs, "were a source of international law for League members, on condition of their being recognized and applied in practice".[5] "The activity of the United Nations, its General Assembly, and other organs, above all the Security Council", Krylov continued, "may lead to a number of resolutions of these organs being an important source of international law on the aforesaid conditions".[6]

E. A. Korovin wrote in 1957: "Resolutions of international organizations and national organizations, if they have obtained international recognition, may be regarded to a certain extent as a source of international law".[7]

There is in these definitions the correct idea that resolutions of international organizations do not in themselves create norms of international law. To say, however, that resolutions of international organizations are sources of international law if they have been recognized by a State in no way determines the place of these resolutions in the process of forming norms of international law.

F. I. Kozhevnikov expresses a rather different point of view: "Resolutions of the General Assembly as a general rule only have the character of a recommendation. One may consider resolutions of this United Nations organ which are adopted unanimously as going beyond the limits of simple recommendations and as acquiring the significance of legal force".[8] However, the author puts forward no arguments in

[4] V. N. Durdenevskii and S. B. Krylov (eds.), Международное право [International Law] (1947), p. 24.

[5] Ibid.

[6] Ibid., p. 25.

[7] F. I. Kozhevnikov, Международное право [International Law] (1957), p. 9.

[8] Kozhevnikov, "Общепризнанные принципы и нормы международного

support of this thesis. Moreover, the United Nations Charter does not distinguish between General Assembly resolutions adopted unanimously and resolutions adopted by a majority vote as defined by the Charter. Although, as will be shown below, unanimity in adopting General Assembly resolutions has a certain significance, it by no means follows that this in and of itself changes the character of the resolution.

N. M. Minasian suggests that all United Nations General Assembly resolutions which do not contravene the Charter or the basic principles of international law and have been adopted unanimously or by a two-thirds vote, including representation of the three groups of States, are binding on all members of the United Nations,[9] since "the concordant will of States has been expressed therein, only not by signing them (this form has been fixed for treaties), but by voting for them".[10]

It is true that when a United Nations General Assembly resolution is adopted, since each delegation acts in the name of its State, the concordance of the wills of the States which voted for the resolution is present. It does not follow therefrom, however, that a norm of international law results from such concordance. The former arises only when there is a concordance of the wills of States relating to recognition of a particular rule as a norm of international law.

In this case the question is one of the concordance of the wills of States within the framework of an international organization, and the results of such concordance are defined by the charter of this organization. In voting for any resolution relating, for example, to general principles of cooperation in the cause of maintaining international peace and security,

права" [Generally-Recognized Principles and Norms of International Law], Советское государство и право [Soviet State and Law], no. 12 (1959), p. 17. Kozhevnikov later repudiated this view. See Курс международного права [Course of International Law] (2d ed.; 1966), p. 41.

[9] N. M. Minasian, Право мирного сосуществования [Law of Peaceful Coexistence] (Rostov, 1966), p. 325.

[10] Ibid., p. 234.

a State bears in mind that a greater significance may not be attached to its vote than that which is defined by the United Nations Charter.

G. I. Morozov also broadly interprets the provisions of the United Nations Charter relating to General Assembly resolutions. He writes: "If Assembly resolutions fully conform both to the concrete provisions and to the general principles of the Charter, if they were adopted by all members of the United Nations, are there grounds for any doubting their legal nature as sources of law? From our point of view, a negative answer should be given to this question. In ratifying the Charter, member States of the United Nations recognized it as binding on themselves; they recognized thereby the binding nature of the resolutions of its organs adopted in strict conformity with the procedure provided by the Charter and the principles proclaimed therein".[11]

There is a contradiction here between the first and last theses. The purport of the first thesis is that Assembly resolutions are binding within the framework provided by the United Nations Charter. And this is correct. The purport of the last thesis is that since the Charter is binding upon member States, all resolutions adopted in conformity with the procedure established by the Charter and corresponding to the principles of the Charter are binding. The Charter provisions relating to the legal force of the resolutions of individual organs are lost sight of here. The jurisdiction of the organs is defined not only by the principles and purposes of the Organization, but above all by the specific Charter provisions concerning such jurisdiction (see Chapter XIV).

In G. P. Zadorozhnyi's view, it is absurd not to regard United Nations General Assembly resolutions as sources of international law since, in his words, "at any international conference a lesser number of States would be sufficient to

[11] G. I. Morozov, Организация Объединенных Наций [The United Nations] (1962), pp. 217-218.

create a new norm of international law".[12] This argument is, however, completely unfounded, since international conferences do not create norms of international law but can be only stages in the process of creating such norms.

We note in passing that confusion on the question of United Nations General Assembly resolutions frequently is aggravated by stating the question incorrectly: are General Assembly resolutions sources of international law or not? In answering the question states in this way, the position of the author of the present work, for example, sometimes is characterized as not recognizing General Assembly resolutions as sources of international law.[13] Whereas, in our view, General Assembly resolutions, being, as a rule, recommendations, may enter the process of forming norms of international law.[14]

As will be shown below, the basic orientation of Soviet international legal doctrine on this question proceeds from the position that General Assembly resolutions are recommendations, except those which under the Charter have a binding character.

In bourgeois international legal doctrine there is a concept, which, it is true, is not widespread, that ascribes to United Nations General Assembly resolutions legal qualities they do not have. Thus, the American Commission to Study the Organization of Peace, under the chairmanship of C. M. Eichelberger, expressed the view that to a certain extent the General Assembly approximates a legislative organ. "Resolutions such as those described", says the Seventeenth Report of the Commission, "when adopted almost unanimously, are likely to be observed. If so, they are eventually recognized as binding

[12] G. P. Zadorozhnyi, Мирное сосуществование и международное право [Peaceful Coexistence and International Law] (1964), pp. 326-327.

[13] See, for example, S. A. Malinin, "О критериях правомерности резолюций Генеральной Ассамблеи ООН" [On Criteria of the Lawfulnexx of United Nations General Assembly Resolutions], Правоведение [Jurisprudence], no. 2 (1965), p. 114.

[14] G. I. Tunkin, Вопросы теории международного права [Questions of the Theory of International Law] (1962), pp. 130-136.

upon the Members".[15] Further on, the report contains a highly significant reservation: "Despite its growing authority, there is a gap between the General Assembly as at present constituted and a full-fledged legislative body".[16]

Professor P. Reuter suggests that resolutions of international organizations are "unilateral acts" and that such acts "possess to a varying but never an insignificant degree the character of authority (*d'autoritŭ*) over governments and States, and sometimes over specific individuals".[17]

Some Western authors believe that United Nations General Assembly resolutions are not "nonbinding" and at the present time are obliterating the distinction between such resolutions and international treaties from the standpoint of their legally binding nature. Professor E. Schwelb, of Yale University, writes: "In any case, after the 1960 Declaration [the Declaration on Granting Independence to Colonial Countries and Peoples – *G.T.*] became a fact, there are international documents which, although not concluded or ratified as treaties, are not `nonbinding'. One can say that they comprise a third category".[18] Thereupon the author asserts that the difference between treaties and resolutions of international organizations is being obliterated.[19]

Professor R. Falk, of Princeton University, in speaking about United Nations General Assembly resolutions, is of the following opinion: "The main point is that the traditional dichotomy between what is obligatory and what is permissive is

15 *New Dimensions for the United Nations: The Problems of the Next Decade. Seventeenth Report of the Commission to Study the Organization of Peace* (1966), p. 22.

16 Ibid.

17 P. Reuter, "Principes de droit international public", *Recueil des cours*, CIII (1963), 578.

18 E. Schwelb, "Neue Etappen der Fortentwicklung des Völkerrechts durch die Vereinten Nationen", *Archiv des Völkerrechts*, XIII (1966), 25-26.

19 Ibid., p. 44.

crumbling and that therefore international lawyers need a more adequate ... theory of legal obligation ...".[20]

Basically, however, Western international legal doctrine adheres to the view that United Nations General Assembly resolutions are recommendations except for those, of course, which under the Charter have a binding character.

"It should be noted above all", A. Verdross writes, "that each organ can adopt lawful decisions only within the constraints of its power. Therefore, if the General Assembly on the basis of the United Nations Charter may direct only recommendations to States, such resolutions may be neither binding nor quasi-binding".[21]

"Whatever political or moral force such recommendations of the General Assembly may claim, they are not legally binding", writes G. Schwarzenberger.[22]

Professor M. Virally, whose previously expressed views on this question were less definite",[23] now says the following: "Resolutions of the General Assembly incorporating declarations of ... principles are not in themselves creative of new rules of international law ... The General Assembly has no general legislative power".[24]

[20] R. A. Falk, "New Approaches to the Study of International Law", *American Journal of International Law*, LXI (1967), 487.

[21] A. Verdross, "Kann die Generalversammlung der Vereinten Nationen das Völkerrecht weiterbilden", *Zeitschrift für auslandishes öffentliches Recht und Völkerrecht*, XXVI (1966), 693.

[22] G. Schwarzenberger, *A Manual of International Law* (5th ed.; 1967), p. 289.

[23] M. Virally, "La valeur juridique des récommendations des organisations internationales", *Annuaire français de droit international*, II (1956), 87-88.

[24] M. Sørenson, ed., *Manual of Public International Law* (1968), p. 162; see also A. J. P. Tammes, "Decisions of International Organs as a Source of International Law", *Recueil des cours*, XCIV (1958), 338-339; A. Malintoppi, *Le raccomandazioni internazionali* (1958), pp. 359-360; M. Sørenson, "Principes de droit international public", *Recueil des cours*, CI (1960), 100; D. P. O'Connell, *International Law* (1965), I, 27; A. Sereni, *Diritto internazionale* (1960), II(2), p. 1044; I. Brownlie, *Principles of Public International Law* (1965), p. 535; S. Bastid, *Droit international public: Le droit des organizations internationals* (n.d.), p. 304; Lino di Qual, *Les éffets des resolutions des Nations Unies* (1967),; G. Castaneda, *Legal Effects of United Nations Resolutions* (1969); C. Rousseau, *Droit international public* (1970), I, 438-441.

Some Western jurists hold the view that the legal force of a General Assembly resolution depends upon the intention of the States who voted for this resolution. Thus, an American jurist, F. Sloan, in acknowledging that as a rule General Assembly resolutions do not create legal obligations, says that if a State which voted for a resolution intended to bind itself legally, the resolution in this case imposes legal obligations on it.[25] An English professor, D. Johnson, adheres to the same view.[26]

On this same plane an English jurist, F. Vallat, says that "Delegations acting without special authority from their governments are limited by the provisions of the Charter. They cannot bind their governments except so far as the Charter allows. If by their votes or their speeches they purport to bind their governments, they do so not by virtue of their position as delegates to the General Assembly but by virtue of some extraneous authority from their governments".[27]

However, in voting for a resolution in the General Assembly, States act within the framework of the Charter, and irrespective of their intention, a resolution may have only that force which is provided by the Charter.[28] Recognition by States of a General Assembly resolution having the character of a recommendation as being binding is a special act not connected with voting on the resolution and goes beyond the limits of the Charter.[29]

25 See F. B. Sloan, "The Binding Force of a 'Recommendation' of the General Assembly of the United Nations", *British Year Book of International Law,* XXV (1948), 22, 31.

26 D. H. N. Johnson, "The Effect of Resolutions of the General Assembly of the United Nations", ibid., XXXII (1955-1956), 121.

27 F. A. Vallat, "The Competence of the United Nations General Assembly", *Recueil des cours,* XCVII (1957), 230.

28 See Verdross, "Kann die Generalversammlung der Vereinten Nationen das Völkerrecht weiterbilden", p. 693.

29 See S. Bastid, "Observations sur une 'étap' dans le dйveloppement progressif et la codification des principes du droit international", *Recueil d' йtudes de droit international en hommage à Paul Guggenheim* (1968), p. 145.

In the opinion of Professor Lauterpacht, a former member of the International Court, United Nations General Assembly resolutions are in the nature of recommendations, and "... although on proper occasions they provide a legal authorization for Members determined to act upon them individually or collectively, they do not create a legal obligation to comply with them".[30]

The legal force of the resolutions of a particular international organization is defined by the particular acts on the basis of which this international organization exists and operates.

In this connection it is necessary to distinguish two aspects of the jurisdiction of an international organization and its organs: a thematic competence defining the questions subject to the jurisdiction of the organization, and a jurisdictional competence defining the legal force of acts of the organization relating to individual questions which fall within its thematic competence.

Further, one should never identify the legally binding nature of General Assembly resolutions or the resolutions of other international organizations with their lawfulness. Establishing the lawfulness of a resolution, that is, its conformity to the requirements of the charter of an international organization, is only to establish its juridical validity. After this, it is still necessary to ascertain whether a lawful resolution is legally binding or is a recommendation.[31]

One can not concur, for example, with the Nigerian professor T. O. Elias, who regards all United Nations General Assembly resolutions on questions enumerated in Article 18(2)

[30] International Court of Justice, Reports of Judgments, Advisory Opinions and Orders, *Nottebohm Case (Liechtenstein v. Guatemala), Second Phase, April 6, 1955* (1955), p. 115.

[31] S. A. Malinin, in particular, has identified the lawfulness with the legally binding nature of a United Nations General Assembly resolution. See S. A. Malinin, Правовые вопросы разоружения [Legal Questions of Disarmament] (1966), pp. 134-138.

of the United Nations Charter as legally binding on States.[32] Among the important questions mentioned in Article 18(2) are both questions regarding which the General Assembly may take binding decisions and those regarding which it may only adopt recommendations. The text of Article 18(2) says within this category of questions are "re- commendations in respect of the maintenance of international peace and security", which are just recommendations. But eight questions are enumerated in this point with regard to which the General Assembly adopts binding resolutions (for example, elections of permanent members of the Security Council, admission of new members, and so forth). One must bear in mind that not every binding directive is a norm of law.

Under the United Nations Charter, the General Assembly, just as other United Nations organs except the Security Council – which raises a special question – adopts binding resolutions only with regard to a narrow circle of matters, primarily organizational and financial.

Thus, the General Assembly adopts its own rules of procedure (Article 21 of the Charter), establishes the procedure of appointing and discharging the staff of the United Nations (Article 101[1]), approves the budget of the Organization and the apportionment of expenses among members in conformity with Article 17 of the Charter, admits States as members of the United Nations upon the recommendation of the Security Council (Article 4), and has the right to adopt a resolution suspending the rights of a United Nations member (Article 5) or expelling it from the Organization (Article 6). The General Assembly approves trusteeship agreements (Articles 16, 79, 85), agreements between the United Nations and specialized agencies (Article 63), and so forth. Lawful General Assembly resolutions concerning a broader circle of

[32] T. O. Elias, "Modern Sources of International Law", in W. Friedmann, L. Henkin, and O. J. Lissitzyn, eds., *Transnational Law in a Changing Society: Essays in Honor of Philip C. Jessup* (1972), p. 46.

questions regulating the "internal law" of the United Nations have the same significance.[33]

With regard, however, to basic questions of its activity which concern relations of States with the United Nations or of States *inter se*, the General Assembly, as provided by Article 10 of the Charter, only makes recommendations.

The distinction between recommendations and legally-binding resolutions consists in the fact that the first is a suggestion to States, whereas the second imposes legal obligations on States.

Soviet international legal doctrine basically adheres to the view of which we have spoken, that United Nations General Assembly resolutions are of a recommendatory character.[34]

An analogous point of view predominated in the literature of other socialist countries.[35]

[33] For greater detail see Malinin, "О критериях правомерности резолюций Генеральной Ассамблеи ООН" [On Criteria of Lawfulness of United Nations General Assembly Resolutions], pp. 115-116; F. Durante, *L'Ordinamento interno delle Nazioni Unite* (1964); D. I. Fel'dman and M. V. Ianovskii, Генеральная Ассамблея ООН [United Nations General Assembly] (Kazan, 1968), pp. 31-78.

[34] See G. I. Tunkin, Основы современного международного права [Fundamental Principles of Contemporary International Law] (1956), p. 13; D. B. Levin, Основные проблемы современного международного права [Basic Problems of Contemporary International Law] (1958), p. 103; P. I. Lukin, Источники международного права [Sources of International Law] (1960), p. 110; A. N. Talalaev, Юридическая природа международного договора [Legal Nature of the International Treaty] (1963), p. 143; Kozhevnikov (ed.), Курс международного права [Course of International Law], p. 41; I. I. Lukashuk, Источники международного права [Sources of International Law] (Kiev, 1966), pp. 81-94; V. M. Chkhikvadze and others (eds.), Курс международного права в шести томах [Course of International Law in Six Volumes] (1967), I, 194; Fel'dman and Ianovskii, Генеральная Ассамблея ООН [United Nations General Assembly], pp. 77-78; G. K. Efimov, Генеральная Ассамблея ООН [United Nations General Assembly] (1969), p. 86.

[35] See, for example, M. Bartos, "Odluke medunarodnikh tela u sistemu pravnikh izvora", *Medunarodni problemy*, V, no. 4 (1953), pp. 12-27; P. Radoinov, "Правната сила на актовете на Общото Събрание на ООН", *Известия на Института за правни науки*, XIV, no. 2 (1964), p. 79; M. Lachs, "Le rôle des organisations internationales dans la formation du droit international", *Mülanges offerts à Henri Rolin: Problumes de droit des gens* (1964), pp. 165- 166; V. Pĕchota, *Mnohostrannü mezinárodni smlouvy a přistup k nim* (1965), p. 16; H. Bokor-Szegó, "The International Legal Content of the Right of Self- Determination as Reflected by the Disintegration of the Colonial System", in Hungarian International Law Association, *Questions*

The practice of States leaves no doubt that they regard General Assembly resolutions which contain rules for the conduct of other States as recommendations. Actually, in those instances when States desired to attach a binding character to norms formulated in such resolutions, a resolution on working out a draft international treaty on the basis of the respective resolution (or declaration) was adopted. As examples, one may cite the Universal Declaration of Human Rights, on the basis of which the covenants on human rights were worked out, the Declaration of the Elimination of All Forms of Racial Discrimination, and the Declaration of Legal Principles Governing the Activities of States in the Exploration and Use of Outer Space, on the basis of which a convention and treaty respectively were worked out.

The viewpoint of the government of the USSR on this question was set forth in the "Memorandum of the Government of the USSR on the Procedure of Financing the Operations of the Emergency United Nations Forces in the Middle East and the United Nations Operations in the Congo" sent to the International Court on 15 March 1962. The Memorandum states: "... U. N. General Assembly resolutions, as is provided for in Article 10 of the Charter, have the character of recommendations and are not binding upon States. Member States of the United Nations themselves define their attitude toward such resolutions. All measures which arise out of General Assembly resolutions also bear only a recommendatory character and cannot create legal obligations for member States of the Organization".[36]

It is necessary, however, to say a special word about those United Nations General Assembly resolutions which themselves represent an interpretation of the United Nations Charter. Although the Charter contains no special provisions on

---

of International Law (1966), p. 17; S. Nahlik, *Wstep do nauki prawa miedzynarodwego* (1967), p. 417; A. Basak, *Decisions of the United Nations Organs in the Judgments and Opinions of the International Court of Justice* (1969), pp. 74-102.

[36] For the text of the Memorandum, see Международная жизнь [International Life], no. 5 (1962), p. 158.

this score, the report of Committee 2 of Commission IV of the San Francisco Conference, which has been referred to previously, says that if an interpretation of the Charter given by a particular United Nations organ is generally accepted, it acquired binding force.[37] This rule is followed in United Nations practice. One can, therefore, regard a General Assembly resolution relating to the interpretation of a particular provision of the United Nations Charter and adopted by the votes of all United Nations members as binding.

But as I. I. Lukashuk has justly remarked, and according to the said report of Committee 2, "an interpretation of the Charter acquires binding force not because it is contained in a resolution, but in consequence of the fact that it is generally recognized".[38]

A. Verdross says that he can not agree with my view because "any authentic interpretation of a legal norm may proceed only from the authority which created it, or from a superior authority, or perhaps as a result of a procedure which has been determined by these authorities. We find such a procedure for the present case in Articles 108 and 109 of the United Nations Charter".[39]

In reality, the interpretation of a particular provision of the United Nations Charter becomes binding only when it has been recognized by all or almost all United Nations members, including the permanent members of the Security Council. Its legally binding nature is determined by such recognition, which may be expressed by various means, particularly by custom. Voting for a resolution which gives an interpretation of the Charter is one method of such recognition, and a resolution

[37] United Nations, *Documents of the United Nations Conference on International Organization* (1945), XIII, 710.

[38] Lukashuk, Источники международного права [Sources of International Law], p. 92.

[39] Verdross, "Kann die Generalversammlung der Vereinten Nationen das Völkerrecht weiterbilden", p. 695.

adopted unanimously is testimony to universal recognition of the respective interpretation.

As regards the Security Council, it may take decisions binding upon members of the United Nations. Article 25 of the Charter provides: "The Members of the United Nations agree to accept and carry out the decisions of the Security Council in accordance with the present Charter". These decisions, however, are by their nature executive resolutions which do not have the purpose of creating general norms of conduct.

At the same time, resolutions of international organizations, above all resolutions of the General Assembly and Security Council adopted in conformity with the provisions of the United Nations Charter, may enter into the process of norm-formation and play a definite role in forming new principles and norms of international law and in affirming, strengthening, developing, and interpreting existing principles and norms.

Resolutions of the Security Council adopted in conformity with the Charter may in a number of instances create a specific practice or contribute to the formation of an international practice that can crystallize into a rule of conduct and therefore be a definite stage in the process of forming a customary norm of international law. Practice does not, however, always lead to the formation of a rule of conduct, and a rule of conduct, if it is formed, does not necessarily become a legal norm. The importance of Security Council decisions goes beyond the limits of the Charter and relates to the formation of customary norms of international law. But it nonetheless is very real.

Resolutions of the General Assembly influence the de- velopment of international law by two means: within the framework of the Charter and in the process of creating norms of international law by way of custom.

The General Assembly, as well as the respective agencies of other international organizations, frequently approve the texts of international treaties.

Resolutions of international organizations adopting the texts of agreements enter into the process of concluding them. But a resolution of an international organization confirming the text of a treaty does not complete the process of forming a norm of international law and does not as such lead directly to the emergence of such a norm.

As regards the recommendatory resolutions adopted by the General Assembly, within the framework of the Charter such resolutions are recommendations and, as already pointed out, do not impose legal obligations on members.

But resolutions of the General Assembly and, to a lesser degree, the resolutions of other organizations play a specific role in the process of forming norms of international law by way of custom.[40] Recommendatory resolutions of international organizations, above all resolutions of the General Assembly adopted in conformity with the Charter and for which votes have been cast by States of the two systems (this is very important, since the question is the formation of norms of general international law), play an important role in the very process of forming customary norms of international law.

Specific rules, norms for the conduct of States, are formulated in General Assembly resolutions. They still are not norms of international law, but in the future they can become such by the same means as customary norms of international law are formed.

As already has been pointed out, however, the fact that a norm of any act later becomes a norm of international law is, in and of itself, not sufficient to consider this act as entering into the process of forming a norm of international law. There are more than a few norms of international law which were formulated for the first time, for example, in acts of national legislation, but this alone is no basis for including national

[40] See R. Higgins, *The Development of International Law Through the Political Organs of the United Nations* (1963), pp. 2-7; K. Wolfke, "Practice of International Organizations and Customary International Law", *Polish Yearbook of International Law 1966/1967* (1968), I, 183-194.

legislative acts in the process of international norm-formation. The process of becoming a norm of international law begins only from the moment when the norm begins to be created as a norm of international law, that is, when the process acquires an interstate character.

It is obvious in this instance that the process of forming a rule of conduct which already has been fixed in a resolution of an international organization has an international character. What place do recommendatory resolutions of international organizations occupy in the process of forming customary norms of international law?

Usage as a stage in the formation of a customary norm of international law reflects the practice of States, which frequently is absent in resolutions of the United Nations General Assembly or other international organ. Consequently, in this respect usage stands, as a rule, farther ahead in the process of norm-formation than a resolution of an international organization. At the same time, the concordance of the wills of States which takes place in a General Assembly resolution, even though it does not go beyond the limits of a recommendation, expresses the wish of States that members of the organization act in conformity with the norms of the resolution. This element places a resolution farther ahead than usage in the process of forming customary norms of international law.

The subsequent development depends above all upon the extent to which a norm contained in a resolution conforms to the law of societal development, to the real co-relation of forces. The results of voting are an indicator here. Therefore, resolutions of the United Nations General Assembly adopted unanimously or by the majority stipulated in the Charter, including States of the two systems, may signify the birth and formation of those new principles and norms of international law which are proclaimed in such resolutions. One may regard as such resolutions, for example, the resolutions of the General Assembly on the question of the regulation and reduction of armaments, beginning with the resolution of 14 December 1946 (41/I), on general and complete disarmament, beginning with the resolution of 20 November 1959 (1378/XIV), on the prohibition of war propaganda of 3 November 1947 (110/II), on recognizing Africa as a nuclear-free zone of 24 November 1961 (1652/XVI),[41] on strict compliance with the prohibition of the threat or use of force in international relations and the right of peoples to self-determination of 30 November 1966 (2160/XXI), and a number of others.[42]

Similar resolutions may be stages in the process of creating customary norms of international law – stages, however, which do not complete the process of norm-formation and therefore do not lead directly to the emergence of a norm of international law. As is common in the process of forming customary norms of international law, their further development may slow down temporarily or forever. In the latter case, the process will not be completed and will not lead to the formation of a norm of international law. But it can continue and be completed by States recognizing rules established in General Assembly resolutions as norms of international law.

Resolutions of the United Nations General Assembly also frequently are means of declaring or interpreting prevailing principles and norms of international law.

When a resolution of the General Assembly or of another international organ is in the nature of declaring the existence of a particular norm of international law, it has, naturally, a declarative character. But in international law, where frequently there are disputes over whether a particular norm of international law exists or not, the significance of such resolutions, if States of different social systems have voted for them, can not give rise to doubt. This also is true of resolutions interpreting prevailing principles and norms. Although under the United Nations Charter these and other resolutions are

[41] For greater detail, see O. V. Bogdanov, Всеобщее и полное разоружение [General and Complete Disarmament] (1964); Malinin, Правовые основы разоружения [Legal Foundations of Disarmament].

[42] For greater detail, see Fel'dman and Ianovskii, Генаральная Ассамблея ООН [United Nations General Assembly], pp. 80-191.

in the nature of recommendations, on a broader plane there is every reason to anticipate that the declaration of the existence of a norm or its interpretation contained in such resolutions will be accepted in practice and be confirmed as legally binding by means of custom.

The voting of States for a General Assembly resolution which represents a declaration or interpretation of prevailing principles and norms of international law is an affirmation of the previously existing agreement that was embodied in the prevailing principles and norms, as to which there is a question in a specific case.

Moreover, for a number of States, voting for such a General Assembly resolution may be the first instance of their expressing recognition of the respective principles and norms as norms of international law or recognition of the interpretation of the principles and norms set forth in the resolution.

As an example of a General Assembly resolution which contains a declaration or interpretation of prevailing principles and norms of international law, one may mention in the General Assembly Resolution (95/I) of 11 December 1946 on the principles of in- ternational law recognized by the charters and judgments of the Nuremberg and Tokyo tribunals, which say that the General Assembly "affirms the principles of international law recognized by the Charter of the Nuremberg Tribunal and sanctioned by the judgment of that Tribunal".

Also included in this category are the basic provisions of the Declaration on Granting Independence to Colonial Countries and Peoples (Resolution 1514 (XV), resolution 1653/ XVI of 24 November 1961, which says that "the use of nuclear or thermonuclear weapons contravenes norms of international law and the law of humanity", the Declaration on Principles of International Law Relating to Friendly Relations and Cooperation Among States in Accordance with the Charter of the United Nations (Resolution 2625(XXV) of 24 October 1970), and a number of other resolutions of the General Assembly.

It is necessary to bear in mind in this connection that the question of whether a specific resolution or certain provisions of a resolution are a declaration or interpretation of prevailing principles and norms of international law must be decided not on the basis of philological formulations, which might be accidental, but on the basis of the true meaning of the resolution. The resolution must testify to the expression of recognition (primarily or secondarily) by the States which voted for it of the provisions set forth in the resolution as norms of international law.

It must be emphasized that in these instances the binding force of the provisions contained in the resolution is based not on the resolution itself, which can not have a greater force than is provided for by the United Nations Charter, but on the agreement of States who voted for the resolution, which is characteristic of the process of creating and modifying norms of international law by means of custom.

The fact that as a rule the General Assembly can adopt only recommendations dealing with the most important issues of United Nations activities is one of the most important manifestations of the legal nature of the United Nations (see Chapter XV).

2. Recommendations of Specialized International Organizations

The legal nature of recommendations of specialized agencies whose constitutions provide for the adoption of such re- commendations addressed to member States is of considerable interest.

The provisions of constitutions of the specialized agencies on this question are not identical. Thus, for example, the constitutions of the International Civil Aviation Organization and of the World Meteorological Organization speak of standards and recommended practice, which in essence means regulations in the first case and recommendations in the second.

The question of recommendations has been formulated most precisely in the constitutions of the International Labor Organization and UNESCO. The Constitution of the International Labor Organization says that a recommendation adopted by the General Conference of the ILO "will be communicated to all Members for their consideration with a view to effect being given to it by national legislation or otherwise" (Article 19[6]). The UNESCO Rules of Procedure provide that in recommendations the "General Conference formulates principles and norms for the international regulation of any particular question and invites Member States to take whatever legislative or other steps may be required – in conformity with the constitutional practice of each State and the nature of the question under consideration – to apply the principles and norms aforesaid within their respective territories".[43]

Member States are not legally bound to fulfill recommendations. But the constitutions of a number of specialized agencies provide that if a recommendation is adopted, the member States, irrespective of their attitude toward the given recommendation, shall be bound to undertake the specific actions. Thus, according to the Constitution of the International Labor Organization, each member of the Organization is obliged within twelve or, in an extreme case, eighteen months, to submit this recommendation to the respective competent authorities for the purpose of taking decisions pursuant thereto and to notify the Director-General of the ILO about this decision. At the same time, member States are obliged, according to the Constitution of the ILO, periodically to notify the Director-General of the ILO with regard to the state of their legislation and practice concerning matters touched upon in the recommendation (Article 19(6),

[43] The Rules of Procedure concerning recommendations made by the General Conference to member States and to the adoption of international conventions by the General Conference were confirmed by the General Conference at its fifth session, and amended at the seventh session. Сборник правил по созыву и проведению конференций [Collection of Rules on Convocation and Holding of Conferences] (1964).

paras. b, c, d). The submission by member States of information concerning measures which they have taken to effectuate recommendations approved by the General Conference also is provided for by the Constitution of UNESCO (Article VIII, as well as Articles XV and XVI of the Rules of Procedure relating to recommendations and conventions).

The legal nature of recommendations of international organizations has given rise to more than a few disputes. Thus, Professor M. Virally, although he points out that "from a strict legal viewpoint its addressee ... is not bound to apply it and even is not bound to keep its existence in mind",[44] nevertheless suggests that if a State executes a recommendation adopted by an international organization, it fulfills its obligations and, in the event of nonfulfillment, it is "guilty" before the organization.[45]

In the view of Professor P. Vellas, of Toulouse University, the recommendations of specialized agencies "possess a considerable socio-juridical power of applicability".[46]

The legal adviser of UNESCO, H. Saba, speaks of "nonratified norms", by which he means recommendations,[47] clearly un- derestimating the difference existing between conventions and recommendations adopted by international organizations.

It is important, above all, in our view, not to confuse the actual effectiveness of recommendations of international organizations with their legally binding nature. Not only legal norms may be effective. The effectiveness of a norm as such does not make it legal. Moral norms in a number of instances are more effective than certain legal norms, but they continue to remain moral norms.

[44] Virally, "La valeur juridique des récommendations des organisations internationales", pp. 83-84.

[45] Ibid., pp. 87-88.

[46] P. Vellas, *Droit international public: institutions internationales* (1967), p. 214 ["... d'une force d'applicabilité socio-juridique considerable"].

[47] H. Saba, "L'Activité quasi-législative des institutions specialisées des Nations Unies", *Recueil des cours*, CXI (1964), 660.

The assertion that the legal force of recommendations of such international organizations as the International Labor Organization, UNESCO, and certain others consists in the fact that in consequence of their adoption States are bound to perform certain actions also is incorrect. The respective obligations are fixed in the articles of the constitutions of these organizations, and these articles begin to operate when a specific legal fact takes place: the adoption by an international organization of a particular recommendation. The duty to submit a recommendation for the consideration of competent agencies to communicate the results of the consideration to the international organization, to submit information on matters touched upon in the recommendation, has been provided for by the constitutions of these international organizations. It is true that a recommendation adopted in such organizations defines the extent of the information to be submitted by all member States. In prescribing a specific form of State action, however, the norms of a recommendation are not legally binding upon them. Each State decides for itself whether to act in accordance with the recommendation or not.

Moreover, in contrast to regulations, recommendations – to which we refer here – do not have the purpose of creating international obligations of States. If a State has adopted a regulation, it is bound to it as an international treaty. If a State effectuates the norms of a recommendation, it does not by virtue thereof become bound by international obligations.

The real effectiveness of the norms of recommendations, that is, the degree of their influence on the conduct of States, is another question. The more a recommendation of an international organization is responsive to the pressing requirements of the cooperation of States in a given sphere, the higher its effectiveness. One must concur with Professor Vellas that recommendations of international organizations relating to cooperation in economic, scientific, and technical domains have, in a number of instances, very great effectiveness.[48]

[48] Vellas, *Droit international public: institutions internationales*, p. 214.

The role of normative recommendations of specialized international organizations undoubtedly is growing in international relations. Therefore, ascertaining their legal nature and true role is of both theoretical and practical importance.

3. Decisions of the International Court and of International Arbitration Tribunals

There are two opposing points of view in bourgeois legal literature on the significance of decisions of international courts and arbitral tribunals as sources of international law.

One viewpoint, expressed most frequently in "common law" countries, exaggerates the role of judgments of the International Court. Thus, Lauterpacht, in a detailed work, *The Development of International Law by the International Court,* whose second edition appeared in 1958, writes the following with regard to decisions of the International Court: "They state what the law is. Their decisions are evidence of the existing rule of law. That does not mean that they do not in fact constitute a source of international law. For the distinction between the evidence and the source of many a rule of law is more speculative and less rigid than is commonly supposed ... insofar as they show what are the rules of international law they are largely identical with it".[49]

In noting that there is no legislative body in international relations, G. Fitzmaurice, an English jurist who was a member of the International Court, writes: "The international community is therefore peculiarly dependent on its international tribunals for the development and clarification of the law, and for lending to it an authority more substantial and less precarious than can be drawn from the often divergent or uncertain practice of States, or even from the opinions of individual publicists, whatever their repute".[50]

[49] H. Lauterpacht, *The Development of International Law by the International Court* (2d ed.; 1958), p. 21.

[50] G. Fitzmaurice, "Hersch Lauterpacht: The Scholar as Judge", *British Year Book of International Law*, XXXVII (1961), 14.

Another English jurist, C. W. Jenks, declares in a summary discussion in which he draws an analogy with the development of the English judicial system: "International law now has its supreme Court and that supreme Court is approaching with judicial statesmanship the task of giving a new vitality to the law".[51] And further, in developing Lauterpacht's idea, Jenks says that "in respect of a widening range of questions the Court is progressively substituting judicial precedent for formless and debatable custom".[52]

On the same plane, an Australian jurist, O'Connell, asserts that "As the judge in the common law system plays a fundamental role in the formulation of general principles, in their application and modification by reference to contingent circumstances, in extension by analogy and deduction from accepted hypothesis, so does the judge in the system of international law".[53]

This concept finds no support in the provisions of the Statute of the International Court. Article 38 of the Statute says that the Court shall be obliged to decide disputes submitted to it on the basis of international law. With regard to the specific sources to be applied by the Court, Article 38(1)(d) says that the Court shall apply "subject to the provisions of Article 59, judicial decisions and the teachings of the most highly qualified publicists of the various nations, as subsidiary means for the determination of rules of law". Article 59 of the Statute provides: "The decision of the Court has no binding force except between the parties and in respect of that particular case".

It by no means follows that decisions of the Court "are evidence of the existence of a rule of law". This concept, arising out of Anglo- American "common law" doctrine, is inapplicable

[51] C. W. Jenks, *The Common Law of Mankind* (1958), p. 181.

[52] Ibid., p. 180. For greater detail, see C. W. Jenks, *The Prospect of International Adjudication* (1964).

[53] O'Connell, *International Law*, I, p. 28; an Israeli jurist trained in England, S. Rosenne, says that the International Court has become a "powerful instrument for the progress" of international law. See S. Rosenne, *The Law and Practice of the International Court* (1965), II, 607.

to international law. To ascribe such a role to the International Court is to go beyond the provisions of its Statute.

Lauterpacht asserts that judgments of the Court also are international law. He equates them, therefore, to international treaties and customs enumerated in Article 38(1) (a) and (b) of the Statute. But if the Statute says that the Court shall apply international treaties and international custom as part of international law by which it must be guided, the Statute says otherwise with respect to judicial decisions. They may be used only as one of the subsidiary means for determining the existence or absence of a particular norm of international law. It also must be noted that the Statute places judicial decisions on the same level as doctrine.

Lauterpacht goes further, asserting that the Court may regard its decisions as an expression of international law notwithstanding the provisions of the Statute. "They are not binding *upon States*. Neither are they binding upon the Court. However, no written provisions can prevent them from showing authoritatively what international law is, and no written rule can prevent the Court from regarding them as such".[54]

If the Court regarded its decisions as an embodiment of international law and consequently as binding upon States, this would expressly contravene its Statute. But the International Court, as any other international organ, was created on the basis of agreement: the United Nations Charter and the Statute of the Court. The powers and functions of an international organ, particularly of the International Court, are defined by its Statute, and the Court can not pretend that greater significance is attached to its decisions than has been established by the Statute of the Court.

There is no basis for presupposing that the Statute of the International Court has been changed by customary means on

[54] Lauterpacht, *The Development of International Law by the International Court*, p. 22.

the basis of the general agreement of United Nations members, and even Lauterpacht himself does not say this.

Another point of view expressed in bourgeois literature with regard to judicial decisions is that they are not sources of international law. Thus, Professor A. Verdross, in combining judicial decisions and doctrine, says: "Judicial decisions therefore can never be guided exclusively by an individual prior decision or by doctrine. It can use a prior decision and doctrine in order to ascertain whether a norm of international law is not sufficiently clear. Therefore, judicial practice and doctrine are not independent sources of international law; they are only subsidiary sources of law which serve to help understand doubtful provisions of law".[55]

Citing Article 59 of the Statute of the International Court, H. Kelsen writes that a "decision of the Court can not have the character of a precedent".[56]

In Oppenheim's treaties *International Law* edited by Lauterpacht we read: "In the absence of anything approaching the common law doctrine of judicial precedent, decisions of international tribunals are not a direct source of law in international adju- dications".[57]

"Decisions of international courts or tribunals", writes G. Schwarzenberger, "do not have the effect of precedents in the technical sense of English law ... such authority as international decisions may claim is purely persuasive".[58]

The majority of Soviet writers adhere to the view that decisions of the International Court and international arbitral tribunals

55 Verdross, *Международное право*, pp. 164-165.

56 Kelsen, *Principles of International Law*, p. 394.

57 L. Oppenheim, *International Law*, ed. H. Lauterpacht (8th ed.; 1955), I, 31.

58 Schwarzenberger, *A Manual of International Law*, p. 255; Waldock expresses a view close to this. See H. Waldock, "General Course on Public International Law", *Recueil des cours*, CVI (1962), 91; Brownlie remarks that "the Court applies law and does not make it". Brownlie, *Principles of Public International Law*, p. 17.

are not a means of creating or modifying its norms,[59] but are subsidiary sources.

Article 38 of the Statute of the International Court provides that the Court, in considering disputes submitted to it by States, shall act "in accordance with international law". It is not empowered to make changes in prevailing international law, but should be guided by it. The Statute expressly rejects the concept of "judicial precedent", establishing in Article 59 that "the decision of the Court has no binding force except between the parties and in respect of that particular case". With this reservation, the International Court can use its decisions "as subsidiary means for the determination of rules of law". Consequently, according to the Statute of the International Court, its decisions are not part of the process of creating or modifying norms of international law.

What role do decisions of the International Court have on the broader plane of forming norms of international law? The International Court does not consist of representatives of States. It is composed of persons elected by representatives of States. It is composed of persons elected by representatives of States (respectively, in the Security Council and General Assembly of the United Nations), but who act as "independent judges" (Article 2 of the Statute). Decisions of the Court reflect the opinion of the members of the Court, who are specialists in international law. This brings decisions of the Court closer to doctrine, and not without reason does the Statute of the Court speak of judicial decisions and teachings of international law simultaneously.

[59] See, for example, E. A. Korovin, Международное право [International Law] (1951), pp. 17-18; Kozhevnikov (ed.), Международное право [International Law], p. 9; Levin, Основные проблемы современного международного права [Basic Problems of Contemporary International Law], pp. 102-102; G. P. Kaliuzhnaia and D. B. Levin, Международное право [International Law] (1960), p. 32; Kozhevnikov (ed.), Курс международного права [Course of International Law], pp. 41-42; Lukashuk, Источники международного права [Sources of International Law], pp. 95-96; Chkhikvadze and others (eds.), Курс международного права в шести томах [Course of International Law in Six Volumes], I, 195; L. A. Modzhorian and N. T. Blatova (eds.), Международное право [International Law] (1970), p. 60.

But the International Court is at the same time one of the principal organs of the United Nations, fulfilling its judicial functions in conformity with the United Nations Charter and its own Statute. It considers cases submitted to it by States and whose parties are States. Decisions of the Court are binding upon the parties to the case, and the United Nations Charter provides that the parties shall be bound to comply with such decisions (Article 94).

These specific features are the basis for considering that decisions of the International Court enter into the process of norm- formation as part of international practice in that they relate to the declaration of the existence of norms of international law or their interpretation. This practice, it is true, can not be placed on the same level with State practice, since the International Court is not composed of representatives of States.

Inasmuch as this is so, what has been said previously with regard to the formation and modification of norms of international law by way of custom is applicable to decisions of the International Court. As part of international practice, decisions of the International Court can lead to completion of the process of norm-formation by their being recognized by States and being consolidated in international law. Of course, only those decisions of the International Court for which judges representing the different social and legal systems have voted and which frequently are cited in the practice of relations among States actually have a chance of being consolidated.[60]

Regrettably, however, if one takes the practice of the International Court as a whole, we find more than a few

[60] In its decision of 18 December 1951, in the Anglo-Norwegian fisheries disputes, for example, the International Court expressed the view that the so-called ten-mile rule upheld by England – that the waters of bays and gulfs may be considered to be internal waters of a coastal State only if the breadth of the aperture of such bays and gulfs does not exceed ten miles – is not a principle of international law. This position was consolidated in the 1958 Convention on the Territorial Sea and Contiguous Zone, which provided that the waters of bays and gulfs, the breadth of whose aperture does not exceed twenty-four miles, shall be considered internal waters of the coastal State. Thus, the 1958 Convention establishes not a ten-mile, but a twenty-four mile rule.

decisions that do not correspond to prevailing international law, decisions in which a one-sided interpretation of the latter is reflected.[61]

The considerations set forth above also relate basically to awards of international arbitral tribunals created by agreement between two or more States to consider interstate disputes. However, in carrying less weight for wholly understandable reasons than decisions of the International Court, the awards of international arbitral tribunals stand, in comparison with the former, closer to international legal doctrine.

4. National Legislation and Decisions of National Judicial Instances

National legislative acts, as well as decisions of national courts, can be, first and foremost, one of the means of establishing norms of international law. Their role is defined by the fact that norms of international law are created by means of agreement among States. National legislation and decisions of national courts can in a number of instances be regarded as expressing recognition by a specific State of a particular rule as a norm of international law.

National courts are agencies of a State and, as Lauterpacht correctly points out, "their decisions within any particular State, when endowed with sufficient uniformity and authority, may be regarded as expressing the *opinio juris* of that State".[62]

A clarification, however, is necessary. Judicial decisions, although on questions concerning international relations, can

[61] For example, the decision relating to the recognition of consular jurisdiction in the Franco-American case on the rights of American nationals in Morocco, and others. S. B. Krylov, Международный суд [International Court] (1958). One also should mention in this connection the 1962 advisory opinion in the case of certain expenses of the United Nations and the 1966 judgment in the Southwest Africa case. See M. Iuranov, "Отказ в правосудии (Решение Международного Суда по делу о Юго-Западной Африки)" [Denial of Justice (Judgment of International Court in South-West Africa Case)], Советское государство и право [Soviet State and Law], no. 5 (1957), pp. 45-54.

[62] Lauterpacht, *The Development of International Law by the International Court*, p. 20.

all the same have significance only within the limits of the national law of a given State. In order to have significance for international norm- formation, such a decision must express, just as the legislative act of a State, the acceptance or recognition of a particular rule as a norm of international law.[63]

The role of national legislation and of decisions of national courts is not limited to the fact that they have significance for establishing the existence of principles and norms of international law. The said acts can, for example, contain proposals to other States, an expression of readiness on the part of a given State to recognize a particular rule as a norm of international law on condition that other States will agree to act in an analogous manner. In this respect the Dekret on Peace of 8 November 1917 is especially characteristic, wherein the Soviet State advanced a whole series of international legal principles, first and foremost the principle of the prohibition of aggressive war, the principle of the criminality of such war, the principle of self-determination of nations, and others. This was not just the formulation of the policy of a socialist State, but also a proposal to all other States to recognize these principles as principles of international law.[64]

The actions of a State in the person of its legislative or judicial agencies can, as already has been pointed out, also signify recognition on the part of a state of a norm being formed or already prevailing as a norm of international law as regards the State concerned.

Therefore, in both the first and second instance the actions of a State can be part of the process of forming a customary norm of international law.

[63] K. Strupp speaks of the need for a decision to express *opinio juris gentium*. K. Strupp, "Règles générales du droit de la paix", *Recueil des cours*, XLVII (1934), 307-308.

[64] For greater detail, see N. V. Mironov, Советское государство и международное право [Soviet State and International Law] (1968).

CHAPTER VI. DOCTRINE AND THE OPINIONS OF SOCIAL ORGANIZATIONS

1. *International Legal Doctrine*

In the nineteenth and even at the beginning of the twentieth century, many jurists regarded international law as, to a significant extent, "doctrinal" law, the law of "scholars". They ascribed to the science of international law not just the role of declaror, but also the role of creator, of its norms. J. C. Bluntschli, for example, called treatises of international law the "surrogate of legislation in which private persons who know the law expound and systematize prevailing legal norms".[1]

There is no doubt that doctrine previously played a significantly larger role as a source of international law than at the present time.

The opinions of authoritative specialists on international law of various countries are now one means of establishing the existence or absence of a particular norm of international law, as well as of interpreting them.

Article 38 of the Statute of the International Court provides that in deciding cases the Court may apply "the teachings of the most qualified publicists of the various nations, as a subsidiary means for the determination of the rules of law".

Taking into account the various difficulties which frequently arise when establishing the existence of or interpreting norms of international law (especially with regard to customary norms), the science of international law often renders important service in this area.

At the same time, there is no doubt that as State practice becomes more accessible as a result of the publication of various kinds of diplomatic and other State documents, as well as of decisions of international organizations and international courts, the role of doctrine as a means of establishing the

[1] J. C. Bluntschli, *Das moderne Völkerrecht der civilisirten Staten* (2d ed.; 1872), p. 7.

existence of norms of international law and of interpreting them is tending to diminish.[2]

The scientific investigations of international lawyers are not part of the process of international law-making, although they exert some influence upon it. There is virtually complete agreement in Soviet legal literature on this question. The overwhelming majority of bourgeois international lawyers also adhere at present to the view that international legal doctrine is not a method of creating norms of law, but plays only that subsidiary role defined in Article 38 of the Statute of the International Court.[3]

It is characteristic that even the International Court, as H. Waldock notes, never has cited international legal doctrine in its judgments, although, as he correctly suggests, this does not mean that doctrine exerts no influence upon these judgments.[4]

If it is of a progressive character, the science of international law may have a material impact upon the development of international law. In uncovering the laws of societal development, in noticing and supporting new trends or progressive new principles and norms which may not be completely formulated, in waging a struggle against everything obsolete which impedes social progress, and in unmasking reactionary forces clinging to obsolete principles and norms that inhibit the progressive development of international law, science may contribute significantly to its development.

[2] L. Oppenheim, *International Law*, ed. H. Lauterpacht (8th ed.; 1955), I, 33.

[3] For example, see A. Verdross, Международное право [International Law], transl. from 3d ed. by F. A. Kublitskii and R. L. Naryshkina, ed. G. I. Tunkin (1959), p. 165; Oppenheim, *International Law*, I, 33. An Italian professor, R. Ago, essentially ascribes a law-creating role to [legal] science. See R. Ago, "Positive Law and International Law", *American Journal of International Law*, LI (1957), 691- 733.

[4] See H. Waldock, "General Course on Public International Law", *Recueil des cours*, XVI (1962), 95-96.

2. Opinions and Resolutions of Social and Scientific Organizations

At the present time, there are a significant number of international and national social and scientific organizations which either are specially concerned with questions of international law or from time to time express views on such questions. These organizations are highly diverse both by their character and their social significance. Among them are congresses of advocates of peace representing hundreds of millions of people, and also organizations such as the World Federation of Trade Unions, a very broad mass organization. On the other hand, there are such legal organizations as the International Association of Democratic Jurists (IADJ), a broad organization of jurists, the Institute of International Law, whose membership under the existing statute may not exceed 130 persons, international legal specialists from various countries, and the International Law Association, numbering several thousand persons, far from always international legal specialists. There also are a large number of national organizations for questions of international law.

From the standpoint of the process of international norm- formation, these organizations all have in common the fact that they are not agencies reflecting the will of States. Their views and resolutions therefore do not enter into the process of international norm-formation.

But these organizations are so diverse that their impact upon the process of creating international legal norms also is highly diverse.

Draft conventions, resolutions, and so forth prepared by special legal organizations (as for example, the Institute of International Law, the International Law Association, and others) occupy the same place with regard to the process of norm-formation in general as does international legal doctrine.

The resolutions of mass international organizations which express the opinion of broad circles of the public have another significance. While perhaps not always formulating a particular provision of international law with sufficient precision, they express the aspirations of peoples which governments can not fail to take into account. Of the mass international organizations one should especially single out the movement of the advocates of peace. This movement, taking as its basic task the struggle for the maintenance and strengthening of peace, devotes great attention in international law as a means of struggle for peace. In their resolutions and appeals, organs of the movement of advocates of peace, expressing the will of hundreds of millions of progressive people, raise vital questions of contemporary international relations and international law, as, for example, the problem of disarmament, prohibition of war propaganda, definition of aggression, and others.[5]

[5] On this question see M. I. Lazarev, Конгресс народов в защиту мира и основные принципы международного права [Congress of Peoples in Defense of Peace and Basic Principles of International Law] (1953); N. Ul'ianova, "Межнародноправовое значения документив всевитнього руху прихильников миру" [International Legal Significance of Documents of Universal Movement of Supporters of Peace], Радянське право [Soviet Law], no. 3 (1959), pp. 21-27; V. M. Chkhikvadze, Борьба за мир – неодилимое движение современности [Struggle for Peace -- Invincible Movement of Modern Times] (1969).

CHAPTER VII.
THE PROBLEM OF "GENERAL PRINCIPLES OF LAW"

The problem of "general principles of law" was and still is the subject of lively discussion chiefly in connection with Article 38(1)(c) of the Statute of the Permanent Court of International Justice and, at present, the Statute of the International Court.

This problem has occupied a very large place in international legal literature, primarily in consequence of the endeavours of the followers of new natural law concepts, who have attempted to find support for their own theoretical constructions in the Statute of the Permanent Court of International Justice.

Some representatives of the "law of precedent" see a tendency in this provision of the Statute of the International Court to enlarge the role of the international court and an attribution of functions thereto which resemble the law-making functions of courts in "common law" countries.[1]

Other bourgeois authors, believing that "general principles of law" do not have a significant place in international law, point out that the Permanent Court of International Justice not once has referred in its decisions to the corresponding paragraph of its own Statute which speaks of "general principles of law".[2]

The majority of bourgeois authors, citing the *travaux prŭparatoires* of the Commission of Jurists for Drafting the Statute of the Permanent Court of International Justice of the League of Nations, adhere to the view that Article 38 of the Statute of the International Court of the United Nations

[1] Lauterpacht said that Article 38(1)(c) of the Statute is an important landmark in the history of international law. See L. Oppenheim, *International Law*, ed. H. Lauterpacht (8th ed.; 1955), I, 30.

[2] J. Basdevant, "Règles générales du droit de la paix", *Recueil des cours*, LVIII (1936), 503; C. Rousseau, *Principes généraux du droit international public* (1944), I, 897-898; Rousseau, "Principes de droit international public", *Recueil des cours*, XCIII (1958), 485.

has in mind principles of national legal systems common to all "civilized States".

As regards the character of these principles and their place in international law, there are greatly differing opinions in bourgeois international legal literature.

In D. Anzilotti's view, the "general principles of law" mentioned in Article 38 of the Statute of the Permanent Court of International Justice are now in Article 38 of the Statute of the International Court are, first and foremost, general principles of international law, and then the principles recognized in the legislation of all countries. As principles of national legal systems, they are not part of international law. However, says Anzilotti, such principles may be used by an international court as material for the creation of a norm of international law.[3]

Another Italian writer, G. Morelli, believes that Article 38 of the Statute of the International Court does not speak about principles of international law. He goes on to add: "The question is the criteria which should guide the Court in rendering a decision in the event it declares that neither a customary nor conventional rule exists that is applicable to the instance being considered".[4] In this event, according to Morelli, the decision of the Court is to be based on nonlegal principles. A norm of international law is created not by general principles, but by judges on the basis of general principles extracted from national legal systems.

According to Anzilotti and Morelli, therefore, Article 38 of the Statute of the Permanent Court of International Justice and of the Statute of the International Court has empowered the Court to create norms of international law from the principles of national legal systems. Such an interpretation can and could have been defended previously on the basis of

[3] D. Anzilotti, *Corso di diritto internazionale* (3d ed.; 1928), pp. 106-107.

[4] G. Morelli, "Cours général de droit international public", *Recueil des cours*, LXXXIX (1956), 470-471; Morelli, *Nozioni de diritto internazionale* (3d ed.; 1951), p. 44.

the text of Article 38 of the Statute of the Permanent Court of International Justice, although it would not have conformed to the general spirit of the Statute, but at the present time, since as a result of the International Court it indicates precisely that the Court settles disputes "in accordance with international law", this interpretation clearly has become incorrect. The Court does not create international law; it applies it.

Proponents of the "pure" theory of law are partial to the view that "general principles of law" are not an autonomous source of international law.

The leading representative of this theory, Professor H. Kelsen, doubts the possibility that principles "... common to the legal orders of the civilized nations ..." exist, pointing to the ideological differences existing among States. Digressing to the doctrine of "gaps" in international law, he points out that any international dispute can be settled on the basis of treaty or customary international law. Consequently, the reference to "general principles of law" is superfluous. He also supports this conclusion by citing Article 38 of the Statute, pursuant to which the Court must decide cases "in accordance with international law". "Hence it might be argued", he says, "that `the general principles of law' are applicable only if they are part of international law, and this means part of the law referred to in clauses (a) and (b) of Article 38. Then, clause (c) is superfluous".[5]

At the present time, two viewpoints on the question of the character of "general principles of law" are most prevalent in bourgeois international legal literature: the moderate normativistic and the natural law.

As representatives of the first point of view, one can take a Swiss professor, P. Guggenheim, who, it seems to us, is moving away more and more from the "pure theory of law", and a French professor, C. Rousseau.

[5] H. Kelsen, *Principles of International Law*, ed. R. W. Tucker (2d ed.; 1967), p. 540.

Professor Guggenheim writes with regard to Article 38 of the Statute of the International Court: "The most important international law code of procedures, therefore, admits the existence of a third group of norms as a base for judicial decisions. As we already have pointed out, in considering the question of gaps there is no technical necessity for such an expansion of the legislative procedure. Since gaps do not exist in international law, founded upon customary and conventional law, any dispute submitted to the jurisdiction of an international court can be settled. There is no place therefore, for a *non liquet*".[6]

The inclusion in the Statute of a reference to "general principles of law", that is, principles applied *in foro domestico*, says Guggenheim, arose out of the desire to fill gaps and, for this purpose, to enlarge the rights of the Court.[7]

There is no doubt, continues Guggenheim, that all general principles of law whose application is expressly provided for in agreements on arbitration and judicial settlement enter into conventional law. But even in those instances when this was not so, certain international arbitrators at their own initiative applied general principles of law from the domain of national private or public law. The validity of these principles in such cases can be proved within the body of customary law. "Therefore", the author concludes, "general principles of law are based either on conventional or customary law".[8]

In the opinion of Guggenheim, who cites international judicial and arbitral practice in this connection, not all general principles of law which are part of the various legal systems are included in international law. "Only a very insignificant number of such principles have been incorporated into the international legal order".[9]

6 P. Guggenheim, *Traité de droit international* (2d ed; 1967), I, 292.

7 Ibid., pp. 295-296.

8 Ibid., p. 298.

9 Ibid.. In his work *General Principles of Law as Applied by International Courts and*

C. Rousseau writes: "By means of custom and treaty, States themselves define the extent of their rights and duties. But they also may be limited by the fact that they recognize by general consent that specific legal principles which already exist in other spheres of law will be applied in their mutual relations".[10] In international judicial and arbitral decisions, Rousseau says, general principles of law mean the "principles which are common to the legal systems of the various civilized States".[11]

Citing, just as other bourgeois writers, the *travaux prŭparatoires* relating to the drawing up of the Statute of the Permanent Court of International Justice, he adheres to Phillimore's view that general principles of law are those principles "accepted by all nations *in foro domestico*", and to La Pradelle's view that these are the "principles on which national law is based".[12]

Rousseau suggests that in Article 38 of the Statute of the Permanent Court of International Justice the question was one of the "principles common to the domestic legal order and the international legal order", "of the law in general (*du droit sans ŭpithute*), embracing both international and domestic law".[13] An analysis of international judicial and arbitral decisions, Rousseau says, leads to the conclusion that "general principles of law are a specific and distinct source of international law".[14] Any other conclusion, in Rousseau's opinion, would lead to the

---

Tribunals, B. Cheng, in maintaining that "... the essence of general principles of law is the fact of their being common to all legal systems", is obliged to acknowledge that "international custom or customary international law, understood in a broad sense, may include all that is unwritten in international law, *i.e.*, both custom and general principles of law". B. Cheng, *General Principles of Law as Applied by International Courts and Tribunals* (1953), pp. xv, 23.

[10] C. Rousseau, *Principes généraux du droit international public*, I, 890; Rousseau, *Droit international public* (1970), I, 371-375.

[11] Ibid.

[12] Ibid., p. 892.

[13] Ibid., p. 901.

[14] Ibid., p. 913.

view that the reference in the Statute to general principles of law is superfluous.[15]

Rousseau suggests that "general principles of law" include not only principles common to the various national legal systems, but also general principles of international law which "do not coincide either with conventional or with customary rules".[16]

In the opinion of Verdross, who is a representative of the modern natural law orientation, "general principles of law" are those similar provisions which underlie the legal systems "of civilized peoples". They are a reflection of natural law – not principles of natural law directly, but those principles which have already been reflected positively in the prevailing legal systems of States.[17]

Verdross believes that "general principles of law" rest upon a general legal consciousness. One must distinguish them from general principles of international law in "the narrow sense", since "general principles of law" are not reflected in either treaties or custom.[18] International law, he says, "is not exhausted by treaty or customary international law; general principles of law should be added to them".[19]

Verdross maintains that "general principles of law" are the basis of all international law. At the same time, they form a constituent part thereof and are applied in those instances when positive international law does not contain principles and norms applicable to a particular case.[20]

15 Ibid., p. 925.

16 Ibid., p. 914.

17 A. Verdross, Международное право [International Law], transl. from 3d ed. by F. A. Kublitskii and R. L. Naryshkina; ed. G. I. Tunkin (1959), p. 45; Verdross, *Völkerrecht* (5th ed.; 1964), pp. 23-24.

18 Ibid., respectively, pp. 160, 147.

19 Ibid., respectively, pp. 164, 151.

20 Ibid., respectively, pp. 43-44, 22.

It is Verdross's view that Article 38 of the Statute of the International Court has in view "not all legal norms of the various States which happen to coincide, but only those principles of law which rest upon common legal ideas and which can be carried over into interstate relations".[21] The author admits the possibility of deciding disputes between States on the basis not only of conventional and customary norms, but also of solely "general principles of law".[22]

Another representative of the modern natural law orientation, Le Fur, asserts that although "general principles of law" are not directly principles of natural law, the number of which is very limited, they arise directly form natural, or objective, law. Both general principles and natural law have as their initial basis the concept of justice and morality, which is common and, one can say, natural for man. In order to become "general principles of law", principles of natural law must find their positive expression in the national law of the "civilized States".[23]

The majority of Soviet writers are of the opinion that Article 38(1)(c) of the Statute of the International Court does not have in view a special source of international law, a special form of creating norms of international law. "General principles of law" can only be principles of international law.

V. M. Koretskii suggests that "general principles of law" are "general (or fundamental) principles of *international* law".[24] In developing this idea, Academician Koretskii goes on to say: "Article 38 of the Statute of the International Court

[21] Verdross, *Völkerrecht*, p. 148. In this edition the position is given differently from that which was translated into Russian.

[22] Verdross, Международное право [International Law], pp. 163-164; Verdross, *Völkerrecht*, p. 150.

[23] L. Le Fur, "La coutume et les principes généraux du droit comme sources du droit international public", *Recueil d'études sur les sources du droit en l'honneur de François Geny* (1935), III, 368; Le Fur, "Règles générales du droit de la paix", *Recueil des cours*, LIV (1935), 205.

[24] V. M. Koretskii, "Общие принципы права" в международном праве ["General Principles of Law" in International Law] (Kiev, 1957), p. 45.

(which also contains a reference to `the general principles of law recognized by civilized nations') just begins with a statement of the duty of the Court "to decide in accordance with international law such disputes as are submitted to it'. Consequently the Court is bound to apply principles of international law, but by no means principles of domestic law of individual States".[25]

Professor V. N. Durdenevskii also believes that "general principles of law" are "by their very nature the most fundamental provisions of international customary law".[26] He includes the five well-known principles of peaceful coexistence and certain other principles of international law among them.

This question is treated somewhat differently by Professor D. B. Levin. While not characterizing "general principles of law" as a whole, he points out that the "fundamental principles of international law occupy an important place among them", after which he limits himself to an analysis of these "fundamental principles".

In Levin's view, the fundamental principles of international law are, on one hand, the "normative ideas underlying the entire system of international law". As an example of such normative ideas he cites the "principles of sovereignty and equality of States", and "the principles of freedom of the seas or the inviolability of diplomatic representatives".[27]

[25] Ibid., pp. 45-46.

[26] V. N. Durdenevskii, "Пять принципов" [Five Principles], Международная жизнь [International Life], no. 3 (1955), p. 45; see also Durdenevskii and S. B. Krylov (eds.), Международное право [International Law] (1947), pp. 26-27; E. A. Korovin (ed.), Международное право [International Law] (1951), p. 17; G. I. Tunkin, Основы современного международного права [Fundamental Principles of Contemporary International Law] (1956), p. 4; F. I. Kozhevnikov (ed.), Международное право [International Law] (1957), p. 8; N. M. Minasian, Сущность современного международного права [Essence of Contemporary International Law] (Rostov-on-Don, 1962), p. 177. This problem unaccountably was passed over in V. M. Chkhikvadze and others (eds.), Курс международного права в шести томах [Course of International Law in Six Volumes] (1967), I.

[27] See D. B. Levin, Основные проблемы современного международного права [Basic Problems of Contemporary International Law] (1958), p. 100.

We note at once that the provisions cited by Levin as examples of "normative ideas" are principles of international law, that is, the most general norms from which arise, however, specific rights and duties of States. These, consequently, are not ideas, but legal norms.

"On the other hand", says Levin, "fundamental principles of international law are one of the forms of reflecting and consolidating international law, organically linked with the specific peculiarities of the latter, and above all with the fact that norms of international law are established by way of the concordance of the wills of States on the basis of general principles, written or unwritten, which they have previously recognized. In this sense fundamental principles of international law are one of the sources of international law".[28]

The author does not show, and it is doubtful in general whether one could demonstrate, that if the basic peculiarity of international law is that its norms are created by the concordant wills of States, the "fundamental principles of international law" can be regarded as an independent source of international law side by side with treaty and custom. He himself speaks of fundamental principles as "general principles which they (States) have previously recognized", that is, consequently, of principles which entered into international law either by custom or by treaty.

P. I. Lukin suggests that "general principles of law are those principles consolidated in the legislation of all member States of the United Nations or in the legislation of the majority of the most important States in each one of the basic legal systems of the world".[29] But at the same time he says that as a result of the difference of socio-economic systems, it is impossible in the majority of cases to establish such general principles".[30]

[28] Ibid., pp. 100-101.

[29] P. I. Lukin, Источники международного права [Sources of International Law] (1960), p. 100.

[30] Ibid.

M. Bartos, a Yugoslav professor, suggests that "general principles of law" in international law are by their origin the "general principles and general institutions of law recognized by civilized nations",[31] having, as one can suppose from the author's conception, a normative character. Bartos, however, emphasizes that as soon as such principles have entered into international law, they break off from municipal law and "in the future fully share the fate of the system of international law".[32]

In speaking of "general principles of law", one must point above all to the fact that the enormous bourgeois literature on this question was and is based primarily upon Article 38 of the Statute of the Permanent Court of International Justice and on the materials of the Committee of Jurists of the League of Nations for the preparation of this Statute.

Meanwhile, the Statute of the International Court of the United Nations is a new international agreement. This agreement was created in different conditions than the Statute of the Permanent Court of International Justice, and one should not attach to the provisions of the Statute of the International Court that significance which the Committee of Jurists attached in 1920 to the analogous provisions of the Statute of the Permanent Court of International Justice.

The meaning which was placed in this point by the drafters of the Statute of the Permanent Court of International Justice is only of historical importance for an understanding of the corresponding provision of the Statute of the International Court. Evidently the drafters, representing different types of bourgeois law, had in mind expanding the possibilities for the Court in deciding cases by granting it the right to refer to principles common to the national legal systems of bourgeois States. However, this is not important in interpreting Article 38(1)(c) of the Statute of the International Court, but rather that

31 M. Bartos, "Transformation des principes généraux en règles positives du droit international", in V. Ibler, ed., *Mélanges offerts à Juraj Andrassy* (1968), p. 1.

32 Ibid., p. 2.

which the States represented at the San Francisco Conference, where this Statute was adopted and signed, had in mind. A sufficient reference point for this is the fact that a very important provision was inserted into Article 38 of the Statute of the International Court, that the Court "is to decide in accordance with international law such disputes as are submitted to it ...".[33]

There is no doubt that this is of material importance in interpreting Article 38(1)(c) of the Statute of the International Court. Above all, the unfoundedness of the concept that "general principles of law" are principles of national legal systems "common to all civilized States" becomes obvious.

One can not fail to note that there have been and are attempts to use this concept, irrespective of the wish or desire of the scholars and jurists who support it, against the socialist States and the new Asian and African States. The basic leading principles of the leading capitalist powers as, for example, the doctrine of "acquired rights", adequate compensation for nationalized property of aliens, and others usually are included among the "general principles of law", and they are proclaimed to be common to "civilized peoples". Here in manifested the desire to use "general principles of law" in order to proclaim principles of the bourgeois legal system to be binding upon all.[34] Such efforts are juridically unjustified and politically harmful, for they can lead only to an aggravation of relations among States.[35]

[33] See S. B. Krylov, История создания ООН [History of Creation of United Nations], ed. G. I. Tunkin (1960), p. 228.

[34] See Koretskii, *"Общие принципы права" в международном праве* ["General Principles of Law" in International Law].

[35] It is very doubtful that Abi-Saab's view reflected the true situation. He writes with regard to general principles of law: "This source of international law is very important from the point of view of the newly independent States. It is through it that they hope their legal systems will contribute to the development of international law". G. M. Abi-Saab, "The Newly Independent States and the Rules of International Law: An Outline", *Howard Law Journal*, VIII (1962), 109. The experience of the International Law Commission, of the Sixth Committee of the General Assembly, and of international conferences in our view shows that the new States attach primary importance in this respect to the international

The attempts to justify the inclusion of the said "principles" among the "general principles of law recognized by civilized nations" by references to judicial and arbitral decisions are scientifically unfounded. First and foremost, the judicial and arbitral practice which bourgeois writers cite in the practice of a specific group of bourgeois States. It is not "general" in the sense that this must be understood at the present time, and it has not been recognized as a legal norm by States of the two systems.

The viewpoint of the majority of Soviet international lawyers, as noted above, correctly emphasizes, in counterbalance to the predominant bourgeois doctrine, that the existence of similar principles in national legal systems, even though of all States, does not signify that they therefore have effect in international law; any provision, in order to be applied in international law, must enter by treaty or customary means. But as regards equating "general principles of law" with general principles of international law, this seems to us to be unjustified.

It is no accident that Article 38(1)(c) of the Statute of the International Court – and the Statute is a virtually universal international treaty – speaks not of "general principles of international law" but of "general principles of law". Professor C. Rousseau is right in stating that the question is one of the principles of law in general, of the principles common not only to national legal systems but also to international law as a special system of law.

But the question arises whether in contemporary conditions of the existence of States not only with different but also with opposed socio-economic systems there can exist normative principles common to socialist law and to bourgeois law. One must say very definitely that normative principles which would be common to the two opposed systems of law, socialist and bourgeois, do not exist. The principles of these legal systems, even in those instances when externally they appear to be

treaty. See R. Ago, "La codification du droit international et les problèmes de sa realisation", *Mélanges Guggenheim*, p. 109.

identical, are fundamentally distinct by virtue of their class nature, role in society, and purposes. Since a norm of law is not a "pure" rule of conduct deprived of social content, the externally (or technically) similar principles or norms of the said legal systems of this kind are different, and not identical, norms.

This does not mean that the norms of the opposed types of law have nothing in common. The content of a norm of law is formed from a rule of conduct and a purpose, which naturally always has a social and not a technical character. A legal norm is not simply a rule of conduct; it always is purposeful. In addition, to characterize the essence of a legal norm one must take into account the social consequences of its operation. Norms of socialist and bourgeois law are fundamentally distinct by virtue of their content and essence. But rules of conduct as part of the content of the corresponding norms of socialist and bourgeois law very frequently are identical.

This generally has a certain significance for the formation of norms of international law. The existence of externally identical principles and norms in different systems of national law frequently leads to the emergence of corresponding principles and norms of international law. It is possible, for example, to mention such principles of international law as the principle of State sovereignty, the principle of State sovereignty over territorial waters, many norms of the covenants of human rights, especially the covenant on civil and political rights, and so forth.

The principles of national legal systems exert great influence upon the development of international law, but they can not be principles of the latter. The juridical and social nature of norms of national legal systems and norms of international law are different. The principles and norms of a national legal system reflect the will of the ruling class of a given State (in the USSR – the will of the whole people), whereas the class content of norms of international law is different; norms of international law can not reflect the will of the ruling class of a single State. Norms of national law can be changed by a State at its discretion, so that principles which are "common" to various national legal systems today can cease to be such tomorrow. And, finally, the principles of a national legal system are binding only within the limits of that system, since a State can not promulgate international norms which are legally binding upon other States.

The normative principles of national legal systems can be material for the creation of corresponding principles of international law. But the principles of international law which have arisen in this way and which externally are frequently very similar to principles of national law are in fact, as pointed out above, otherwise; their content and essence are changed.

The conclusion is, therefore, that there can not exist normative legal principles which would be common to socialist and bourgeois law, nor normative legal principles which would be common to contemporary international law and to national systems of law.

There are, however, general legal concepts, logical rules, modes of legal technique, which are used in interpreting and applying law in general, both international and national, irrespective of the social essence of the law. This kind of "principle" is not normative and does not establish rights and duties, but it is necessary for an understanding of the co-relation of norms of law and their social content. Among such rules are, for example: *lex specialis derogat generali, lex posterior derogat priori, nemo plus juris transferre potest quam ipse habet*, and others.

Although this kind of provision is legal, it is not in essence a norm of law. Therefore it is doubtful whether there are scholarly and practical grounds for C. W. Jenks's appeal "to develop from the common elements in these legal systems, all of which are still in process of evolution, a universal legal order ..."[36] or H. Waldock's thesis that "general principles of law" are the "common law of the international community".[37]

[36] See C. W. Jenks, *The Common Law of Mankind* (1958), p. 169.

[37] H. Waldock, "General Course on Public International Law", *Recueil des cours*, CVI (1962), 54.

The next question is: how do the said non-normative provisions common to existing national legal systems enter into international use:

(1) are they a "reservoir" from which the International Court or other international instances can draw upon when necessary?[38]

(2) or does Article 38(1)(c) of the Statute of the International Court mean that the provisions common to different national legal systems become applicable in international law only by virtue of that fact?[39]

(3) or do such principles common to different national systems of law, although non-normative before being applied in international law, enter into it through the usual processes of forming norms of international law: treaty or custom?[40]

If the International Court at its discretion could draw from national legal systems the principles which in the opinion of the respective writers are normative, it would possess law-creating functions. But, as has been shown above, the Court does not possess such powers.

The second point of view also can not be deemed to be justified. If one presumes that Article 38(1)(c) of the Statute of the International Court means the inclusion in the system of international law of all principles common to the various national legal systems, it should be borne in mind that the respective writers have normative principles in mind and consider as common all those which contain identical rules of conduct – which clearly does not correspond to reality. Numerous principles of national legal systems which from the viewpoint of these authors should be regarded as

38 *Ibid.*, p. 56; S. Nahlik, *Wstep do nauki prawa miedzynarodwego* (1967), p. 382.

39 See Rousseau, *Principes généraux du droit international public*, I, 890.

40 See Guggenheim, *Traité de droit international public*, I, 298; M. Genovski, Основи на международното право [Fundamental Principles of International Law] (1966), p. 26.

common are not applied in international law at all (for example, electing members of legislative organs, the right of individuals to resort to a court, and so on). If not all principles which in the view of these authors are common to national legal systems are to be applied in international law, then the question arises: who selects which to apply and which not? The point of view being considered does not answer this question.

Even if one takes the non-normative provisions to which we have referred that are common to the various national legal systems, far from all can be applied in international law. Thus, for example, such a general provision as *nemo judex in sua causa* is not applicable in international law since there is no compulsory international jurisdiction here.

"General principles of law" are those principles not only common to national systems of law but also simultaneously peculiar to international law. The statement that a given principle is common to national legal systems does not make this principle a "general principle of law", that is, of law in general. It is still necessary to prove that this principle also is peculiar to that special system of law which is called international law. Only if there is an affirmative response to this question can such a principle be considered "common" to any law, a "general principle of law".

But how can a particular provision, even a non-normative one which has significance for the application of a norm, "become applicable" in international law? Obviously only by its being recognized by States as "applicable in international law", or, that is to say, through an international treaty or international custom.[41]

In interpreting the respective provision of the Statute of the International Court, attention is usually called to its first part, "general principles of law", and insufficient attention is devoted to the second part, "recognized by civilized nations". To be applicable in in- ternational law, the

[41] See M. Diez de Velasco, *Instituciones de derecho internacional publico* (1973), p. 138.

corresponding "general principles of law" must be recognized by States as "being applicable in international law", which, as pointed out previously, occurs either by international treaty or by international custom.

Consequently, in our view, "general principles of law" are those non-normative provisions common to national legal systems and to international law which, however, have significance for applying norms of prevailing law; they usually are formed in national law (but nothing prevents them from being formed in international law as well) and enter into international law through treaty or custom.

This interpretation means that Article 38(1)(c) of the Statute of the International Court has in view not a special "source" of international law, but specific juridical provisions, here called principles, which are non-normative.

* * *

Therefore, two means of forming, developing, and modifying norms of general international law exist: treaty and custom. There also are subsidiary processes (resolutions of international or- ganizations, international courts, and arbitral tribunals; national legislation; and decisions of municipal judicial instances) which are specific stages in the process of forming norms but which do not lead to its completion.

At the same time, another means of creating international legal norms has emerged in contemporary international law. We have in mind the binding resolutions of international organizations. In this case international legal norms are created by their being adopted by a majority of members of an international organizations, which has a certain external similarity to municipal legislation. Such international legal norms, however, are created on the basis of the agreement of States, that is, on the basis of the charter of the international organization. Moreover, although such resolutions are binding upon all member States of the organization, also including the States which voted against their adoption, a member

State of an international organization legally can avoid the application of any such resolution to it by withdrawing from the organization.

PART III.
THE LEGAL NATURE AND ESSENCE OF CONTEMPORARY GENERAL INTERNATIONAL LAW

CHAPTER VIII. THE LEGAL NATURE OF AGREEMENT AS THE MODE OF CREATING NORMS OF INTERNATIONAL LAW

1. The Bourgeois Doctrine of "Agreement"

Principles and norms of international law are created, modified, and liquidated as a result of agreement between States. This agreement is embodied either in the form of an international treaty or of an international custom.

The doctrine that only agreement of States can create binding norms of international law has its own history, which must be dwelt upon briefly in order to show what the theory we set forth has in common with the bourgeois concept of agreement and how it is distinctive from the last.

Hugo Grotius and a number of writers of the eighteenth and nineteenth centuries who followed him believed that the so-called positive international law, in which they included both conventional and customary law, is created, in contrast to natural law, by the general consent of States.[1]

According to Grotius, all law, including international law, is partially natural law and partially law created by will (*jus voluntarium*). Natural law is "the dictate of right reason". Instituted law, or law created by will, has will as its source; it may be instituted by the will of God or by the general consent of peoples.[2]

The latter law also received the appellation "positive" law from subsequent writers. Vattel already distinguishes natural or "necessary" law from "positive" law established by the general consent of peoples.[3]

[1] See H. Grotius, О праве войны и мира [On the Law of War and Peace], transl. A. L. Sakketti; ed. V. N. Durdenevskii (1959), Book 1.

[2] Ibid., Book 1, chap. 1, XI, 2; XIII, XIX, 1; XV, 1.

[3] See E. de Vattel, Право народов [Law of Nations], ed. V. N. Durdenevskii (1960), pp. 27, 34; R. J. Phillimore, *Commentaries on International Law* (3d ed.; 1879), p. 38; F. F. Martens, Современное международное право цивилизованных народов [Contemporary

The ideas of bourgeois revolutions resounded in the natural law conceptions of that time; they were directed against feudal law, which did not correspond to the dictates of "right reason". They advanced "reasonable" principles which, although progressive in comparison with the feudal orders, were in reality only principles of a new exploitative society.

With the completion of the bourgeois struggle against feudalism, its revolutionary ardor dried up, natural law theory was rejected as having performed its service, and the positivist orientation, called upon to be the basis of bourgeois reality, became predominant in bourgeois legal science.

The concept that agreement between States is the legal basis of all international law was widely disseminated in the domain of theory during the second half of the nineteenth and the beginning of the twentieth centuries. This doctrine proceeded from the fact that since sovereign States are entering into international relations, under these conditions the sole mode of creating norms binding upon subjects of law is agreements between them.[4]

The bourgeois doctrine of agreement as a means of creating norms of international law correctly reflects one aspect of reality – namely, that agreement between States is the sole mode of creating principles and norms of international law. But the doctrine being considered did not correctly analyse the process of forming a norm, its essence, and frequently limited itself to a purely dogmatic approach, declining in general to undertake an investigation of this question.

In carrying over categories of municipal law into international law, Triepel proceeds in his widely known work *Völkerrecht und Landesrecht* from the premise that in international law only a

---

International of Civilized Peoples] (1882), I, 11.

[4] See H. Triepel, *Völkerrecht und Landesrecht* (1899), pp. 32, 75, 83ff.; D. Anzilotti, *Corso di diritto internazionale* (3d ed.; 1928), I, 43, 63ff.; T. Perassi, "Teoria dommatica delle fonti di norme guiridiche in diritto internazionale", *Rivista di diritto internazionale*, XI (1917), 220; L. Oppenheim, *International Law* (4th ed.; 1928), pp. 18-19; K. Strupp, "Les règles générales du droit de la paix", *Recueil des cours*, XLVII (1934), 307.

higher will which stands above the wills of individual States can create norms binding upon a State. This will is formed as a result of agreement between States. Agreement creates a "common will" (*Gemeinwille*), which is the result of the fusion of identical wills of various States. In Triepel's view, the common will stands higher than the will of an individual State, is a supranational will, and as such serves as a source of legal norms binding upon States.[5]

Consequently, according to Triepel, the legal nature of agreement as a means of creating norms of international law consists in the fact that identical wills of States are fused into a "common will", which is a higher will.

Of the writers of recent decades who adhere to this point of view, one could mention Séfériades, who wrote in 1936: "In our view, international law as a whole has as its basis not the individual sovereign will of a State (Jellinek), even with an unsustainable qualification relating to self-limitation, but the wills of States as coinciding wills which, once unified, can not be separated ... This union of wills forms a higher will ...".[6]

In Anzilotti's opinion, agreement is an expression of a united will (*concorde volontà*). This will creates a norm of international law. Anzilotti's "united will", just as Triepel's, is the result of the fusion of the wills of individual States. But, as Anzilotti himself pointed out, he, in contradistinction to Triepel, seeks the source of norms not in some "higher will" standing above

[5] Triepel, *Völkerrecht und Landesrecht*, p. 32; Triepel, having worked out the concept of a common will in detail, which he regards as higher than the wills of States with respect to those participating in the creation of the "common will", was not the initiator of this notion. It is already completely evident in Grotius. Among the writers who preceded Triepel one also can mention A. W. Heffter, who thirty years before Triepel wrote: "... prevailing law is created for independent States only through a common will (*consensu*) ...". A. W. Heffter, *Das europäische Völkerrecht der Gegenwart auf den bisherigen Grundlagen* (5th ed.; 1867), p. 4.

[6] S. Séféraides, "Aperçu sur la coutume juridique internationale et notamment sur son fondement", *Revue générale de droit international public*, X (1936), 145; H. Heller, *Die Souveranität* (1927), pp. 122-124.

the will of individual States, but in a "basic norm" which obliges States to fulfill international agreements.[7]

Thus, if Triepel, in attempting to bring international law within the characteristics of national law, considered a norm of international law to be a product of a higher will with regard to States, then Anzilotti treats an agreement which creates norms of international law differently. The "general will" reflected in an agreement is used by Anzilotti essentially only as a characteristic of agreement and not as a basis for the emergence of a norm of international law. A norm of international law emerges because there exists a "basic norm" binding a State to fulfill international agreements – *pacta sunt servanda*. Anzilotti's theory, in contrast to Triepel's, emphasized the coordinate character of international law.

Another Italian international lawyer, T. Perassi, rejects both the concept of a "higher will" and the concept of a "common will". These theories, he says, would be admissible if it were possible to represent agreement as a juridical act which, although the result of a coincidence of the wills of individual States, relates to a specific subject, in contrast to States. Since, however, this is impossible, one can not accept the view linked with the concept of a higher collective will that norms of international law are "commands".[8]

Perassi closes his investigation with the assertion that in international law agreement is a "source of legal norms". He refuses to go farther, even to merely investigate the legal nature of agreement. Norms of international law, says Perassi, are created by agreement between States, but why an agreement creates a norm of law this jurist is unable to say; the question exceeds the bounds of legal research, which he understands to be purely dogmatic research.[9]

[7] Anzilotti, *Corso di diritto internazionale*, pp. 43, 63, 64ff.

[8] Perassi, "Teoria dommatica delle fonti", pp. 291-292.

[9] Ibid., pp. 201ff.

Agreement itself is characterized by Perassi as the result or embodiment of the coincidence of wills. "Agreement", he says, "is an act having international relevance; the coincidence of the wills of two or more States is essential to agreement".[10]

Proponents of natural law concepts which have been widely propagated during the last half-century (see Chapter IX) acknowledge agreement as a means of creating norms of international law only for treaty norms. But treaty law in their view rests upon natural law, which does not depend upon the will and agreement of States.

The principal objective role of contemporary international legal concepts of natural law consists of undermining the consensual basis of international law and thereby creating greater possibilities for an international legal justification of the imperialist policy of *diktat,* coercion, and military adventurism.

One also encounters at the present time proponents of the concept of agreement as the sole means of creating norms of international law, but they are not numerous.[11]

[10] Ibid., p. 290. Giuliani also opposes interpreting the "collective will" as a "superior will". A superior will, he says, "presupposes the material and social supremacy of the organism or organisms to which this will appertains. But this does not give agreement". The "collective will of a State" simply means the "agreement of wills" (*accordo di volontà).* See M. Giuliani, *La communita internazionale e il diritto* (1950), p. 81.

[11] K. Strupp wrote: "If States are equal and if a supreme authority does not exist to dictate laws to them, nor a power of majority rule, one only can come to a single conclusion: there is no international law without coincident wills, without a treaty". Strupp, "Règles générales du droit de la paix", p. 301. C. Hyde says: "The basis of the law, that is to say, what has given to some principles of general applicability the quality or character of law, has been the acquiescence of the several independent States which were to be governed thereby". C. C. Hyde, Международное право [International Law], transl. from 2d rev. ed. by I. S. Shokhor, ed. V. N. Durdenevskii (1950), I, 50. C. Rousseau writes that in international law "the agreement of States is the sole means of creating legal norms. Here the elaboration of any legal rule depends upon the agreement of the subjects whose relations this rule is intended to regulate". C. Rousseau, *Droit international public* (1953), P. 11; see also M. J. Sierra, *Tratado de derecho internacional publico* (2d ed.; 1955), p. 24; A. Ulloa, *Derecho internacional publico* (4th ed.; 1957), I, 51-52; L. M. Moreno Quintana, *Tratado de derecho internacional* (1963), I, 71.

2. *Agreement as the Result and the Embodiment of the Concordance of the Wills of States*

The bourgeois conception of agreement contained a rational core – namely, the proposition that agreement between States is the sole mode of creating norms of international law. It was based upon the special character of the subjects whose relationships are regulated by international law.

This conception was closely linked with the ideas of bourgeois liberalism inherent in the premonopolistic stage of the development of capitalism. It was derived from the principle of equality of States, inspired in the majority of instances by the idea of the "rule of law" in international relations, which, of course, was understood only as relations among "civilized" States.

Being characterized by a formalistic dogmatic approach to the question, however, the bourgeois concept of agreement has not uncovered the essence of agreement as a mode of creating norms of international law, has passed over those processes of struggle and cooperation which take place in creating norms of international law, and has not shown the social essence of international law.

What is the legal nature of the agreement of States creating a norm of international law?

Let us examine what occurs in the process of forming agreement between States during the creation of a norm of general international law. This can be followed most easily in the example of concluding a treaty. At international conferences for the conclusion of general international treaties, there always exist more or less significant differences between the conference. In the course of the conference, at sessions, during unofficial meetings of delegates, and frequently even outside the conference place (through normal diplomatic channels or special meetings between representatives of States), the concordance of the wills of States takes place, usually by means of mutual concessions.

During the work of the conference, each delegation or group of delegations strives to have its or their joint international legal position reflected as much as possible in the draft treaties which must be adopted by the conference. The result fixed in the text of the treaty as a rule differs to a greater or lesser degree from that which each State taking part in the negotiations to conclude the treaty had proposed.

The concordance of the wills of States in the process of creating norms of international law is the struggle and cooperation of States. In this struggle, a State itself seeks allies first among States whose international legal position is close to the international legal position of the State or group of States concerned.

At the same time, any international conference to work out norms of international law, if the States participating in it have been inspired by the aspiration to reach a decision on the questions raised, includes the cooperation of States. This cooperation naturally takes place not only among States whose international legal positions coincide or are close, but also to some extent among all participants in the conference.

Of course, the degree of such cooperation between various States is far from identical. Without cooperation, however, as a rule one can not create a norm of international law whose general recognition can be relied upon. By means of mutual concessions States attempt to come to an agreed decision acceptable to the participants. This process in the majority of instances is exceedingly difficult and slow, but quite necessary.

Attempts to resolve this kind of question by voting without sufficient efforts to bring the wills of States into concordance usually only harm the cause. Apart from that, such attempts lead to an aggravation of relations among States, and they practically never promote the development of international law. A norm created by such means that is unacceptable to a significant number of States has little effect and, in addition, its adoption terminates, at least temporarily, the searches for a more perfect norm acceptable to the overwhelming majority of States.

The process of creating a customary norm of international law is rather more complex. The essence of this process, however, also consists in the concordance of the wills of States relating to the recognition of a particular rule as a norm of international law (see Chapter VI).

The concordance of the wills of States in the process of creating a norm of international law affects both rules of conduct and its recognition as a legal norm. These are two aspects of the process of norm-formation which frequently are not coincidental or chronological. Confusing them, as we shall show below, can lead to material mistakes.

As a rule, the concordance of the wills of States relating to a rule of conduct takes place first – by means of either treaty or custom – in forming norms of international law. In the creation of treaty norms, this occurs by means of negotiations, in discussions at international conferences, and in international organizations, and is completed by adopting the text as final. This completes the concordance of the wills of States relating to the content of the treaty norm of international law,[12] but it does not finish the process of its coming into being. It is true, States act in this case as though the rule of conduct fixed in the text of the treaty will become a norm of international law in the future. But the concordance of the wills of States relating to the content of a treaty norm still does not make it binding upon States.

The second aspect is the concordance of the wills of States relating to recognition of a rule of conduct as a norm of international law. Completion of this process may or may not coincide with the first. Thus, for example, when a treaty enters into force from the moment it is signed and the signing of the treaty is not preceded by initialling, the two aspects of the process coincide chronologically.

[12] The institute of reservations to multilateral treaties is an exception to the general rule.

When the treaty is subject to ratification, these two aspects of the process do not coincide. The acts completing the concordance of the wills of States relating to the content of the respective norms in this case will be the initialling or signature, and the acts completing the concordance of the wills of States relating to recognizing the respective rules as norms of international law, by the exchange of instruments of ratification or their transfer to the depositary.

The provisions of a treaty also may contain other conditions for the process of creating norms of this treaty to be completed. In multilateral international treaties this is most commonly a specific number of ratifications needed for the treaty to enter into force.

The two aspects of the process of norm-formation appear, as a rule, even more distinctly in the formation of customary norms of international law. The first part of the process of forming a customary norm of international law as a rule leads only to the formation of a usage. The rule of conduct already has emerged, its content has been defined, and States take this rule into account in their actions. Therefore, the concordance of the wills of the States as regards the content of the norm already exists.

But, as already has been pointed out, in order to complete the process of forming a customary norm of international law, the usage must be recognized by States as a norm of international law. The recognition by States of a usage as a norm of international law is an expression of the wills of States. If a number of States or many States, or all States, recognize a particular usage as a norm of international law, this means the concordance of the wills of these States has occurred with regard to such recognition, and the process of creating a customary international legal norm has been completed.

The process of bringing the wills of States into concordance with regard to the content of a rule of conduct does not always lead to this rule being recognized as a norm of international law. The process may stop at the first stage, and in this event the respective rule does not become an international legal norm. Such, for example, are norms of a treaty which has not entered into force.

Those resolutions of the United Nations General Assembly which are not binding also may serve as an example of the concordance of the wills of States regarding the content of a rule of conduct without a concordance of wills regarding recognition of this rule as a norm of international law.

Thus, not every concordance of the wills of States leads to the formation of a norm of international law, that is, to an agreement concerning recognition of the respective rule as a norm of international law.

One must mention in this connection the logical error which some opponents of the concordance of wills theory make. They assert, for example, that the theory of the concordance of the wills is of no use because there are unlawful treaties which embody the concordance of wills of the respective States but do not give a norm of international law.

In logic, this error is called a paralogism. In the present case, this error emerges as follows: a norm of international law is the result and expression of the concordance of the wills of States; a treaty is the result of the concordance of the wills of States; therefore, it is a norm of international law. But if every norm of international law is the result and expression of a concordance of wills, then not every concordance of wills gives a norm of international law.

It already has been said that the concordance of the wills of States may not lead to the formation of a norm of international law because it does not include the concordance of such wills regarding the recognition of the corresponding rule as a norm of international law.

Even when, however, there are both elements, to wit, the concordance of the wills of States regarding the content of the respective rule and the concordance of the wills of States regarding its recognition as a legal norm, the process may not lead to the formation of a norm of international law. This occurs when, for example, a treaty, according to international law, is void.

Of course, this instance also is covered by the afore cited proposition that a norm of international law is the result and expression of the concordance of the wills of States, but not any concordance of the wills of States leads to the formation of a norm of international law.

For agreement and, therefore, for the formation of a norm of international law it is not mandatory that the wills of the States participating in the agreement be identical and fused into a single will.

If we take as an example the creation of norms of contemporary general international law, the wills of different and even opposed class natures (socialist and capitalist States), manifesting the purposes which the various States set, collide here in the process of norm- creation.

At the same time, these wills have something in common. V. I. Lenin pointed out that a "will is sometimes unified in one respect and nonunified in another".[13] In this case, the wills of socialist and capitalist States hold in common the fact that they are directed at the same time toward the creation of a specific international legal norm; they are concordant both with regard to the content and to the recognition of a specific rule as a norm of international law, that it comprises an agreement giving a norm of law.

Despite the absence of identity in the wills of States which take part in an agreement relating to the creation of a norm of general international law, and despite the fact that they are not fused into one, the agreement takes place and a norm of international law emerges. Therefore, neither identity of

[13] V. I. Lenin, "Две тактики социал-демократии в демократической революции" [Two Tactics of Social-Democracy in a Democratic Revolution], Полное собрание сочинений [Complete Collection of Works] (5th ed.; 1960), XI, 73 [First published at Geneva, July 1905 – *WEB*].

wills nor their fusion is an essential feature of agreement as a means of creating norms of international law.

The identity and fusion of the wills of States participating in the creation of norms of international law is not precluded, but it is not an essential element of the agreement embodied in a legal norm.

The concordance of the wills of States includes the interconditionality of wills, reflected in the fact that the consent of a State to recognize a particular norm as a norm of international law is given on condition of analogous consent by another or other States.[14]

Thus, agreement as a mode of creating norms of international law is the result and expression of the concordance of the wills of States.[15]

3. *The International Legal Positions of States and Concordant Wills Reflected in Norms of International Law*

The international legal position of a State includes the general attitude of a State toward international law, its

[14] See D. B. Levin's review of G. I. Tunkin, Вопросы теории международного права [Questions of Theory of International Law] (1962), in Советский ежегодник международного права 1963 [Soviet Yearbook of International Law 1963] (1964), pp. 552-553; G. Schirmer, *Universalität völkerrechtlicher Verträge und internationaler Organisationen* (1966), p. 83.

[15] In speaking of the distinction between the Soviet concept of the concordance of wills and the old bourgeois concept of agreement, Professor Suzanne Bastid remarks that according to the new concept, the wills do not merge into one but are directed toward attaining a single goal, and that the "wills have been interconditioned". See S. Bastid, *Grands problèmes politiques contemporains* (1961), pp. 249-250. Professor P. Ziccardi notes that "it is not accurate to regard this doctrine of sources [that is, the said Soviet concept – *G.T.*] as strictly voluntaristic in the usual meaning of this word. [Reviewing the French translation of Tunkin's Вопросы теории международного права [Questions of Theory of International Law], *Communicazione e studi*, XII (1966), 922. Professor C. Chaumont, in adhering to this concept as a whole, points out that "agreement does not imply that the content of wills is identical". C. Chaumont, "Cours general de droit international public", *Recueil des cours*, CXXIX (1970), 379. However, the majority of bourgeois jurists, in approaching this question formalistically, mistakenly believe the Soviet concept to be a simple revival of the old notion of agreement. See, for example, A. Verdross, *Völkerrecht* (5th ed.; 1965), p. 138; R. Quadri, *Diritto internazionale publico* (4th ed.; 1963), p. 94; Quadri, "Cours générale de droit international public", *Recueil des cours*, CXIII (1964), 322-323.

progressive development, and the observance of principles and norms; its notion of the character of international law; its role in society; the principles and norms for whose introduction into international law a State struggles; its understanding of the principles and norms of prevailing international law; and so forth. To put it briefly, the international legal position of a State includes its viewpoint with regard to all questions of international law expressed not only in its statements, but above all in its real conduct, in its actions.

Of course, in the creation of particular norms of international law that part of the international legal position of a State which relates directly to the particular question is of greater importance.

In the process of creating norms of general international law, treaty or customary, the international legal positions of various States collide, and the process of bringing these positions into concordance occurs – the concordance of the wills of States, which may lead to the creation of an international legal norm.

What happens to the international legal position of a State in this process, and what is the co-relation between the concordant will of a State reflected in a norm and its international legal position?

The international legal position of a State can be subjected to change in the course of creating a norm of international law. Frequently at an international conference, where the positions of other States become well-known, the delegation of the respective State comes to the conclusion that the initially contemplated international legal position of that State must be changed with regard to a particular question.

Of course, when an international legal position of a State is initially formed, it takes into account the known or presumed international legal positions of other States, as well as the peripetia of the impending struggle. But an international legal struggle is formulated by people who can not take into account all circumstances, who make mistakes in evaluating them, who proceed on the basis of incorrect assumptions about the course of the conference, and so forth. If there later appear new circumstances or if new appraisals of facts arise, this may lead to a change in the international legal position of a State with regard to particular questions of international law.

Under these conditions, the concessions made by this State in the search for a compromise acceptable to all can be the result of a change in the international legal positions of this State.

But concessions in the process of creating a norm of international law also can occur without changing the international legal position of a State. A State may reach a compromise on particular questions but, as before, consider that it would be better to do otherwise and to uphold those principles and norms which it previously favored.

Even the adoption of a compromise proposal as a norm of international law binding upon the State concerned does not prevent this State from continuing to favor the adoption of another norm which, from its viewpoint, is more advisable and necessary.

As example is the 1963 Moscow Treaty on the prohibition of nuclear testing in three spheres. The Soviet Union, which before the conclusion of this treaty favored the complete prohibition of all nuclear tests, came to adopt the compromise proposal to prohibit nuclear tests in the atmosphere, in outer space, and under water, supposing that this treaty would serve the cause of peace. Participation in the Moscow Treaty, however, does not prevent the Soviet Union nor any other party to this treaty from continuing to achieve the prohibition of all nuclear tests and the conclusion of an appropriate agreement for this purpose.

Thus, the concordant wills of States reflected in a norm of international law do not always and even as a rule do not fully reflect the international legal position of the respective States.

4. *The Unfoundedness of the Concept of the "Fundamental Norm"*

The bourgeois doctrine of agreement, having correctly established that agreement between States is the sole means of creating norms of international law, has gone in a vicious circle as a result of a dogmatic approach to the question. If agreement is the sole means of creating norms of international law, say bourgeois jurists, the binding force of its norms rests upon the international legal principle or norm *pacta sunt servanda*. But on what is the legal force of this principle based? If one says that it is based on agreement, a new question arises: on what is the legal force of that agreement based? This juridical construction did not answer the question and went on *ad infinitum*.

They began to search for a way out in a certain hypothetical "fundamental norm" as the base point from which international law, and even law in general, emanated. The "fundamental norm" was regarded as a postulate, unavoidable for any legal system, a hypothetical norm beyond which legal research can not go.

D. Anzilotti, who was the first to extensively work out the bourgeois concept of agreement as the single mode of creating norms of international law in *Corso di diritto internazionale*, first published in 1912, writes: "Any legal system consists of norms whose binding force originates in a fundamental norm and to which, directly or indirectly, all norms of this system are reduced". The fundamental norm defines, therefore, what norms comprise the particular legal system and reduces them to a unity. The international order is characterized by the fact that the principle *pacta sunt servanda* is not based, as is the case in municipal law, upon a higher norm; it is itself the higher norm. The norm that "states must respect the treaties contracted by them" is, thus, a formal criterion which distinguishes the norms of which we are speaking from other norms and which reduces them to a unified system; all norms, and only the norms, which come down to the said principle as a necessary and exclusive source of their binding force relate to the category of norms of which we are speaking.

These norms constitute international law or, that is to say, "the legal order of the community of States".[16]

Since, says Anzilotti, sovereign States act in the international community, the norms of law prevailing among States only can be the result of agreement among equals.[17]

The principle *pacta sunt servanda* as a "fundamental norm" has no juridical basis, in Anzilotti's view, although this does not preclude its basis from an ethical, political, or other viewpoint. "This principle", Anzilotti says, "precisely because it is a fundamental norm of which we are speaking, is not subject to further proof from the viewpoint of the norms themselves. It must be regarded as an objective absolute value, or, that is to say, as a primary and unprovable hypothesis which necessarily comes down to this, just as any other order known to mankind. This does not mean that the said principle can not be based upon other viewpoints. It only means that any basis which can be given from another point of view (ethical, political, and so forth), has no relationship with that science which limits itself to the study of the said norms".[18]

T. Perassi develops the same view. Believing that a jurist should not go beyond the limits of "juridical dogmatic", Perassi says that any legal norm presupposes another norm on which the legal significance of the first norm is based. In the final analysis at least one norm concerning the "process of norm-formation" must exist. This is the ultimate point beyond which one can not go without leaving the bounds of international law. This "fundamental norm", Perassi says, should be regarded as a norm of international law, a juridical norm.[19] The "fundamental norm" of international law, in Perassi's view, is the norm by virtue of which agreement represents a "source of legal norms" in international law. This is a postulate which is

16 D. Anzilotti, *Corso di diritto internazionale* (4th ed.; 1955), I, 44-45.

17 Ibid., p. 46.

18 Ibid., pp. 43-44.

19 Perassi, "Teoria dommatica delle fonti", pp. 197-198.

necessary in order to create a juridical theory. At the same time, it is a logical conclusion from the principle according to which for juridical dogmatic "the legal order is a postulate".[20]

H. Kelsen, who rejects the concept of agreement, also comes to a "basic norm" as the norm defining the mode of creating norms of international law. According to Kelsen, norms of law are such because "... their validity is derivable from a higher, that is, a more general norm, as the particular is derivable from the general", or because these norms are created through "acts" by those individuals who have been authorized by a higher norm to create norms.[21] In any case, for Kelsen "the basis of the binding nature of norms can only be a norm".[22]

Beginning with the "lowest norm of international law", Kelsen comes to the conclusion that the basic norm is the principle *pacta sunt servanda.* This is a norm of general international law created by custom. Conventional law, Kelsen says, rests upon customary law. The norm *pacta sunt servanda* is not, therefore, the ultimate "basic norm", since this could only be a norm which is the basis of the binding nature of custom as the foundation of all international law. "The basic norm of international law", Kelsen says, "therefore, must be a norm which countenances custom as a norm-creating fact, and might be formulated as follows: "The States ought to behave as they have customarily behaved".[23] This norm, in Kelsen's opinion, is a "presumed or hypothetical norm".[24]

20 Ibid., p. 201.

21 H. Kelsen, *Principles of International Law,* ed. R. W. Tucker (2d ed.; 1967), pp. 557-558.

22 Kelsen, *Das Problem der Souveranität und die Theorie des Völkerrechts* (2d ed.; 1928), p. 105.

23 Kelsen, *Principles of International Law,* p. 564.

24 Kelsen, "Théorie du droit international public", *Recueil des cours,* LXXXIV (1953), 129; see also G. Morelli, *Nozioni di diritto internazionale* (3d ed.; 1951), pp. 7-11, 28-29.

Kelsen stresses the formal character of the basic norm in his concept. "The basic norm of a positivist pure theory of law is not a norm of justice", he says.[25]

P. Guggenheim adheres very closely to Kelsen's view: "Any legal order", he says, "consists of a system of rules which derive their authority from a fundamental norm to which they all are reduced, directly or indirectly. The fundamental norm defines which norms comprise the given legal order and brings them into unity. Thus, the fundamental norm is the common source of all the rules of international public law".[26]

In the second edition of his *Traité de droit international public,* however, Guggenheim relegates the "fundamental norm" to a much more modest role. "Of course", he says, "the fundamental norm is of interest only on a scientific plane, and that is limited".[27] In explaining this, he writes: "There is no doubt that rules of a higher order, conventional and ... customary, can not be conceived of without some other norm which gives them validity. This fundamental rule is not established by the customary mode of creating norms of law and can not be called a legal norm or a rule of positive law".[28] This, in Guggenheim's view, is a "presumed norm, a hypothesis, which permits us to regard the legal order as a system of prevailing norms, the point of departure for recognizing the validity of legal rules which in fact are applied ...".[29]

In an attempt to combine the normativist concept of a fundamental norm with "natural law" concepts, a West German international lawyers, G. Dahm, asserted that two fundamental norms exist. First and foremost, in his view, the principle *pacta sunt servanda,* which "is not a logical

[25] Kelsen, "Vom Geltungsgrund des Rechts", F. A. Frhr. v. d. Heydte and others, eds., *Völkerrecht und Rechtliches Weltbild: Festschrift für A. Verdross* (1960), p. 165.

[26] P. Guggenheim, *Traité de droit international public* (1953), I, 6.

[27] Ibid., 2d ed. (1967), I, 38.

[28] Ibid., p. 37.

[29] Ibid.

requirement, but a requirement of reason", is a fundamental norm.[30] In believing that the said norm is the fundamental norm of treaty law, he presupposes a second norm for customary law. The latter he formulates as follows: "Law is that corresponding to the will, values, and law-consciousness of the international community and that in general is observed as a norm of practical conduct".[31] The author believes that yet a "third group of rules" should be added to the two fundamental norms of international law – to wit, "rules of international constitutional law".[32] Dahm's entire eclectical construction remains, however, completely unproved and illogical.

The conception of a "fundamental norm" proceeds from a notion of law in general and of international law in particular as a self-contained, exclusive system of legal norms. This is reflected most clearly in the "pure theory of law" of Kelsen and his followers, which is characterized by a complete separation of law from reality.

Proceeding from Kant's philosophical system and delimiting the sphere of "ought" (*sollen*) and the sphere of "reality" (*sein*), Kelsen relegates law to the sphere of the ought, completely divorcing it from other social phenomena. According to Kelsen, norms of law are judgments about what ought to be in contrast to what is. In applying Kantian "pure forms of thought", Kelsen comes to "pure" norms of law which are not dependent upon reality. The domain of law, according to Kelsen, is an exclusive system, divorced from reality. In this domain there exists only a pure legal imperative. Kelsen thereby avoids an investigation of the social content of law in the sphere of empty, nonexistent, "pure" legal norms.

The followers of contemporary natural law and sociological theories criticize the "pure theory of law" chiefly for its being divorced from reality.

30 G. Dahm, *Völkerrecht* (1958), I, 12.

31 Ibid., p. 13.

32 Ibid.

C. de Visscher, for example, says that "of all contemporary doctrines, Professor Hans Kelsen's neo-positivism is the doctrine which is most deliberately and most completely isolated from social reality".[33] "The pure theory of law, de Visscher says, "is a reflection of a certain contemporary tendency which "on the pretext of the requirements of science or unity of method arbitrarily limits the content of law and narrows or distorts legal reality".[34]

A. Verdross, in criticizing the theory which regards international law and law in general as an exclusive world, says that "instead of investigating from the beginning whether positive law is itself an exclusive order, it is simply asserted, purely dogmatically, that it is such an order".[35]

In criticizing positivism, R. Ago, an Italian professor, declares that any theory of international law which reduces international law to "positive law", "in contrast to any forms of abstract, ideal law or law created by thought", goes in a vicious circle. Positivism believes that all norms of law are created by authority. "Now", R. Ago says, "the 'competence' of the authority creating law has no sense if it is not a legal competence established by law; if, in turn, law can only be the product of the law-making activity of a 'competent' authority, there is clearly a vicious circle from which legal positivism cannot escape".[36]

But a critique of normativism from the position of contemporary natural law and sociological orientations does not and can not reveal its basic flaws.

Contemporary normativism, which represents a combination of positivism and neo-Kantianism, is one of the varieties of

[33] C. de Visscher, *Théorie et réalites en droit international public* (2d ed.; 1955), p. 90.

[34] Ibid., p. 91.

[35] A. Verdross, Международное право [International Law], transl. F. A. Kublitskii and R. L. Naryshkina; ed. G. I. Tunkin (1959), p. 42; see also J. Stone, "Problems Confronting Sociological Inquiries Concerning International Law", *Recueil des cours,* LXXXIX (1956), 89.

[36] R. Ago, "Positive Law and International Law", *American Journal of International Law*, LI (1957), 702.

reactionary bourgeois legal doctrine attempting to mask the exploitative essence of bourgeois State and law by carrying formalism to an extreme and being divorced from reality".[37]

The attempt to represent law as an exclusive system, divorced from reality, and to seek an explanation of law in law itself is wholly unfounded. The universal relationship of phenomena is itself a law in nature and society. International law has not been partitioned off from other social phenomena by an impassable barrier. The futility of attempts to find an explanation of law in general and international law in particular in law itself is demonstrated by the concept of the "fundamental norm". The attempt to base the binding force of norms of international law or, that is to say, the attempt to explain law as a social phenomenon without going beyond the domain of law, also has proved to be impossible. The "fundamental norm" tears apart the Kelsenian "legal sphere", goes beyond the limits of law, and undermines the basic positions of normativism.

The doctrine of the "fundamental norm" is purely a logical construction which does not correspond to reality. This concept is not in a position to explain the historical development of international law and the real-correlation of the norms of international law itself, as well as of international law and other social phenomena.

If the "fundamental norm" is regarded as a *conditio sine qua non*, one can agree that contemporary international law can not be conceived without the norm *pacta sunt servanda*. But there also are other important norms of international law without which it is unthinkable – for example, the principle of State sovereignty. Contemporary international law is inconceivable without this principle.

Of course, the significance of various principles and norms of international law is not the same. There are principles and norms which have paramount importance for ensuring peace and developing friendly relations among States. Other principles

[37] See D. B. Levin, О современных буржуазных теориях международного права [On Contemporary Bourgeois Theories of International Law] (1959), p. 12.

and norms, of lesser significance, regulate relations between States on less important questions. There are fundamental principles without which contemporary international law is inconceivable.

But if it is correct that the existence of contemporary international law is impossible without a particular principle, this still does not mean that this principle is a "fundamental norm" in the sense that all international law rests upon it and proceeds therefrom. Such also is the position with the norm *pacta sunt servanda*.

Norms of international law are created as a result of agreement of States. But this does not mean that international law is based on the principle *pacta sunt servanda* as some "fundamental" or primary norm. In reality, the development of international law has not proceeded at all from such a "fundamental norm". As regards the principle *pacta sunt servanda,* this principle developed as a customary norm together with other norms of international law. It is closely linked with such principles of international law as the principle of respect for State sovereignty, the principle of equality, and others. These principles, together with other basic principles of contemporary international law, are interconnected and interconditional. They are a reflection and a juridical consolidation of the fact that sovereign States act in international relations, and this ultimately is determined by the degree of the development of production forces and the production relations corresponding thereto.

CHAPTER IX. THE CHARACTER AND ESSENCE OF CONTEMPORARY GENERAL INTERNATIONAL LAW

1. Bourgeois Science on the Social Nature of International Law

The problem of the essence of contemporary international law is of great interest on both a theoretical and practical political plane.

Bourgeois legal science denies the class character of the law of capitalist society and conceals its exploitative essence. It seeks the social content of law in categories which it characterizes as common to all nations, to all mankind. The same picture is to be observed, naturally, in the bourgeois theory of international law.[1]

The positivists, including proponents of the theory of agreement as the sole mode of creating a norm of international law (Triepel, Anzilotti, Perassi, and others), have refused to investigate the social nature of norms of international law, saying that this is not a matter for legal science.

During the period of imperialism, positivism in bourgeois legal science is degenerating into pure normativism. Thus, normativism in the form of Kelsen's "pure theory of law" is characterized by the complete separation of law from other social phenomena. According to Kelsen, as already has been pointed out, the sphere of law is exclusive, divorced from the true reality of the system. By this means, Kelsen avoids investigating the social content of law in the sphere of nonexistent, "pure" legal norms.

At the same time, there has been a definite digression from positivism in the bourgeois theory of law and a rebirth

[1] On bourgeois concepts of international law, see D. I. Baratashvili, Американские теории международного права [American Theories of International Law] (1956); D. B. Levin, О современных буржуазных теориях международного права [On Contemporary Bourgeois Theories of International Law] (1959).

of natural law concepts during the period of imperialism, especially during the general crisis of capitalism after the Great October Socialist Revolution.

The representatives of contemporary natural law theories seek the social content of international law in the "idea of law", "justice", "reason", the "idea of order", "conscience", and so forth.[2]

In the opinion of Professor A. Verdross, who proceeds from Hegelian philosophy, the essence of law consists in the "idea of law" or, that is to say, in the idea of a "world order". The purpose of any legal order is the prohibition of the use of force. This is a basic "general value". Its normative expression is the "idea of law", the essence of which lies in the idea of "world order". Citing Aristotle and Thomas Aquinas, Verdross says that the idea of law in its subsequent development is transformed into the idea of "moral society", since the prohibition of the use of force is insufficient to secure lasting peace. For this it is also necessary that the fundamental rights of all members of the community be secured; otherwise people will be forced to resist tyranny. Herein also lies the "essence of the idea of international law".[3]

The link between the "idea of law" and the natural law of Verdross is ambiguous. The "idea of law" is embodied first of all in natural law, which is conceived as a law corresponding to the moral nature of man as he exists in the real world. Some features of human nature remain constant, whereas others change. Therefore, one can not work out an immutable and complete system of natural law.[4]

"Positive" law, in Verdross's view, is based on a higher legal order, which is natural law. Norms of "positive" law operate

[2] On contemporary concepts of natural law, see G. P. Zhukov, Критика естественно-правовых теорий международного права [Critique of Natural-Law Theories of International Law] (1961).

[3] See A. Verdross, Международное право [International Law], transl. from 3d ed. by F. A. Kublitskii and R. L. Naryshkina; ed. G. I. Tunkin (1959), p. 35.

[4] Ibid., p. 40.

only within the limits of prescriptions of natural law, within the limits defined by the "idea of law".[5] E. Sauer, a West German professor, also sees the essence of law in the "idea of law", which he identifies with "justice".[6]

It is wholly obvious that the "idea of law", as representing "order" or "world order" in general, does not correspond to reality.

Another representative of contemporary natural law theories, L. Le Fur, sees the basis and social content of international law in "justice". He says that natural law, which in his view and that of a number of other bourgeois jurists is the basis of international law and a constituent part thereof, "has as its ultimate basis the idea of justice and morality which is common and, one can say, natural to all people".[7]

R. Redslob maintains that international law consists of "ideal and positive law", wherein "ideal law" stands higher than "positive law" "Ideal law" is established by "human conscience" and defines the "highest values". It springs from the internal conviction of the subject of a duty and is a "categorical imperative".[8]

B. Smyrniadis sees the basis of international law in "international morality insofar as it is responsive to the conscience of the civilized world".[9]

[5] Ibid., p. 37.

[6] E. Sauer, *Grundlehre des Völkerrechts* (3d rev. ed.; 1955), p. 2.

[7] L. Le Fur, "La coutume et les principes généraux du droit comme sources du droit international public", *Recueil d'etudes sur les sources du droit en l'honneur de François Geny* (1935), III, 368; Le Fur, "Règles générales du droit de la paix", *Recueil des cours*, LIV (1935), 205.

[8] R. Redslob, *Traité de droit des gens* (1950), pp. 62-63.

[9] B. Smyrniadis, "Positivisme et morale internationale en droit des gens", *Revue générale de droit international public*, XXVI (1955), 116. See also R. Laun, "Naturrecht und Völkerrecht", *Jahrbuch für internationales Recht*, IV (1954), 32. Laun expressly identifies "natural law" with morality.

M. Sibert, a French professor, draws from "human reason" the principles of "theoretical, rational, natural law" which, in his view, are the basis of all international law.[10]

A West German jurist, E. Kaufmann, believes that "objective reason" should be recognized as the single true "source" from which law springs.[11]

One frequently encounters the echoes of medieval theories of the divine character of international law which proclaim the will of God or a substance created by God to be the content of "natural" law. A Spanish jurist, J. S. de Erice y O'Shea, states that "law comes to us from God".[12] An Italian jurist, G. del Vecchio, says that the "idea of justice" which lies at the base of law in general, including international law, "consecrates the dignity of the human being in that there is therein an absolute, thanks to the divine imprint ...".[13] Verdross says that the "unity of the legal consciousness of mankind commanded by the Creator" lies at the basis of law.[14]

In essence the natural law theory inevitably leads to religion in one form or another. Believing that natural law does not depend upon the wills of people, is not created by people, the proponents of these theories take the path which leads to a religious explanation of the origin and content of law. They either end in ultimate logical conclusions which refer expressly to God as the ultimate Creator of law or they do not reach the end but stop halfway, which all the same leads to religion.[15]

[10] M. Sibert, *Traité du droit international public* (1951), I, 9.

[11] E. Kaufmann, "Règles générales du droit de la paix", *Recueil des cours,* LIV (1935), 319.

[12] J. S. de Erice y O'Shea, *Derecho diplomatico* (1954), I, 18-19.

[13] G. del Vecchio, *Il diritto internazionale e il probleme della pace* (1956), p. 26.

[14] Verdross, Международное право [International Law], p. 46.

[15] A Swiss professor, R. L. Bindschelder, correctly points out that "natural law" can in any case only be a law established by the will of a superhuman authority. See R. L. Bindschelder, "Zum Problem der Grundnorm", in F. A. Frhr. v. d. Heydte and others, eds., *Völkerrecht und rechtliches Weltbild: Festschrift für*

Bourgeois scholars usually explain the rebirth of natural law theories as a reaction to normativism, especially the normativism of the "Vienna school" carried to an extreme, which, they say, has proved to be completely inadequate for an explanation of international legal phenomena.[16]

There is no doubt that the exposure of the defects of normativism and its scientific unfoundedness was one reason for the departure of bourgeois science from normativist positivism. But the principal reason, of course, is not this. There were serious social reasons which first and foremost also explain the digression of bourgeois jurists from positivism and the rebirth of natural law conceptions.

As Professor G. Schwarzenberger correctly remarks, the primary role of natural law conceptions is to "justify action that by positive law is illegal ...".[17]

If during the period of bourgeois revolutions natural law conceptions were part of the ideology of the bourgeoisie, who fought against feudalism and played a progressive role, then under contemporary conditions the reactionary bourgeoisie refers to "natural law".

In proclaiming "natural law" to be the basis of "positive" law and part of international law in general, bourgeois jurists, willingly or not, give imperialism the opportunity to cite in justification of its aggressive actions abstract, admittedly different, interpretations of "natural law" principles derived from the "nature of man", from the ideas of justice, and so forth. It is characteristic that in our time aggressive circles more often prefer to resort to references to "justice" which correspond to the interests of monopolies, and not to generally-recognized principles and norms of international law.

A. Verdross (1960), p. 164. See also Kelsen, "Die Grundlage der Naturrechtslehre", *Osterreichische Zeitschrift für öffentliches Recht*, XIII (1963), 35-37.

16 See, for example, C. de Visscher, *Théories et réalites en droit international public* (2d ed.; 1955), p. 90; G. Dahm, *Völkerrecht* (1958), I, 11.

17 G. Schwarzenberger, *The Inductive Approach to International Law* (1965), p. 186.

In comparing the natural law theories with normativism on a theoretical plane, it is necessary to point out that if the divorcing of law from other social phenomena is characteristic of normativism, then confusing them is peculiar to natural law theories. One or the other leads to a distortion of the essence of law in general, and of international law in particular.

However, the attempts of various bourgeois sociological schools (solidarism, realism, personalism, and such) to overcome the excesses of normativism and natural law theories and to find a median point have not been crowned with success either. The problem rests in the final analysis upon recognizing the class character of law, which bourgeois science can not accept. In rejecting normativism, therefore, bourgeois sociological concepts of international law are forced in one way or another to resort to natural law theories. As D.

D. Levin correctly says, "a natural law tinge is peculiar to some extent to virtually all bourgeois sociological theories of international law".[18]

Solidarism, for example, seeks the basis of law in general and of international law in particular in "social solidarity". One of the founders of solidarism, L. Duguit, despite the reality of bourgeois society, declares "social solidarity" to be the basic principle of social life. Solidarity, in Duguit's view, is supposedly a natural law of human society arising out of the nature of man. Law is an embodiment of social solidarity. "Man lives in society", says Duguit, "and can live only in society; society exists only thanks to the solidarity which links the individuals that comprise it. Consequently, the rule of conduct is made binding by the very force of things for man in society, which can be formulated as follows: to do nothing that would cause damage to social solidarity in one of its two forms, and to do everything that can be done to effectuate and develop mechanical and organic social solidarity. All objective law is summarized in this formula, and a positive law, to be

[18] Levin, О современных буржуазных теориях международного права [On Contemporary Bourgeois Theories of International Law], p.26.

lawful, must be a reflection, development, or application in practice of this principle".[19]

G. Scelle, developing this concept in the sphere of international legal theory, believes "social solidarity" to be the basis and essence of any law.[20]

In declaring "social solidarity" to be the basis of law, the solidarists further confuse the laws of societal development (as they understand them, of course) with law and thus come to the position of natural law theory.

In an enquiry into the question of the formal sources of international law, published in 1937, one of the proponents of solidarism, the French professor Scelle, maintained that the laws of societal development are "objective law" (*droit objectif*), law in the juridical sense. According to Scelle, this objective law comprises the basis of law. He wrote: "The validity of positive law is based upon its conformity to the "laws of causality" of the existence of society. This primary legal basis we call objective law because it can not contain any subjective element, for it still has not been perceived, interpreted, or desired by human intelligence. On the contrary, once human intervention begins, it does not limit itself to perceiving and interpreting; it evaluates; it attempts to direct and to use the source of law for itself, as a result of which a subjective element is introduced. To the element of necessity is added the element of will; to the element of causality, finality; and, doubtless, to the discovery, error. All positive law is to some extent a distortion of objective law and therefore is imagined to be an imperfect juridical product. It may even happen that a source will be so distorted

[19] L. Duguit, Конституционное право, общая теория государства [Constitutional Law, General Theory of the State], transl. A. Iashchenko, V. Krasnokutskii, and B. Syromiatnikov. Preface to Russian translation by P. Novogorodtsev and the author (1908), p. 18.

[20] G. Scelle, "Essai sur les sources formelles du droit international", *Recueil d'études sur les sources du droit en l'honneur de François Geny*, III, pp. 400- 401. Professor G. Perrin, of the University of Lausanne, speaks of "international solidarity". See G. Perrin, "Le fondement et les limites du droit des gens", *Schweizerisches Jahrbuch für internationales Recht*, XII (1955), 43.

by the subjectivity of its interpreters that it will cease to be law and become nonlaw; positive law may be antijuridical".[21]

However, in the *Cours de droit international public* which appeared in 1948, Professor Scelle expresses himself less definitely and more cautiously on this question. Already he does not maintain that the laws of causality are laws in the juridical sense; he says that a material source of law is the "legal potential" of society which corresponds to "social necessity". Norms of law arise from this material source. International law, he asserts, can be explained only by proceeding from the social factors of international life, which themselves are the result of the "laws of causality".[22]

The laws of societal development, that is first and foremost the laws of the development of the economic structure of society, exist independently of the will and desire of people. People can come to know these laws, to use them in their own interests to the extent this is possible, but they can not abolish them. The laws of societal development are reflected in the principles and norms of international law, but they themselves are not legal norms.

The inability of bourgeois legal science to expose the essence of law in general and of international law in particular is determined by its class character, by the limits of the world outlook of the ruling class. As we have seen, bourgeois legal science either refuses to investigate the social nature of law in general or does not seek it where it in fact exists. It is not in a position to escape from the vicious circle because of its class character. To expose the class nature of bourgeois law would mean that bourgeois science would oppose this law – that is, would cease to be bourgeois science.

21 Scelle, "Essai sur les sources formelles du droit international", p. 401.

22 Scelle, *Manuel de droit international public* (1948), p. 9.

2. *The Societal Laws of the Development of International Law*

(a) *The laws of the development of society and international law.* Marxist-Leninist theory, as a genuinely scientific theory, allows us to analyze the complex system of interconnections of social phenomena, to separate major links from minor, primary from secondary, to establish the dependence of the partial laws of development of individual social phenomena from the general laws of development of human society. "In extending and developing philosophical materialism", Lenin wrote, "Marx completed and enlarged its cognition of nature to a cognition of *human society*. Marx's *historical materialism* was the greatest triumph of scientific thought. The chaos and arbitrariness which had rules until then in the views of history and politics were strikingly changed by the integral and harmonious scientific theory showing how there develops from one structure of social life, in consequence of the growth of productive forces, another higher structure – for example, from serfdom grows capitalism".[23]

Applied to international law, historical materialism makes it possible to ascertain its place in the system of social phenomena, to establish the dependence of its development on the basic laws of the development of human society, and to reveal the specific de- velopmental laws of international law.

International law, just as law in general, is a category of the superstructure. Therefore, the general law of the development of human society having the closest relationship to international law is the law of the dependence of the social superstructure on the base; that is, the economic structure of society.

In formulating this law, Marx wrote in the preface to *A Critique of Political Economy*: "In the social production of their life people enter into specific, necessary relationships irrespective of their

[23] V. I. Lenin, "Три источники и три составных частей марксизма" [Three Sources and Three Constituent Parts of Marxism], Полное собрание сочинений [Complete Collection of Works] (5th ed.;, 1961), XXIII, 44 [First published in Просвещение [Enlightenment], no. 3 (1913) – *WEB*].

will, production relations which correspond to the specific degree of development of their material production forces. The aggregate of these production relations comprises the economic structure of society, the real base on which the legal and political superstructure rises and to which the specific forms of social consciousness correspond. The means of production of material life condition the social, political, and spiritual processes of life in general. The consciousness of people does not determine their being, but, on the contrary, their social being determines their consciousness. At a certain stage of their development, the material production forces come into contradiction with the existing production relations, or – this is merely a legal expression of the latter – with the relations of ownership within which they had developed up to then. From the forms of development of production forces these relations are transformed into their fetters. Then comes an epoch of social revolution. With a change of economic base, there occurs more or less quickly an upheaval in the entire enormous superstructure".[24]

State and law, as part of the superstructure, change with a modification of the base, and the State and law correspond to each socio-economic formation. How does this law of the dependence of the superstructure on the base operate with regard to international law? In contemporary conditions there exist two fundamental bases: the capitalist and the new socialist base coming to replace it. And at the same time there exists a general international law common to the socialist and capitalist States.

The critics of Marxist-Leninist international legal theory attempt to assert in this connection that Marxism is in no position to explain the existence of contemporary general international law and that supposedly the application of Marxist theory to international law leads to the conclusion that two international laws exist.

[24] K. Marx and F. Engels, "К критике политической экономии" [On a Critique of Political Economy], Сочинения [Works] (2d ed.; 1959), XIII, 6-7.

Thus E. McWhinney, a Canadian professor, writes: "Since law is, in Marxist terms, a product of the market-place and each economic system thus gets the body of law appropriate to its state of economic development, how may two economic systems – capitalism and communism – yield identical bodies of international legal doctrine? Or, putting it in more traditional Marxist language, if international law, like national law, belongs to the superstructure and is determined uniquely by the base of production relationships, how can radically different (Capitalist and Communist) economic bases yield the same superstructure of international law?"[25]

The trouble with these critics of the Marxist-Leninist theory of international law lies in the fact that, just as the many other critics of Marxism who existed before them, they attempt to represent Marxist-Leninist theory as a form of vulgar materialism. Their assertion that Marxist-Leninist theory supposedly considers any phenomenon of the superstructure as directly determined by the economic system of society, as representing a simple reflection of economic relations, is nothing other than the fruit of their own imagination.

What Engels said nearly eighty years ago on the subject of distortion of Marxism is wholly applicable to these critics. In a letter to J. Bloch of 21-22 September 1890 Engels wrote: "... According to the materialist conception of history, the *ultimately* determining element in history is the production and reproduction of real life. More than this neither Marx nor I have ever asserted. Hence if somebody twists this into saying that the economic element is the *only* determining

[25] E. McWhinney, *"Peaceful Coexistence" and Soviet-Western International Law* (1964), p. 46; see also J. B. Quigley, Jr., "The New Soviet Approach to International Law", *The Harvard International Law Club Journal*, VII (1965), 8; H. Kelsen, *The Communist Theory of Law* (1955), p. 148; W. Friedmann, *The Changing Structure of International Law* (1964), p. 327; B. Ramundo, *The Soviet (Socialist) Theory of International Law* (1964), p. 57; the review of the French edition of my book Вопросы теории международного права [Questions of Theory of International Law] by Ivo Lapenna in *International and Comparative Law Quarterly*, XIV (1965), 1427-1428; B. Dutoit, *Coexistence et droit international à la lumière de la doctrine Soviétique* (1966), pp. 75, 164; J. L. Hildebrand, *Soviet International Law* (1969), p. 67.

one, he transforms that proposition into a meaningless, abstract, senseless phrase. The economic situation is the basis, but the various elements of the superstructure – political forms of the class struggle and its results, to wit: constitutions established by the victorious class after a successful battle, and so forth, juridical forms, and even the reflexes of all these actual struggles in the brains of the participants, political, juristic, and philosophical theories, religious views and their further development into systems of dogma – also exercise their influence upon the course of the historical struggles and in many cases preponderate in determining their *form*. There is an interaction of all these elements in which, amid all the endless host of accidents ... the economic movement finally asserts itself as necessary. Otherwise the application of the theory to any period of history would be easier than the solution of a simple equation of the first degree".[26]

The view has been expressed in Soviet international legal literature that two groups of international legal principles and norms exist which correspond to the two socio-economic systems, but as we pointed out in 1956, this view was never shared by the majority of Soviet international lawyers.[27]

In fact, only Marxist-Leninist theory allows us to explain scientifically both the existence of contemporary general international law and its social nature. The Marxist-Leninist theory of international law, in revealing the mechanism of its development on the basis of the general tenets of historical materialism, shows why, despite the existence of two diametrically opposed bases, general international law exists and why these bases influence it.

The emergence of a new social system and the existence of two opposed social systems does not mean that they

[26] K. Marx and F. Engels, Избранные произведения в двух томах [Selected Works in Two Volumes] (1948), II, 467-468.

[27] See G. I. Tunkin, "Мирное сосуществование и международное право" [Peaceful Coexistence and International Law], Советское государство и право [Soviet State and Law], no. 7 (1956), p. 5.

are isolated from one another. The intensity of international economic as well as of other ties is increasing with the growth of the production forces of human society and with the development on this basis of a world division of labor. The division of the world into two opposed social systems, the formation of two world markets, has not stopped this objective world process, although it has introduced much that is new into it (see Chapter XIII).

This general societal law is the major objective premise of the peaceful coexistence of States with a diametrically opposed social system and of general international law. At the same time, it is necessary to emphasize that the very possibility of peaceful coexistence of the socialist and capitalist States immediately conditions the possibility of the existence of general international law,[28] since the basic contradictions of contemporary international relations lies in the relations between States of the two systems.

In proving that at the basis of societal development lies the development of its production forces, which at each stage of their development correspond to a specific economic structure of society, and in showing how in connection with the development of production forces the international division of labor develops and international economic and other international ties expand, and that in contemporary society these ties acquire legal forms – Marxist-Leninist theory creates a firm basis for international legal theory.

The conception of the concordance of wills of States (or agreement) as a mode of creating norms of contemporary international law, widely accepted in the Soviet science of international law, helps to reveal on the basis of the general tenets of the Marxist-Leninist theory of law the specific mechanism of the influence of the economic structure of society upon the development of international law – that is, the mechanism

[28] Tunkin, Основы современного международного права [Fundamental Principles of Contemporary International Law] (1956), p. 7.

of the influence of the two bases upon contemporary international law.

As already has been pointed out, norms of contemporary international law are created and changed on the basis of agreement between States. This agreement embraces the concordant wills of States relating to the content of a particular rule of conduct and to its being recognized as a norm of international law.

Marxist-Leninist theory reveals the class content of the will of a State, showing that this will in a society with antagonistic classes is the will of the economically and politically ruling class in the particular society, and under socialism the will of the entire people led by the working class.[29]

The content of the will of a State – that is, its international legal position – is formed under the influence of the entire aggregate of the conditions of the existence of the ruling class in a State, and under socialism, of the entire people. The economic structure of society is the primary base which defines in the final analysis the international legal position of a State in its primary features.

In reality, the economic structure determines the class nature of a State, the fundamental principles of its internal and foreign policy, the major features of its national law, and all other parts of the superstructure. This general societal law is the main societal law. But this does not mean that it is possible to "directly infer" the international legal position of a particular State from the economic structure of society.

[29] On class will and State will in connection with the creation of norms of law see D. A. Kerimov, Свобода, право и законность в социалистическом обществе [Freedom, Law, and Legality in a Socialist Society] (1960); P. S. Romashkin and others (eds.), Теория государства и права [Theory of State and Law] (1962); Общая теория советского права [General Theory of State and Law] (1966); A. I. Denisov (ed.), Теория государства и права [Theory of State and Law] (1967); V. M. Chkhikvadze, Государство, демократия, законность [State, Democracy, Legality] (1967); N. G. Aleksandrov (ed.), Теория государства и права [Theory of State and Law] (1968); A. F. Shebanov, Форма советского права [Form of Soviet Law] (1968); R. L. Bobrov, Основные проблемы теории международного права [Basic Problems of Theory of International Law] (1968).

Forming an international legal position, that is, the content of the will of a State, is a complex process in which the economic structure of society and its societal laws exert a determinative influence. Various parts of the superstructure, however, also exert influence upon the formation of the international legal position of a State: ideology, national law, international legal doctrine, and so forth. One cannot reduce to a basic societal law nor "infer" the will of a State nor the will of its ruling class in each individual instance from the economic structure of society without taking other influences into account. At the same time, it is possible to gain an understanding of this process only by proceeding from the societal laws of the co-relation of base and superstructure.

The economic structure of human society in our days is characterized by the existence of two opposed world economic systems whose development occurs pursuant to directly opposed laws. Each of these systems exerts influence on general international law. One cannot agree with the view repeatedly expressed in Soviet literature that international economic relations are the basis of international law. International economic relations are secondary and therefore cannot be regarded as a special basis of any category of the superstructure.

Thus, the influence of the economic structure of society and its societal laws affects the process of creating norms of international law through the will of a State, since the content of this will basically is determined by the economic conditions of the existence of the ruling class in a given State. The economic structure of society exerts a decisive influence in the process of creating norms of international law upon the wills of States not only through "direct action" but also through other categories of the superstructure, whose operation in general can not go beyond the limits determined by the economic structure of society.

(b) The unfoundedness of the bourgeois concept of ubi societas ibi jus. The denial of the class character of law leads bourgeois science

to the maxim "where there is society, there is law" (*ubi societas ibi jus*). Law and society, say bourgeois jurists, are indivisible. Human society is impossible without law. Law is represented as an a historical category, independent of the social system and peculiar to any human society.

Thus, G. Fitzmaurice, an English jurist and member of the International Court, writes: "The view that seems to be closest both to the realities of the matter and to the historical facts is the `social' view, or in other words the idea embodied in the maxim *ubi societas ibi jus*. This maxim is more than a statement of mere fact ... It is not simply that where society is found, law is found, but that it must be so found – that law is a necessary condition of the existence of society as such – which is to say a necessary condition of any systematized form of inter-relationships".[30]

The maxim *ubi societas ibi jus,* which for a century has been accepted by bourgeois and even prebourgeois legal science as an axiom, is unfounded. Marxist-Leninist theory has shown that there was a time when human society knew neither a State nor law, although there were specific rules of conduct then. The development of production forces led to the emergence of private ownership of the means of production. The possibility of appropriating another's labor, of the exploitation of man by man, was created. Private ownership of the means of production was the basis for the development of inequality among the various groups of human society, the division of society into classes. The State arose as the organ of the economically dominant class in society, as the organ strengthening and consolidating its domination. Together with the State, law emerged, which was distinguished from the rules of conduct which had existed in the prestate society primarily by the fact that it reflected the will not of all society but only of the ruling class and that it was directed at maintaining and developing the social orders favorable and advantageous to this ruling class. Fulfillment of these new norms, legal norms, by members

30 G. Fitzmaurice, "The General Principles of International Law Considered from the Standpoint of the Rule of Law", *Recueil des cours*, XCII (1957), 38.

of society was ensured when necessary through coercion applied by agencies of the State.

When there was no law in general, there could be no international law. Since law emerged as a result of the division of society into classes and of the rise of the State, in the beginning it was national law. In the course of time, international law regulating relations among States began to be formed. The same basic reasons which led to the formation of national law also gave rise to the emergence of international law.

International law, just as national law, inheres in a class society. But class society, as has been proved by the basic tenets of Marxism, represents merely a certain stage in the development of human society, which also had existed where there were no classes. This society was characterized by a low level of the development of production forces. A high development of the production forces of society also inevitably leads to the disappearance of classes, of the State, and of law.

Mankind is approaching a new organization of society which will not have law, and consequently, not international law. This, of course, does not mean that the society of the future will have no rules of conduct. A highly-organized human society, as communist society will be, inevitably presupposes the existence of rules of conduct.

Bourgeois science errs in accepting any rules of conduct, in- cluding rules of conduct in tribal society, as norms of law. The maxim "where there is society, there are rules of conduct" would be correct, but the maxim "where there is society, there is law" (*ubi societas ibi jus*) is incorrect. The rules of conduct which will exist in communist society will by their nature be different from norms of law.

The maxim "where there is society, there is law" is closely linked with the widespread thesis in bourgeois legal science that law is a reflection of "community": community of interests, community of ideology, and so forth. As confirmation of this thesis, many bourgeois scholars point out that the existence of law in general and of international law in particular would be impossible without a specific community among people. Of course, the existence of human society, and therefore of law, is inconceivable without a specific community among people. But it does not follow from this that the community is the reason for the emergence of law or is reflected in law. History shows exactly the opposite: in preclass society, where this community was more significant, there was no law, and law appears only with the emergence of class contradictions, with the disturbance of the tribal community.

(c) International law and international organization. The notion of law as a nonclass system of norms common to all mankind leads bourgeois science to the conclusion in the domain of international legal theory that international law is developing along the same path as national law and is now at an elementary stage of development which national law has long since undergone. They therefore call international law a "primitive" law which, however, is developing in the same direction as national law has developed, to wit, in the direction of centralization. Some, but far from all bourgeois jurists, go further, believing that international law will become a "real" law only with the creation of a world State or an approximation of a world State (see Chapter XIV).

D. Anzilotti has said that norms of international law possess the character which norms of social groups had during the period receding the emergence of State organization, and that in comparison with municipal law, international law is "incomplete and imperfect".[31] It is true that Anzilotti pointed out in this connection that norms of international law could not be otherwise and that the emergence of a world federation "would actually mean the end of international law, which would be superseded by the internal public law of the new State".

In Kelsen's view, the basic difference between national and international law lies in the fact that the first is a centralized and

[31] D. Anzilotti, *Corso di diritto internazionale* (4th ed.; 1955), I, 47.

the second is a decentralized and therefore primitive legal system.[32] Kelsen maintains that so long as the sovereignty of States is recognized, international law can not leave this "primitive condition". He calls for the liquidation of State sovereignty and the creation of a "world State" which would ensure the "development and application of international law".[33]

In developing the same concept of the uniform path of development of international and national law, Professor J. Kunz says that the "private wars" of the Middle Ages were eliminated by means of centralization. The same course must be followed in international relations. The progressive development of international law can not be brought about merely by treaties. "This can only be brought about", Kunz says, "by political action, changing the actual sociological conditions on which the present international community is based ... A more advanced international law must be based on the full recognition by States of the primacy of international law and on enforceable sanctions both for the maintenance of peace and security and for the enforcement of international law in general by organs of the international community".[34]

Lauterpacht gives a very thorough exposition of this concept in one of its extreme variants in Oppenheim's *International Law*. He writes: "The historic idea of a 'general international organisation', an idea prominent in the legal and political thought of the past three centuries, connotes an association of States of potentially universal character for the ultimate fulfillment of purposes which, in relation to individuals organised in political society, are realised by the State. The achievement of these purposes, which are outlined below, is as essential to the Law of Nations as it is to the internal law of

[32] H. Kelsen, *Principles of International Law*, ed. R. W. Tucker (2d ed.; 1967), p. 20.

[33] Ibid., pp. 189-190; Kelsen, *Das Problem der souveranität und die Theorie des Völkerrechts (2d ed.; 1928), p. 320.*

[34] J. Kunz, "Sanctions in International Law", *American Journal of International Law*, LIV (1960), 347.

the State. Failing their accomplishment, or an attempt at their accomplishment, International Law must be deemed to dwell in the realm of a twilight existence in which its very claim to be considered as a system of law is precarious and controversial. To that extent, which is fundamental in its scope and nature, the cause of International Law is identical with that of a general political organisation of mankind as distinguished from organs of international administration and co- operation for particular purposes. For it is only under the shelter of and through such general organisation endowed with overriding and coercive power for creating, ascertaining, and enforcing the law that International Law can overcome its present imperfections. For this reason it is proper that the constitution of international society – such as was embodied in the Covenant of the League of Nations and is now embodied in the Charter of the United Nations – should be studied by reference to its approximation to these essential objects of any political society under the rule of law".[35]

An American professor, P. Jessup, asserts still more categorically that international law can be transformed into real law only if a world government is created. Jessup writes: "Until the world achieves some form of international government in which a collective will takes precedence over the individual will of the sovereign state, the ultimate function of law, which is the elimination of force for the solution of human conflicts, will not be fulfilled".[36]

One should dwell first and foremost upon the general societal laws of the development of international and municipal law. There is no doubt that such societal laws exist. Among them, for example, is the societal law reflecting the fact that at a certain stage of development of human society there was neither municipal nor international law and that in the future,

[35] L. Oppenheim, Международное право [International Law], transl. from 6th ed.; ed. S. B. Krylov (1948), I(1), p. 340.

[36] P. Jessup, *A Modern Law of Nations* (1968), p. 2.

at a very high stage of the development of human society, there also will not be such.

The existence of certain general societal laws of the development of international and municipal law, however, does not mean that international law does not have its own specific societal laws of development. Attempts to approach international law with the yardstick of national law are scientifically unfounded, since the specific nature of the phenomenon being investigated is not taken into account. International law is a distinctive law.

The principal peculiarities of international law arise from the fact that it regulates first and foremost, and primarily, the relations between sovereign States. In taking exception to the argumentation of proponents of a "world State", some specialists on international law in the West, not without justification, point out that the creation of a "world State" would mean the elimination of international law, since in this event international law would be superseded by the municipal law of the "world State".[37]

The major peculiarities of international law as law regulating the relations between sovereign States are determined by the societal laws of historical development. The existence of sovereign States at the present time is not dependent upon the will or desire of individual persons. It is not that governments do not wish to part with sovereign authority, as the proponents of eliminating State sovereignty (Kelsen, Scelle, and others) so frequently lament. The existence of sovereign States is conditioned by the historical societal laws of our epoch.

As regards the link between the development of international law and the development of international organization, there is no doubt that during the period after the First and especially after the Second World War, one observes a tendency to expand

[37] See, for example, Anzilotti, *Corso di diritto internazionale*, I, 47; H. Drost, *Grundlagen des Völkerrechts* (1936), p. 2; H. A. Smith, *The Crisis in the Law of Nations* (1947), p. 22; G. Sperduti, "Osservazioni sulle basi sociali dell'ordinamento internazionale", *Rivista di diritto internazionale*, XXXVIII (1955), 3-16; Verdross, *Международное право*, pp. 24-25.

the role of international organizations both in developing international law and in ensuring compliance with its norms.[38]

International organizations now play an important role in creating norms of international law and ensuring supervision over compliance with them, and strongly influence the conduct of States for the purpose of having them comply with norms of international law. There is every reason to suppose that this role of international organizations will grow in the future.

But there are no grounds to believe that international organizations can be transformed into the likeness of a State authority and fulfill the same or similar functions in creating and ensuring compliance with norms of international law which agencies of State authority fulfill with regard to national law (see Chapter XV).

A world State represents a serious danger to international law. From the concept that only the creation of a world State can make international law a "real" law, it is only one step to completely denying the validity of contemporary international law and recognizing as hopeless all attempts to enlarge its role in ensuring peace and averting war. In reality, if one believes that enhancing the effectiveness of international law is inseparably linked with the creation of a world State, which under contemporary conditions is impossible, the future prospects for the development of international law would be very auspicious.

In fact, however, this is not so at all. Enhancing the role of international law in international relations occurs not by moving toward a world State and eliminating State sovereignty, but as a result of developing and strengthening

[38] See Chapters IV and V. Professor Bourquin is correct in noting this new fact, although he somewhat exaggerates its significance. He writes: "Whereas the functioning of international law previously was based on the actions of States, it now rests to a significant extent on international organizations such as the United Nations and the numerous specialized agencies grouped around it". M. Bourquin, "L'Humanisation du droit des gens", *La technique et les principes du droit public: études en l'honneur de G. Scelle* (1950), I, 48.

the basic principles and norms of prevailing international law, introducing new principles and norms therein aimed at the development of international cooperation and ensuring the peaceful coexistence of States on the basis of equality, respect for sovereignty, and noninterference in internal affairs.

Since the existence of sovereign States is a historic societal law of our epoch, only agreement between these sovereign States is and can be the basic legally binding nature of norms of international law. Agreement of States on the basis of equality as a mode of creating norms of international law continues to remain the characteristic feature of the development of international law in our epoch.

In comparison, moreover, with the preceding period, this situation is being consolidated and is developing. If previously the great imperialist powers frequently declared to be generally recognized norms those norms which they themselves had established, and imposed these norms upon the weaker States, at the present time any attempts of imperialist States to impose norms advantageous to them as norms of international law not only are unlawful but are doomed to failure beforehand.

3. Modification of the Character and Essence of General International Law During the Past Half-Century

The question of evaluating the changes which have taken place in international law since the Great October Socialist Revolution is not just of theoretical interest. It arises, in particular, during the discussion in the United Nations of the most important questions of the progressive development of international law and its codification, wherein the international legal positions of the States of the two systems are in conflict.

(a) Fundamental changes in general international law after the Great October Socialist Revolution. Under the influence of the growing might of the forces of socialism, of the national liberation movement, and of all the forces of democracy and progress,

international law has undergone material changes since the Great October Socialist Revolution. The attempt of German fascism and Japanese imperialism to destroy international law and to replace it with delirious ideas of the dominance of a superior race brought forth the unity of all progressive forces. This general democratic upsurge not only led to the rout of fascism, militarily and in the realm of ideas, but also ensured a significant development of international law, reflected above all in the United Nations Charter.

The fundamental principles of international law, that central part which has the greatest significance from the viewpoint of ensuring international peace, the independence of peoples, and the development of international cooperation and which first and foremost determines the fact of international law (see Chapter III), have changed fundamentally during the past half-century.

The changes which have occurred in international law naturally have affected all of its branches and institutes, the changes in individual branches of international law being above all the consequence of the change in the fundamental principles. Thus, in the domain of responsibility, whose importance in the general system of international law is difficult to underestimate, there has been an extension of international legal responsibility for war and its consequences (see Chapters XVII and XVIII).

Together with this there arose a new important institute of international law: responsibility of individuals for crimes against humanity, as they have been defined in the Statute and Judgment of the International Military Tribunal in Nuremberg.

Significant changes have taken place in the law of treaties. Contemporary international law declares void international treaties imposed upon a State through the unlawful use of force or those which contravene principles of international law having the character of *jus cogens* and recognizes a special status for treaties concluded with regard to an aggressor State.[39]

In the domain of sources of international law, the international treaty has become the principal source. Resolutions of international organizations, and especially of the United Nations, are playing larger and larger roles in the process of forming norms of international law.

In the domain of subjects of international law, new entities have emerged which are different from States, the traditional subjects of international law. These are international organizations, as well as nations fighting for their independence. International organizations possess a limited status as subjects of international law, but they are playing an ever greater role in international relations.

In ambassadorial law there has been a trend toward expanding the group of persons who enjoy diplomatic immunity and privileges. Thus, according to the 1961 Vienna Convention on Diplomatic Relations, together with diplomats, the basic diplomatic privileges are accorded to administrative and technical personnel of diplomatic representations and, to a certain extent, also to service personnel.[40]

Material changes also have taken place or are occurring in the law of neutrality. In recent years many States, especially new States of Asia and Africa, adhere to a policy of neutrality. The international legal formulation of this policy, in consequence whereof international obligations arise for the respective State, is taking place, as L. A. Modzhorian correctly points out, through unilateral declarations of a State wishing to adhere to a policy of neutrality, tacitly or expressly recognized by the remaining States and through bilateral or multilateral agreements.[41]

39 See Articles 52, 53, and 75 of the 1969 Vienna Convention on the Law of Treaties.

40 Article 37, Vienna Convention on the Law of Treaties. V. K. Sobakin (comp.), Современное международное право: сборник документов [Contemporary International Law: Collection of Documents] (1964), pp. 310-311.

41 L. A. Modzhorian, Основные права и обязанности государств [Basic Rights and Duties of States] (1965), p. 42.

The content of the status of a permanently neutral State has changed in connection with the change of the international situation and of international law. Neutrality in time of war has acquired primary importance in general. These new phenomena in the domain of neutrality mark a significant change in this branch of international law.[42]

The intensification and deepening of international ties, determined first and foremost by the development of productive forces and the international division of labor, has led to the emergence of new areas of international legal regulation.

The origin of a branch of international law which might be called the law of international security has enormous, but to a significant extent still potential, importance. Included within it are, first and foremost, international legal questions of disarmament, the prohibition of the testing of nuclear weapons, the creation of nuclear- free zones, the nonproliferation of nuclear weapons, collective security, and others.

A new branch of international law is developing which by analogy with sea and air law is called space law.[43]

The growth of the number and the expansion of the jurisdiction of international organizations has led to the emergence of a branch of international law which usually is called the law of international organizations. This law partially relates to general international law and partially is the law of individual international organizations.

Norms of international public law affecting commercial and other economic relations among States are developing rapidly, and thus international economic law is being formed.

A branch of international law known by the name "international labor law", whose norms determine the rights and duties of States in the domain of regulating labor conditions,

[42] For greater detail see B. V. Ganiushkin, Нейтралитет и неприсоединение [Neutrality and Non-Accession] (1965); O. I. Tiunov, Нейтралитет в международном праве [Neutrality in International Law] (1968).

[43] See G. P. Zhukov, Космическое право [Law of Outer Space] (1966).

has developed significantly. This branch of international law is embodied chiefly in conventions of the International Labor Organization.[44]

The profound changes which have occurred in international law since the Great October Socialist Revolution, above all under the influence of the changes which it wrought in the world and the ideas it advanced, lead to the conclusion that the question is not one of partial changes, but of those which are changing materially the entire character and essence of international law.

International law before the Great October Socialist Revolution, which we call the old international law, was essentially the law of the strong; it recognized and legally consolidated the domination of force in international relations.[45] This has emerged most clearly in such principles, for example, as the "right of a State to wage war", the "right of the victor", and others. If a State were sufficiently strong and could count upon victory, it always had the legal possibility of using the "right to wage war" and to resort to war in order to satisfy its actual or imaginary claims against another State. Moreover, victory in war allowed the victor to exceed the limits of the claims previously submitted (see Chapters XVII and XVIII). International law sanctioned that which was obtained by force.

Contemporary international law prohibits resort to war, prohibits the use or threat of force against the territorial integrity and political independence of any State or by any means incompatible with the purposes of the United Nations. States are obliged to settle their disputes only by peaceful means.

[44] See S. A. Ivanov, Проблемы международного регулирования труда [Problems of International Regulation of Labor] (1964); I. Szaszy, *International Labour Law* (1968).

[45] Professor E. B. Pashukanis was correct in speaking with regard to this international law that "with its help they divide the loot". See E. B. Pashukanis, Очерки по международному праву [Essays on International Law] (1935), p. 9.

Thus, the new international law prohibits aggressive war, is an instrument of the struggle for peace. Already the emergence of the principle of nonaggression has modified the character of international law to a significant extent.[46] In its subsequent development international law swung its face still more toward peace.

The old international law recognized two equal conditions of relations between States: a state of peace and a state of war. A significantly greater place was given to questions of war than to questions of peaceful relations.[47] Of the numerous international conventions concluded in the second half of the nineteenth and beginning of the twentieth centuries, the overwhelming majority treat the law of war. Thus, of fourteen documents (thirteen conventions and one declaration) signed at the Second Hague Peace Conference in 1907, only two concerned peaceful relations between States. All the other documents were devoted to the law of war.

At the present time, the unleashing of war is the most flagrant violation of international law, entailing not only the grave responsibility of the aggressor State but also the personal criminal responsibility of the persons guilty of the war. A state of war has ceased to be a "normal" state of relations between States in international law; it is the result of the gravest violation of international law.

More and more attention is being devoted to questions of regulating and strengthening peaceful relations between States. In contrast to what was previously, the majority of

[46] An American professor, C. Eagleton, in stressing the significance of the princpiles of the prohibition of aggressive war in international law, drew exceedingly far-reaching and incorrect conclusions. He wrote: "To deny to a state the right to make war is a change of fundamental character from which many consequences flow. The law of war and the law of neutrality would disappear – if they already have not disappeared. The means for peaceable settlement of disputes would have to be strengthened so that a community of decision would replace the right now claimed by each state to judge its own disputes. Thus the very foundations of international law are being changed". C. Eagleton, "Ferment or Revolution?" *American Journal of International Law*, L (1956), 920.

[47] In Grotius' celebrated work *On the Law of War and Peace* published in 1625 the "law of war", as is well-known, is given priority.

international conventions concluded since the Second World War are devoted to peaceful relations between States.

Under contemporary international law, war is not a duel, a contest between equal parties. The parties are not in an identical legal situation: one party, the aggressor, has committed the gravest breach of law, having unleashed a war, and is waging the war in violation of international law; and the other party is waging the war in self-defense, that is, on the basis of international law.

Elimination of the "right of a State to wage war" and the emergence in international law of the principle of nonaggression has led to the liquidation of the "right of the victor" and the institute of conquest and to the expansion of the principles of State responsibility for war and its consequences (see Chapter XVIII).

The old international law contained norms and institutes which were an instrument of the colonial enslavement of peoples and which consecrated and juridically strengthened the colonial regime and other forms of the dependence and exploitation of peoples. The right to acquire "no man's" territory (the rights of the indigenous populace of underdeveloped countries not being taken into account), the right of conquest, spheres of influence, institutes of colonial law, the regime of the protectorate, and others related to this category of norms and institutes of international law. These norms and institutes existed side by side with democratic principles and norms of the old international law while being in sharp contradiction with them.

Despite its imperfections, especially in the struggle against various forms of neocolonialism, contemporary international law as a whole is anticolonial. With the recognition of the principle of self- determination of nations as a generally accepted principle of inter- national law, the latter has turned against the colonial system. From ameansofenslavingpeoples,ithasbecomeaninstrumentofstruggleforthe liberation of peoples of colonies and dependent countries. Colonial- ism contravenes the very bases of contemporary international law.

The idea of the equality of all peoples, irrespective of race, language, religion, and so forth, is being consolidated more and more in international law.

The idea of the equality of the two systems together with the equality of States irrespective of their social system is winning recognition. The realization that any attempts to decide international questions on a plane unacceptable to the socialist countries are futile and harmful to the cause of peace and that agreement between States of the two systems is the sole means of deciding such questions is forcing its way more and more into international organizations and international conferences.[48]

The old international law was primarily a law of the so-called "civilized" or "Christian" States. The enormous continent of Africa and an important part of Asia had not entered into international relations, being the object of colonial oppression and exploitation. "Only the Christian States and their colonies belong to the sphere of international relations", wrote Professor M. Kapustin, of Moscow University.[49] "The spatial operation of international law", said Professor F. Martens, of Petersburg University, "is limited just to those peoples who recognize the basic principles of European culture and are worthy of the name of educated peoples".[50]

In consequence of the breakup of the colonial system of imperialism, there has been an expansion of the spatial sphere

48 See R. L. Bobrov, "Принцип равноправия двух систем в современном международном праве" [Principle of Equality of Two Systems in Contemporary International Law], Советское государство и право [Soviet State and Law], no. 11 (1960), pp. 42-50.

49 M. Kapustin, Обозрение предметов международного права [Survey of Subject-Matter of International Law] (1856), II, 41.

50 F. F. Martens, Современное международное право цивилизованных народов [Contemporary International Law of Civilized Peoples] (2d ed.; 1887), p. 180.

of the operation of international law. On this basis, international law more and more is becoming a universal law.

Contemporary international law precludes discrimination against States on the basis of such criteria as being "civilized" or "uncivilized", "Christian" or "non-Christian". The reference to "civilized" nations encountered in the Statute of the International Court now seems to be an obvious anachronism.

The essence of contemporary general international law also has changed. The expression "general" in this case is of material significance, since taken as a whole contemporary international law has no single class essence. One must distinguish in this respect between general international law and local international legal norms, whose essence in many instances differs from the essence of general international law.

The Marxist-Leninist theory of law considers the essence of law (as regards national law) to be the "general will of a particular class expressed therein".[51] This proposition is generally recognized in Soviet legal science.

Norms of international law are created not by one State, but by States; they reflect the concordant wills of States. The co-relation of the wills of States which participate in creating norms of international law with the wills of peoples depends upon the character of each individual State. The will of a capitalist State always is the will of its ruling class, determining, of course, the entire aggregate conditions of the existence of this class, including the struggle of the working class and all the working people. The will of the Soviet State of the whole people is the will of the entire Soviet people led by the working class; in contrast, in the international arena to the will of the ruling classes of capitalist States, it is the will of the toiling classes.

[51] Chkhikvadze, Государство, демократия, законность [State, Democracy, Legality], p. 293.

In the process of creating norms of international law, the wills of various States, above all the wills of States whose class essence is opposed, come into conflict. The process of creating norms of international law is the process of the struggle and cooperation of States, and naturally, being the result of this process, norms of international law themselves bear its imprint.

The creation of norms of international law takes place in specific juridical forms peculiar to contemporary international law, through the concordance of the wills of States as sovereign and equal subjects completed by an agreement fixing the content of a norm and recognizing it as a norm of international law. In this process the wills of States judicially are of equal importance. As Professor L. A. Aleksidze has noted correctly, one cannot speak on the juridical plane about whose will has prevailed in the process of creating a norm of international law, since the question is one of agreement of sovereign States on the basis of equality.[52]

As already has been pointed out, however, the actual influence of different States and groups of States in the process of creating norms of international law is far from identical.

The content and essence of norms of general international law, being the result of the norm-formation process, depend not only upon the actual situation (for example, the co-relation of forces at a conference, the influence of public opinion, the skill of diplomats, and so forth) but also upon the legal aspect of this process. The co- relation of forces upon a specific question of international law, of course, is of primary importance. But despite the preponderance of forces of a particular group of States, a norm of international law can not be created by the dictate of this group of States; it emerges only in consequence of agreement of States on the basis of equality.

[52] L. A. Aleksidze, "О классовой природе современного международного права" [On the Class Nature of Contemporary International Law], Советское государство и право [Soviet State and Law], no. 6 (1967), pp. 56-58.

The existence of States belonging to two opposed social systems creates specific limits for agreements between them. And since only those international legal norms which embrace the agreement of all States are norms of contemporary general international law, the norms of general international law, therefore, may not exceed the said limits.

This means that norms of contemporary general international law cannot be socialist, since agreement on this basis between socialist and capitalist States is impossible. Socialist international legal norms can be created only in relations between socialist States. On the other hand, norms of contemporary general international law cannot be an embodiment of an imperialistic policy, since agreement between socialist and capitalist States also is impossible on this basis.

The principles and norms of contemporary general international law as a whole are of a general democratic character, since agreement between socialist and capitalist States is possible only on this basis.[53] The notion of being generally democratic, however, is a very broad concept. The degree of the democratic nature of specific norms of international law is determined by the influence which has been exerted on the creation and development of such norms by the forces which favor the progressive development of international law and the forces which impede such progress.

The social consequences which regulate the influence of this system of law upon the corresponding social relations have important significance for the characteristic features of the content and essence of international law. A. A. Piontkovskii undoubtedly is right that one cannot consider norms of law while ignoring legal relations, although one can not agree with his thesis that the regulating influence of norms of law always is realized through legal relations.[54]

53 See Tunkin, Основы современного международного права [Fundamental Principles of Contemporary International Law], p. 8.

54 See A. A. Piontkovskii, "О некоторых вопросах советской правовой науки на современном этапе" [On Certain Questions of Legal Science at the Contemporary

The regulating influence of contemporary general international law is such because it was formed and is developing further under the decisive influence of the socialist States, the developing countries, and the other forces of peace and socialism, and as a whole is aimed at ensuring peace and peaceful coexistence, at the freedom and independence of peoples, against colonialism in all of its manifestations, and at the development of peaceful international cooperation in the interests of all peoples. Contemporary international law promotes the progress of human society, and this progress inevitably is linked to socialism, leads to socialism, and facilitates the struggle for socialism.

Contemporary general international law can be defined as the aggregate of norms which are created by agreement between States of different social systems, reflect the concordant wills of States and have a generally democratic character, regulate relations between them in the process of struggle and cooperation in the direction of ensuring peace and peaceful coexistence and freedom and independence of peoples, and are secured, when necessary, by coercion effectuated by States individually or collectively.

The changes which have taken place in international law in the post-October period give reason to speak of a new[55] contemporary international law which can be called briefly the law of peaceful coexistence and self-determination of peoples.

Some bourgeois international lawyers attempt to represent the concept of the *new international law* advanced by Soviet jurists as an appeal to cast aside existing international law and to

---

Stage], Советское государство и право [Soviet State and Law], no. 2 (1964), p. 42; see also S. N. Bratus', "Содержание и форма права" [Content and Form of Law], *Ученые записки всесоюзного научно-исследовательского института Советского законодательства* [Learned Papers of All-Union Scientific Research Institute of Soviet Legislation], XIV (1968), 38.

55 See R. L. Bobrov, "Великая Октябрьская социалистическая революция" [Great October Socialist Revolution], Правоведение [Jurisprudence], no. 1 (1957), p. 87.

replace it with another,[56] or assert that one could recognize contemporary international law as new only if all or the majority of its principles and norms differed fundamentally from the principles and norms of the international law which previously existed.[57] Both assertions are completely unfounded.

First, the conception of a new international law in no way calls for a repudiation of prevailing international law. Just to the contrary. According to this concept, international law has undergone such progressive substantive changes that prevailing international law should be classified as new. And since from the viewpoint of this concept this new international law basically is responsive to the requirements of contemporary international relations, the principal task is to ensure strict compliance with prevailing international law by States.

On the other hand, this concept in no way diminishes the significance of the further progressive development of international law. If contemporary international law already is not a "traditional" or "classical" international law, if it has already become an important means of ensuring peace, the independence of peoples, and the development of equal international cooperation, this naturally does not signify that such means do not need further improvement. In noting the new progressive phenomena in international law and in showing how social forces have ensured this progress, this concept facilitates finding the paths and methods for the further progressive development of international law.

Recognition of contemporary international law as new does not mean, further, that it thereby is treated as having nothing in common with the old international law. The new international law has emerged as a result of the gradual

[56] See, for example, F. Vallat, "International Law – A Forward Look", *Yearbook of World Affairs*, XVIII (1964), 248.

[57] See, for example, the speech of the United States representative, F. Plimpton, in the Sixth Committee of the United Nations General Assembly. Doc. No. A/ C.6/SR.722 (XVI), 1 December 1961.

accumulation of quantitative changes which have been turned into qualitative.

It would, of course, be a simplification to believe that the new international law emerged after the Great October Socialist Revolution as a *deux ex machina,* that the October Revolution liquidated the old international law and created a new one. The question is not one of national but of international law, whose norms are created on the basis of agreement between States. The new revolutionary international legal ideas and principles advanced by one or several States can not, consequently, change existing international law at once.

The changes which led to the transformation of the old international law into a qualitatively new one were the result of a prolonged and persistent struggle of the Soviet State, of other socialist countries, and of the new States which have emerged on the ruins of the colonial system, a result of the struggle of all progressive forces. The October Revolution was the beginning of the formative period of the new international law, and not its completion. It put forth the international legal ideas and principles which exerted and continue to exert a decisive influence upon the development of international law.

Classifying contemporary international law as new does not mean that one thereby recognizes only that which is new and casts aside everything that is old in international law. Some principles and norms of the old international law actually have been liquidated and replaced by new progressive principles and norms. Other principles and norms have remained, but have undergone more or less substantive changes. Several important principles and norms relating to new domains of international legal regulation have emerged. The general character and essence of international law has changed.

The emergence of a qualitatively new international law is a negation of the old quality. But every dialectical negation is a moment of development; there is not only a destruction of the old, but a retention in the new of the positive content of the former level of development.

As already has been pointed out, despite the significant changes in international law that took place after the Great October Socialist Revolution which were reflected not only in a change of its principles and norms but also in a qualitative change of the social consequences of its operation and its essence, contemporary international law needs to be further improved. This improvement of international law can be ensured only by the resolute struggle of the forces of socialism and progress against the forces of reaction and war.

The struggle goes on for the further progressive development of international law and for the enhancement of its effectiveness in order to make it a more efficacious means of ensuring peace and the development of friendly relations between States, of freedom and the independence of peoples.

There are many domains of international law in which one can expect further progressive development in the immediate future. Codification of the law of treaties has been carried out. A convention on the law of treaties was adopted at the 1968-1969 Vienna Conference which, as a whole, is a significant step forward in developing this most important branch of international law. The prerequisites have matured for settling a number of new urgent problems of the international law of the sea, particularly problems relating to the conservation of marine resources, exploitation of the wealth of the seabed, the regime of the high seas, and so forth.

The branch of international law relating to the protection of human rights is developing. An important event in this domain is the adoption by the United Nations General Assembly on 21 December 1965 of an international convention on the elimination of all forms of racial discrimination, and on 16 December 1966 of the covenants on human rights.

There are possibilities for the progressive development of a number of other branches and institutes of international law: international labor law, the law of international trade, State succession, responsibility, and air law.

With regard to questions of international law relating directly to the maintenance of international peace and ensuring the independence of peoples, that is, the fundamental questions of international law, the struggle of the two orientations in international politics is so intense that movement forward is proceeding very slowly. In this domain, however, one can not such positive phenomena as the 1963 Moscow treaty on the prohibition of nuclear tests in three spheres; the treaty on the principles of the activity of States in exploring and exploiting outer space, including the moon and other celestial objects, signed in 1967; and the treaty on the nonproliferation of nuclear weapons, signed in 1968.

As already pointed out, the raising of the question of the codification and progressive development of the basic principles of contemporary international law by the socialist and some developing countries in the United Nations has itself aroused the embittered resistance of the imperialist powers. These principles comprise the most important part of international law, and with them come the concerns of States in the major questions of foreign policy. The basic principles of contemporary international law are aimed at ensuring peace, peaceful coexistence, and the independence of peoples, and therefore the imperialist powers impede in every possible way the work concerning their further development. Despite the fact that definite positive work has been done since the adoption of the decision to work out these principles by the General Assembly in 1961, serious pressure is required on the part of all peace-loving forces to compel the imperialist forces to go forward on this question.

A serious struggle is in prospect for the further development of anticolonial provisions of international law applicable to the new situation created as a result of the breakup of the colonial system. Norms directed against methods of neocolonialism are contained in various branches of international law (basic principles, law of treaties, law of international trade, and so forth). The further development of these kinds of principles and norms will be promoted by ensuring the economic and political independence of the developing countries and their economic and social progress.

It follows from what has been said above that the struggle for compliance with the principles and norms of international law acquires special significance under contemporary conditions.

The perfecting of specific international mechanisms (international organizations, various means for the peaceful settlement of international disputes, and others), distinct from municipal mechanisms and created by taking into account the complex character of the contemporary international situation, can be an important factor for increasing the effectiveness of international law.

The decisive prerequisite for the efficacy of international law, however, is the growth of the might, organization, and activeness of all forces of the world, State and social.

(b) *The position of bourgeois practice and doctrine on the question of changes in international law.* The concept that international law has undergone a fundamental transformation was characteristic of the international legal position of the imperialist powers immediately after the end of the Second World War. Interpreting this transformation in their own way, they maintained that international law, if it had not already, then was close to rejecting the sovereignty of States, to recognizing individuals as subjects of international law, to transforming an international organization into some likeness of a superstate, and to sanctioning broad interference in the internal affairs of States. They calculated that it would be advantageous to them to direct the development of international law in this way and, with the aid of the United Nations, to use it in the struggle against the socialist countries and the national liberation movements in the colonies.

Reality, however, cruelly deceived their expectations. The formation of the world socialist system and the rapid growth of its influence on international affairs, the disintegration of the colonial system, and the emergence of dozens of new States which, as a rule, favor peace, the growth of the international revolutionary movement of the working class, and the unfolding of the people's struggle for peace frustrated the plans of the imperialists. Their predominant position in the United Nations was undermined. The development of international law did not proceed along the path of liquidating State sovereignty and of expanding the possibilities for interference in the internal affairs of other States, as the imperialists powers supposed, but instead along the path of strengthening the principles of respect for sovereignty and noninterference in internal affairs and other important principles of international law – the introduction into international law of new progressive principles directed against aggression and colonialism and toward the strengthening of peaceful coexistence of States.

Under these conditions, the imperialist States are reconsidering, or rather already have reconsidered, their attitude toward the progressive development of international law and the evaluation of the results of its development. In striving to impede the progressive development of international law, in attempting to drag it backward, they are beginning to deny the existence of substantive changes in international law during the past decades. The old international law seems to them to be significantly more suitable for the policy "from a position of strength" than the new international law, which is aimed at strengthening peaceful coexistence.

This new orientation has been manifested very precisely, in particular, in the position of the delegations of the United States and its allies during the discussion of the question of the future work of the United Nations in the field of the codification and progressive development of international law at the Sixteenth Session of the United Nations General Assembly, as well as in many other instances (law of treaties, convention on the elimination of all forms of racial discrimination, questions of sovereignty over natural resources, and so forth). In objecting to the evaluation of the results of the development of international law after the Great October Socialist Revolution given in a speech of the Soviet Representative in the Sixth Committee of the United Nations General Assembly, the American delegate actually developed the thesis that material changes have not taken place in international law during this period and that international law remains basically as it was fifty years ago.

The delegations of the Soviet Union and other socialist countries, as well as the majority of delegations of the nonsocialist countries which are not members of aggressive military blocs of the Western powers, proceeded from the fact that important changes have taken place and are taking place in international law which should be reflected and formulated in undertaking the codification of the principles of peaceful coexistence, that is, the basic principles of international law. The imperialist powers and the participants in their aggressive blocs, relying upon the thesis advanced by the United States delegate, attempted to prevent the adoption of a draft resolution proposed by a number of socialist and neutral countries on the codification of the basic principles of peaceful coexistence. Seeing, however, that this proposal had the support of the overwhelming majority of delegations, and feeling the weakness and unpopularity of their position, the Western powers were obliged to vote for the resolution, which provides that the General Assembly at its Seventeenth Session will consider the principles of international law concerning the development of friendly relations and cooperation among States.[58]

The predominant bourgeois doctrine of international law reflects the said policy trends of the imperialist powers. It is characterized by the nonrecognition of a number of new important principles and norms which have emerged in international law during the past half-century and a denial of a material change in international law as a whole. The tendency to regard law as the sum of technical norms, the denial of the class character of law, recognition of the evolution and the denial of the revolutionary changes, and a view of the history of

[58] G. A. Res. 1686 (XVI), 18 December 1961.

law in general and of international law in particular as a single stream of development of juridical thought lead bourgeois international lawyers to recognize only more or less significant but not fundamental changes in general international law.

It is true that some bourgeois jurists believe material changes have occurred in international law and even speak of a "new international law". Naturally none of them, however, links these changes with the new epoch in the history of human society opened by the Great October Socialist Revolution. At the same time, they frequently attach exaggerated importance to secondary phenomena and frequently see material changes where such changes have not actually occurred.

A. Alvarez, the well-known Chilean international lawyer, for example, remarks in his book *Le droit international nouveau* that international law "has undergone, since the middle of the nineteenth century and especially since 1939, changes which affected not merely details but also, and especially, its substantive elements, its structure, so that at the present time it is essentially different from classical international law".[59]

The cause of change in international law Alvarez sees in the change of the living conditions of peoples, in the emergence of a "new social regime" – a "regime of interdependence".[60] The old international law, says Alvarez, rested upon an individualistic regime, when the individual was regarded as something divorced from social life. Now the individual is considered to be a part of society, that is, part of a higher organization. Society has its own personal interests; it gives birth to "general interest". Law, both national and international, must be based upon this new regime, and States must have not only those rights and duties which arise from their expression of will but also those which arise from the general interest.[61]

[59] A. Alvarez, *Le droit international nouveau dans ses rapports avec la vie actuelle des peuples* (1959), p. 409.

[60] Ibid., p. 313.

[61] Ibid., p. 314.

The "*regime of social interdependence* gives birth to a new conception of international law, a *law of social interdependence*". This "new international law", Alvarez continues, "strives not only to delimit the rights of States ..., but also, and especially, to harmonize them, taking into account the general interest".[62]

Alvarez correctly notes the intensification of the inter- dependence of States caused by the expansion and deepening of international ties and the growing influence of these processes upon international law. But the development of international ties he considers one-sidedly, without taking into account the real moving forces and contradictions. He therefore pays attention only to one facet of the influence of these ties on international law, without noting that there is reflected in international law not just the growing interdependence of States but also the inevitable struggle between them, the struggle between the socialist and capitalist States, the struggle of the new States against imperialism, and the struggle of the forces of peace and socialism as a whole against the forces of reaction.

An English jurist, C. W. Jenks, appeals for the creation of a new international law, a "common law of mankind" from the common elements of national legal systems. "We must seek to develop", he writes, "from the common elements in these legal systems [having in mind the basic national legal systems of the modern day – *G.T.*], ... which are still in process of evolution, a universal legal order which gives reasonable expression to our sense of right and justice".[63] As has been shown above, however, norms of international law are created differently than Jenks suggests.

Professor W. Friedmann, of Columbia University, suggests that "many profound changes that have affected ... international law to such an extent that it is today something

[62] Ibid., p. 606.

[63] C. W. Jenks, *The Common Law of Mankind* (1958), p. 169.

very different even from what it was a generation ago".[64] The primary difference between contemporary international law and "traditional", in Friedmann's view, lies in the fact that a new important part, which he calls "co- operative international law", has emerged. The "traditional" part of contemporary international law is predicated on the conflict of national interests, whereas "co-operative international law" requires a community of those interests.[65]

While noting correctly some new phenomena in international law, in particular the expansion of its operative sphere in connection with the emergence of new States, the emergence of new branches of international law, of principles obliging States to cooperate with each other in the interests of peace, and so forth, Friedmann, however, passes over the most important change in international law. He does not note the emergence of such important principles as the principle of the prohibition of the use of force, the principle of self- determination of peoples and nations, the principles of peaceful coexistence, the criminality of aggressive war, and responsibility of individuals for crimes against humanity.

One must agree with Friedmann when he speaks of the increasing importance in contemporary international law of the principles and norms regulating the cooperation of States in various fields. However, the division of international law into two parts, which he suggests, one of which would be based upon a conflict of interests, and the second, upon their community, does not correspond to reality. Struggle and cooperation between States in international relations and in international law, reflecting the contradiction and community of interests, exist simultaneously and mutually penetrate each other: struggle does not preclude cooperation; cooperation premeates struggle.

An American professor, Quincy Wright, also speaks of the "new international law". But he limits himself to noting the

[64] Friedmann, *The Changing Structure of International Law*, p. vi.

[65] Ibid., p. 367.

emergence in international law of such new important provisions as the prohibition of aggressive war; the principle of self-determination of peoples; the principle of respect for human rights; the legal personality of international organizations.[66]

E. Giraud, a French professor, writes that there is a "radical difference" between international law as it was before the League of Nations and contemporary international law.[67] He notes in this connection only one basic change, to wit, the emergence of the principle of the prohibition of the use of force, which "represents enormous progress on the path to creating a true international legal order".[68]

L. Henkin, an American professor, also speaks very convincingly of the enormous significance of the principle of the prohibition of the use of force in international relations: "After hundreds of years", he writes, "nations finally agreed on a legal principle against national force in order to add the influence of law as a further deterrent to war. It would be tragic if nations allowed force to descend again to the level of national political interest as each nation saw that interest".[69]

For bourgeois international legal doctrine as a whole, however, the nonrecognition of many substantive changes and of the fundamental difference of contemporary international law from that previously existing is characteristic.

The followers of "political realism" have primacy of place in this respect. Thus, Professor Hans Morgenthau, in refusing to see any substantive changes in international law, suggests that it is primitive and resembles the law which prevails in some preliterate societies, for example, the Australian aborigines or the

66 Q. Wright, *The Role of International Law in the Elimination of War* (1961), pp. 27-29.

67 E. Giraud, "L'intérdiction du recours à la force", *Revue générale de droit international public*, XXXIV (1963), 501-544.

68 Ibid., p. 511.

69 L. Henkin, "International Law and the Behaviour of Nations", *Recueil des cours*, CXIV (1965), 276.

Yurok tribe of northern California.[70] The French sociologist, R. Aron, writes that no progress has occurred in international law.[71] R. Laun, a West German professor, maintains that international law always has been recognized and is now recognized as a "right to dominate" based upon the so-called "law of the strongest".[72] Professor G. Schwarzenberger, of the University of London, the major representative of "political realism" in Western European international legal doctrine, although in his work *The Inductive Approach to International Law* he takes some steps toward recognizing material changes in international law,[73] basically retains his previous position which he formulates as follows: "In the spheres that from the point of view of power, matter most, organised post-1945 world society distinguishes itself primarily from pre-1914 international society by its wider use of two-level politics or power politics in disguise".[74] Schwarzenberger does not deny the emergence of many new important principles in international law, such as, for example, the principle of the prohibition of aggressive war, the principle of the prohibition of the use of force in international relations, and so forth, but he unjustifiably suggests that these new principles and norms are not universal, that they are not binding upon all States, and therefore they have not changed general international law, although they have narrowed the sphere of its actual application.

The majority of other bourgeois international lawyers also tend to deny, although less clearly so, the fundamental changes in international law. Thus, in the opinion of the well-known Belgian professor, C. de Visscher, the major change in

[70] H. Morgenthau, *Politics Among Nations* (3d ed.; 1962), p. 278.

[71] R. Aron, *Paix et guerre entre les nations* (3d rev. ed.; 1960), p. 278.

[72] R. Laun, "Le droit des peuples à disposer d'eux-memes", *Annuaire des Anciens Auditeurs de l'Academie de droit international de la Haye*, XXVIII (1958), 99.

[73] Schwarzenberger, *The Inductive Approach to International Law*, p. 185;; Schwarzenberger, *International Law and Order* (1971), p. 19.

[74] Schwarzenberger, *The Inductive Approach to International Law*, p. 188.

international law lies in the fact that the United Nations Charter attaches great importance to respect for human rights, which, in his view, are the basis of the "international order".[75] But at the same time, de Visscher notes that the "human rights so frequently mentioned in the United Nations Charter, have a place there which is at once eminent and ill-defined".[76] De Visscher does not attach great importance to the emergence in international law of such an important principle as the principle of the prohibition of the use of force,[77] and he decisively rejects the existence of the principle of self-determination of peoples.[78]

The most authoritative bourgeois treatises which have appeared in recent years, the authors of which are proponents of various orientations in bourgeois international legal doctrine, go in the same direction. In them, as has been previously mentioned in part, we sometimes find a general denial of any basic changes in international law, more frequently a recognition of only some of them, but never do we see an evaluation of contemporary international law as a qualitatively new international law.

Thus, Professor A. Verdross regards the principle of self-determination of peoples as one of the important principles of contemporary international law,[79] and he notes the importance of the principle of the prohibition of aggressive war, although he suggests that reprisals with the use of armed force are permitted by general international law.[80] The emergence of a new international law, however, he sees in the "law of an organized international society", which in general

[75] Visscher, *Théories et réalites en droit international public*, pp. 158-162.

[76] Ibid., p. 162.

[77] Ibid., p. 359.

[78] Ibid., p. 166.

[79] Verdross, *Völkerrecht* (5th ed.; 1964), p. 576.

[80] Ibid., p. 426.

Verdross considers to be different from contemporary general international law.[81]

P. Reuter, a French professor, sees the primary change in international law in the emergence of certain features of international society based upon a community of interests. From the viewpoint of the structure of international society, the basic element, in Reuter's view, lies in the development of international organization, in consequence of which "the latter has been transformed from an unorganized international society into a partially organized one".[82] In emphasizing, however, that the organization of international society is of an "exceedingly superficial character", Reuter comes to the conclusion that in general, despite certain changes, the fundamentals of international law as a whole remain as before.[83]

There is nothing in the treatise of the Italian professor, R. Quadri, about new principles of international law. Quadri denies the existence of the principle of the prohibition of the use of force in contemporary international law. Believing that the principles of the United Nations Charter are provisions of a "special legal order", he maintains that "the right of a State to wage war" is a norm of general international law at the present time.[84]

In his "General Course on Public International Law", an English professor, H. Waldock, while recognizing that significant changes have taken place in international law, among which he includes the prohibition of aggressive war, a partial prohibition of the use of force in general, as well as the international responsibility of individuals for crimes against

[81] Ibid., p. 661.

[82] P. Reuter, "Principes de droit international public", *Recueil des cours*, CIII (1961), 457.

[83] Ibid., pp. 457-458.

[84] R. Quadri, *Diritto internazionale publico* (4th ed.; 1963), p. 23; see also R. Monaco, *Manuale di diritto internazionale publico* (1960), pp. 414-425; A. Sereni, *Diritto internazionale* (1956), I, 68.

humanity,[85] at the same time passes over the other important new principles of international law in silence.

We find virtually a complete denial of substantive changes in international law in the three-volume treatise of the Argentine professor, L. M. Moreno Quintana. He speaks, for example, of the 1928 Pact of Paris, in which the parties renounced resort to war for the settlement of international disputes, but he does not mention at all the fact that this international treaty was an important landmark in formulating the very important generally-recognized principle of international law prohibiting aggressive war. Moreno Quintana only notes pessimistically that the "absence of sanctions for those who violate this pact deprived the document of any effectiveness". He denies the existence in contemporary international law of norms providing for the criminal responsibility of individuals for crimes against humanity, calling the Nuremberg and Tokyo trials of the major war criminals precedents "deserving regret".[86]

A Peruvian professor, A. Ulloa, although he notes the im- portance of the United Nations Charter and other international treaties for the progressive development of international law in his two-volume treatise on international law,[87] believes at the same time that its basic principles have not changed. "The basic principles of international law", he says, "survived the war".[88] Ulloa in essence denies the existence of the principle of the prohibition of the use of force in contemporary international law.[89] He recognizes the existence of the principle of self-determination of peoples and emphasizes

85 H. Waldock, "General Course on Public International Law", *Recueil des cours*, CVI (1962), 236-237.

86 L. M. Moreno Quintana, *Tratado de derecho internacional* (1963), II, 401.

87 A. Ulloa, *Derecho internacional publico* (4th ed.; 1957), I, 82.

88 Ibid., p. 79.

89 Ibid., pp. 283-284.

its significance, but he sees nothing new in comparison with the "principle of nationality".[90]

A West German professor, F. Berber, recognizes that the prohibition of the use of force in relations between States is not an actual generally-recognized norm of international law.[91] He emphasizes that the emergence of the principle of aggressive war as a result of the conclusion of the Briand-Kellogg Pact was a genuine "revolution" in international law.[92]

At the same time, Berber resolutely refuses to recognize the existence in international law of the responsibility of individuals for crimes against peace and, to a certain extent, for crimes against humanity. He maintains that the Nuremberg International Military Tribunal could judge the Nazi leaders only for war crimes and partially for crimes against humanity, but he denies the legality of the provisions of the Statute and the Judgment of the Tribunal with respect to crimes against peace".[93] This type of crime, Berber declares, "international law did not know before 1945 and does not know at the present time".[94] Berber goes farther, asserting that if the principle of responsibility for crimes against peace had become a norm of general international law, then "this was not a step forward in international law" and "was not a constructive contribution to the cause of averting war" supposedly because the rulers of every belligerent State would play to win the war in order to avoid being put in the dock, and this would only lead to a prolongation of wars.[95]

[90] Ibid., pp. 130-152.

[91] F. Berber, *Lehrbuch des Völkerrechts* (1962), II, 38.

[92] Ibid., p. 36.

[93] Ibid., pp. 254-257.

[94] Ibid., p. 257.

[95] Ibid., pp. 262-263.

Berber denies the existence in contemporary international law of the principle of the self-determination of peoples, as well as the emergence of other new important principles.[96]

The general conclusion is that, despite the existence of certain progressive tendencies, bourgeois international legal science as a whole has lagged behind the development of events and does not reflect many substantive changes which have taken place and are taking place in international law during recent decades, not to mention the fact that it does not notice the profound transformation of the general character and essence of international law.

4. The Question of an "Intermediate Status" Between War and Peace

The numerous conflicts created by imperialists in various parts of the globe (the Anglo-French-Israeli aggression against Egypt in 1956, the American aggression in Vietnam, which already has lasted several years, Israeli aggression against the Arab States, and so forth), as well as the tense state of international relations conditioned by the policy "from a position of strength", the arms race, and the creation of military blocs and military bases directed against the socialist and other peace-loving States, have served as the basis for proposals to reform contemporary international law by introducing into it a third, so-called "intermediate status" between peace and war.

Professor P. Jessup, having set forth the concept of an "intermediate status" in greatest detail, defines its basic features as follows:[97]

Hostility and strain exist in relations among States. Recalling the practice of the Turkish Empire prior to the middle of the eighteenth century not to make treaties of peace with Christian

[96] Ibid., I, 75ff.

[97] P. Jessup, "Should International Law Recognize an Intermediate Status between Peace and War", *American Journal of International Law*, XLVIII (1954), 100-102.

States, but only armistices because the Koran forbade peace treaties with infidels, Jessup suggests this practice is one of the elements of the "intermediate status";

The issues between the parties are so fundamental and deep-rooted that no solution of a single question could terminate them;

At the same time the parties have no intention or, at least, decision to resort to war in order to solve the disputed questions.

Jessup proposes to legitimize this state, inserting it between "peace" and "war". He says in this connection that international law should not be divorced from reality and that it should be brought into conformity with the real international situation.

First, what status does it have under prevailing international law? The answer to this question must be definite and categorical: contemporary international law knows no "intermediate status".

International tension is not a normal state from the standpoint of international law. The "cold war" policy which caused this condition contravenes international law and is linked to serious violations of it. This policy creates no juridical status whatever that could be sanctioned by contemporary international law.[98]

Somewhat distinct from the concept of an "intermediate status" but close to it is the concept of a "status mixtus". Proponents of this concept maintain that there is no precise delimitation between peace and war and that an "intermediate" or "mixed" status exists which is characterized by the fact that one observes the use of armed force by some States against others side by side with peaceful relations.

An English professor, G. Schwarzenberger, wrote during the Second World War that international practice supposedly created

[98] Professor Verdross says that it is impossible to prove the existence of special legal norms corresponding to "cold war". See Verdross, Международное право [International Law], pp. 111-112.

legal norms which related neither to the law of peace nor the law of war, but represent a *status mixtus*. "The doctrine of war as a status and objective phenomenon", he says, "breaks down over the reality of the *status mixtus*. This status is not separated from those of peace and war by any objective tests. States contend by power in peace and war. In the state of peace, they are limited to the use of economic and political power. In the *status mixtus*, they supplement these forms of power by the use of military power. In the state of war, they use all available forms of power. It betrays an over-estimation of the difference between political and economic power as compared with military power, to imagine that, within a system of power politics, there is any qualitative difference between the states of peace and war".[99]

In his review of the French edition of *Вопросы теории международного права*,[100] Professor Schwarzenberger insists that in his 1943 article and at the present time he had and has in view the "lack of any objective distinction between states of peace and war in an *unorganized* international society, *i.e.*, primarily under international customary law", and that the situation has changed "in contemporary international law under the Charter of the United Nations ...".[101]

One can only welcome this remark of Professor Schwarzenberger. If, however, his position on this question were to be wholly clear, one must bear in mind that according to Schwarzenberger's theory, two international laws exist at the present time: general, or universal, international law, which is customary law, and the law of the United Nations, which is not general international law. It is true that in his recent works Schwarzenberger calls the principles of the United Nations Charter "near-universal" law.[102]

[99] Schwarzenberger, "Jus pacis ac belli?", *American Journal of International Law*, XXXVII (1943), 474.

[100] Tunkin, *Droit international public: problèmes théoriques* (1965).

[101] *Yearbook of World Affairs*, XX (1966), 293.

[102] See Schwarzenberger, *The Inductive Approach to International Law*, p. 112.

But general international law continues to exist side by side with the principles of the United Nations Charter according to Schwarzenberger's theory, and all the changes which have occurred in international law during the past fifty years have not affected it; the "right of a State to wage war", the "right of the victor", "de bellatio", and so forth, exist in it as formerly.[103]

An Argentine professor, L. M. Quintana, in identifying himself with Schwarzenberger's concept as regards the "status mixtus", suggests for his part that it should be called a neutral state (*estado neutro*) in which "there is neither war nor peace" (*no hay ni guerra ni paz*).[104]

Schwarzenberger's assertion that there is no precise boundary between peace and war under international law could find some basis in international law before the Great October Socialist Revolution, which recognized the "right of a State to wage war". The old international law permitted not only war, but also armed reprisals and the so-called pacific blockade, which were not regarded as war.

Even after the prohibition of aggressive war pursuant to the 1928 Pact, there remained the loophole of justifying war by pretending it was something else, to which the imperialist powers frequently also resorted. It is well-known that the colonizers preferred to call the wars they wages for the purpose of enslaving colonial peoples "police actions", "reprisals", "armed conflict", and so forth, and thereby to show that such actions do not fall within the effect of the Pact of Paris.

The situation changed with the adoption of the United Nations Charter, which prohibits not only aggressive war, but also the use or threat of force against the territorial integrity and political independence of any State or by any other means inconsistent with the purposes of the United Nations. As already

[103] Schwarzenberger, *International Law as Applied by International Courts and Tribunals: The Law of Armed Conflict* (1968), II, 54, 63.

[104] L. M. Moreno Quintana, "El Tercer Estado del derecho intrnacional", *Bibliotheca Grotiana* (1954), II, 39.

has been pointed out, these norms at the present time are norms of general international law. The use of force contravening the provisions of the United Nations Charter is not only a violation of the Charter, but also of general international law.

One must agree with Professor Lachs, who writes: "International law does not know nor recognize any intermediate status between war and peace. The precise delimitation of these two institutes was recognized long ago, when war still was a legal means of settling international conflicts. The emergence of this dividing line is justified even more at the present time, when aggressive war has been prohibited, when this line must represent the border between law and no law. The obliteration of this border not only is without legal justification, but it plays into the hands of those for whom the prohibition of an annexationist war is politically disadvantageous".[105]

There is still the third variant of the theory of the "intermediate status" advanced by an American professor, M. S. McDougal. McDougal believes that there exists in international law not one "intermediate status", but a countless number of such states. "Between the polar extremes, that is, between the lowest and the highest level of coercion", he says, "there exist not one intermediate stage, but a countless number of stages, and in using the concept `war' and `peace' and other concepts the decision-maker has not two or three, but a large number of positions to which he may refer".[106]

It is correct, of course, that norms of international law juridically tolerate various concrete situations within certain limits. As any legal norms, they presuppose a certain possibility of freedom of action within the limits of these norms. But the diversity of concrete relations between States by no means

105 M. Lachs, Женевские соглашения 1954 года об Индо-Китае [Geneva Agreements of 1954 on Indo-China] (1955), p. 180.

106 M. S. McDougal, "Peace and War: Factual Continuum with Multiple Legal Consequences", *American Journal of International Law*, XLIX (1955), 67.

signifies that every such specific legal state is reflected in general international law as some special status.

McDougal's assertion that there are a countless number of intermediate stages between peace and war among which there is no precise boundary does not correspond to contemporary international law.

We now consider the suggestion of an "intermediate status" *de lege feranda*. It follows from the aforecited statements of Jessup that he only is suggesting that an "intermediate status" be established, and he does not maintain that it is provided for by prevailing international law.

International law, of course, can not be divorced from reality, but this in no way means that it must juridically legitimize any practice of particular States in international relations. That is why it is important to explain toward what practice the proposal of an "intermediate status" is oriented, perhaps, besides, irrespective of the subjective wishes and intentions of the authors and advocates of this proposal.

The proposal to introduce an "intermediate status" into international law is aimed essentially at legitimizing the tension in international relations, the distrust among States which has existed since the Second World War, and to legitimize the policy "from a position of strength", the state of "cold war", and even (in its extreme variants) armed aggression.

It is possible that some proponents of the "intermediate status" sincerely believe in the advisability of introducing this new juridical state into international law because it is much better than war. But the state of international tension is fraught with events which could lead to war. "In addition to the moral necessity of peace", stated the Prime Minister of India, Nehru, at the 1960 session of the United Nations General Assembly, "every practical consideration also leads us to this conclusion because, as everyone knows, one must make a choice now, in our atomic age, between the complete destruction and perishing of civilization, on one hand, or some form of peaceful coexistence between countries, on the other. There is no middle path".[107]

The initiators and organizers of the "cold war" themselves have pointed to the danger. The former United States Secretary of State, John Foster Dulles, said: "There is today what is called a 'cold' war. There is a struggle going on which is worldwide in scope. The danger constantly exists that that struggle could break from the so-called cold war into a hot war".[108]

The sanctioning of an "intermediate status" by international law would mean a step backward in the development of international law. It would be essentially substituting a state of "cold war", a state which also would legalize many instances of armed aggression, for peaceful coexistence.

The proposal to introduce an "intermediate status" does not correspond to the societal laws of the development of contemporary international law. Under the influence of the growing forces of peace and progress, international law has a tendency to move forward, and not backward; it is becoming a more and more improved and effective means of developing and strengthening peaceful coexistence.

107 "За мирное сотрудничество всех стран" [For Peaceful Cooperation of All Countries], Правда [Pravda], 6 October 1960, p. 3.

108 J. F. Dulles, "Tasks and Responsibilities of the Foreign Service", *Department of State Bulletin*, XXXIV (1956), 588.

PART IV.
INTERNATIONAL LAW, FOREIGN POLICY, AND DIPLOMACY

The co-relationship of international law, foreign policy, and diplomacy has three aspects: the influence of foreign policy upon the development of international law; the converse influence of international law upon the foreign policy of a State; and the use of international law by States as a support for foreign policy.

CHAPTER X. THE INFLUENCE OF FOREIGN POLICY AND DIPLOMACY UPON THE DEVELOPMENT OF INTERNATIONAL LAW

Norms of international law are created in the process of relations among States as a result of a clearly expressed or tacit agreement among them. In this process each State defends specific principles and has its own international legal position, which may coincide with or be different from the positions of other States. The position of a State on questions of international law is a part of its foreign policy position. Norms of international law regulate relations between States and affect the interests of a State, so it is natural that the international legal position of each State is derived from those principles upon which the foreign policy of the particular State is based in general and pursues the same goals as the foreign policy as a whole.

In the process of creating new or of changing prevailing norms of international law, each State strives to have the principles of its foreign policy reflected and secured as fully as possible in norms of international law. That is to say, each State strives to have its position reflected as fully as possible in norms of international law which are in the course of being elaborated.

Although not the only means, diplomacy is the most important means of effectuating foreign policy. It may be defined as activity (including the content, modes, and methods of the activity of general and special State agencies of foreign relations) of heads of States, of governments, of departments of foreign affairs, of special delegations and missions, and of diplomatic representations appertaining to the effectuation by peaceful means of the purposes and tasks of the foreign policy of a State.[1]

One would not err in saying that diplomacy plays the primary role in the process of creating norms of international law.

[1] See D. B. Levin, Дипломатия [Diplomacy] (1962), pp. 14-15.

This proposition applies to the formation of international legal norms by either conventional or customary means.

The process of forming norms of international law by means of treaty, irrespective of what questions a specific treaty touches upon, is essentially and on the whole a diplomatic process. It commences with negotiations between States, discussions at conferences and in organs of international organizations, and so forth. In the broadest sense of the word, all of this is negotiation, although in each instance the form may be different. This initial stage of the process of concluding an international treaty is the most important and decisive. The content and form of agreements between States are formed precisely at this stage; that is to say, a concordance of the wills of States occurs with regard to the normative content of the treaty.

Negotiations concerning the conclusion of an international treaty, as well as those appertaining to other questions, in whatever form they are conducted, themselves represent the diplomatic process. They occupy such a large place in diplomacy that the latter frequently is defined narrowly as "the art of conducting negotiations and concluding treaties between States".[2]

W. Garden wrote in his voluminous treatise on diplomacy that: "Diplomacy in the broadest sense of the word is the science or the art of negotiations".[3] "Diplomacy", says C. Calvo, "is the science concerning the relations which exist between various States ..." or "simply the art of negotiations".[4] In his well-known book *Diplomacy*,

H. Nicholson takes as the point of departure for his investigation of questions of diplomacy the definition given

[2] Большая Советская Энциклопедия [Great Soviet Encyclopedia] (2d ed.; 1949-58), XIV, 405.

[3] [W. Garden], *Traité complet de diplomatie, our théorie générale des relations exterieures des puissances de l'Europe* (1833), I, 1-2.

[4] C. Calvo, *Dictionnaire de droit international public et privé* (1885), I, 250.

in the *Oxford Dictionary of the English Language,* which says: "Diplomacy – the conduct of international relations by means of negotiations; a method with whose aid these relations are regulated and conducted by ambassadors and envoys; the work or art of a diplomat".[5]

The positions of different States, their wills, are brought into concordance, usually by means of mutual concessions, precisely during the course of negotiations concerning the conclusion of an international treaty and in the process of diplomatic activity connected with such negotiations. These concordant wills are reflected in the norms of the international treaty.

The subsequent stages of the process of concluding an international treaty (signature, ratification, exchange or deposit of instruments of ratification, and others) also are linked to a significant degree with diplomatic activity.

Customary norms of international law grow out of the practice of relations between States and of the foreign policy actions of States. Since diplomacy occupies the primary place in the foreign policy activity of a State, it is natural that customary norms of international law are formed to a significant extent in the process of diplomatic activity.

The role of foreign policy and diplomacy is even more significant in the final stage of the process of creating a customary norm of international law. Recognition by States of existing practice as a norm of international law occurs, as a rule, by means of conclusive actions and, consequently, first and foremost of foreign policy, especially diplomatic, actions.

At the same time, it must be noted that diplomacy is not the only means of the foreign policy of States. At present, the framework of relations between States has been expanded significantly in comparison with the nineteenth and beginning of the twentieth centuries. These relations embrace such new domains as scientific and technical cooperation, and

[5] H. Nicholson, Дипломатия [Diiplomacy] (1941), p. 20.

so forth.[6] But if the domain of foreign policy and the domain of diplomacy previously coincided during peacetime, foreign policy now includes many questions which go beyond the bounds of diplomacy.

The extent to which the foreign policy and diplomacy of a specific State influence the development of international law depends upon a number of circumstances.

Norms of international law formed in the process of the struggle and cooperation of States are the result of a clash of different foreign policy aspirations, of the clash and the concordance of the wills of different States. Sovereign States are involved in the process of forming norms. The wills of States which clash during the creation of norms of international law juridically are of equal significance. But, of course, the actual influence of such wills is not identical.

The actual situation is such that in international relations in general and in the creation of norms of international law in particular the great powers play a special role. On the juridical plane, the principles of respect for State sovereignty and of the equality of States, which are an important means of defending the independence of weak States from the encroachments of strong powers, ensure at the same time a special role for the great powers in the process of creating norms of international law.

A new international legal norm may not, by virtue of the sovereign equality of States, be imposed upon any one State. Consequently, it also may not be imposed upon a great power. Therefore norms which are not recognized by the great powers, or even some of the great powers, would not bind them. This means that the sphere of operation of such norms would be so limited that one could not say such norms had real importance. This circumstance has special significance in those instances when one speaks of norms relating directly to the maintenance of international peace and security, since

6 For greater detail, see Levin, Дипломатия [Diplomacy], p. 26ff.

the real means of ensuring peace and, at the same time, the instruments of war, are first and foremost in the hands of the great powers. Therefore, practice frequently takes the course of a preliminary agreement on questions among the great powers, since the absence of agreement among them renders useless, and sometimes even harmful, the adoption of decisions concerning international problems of a general order.

The influence of a State's foreign policy and diplomacy upon the development of international law depends primarily upon the character of foreign policy and diplomacy and the character of international legal principles which this State adduces and advocates.

The general line of the development of international law is determined by the laws of societal development. A State which advances international legal principles not corresponding to these laws of societal development and, consequently, to a general line of international legal development which is inconsistent with the expectations of peoples, can not be expected to exert substantial influence upon the development of international law.

In carrying out the policy "from a position of strength", imperialist powers, for example, attempt to prove that the use of force by one State against another is admissible under contemporary international law at least "to protect the life and property of its citizens",[7] or under other pretexts. The purpose is to justify the acts of aggression which are committed systematically by imperialist States even after the adoption of the United Nations Charter. However, there exists in contemporary international law a generally-recognized principle which prohibits the use of force and even the threat of force by a State against the territorial integrity and political inviolability of another State or by any means incompatible with

[7] Thus, for example, the United States Government referred to the need to "protect the lives of American citizens" in order to justify armed intervention in the Dominican Republic in 1965. See R.-J. Dupuy, "Les États Unis, l'O.E.A. et l'O.N.U. a Saint-Domingue", *Annuaire français de droit international*, XI (1965), 75-76.

the purposes of the United Nations. Undoubtedly, such efforts to justify aggression and to drag international law backward are doomed to failure.

Other examples of such reactionary tendencies are the support for colonialism by proponents of the policy "from a position of strength", the attempts to deny the principle of self-determination of peoples as a principle of contemporary international law, as well as efforts to transform this principle into an empty shell. But life condemns to failure the foreign policy and diplomacy of States which support such tendencies. Despite their vain attempts, the principle of self-determination of peoples is being strengthened and implemented.

The policy "from a position of strength" also has sustained a defeat in many other areas of international law. Thus, at the First Conference on the Law of the Sea in 1958 proponents of this policy failed in their efforts to impose a three-mile breadth of territorial waters on other States as a norm of international law. At the Second Conference on the Law of the Sea in 1960, even though the United States used every means of pressure to their fullest upon the small States, the proponents of the policy "from a position of strength" again failed to effectuate their proposal, this time for a six-mile breadth of territorial waters.

The policy of imposing norms of international law with the aid of economic and political pressure, threats, and bribery are an integral part of the policy "from a position of strength" and suffer one failure after another.

CHAPTER XI.
THE INFLUENCE OF INTERNATIONAL LAW ON FOREIGN POLICY AND DIPLOMACY

International law, just as national law, influences the social relations which it regulates. This authority is effectuated by means of normative influence upon the conduct of subjects of international law.

The principles and norms of international law determine the rights and duties of States and of other subjects of international law. Hence, there are two types of links among foreign policy, diplomacy, and international law: (a) as concerns the obligations of States, international law acts as a limitation with regard to foreign policy and diplomacy; (b) as concerns rights, it, on the contrary, acts as a means of or support for foreign policy and diplomacy.[1]

It must be mentioned, however, that this contrast is not absolute. There is an element of limitation not only in a legal duty, but also in a subjective right, since every right is a limited right.

The general character of the influence of international law on relations between States and, consequently, on the foreign policy of individual States and their diplomacy, is determined by the character of a given specific international law which, as any law, may promote or impede the progressive development of society. Of course, law, including international law, can not stop the process of societal development, and if law sharply contravenes the laws of societal development, it inevitably yields to these objective laws. Then new norms come to replace the obsolete norms.

Contemporary international law is the law of peaceful coexistence and of the free development of peoples. The

[1] Professor M. Virally expressed this proposition vividly in the following words: "Depending upon what it is used for [law – *G.T.*], a subject of law sees the system of law either as directed against it or as being at its service". M. Virally, "Le phénomene juridique", *Revue du droit public et de la science politique en France et à l'étranger*, LXXXII (1966), 11.

character of the influence of contemporary international law on the international relations, foreign policy, and diplomacy of States for the purpose of ensuring the peaceful coexistence and freedom of peoples is also determined by this.

How effective is the influence of international law on the foreign policy and diplomacy of States?

We already have considered the theory that contemporary international law is "ineffectual" and "primitive", and "true" international law will be possible only if a world State, or something closely approximating this, is created (see Chapter IX). An exaggeration of the role of compulsory jurisdiction, which frequently is portrayed as a panacea for all international ills, in particular has been linked with this conception.[2]

The possibility of applying State coercion in order to ensure compliance with norms is one of the important distinctive features of law, including international law. It is common knowledge, however, that coercion in international law, by virtue of the peculiarities of this law, is less effective than coercion in national law. But it should be borne in mind that the real influence of a legal norm on the conduct of subjects of law is not determined only by the possibility of coercion.

As regards the influence of international law on the foreign policy of States, it also depends to a significant degree upon the moral authority of norms of international law, this being determined primarily by the extent to which such norms correspond to the innermost desire of the peoples to ensure peace.

In general, the effectiveness of the influence of contemporary international law on the foreign policy of States is determined by the co-relation of the forces of peace and war in the international arena. Since international law as a whole aims to ensure peace and peaceful coexistence, the forces which are

[2] See G. I. Tunkin, Идеологическая борьба и международное право [Ideological Struggle and International Law] (1967), pp. 158-166.

supporting peace are, at the same time, the forces supporting international law. Therefore, the effectiveness of the influence of international law upon the conduct of subjects of law depends primarily upon the might and the activeness of all the forces of peace.

In this respect it is very important to have definite criteria which would show the real attitude of a State toward international law in order to have a more accurate idea of the positions of States on this question. The co-relation between the principles of a State's foreign policy and the principles of contemporary international law is such a criterion.

The foreign policy of a State is connected closely with its domestic policy, as though it were a continuation thereof. The general foreign policy line of a State is determined primarily by the bases of its social system, of the class nature of the State. "The nature of a socialist system", writes Academician V. M. Khvostov, "is the opposite of the nature of capitalism. Hence the contrast of the foreign policy of socialism with the policy of imperialism; hence, also the struggle of the two lines in international politics which has been waged in the world arena already for half a century".[3] At the same time, a State formulates its foreign policy by taking into account the changing domestic and international situation.

From the viewpoint of foreign policy, all States of the world may be broken down at the present time into three groups: (1) socialist States; (2) States which are participants in the military blocs of the Western powers; (3) new States which arose from the ruins of the colonial system. What is the co-relation of the principles of foreign policy of States from each group with the principles of contemporary international law?

Contemporary general international law aims at ensuring the peaceful coexistence of all States, primarily the States

[3] V. Khvostov, "Советская внешняя политика и ее воздействие на ход истории" [Soviet Foreign Policy and Its Impact on the Course of History], Коммунист [Communist], no. 10 (1967), p. 81.

of two opposed social systems, and at ensuring the free development of peoples.

The struggle for the peaceful coexistence of States with different social systems and the struggle for the freedom and independence of peoples are immutable characteristics of the foreign policy of the Soviet State as a genuinely socialist foreign policy. The same applies to the foreign policy of other States of the socialist commonwealth.

In accordance with the policy of peaceful coexistence which the socialist States are pursuing, they consistently favor compliance with the principles and norms of international law. This policy has been affirmed in numerous bilateral and multilateral documents, in practical proposals which the socialist States have made in international organizations and at conferences, and in all of the international actions of these States.

Thus, there are no contradictions between the principles of foreign policy of the socialist States and contemporary international law. The tendency to violate international law is not, therefore, characteristic of the foreign policy of socialist States. On the contrary, States of the socialist camp act as a basic bulwark of contemporary international law.

The new States which have emerged as a result of the liberation of colonies are confronted with enormous problems of developing their economy, of raising the living standard and culture of their peoples, and of strengthening their political and economic independence. Therefore, those new States which are in a position to pursue an independent foreign policy orient it toward peaceful coexistence, the struggle against colonialism and neocolonialism, and the development of equal, mutually advantageous international economic and cultural relations.

Consequently, there also is in this case no contradiction between the foreign policy orientation of States and the principles of contemporary international law. Of course, we have in mind prevailing international law and not the law of the past or the so-called "classical" international law against which certain representatives of the developing countries aim their arrows, mistakenly accepting, under the influence of Western international legal doctrine, this "classical" international law for prevailing international law.

The policy pursued at the present time by a group of countries which includes the imperialist powers and their allies in aggressive military blocs is known as the policy "from a position of strength". This policy relies upon force, upon armed force; the arms race, the organization of aggressive military blocs and military bases, war propaganda, and the maintenance of international tension are an integral part of it. Being screened by preposterous references to a military threat on the part of the Soviet Union, it in fact expressly reflects the interests of the largest monopolies which make a fortune on the arms race and are prepared to use armed force in order to maintain their domination both within their own States and in other countries.

Reliance upon the use and threat of force as an instrument of foreign policy contravenes the fundamental principles of contemporary international law. Therefore, the policy "from a position of strength" and "cold war" diplomacy contain a constant tendency to violate international law and the desire to move international law to the side.[4]

As the most recent examples of the manifestation of this tendency, one may cite the aggression of England, France, and Israel against Egypt in 1956, the United States' intervention in Lebanon and Jordan in 1958, Belgian aggression in the Congo, United States' intervention against Cuba in 1961, interference of the United States in the internal affairs of Laos, armed

[4] Hans J. Morgenthau writes: "... rarely has history witnesses a more relentless drive toward expansion, more oblivious of risks, and more ruthless in brushing obstacles aside than that of the United States. The Westward expansion of the U.S. would have been impossible without the violation of the treaties guaranteeing the Indians their land. And thus, those treaties had to be broken ... When ... economic, military or political pressure was not sufficient, we did not hesitate to go to war". H. J. Morgenthau, reviewing D. Perkins, *The American Approach to Foreign Policy*, in *The New Republic*, 19 May 1952, p. 20.

intervention of the United States in the Dominican Republic in 1965, Israeli aggression against the Arab States in 1967, and especially the war of the United States against the Vietnamese people.

The contradiction between the foreign policy of imperialist States and international law reflects the contradictions between the aggressive essence of imperialism and the limited possibilities of effectuating imperialist plans.[5] This contradiction between the policy of imperialist States and international law now is being crystallized in the course of forming norms of international law. In contemporary conditions, when the international legal principles adduced in the process of forming norms by States that support the policy of peaceful coexistence enjoy the powerful support of peoples, imperialist States frequently conceal their true objectives and, in a number of instances regarding the acceptance of new democratic provisions of international law, go beyond that which corresponds to the real principles of their foreign policy. In so doing imperialist governments usually believe that they will manage to get around these norms and to distort their intent by way of interpretation, and so forth.

The so-called realist orientation in the theory of diplomacy and international law is a reflection of the policy "from a position of strength" and "cold war" and of attempts theoretically to justify it which, however, unwittingly reveal the contradiction between this policy and international law. This orientation has been rather broadly propagated in the United States, and its echoes also are noticeable in certain other countries.

The essence of the "realist" orientation consists of the following: international relations are relations of power. Events occurring in international relations are "power processes". An aspiration to dominate is a characteristic feature of international relations. The realist approach to

[5] See A. Sovetov, "Особенности современного международного развития" [Peculiarities of Contemporary International Development], Международная жизнь [International Life], no. 11 (1960), p. 16.

foreign policy means that one must achieve one's objectives in foreign policy by any means, without taking into account principles of law and morality.

One of the most zealous proponents of this conception is an American professor, Hans J. Morgenthau, who in criticizing the "legalistic approach" to problems of international politics actually calls upon diplomacy to put international law aside and to be guided in its actions only by the co-relation of power.

The societal laws of the development of international relations Morgenthau attributes to human nature. "Political realism", he writes, "believes that politics, like society in general, is governed by objective laws that have their roots in human nature".[6] "International politics", says Morgenthau, "like all politics, is a struggle for power".[7] The "aspiration for power", he continues, "being the distinguishing element of international politics, as of all politics, international politics is of necessity power politics".[8]

The aspiration to dominate which supposedly arises out of human nature is declared to be a societal law of international relations since it is a peculiarity, Morgenthau maintains, of any human association. "The tendency to dominate", Morgenthau writes, "in particular, is an element of all human associations, from the family through fraternal and professional associations and local political organizations, to the State".[9]

Although Morgenthau defines "power" in sufficiently vague terms as "man's control over the minds and actions of other men",[10] in fact the idea that the armed strength of States is the power which must be taken into account in international relations runs throughout the author's entire discussion.

[6] Hans J. Morgenthau, *Politics Among Nations* (3d ed.; 1960), p. 4.

[7] Ibid., p. 27.

[8] Ibid., p. 31.

[9] Ibid., p. 34.

[10] Ibid., p. 29.

In asserting that international law is a primitive law resembling the law that exists in certain preliterate societies, such as the Australian aborigines and the Yurok of Northern California, Morgenthau comes to deny the regulatory role of international law.[11]

In Morgenthau's view, the task of diplomacy is fourfold. Diplomacy must: (1) determine its objectives in the light of the power actually and potentially available for the pursuit of these objectives; (2) assess the objectives of other States and the power actually and potentially available for the pursuit of these objectives; (3) determine to what extent these different objectives are compatible with each other; (4) employ the means suited to the pursuit of its objectives.[12] What means may diplomacy employ? "The means at the disposal of diplomacy", says Morgenthau, "are three: persuasion, compromise, and threat of force".[13]

Thus, according to Morgenthau, diplomacy must take only power into account; international law has no place in his theory. We also note that the "threat of force", which Morgenthau regards as one of the means of diplomacy, is prohibited by contemporary international law (Article 2(4), United Nations Charter).

Reality notwithstanding, Morgenthau maintains that diplomacy suffers defeat supposedly because it attaches too great a significance to the legal aspect of international events. "The old diplomacy has failed", he writes, "it is true, but so has the new one. The new diplomacy has failed and was bound to fail, for its legalistic tools have no access to political problems to be solved".[14]

The former Minister of External Affairs and then Prime Minister of Canada, Lester Pearson, advocates an analogous

[11] Ibid., p. 278. See also Morgenthau, *In Defense of the National Interest* (1951), p. 136.

[12] Morgenthau, *Politics Among Nations*, pp. 539-540.

[13] Ibid., p. 541.

[14] Morgenthau, *Politics in the Twentieth Century* (1962), I, 358.

theory in his book *Diplomacy in the Nuclear Age*. In glorifying power politics, he does not leave a place for international law in international relations or in diplomacy. He appeals for the "collection and use of force" as a backing for diplomacy.[15] Pearson maintains that in the nuclear age "our immediate and temporary protection from these grim consequences of our own genius requires the possession of overwhelming, destructive power".[16] At the same time, Pearson is compelled to recognize that this concept operates in a vicious circle because an attempt to obtain overwhelming supremacy in armaments gives birth to an arms race, and the ending can not be a happy one.[17]

The eminent propagandist of the "policy of strength", George Kennan, the former United States ambassador to the USSR, in criticizing a "legalistic" and "moralistic" approach to international problems, lays bare completely the contradiction between this policy and international law. He asserts that international law not only is ill- suited as a means of regulating international problems, but that even attempts to use it for such purposes are harmful; he calls international law a "legal straitjacket", while recognizing that it inhibits effectuation of the "policy of strength". "The national State pattern," he says, "is not, should not be, ... a ... static thing. By nature, it is an unstable phenomenon in a constant state of change and flux. History has shown that the will and the capacity of individual peoples to contribute to their world environment is constantly changing. It is only logical that the organizational forms (and what else are such things as borders and governments?) should change with them. The function of a system of international relationships is not to inhibit this process of change by imposing a legal straitjacket upon it but rather to facilitate it; to ease its transitions, to temper the asperities to which it often leads, to isolate and moderate the conflicts to which it gives rise, and to see that these conflicts do not assume forms too unsettling

15 L. B. Pearson, *Diplomacy in the Nuclear Age* (1959), pp. 63-65.

16 Ibid.

17 Ibid., p. 65.

for international life in general. But this is a task of diplomacy, in the most old-fashioned sense of the term. For this, law is too abstract, too inflexible, too hard to adjust to the demands of the unpredictable and the unexpected".[18]

And thus the slogan: international law is unsuitable as a means of regulating international problems; it even impedes their regulation. Hail diplomacy without international law![19]

The majority of American international lawyers nonetheless do not accept the theory of the "realists". They also, however, do not oppose these concepts with any serious criticism. Some limit themselves to complaints against the diminished role of international law;[20] others make serious concessions to the theory of the "realists", sometimes sliding down to their position to a significant degree;[21] still others, McDougal for example, in polemicizing with the "realists" reach essentially the same conclusions by other means or come very close to the theory of the "realist" orientation.[22]

[18] G. F. Kennan, *American Diplomacy 1900-1950* (1951), p. 98.

[19] Some American international lawyers point out that a disregard for international law in United States foreign policy was excluded from the list of subjects in which persons entering the American foreign service are examined, as well as excluded from the curricula of law schools and replaced by a course in "international relations". J. Kunz, "The Swing of the Pendulum: From Overestimation to Underestimation of International Law", *American Journal of International Law*, XLIV (1950), 139; C. T. Oliver, "Historical Development of International Law", *Recueil des cours*, LXXXVIII (1955), 424. On the "realist" orientation see also D. B. Levin, "Об основных направлениях современной буржуазной науки международного права" [On the Basic Orientations of the Contemporary Bourgeois Science of International Law], Советский ежегодник международного права 1959 [Soviet Yearbook of International Law 1959] (1960), pp. 88-119; Levin, О современных буржуазных теориях международного права [On Contemporary Bourgeois Theories of International Law] (1959).

[20] See, for example, Oliver, "Historical Development of International Law", pp. 424-427.

[21] Thus, for example, Professor Pitman Potter, in appealing for an enhanced role of international law in international relations, at the same time leans towards the "realist school" in justifying "ultra and extraordinary actions". See P. Potter, "The Need for a Return to International Law", *American Journal of International Law*, XLV (1951), 540; Potter, "Legal Aspects of the Situation in Korea", ibid., XLIV (1950), 712.

[22] See, for example, P. Jessup, *The Use of International Law* (1959), pp. 9-10ff.

Representatives of the "pure" theory of law, Professors H. Kelsen and J. Kunz, have opposed the "realist" orientation somewhat more resolutely. In speaking of the so-called "political approach" to international law, Kelsen is completely correct in saying: "This view is in my opinion nothing but an attempt to justify the nonapplication of the existing law in case its application is in conflict with some interest, or rather, with what the respective writer considers to be the interest of his State".[23]

In criticizing "neorealism", Professor J. Kunz points out that it actually leads "to a denial of international law". "In reaching such conclusions", he says, "the so-called neorealism becomes completely unrealistic, and should be combatted very energetically".[24]

In another of his works, Kunz expresses an interesting view linking nihilistic concepts of the "realists" with the crisis of the capitalist system, or, as he prefers to express it, the crisis of "Western Christian culture". He writes: "Under the modern 'realistic' conception, international law as such is denied; it is held by preachers of a 'national self-interest' that in international relations 'legal questions largely are irrelevant'. This attitude must lead to a lower and lower respect for the rule of the law. This attitude is itself the outcome of the deep-seated crisis of our Western Christian culture, which is now struggling for its very survival. Of that total crisis, the crisis of international law is only one facet".[25]

The criticism of international law by "realists" is scientifically unfounded and rather reminds one of the seeking out of plausible pretexts to get rid of international law and untie the hands of power politics.

23 H. Kelsen, *Principles of International Law*, ed. R. W. Tucker (2d ed.; 1967), p. x.

24 J. Kunz, "La crise et les transformations du droit des gens", *Recueil des cours*, LXXXVIII (1955), 38.

25 Kunz, "The United Nations and the Rule of Law", *American Journal of International Law*, XLVI (1952), 504.

Indeed, the "realists" criticism of the "legalistic approach" to international problems actually is in no way directed against a legalistic approach, but only against a formal, normativist approach.

As has already been said, in legal science normativism is characterized by the isolation of law from that basis on which it arises and develops, from the economic system of society, from its class structure and policy. In the normativists' conceptions, norms of law in general and norms of international law in particular are "pure", are technical rules of conduct devoid of social content. The unfoundedness of normativism has been proved by life; it has been subjected to sharp criticism both in socialist and in capitalist countries. In addition, the application of law in general and of international law in particular requires a knowledge not only of law, but also of the actual circumstances of the case. Law regulates exceedingly complex relationships, and naturally the application of a legal norm as a general rule to a concrete social relationship can not be simply a mechanical process. The practice of applying national law, and also of in- ternational law, is convincing evidence of this.

A legal approach and a formal approach to questions are not one and the same thing. Proponents of the "realistic" orientation attempt to pass a formal, normativist approach to law and to its application as a legal approach in general and, in refuting normativism, assert that they thereby are proving the unfoundedness of a "legal approach" to international problems. But normativism has already fallen without the participation of the "realists". As regards the present reasonable legal approach to international problems, the arrows of the "realists" are going wide of the mark.

Is international law useful as a means of regulating relations among States or, as the "realists" maintain, does it only obstruct the regulation of international problems? Let us raise the question more concretely. Do those limitations or, expressly it juridically, those obligations which the following principles of international law impose upon States benefit the cause of peace and the development of international cooperation: the prohibition of the use of force in international relations; the obligation to resolve all international disputes only by peaceful means; respect for State sovereignty; equality of States; noninterference in the internal affairs of other States; self-determination of peoples; conscientious fulfillment of international obligations; and the guarantee of basic human rights? Or the obligations derived from such norms of international law as State sovereignty over its territorial waters, immunity of the premises of a diplomatic representation, inviolability of the person of a diplomat, and so forth? The answer to this question has been given by life itself. The practice of international relations shows that ignoring international law, that is, ignoring those limitations which international law places upon foreign policy and diplomacy, is peculiar to States which adhere to the policy "from a position of strength", leads to an aggravation of the international situation, and is fraught with military conflicts.

The basic thesis of the "realistic" orientation, consisting in the fact that the societal law of contemporary international relations is a struggle for domination, for the domination of one State over another, of one people over another (*bellum omnium contra omnes*), is false and unscientific. Power decides the outcome of this struggle; the destiny of the weak is subordination to the stronger; it is a societal law that the strong subdue and, consequently, exploit the weaker.

Hence hysterical appeals to strengthen the means for subduing and enslaving other peoples and, above all, to build up the military potential, primarily the nuclear potential, of the Atlantic bloc and other aggressive military alliances. It is not difficult to note that the concept of the "realists" reproduces the basic features of the foreign policy of the imperialist States.

The theoretical unfoundedness of the "realist" orientation is determined first and foremost by the fact that certain societal laws of international relations claimed by them to be universal are in fact only societal laws of imperialism. The aspiration to dominate and subject other peoples is in no way peculiar to the foreign policy of the socialist countries. It also is not peculiar to the policy of neutralist States. The argumentation of the "realists" that the aspiration to dominate is a characteristic feature of foreign policy in general is intended to whitewash the policy "from a position of strength" and to slander the foreign policy of the States of the socialist system. The societal laws of the capitalist system are claimed by "realists" to be the societal laws of the development of international relations in general, whereas the capitalist system not only has ceased to be the only system in the world but also is no longer the most influential system. A new, higher social system, the system of socialism, transformed into the decisive factor of world development, is being developed and strengthened side by side with the capitalist system.

"Political realism" emasculates social content from inter- national politics, attempting to represent international relations as a game of some abstract forces which have no class content. Morgenthau speaks in this connection about "perennial forces" that have shaped the past and will determine the future of human society.[26]

This philosophical premise is used by proponents of "political realism" to resort to such a political sleight-of-hand as identifying the policy of the Soviet Union with the policy of Tsarist Russia. Thus, Professor F. M. Schumann writes: "During the time of the tsars, the world mission of Russia and its world pretensions were represented by the Orthodox Church, and later by pan-slavism, just as now, under the Soviets, they are represented by 'international communism'".[27] The same notion is voiced in G. Kennan's article "Peaceful Co- existence: A Western View".[28]

[26] Morgenthau, *Politics Among Nations*, p. 10.

[27] F. M. Schumann, *The Cold War: Retrospect and Prospect* (1962), p. 11.

[28] G. F. Kennan, "Peaceful Coexistence: A Western View", *Foreign Affairs*, XXXVIII (1960), 178-180.

This attempt of the "realists" to operate with abstract and perennial categories such as "power processes" and "perennial forces" as categories devoid of social content is wholly unfounded. Abstract forces which are distinguished from one another only by quantitative indicators do not operate in international relations. States are the primary actors in the international arena: socialist and capitalist States, and the new States which have arisen in consequence of the liberation of the colonies. If one limits oneself to a comparison only of socialist and capitalist States, then their class nature is opposed, and the foreign policies which they pursue are fundamentally distinguished one from the other by their social content.[29] This, of course, does not mean that there can be nothing in common between these two policies; both socialist and, in a number of instances, bourgeois foreign policy can, for example, be a policy of peaceful coexistence, this is, be directed toward ensuring peace and developing cooperation among States for these purposes.

The "realistic" orientation, in pretending to the role of the most modern doctrine, in fact is a captive of the obsolete concepts of the German school of *Machtpolitik* of the second half of the nineteenth century. In preaching the dominance of power in international relations, it does not take into account the enormous changes in the international situation which have occurred during the period of the coexistence of the two systems.

The downfall of the policy "from a position of strength" is the best evidence of the unfoundedness and the unrealistic nature of the concepts of the "realists" concerning the co-relation of foreign policy and international law in our day.

International law is a system of legal norms which are subject to being complied with by States. It consequently must

[29] A French professor, R. Bosc, correctly points out in criticizing Morgenthau's conception that Morgenthau evidently believes "States are interchangeable or their reactions to events are identical; he distinguishes only between strong and weak States". R. Bosc, *Sociologie de la paix* (1965), p. 23 ["... il ne connait que des États forts et des États faibles"].

be a guiding principle for diplomacy. There can not be peaceful coexistence without compliance with the norms of international law.

In our epoch of unprecedented technological progress, which has opened up to mankind enormous inexhaustible reserves if energy and at the same time has led to the creation of weapons whose destructive force exceeds man's imagination, in the epoch of the beginning of space navigation, compliance with the norms of international law by States is becoming a necessity dictated by the common interests of all mankind. Violations of international law can lead to the catastrophic consequences of a world nuclear war, which would affect all persons and all States.

The need to struggle for compliance with the principles and norms of international law by States is entering more and more into the consciousness of peoples, especially those peoples which have endured all of the burdens, deprivations, and sufferings brought down upon them by the Second World War, those who experienced the horrors of Nazism. It is no wonder that "political realism" does not find any wide propagation in Europe, but prospers primarily in the United States, on whose cities and villages not one bomb fell during the Second World War and whose land was not trampled by the filthy boots of the fascist "supermen".

The need to enhance the role of international law in international relations was emphasized in United Nations General Assembly Resolution 1505 (XV) of 12 December 1960 concerning future work in the field of the codification and progressive development of international law. This resolution points out that "... conditions prevailing in the world today give increased importance to the role of international law – and its strict and undeviating observance by all governments – in strengthening international peace, developing friendly and co-operative relations among the nations, settling disputes by peaceful means and advancing economic and social progress throughout the world".

The General Assembly Resolution 1686 (XVI) of 18 December 1961 on the same question notes that "... important role of codification and progressive development of international law with a view to making international law a more effective means of furthering the purposes and principles set forth in Articles 1 and 2 of the Charter of the United Nations".

With the growth of the forces of peace, which are coming out for undeviating compliance with the principles and norms of international law, the influence of international law on the foreign policy and diplomacy of States is increasing. The task is for the unified forces of the mighty socialist camp, the peace-loving nonsocialist States, the international working class, and all forces upholding the cause of peace, to ensure compliance with the principles and norms of international law, above all its fundamental principles, and not to permit a world war.

CHAPTER XII.
INTERNATIONAL LAW AS A SUPPORT FOR FOREIGN POLICY

As already has been pointed out, in determining the legal duties of States international law fixed specific limits for their foreign policies and diplomacy. On the other hand, in fixing the rights of States, it opens the possibility of States using international law in the interests of their foreign policy and diplomacy. The preceding Chapter was devoted primarily to the first aspect; the present Chapter, to the second.

The fact that States strive to rely upon international law in effectuating their foreign policy and diplomacy can not be doubted. The foreign policy documents of various States are replete with references to international law in general and to individual principles and norms.

International law is not only a legal, but also an important political and moral factor. The foreign policy action of a State which rests upon international law acquires by virtue thereof not just legal, but also political and moral advantages.

An analysis of the question of the possibility of States using international law for the purpose of achieving the goals of their foreign policy must begin with the process of forming norms of international law, which are created in the course of the struggle and cooperation of States as a result of agreement between them. As already has been pointed out, each State participating in the process of creating, developing, and modifying norms of international law very naturally seeks to have its international legal position, as part of its foreign policy program as a whole, be reflected as fully as possible in the working out of norms of international law. That is to say, each State seeks to have the legal principles which it upholds recognized by other States as norms of international law.

Thus, the very process of creating norms of international law is being used by States for the purpose of achieving certain goals of their foreign policy.

We shall now consider the possibility of using prevailing international law as an instrument of the foreign policy of States.

International law determines the rights and duties of States. It is natural that in its foreign policy and diplomacy every country has the possibility in specific instances of relying upon international law, of upholding its rights, and of demanding the fulfillment of obligations by other States.

This, of course, does not mean that international law can be an instrument of any policy. Norms of international law can be used as an instrument of the foreign policy of individual States only within the limits defined by the content of these norms, that is, the content of the agreement between States in consequence of which a particular norm of international law has emerged, developed, or been modified.[1]

As a whole, contemporary international law is directed at ensuring the peaceful coexistence of States, at developing cooperation between them in the interests of peace.

Of the two basic orientations in foreign policy which presently exist – the policy "from a position of strength" and the policy of peaceful coexistence – only the latter corresponds to the general character of international law.

The policy "from a position of strength" and the arms race connected therewith, the knocking together of aggressive military blocs leading not to peace but to war, contravene international law. And if references to international law frequently are encountered in practice for the purpose of justifying the policy "from a position of strength", it should not follow from this, of course, that contemporary international law can be used in support of such a policy. Such efforts as, for example, the attempts to justify the aggression of England, France, and Israel against Egypt, or the aggression of Belgium against the Congo, or the aggression of the United States in Vietnam, have no basis whatever in international law.

1 See G. I. Tunkin, Основы современного международного права [Fundamental Principles of Contemporary International Law] (1956), p. 8.

International law can be a support only for that foreign policy whose principles conform to international law. In this case, a State may rely upon international law. The policy of peaceful coexistence and of the liberation of peoples from the colonial yoke is such a policy. In conformity with the nature of contemporary international law, it is an instrument in the hands of peace-loving States and peoples in the struggle for strengthening peace and averting a new war, for the freedom and independence of peoples.

Thus, international law is, on one hand, a system of norms binding upon States and regulating the conduct of States; and on the other, within defined limits a support (or, in a specific sense, an instrument) of the policy of such States. These are two aspects of one and the same phenomenon.

The existence of the aforesaid two contradictory aspects of international law usually confuses many bourgeois jurists. Corbett's book, *Law in Diplomacy,* which appeared in 1959, can serve as one example of how unresolved the problem of the co-relation of international law and foreign policy is for some of them. Corbett blames Soviet science for the fact that it does not consider it necessary to reconcile the concepts of law as an instrument of policy and law as a system of norms regulating relations among States. If, says Corbett, international law is the aggregate of norms regulating relations among States, then it consequently in some measure controls the conduct of governments. "But", Corbett continues, "... international law, if it is to regulate, must operate as a limitation upon, rather than a tool of, national aims and practice. If it is an objective regulating device, it cannot at the same time be subservient to the passing purposes of governments".[2]

The fact is, however, that the dual role of international law as a "regulator" and as a "support" or "instrument of policy" of the subjects of law reflects reality. It, as already has been pointed out, is determined by the content of norms of international law which, just as norms of national law, influence

[2] P. Corbett, *Law in Diplomacy* (1959), p. 101.

the conduct of subjects of law by defining their rights and duties.

If international law is a support or instrument of foreign policy, this does not mean that a State may take international law into its own hands and, as a sculptor from clay, fashion from it that which is necessary. Norms of international law are the result of agreement between States, and an individual State can not change them at its discretion.

One can not, therefore, concur with Professor D. B. Levin's view that "in applying norms of international law, diplomacy fills them with concrete political content, according to which the purport and the entire significance of such norms may be changed ... It has happened more than once that some of these provisions and norms of international law have served directly opposite purposes. The most progressive principles and institutes of international law can in the hands of reactionary diplomacy be transformed into an instrument of a reactionary policy".[3]

D. B. Levin's view can be based only on one of the following presuppositions: (a) norms of international law are technical rules which have no social content; (b) although norms of international law have their own content, a State may take just the form from such norms and pour new content therein. Neither the first nor the second presupposition can be accepted.

Norms of international law are not empty forms to which every State may bring a particular content. As any legal norm, a norm of international law has its own form and content.

[3] D. B. Levin, *Дипломатический иммунитет* [Diplomatic Immunity] (1949), p. xiii; the same thought, in a less specific form, is in E. A. Korovin (ed.), Международное право [International Law] (1951), p. 12. This question, in our view, is treated more correctly but also not completely accurately in D. B. Levin's article "К вопросу о соотношении дипломатии и международного права в свете принципа мирного сосуществования" [On the Question of the Correlation of Diplomacy and International Law in Light of the Principle of Peaceful Coexistence], Советский ежегодник международного права 1960 [Soviet Yearbook of International Law 1960] (1961), p. 113; Levin, *Дипломатия* [Diplomacy] (1962), pp. 151-152.

The latter is determined by the content of that agreement in consequence of which this norm exists (see Chapter IX).

An individual State can not introduce new content into a norm of international law. Changing the content of a norm of law is to change the norm, which is not possible as a result of the unilateral actions of a State, but by virtue of agreement among States. No single *power* can change a norm of international law in a unilateral manner.

The concept that a State may take from norms of international law only their form was expressed by E. B. Pashukanis in his day. In his exceedingly contradictory argumentation Pashukanis in fact asserted that the Soviet State "applied a number of forms" of international law and that there was only an external resemblance between the institutes of international law applied by the Soviet State and the institutes applied by bourgeois States. In Pashukanis's view, general international law exists side by side with this.[4]

Form without content, however, is not a norm. A State can not take only the form of an international legal norm, place new content therein, and assert that this is a norm of international law. Such a norm would be some sort of new norm but, naturally, not an international legal norm, since one State can not create norms of international law.

If one admits that every State can introduce changes into norms of international law by its unilateral actions the latter, as an objective system of norms regulating relations among States, disappears, and an external law of individual States emerges in its place.

Norms of international law have their own content which, of course, can be changed in the course of international relations by treaty or custom. Such change always occurs in consequence of agreement between States, in the process of

[4] See E. B. Pashukanis, Очерки по международному праву [Essays on International Law] (1935), pp. 16- 17.

whose formation the unilateral actions of States, as already pointed out, play a role.

Even though States may use international law as a support for foreign policy, this does not mean that international law is merged with policy. Mixing international law with policy inevitably leads to a denial of the normative character of international law, that is to say, to a denial of international law, which becomes buried in policy and vanishes as law.

Professor McDougal's concept of the policy approach to international law is an example of this kind of mixing or blending of foreign policy and international law.

Although McDougal also criticizes Kennan, Morgenthau, and Schwarzenberger for exaggerating the importance of "naked force" in international relations, he comes – it is true, by other paths – to essentially the same conclusions with regard to the role of international law as do the authors whom he criticizes. If Kennan and Morgenthau rather openly and unceremoniously cast international law aside and call upon diplomacy not to take it into consideration, McDougal, while not denying the importance of international law in so many words and sometimes also stressing it, in fact drowns international law in policy. In consequence thereof, international law in McDougal's concept is devoid of independent significance as a means of regulating international relations; it disappears into policy and, moreover, is transformed into a means of justifying policies which violate international law.[5]

Just as Kennan and Morgenthau, McDougal criticizes a "legalistic approach" to international problems. To him, international relations also represent first and foremost "power processes".[6] "World power processes", or, to express it in everyday language, international relations are, in McDougal's view, "processes of coercion". McDougal speaks of the

[5] M. S. McDougal, "International Law, Power, and Policy: A Contemporary Conception", *Recueil des cours*, LXXXII (1953), 137-259.

[6] Ibid., p. 171.

"complex process of coercion in the contemporary world arena", of the "great variety and differing intensities of the events in the coercion process".[7]

McDougal declares to be unfounded the view that international law is a system of legal rules regulating the relations among States. This notion of international law leads, McDougal asserts, "too many people to make sharp and unreal distinctions between law and policy ...". Too often it is assumed that "technical rules which are to constitute international law" can resolve the question of what ought to be done.[8]

The author's scornful gesture toward "technical rules" (although, of course, norms of international law are not technical rules) should be noted; it brings McDougal very close to Kennan.

McDougal concentrates his attention on so-called "decision-making", by which he means the process of formulating and effectuating foreign policy.

What is the role of international law in this process? Does McDougal believe that in making a decision one must take international law into account, comply with the norms of international law? Not at all.

McDougal maintains that the application of "common rules" of international law requires a "policy choice". Consequently, in the author's view, it is not necessary to take into account and comply with norms of international law in making policy decisions, but on the contrary, one must begin by "choosing a policy". The author bases the necessity of the preliminary "policy choice" on the fact that in applying a norm of international law there may be varying opinions as to what ought to be done.[9]

[7] M. S. McDougal and F. Feliciano, *Law and Minimum World Public Order* (1961), p. 7.

[8] McDougal, "International Law, Power and Policy", p. 144; see also O. J. Lissitzyn, *International Law Today and Tomorrow* (1965), pp. 39-40; M. A. Kaplan and N. B. de Katzenbach, *The Political Foundations of International Law* (1961), p. 231.

[9] Ibid., pp. 152-153.

As regards international law, it is by no means clear what role the author assigns to it in the "policy choice". Since the "policy choice" precedes the application of the norm of international law, this "choice" obviously is made independently of the existing norms.

McDougal asserts that the process of "decision-making" is a process in which norms of international law are created, interpreted, and reinterpreted.[10] But the "decision-making" process consists of unilateral actions of States. Consequently, according to McDougal, every States creates international law in the process of "decision- making". The author does not say this expressly, but this conclusion inevitably springs to mind. Not without reason does McDougal maintain that in his concept the dispute as to whether the "decision- maker" applies international law or national law is futile.[11]

In any event, for McDougal the role of international law consists not in defining the limits of possible or proper conduct of States. "The realistic function of those rules [that is, norms of international law – *G.T.*] considered as a whole", writes McDougal, "is, accordingly, not mechanically to dictate ... decision but to guide the attention of decision-makers to significant ... factors in typical ... contexts of decision, to serve as summary indices to relevant crystallized community expectations, and, hence, to permit creative and adaptive, instead of arbitrary and irrational, decisions".[12]

McDougal is right that international law, just as national law, in the majority of instances does not and can not determine specific foreign policy actions of States. These actions are determined by numerous factors, including international law (see Chapter VIII). But international law is a very specific, though not determinative, factor. The specific feature of this determinant of foreign policy consists in the fact that

10 Ibid., pp. 182-183.

11 Ibid., p. 184.

12 McDougal and Feliciano, *Law and Minimum World Public Order*, p. 57.

international law, while not determining specific decisions of States, fixed the limits of possible or proper decisions by establishing the rights and duties of States.

McDougal denies precisely this. To him, law does not limit a State in effectuating its foreign policy and diplomacy, but only serves it; the limits of propriety disappear, and the limits of possible conduct are expanded to any limits necessary to effectuate the policy.

Professor Roger Fisher, of Harvard University, is completely correct in writing as follows: "Seeking a realistic analysis of the decision process, McDougal finds that the deciders are not actually bound by rules and prescriptions but rather have them at their disposal. Decision-makers, he discovers, come out any way they want to an dhow they will want to depends upon their biases and policy objectives. McDougal welcomes this fact with open arms".[13]

But McDougal does not stop here; he goes farther. He imperceptibly leaves international law to the side and crosses over to a purely subjective "postulating the base values of international law ...". He proclaims nine such "values" (respect for human dignity, free access to "wealth processes", and so forth).[14] These precepts postulated by the author are declared to be the bases of an "international law of human dignity". The said "base values" should, in McDougal's view, be the criteria for evaluating the foreign policy of States and the guiding principles of this policy.[15] "Decisions", that is to say, the policy of States, should correspond to these "values", and not to norms of prevailing international law.[16]

[13] R. Fisher, "Law and Policy in International Decisions", *Science*, CXXXV (1962), 659.

[14] In his passing and far from complete critique of McDougal's conception, an Australian professor, J. Stone, is correct in pointing to the purely subjective character of these "base values". See J. Stone, "Problems Confronting Sociological Enquiries Concerning International Law", *Recueil des cours*, LXXXIX (1956), 73.

[15] McDougal, "International Law, Power and Policy", p. 190.

[16] Ibid., p. 183.

McDougal does not prove and does not even attempt to prove that the "values" which he has proposed are generally-recognized principles of international law. However, even if the question were one of such principles, one could not concur with the assertion that States must be guided only by these extremely broad general principles, not taking into account the concrete norms of international law. International law as an objectively existing system of norms disappears.

Such is the objective orientation of McDougal's conception. But the actual aim of the author is otherwise: to present the policy of the United States as equivalent to contemporary international law, as international law itself. One must agree with Professor S. V. Anderson, of the University of California, who characterizes the essence of McDougal's concept as follows: "Law is policy. Policy is human dignity. Human dignity is fostered in the long run by the success of American foreign policy. Therefore, law is the handmaiden of the national interests of the United States (Other countries will substitute their own national policy in place of the American). It is clear that such 'law' does not regulate behavior: it does not restrain, but liberates. Law becomes merely an increment to power".[17]

It is no wonder that McDougal and his supporters attempt to justify with references to "international law" any violations of this law by the United States, particularly the American intervention in the Dominican Republic in 1965 and especially the aggressive war of the United States in Vietnam.[18]

Moore, for example, in his article in the *American Journal of International Law*, invokes the spirit of McDougal's concept in searching for a justification of American aggression in Vietnam not in the "black-letter rules" of international law. He writes: "Lawfulness of assistance to either faction [that

[17] S. V. Anderson, "A Critique of Professor Myres S. McDougal's Doctrine of Interpretation by Major Purposes", *American Journal of International Law*, LVII (1963), 382.

[18] See J. N. Moore and J. L. Underwood, in collaboration with M. S. McDougal, *The Lawfulness of United States Assistance to the Republic of Vietnam* (May 1966), mimeo.

is, to the South Vietnamese authorities – *G.T.*] must be determined in reference to genuine self- determination and the requirements of minimum world public order, not in blind reliance on black-letter rules ...".[19]

Professor W. Friedmann, of Columbia University, with complete justification, says sarcastically with regard to such argumentation that "in the absence of third-party determination,

`minimum world public order' means, Humpty-Dumpty-like, what the policy-maker wants it to mean, a catch-all phrase to justify whatever action the writer wishes to justify".[20]

Professor Richard A. Falk, of Princeton University, who identifies himself with the basic positions of McDougal's concept although he also criticizes him on many questions, says in justification of McDougal's concept, having in mind foreign policy decision- makers: "Rational actors use every means at their disposal, including law, to maximize their values".[21] However, he also is forced to disassociate himself from McDougal on the question of States using international law as an instrument of their policy. "McDougal, in my judgment", he writes, "confirms the auto-interpretive role [of law – *G.T.*] of national elites so as to virtually nullify the distinction I deem crucial between the impartial application of law and its adversary use".[22]

Were McDougal to have limited himself to the assertion that States use international law as an objectively existing system of legal norms in order to achieve the goals of their foreign policy, then, as was said previously, there would be no dispute. But in McDougal's concept the State, first of all, can, in being guided

[19] J. N. Moore, "The Lawfulness of Military Assistance to the Republic of Viet-Nam", *American Journal of International Law*, LXI (1967), 31.

[20] W. Friedmann, "Law and Politics in the Vietnamese War: A Comment", ibid., LXI (1967), 783.

[21] R. A. Falk, *Legal Order in a Violent World* (1968), p. 87.

[22] Ibid., p. 7.

by "overriding values", pay no attention to international law, but if it wishes to use it, then to interpret it in such a way as is suitable for the achievement of its goals.

From a political point of view, McDougal's concept objectively is directed toward clearing international law out of the way, clearing a path for the policy whose effectuation this law impedes, that is to say, for an aggressive policy.

McDougal's concept is based on the positions of "political realism" which, as we already have pointed out, calls to mind the basic features of German concepts of *Machtpolitik* of the second half of the nineteenth century. In its basic legal orientation, this concept also is not new. Its roots stretch out from German concepts of external State law which, in turn, were closely linked with the said theories of *Machtpolitik*.

McDougal's concept, the core of which consists in the fact that international law is fused with policy, is scientifically unfounded.

International law, just as national law, while closely linked with policy, does not merge into it. Its principles and norms are created in the process of relations between States under the influence of their foreign policy as a result of agreement. As soon as it has been crystallized in the political cauldron of relations among States, a norm of international law becomes a special category, a legal category. It takes on an independent existence, and, although it can never be divorced from policy, nevertheless, without losing political significance, it becomes a special social phenomenon distinct from policy.

PART V. THE LEGAL NATURE OF CONTEMPORARY GENERAL INTERNATIONAL ORGANIZATIONS

CHAPTER XIII.
THE LAWS OF SOCIETAL DEVELOPMENT AND INTERNATIONAL ORGANIZATIONS

One of the characteristic features of contemporary international relations is the rapid development of and increase in the role of interstate organizations. We cannot consider all of these organizations though, as will be pointed out below, but while we so limit ourselves we are fully aware at the same time of the large and ever growing role of the so-called nongovernmental international organizations. Obviously, however, the nature and functions of these organizations have a special character, and they must be the subject of an independent investigation.[1]

International organizations have become a permanent and very important phenomenon of international life. Contemporary in- ternational (intergovernmental, interstate) organizations are created by States through the conclusion of international treaties. They are specific entities in the fabric of international relations which, though elevated above them structurally, are intertwined in these relations and constitute a distinctive part thereof. International organizations are not situated above international relations, but are within the system of these relations. Relations between States permeate international organizations, which represent a specific form of such relations.

The increase in the number and the expansion of the functions of international organizations are changing the structure of international relations. International organizations are drawing to themselves a significant number of questions of a direct bilateral or multilateral character which previously were dealt with in relations between States. Relations between States relating to questions falling within the jurisdiction of the respective international organization are handled by this

[1] On this question, see G. I. Morozov, Международные огранизации [International Organizations] (1969); A. S. Beliakov (ed.), Международные неправительственные орнанизации: справочник [International Non-Governmental Organizations] (1967).

organization. That is to say, in these instances an international organizationisasthoughitwerestandingamongStates, and the links among States pass in such instances through the more or less complex mechanism of this international organization.

The development of international organizations has meant the development of new methods of resolving international problems and an increase in the importance of these new methods in comparison with traditional methods. These new methods are highly diverse and are characterized in general by the application of the various mechanisms of international organizations.

In connection with the growth of the role of international organizations in contemporary international relations, the question of their legal nature, by which we mean their most important international legal features, acquires great theoretical and practical importance.

An international organization – is an institution of modern human society. The basic features of this institution, therefore, including its legal nature, are determined by the laws of societal development.

At the present time there exist two opposed social systems in the world: socialist and capitalist. Consequently, side by side with the general laws of societal development there also operate specific laws of development peculiar to each of the two opposed social systems. In addition, there exist specific societal laws for the development of countries which have come to be called "developing", although one must bear in mind that they do not represent a single group in terms of the direction of their social development, but can be broken down into two categories: countries developing along a capitalist path, and countries developing along a noncapitalist path.

The legal nature of general international organizations in which States of opposed social systems take part is determined in the final analysis by both the general laws of societal development and by the clash of specific laws peculiar to each of the existing social systems. Moreover, the legal nature of international organizations in which States of only one social system take part are formed under the decisive influence of the laws peculiar to that system and the general laws of societal development.

It is exceedingly important, therefore, for a correct scientific analysis of the legal nature of international organizations to distinguish international organizations whose membership in its social aspect is different.

Moreover, many bourgeois international lawyers analyze the legal nature and the long-term development of international organizations on the basis of composite data relating both to general and to Western European international organizations.[2]

Of course, the comparison of local international organizations *inter se*, as well as their comparison with general international organizations, is not only possible but is also necessary in the course of scientific research. The objection is not to the comparison, but to the mixing; for example, the inclusion of features peculiar to some local international organizations whose members are of the same social composition or ascribing to general international organizations trends of development peculiar to such local organizations.

Under contemporary conditions one must bear in mind at least the following basic categories of international organizations: general international organizations and local international organizations.

In the present work we limit ourselves to considering the legal nature of general international organizations.

In our view, those general laws of societal development peculiar to several socio-economic formations, such as the internationalization of economic, political, scientific, and cultural life, as well as the existence of sovereign States, exert a formative influence upon the legal nature of

[2] See, for example, I. Detter, *Law Making by International Organizations* (1965), pp. 319-329; D. W. Bowett, *The Law of International Institutions* (1964), pp. 273ff.

contemporary general international organizations. The clash of the developmental laws of the two opposed socio-economic systems, concretely reflected in the clash of the foreign policies of socialist and capitalist States in international organizations, has special significance for the character of contemporary international organizations. The law of decolonialization materially influences the character of contemporary international organizations. As a result of the breakup of the colonial system and the emergence in international organizations of a large number of new States formed in consequence of the liberation of the colonies, the co-relation of forces in international organizations has materially changed, and this can not but affect their further development.

1. The Internationalization of Economic Life and International Organizations

The development of the production forces of human society is accompanied by a deepening and an expansion of the international division of labour which, in its turn, is an important condition and indicator of the development of production forces.[3]

The international division of labour, which is specialization and cooperation on an international scale, embraces an ever wider sphere of human activity – first and foremost, production and consumption, science and technology, and economic life in general. This division of labor assumes the appearance of economic, scientific, technical, and other ties between States in various spheres of human activity.

The process of the internationalization of economic life first acquires significant depth and a tendency to become world-wide under conditions of capitalism. "The bourgeoisie", said Marx and Engels in the *Manifesto of the Communist Party*, "have made the production and consumption in all countries cosmopolitan by exploiting the world market ... In place of the old local and

[3] For greater details, see E. T. Usenko, Формы регулирования социалистического международного разделения труда [Forms of Regulation of Socialist International Division of Labor] (1965), pp. 9-40.

national seclusion and self- sufficiency, we have intercourse in every direction, universal interdependence of nations. As in material, so also in intellectual production".[4] And sixty years later, in 1913, Lenin wrote: "Developing capitalism knows two historical tendencies on the national question. The first: the awakening of national life and national movements, the struggle against any national oppression, the creation of national States. Second: the development and quickening of any relations among nations, the breaking of national partitions, the creation of an international unity of capital, of economic life in general, of politics, of science, and so forth.

Both tendencies are the essence of the world law of capitalism. The first predominates at the beginning of its development; the second characterizes mature capitalism moving toward its transformation into a socialist society".[5]

The emergence of the first socialist State in the world and then of the world system of socialism, the division of the world into two opposed social systems, the struggle between these systems in the course of which the leading system – the socialist – supplants the other already obsolete system, have not stopped the world process of the internationalization of economic life, as well as the internationalization of other aspects of societal life. There is not and could not be a force which could eliminate world economic relations, and the attempts of the imperialists to cut the Soviet State out of this system inevitably were doomed to failure. "There is a force greater", said V. I. Lenin, "than the desire, will, or decision of any of the hostile governments or classes; this force is general world economic relations, which compel them to enter upon the path of intercourse with us".[6]

[4] K. Marx and F. Engels, "Манифест коммунистической партии" [Manifesto of the Communist Party], Сочинения [Works] (2d ed.; 1955), IV, 427-428.

[5] V. I. Lenin, "Критические заметки по национальному вопросу" [Critical Remarks on the National Question], Полное собрание сочинений [Complete Collection of Works] (5th ed.; 1961), XXIV, 124.

[6] Lenin, "О внутренней и внешней политике республики: отчет ВЦИК и СНК 23 декабря [1921]" [On the Internal and Foreign Policy of the Republic:

The two social systems are not and can not be isolated from each other in the domain of economics or politics, nor in other spheres. At the present time, two world markets, socialist and capitalist, developing according to their own special laws, have been formed on the basis of the two social systems. But a world division of labour and a world market exists and is developing together therewith.[7]

The production forces of human society at the present time exist first and foremost as the production forces of individual States. Therefore, links among these national complexes of production forces take the form of international links, that is, links going beyond the bounds of States.[8]

International economic relations are production, secondary economic relations,[9] and the State complexes of production forces and the production relations existing in each State which correspond thereto are primary with regard to international economic relations.

It is natural, therefore, that the character and essence of international economic links at the present time are not of the same kind; they are determined basically by the character and essence of the social systems of the States among which such links occur. Consequently, in speaking of the internationalization of economic life and the development of international economic relations on a world scale, one should bear in mind the contradictions among the various elements of this system.

Report of the All-Russian Central Executive Committee and Council of People's Commissars of 23 December], Полное собрание сочинений [Complete Collection of Works], XLIV, 304-305.

[7] For greater detail, see M. V. Senin, Развитие международных экономических связей [Development of International Economic Links] (1968), pp. 48-49.

[8] For greater detail see Usenko, Формы регулирования социалистического международного разделения труда [Forms of Regulation of Socialist International Division of Labor]; see also R. L. Bobrov, Современное международное право [Contemporary International Law] (1962), p. 54.

[9] See Marx and Engels, Сочинения [Works], XII, p. 735.

International economic relations serve as an important developmental base for other international relations: political, cultural, and others. Whereas international economic relations are a base category, then these other international relations are of a superstructure character. But it would be incorrect to regard these latter as a superstructure only above international economic relations, as Professor R. L. Bobrov has correctly noted.[10]

Since international economic relations are, as already has been pointed out, secondary, their influence upon other international relations is a secondary influence with regard to the base. In addition, it is not the sole influence relating to the case. International relations of a superstructure character do not experience the influence of the economic system of various States only through international economic relations. The economic system of individual States influences the foreign policy of these States (and therefore international relations of a superstructure character) both directly and through national categories of the superstructure. Through these two channels, the fundamental base complexes, that is, the economic systems of individual States, influence international relations of a superstructure character, as well as contemporary international organizations and international law.

The intensification of the internationalization of economic and other aspects of life, reflected in the intensification of international economic, scientific, technical, and other ties, inevitably leads to an increasing number of questions which can not be resolved successfully on a bilateral or narrowly regional basis, but require the participation of all or a significant number of States. This is reflected in particular in the increased number of multilateral treaties in which a large number of States participate.

Another aspect of the development of economic and other international ties is the complexity of the questions which

[10] Bobrov, Современное международное право [Contemporary International Law], pp. 16-17.

arise in the course of effectuating such ties and the emergence of the need to create permanent international mechanisms which concern themselves with such questions. This leads to the creation of international organizations as agencies of State cooperation for the purpose of settling the said questions.

Such organizations arise primarily in those areas of international relations where they are engendered by the requirements of economic, scientific, and technical ties. These were, for example, the International Telegraphic Union, founded in 1865, the Universal Postal Union, created in 1875, and so forth.

The functions of these international organizations at first were very limited. A significant growth in the number of participants in international organizations, however, and the need to ensure the operative resolution of questions leads to an expansion of the rights and powers of international organs in settling such questions, of course, within the bounds defined in each individual instance by the statute of the organization. The expansion of the competence of international organizations takes place, therefore, both along the line of expanding the circle of questions over which it has jurisdiction and along the line of expanding the powers of the international organs in settling these questions.

With the intensification and complication of international ties, the number of international organizations also grows. Together with international organizations in the sphere of economic, scientific, and technical cooperation, international organizations in the domain of culture, education, and even international organizations for questions of peace and security are emerging.

Thus, the intensification of the internationalization of economic and other areas of contemporary social life leads to the creation of international organizations in various domains of international ties, to an expansion of their functions and powers, and to an increase of their role in international relations generally.

However, both the character of internationalization itself and the other laws of societal development, acting in another direction, define the perimeters of this process.

2. Coexistence of the Two Opposed Social Systems and International Organizations

The most important law of societal development of our epoch is the existence of two opposed social systems developing according to different laws, and the struggle between them, in which a new social system is superseding the old system.

General international organizations are created and function on the basis of agreement between States of different social systems, and therefore what has been said earlier about the link between international law and peaceful coexistence also is applicable to the co-relation of international organizations and peaceful coexistence. General international organizations can develop only on the basis of peaceful relations, relations of peaceful coexistence between States with different social systems. The events of the Second World War graphically confirmed that war destroys general international organizations, undermining the only basis on which they can exist and develop. At the same time, the postwar period has shown no less convincingly that the development of international relations along the line of peaceful coexistence promotes the development and activity of general organizations, especially the United Nations, and the atmosphere of "cold war" retards their development and reduces the effectiveness of their activity.

The struggle of the two opposed systems in contemporary general international organizations generally manifests itself as the struggle of two foreign policy orientations opposed by virtue of their class essence: the foreign policy of socialist States and the foreign policy of the imperialist powers and their allies. The policy of the socialist States in international organizations is first and foremost a policy of peaceful coexistence. On this plane it is shared by many developing and even capitalist countries. The policy of the imperialist States and their allies generally is characterized by a rejection of peaceful coexistence and by aggressive aspirations against the socialist States. Under these conditions, only a struggle of States, and on a broader plane, of all forces favouring peaceful coexistence, ensures as a whole the position that contemporary general international organizations are organs of peaceful coexistence.

This is reflected first and foremost in the charters of general international organizations. These charters define as the basic purpose of the respective general international organizations either the maintenance of peace and struggle against the threat of war (the United Nations) or assistance in achieving this purpose (the specialized international organizations).

The United Nations Charter proclaims that the United Nations has as its purpose "to maintain international peace and security and for this purpose to take effective collective measures to prevent and eliminate a threat to the peace and to suppress all acts of aggression or other breaches of the peace, and to promote through peaceful means, in conformity with the principles of justice and international law, the reconciliation or settlement of international disputes or situations which might lead to a breach of the peace" (Article 1).

Article 1 of the Constitution of UNESCO says: "The purpose of the Organization is to contribute to peace and security by promoting collaboration among the nations through education, science and culture in order to further universal respect for justice, for the rule of law and for the human rights and fundamental freedoms which are affirmed for the peoples of the world, without distinction of race, sex, language or religion, by the Charter of the United Nations".

The Constitution of the International Labour Organization, as amended after the Second World War, says that the activity of the organization should promote the "securing of the permanent peace" (Preamble).

A second aspect of peaceful coexistence is the development of international cooperation in economic, political, cultural, and other spheres, which under contemporary conditions is a very important condition for maintaining international peace. Thus, for example, considerable attention is given to the development of international cooperation in various domains of the activity of the United Nations, whose basic task is to maintain international peace and security.

The development of cooperation between States in the respective special fields is the principal task of international organizations for specialized questions.

It already has been pointed out that struggle and cooperation in the international arena mutually permeate each other. But the co- relation between them in various international organizations is not the same. The fact is that contradictions between States, and especially between States of different social systems, affect various domains of international cooperation to varying degrees.

The closer the questions of the respective international organization to the peculiarities of the social and State system and bases of foreign policy of States of the two systems, the sharper is this struggle. The questions of disarmament, of the eradication of colonialism, of the elimination of racial discrimination, and of human rights, and so forth, may serve as examples.

In fields which do not directly affect the peculiarities of the economic system, the possibilities for States of different social systems are broader, and the struggle between them less acute. Examples of such organizations are the Universal Postal Union, International Telecommunications Union, World Meteorological Organization, Intergovernmental Maritime Consultative Organization, World Health Organization, and so forth.

Virtually the entire range of existing international contradictions are reflected in the United Nations as a universal international organization of a political character. In comparison with other international organizations, the tension of political struggle here is significantly higher.

The thesis that struggle and cooperation of States occurs in contemporary general international organizations, nut just of States of different social systems but also of States in general, is merely a statement of fact. Appeals to make contemporary general international organizations only organs of cooperation, and reproaches directed to Soviet and other scholars who speak of struggle, can not serve the cause of peace and the development of international cooperation. In distorting the real situation in international organizations, such appeals disorient the forces of progress. The real situation is that only the struggle of progressive forces in contemporary general international organizations can ensure and, to the extent of their growing might, is ensuring that the activity of such international organizations actually makes a contribution to the cause of peace and the development of international cooperation.

The presence in the membership of contemporary general international organizations of States of the two opposed social systems and the struggle between them affects the sphere of operation and competence of international organizations in two contrary directions.

The sphere of activity of international organizations, which are created on the basis of agreement between States and operate on the basis of understandings between them, includes only questions upon which agreement between States is possible. Therefore, questions of the peculiarities of a social system and questions of ideology, upon which agreement is impossible, are outside the sphere of activity of contemporary general international organizations. This objective law of societal development limits the sphere of activity and the competence of contemporary general international organizations.

The United Nations is an example. The principal task of the United Nations is the maintenance of international peace and security. The basic causes of wars are found in the nature of the capitalist social system. As V. I. Lenin has pointed out, "war is not a contradiction with the fundamentals of private ownership, but a direct and inevitable development of these fundamentals".[11] The United Nations, however, does not and can not assume as its task the liquidation of these basic causes of was, since these are questions of a social system that lie outside the competence of the United Nations. But in addition to these basic causes of international wars, there are numerous direct causes of international conflicts and wars, and the sphere of activity of the United Nations is limited in questions of the maintenance of international peace and security to precisely this domain.

In domains which are closely linked with the peculiarities of the economic system of States of the two systems, the creation of general international organizations is much more difficult. Among such organizations are, for example, the International Bank for Reconstruction and Development, created in 1945, the International Monetary Fund, formed in the same year, the International Finance Corporation, organized in 1957 – in which the USSR does not participate. Of course, it is of no little significance here that the imperialist powers, and above all the United States, from the very beginning transformed these organizations into an instrument for effectuating their own policy.[12]

Together with the limited function which we have considered, the law of societal development also operates in the direction of expanding the sphere of activity and the competence of international organizations. The policy of the socialist States in international organizations, supported by many nonsocialist countries, contemplates that international organizations are genuine organs of peace and international cooperation on the basis of equality and independence of peoples. The socialist States are struggling against attempts of imperialist powers to transform international organizations into

[11] Lenin, "О лозунге соединенных штатов Европы" [On the Slogan of United States of Europe], Полное собрание сочинений [Complete Collection of Works], XXVI, p. 353.

[12] G. I. Morozov and others (eds.), Специализированные учреждения ООН [Specialized Agencies of the United Nations] (1967), pp. 196-277; K. Ia. Chizhov, Международные валютно-финансовые огранизации капитализма [International Currency and Financial Organizations of Capitalism] (1968), pp. 14-15.

an instrument of aggression and imperialist policy. Therefore, the growth of the influence of the socialist States in international organizations promotes the normalization and expansion of the activity of international organizations.

To illustrate this situation it suffices to list a number of important problems with which contemporary international organizations have engaged themselves as a result of the efforts of the socialist countries and other progressive forces: problems of peaceful coexistence, the liquidation of colonialism, disarmament, economic assistance to less developed countries, the elimination of racial discrimination, the codification of international law, human rights, and so forth.

3. *The Breakup of the Colonial System and International Organizations*

One of the most important laws of societal development in our day is the breakup of the colonial system. The colonial system could not exist for long in the new epoch opened by the Great October Socialist Revolution, in an epoch of a general upsurge in the struggle against the exploitation of man by man, since colonialism is the most detestable manifestation of such exploitation.

The influence of this law of societal development upon international organizations can be divided into two stages: the first stage precedes the formation of independent States as a result of the national liberation struggle; the second follows the formation of a significant number of such States. During the stage of struggle for the liberation of colonies, of all the forces which wages this struggle only the socialist States participated directly in the process of the creation and of the activity of international organizations. During the second stage, a greater and greater number of the new States which emerged in consequence of the liberation of the colonies aligned themselves with the socialist States. This substantially changed the situation, since the national liberation movement had the opportunity to exert a more direct influence in international organizations through these States.

And here the laws of societal development were transformed into life through the struggle of progressive forces against the forces of reaction. This struggle was especially sharp during the creation and in the course of the activity of the United Nations, which inevitably had to place the problem of decolonization on the agenda.

The struggle of progressive forces against the forces of reaction was intertwined with interimperialist contradictions and struggle. During the Second World War, this struggle was especially acute between the United States and England. The imperialist circles of England, fearing that the upsurge of the national liberation movement and the growth of the international influence of the Soviet Union could lead to England's losing her colonies, strove so that the future international organization would be at least a factor holding in check the struggle of colonial peoples for their independence. Meanwhile, American monopolies reckoned that as a result of the breakup of the English and French colonial empires they would manage to establish their own dominance in the former English and French colonies and thus expand their sphere of exploitation. The United States, therefore, favoured proposals aimed at undermining the colonial domination of England and France but at the same time would guarantee against an "excessive" scope of the national liberation struggle of the colonial peoples, which in this case inevitably would be transformed into a struggle against any colonizers.

Precisely this aspiration underlay the proposals on the colonial question advanced by the United States. The draft declaration on the colonial question which was submitted by United States Secretary of State, Cordell Hull, at the Moscow Tripartite Conference of Ministers of Foreign Affairs on 24 September 1943 said that the United Nations must be responsible for the future of the colonial countries and must prepare these countries so that "they might become qualified for independent national status". It was pointed out in the draft declaration that every country having a "political tie with colonial peoples" should "progressively grant self-government to colonial peoples ... in the light of the various stages and preparedness for independence", should "fix at the earliest practicable moments the dates when each colonial people shall be accorded the status of full independence within a system of general security". It was proposed to create an "international trusteeship organization" consisting of the representatives of the United Nations which would operate through regional commissions composed of representatives of countries "having substantial interests in the respective areas".[13]

This proposal of the United States met with the resolute opposition of Great Britain. In March 1943, when the said draft declaration was sent by Hull to English Foreign Secretary, Anthony Eden, during a visit of the latter to Washington, the English treated it more than coldly. Thereafter, the Americans persistently sought the consent of the English to publish the declaration with regard to the colonial question, but the latter no less persistently avoided a discussion of this declaration, which was aimed at the Achilles heel of the British Empire.[14]

At the San Francisco Conference, however, where the Soviet Union strove so that the new international organization, in contrast to the League of Nations, would be an organ promoting the liberation of colonies and not impeding the self-determination of peoples, the United States to a significant extent actually united itself with England and the other colonial powers against the Soviet proposals. As a result thereof, the provisions of the United Nations Charter on the system of trusteeship and on non-self-governing territories were of a somewhat contradictory character, although no doubt remained that the question was one of ultimately granting to all peoples the possibility of effectuating their right to self-determination and that the Organization and its members must "develop friendly

[13] S. B. Krylov, История создания ООН [History of Creation of United Nations], ed. G. I. Tunkin (1960), pp. 21-23.

[14] See C. Hull, *The Memoirs of Cordell Hull* (1948), II, 1234-1238.

relations among nations on the basis of the principle of equality and the self-determination of peoples" (Article 1).

The development of the national liberation movement broke the resistance of the colonial powers, who had attempted to use certain "overly cautious" provisions of the United Nations Charter with respect to decolonization for their own purposes. Under the influence of events and in consequence of the increased weight of the anticolonial forces, anticolonial tunes echoed more loudly in the resolutions of the United Nations, although the imperialist States impede the realization of these resolutions to a significant degree.[15]

At the present time, about half of the members of general international organizations are from States formed as a result of the breakup of the colonial system. These basically are economically less-developed countries with small populations. The struggle for economic and cultural developments, for strengthening political and economic independence against the attempts of imperialists to take advantage of the economic weakness of these States in order to impose new forms of

[15] For greater detail on the colonial question in the United Nations, see Krylov, История создания ООН [History of Creation of United Nations]; D. I. Baratashvili, За свободу и независимость народов [For Freedom and Independence of Peoples] (1960); Baratashvili, Новые государства Азии и Африки и международное право [New States of Asia and Africa and International Law] (1968); L. A. Modzhorian, "Распад колониальной системы империализма и Организации Объединенных Нации" [Collapse of Colonial System of Colonialism and the United Nations], Советский ежегодник международного права 1960 [Soviet Yearbook of International Law 1960] (1961), pp. 121-140; Modzhorian, Колониализм вчера и сегодня [Colonialism Yesterday and Today] (1967); G. I. Morozov, Организация Объединенных Наций [The United Nations] (1962), pp. 426-491; L. V. Speranskaia, Принцип самоопределения в международном праве [Principle of Self-Determination in International Law] (1961); R. A. Tuzmukhamedov, Национальный суверенитет [National Sovereignty] (1963); Tuzmukhamedov, "ООН и ликвидация колониализма" [United Nations and Liquidation of Colonialism], Советский ежегодник международного права 1964-1965 [Soviet Yearbook of International Law 1964-1965], pp. 48-57; N. V. Chernogolovkin, Крушение колониализма и международное право [Collapse of Colonialism and International Law] (1963); S. Krasil'shchikova, ООН и национально-освобительное движение [United Nations and National-Liberation Movement] (1964); G. B. Starushenko, Нация и государство в освобождающихся странах [Nation and State in Liberated Countries] (1967); L. Antonowicz, *Likwidacja kolonializmu za stanoviska prawa miedzynarodowego* (1964); R. Arzinger, *Das Selbstbestimmungsrecht im allgemeinen Völkerrecht* (1966).

subordination and exploitation (neocolonialism), are the most important problems of these States. The new States, naturally, bring their needs to international organizations. They demand with complete justification that the international organizations, and above all the United Nations, devote more attention to the problems affecting that portion of mankind which up to now had not entered directly into the international arena.

At the same time, the new States manifest great concern about general questions of the maintenance of international peace and security, not only because atomic war threatens existing human civilization in general, but also because international peace and the development of international cooperation are the best basis for their internal development and facilitate their struggle to strengthen political and economic independence.

General international organizations are becoming more universal not only in form, but also in substance. The attainment of complete universality is obstructed by the policy of certain imperialist powers who, on the one hand, persistently do not admit some socialist States to general international organizations, and on the other, prevent the realization of the right to self-determination by peoples of the remaining colonies (for example, South-West Africa, Angola, and others).

The emergence in international organizations of a large number of new States exerts a salutary influence upon their activity. This leads first and foremost to the fact that the problems of the activity of many international organizations now are being subjected to material changes. Questions of economic and cultural development of the new States, problems of health in these countries, and so forth occupy a larger place in the work of international organizations.

The co-relation of forces in international organizations has changed materially. Thus, for example, whereas previously in the General Assembly of the United Nations the imperialist powers had a firm majority of two-thirds of the votes and could pass any resolution advantageous to them, now the situation is different. This majority is no more, although now the imperialist powers still frequently manage, using various forms of pressure on small States, to pass resolutions clearly contrary to the United Nations Charter (for example, on leaving American armed forces in South Korea, on the representation of China, and so forth). At the same time, in the majority of instances relating to the most important questions the imperialist powers find themselves in a minority (for example, the 1960 Declaration on Granting Independence to Colonial Countries and Peoples and the 1961 General Assembly resolution on banning the use of nuclear weapons). This situation frequently leads to the imperialist powers sometimes being compelled, in order to avoid being placed in a politically disadvantageous position, to vote for resolutions against which they resolutely struggled. Of course, they have in mind in this connection to obstruct the effectuation of these resolutions in the future. The General Assembly resolution adopted at the beginning of 1961 on the question "Consideration of the Principles of International Law Concerning Friendly Relations and Cooperation of States in Accordance with the United Nations Charter", for which the imperialist powers voted but whose implementation they have stubbornly prevented, is an example.

4. The Existence of Sovereign States and International Organizations

One of the most important laws of the development of mankind in our epoch which has direct relation to international organizations is the existence of sovereign States.

This law of societal development can be felt in all international organizations. Its basic manifestation is the principle of sovereign equality of the member States, which is itself the guiding principle of the structure and activity of contemporary general international organizations.

The sovereignty of member States of an international organization is reflected first and foremost in the fact that contemporary general international organizations are created and operate on the basis of charters which are international treaties concluded by sovereign States.

It is true that there are certain new phenomena in this domain. The inevitable expansion of the functions of international organizations leads in numerous subsidiary organs being created with them which in a number of instances operate to a certain extent as autonomous international organizations, although subordinated to the international organizations which created them (for example, the regional economic commissions of the United Nations for Europe, Asia and the Far East, Latin America, and Africa).

The most significant innovation is the creation of an Organization for Industrial Development. The decision to create this organization was adopted by the United Nations General Assembly in Resolution 2089 (XX) of 20 December 1965. The Twenty-first Session of the General Assembly confirmed the Charter of this organization.[16] According to these resolutions, the United Nations Organization for Industrial Development, "established as an organ of the General Assembly, shall function as an autonomous organization within the United Nations...".[17] Resolution 2152 (XXI) determines that the principal organs of the Organization will be the Industrial Development Board, consisting of forty-five members, elected by the General Assembly from the members of the United Nations, members of specialized agencies, and members of the International Atomic Energy Agency.

It is pointed out in this resolution that decisions of the board will be taken by a simple majority of those present and voting (point 9). It further determines that the expenses for administrative and research activities will be included in the regular budget of the United Nations, and operational expenses will be met from other sources (points 20, 21, and 22 of the resolution).

[16] G. A. Res. 2152 (XXI), 17 November 1966.

[17] Ibid.

Despite these peculiarities of the creation of the United Nations Organization for Industrial Development, it would be incorrect in this instance not to note the treaty basis of this organization. It is an international organization of a secondary order, an organ of an already existing international organization created by an international treaty. It is one of the subsidiary organs of the General Assembly, whose creation is provided for by Article 22 of the United Nations Charter. The fundamental legal basis of such an international organization, even if it is called "autonomous", is the treaty by which the primary international organization was created, in this case, the United Nations Charter.

In reality, the existence of such a subsidiary organization depends completely upon the existence of this basic international treaty and the international organization which has given birth to the said subsidiary organization.

An important manifestation of the sovereignty of member States is the general proposition that any amendment of the charter of an international organization can not become binding upon a member State of the organization without its consent (see Chapter XV).

The principle of sovereignty is further manifested in the fact that the organs of general international organizations endowed with the right to adopt decisions consist of the representatives of the member States acting in accordance with the instructions of their governments. This is a very important feature of contemporary international organizations.

The fact that resolutions of general international organizations, with certain exceptions, have the character of recommendations and are not legally binding upon members of the organization also is a manifestation of the principle of sovereignty (see Chapter V).

Finally, in all general international organizations, member States have the right to withdraw from the organization (see Chapter XV).

CHAPTER XIV. THE BASIC FEATURES OF THE LEGAL NATURE OF GENERAL INTERNATIONAL ORGANIZATIONS. THE CHARTER AS THE BASIS OF AN ORGANIZATION'S ACTIVITY

1. Charters of International Organizations: Treaties or Constitutions?

The question of the legal nature of charters of international organizations is undoubtedly of great theoretical and practical interest. Is a charter of an international organization an international treaty *sui generis* or is it a constitution of an international organization, similar to the constitution of a State?

According to constitutional theory, charters of contemporary international organizations, and above all of the United Nations, are constitutions or are basically constitutions and only partially international treaties, and therefore the provisions of the law of treaties are nonapplicable or virtually nonapplicable to them. The basic idea of this theory, which is oriented toward American and English constitutional practice, is that the charters of international organizations as constitutions are "flexible" documents from whose provisions one may digress in practice, and this digression will not be a violation, but a modification of these charters.

"And as formal amendments of an international constitutional document, such as the U.N. Charter", writes an American professor,

W. Friedmann, "are almost impossible to achieve, the adjustment generally proceeds by the consolidation of practices or by *de facto* revisions. Thus a whole body of parliamentary law has been developed in the United Nations, a formalized interplay between the various named organs of the United Nations, and the Committees set up by them. The text of the Charter would, for example, entirely fail to account for the *de facto* shift in the relative competencies of the Security Council and the General Assembly ... The United for Peace

Resolution of 1950 can be regarded as an indirect amendment of the Charter, transferring certain functions from the Security Council to the Assembly without the complex process of amendment provided by the Charter itself ...".[1] In drawing a parallel between the United Nations Charter and the United States Constitution, the author writes further: "National constitutions, notably that of the United States, have also been greatly moulded by the interplay of social change, legal practices, and legal interpretations".[2]

E. Jimenez de Arechaga, a Uruguyan professor who entitled his book *Derecho constitucional de las Naciones Unidas*, characterizes as follows the constitutional theory as it concerns the United Nations Charter. Attempting at the outset to justify the legality of Resolution 377(V) of 3 November 1950, "Uniting for Peace", with references to the provisions of the United Nations Charter, and then in fact recognizing that such a justification is impossible, he writes: "This constitutional development shows that the Charter is an international document which is not static and which has demonstrated that it possesses to a high degree the quality of a constitution in adapting itself to unexpected changes and new circumstances. It is possible to assert that few national constitutions have undergone in the process of their application such important and rapid changes as has the United Nations Charter ...".[3]

There is no doubt that the constitutional theory is worked out and propagandized strenuously in the West because it is aimed at justifying the numerous violations of the charters of general international organizations, and above all of the United Nations, which did and do occur under the pressure of the imperialist powers. Herein is the political significance of this theory.

1 W. Friedmann, *The Changing Structure of International Law* (1964), p. 153.

2 *Ibid.*, p. 154.

3 E. Jimenez de Arechaga, *Derecho constitucional de las Naciones Unidas* (1958), p. 204.

The legal argumentation in justification of this theory is worked out most thoroughly in S. Rosenne's article "Is the Constitution of an International Organization an International Treaty?"[4]

Professor Rosenne asserts that the application of the law of treaties to the charters of international organizations reveals a whole series of basic departures from the general law of treaties.[5] These departures he sees in the following issues: admission to an organization in comparison with accession to a treaty;[6] reservations to an instrument in those instances when the instrument contains no provisions regarding reservations;[7] suspension of membership in an international organization, expulsion from an organization, withdrawal from it;[8] amendment of charters;[9] interpretation of charters.[10]

The author then draws, though cautious in form, very far- reaching conclusions. In essence Rosenne maintains that although by their origin the charters of international organizations are international treaties, as regards their operation they are basically not treated as treaties. "The question", he writes, "whether the constitution of an international organization is itself an international treaty does not permit of an unqualified answer. The reply will depend on the circumstances in which the question is raised. There is no room for doubt that the process by which a State forms its will to be a member of an international organization on its internal plane, by which it expressed that will on the international plane,

[4] S. Rosenne, "Is the Constitution of an International Organization an International Treaty?" *Communicazioni e studi,* XII (1966), 21-89.

[5] Ibid., p. 50.

[6] Ibid., p. 55.

[7] Ibid., pp. 58-64.

[8] Ibid., p. 64.

[9] Ibid., pp. 64-65.

[10] Ibid., pp. 67-80.

both come within the normal scope of the law of treaties, domestic and international as the case may be".[11]

But with regard to the operation of the charter of an international organization, Rosenne says the following: "The fact that so many cardinal aspects relating to the very essence of the legal relationships created by membership in an international organization and participation in its constituent instrument are in practice governed by principles and rules fundamentally different from those applicable to the corresponding aspects of participation in multilateral treaties must raise serious doubts as to whether the constituent instruments of international organizations are of the same *genus*, in international law, as multilateral treaties".[12]

The author specially dwells in detail on interpreting the United Nations Charter, showing that the International Court in "appropriate instances" has applied methods of interpreting the Charter which are characteristic of national constitutions and not of international treaties.[13] But one immediately notes that Rosenne does not even make an attempt to prove in this connection that such practice conforms to international law and is not a violation thereof. The emphasis upon the problem of interpretation is completely understandable since even the "United for Peace" resolution and the practice based thereon in the majority of instances are claimed by Western authors to be based upon an interpretation of the United Nations Charter.[14]

Upon closer examination of the arguments advanced by Professor Rosenne in justification of the conclusion concerning the nonapplicability or the basic nonapplicability of the law of

[11] Ibid., p. 86.

[12] Ibid., p. 66.

[13] Ibid., pp. 70, 79.

[14] See L. Goodrich, *The United Nations* (1958), p. 168; Arechaga, *Derecho constitucional de las Naciones Unidas*, pp. 204-205.

treaties to the charters of international organizations, there are insufficient grounds for such a conclusion.

The charters of international organizations are international treaties having certain peculiarities, treaties *sui generis*. The statute of an international organization, in contrast to the usual multilateral international treaty, creates a permanent international entity which functions on its basis. It defines not only the rights and duties of States-parties to the treaty, but also the purposes and tasks of the organization, being an international organism distinct from States, the functions and competence of organs of the organization, the mutual relations between the organization and the member-States, and so forth. In other words, the statute of an international organization is a more complex phenomenon than the ordinary multilateral treaty.

It is natural, therefore, that the conclusion, and especially the operation of an international treaty such as the charter of an international organization, has certain peculiarities. However, all the basic provisions of the law of treaties are applicable to the charters of international organizations, in a number of instances with insignificant changes. In particular, the following provisions of the law of treaties are applicable to them: the conclusion and entry into force of multilateral treaties, except for certain provisions relating to reservations; the invalidity of treaties; the amendment and interpretation of treaties; the operation of international treaties; the operation of international treaties; and above all the basic principle of this section of the law of treaties – *pacta sunt servanda*; the significance of treaties for third States; and so forth. It is necessary to remark once again that the application of individual norms of the law of treaties relating to the said sections may reveal the need to adapt some of them. The International Law Commission therefore acted correctly in having included in the final draft of the law of treaties Article 4, which says: "The application of the present articles to treaties which are constituent instruments of an international organization or are adopted within an international organization shall be subject to any relevant rules of the organization".[15]

In so doing the Commission by no means proceeded from those considerations ascribed to it by Professor Rosenne, who welcomes the first paragraph of this article as supposedly signifying recognition in principle of the inapplicability of the law of treaties to the charters of international organizations.[16] The text of the article itself testifies to the contrary. The article speaks, first, of treaties "which are constituent instruments of international organizations", that is, the Commission believes such charters to be international treaties. Second, the article said "the application of the present articles to treaties which are constituent instruments of international organizations ...," that is, the Commission proceeded from the fact that as a whole the draft articles are applicable to the charters of international organizations, with the exception, of course, of those instances when an international organization has its own rules regarding a given concrete question.

Thus, the charters of international organizations are a special category of international treaties. The attempt to ascribe certain features of State constitutions to the charters of international organizations has no justification, since international organizations are qualitatively different from States.

2. *The Jurisdiction of International Organizations*

The numerous violations of the United Nations Charter which have taken place under the influence of imperialist States have led to the emergence of various legal constructions having the purpose to justify these violations. Since these violations of the Charter were connected primarily with a violation of the competence of the United Nations in general and the distribution

[15] United Nations, *Yearbook of the International Law Commission 1966* (1967), II, 191.

[16] Rosenne, "Is the Constitution of an International Organization an International Treaty?", p. 87.

of such competence among the organs of the United Nations, these constructions have endeavoured to prove the possibility of freely manipulating this competence.

Among such constructions are the theory of "inherent jurisdiction" and the theory of "implied powers" of international organizations.

(a) The concept of "inherent jurisdiction". The content of the concept of "inherent jurisdiction" (*compétence inhérente*) of international organizations amounts in its general features to the following. The practice of the United Nations and other international organizations, say the proponents of this concept, shows that their activity goes beyond the limits provided by their charters. From this the conclusion is drawn that a generally-recognized norm of international law exists to the effect that international organizations have "inherent jurisdiction", meaning that any international organization can undertake activities necessary to achieve its purposes irrespective of the specific provisions of the organization's charter.

The concept of "inherent jurisdiction" of international organizations was reflected in particular in the opinion of the International Court of 20 July 1962 on the question of certain expenses of the United Nations. The opinion of the Court says that "when the Organization takes action which warrants the assertion that it was appropriate for the fulfillment of one of the stated purposes of the United Nations, the presumption is that such action is not *ultra vires* the Organization".[17]

F. Seyersted, a Norwegian jurist who is a staunch advocate of the concept of "inherent jurisdiction", defines it as follows: "The legal capacity of intergovernmental organizations to perform sovereign' and international acts is, like that of States, not confined to what can be positively deduced from their constitutions, but comprises all acts which are not

[17] International Court of Justice, Reports of Judgments, Advisory Opinions and Orders, *Certain Expenses of the United Nations, Advisory Opinion of July 20, 1962* (1962), p. 168.

precluded by their constitutions and which do not impose new obligations upon parties who are not subject to their jurisdiction. If the constitution does not define the matters with which the Organization can deal, as is the case of the Nordic Council, then it can deal with any matter. And if the constitution does not preclude certain types of acts or *exhaustively* enumerate the acts which the Organization may perform, as very few constitutions do, then it can perform any type of acts. And so it can if there is no constitution. This principle of inherent capacities reflects more adequately the position as it is in practice".[18]

In application to the specific question of creating United Nations armed forces, the same author reasons as follows: "... it is submitted that the United Nations has the legal competence to establish military forces even in the absence of specific authority therefor in the Charter ... This is an inherent capacity of the organization ... The capacity is well within the scope of the first purpose of the United Nations, which is stated in Article 11 of the Charter ...".[19]

In stating correctly that the practice of contemporary international organizations often goes beyond the provisions of their charters, the proponents of this concept draw unjustified legal conclusions therefrom.

Can one draw from the fact of the existence of the practice of going beyond the limits of the provisions of charters of international organizations the conclusion that a generally-recognized norm of international law exists with regard to the "inherent competence" of international organizations? How could such a norm arise?

As already has been said, a customary norm of international law arises from international practice in consequence of the recurrent actions of States. Practice in and of itself, however,

18 F. Seyersted, "International Personality of Intergovernmental Organizations", *Indian Journal of International Law*, IV (1964), 55.

19 Seyersted, "Can the United Nations Establish Military Forces and Perform Other Acts Without Specific Basis in the Charter?" *Österreichische Zeitschrift fur öffentliches Recht*, XII (1962), 214.

is not yet a norm of international law. The process of forming a customary norm of international law is completed only with the recognition by States of a customary rule as a norm of international law.

Proponents of "inherent competence" make a logical generalization from individual facts and declare it to be a norm of international law. But the norm logically inferred, even if the conclusion itself is sufficiently justified, still is not a norm of law. In order to become a norm of international law, this logically inferred norm must be recognized by States as a legal norm. In this case, such recognition by States of the said norm does not exist, and not a single proponent of "inherent competence" attempts to show the contrary. It is obvious that member States of various international organizations agree in individual instances, albeit tacitly, to a respective international organization performing particular actions not expressly provided for by its charter. States do this not by virtue of legal duty, which would arise form them from the said norm if it existed, but by virtue of a free expression of will.

Thus, norms of general international law relating to "inherent competence" of international organizations do not exist.

This concept also does not find a basis in the charters of general international organizations. There are no general international organizations whose charters would empower the international organizations to use any means to achieve the purposes stipulated in their charters. Nor are there such provisions even in the charters of Western European organizations which have specific features of supranationality.

Contemporary general international organizations are created by States, and only States may define the character of eachorganization created by them, the purpose it will strive to accomplish, and the means which they place at the disposal of this organization. All this is done by concluding an international treaty – the charter of theorganization.

C. M. Chaumont, a French professor, properly emphasizes that "the creator States of an organization conclude an agreement not only regarding the nature of its purposes, but also regarding the means for accomplishing these purposes".[20]

Meanwhile, it follows from the concept of "inherent competence" that an international organization created by treaty between States is immediately separated from its base.

Since the charters of international organizations are international treaties, the concept of "inherent competence" contravenes the basic principle of the law of treaties – *pacta sunt servanda*. It follows from this principle that States should fulfill their obligations in good faith according to the charter of the international organization, that more should not be required of member States than is provided by the charter, and that member States have the right to require that the organization act in conformity with its charter.[21]

The concept of "inherent competence" contravenes the principles of interpreting international treaties. Article 31(1) of the 1969 Vienna Convention on the Law of Treaties establishes: "A treaty must be interpreted in good faith in conformity with the ordinary meaning of the provisions in the context of the treaty and in light of the subject and purpose of the treaty".

Meanwhile, the concept of "inherent competence" ascribes a certain magical force wrested from the context of the treaty to the purposes of the treaty, transforming them into something independent and essentially superseding the entire treaty. As the member of the International Court, V. M. Koretskii, noted, such a presumption with respect to the purposes of a treaty

[20] C. M. Chaumont, "La signification du principle de specialité des organizations internationales", *Mélanges offerts à Henri Rolin: Problèmes de droit des gens* (1964), p. 59.

[21] It was pointed out in a Letter of the French Government to the International Court on 15 February 1962: "Member States of the United Nations, whether original members or not, have subscribed to the obligations of the Charter, but nothing more. The Charter is a treaty, by which States have limited their jurisdiction only to the extent that they have consented". International Court of Justice, Pleadings, Oral Arguments, Documents, *Certain Expenses of the United Nations (Article 17, Paragraph 2, of the Charter). Advisory Opinion of 20 July 1962* (1962), p. 133.

would signify a return to the long condemned maxim "the ends justify the means".[22]

Finally, the concept of "inherent competence" contravenes the legal nature of contemporary international organizations. One must cite on this occasion the words of a member of the International Court, at the time the President of the Court, Winiarski, contained in his dissenting opinion regarding the Advisory Opinion of the International Court on certain expenses of the United Nations. "The Charter", declared Winiarski, "has set forth the purposes of the United Nations in very wide, and for that reason too indefinite terms. But – apart from the recourse, including the financial resources of the Organization it does not follow, far from it, that the Organization is entitled to seek to achieve those purposes by no matter what means. The fact that an organ of the United Nations is seeking to achieve one of those purposes does not suffice to render its action lawful. The Charter, a multilateral treaty which was the result of prolonged and laborious negotiations, carefully created organs and determined their competence and means of action.

"The intention of those who drafted it was clearly to abandon the possibility of useful action rather than to sacrifice the balance of carefully established fields of competence, as can be seen, for example, in the case of the voting in the Security Council. It is only by such procedures, which were clearly defined, that the United Nations can seek to achieve its purposes. It may be that the United Nations is sometimes not in a position to undertake action which would be useful for the maintenance of international peace and security or for one or another or the purposes indicated in Article 1 of the Charter, but that is the way in which the Organization was conceived and brought into being".[23]

The nonconformity of the jurisdiction of the United Nations to the purposes proclaimed in its Charter is by no means the

[22] International Court of Justice, *Certain Expenses of the United Nations*, p. 268.

[23] Ibid., p. 230.

result of the lack of foresight of the founders of this international organization, but, as already pointed out (see Chapter XIII), a manifestation of the nature of contemporary international organizations.

The concept of inherent competence, supposedly guided exclusively or basically by the purposes proclaimed in the charter of an international organization, fundamentally contravenes the legal nature of contemporary general international organizations as interstate formations of peaceful coexistence.

(b) The concept of "implied powers". The concept of "implied powers" (*compétence implicite*) of international organizations frequently is interpreted so broadly that it closely approximates the concept of "inherent competence".

In the Advisory Opinion of the International Court in the case concerning reparation for injuries suffered in the service of the United Nations this concept was formulated as follows: "Under international law, that the Organization must be deemed to have those powers which, although not expressly provided in the Charter, are conferred upon it by necessary implication as being essential to the performance of its duties".[24] The Court referred in this connection to the Advisory Opinion of the League of Nations Permanent Court of International Justice of 23 July 1926.[25]

In substantiating this position, the International Court referred to the presumption of the conformity of jurisdiction to the purposes and functions of an organization, that is to say, to the "principles of effectiveness", coming close to the concept of "implied competence". "It must be acknowledged", the Court maintains in this Advisory Opinion, "that its members, by entrusting certain functions to it, with the attendant duties

[24] International Court of Justice, Reports of Judgments, Advisory Opinions and Orders, *Reparation for Injuries Suffered in the Service of the United Nations, Advisory Opinion of April 11, 1949* (1949), p. 182.

[25] Ibid., pp. 182-183.

and responsibilities, have clothed it with the competence required to enable those functions to be effectively discharged".[26] The Court added that the "rights and duties of an entity such as the Organization [the United Nations – *G.T.*] must depend upon its purposes and functions as specified or implied in its constituent documents and developed in practice".[27]

The concept of "implied powers" was applied by the Western powers to justify General Assembly resolution 377(V), "Uniting for Peace".

This resolution maintains, first, that it should be implied that if an organ has not undertaken necessary actions provided for by the United Nations Charter, another organ may assume the fulfillment of these duties. "... Failure of the Security Council to discharge its responsibilities on behalf of all the Member States ... does not relieve Member States of their obligations or the United Nations of its responsibility under the Charter to maintain international peace and security".

The conclusion is drawn from this that another organ, to wit, the General Assembly, can assume, in the event the Security Council fails to act, the adoption of appropriate measures, including the "use of armed forces, when necessary, to maintain or restore international peace and security".[28] The conclusion concerning the "implied power" of the General Assembly was formulated as follows in the resolution: "... discharge by the General Assembly of its responsibilities in this respect calls for possibilities of observation which would ascertain the facts and expose aggressors; for the existence of armed forces which could be used collectively; and for the possibility of timely recommendation by the General Assembly to Members of the United Nations for collective action which, to be effective, should be prompt".

[26] Ibid., p. 179.

[27] Ibid., p. 180.

[28] G.A. Res. 377(V), 3 November 1950.

The concept of the "implied powers" of international organizations and their organs as set forth in the above advisory opinion of the International Court of 1949 and in the illegal United Nations General Assembly resolution 377(V) lay at the basis of bourgeois doctrine on this question. In its turn, this doctrine resorts to the concept of "implied powers" generally to justify the "Uniting for Peace" resolution and the actions undertaken on the basis of this resolution.

Thus, Professor L. Goodrich maintains on this plane that the General Assembly "has at least a 'residual responsibility' of its own".[29] Professor de Arechaga also speaks of the "residual functions" (*la reserva de funciones*) of the General Assembly of the United Nations.[30] "Taking effective collective measures to suppress aggression", he writes, "is within the limits of the Charter, one may say, in the center of the Charter. It obviously follows from this that the General Assembly can discuss and recommend the taking of effective collective measures to suppress aggression".[31]

D. W. Bowett, an English professor, in devoting an extensive monograph to the question of United Nations armed forces, raises the question: "Is it necessary at all to locate specifically in the Charter provisions for the constitutional authority of the United Nations Forces? In other words, cannot a more general argument for their legality be relied upon?"[32] And of course the author answers this question affirmatively, resorting to the concepts of "inherent" and "implied" competence as they have been formulated in the advisory opinions of the International Court in question.[33]

In formulating a broad concept of "implied powers", bourgeois jurists in fact maintain that there exists a norm of

[29] Goodrich, *The United Nations*, p. 177.

[30] Arechaga, *Derecho constitucional de las Naciones Unidas*, p. 197.

[31] Ibid., p. 198.

[32] D. W. Bowett, *United Nations Forces* (1964), p. 307.

[33] Ibid., pp. 307-311.

international law according to which one should imply that member States of an international organization have granted it that competence which is necessary to effectuate the purposes and functions of the organization. Bowett defines "implied powers" as those powers "which may reasonably be deduced from the purposes and functions of the organisation in question".[34]

Professor B. Rouyer-Hameray, of the University of Strasbourg, writes: "One should suppose that the authors of an agreement or treaty intended to create norms which in practice could operate. It is necessary, therefore, to presume an intention to create everything necessary for their effective operation: if States have created an international organization, they intended to create everything necessary for it to function...".[35]

A. Sereni, an Italian professor, in declaring that the question of "implied powers" is one of interpreting the charter of an international organization, actually comes to assert that there is a generally obligatory norm of international law regarding "implied powers". "The determination of the implied powers of international organizations", wrote Sereni, "is, therefore, the result of interpretation, although also an extension, of the constitution of the organization, and not a process of creating new norms ...".[36]

In this connection, however, Sereni places in such interpretation a content which transforms it into the creating of new norms even in violation of the organization's charter. "With the exception of provisions contained in the constitution", he says, "any organization has the implied power to interpret the constitution for the purpose of determining its own competence as regards its purposes and functions and therefore

[34] Bowett, *The Law of International Institutions* (1964), p. 275.

[35] B. Router-Hamaray, *Les competences implicites des organisations internationales* (1962), pp. 80-81.

[36] A. Sereni, *Diritto internazionale* (1960), II, 980.

to establish the extent of its own competence".[37] The author even admits, although by way of exception, that such a determination of the jurisdiction of the organization also can be effectuated by an organ not entrusted by the charter with the functions regarding which a question may arise in a concrete instance.[38]

Of course, it is virtually impossible to provide clauses for all possible instances of future activity in the charters of international organizations, especially in the charter of an organization such as the United Nations, whose functions are exceedingly broad and diverse. Therefore, in working out the charters, the parties inevitably presuppose that a number of questions of the activity of an international organization, not of course the major questions, remain to be decided on the basis of the charter provisions in the process of the functioning of the organization. On this level, one may speak of "implied powers".

"Implied powers" is not a norm of general international law. What has been said before about the absence in international law of norms concerning "inherent competence" also relates generally to the "implied powers" of international organizations. The 1949 opinion of the International Court and the majority of bourgeois jurists go father than what corresponds to contemporary international law. On this plane, the view of the member of the International Court, G. Hackworth, expressed in is dissenting opinion in this case, deserves attention, although one can not completely agree with it. Warning of the danger of a broad interpretation of "necessary implication", Hackworth declared: "There can be no gainsaying the fact that the Organization is one of delegated and enumerated powers. It is to be presumed that such powers as the Member States desired to confer upon it are stated either in the Charter or in complementary agreements concluded by them. Powers not expressed cannot freely be implied. Implied powers flow from

37 Ibid., p. 985.

38 Ibid.

a grant of expressed powers, and are limited to those that are `necessary' to the exercise of powers expressly granted".[39]

Professor Chaumont defines the "implied powers" (*pourvoirs implicites*) of an international organization as follows: "By implied powers are understood those powers which, while not textually provided for by the creators of the organization, have been recognized or accepted by member States within a certain period of the life of the organization as auxiliary or subordinate means to accomplish the permanent ends for which the organization was founded".[40]

Here, however, the question is actually one of the creating of new, subordinate, and more precise norms through additional agreements among the members.[41]

Thus, "implied powers" of international organizations can occur. The question of the existence and extent of such jurisdiction in each individual instance is a question of interpreting the charter of the respective international organization with those additions and changes which might have been formed in the course of its activity on the basis of agreement of the members of the given organization.

The general rules of interpreting international treaties, with those possible changes which may exist within the framework of the respective international organizations, apply to interpreting the charters of international organizations. This has been recognized repeatedly by the International Court, and the practice of the international organizations themselves;

[39] International Court of Justice, *Reparation for Injuries Suffered in the Service of the United Nations*, p. 198.

[40] Chaumont, "La signification du principe de specialité des organisations internationales", p. 59.

[41] On this plane, P. Reuter believes the adoption by international organizations of "executive regulations by which organs of an international organization clarify obligations defined in the charters without broadening them" is a manifestation of "implied powers". As an example, he mentions the United Nations General Assembly resolution establishing rules for registering international treaties at the United Nations. P. Reuter, *Institutions internationales* (4th ed.; 1963), p. 215.

and international legal doctrine proceeds from this. Thus, in the 1962 advisory opinion on the question of certain expenses of the United Nations, the International Court again confirmed the proposition, although in its conclusions it actually moves far away from it. The Court pointed out: "On the previous occasions when the Court has had to interpret the Charter of the United Nations, it has followed the principles and rules applicable in general to the interpretation of treaties, since it has recognized that the Charter is a multilateral treaty, albeit a treaty having certain special characteristics".[42]

The interpretation of an international treaty is the establishment of the result of the concordance of the wills of States as it was expressed in the treaty. Interpretation of a treaty includes also an elucidation of the concordance of wills with regard to what was implied but was not precisely expressed in the treaty text and the accompanying documents. If certain changes and additions have been made in the treaty in the course of applying it, then naturally the interpretation of a treaty at a particular moment will also embrace the concordance of the wills of the parties to the treaty which has occurred in connection with such additions and changes.

One should above all reject the concept of interpretation which attaches exaggerated significance to the purposes and functions proclaimed in the charter of an international organization at the expense of diminishing the significance of the specific provisions of the charter.

Without treating in detail the problems of interpreting international treaties, it is necessary to point out that implied powers can not be sought in the charter of every international organization. As A. D. McNair justly points out, "many treaties contain express conditions, and in some treaties conditions are implied".[43] But the author, not without justification, warns against an enthusiasm for "implying". "Conditions", he says,

[42] International Court of Justice, *Certain Expenses of the United Nations*, p. 157.

[43] A. D. McNair, *The Law of Treaties* (1961), p. 436.

"should be implied only with great circumspection, for if they are implied too readily, they become a serious threat to the sanctity of a treaty".[44]

The "implied power" of an international organization in reality exists when in order to effectuate the competence clearly granted to the organization as a whole or its organ (but not generally to effectuate the purposes and functions of the organization) it is necessary to resort to actions which not only do not contravene the charter of the organization but also are customary in international practice.

Thus, for example, if the charter of an organization provides for the organization's rendering assistance to States in a specific field but is silent about the possibility of the organization's concluding agreements with the respective States, one can suppose with assurance that the conclusion of such agreements is an "implied power" of this organization. The conclusion of such agreements not only is necessary to effectuate a specific competence of the organization, but is at the present time a normal means of formalizing such relations between States and international organizations.

3. Change of the Charters of International Organizations

The most important feature characterizing the legal nature of contemporary general international organizations and their charters is the fact that no changes of these charters become binding upon member States without their consent.

In this domain there are a number of new phenomena. The previous requirement of the unanimity of members of the organization has passed away; it no longer is applied either at the stage of adopting amendments to charters of international organizations nor at the stage of their entry into force. According to the charters of the majority of contemporary general international organizations, amendments to charters are adopted by two-thirds of the votes of the organization or special conferences where all members of the organization

[44] Ibid. [The Russian text reads: "... to the stability of treaties" – *WEB*].

are represented. Amendments usually enter into force after their ratification or adoption by two-thirds of the members of the organization; in some organizations this majority must include specific members of the organization; in the United Nations – all permanent members of the Security Council; in the International Labour Organization, five of the ten members of the Council included in the category of basic industrial powers.

An amendment to the charter of an international organization ratified or adopted by the requisite majority of members of the organization usually, but not always, enters into force for all members of the organization (United Nations, International Labour Organization, World Health Organization). Sometimes this rule is applied only with respect to less significant amendments to a charter, whereas the more important amendments enter into force after their adoption by two-thirds of the member States and only for those States which have accepted these amendments (World Meteorological Organization).

The constitutions of UNESCO and of the Food and Agricultural Organization go the farthest on this level. Article XIII(1) of the UNESCO Constitution reads: "Proposals for amendments to this Constitution shall become effective upon receiving the approval of the General Conference by a two-thirds majority; provided, however, that those amendments which involve fundamental alterations in the aims of the Organization or new obligations for the Member States shall require subsequent acceptance on the part of two-thirds of the Member States before they come into force". Amendments to the Food and Agricultural Organization Constitution are adopted by the Conference by two-thirds of the States voting on condition that the majority of those who voted for the amendment constitute more than half of the members of the organization. An amendment not involving new obligations for members of the FAO enters into force immediately, unless otherwise provided in the conference resolution adopting the amendment (Article 19).

Thus, in both UNESCO and the FAO some amendments to the constitution of the organization enter into force after their adoption by an organ of the organization without subsequent ratification or approval by member States.

It would be incorrect to deprecate the importance of these new phenomena in the question of amending the charters of international organizations. But at the same time, one can not lose sight of the fact that all these changes leave the basic process of changing the charters of international organizations unaffected – the concordance of the wills of States. Any amendment to the charter of a general international organization can not become binding upon member States of the organization without its consent, explicitly or tacitly expressed. This also is applicable to those instances when, according to the charter of an international organization, amendments to the charter which have been adopted or for which two-thirds of the members of the organization have expressed themselves enter into force for all members of this organization.

If a State does not consider it possible to adopt a charter amendment which is entering into force, it has according to the provisions prevailing in contemporary general international organizations either the right to withdraw from the organization (the United Nations and the majority of specialized agencies) or is considered automatically to have left the organization (the International Civil Aviation Organization) and the Intergovernmental Maritime Consultative Organization). In some specialized agencies of the United Nations (ICAO, IMCO), continuation of membership in the organization for States who have not ratified an amendment which has entered into force is allowed with respect to specific amendments, that is to say, a different legal regime for member States is permitted.[45]

[45] For greater detail, see R. Zacklin, *The Amendment of the Constitutive Instruments of the United Nations and Specialized Agencies* (1968), pp. 161- 166; E. Yemin, *Legislative Powers in the United Nations and Specialized Agencies* (1969).

The question of the possibility of changing the charters of international organizations by subsequent practice, that is, by means of custom, is much more complex. In order to ignore or, first and foremost, to justify the violations of the United Nations Charter which have taken place under the pressure of Western powers, many bourgeois international lawyers frequently speak of the practice of the United Nations and other international organizations as something which must be followed in the future as well, almost forgetting about the charters of these organizations. In analyzing this practice, they mix together lawful acts with actions which are a violation of the charters, and they come to the more or less identical conclusion that the practice of an international organization can change its charter. The view of L. Goodrich, of Columbia University, relating to the practice of the United Nations is characteristic. "In actual practice", writes Goodrich, "the structure of power and influence in the United Nations has been quite different from what was initially envisaged. The Charter itself has not been amended. The composition, functions, and powers of organs have remained the same on paper. But in the course of the day-to-day interpretation and application of these provisions, a quite different system of power relationships has emerged from that which was anticipated at the time the Charter was approved in San Francisco".[46]

We have spoken previously (see Chapter IV[3]) about the possibility of changing an international treaty through custom being applicable in principle also to the charters of international organizations. In admitting the possibility of the change and development of a treaty through custom, however, one must be cautious, since the question is one of the subsequent agreement of the parties not clearly expressed changing a clearly-expressed agreement which has been embodied in the treaty. To establish the existence of an agreement not clearly expressed, naturally, is more difficult. In addition, an agreement not clearly expressed in this case is an

46 Goodrich, *The United Nations*, p. 115.

exception with regard to the provisions concerning a change of the treaty which are fixed in the treaty itself.

Special caution must be shown in appraising the practice of international organizations. The fact is that the question here is one of a permanently functioning entity where there may occur, as the experience of the United Nations illustrates, recurrent practice which was simply a violation of the United Nations Charter and in no way a change thereof.

From that which was said in Chapter IV(3) below about treaties in general being applicable to the charters of international organizations, it follows that the amendment through custom of certain provisions of the charter of an international organization which are not basic is possible in those instances when: (a) a practice has been formed in a given international organization with which all members of this organization have agreed; (b) this practice is evidence of an agreement of members of the organization to amend the respective provisions of its charter.

The basic element is that the charter of an international organization, being an international treaty, can be amended only by States-parties to this treaty, and not by the international organization itself, created by the treaty. The subsequent practice of an international organization is at the same time the practice of States, since the actions of an international organization are basically determined by the actions of member States of this organization. If such practice is evidence of the existence among participants in the organization of an agreement concerning the making of certain changes to the previously constituted agreement of these States expressed in the charter of the organization, then, as already has been pointed out, such agreement achieved through custom may not change the basic provisions of the treaty, that is, in the present case the charter of the international organization.

What has been said seems to us to reflect existing practice, which also testifies to the fact that this does not relate to the provisions of charters affecting the bases of a particular international organization.

The practice of the United Nations Security Council on the question of the abstention of permanent members of the Council is a clear example of the modification of the charter provisions of an international organization by subsequent practice which corresponds to the said requirements. As is well-known, according to Article 27(3) of the United Nations Charter, decisions of the Security Council concerning all questions of a nonprocedural character are considered to be adopted when nine members of the Council (previously seven) have cast their votes for them, including the concurring votes of all its permanent members. This point does not provide for cases when the permanent members abstain from voting on nonprocedural questions.

In practice the Security Council, as a result of the clearly expressed or tacit consent of the members of the Council, has established the rule that the abstention of a permanent member of the Security Council during a vote is not regarded as a negative vote and does not prevent the adoption of the decision.

Logically, this rule emanates from the fact that every permanent member of the Security Council has the opportunity to determine its attitude toward the resolution being discussed and to vote for it, if it supports it, or to abstain, if it does not support its adoption but nevertheless has no objection to its being adopted, or to vote against if it objects to the given decision.

The said rule, formed in the practice of applying Article 27 of the United Nations Charter, introduces some change into this Article. Tacitly adopted by the member of the United Nations, it has been completely consolidated in the practice of the Security Council's work.

On the other hand, General Assembly Resolution 377(V) of 3 November 1950 (the so-called "Uniting for Peace" resolution), as it does not correspond to the aforesaid requirements, is a violation of the Charter and not a modification thereof. This resolution has the purpose of amending the basic provisions of the Charter (the principle of the unanimity of the permanent members of the Security Council, the co-relation of the competence of the General Assembly and the Security Council, and so forth), and many States resolutely opposed it, including one permanent member of the Security Council. Meanwhile, even the provisions of the Charter relating to changes of the Charter provide that no change of the Charter may occur without the consent of all the permanent members of the Security Council.

One can not concur with J. Castaneda, a Mexican jurist, who, while proceeding from theoretical propositions that on the whole are correct, permits inaccuracies in stating the facts and in consequence thereof comes to the unjustified conclusion that all members of the United Nations, supposedly including the Soviet Union, agreed with the "Uniting for Peace" resolution, as a result whereof this resolution modified the United Nations Charter. Castaneda writes: "The thesis which will be here sustained is that the United-for-Peace resolution could not, by itself, have the legal consequences of altering the collective security system of the Charter, but that it was the starting point, as well as the nucleus of a rule shaped during the subsequent years, through the conscious and repeated acquiescence of it, either tacit or stated, of all groups of United Nations Members; and that by virtue of this rule, the legal situation prevailing at present as regards the collective security system of the United Nations is different in an appreciable degree and in several aspects, from the original Charter's system".[47]

The argumentation adduced by the author in evidence of this thesis amounts to the following: The "Uniting for Peace" resolution was approved by the General Assembly with the votes of all members of the United Nations except the socialist States. On the other hand, on the question of intervention in Europe, the socialist States voted for a number of resolutions adopted by the General Assembly. Only Israel voted against the

[47] J. Castaneda, "Certain Legal Consequences of the Suez Crisis", *Revue Egyptienne de droit international*, XIX (1963), 3.

key resolution in the General Assembly. As the States which voted against or abstained on the resolutions regarding the invasion of Egypt had previously voted in favour of the "Uniting for Peace" resolution, it can be said that after the Suez crisis not a single member of the United Nations was left who at one time or another had not approved the "Uniting for Peace" resolution and, therefore, had not accepted juridically its necessary impli- cations.[48]

The author, however, lost sight of exceedingly important facts: the Soviet Union voted in 1956 only for those General Assembly resolutions which contained appeals to the belligerents to reach a cease-fire agreement, recommendations to all United Nations members to refrain from deliveries of arms to the area of military activities [Resolution 997(E-1)], appeals to Israel, England, and France to withdraw their forces from Egyptian territory [Resolution 1002(E-1)], and so forth. In abstaining from the resolutions concerning the creating of emergency armed forces and their functioning [Resolutions 998, 1000(E-1)], since the State being subjected to aggression considered the creating of such forces useful, the Soviet Union set forth its position on this question precisely. The Representative of the Soviet Union, V. Kuznetsov, stated at the 567th Session of the First Emergency Session of the General Assembly on 7 November 1956 the following: "As regards the creation and stationing on Egyptian territory of an international police force, the Soviet delegation is obliged to point out that this Force is being created in violation of the United Nations Charter.

"The General Assembly resolution on the basis of which it is now proposed to form this Force is inconsistent with the Charter. Chapter VII of the Charter empowers the Security Council, the Security Council only, and not the General Assembly, to set up an international armed force and to take

[48] Ibid., p. 9; see also I. Detter, *Law Making by International Organizations* (1965), p. 39. In a review of this book H. Blix says Detter's comments that during the 1956 Suez Crisis the Soviet Union supposedly agreed that Resolution 377(V) "does not correspond to reality". H. Blix, "The Beginnings of International Regulation", *Cooperation and Conflict*, I (1966), 109.

such action as it may deem necessary, including the use of such a force, to maintain or restore international peace and security".

The position of the Soviet State, therefore, was expressed sufficiently clearly: the Soviet Union expressly declared that the creation and use of armed forces on the basis of a General Assembly resolution is a violation of the United Nations Charter.

The Soviet Union repeatedly opposed and protested against other measures contravening the Charter, in particular measures concerning the operation of the armed forces and their financing.[49]

The interpretation which R. Zacklin gives of the proposal of the Soviet Government made in June 1967 to convene an emergency session of the General Assembly also is untrue.[50] The Soviet Government declared in this proposal that it considers it essential that the General Assembly, in accordance with Article 11 of the United Nations Charter, consider the situation which has arisen and adopt a decision designed to bring about the liquidation of the consequences of aggression and the immediate withdrawal of Israeli forces behind the armistice lines.[51]

[49] See, in particular, the Memorandum of the USSR Government to the International Court on the Procedure of Financing the Operations of the United Nations Emergency Force in the Middle East and the United Nations Operations in the Congo, in International Court of Justice, Pleadings, Oral Arguments, Documents, *Certain Expenses of the United Nations*, pp. 270-274; the Memorandum of the Government of the USSR Regarding Certain Measures to Strengthen the Effectiveness of the United Nations in the Safeguarding of International Peace and Security, Doc. No. S/5811, 10 July 1964; the Memorandum of the Ministry of Foreign Affairs of the USSR on the Question of the Financial Situation of the United Nations, Doc. No. A/5729, 11 September 1964; the Memorandum of the Government of the USSR of 16 March 1967, relating to "U.N. Operations for the Maintenance of International Peace and Security", Известия [News], 6 April 1967, p. 1.

[50] Zacklin, *The Amendment of the Constitutive Instruments of the United Nations*, p. 188.

[51] Doc. No. A/6717 [Request for the summoning of an emergency special session of the General Assembly: letter dated 13 June 1967 from the Representative of the USSR to the Secretary-General – *WEB*].

There are not grounds whatever for interpreting this declaration as evidence of the Soviet Union's having recognized Resolution 377(V), as Zacklin claims. There is no reference to this resolution in the declaration of the Soviet Government, and the proposal to convene a special session of the General Assembly could be based on Article 20 of the United Nations Charter. In any case, there is nothing in this statement, nor in other statements of the Soviet Government, giving grounds to interpret them as agreement with the basic provisions of Resolution 377(V) that United Nations armed forces may be created on the basis of a resolution of the United Nations General Assembly.

In a Memorandum of 16 March 1967, the Soviet Government once again confirmed its position on the question of the creation and use of United Nations armed forces. "At the same time", the Memorandum says, "the Soviet Government considers it necessary to emphasize once again that any attempts to revise the provisions of the Charter concerning the use of armed forces in the name of the United Nations or the conditions of financing such operations will encounter a negative attitude on the part of the Soviet Union".[52]

Consequently, the thesis that Resolution 377(V) and the practice based on it have introduced changes into the Charter of the United Nations is unjustified. This resolution has left a dark stain on the history of the United Nations as a flagrant violation of the basic principles of this organization.

One must agree with Professor M. Seara Vasquez (Mexico) that the "Uniting for Peace" resolution was an "attempt against the very concept of the Organization", violated the basic provisions of the United Nations Charter, and therefore is void *ab initio*.[53]

[52] Известия [News], 6 April 1967, p. 1.

[53] M. Seara Vasquez, "Las reformas a la Carta de la Naciones Unidas", *Estudios de Derecho Internacional Homenaje a D. Antonio de Luna* (1968), p. 442.

CHAPTER XV.
THE BASIC FEATURES OF THE LEGAL NATURE OF CONTEMPORARY GENERAL INTERNATIONAL ORGANIZATIONS

(continued)

1. *The Interstate Character of General International Organizations*

The objective process of the internationalization of production and of other aspects of the life of contemporary society is leading, as already has been pointed out, to an expansion of the functions and powers of international organizations. At the same time, laws of societal development, such as the existence of sovereign States and the coexistence and struggle of the two opposed social systems, lead to the fact that both the process of internationalization itself and the expansion of the functions and powers of international organizations are occurring in interstate forms.

Contemporary general international organizations as interstate entities are characterized in general by the following features: they are created by States through the conclusion of international treaties and operate on the basis of such treaties (see Chapter XIV); States remain sovereign and equal both within and without an international organization; the mechanism of an international organization is brought into operation by States; member States have the right to withdraw from the organization; the basic resolutions of international organizations are of a recommendatory nature (see Chapter V).

(a) The principle of the equality of States in international organizations. We already have said that by virtue of the laws of societal development contemporary general international organizations are so structured that member States of such organizations continue to remain sovereign entities (see Chapter XIII).

The question of the application of the principle of equality of States within contemporary international organizations is, theoretically and practically, more complex. In approaching the question formally, some bourgeois jurists come to maintain the "sovereign equality" in general is not compatible with the nature of contemporary international organizations. The principle of equality, they assert, supposedly requires the adoption of resolutions only on the basis of unanimity, whereas unanimity is not now applied in international organizations. Thus, Professor G. Scelle, citing Article 2(1) of the United Nations Charter, which says that the organization is based on the principle of the sovereign equality of all its members, wrote that "philosophically this is impossible, false, and hypo- critical".[1] An international organization, Scelle wrote further, is "incompatible with the system of the unanimity limited even to the five great powers because the principle of `equal sovereignty' implied that a State is bound only by those norms of law which have been signed and ratified by its government".[2]

The application of the principle of equality of States within international organizations, naturally, has its own peculiarities in comparison with general international law. In order to effectuate the purposes and tasks of a respective international organization, its principles, particularly the principle of equality of members, must be so formulated as to best promote the effectuation of the organization's tasks. Therefore, as Professor C. A. Colliard points out, the principle of equality of States "adjusts itself" to the purposes and tasks of the organization.[3] But at the same time, it remains one of the most important principles of the structure and activity of contemporary general international organizations.

The principle of equality signifies above all the equal right of all States to participate in general international organizations

[1] G. Scelle, "Préalable à l'intégration d'une société internationale universelle", *Mélanges Séfériades* (1961), I, 8.

[2] Ibid., p. 9.

[3] See C. A. Colliard, "Quelques réflexions sur la structure et le fonctionnement des organizations internationales", *Mélanges offerts à Henri Rolin: Problèmes de droit des gens* (1964), p. 68.

since such organizations take up questions of interest to all States and their activity affects the rights and interests of all States.[4]

In general international organizations each member State has an equal right to raise questions and put forward proposals for discussion in the organization. Every member has an equal right, in accordance with the organization's charter, to be represented in organs of the organization and to take part in the discussion of issues. In taking decisions, each State has one vote. This is the situation in the United Nations. Of thirteen specialized agencies of the United Nations, to which one should add the International Atomic Energy Agency, which is linked to the United Nations by an agreement on cooperation, only three apply the system of weighted voting: the International Bank for Reconstruction and Development, the International Monetary Fund, and the International Finance Corporation.[5] These international organizations, however, are not actually general international organizations since the socialist States do not participate in them.

Practical necessity has led to the establishment in all general international organizations of a more or less uniform structure: a plenary organ (assembly, congress) in which all States are represented; a particular organ (council) consisting

[4] See G. Schirmer, *Universalität völkerrchtliche Verträger und internationaler Organisation* (1966).

[5] See K. Ia. Chizhov, Международные валютно-финансовые организации капитализма [International Currency and Financial Organizations of Capitalism] (1968). The author very aptly remarks in particular: "The organizers of the International Monetary Fund understood that all member countries would lay a claim to take part in the administration of this institution. At the same time, they were clearly aware that an organ created from equal representatives of all countries would be difficult to use in their own interests. Therefore, the principle of equality was not laid down as the basis of the organization of the IMF, but the recognition of the economic inequality of States, pursuant to which the status of members of the international organization is determined by their economic power. As a result, the organizational form of a joint-stock society was deemed most responsive was deemed most responsive to the requirements submitted by the imperialist States to the International Monetary Fund, since it ensured the predominance of the United States and a small group of other imperialist countries in this international agency" (pp. 15-16).

of representatives of a limited number of members of the organization, and a secretariat. Frequently, a specific number of places in the council of the organizations are allocated to the more important States within the sphere of activity of the organization (Intergovernmental Maritime Consultative Organization,[6] International Labor Organization, International Atomic Energy Agency) or through other means ensure the permanent representation of such States in the council (for example, International Civil Aviation Organization). The permanent members of the United Nations Security Council are expressly indicated in the United Nations Charter.

In the United Nations there also exists the principle of unanimity of the great powers in the Security Council, engendered for exceedingly important reasons: the diverse role of States in international relations, especially in the maintenance of international peace and security; the existence of two opposed social systems and the necessity of guarantees against the United Nations being transformed into an instrument of States of one social system; the need to ensure the effectiveness of decisions of the organization on the maintenance of international peace and security, and so forth.

From the viewpoint of the principle of equality of States, the principle of the unanimity of the great powers in the Security Council is subjected to the most serious attacks. Many writers maintain that the principle establishes the hegemony of the great powers and is incompatible with the principle of the equality of States. Comparing the "right of veto" with the principle of sovereign equality of all members of the United Nations proclaimed in Article 1 of the United Nations Charter. H. Kelsen maintains that "there is an open contradiction between the political ideology of the United Nations and its legal constitution".[7]

[6] Since 1982 this organization is called the International Maritime Organization – *LNS*].

[7] H. Kelsen, *The Law of the United Nations* (1951), p. 277.

Ulloa, a Peruvian professor, states that the Charter is a "step backward" as regards the principle of equality of States.[8] He says, in particular, that the institute of permanent members and the principle of unanimity of the great powers in the Security Council "eliminate the proclaimed principle of international equality".[9]

An Indian author calls the formula of Article 2(1) of the Charter an "empty phrase".[10] "The special privileges of the Great Powers in the Security Council and otherwise", the author writes, "make nonsense of that principle".[11]

To that which has been said about the importance of the principle of unanimity of the great powers in the Security Council as a guarantee against the United Nations being transformed into an instrument of States of one social system, it should be added here that precisely this principle prevents in a specific international situation the hegemony of certain great powers in the Security Council and, consequently, in the United Nations, and is a guarantee of the realization of the principle of equality of member States of the United Nations.[12] In reality, if this principle did not exist, the Security Council could easily be transformed into a dangerous weapon in the hands of the imperialist powers and be used not only against the socialist States, but also, and even most likely, against the weak States of Asia, Africa, and Latin America.

The principle of the sovereign equality of States frequently is referred to in order to justify the claim of the supremacy of the General Assembly in comparison with the Security Council. This idea is one cornerstone of a draft amendment of the United

[8] A. Ulloa, *Derecho internacional publico* (4th ed.; 1957), II, 457.

[9] Ibid., p. 458.

[10] R. Anand, "Sovereign Equality of States in the United Nations", *Indian Journal of International Law*, VII (1967), 200.

[11] Ibid.

[12] See G. I. Tunkin, "The Legal Nature of the United Nations", *Recueil des cours*, CXIX (1966), 1-68.

Nations Charter set forth in the book of two American writers, Grenville Clark and Louis

Sohn, which is so widely publicized in the United States and other countries.[13]

Of course, the United Nations General Assembly, where all members of the Organization are represented, where every member has one vote, and decisions are taken by a majority vote (on important questions by a two-thirds majority), is closer in structure to an international conference than other organs of the United Nations. Therefore the principle of the sovereign equality of States is manifested more directly here. On this plane it was pointed out in an explanatory memorandum of forty-nine Asian and African States on the question of the composition of the General Committee that the General Assembly is the body "reflecting the principle of sovereign equality of all Member States".[14] As already has been said, however, it would be untrue to regard the said principle as not operative in other organs of the United Nations, although there, as an analysis of the provisions of the Charter shows, it adapts itself to the conditions of the activity of contemporary international organizations in general and to the specific peculiarities of the United Nations dictated by the contemporary international situation.

The supremacy of the General Assembly in comparison with the Security Council may seem more advantageous to small States, which have a majority of votes in the General Assembly. Here, however, a consideration of a legal principle divorced from reality, that is, from the real consequence of its operation in a concrete situation, leads to the incorrect conclusion that the supremacy of the General Assembly would strengthen the international organization and would be useful

13 See G. Clark and L. Sohn, World Peace Through World Law (3d ed.; 1966), pp. 35-49. Also see Commission to Study the Organization of Peace, *New Dimensions for the United Nations* (1966).

14 Doc. No. A/5519 (XVIII), 17 September 1963.

for the small States.[15] As Professor M. Virally correctly notes, the idea of "international democracy" and the taking of decisions by a majority of votes of States is a "deceptive" idea.[16]

In reality, if the competence to take decisions on questions of the maintenance of international peace and security requiring action (Article 11), were transferred from the Security Council to the General Assembly, a completely new situation would arise that would represent a danger above all for the small powers. The imperialist powers would have broad opportunities to use the various combinations, to apply the old "divide and conquer" policy, from which small countries have suffered so much in the past.

(b) The right to withdraw from an international organization. The right of member States to withdraw from an international organization is a *conditio sine qua non* of the interstate character of the organization.

The right to withdraw exists in all general international organizations irrespective of whether it is specified in the charter of an international organization. Naturally, it is effectuated in conformity with the provisions of the respective international organization's charter or supplemental agreements of the organization's members.[17]

The constitutions of all specialized agencies of the United Nations, except for the World Health Organization, the Charter of the International Atomic Energy Agency, as well as the

[15] See, for example, Ulloa, *Derecho internacional publico*, II, pp. 457-464; Anand, "Sovereign Equality of States in the United Nations".

[16] M. Virally, *L'O.N.U. d'hier à demain* (1961), pp. 114-115.

[17] On the question of the right to withdraw from an international organization, see in particular S. B. Krylov, История создания ООН [History of Creation of United Nations], ed. G. I. Tunkin (1960), pp. 115-118; E. A. Shibaeva, Специализированные учреждения ООН [Specialized Agencies of the United Nations] (1966), pp. 61-63; L. Goodrich and E. Hambro, *The Charter of the United Nations* (2d ed.; 1949), p. 144; N. Singh, *Termination of Membership in International Organizations* (1958), pp. 23-26, 80-98; N. Feinberg, "Unilateral Withdrawal from an International Organization", *British Year Book of International Law*, XXXIX (1963), 215-218; F. Dehousse, "Le droit de retrait aux Nations Unies", *Revue belge de droit international*, I (1965), 30-48.

charters of the majority, if not all, of the other specialized general international organizations contain provisions on the right of withdrawal from the organization. However, the absence in the charter of an international organization of a reference to the right of withdrawal from the organization can not, of course, be interpreted as the absence of such a right. In his monograph, *Termination of Membership of International Organizations,* an Indian jurist, N. Singh, comes to the correct conclusion that if the charter of an international organization is silent about the right to withdraw from the organization, such a right is presupposed since "anything which is not conceded in favour of the international organization is retained by the member State, which by virtue of its sovereignty must be vested with the residuary juris- diction".[18]

The right of withdrawal also exists in the United Nations, although the Charter is silent about it. However, the San Francisco Conference approved a report of Committee I/2, which spoke of the right of withdrawal from the Organization "for good and sufficient reasons".[19] The Representative of the USSR, A. A. Gromyko, stated in this connection at a plenary session of the Conference that the right to withdraw from the Organization "is a reflection of State sovereignty".[20] The United States delegate, in turn, pointed out that "in an organization of sovereign States it was clear that all members would possess the faculty of withdrawal".[21] Kelsen's view, that the right to withdraw from the United Nations does not exist since it was not specified in the United Nations Charter, is based on a narrower formalistic approach and has no basis in international law.[22] One also can hardly agree with the view of M. Scerni, an Italian professor, who suggests that the right of

18 Singh, *Termination of Membership of International Organizations,* pp. 80- 81.

19 United Nations, *Documents of the United Nations Conference on International Organization, San Francisco, 1945* (1945), VII, 577.

20 Ibid., p. 264.

21 Ibid., p. 265.

22 See Kelsen, *The Law of the United Nations,* pp. 124-129.

withdrawal from the United Nations exists only for instances of amending the Charter, and in all other "exceptional instances" there is only a right "to refuse in some degree to cooperate in the organization".[23]

When in 1965 Indonesia declared its withdrawal from the United Nations, the question of the right to withdraw could not arise in general and, as Professor G. Schwarzenberger correctly pointed out, the question could only be whether the utterances were sufficient grounds for such withdrawal.[24]

However, in this sole instance in United Nations practice, the question did not receive precise legal treatment. The Statement of the Government of Indonesia in 1965 said that "Indonesia has decided at this stage and under present circumstances to withdraw from the United Nations". However, the telegram of the ambassador of Indonesia to the United States to the Secretary General of the United Nations of 19 September 1966 said that the Indonesia Government "has decided to resume full cooperation with the United Nations and to resume participation in its activities starting with the twenty-first session of the General Assembly".[25]

The return of Indonesia to the United Nations occurred without an admission procedure which obviously would have been necessary if Indonesia had withdrawn from the United Nations in 1965.

2. International Organizations as Organs of Peaceful Coexistence

In Chapter XIII we concluded that contemporary general international organizations are organs of peaceful coexistence. How do the general character and purposes of international organizations concretely reflect this is the legal

[23] M. Scerni, "Aspetti giuridici del ritiro dalle Nazioni Unite", *La Comunita Internazionale*, XX (1965), 239.

[24] G. Schwarzenberger, "Indonesia and the U.N.", *The Times*, 11 January 1965, p. 9, col. 5.

[25] *United Nations Juridical Yearbook 1966* (1967), pp. 222-223.

norms defining the composition, structure, and activity of international organizations?

First, the principle of nondiscrimination on the basis of socio-economic systems, arising out of the principle of equality of States, is characteristic of contemporary general international organizations. And in fact the charters of general international organizations do not contain membership limitations tied to the socio-economic system of States. According to the United Nations Charter, "admission to membership of the Organization is open to all peaceloving states ..." (Article 4). This general requirement, arising out of the basic principles of contemporary international law and the purposes of the United Nations, did not contemplate and never has been interpreted as having in view the socio-economic system of a State. The attempts of Western powers not to admit certain socialist States into the United Nations using far-fetched pretexts, but in fact because they were socialist States, were a flagrant violation of the Charter.

A second important principle relating to this aspect of the legal nature of general international organizations is the principle of the distinctive equality of the different social systems. The principle of equality of States is not sufficiently complied with in the structure of the organs and in the activity generally of contemporary general international organizations; it is still necessary to take into account that member States belong to different socio-economic systems. A quantitative approach on the basis of the equality of States is, therefore, inadequate. The question is one that under contemporary conditions is exceedingly important for the activity of any general international organization so that States representing the various social systems take part in working out and deciding various questions of the organization's activity on the basis of equality.

A third juridical aspect of the legal nature of general international organizations as organs of peaceful coexistence is the guarantees against the use of an international organization by States affiliated with one socio-economic system against States belonging to another socio-economic system.

The Soviet side pointed to the importance of this problem in 1925, in connection with the question of the possibility of the Soviet Union's entering the League of Nations. In a Soviet press communique concerning the statement of the People's Commissar of Foreign Affairs of the USSR, G. V. Chicherin, to the German journalist Stein on 17 October 1925, it was said: "The Soviet Government can not subordinate its actions and decisions arising out of the fundamental principles of the Soviet system to the resolutions of a majority of those States which are constructed on completely different bases".[26]

Bourgeois international legal doctrine is silent on this problem. In considering the questions of the functions, competence, and effectiveness of international organizations, bourgeois international lawyers usually ignore the class nature of member States of international organizations, trends in their policy, the struggle which takes place, though to an unequal extent, in various international organizations, the real co-relation of forces, and so forth. In this instance, as in many others, the formalistic approach is a convenient means for avoiding problems and masking the essence of social phenomena.

This danger is especially great with respect to an international organization such as the United Nations. Reality is such that in contemporary general international organizations the socialist States are for the time being an insignificant minority in relation to the total number of member States. The leading capitalist States strive to use general international organizations and, above all, the United Nations against the socialist countries, as well as in the interests of their colonialist or neocolonialist policy. The danger of transforming general international organizations under these conditions into an instrument of capitalist States is very real. The change in

[26] Ministerstvo inostrannykh del SSSR, Документы внешней политики СССР [Documents of Foreign Policy of the USSR], VIII, 633.

the co- relation of forces in the United Nations, as well as in other general international organizations in connection with the entry of a large number of new States which have emerged in consequence of the liberation of the colonies reduces somewhat, but by no means completely removes, this danger.

How to avoid this problem was a cardinal issue when the United Nations was created, although nothing was said expressly about it. As the well-known commentator on the United Nations Charter, Professor L. Goodrich, is forced to acknowledge, at the time when the United Nations was created, the Western powers expected that the West would predominate in it as it had predominated in the League of Nations.[27]

Naturally, the question was one primarily of the Security Council, which under the Charter was endowed with special responsibility in the fundamental and very crucial area of activity of the international organization, in the cause of maintaining international peace and security.

It is well-known how difficult it was to find a satisfactory resolution of this question. It was necessary to ensure the possibility of rapid and effective actions based on the principle of the sovereign equality of States and, at the same time, to take into account their unequal role in international relations. But above all the principal task was to ensure that the organization was not transformed into an instrument of States of one social system.

The two possible extreme solutions were unacceptable. The principle of unanimity of all members of the Council, which had existed in the League of Nations, would have the same parallel effect which it had within the framework of the League of Nations. The taking of decisions by majority vote (simple or qualified) contravened the said principal requirement.[28]

At the suggestion of the American President, Franklin D. Roosevelt, the principle of unanimity of the permanent

[27] See L. Goodrich, *The United Nations* (1959), p. 41.

[28] See Tunkin, "The Legal Nature of the United Nations".

members of the Security Council was finally adopted at the Yalta Conference of the three great powers.[29] According to Article 27 of the Charter, all decisions of the Security Council, with the exception of procedural questions, are considered to be adopted when the votes of seven (at present, nine) members of the Council, including the concurring votes of all permanent members of the Council, have been cast in favor.

Thus, the Yalta formula provided for the adoption of Security Council decisions by a majority vote; however, this majority must include the concurrent votes of the permanent members of the Council. The Statement of the delegations of the four host governments at the San Francisco Conference of 7 June 1945 pointed out that the proposed formula for adopting measures in the Security Council by a majority of seven members makes the activity of the Council less liable to obstruction than it was in the League of Nations, whose rules provided for complete unanimity.[30] The "Yalta formula" took into account the special role of the great powers in international relations. The aforesaid Statement of the host powers at the San Francisco Conference said with regard to this question: "In view of the basic responsibility of the permanent members, one can not expect them under present conditions existing in the world to assume obligations to act in such serious matters as the maintenance of international peace and security in conformity with a decision with which they did not agree. Therefore, for the adoption of decisions by the Security Council by a majority vote to be possible, the sole practical method will be to provide for the unanimity of the permanent members plus the concurrent voice of at least two

[29] For greater detail, see N. A. Ushakov, Принцип единогласия великих держав в Совете Безопасности ООН [Principal of Unanimity of Great Powers in United Nations Security Council] (1965), pp. 34-76; V. N. Fedorov, Совет Безопасности [Security Council] (1965), pp. 58-60.

[30] Cited according to V. N. Durdenevskii and S. B. Krylov (comps.), Организация Объединенных Наций; сборник документов [United Nations: Collection of Documents] (1956), p. 30.

non-permanent members with respect to non-procedural decisions".[31]

This Statement, therefore, emphasized wholly correctly, particularly on the basis of the experience of the Second World War, the special role of the great powers in questions of peace and war.

It was very important, however, that nowhere was this said. The Yalta formula precluded the possibility of transforming the Security Council, and consequently, the entire United Nations, into an instrument of States of one social system. The Yalta formula embraced the principle of peaceful coexistence of States of different social systems. In reality, of the five permanent members of the Security Council, one State, the USSR, was a State of another, a socialist, social system. Decisions of the Security Council, therefore, could be taken only on the basis of the agreement of States of the two opposed social systems.

On this plane, Professor M. Lachs is certainly correct in noting: "The principle of unanimity, which was born towards the end of the war, has today grown in importance and has acquired a new meaning. In a concrete historical situation, it not only reflects the equality of States, but it also stands against any discriminatory practices by one of the dominating political systems in the world today against the other. It means that no important decision can be taken without the agreement and support of the socialist States. This new equality of the political systems is probably the most important feature of international relations today".[32]

The thesis is widely publicized in the West that the adoption of the Yalta formula was a mistake, as a result of which the Soviet veto in the Security Council would not allow the United Nations to fulfill its duties regarding the maintenance of peace

[31] Ibid.

[32] M. Lachs, "The United Nations and Peaceful Co-Existence", *Polish Perspectives*, III, no. 4 (1960), p. 9.

and security.[33] An objective analysis of the operation of the unanimity rule of the great powers shows, however, that the veto of the Soviet Union was a reliable means against the use of the United Nations as an instrument by States of one social system against States of another social system. Thus, in 1946, in connection with the Security Council's consideration of the request of Syria and Lebanon concerning the withdrawal of English and French forces from the territory of these States, the Soviet Union, in supporting this just request, vetoed a draft English and French resolution which actually sanctioned a further stay of foreign forces in Syria and Lebanon. In 1961 the Soviet Union prevented by its veto the adoption of a resolution by the Security Council aimed at supporting colonialist claims of Portugal against India to Goa, Daman, and Diu. The Soviet Union was obliged to use its veto dozens of times against discriminatory proposals of Western powers which had the purpose of admitting to the United Nations States whom they chose and of not admitting other such equal States only because they were socialist States.

It is true that the veto sometimes has been used also by colonial powers in their colonialist interests. One can mention as an example France's vote in 1947 against a proposal of the Soviet Union to create a commission to observe the effectuation of a Security Council resolution regarding the Indonesian question, England's veto in 1963 of the draft resolution of Ghana, Morocco, and the Philippines which called upon the English Government not to transfer authority to the white minority in Southern Rhodesia, and others.

But most frequently of all the imperialist powers, above all the United States, simply have no need to use the veto. They have succeeded in voting down proposals objectionable to them, having the requisite majority of votes in the Security Council. "One of the more persistent myths surrounding the United Nations", writes J. G. Stoessinger, an American professor, "concerns the use of the veto power by the Soviet

33 See, for example, Goodrich, *The United Nations*, pp. 164-176.

Union and the United States. It is an established fact that by late 1965 the Soviet Union had vetoed 103 Security Council resolutions, whereas the United States had yet to cast its first veto. Hence, it is said that the Soviet Union's frequent use of the veto has hampered ... the United Nations by preventing it from acting, while the United States has exercised remarkable self-discipline by never using the veto at all".[34] The author goes on: "To say that the United States has never used the veto power is literally correct, but highly misleading in a broader sense. The implication would be that one superpower had ... put national interest above international considerations while the other had ... subordinated national interests in order to further international co-operation. The fact of the matter is that the United States has not used the veto because it has been able to protect and promote its national interest in other ways. By obtaining majority votes against resolutions it opposes the United States has never been forced to cast a veto. The key to this American `hidden veto' is, of course, the composition of the Security Council.

It is a fact that a majority of the members of the Council have regularly been military allies of the United States".[35]

There are dozens of instances of the use of the 'hidden veto' by the imperialist powers. It was used, for example, in 1946 against a proposal of the Ukrainian SSR concerning the withdrawal of English forces from Greece, in the same year against a Ukrainian proposal concerning the actions of English forces in Indonesia, in 1950 against a proposal of the USSR concerning the withdrawal of American forces from the island of Taiwan and the cessation of aggressive actions of the United States against the People's Republic of China, against a Soviet proposal concerning the cessation of American-Anglo intervention in Lebanon and Jordan in 1958, and in many other instances.

[34] J. G. Stoessinger, *The United Nations and the Superpowers* (1965), p. 3.

[35] Ibid., pp. 13-14.

The Yalta formula, of course, is not ideal. As we have seen, the veto sometimes may be used for reactionary purposes. Nevertheless, the principle of unanimity of the great powers in the Security Council belongs among the fundamental principles of the United Nations, reflecting one of the principal laws of our epoch. The violation of this principle in the practice of the United Nations under the influence of the policy of imperialist powers (especially Resolution 377(V) of 3 November 1950 and the United Nations practice based thereon), therefore, frequently has led to a situation highly dangerous for the cause of peace and for the United Nations itself.

In other general international organizations, to wit, in international organizations for specialized questions, there does not exist an institute similar to the principle of the unanimity of the great powers in the Security Council. As has been pointed out, for a number of reasons there is usually not the bitter struggle in these organizations that takes place in the United Nations. The absence of the said institute in these organizations, however, leads in certain questions, as for example, the admission of members to these organizations, to the capitalist States pursuing a policy of discrimination with respect to certain socialist States. Thus, the German Democratic Republic, the Korean People's Democratic Republic, and the Democratic Republic of Vietnam persistently are not admitted by the Western powers to the United Nations specialized agencies, although the Federal Republic of Germany, South Korea, and South Vietnam are members of these international organizations.

As is evident from the above, the guarantees of which we are speaking still have not been properly developed in general international organizations. Moreover, the need for them up to now has not been adequately realized nor has it been acceptable to speak of this directly. Meanwhile, the future development of general international organizations and the enlargement of their role in ensuring peace and the development of international cooperation, in our view, is linked to a significant degree with the working out and realization of these guarantees.

3. The International Legal Personality of International Organizations

The emergence among the large numbers of intergovernmental international organizations of those which possess international legal personality was a result of the increased role of international organizations in international life. International organizations grew out of international conferences and, as P. Reuter notes correctly, at first were only a continuation of these conferences.[36]

The proposition that international organizations can be, and many are, subjects of international law is, at present, essentially generally recognized, and disputes with regard to this question can be regarded as the legacy of history.[37]

In every legal system there may be various subjects of law. In international law, together with the traditional and still primary subjects of international law, new subjects – international organizations – have emerged. International organizations are an institute of contemporary society, distinct from a State, but it would be incorrect to assert on this basis that they can not be subjects of international law just as it would be incorrect, in acknowledging that international organizations are subjects of law, to equate them to States. International organizations are distinct from the State as a type of subject of international law. Extensive international practice already is evidence of this.

Many international organizations have specific international rights and duties, may by their actions acquire rights and assume legal duties, and bear international legal responsibility for

36 P. Reuter, *Institutions internationales* (4th ed.; 1963), p. 188.

37 On disputes in Soviet international legal literature, see Shibaeva, Правовой статус межправительственных организаций [Legal Status of Intergovernmental Organizations] (1972), pp. 83-88; L. Valki, "The Juristic Personality and Treaty-Making Power of International Organizations", *Questions of International Law* (1968), pp. 285-308.

their actions. In conformity with their charters, international organizations are in specific international legal relations with the member States of these organizations; they conclude international treaties with States and with other international organizations; representations of States frequently are attached to international organizations; sometimes international organizations have representations in States; international organizations exchange representatives between themselves; international organizations are their officials enjoy privileges and immunities on the basis of international law; they bear international legal responsibility in the event unlawful actions are committed; and so forth. That is to say, many international organizations possess international legal personality.

On the other hand, the treaties concluded by international organizations between themselves and with States are distinct from treaties between States; missions of international organizations and missions to international organizations by their functions and in the overwhelming majority of instances by their legal status are different from diplomatic representations;[38] the international legal responsibility of international organizations is far from identical to State responsibility; and so forth.

One must, therefore, concur with the view of the International Court, which in its advisory opinion of 11 April 1949 on the question of reparation for injuries suffered in the service of the United Nations came to the conclusion that: (1) the United Nations is a subject of international law; (2) this does not mean

[38] The functions of permanent missions of States to international organizations sometimes can be more important than the functions of some diplomatic representations, but by their very nature they differ significantly from the functions of the latter. Therefore, the trend toward identifying somewhat the functions of permanent missions with the functions of diplomatic representations which has crept into the commentary to Article 7 of the "Draft Articles on Representatives of States to International Organizations" adopted by the International Law Commission at its Twentieth Session in 1968 seems unjustified. See the "Report of the International Law Commission on the Work of its Twentieth Session", in United Nations, *Yearbook of the International Law Commission 1968* (1968), II, 200.

that the United Nations is recognized as a State, which it certainly is not, or that the legal personality of the United Nations is the same as the legal personality of a State.[39]

(a) The legal basis and extent of the legal personality of international organizations. The question of the legal basis of international organizations as subjects of international law has important theoretical and practical significance. The problem lies first of all in whether the international legal personality of international organizations and its scope are determined by general international law or whether the legal personality of each international organization is based on its charter.

Under contemporary international law, each State is a subject of international law. States as subjects of international law are equal *inter se,* that is to say, all States have the same amount of international legal personality.

The concept of "inherent legal personality" of international organizations has received some attention in bourgeois international legal doctrine recently, especially since the advisory opinion of the International Court of 20 July 1962 on the question of certain expenses of the United Nations. According to this concept, international organizations are subjects of international law on the basis of general international law just as are States, and legal personality inheres in every international organization to the same extent that it inheres in States. The charter of an international organization, under this theory, has significance only in that it may serve the legal personality peculiar to any international organization in conformity with the purposes of the organization.[40]

39 International Court of Justice, Reports of Judgments, Advisory Opinions and Orders, *Reparation for Injuries Suffered in the Service of the United Nations, Advisory Opinion of 11 April 1949* (1949), p. 179.

40 See, for example, F. Seyersted, "International Personality of Intergovernmental Organizations", *Indian Journal of International Law,* IV (1964), 19, 26-27, 48; a more cautious formulation is H. Chiu, *The Capacity of International Organizations to Conclude Treaties, and the Special Legal Aspects of the Treaties Concluded* (1966), p. 21; and even more cautiously in Reuter, *Institutions internationales,* p. 218.

In support of this view one may point to the fact that international organizations very frequently perform legal actions not provided for by their charters. The conclusion is drawn from this that the legal personality of international organizations is not based on their charters, but directly on norms of general international law.

What has been said previously (see Chapter XIV) relating to the unfoundedness of the theory of "inherent jurisdiction" is wholly applicable also to the concept of "inherent legal personality". International reality is such that far from all intergovernmental international organizations are subjects of international law, and the scope of legal personality of those organizations which possess it is very different. The concept of "inherent legal personality", like the concept of "inherent jurisdiction", is in contradiction to the fundamental principles of contemporary international law, in conformity with which the charter of an international organization is the juridical basis of its existence and activity.

The viewpoint of A. Sereni comes to almost the same conclusions as does the concept of "inherent legal personality", although he does not maintain that all international organizations possess legal personality. Sereni, citing Anzilotti, proceeds from the proposition that only the international legal order, that is, general international law, can attach to a particular entity the status of a subject of international law. Since, in Sereni's view, a treaty can not create norms of general international law, it is not in a position to create a subject of international law. In general, he says, an international treaty can not create an international organization. Its emergence is of a factual nature; an international organization exists from the moment it begins to function through its organs. It acquires international legal personality if the functions of its organs may create rights and duties for it under international law. And if an international organization possesses legal personality, this legal personality is equal to the legal personality of all other subjects of international law with which the organization does business.[41] This is purely a speculative construction which, as is obvious from the preceding, is in sharp disaccord with reality.

Norms defining the legal status of international organizations do not exist in contemporary general international law. The fact that international organizations conclude agreements with States in all instances when a question arises of the legal status of the organization, its organs, officials, and so forth, is testimony, in particular, to this. If general international law defined the legal status of international organizations, such agreements would be unnecessary, and if they still were concluded, they undoubtedly would contain references to the respective norms of general international law. At the same time, general international law does not contain norms preventing the allotment of the legal personality to international organizations. The legal personality of an international organization is based on its charter, which also defines the scope of this legal personality.[42]

The frequently cited advisory opinion of the International Court of 11 April 1949 also proceeds in general from this position. It says in this opinion that in order to answer the question of whether the United Nations has such a nature as involves the

41 A. Sereni, *Diritto internazionale* (1960), II(2), pp. 837-852.

42 See G. I. Tunkin, Основы современного международного права [Fundamental Principles of Contemporary International Law] (1956), pp. 17-18; R. L. Bobrov, "О правовой природе Организации Объединенных Наций" [On the Legal Nature of the United Nations], Советский ежегодник международного права 1959 [Soviet Yearbook of International Law 1959] (1960), pp. 229-240; G. I. Morozov, Организция Объедненных Наций [United Nations] (1962), pp. 196-202; A. N. Talalaev, Юридическая природа международного договора [Legal Nature of International Treaty] (1963), p. 27; S. A. Malinin, "О правосубъектности международных организации" [On the Legal Personality of Interntional Organizations], Вестник Ленинградского государственного уни- верситета, [Herald of Leningrad State University] no. 17 (1965), p. 114; I. I. Lukashuk, Стороны в международных договорах [Parties to International Treaties] (1966), pp. 124-125; Shibaeva, Специализированные учреждения ООН [Specialized Agencies of the United Nations], p. 24; V. M. Chkhikvadze and others (eds., Курс международного права в шести томах [Course of International Law in Six Volumes] (1967), I, 160. In the literature of other socialist countries see, in particular, C. Berezowski, *Prawo miedzynarodowe publiczne* (1966), I, 168; P. A. Steiniger, ed., *Völkerrecht* (1966), pp. 112-113; M. Genovski, (2d ed.; 1966), p. 109; Valki, "The Juristic Personality and Treaty-Making Power of International Organizations", p. 299.

capacity to bring international claims, "the Court must first enquire whether the Charter has given the Organization such a position that it possesses, in regard to its Members, rights which it is entitled to ask them to respect. In other words, does the Organization possess international personality?"[43]

The International Law Commission also proceeded from the same position. As a result of the discussion of the question of the capacity to conclude international treaties in 1962, the International Law Commission inserted in draft Article 3 a paragraph of the following content: "In the case of international organizations, capacity to conclude treaties depends on the constitution of the organization concerned".[44]

In discussing the first report in 1963 of the special rapporteur on relations between States and intergovernmental organizations, El-Erian, an Egyptian jurist, almost all members of the International Law Commission who treated the question of the legal personality of international organizations (Tunkin, Yasseen, Ago, Verdross, Gros) expressed the view that there were no norms in general international law defining the legal status of international organizations and that in each concrete instance this position is defined by the charters of these organizations.[45] Professor Verdross, in particular, noted: "... States were at the origin of international law, whereas international organizations were creations of States; their existence rested on agreements concluded between States, and their legal status depended on the content of those agreements".[46]

The view that contemporary international law does not contain norms defining the legal status of international organizations and, therefore, the legal personality of

[43] International Court of Justice, *Reparation for Injuries Suffered in the Service of the United Nations*, p. 178.

[44] United Nations, *Yearbook of the International Law Commission 1962*, II, 164.

[45] Ibid., 1963, I, 299-305.

[46] Ibid., p. 304.

international organizations is based upon the charter thereof is, it seems to us, predominant in Western international legal literature.[47]

The special rapporteur of the International Law Commission for treaties with the participation of international organizations, Professor P. Reuter, laid this correct position at the base of his investigation. In his second report submitted in 1973 to the Commission Professor Reuter points out that "the legal capacity of an international organization depends on the special constitutive act and its corresponding law and not on any norms of general international law".[48]

In its documents the International Law Commission usually employed the formula "international organizations may possess legal capacity". Thus, the report of the Commission on the work of the first part of the Seventeenth Session says that the Commission "recognized that international organizations may possess a certain capacity to enter into international agreements and that these agreements fall within the scope of the law of treaties".[49] The Commission thereby emphasized that a particular international organization may or may not be a subject of international law.

And so the legal personality of an international organization is defined by its charter. But what does this mean? H. Kelsen expressed the view that "if the constituent treaty does not contain a provision conferring expressly upon the community international juridical personality, that is to say, unrestricted legal capacity under international law, the community

[47] See in particular Kelsen, *The Law of the United Nations*, pp. 329-330; Leo Gross, "Expenses of the United Nations for Peace-Keeping Operations", *International Organization*, XVII (1963), 9-10; P. Pescatore, "Les relations extérieures des communautés européenes", *Recueil des cours*, CIII (1961), 27-28; D. W. Bowett, *The Law of International Institutions* (1963), pp. 273, 296; H. Mosler, "Réflexions sur la personalité juridique en droit international public", *Mélanges Rolin*, pp. 243-246.

[48] Second Report on the Question of Treaties Concluded Between States and International Organizations or Among Two or More International Organizations, Doc. No. A/CN.4/271, 15 May 1973, para. 41.

[49] United Nations, *Yearbook of the International Law Commission 1965*, II, p. 158.

has only by those special capacities as conferred upon it by particular provisions".[50] It is completely obvious that such a limited normativist approach does not arise out of the basic provisions of contemporary international law and does not explain the existing practice, which is not disputed by States.

In defining the legal personality of an international organization, attention must be given to possible changes in certain nonbasic provisions of its charter which may have occurred in the course of the organization's activity with the general consent of its members (see Chapter XIV). Thus, for example, if the charter of the organization in general contains no provisions concerning the concluding of international treaties, the organization nonetheless may conclude such treaties with the general consent of the members of the organization. If the practice of concluding treaties by this organization is stabilized and does not raise objections, it will be evidence of the agreement of the organization's members to introduce such an addition to the charter (see Chapter XIV).

The charter of an international organization, as an international treaty *sui generis*, that is, a treaty which is the legal basis for the activity of a permanent international mechanism endowed with powers to adopt decisions, may include "implied" elements of inter- national legal personality such that it may include implied competence in the understanding set out by us above (see Chapter XIV).

Finally, on the basis of and in conformity with the provisions of a charter of an international organization a certain expansion of the scope of the legal personality of an organization is possible through the adoption of decisions by its respective organs if such decisions reflect the agreement of all members of the organization. Thus, for example, the United Nations Charter empowers the organization to conclude international treaties on specific questions. In practice, however, treaties also are concluded with regard to many other questions on the basis of decisions of the respective United Nations organs. And if such

50 Kelsen, *The Law of the United Nations*, pp. 329-330.

practice does not contravene the Charter nor give rise to objections on the part of the members, it may be regarded as evidence of a supplemental agreement resting upon the respective provisions of the Charter.

(b) The legal personality of international organizations and third States. Under contemporary international law the legal personality of States is a legal personality *erga omnes*. It does not require recognition by other States.

The status of international organizations is different, since their legal personality is based upon their charters. The charter of an international organization as an international treaty is binding only upon its members and, therefore, the legal personality of an international organization is binding only upon the members of this organization. For States who are not members of the organization its charter is *res inter alios acta.*[51]

Any State, of course, can recognize the legal personality of an international organization of which it is not a member. Such recog- nition may relate to the legal personality of the given organization in general or only to individual elements (for example, the privileges and immunities of all or only some officials of the organization). The respective obligations for such a State with respect to the given organization, of course, arise not from the charter of this organization but from a special agreement (clearly or tacitly expressed).

The participation of all States in a particular international organization possessing international legal personality or the recognition of the legal personality of such an organization not only by its members but also by all other States makes such an international organization a generally-recognized subject of international law, a subject *erga omnes*. The United Nations

[51] See C. M. Chaumont, "La signification du principe de specialité des organisations internationales", *Mélanges Rolin*, p. 62; Mosler, "Réflexions sur la personalité juridique en droit international public", p. 250; G. Schwarzenberger, *A Manual of International Law* (5th ed., 1967), p. 80.

and the majority of the specialized agencies are such subjects or approximate thereto.[52]

The theory is widely disseminated in bourgeois international legal doctrine that the participation of a majority of States in an international organization makes this organization a subject of international law *erga omnes*. In confirmation of this view the advisory opinion of the International Court of 11 April 1949 on reparation for injuries suffered in the service of the United Nations is usually cited: "... fifty States, representing the vast majority of the members of the international community, had the power in conformity with international law, to bring into being an entity possessing objective international personality, and not merely personality recognized by them alone ...".[53]

This theory, just as the concept which proclaims customary norms of international law recognized by a majority of States are binding upon all States, has no basis in contemporary international law (see Chapter IV).

Still further in this direction is the view that all international organizations possess international legal personality which is legal personality *erga omnes*.[54]

A more moderate point of view on this question is that the number of members of an international organization is of no significance, and any lawfully created international organization possessing international legal personality is a subject of international law *erga omnes*.[55]

[52] See Tunkin, Основы современного международного права [Fundamental Principles of Contemporary International Law], p. 19.

[53] International Court of Justice, *Reparation for Injuries Suffered in the Service of the United Nations*, p 185.

[54] See, for example, Seyersted, "International Personality of Intergovernmental Organizations", pp. 60, 68.

[55] See, for example, Max Sørenson, "Principles de droit international public", *Recueil des cours*, CI (1960), 138-139; Sereni, *Diritto internazionale*, II (20), pp. 843-846.

As evidence of this view, Sørenson refers to the practice of some local international organizations of concluding agreements with nonmember States or with other international organizations. But this practice rather disproves Sørenson's thesis. Is it not true that the conclusion by such organizations of respective international agreements with nonmember States also expands the sphere of operation of their legal personality? Evidently aware of the weakness of this argument, Sørenson says very cautiously that "undoubtedly an international custom is being formed that no third State may contest the legal personality of an international organization established in conformity with the principles of international law for a legal purpose".[56]

In reality, one could speak of the objective legal personality of international organizations only if according to general international law all international organizations respectively established by international legal criteria *ipso facto* were subjects of international law *erga omnes*, as happens with regard to States. But as already has been said, such norms do not exist in contemporary international law.

[56] Sørenson, "Principes de droit international public", p. 139.

CHAPTER XVI.
THE PROBLEM OF A WORLD STATE AND PROSPECTS FOR THE DEVELOPMENT OF INTERNATIONAL ORGANIZATIONS

1. Bourgeois Concepts of a World State

Bourgeois philosophers, politicians, and jurists maintain that the existence of sovereign States is a source of wars and that to make wars impossible it is necessary to create a world State, without affecting, of course, the basic principles of the capitalist system. This abstract scheme, divorced from reality, is advanced persistently in bourgeois international legal literature as the most progressive trend of contemporary political and legal thought, and its opponents are portrayed as reactionaries who have failed to keep pace with life.

At the present time, the concept of the world State has two basic orientations. The first approaches the problem of creating a world State on a logical basis, planning *de lege feranda*. Here is your design of an ideal arrangement which can save you from wars, say proponents of this orientation; take it or leave it. "Before the atomic bomb", writes R. Hutchins, "we could accept the plan of a world State or reject it ... Our slogan must be: a world government is necessary; therefore it is possible".[1]

Proponents of the second orientation maintain that rapid scientific and technical progress and the expansion of international ties, especially in economics and science, gradually are creating the base for a world State. The task is to reconstruct existing international organizations, beginning with economic and scientific, in conformity with this new situation, transforming them into supranational organizations.

The first orientation is abstract and formalistic. Existing international organizations, assert the proponents of this approach, are imperfect; they do not guarantee against the outbreak of wars. States wage war, and therefore to exclude wars it is

[1] R. Hutchins, "Constitutional Foundations for World Order", in S. H. Mendlovitz, ed., *Legal and Political Problems of World Order* (1962), p. 67.

necessary to create a supranational organization which could suppress an attempt by any State to take up arms. But to do this it is necessary that States renounce their sovereignty. If they could be persuaded to renounce their sovereignty and to agree to the creation of a world State, everything would be all right. "The notion of the sovereignty of individual states", wrote H. Kelsen soon after the First World War, "up to now, correctly or incorrectly, has stood in the path of any measures having the purpose to transform the international legal order into an effective organization ...".[2]

Professor P. C. Jessup, a member of the International Court, wrote in 1948 that the sole means of ensuring peace is the creation of an "international government". "There must be organs empowered to lay down rules (a legislature); there must be judicial organs to interpret and apply those rules (a judiciary); and there must be organs with power to compel compliance with the rules (a police force)".[3]

A resolute opponent of State sovereignty, the French professor G. Scelle, in favoring the creation of a world federation, wrote: "If the proposed plan turns out to be inadmissable and the so-called external sovereignty must remain the patrimony of hundreds of States, themselves defining the extent of their discretionary authority, it is better to say together with the poet: 'Lose all hope; we henceforth shall remain at the threshhold of hell'".[4]

Seeing the cause of wars in State sovereignty just as many other bourgeois jurists, an English professor, G. Schwarzenberger, comes to the conclusion that the appearance of the atomic bomb urgently dictates the renunciation of State sovereignty. He writes: "To hold that power politics and war are inevitable consequences of the organization of international society on the

[2] H. Kelsen, *Das Problem der Souveranität und die Theorie der Völkerrechts* (2d ed.; 1928), p. 320.

[3] P. C. Jessup, *A Modern Law of Nations* (1948), pp. 2-3.

[4] G. Scelle, "Préalable à l'integration d'une société internationale universelle", *Mélanges Séfériades* (1961), p. 12.

basis of sovereign States and empires, which, being sovereign, insist on their freedom of armaments, tends to become a commonplace". Evidently, however, the advent of the atom bomb was necessary to induce statesmen to make declarations such as "every succeeding discovery makes greater nonsense of old-time conceptions of sovereignty".[5] Schwarzenberger concludes that the sole answer to the threat of world destruction is the creation of a world federation.[6]

Since the Second World War there have appeared and still appear in capitalist countries, as mushrooms after a rain, various more or less detailed plans for creating a world government or world federation, most frequently by restructuring the existing United Nations Organization.

At the present time, for example, a plan for reforming the United Nations worked out by the American professors Grenville Clark and Louis B. Sohn is being publicized widely. Their book, *World Peace Through World Law,* was issued in the United States in 1966 in a third edition and has been translated into many foreign languages. One must give the authors their due for having invested enormous labor in this work, which contains a draft of a revised United Nations Charter with detailed commentary, as well as plans for disarmament, plans for creating a United Nations military force, suggested changes in the Statute of the United Nations International Court, and other proposals.

At the basis of the entire plan lies, in the words of the authors themselves, "the adoption on a world-wide basis of the measures and institutions which the experience of centuries has shown to be essential for the maintenance of law and order, namely, clearly stated laws against violence, courts to interpret and apply that law and police to enforce it".[7]

[5] G. Schwarzenberger, *The Frontiers of International Law* (1962), p. 312.

[6] Ibid., p. 313.

[7] G. Clark and L. B. Sohn, *World Peace Through World Law* (3d ed.; 1966), pp. xv-xvi.

According to the revised draft of the United Nations Charter proposed by Clark and Sohn, the United Nations would be transformed into the likeness of a world State having its own legislative, executive, and judicial organs, as well as military force.

The supreme organ of the United Nations would be a General Assembly, consisting of representatives elected during a specific transitional period by national legislative organs, and thereafter directly by the people.[8] The number of delegates from each State would depend, although not expressly, upon the size of its population. The delegates would not be representatives of States. The authors suggest a sample apportionment of representation of various States in the General Assembly which would ensure a firm majority to the Western powers and their allies.[9] Decisions of the General Assembly would be adopted by a simple majority of votes.[10]

The General Assembly would enact laws on questions relegated to the competence of the Organization, adopt measures to implement them, create military forces, bring States and individual persons to responsibility for violating laws, and so forth. The laws enacted by the General Assembly would be binding not only upon member States of the Organization, but also directly upon individuals.[11]

The existing Security Council would be transformed into an Executive Council elected by the General Assembly and would be an organ subordinate to it. And here, in contrast to the present situation, Council members would not be representatives of governments, but would act in a "personal capacity". The principle of the permanent Council members is not provided.[12] The General Assembly, and not the Council, would adopt

8 Ibid., pp. 20-25.

9 Ibid., pp. 28-29.

10 Ibid., p. 53 (Article 17).

11 Ibid., pp. 34-39 (Articles 10 and 11).

12 Ibid., pp. 66-83 (Articles 23-27).

measures in the event of a threat to the peace, breach of the peace, or act of aggression. Only when the General Assembly is not in session and the circumstances require that measures be taken immediately would the Executive Council take "provisional" measures, but a session of the General Assembly would have to be convened immediately, to which the Council reported its actions and which decided what measures should be taken.[13]

The General Assembly would establish the procedure for creating a permanent military force of the new Organization. It would be comprised not of national contingents, but of volunteers from the various countries.[14] The military force would be stationed at various points of the globe "in order to facilitate prompt action".[15]

Finally, the plan proposed by Clark and Sohn provides for the establishment of the compulsory jurisdiction of the International Court.[16]

The proposal of the World Association of World Federalists approved at a conference of this Association held in Japan in 1963 may serve as another example of plans to create a world State.[17]

The so-called Tokyo Declaration and Proposals of the Association of Federalists declare that under contemporary conditions "man must choose between world law and world war".[18] "The United Nations", these documents go on to state, "should be transformed into a world federation with universal membership and with limited but adequate powers ...". According to the draft, the world federation would

13 Ibid., pp. 111-113 (Article 39).

14 Ibid., p. 321.

15 Ibid., p. 325.

16 Ibid., p. 337.

17 For the text of the plan, see the *Japanese Annual of International Law*, VIII (1964), 37-43.

18 Ibid., p. 37.

promulgate laws and have a world inspectorate, police forces, and a court with compulsory jurisdiction.[19]

Professor K. S. Tabata of Kyoto University, whose article accompanies the publication of the said documents in the *Japanese Annual of International Law*, explains that the plan prefers to speak of a "world federation" and not a "world State", since the creation of a supranational organization "founded on the present national State system" is envisaged. However, he continues, this plan provides for a significant limitation of State sovereignty.[20]

According to this plan, the United Nations General Assembly would be transformed into a "world parliament". Representation in the parliament would be based on size of population and "other relevant factors".[21] A "world executive council", replacing the United Nations Security Council, would consist of persons elected by the General Assembly, and they would not be representatives of the governments of the member States. The Council would be subordinate to the General Assembly and act according to its instructions. A "federal world force" would be created in order to take measures to implement "provisions of the Charter, the laws enacted thereunder, and the decisions of the International Court of Justice and other organs of the U.N.".[22] A unified citizenship would be established; each citizen of a member State simultaneously would be a citizen of the world federation. The Charter and laws enacted thereunder would extend directly to citizens.[23]

The other orientation which, borrowing certain theses of historical materialism, regards the creation of a world State

[19] Ibid., pp. 37-41.

[20] K. S. Tabata, "World Federation: The Eleventh World Conference of the World Association of World Federalists, Tokyo, 1963", ibid., p. 31.

[21] Ibid., p. 40.

[22] Ibid., pp. 39-40.

[23] Ibid., p. 41.

as an inevitable consequence of scientific and technological development and the expansion of international ties is now much more influential than the dogmatic orientation.

This second orientation found powerful support and authoritative expression in the Encyclical of Pope John XXIII, *Pacem in Terris*, promulgated in 1963. "The progress of science and technology", says the Encyclical, "has ... influenced men to work together and live as one family".[24] The bonds among people and nations have increased sharply. "At the same time the interdependence of national economies has grown deeper, ... so that they become, as it were, integral parts of the one world economy" (p. vi). The social progress, order, and security of one State necessarily are connected with the progress of other States. Under such circumstances, each individual State, if it were isolated from other States, would not be in a position to provide for its own development.

In paying verbal tribute to traditional Catholic natural law doctrine, based on the nature of man created by God, the Encyclical in fact acknowledges the decisive significance of the contemporary development of the production forces of society. In noting that the development of science and technology and of economic and other ties among States leads to the creation of problems which can not be solved successfully either by individual States or by old methods of diplomacy – the conclusion of treaties – the Encyclical points out: "It can be said, therefore, that at this historical moment the present system of organization and the way its principle of authority operates on a world basis no longer correspond to the objective requirements of the universal common good ..." (p. vi).

The conclusion which the Encyclical draws in this connection is that: "Today the universal common good poses problems of world- wide dimensions, which cannot be tackled or solved except by the efforts of public authorities endowed with wideness of powers, structures, and means of the same

[24] *Die Furche*, XIX, no. 17 (1963), Special Supplement: Enzyklika "Pacem in Gerris", p. vi.

proportions: that is, of public authorities which are in a position to operate in an effective manner on a world-wide basis ... such a form of public authority must be established" (p. vi).

This orientation builds its conclusion, therefore, on the fact of the development of economic, scientific, technical, cultural, and other international ties.

Thus, while proceeding from several different basic positions, these two orientations come to the single conclusion of the need to create a world State. Proponents of this concept allege that the sole means of increasing the effectiveness of the United Nations, as well as of other international organizations, in the cause of securing peace and developing cooperation lies in the direction of a world State. They also appeal for all efforts to be directed to this end.

2. Marxism and the Problem of a World State

Bourgeois conceptions of a world State are theoretically unfounded and politically harmful. The claims by proponents of a world State that their concepts are the most progressive have no basis whatever.

These conceptions have been subjected to well-known criteria by a number of bourgeois writers, who call attention first and foremost to the fact that such concepts ignore reality and are impracticable.

An American professor, W. Friedmann, says, for example, with regard to the Clark-Sohn plan that it "ignores the basic social factors of international society". "The only observations directed to the practicability of the proposals", writes Friedmann, "are those made by Mr. Clark in the introduction. They base the practicability of the proposals primarily on the overwhelming destructive force of the new weapons, on a moral reluctance of the average American to engage in mass destruction inherent in nuclear war, and on a world- wide desire to life the burden of competitive armaments. While these are unquestionably factors to be considered, no serious student of international politics and society regards them as the *only* relevant factors".[25]

Professor Q. Wright says that at present "it seems unlikely that the United Nations can develop into anything deserving of name of world federation ...".[26]

Other bourgeois writers also point to the danger of plans to transform the United Nations into a world State.

Thus, for example, M. Bourquin, in summing up the results of a number of investigations devoted to the positions of various States with regard to the United Nations, has remarked that the majority of these works conclude that under present conditions a fundamental restructuring of the United Nations is impossible and that this path is fraught with dangers for the international organization. "In planning for a significant enlargement of the powers of the United Nations", writes Bourquin, "it is too often forgotten that these powers would not be granted to an homogeneous entity whose concern would be only for the general interests of the international community, but would be in the hands of an association of States, each of which would act primarily on the basis of national motives, and would attempt to use those resources which this association makes available to it in the interests of their own policy.

"Legally, the authority of the organization itself would grow, and, therefore, the authority of the community which this organization represents. But this would merely be a fiction, since the powers of the organization are to be effectuated by a majority; both this majority and above all the Powers around which it is formed would benefit from the advantages connected with these changes. In our world, so deeply divided, this would mean transferring a very dangerous weapon into their hands, which could lead to the ruin of the organization instead of strengthening it".[27]

[25] W. Friedmann, *The Changing Structure of International Law* (1964), p. 276.

[26] Q. Wright, *The Role of International Law in the Elimination of War* (1961), pp. 54-55.

[27] M. Bourquin, *L'État souverain et l'Organisation internationale* (1959), p. 32.

Professor C. de Visscher also points to this danger, declaring that a world federation "could be transformed into instruments of the antagonisms that divide the peoples".[28]

And A. Verdross, not without justification, remarks: "Can one truly believe that a minority will agree to subordinate itself to a majority when such different civilizations and economic systems exist in the world? Central authority can function only when a minimum homogeneity exists among the members of society. Otherwise, a State always is threatened with being destroyed by civil war".[29]

The criticism of the concept of a world State by bourgeois international lawyers, however, does not disclose the fundamental reasons of its unfoundedness, which lie in the fact that these are in contradiction to the laws of societal development of our day.

In reality, the first of these orientations in the bourgeois concept of a world State ignores these laws in general, approaching the question with formalistic logic. The second orientation bases its conclusions upon the internationalization of economic life and the development of economic, scientific, technical, cultural, and other ties among States. This is, of course, the most important developmental law of contemporary society, which greatly influences the development of international organizations. But it is not the only law influencing the character of contemporary international organizations (see Chapter XIII).

Marxism-Leninism approaches the problem of a world State from the viewpoint of the interaction of the laws of societal development. As has been shown previously (see Chapter XIII), these laws do not operate in a single direction with regard to the character of contemporary international organizations.

[28] C. de Visscher, *Théories et réalités en droit international public* (2d ed.; 1955), p. 450.

[29] A. Verdross, "Le problème d'une autorité politique mondiale", *Comprendre*, no. 28 (1965), p. 17.

It is necessary to point out that the view, widely held in the West, that the Soviet Union and Soviet jurists oppose a world State, oppose an effective international organization, while Western countries and Western jurists favor a world State in principle and therefore an effective international organization, is completely unjustified.

Marxism-Leninism links the possibility of a world association of nations first and foremost with the liquidation of capitalism as the last exploitative socio-economic formation and with the creation of a socialist society. "The purpose of socialism", wrote V. I. Lenin, "is not only to eliminate the splintering of mankind into petty States and any isolation of nations; is not only the coming together of nations, but also their amalgamation".[30] But in order to create the conditions for this, more than just the liquidation of private ownership and the creation of a socialist State is needed. Lenin pointed out that national and State differences among peoples and countries will last "for a very, very long time even after realization of the dictatorship of the proletariat on a world-wide scale".[31]

Even on the domestic plane in a number of instances socialism inherits from capitalism such deep roots of national discord and economic, political, and cultural inequality that a considerable time is required to liquidate them. In international relations, naturally, the matter is far more complex. Each State represents both a political and an economic unit. With the various historical strata of contradictions between States and between nationalities are associated a number of economic, political, cultural, and other problems.

Within the framework of the world socialist system, however, these differences and contradictions gradually are being overcome on the basis of a new socialist social structure

[30] V. I. Lenin, "Социалистическая революция и право наций на самоопределения" [Socialist Revolution and Right of Nations to Self-Determination], Полное собрание сочинений [Complete Collection of Works] (5th ed.; 1962), XXVII, 256.

[31] Lenin, "Детская болезнь левизны в коммунизме" [Infantile Illness of Leftism in Communism], ibid., CLI, 77 [First published in June 1920 – *WEB*].

and Marxist-Leninist ideology. Various forms of State unions of socialist States are possible on the path to a classless, stateless communist society. The creation of a world federation or another form of uniting free States and nations is conceivable, therefore, only on the path of liquidating private ownership, exploitation, class and national contradictions, on the path of constructing socialism and communism. "A United States of the World (and not of Europe)", wrote V. I. Lenin, "is that State form of union and freedom of nations which we link with socialism, as the complete victory of communism does not lead to the final disappearance of any State, including a democratic State".[32]

The theoretical unfoundedness of bourgeois concepts and plans to create a world State is determined by the basic unfoundedness of bourgeois methodology, which is characterized by the divorcing of the superstructure from the base. A State is regarded as something that can be reconstructed as a cardinal format the will of politicians and jurists irrespective of the economic structure of society. The causes of war, whose liquidation is the *leitmotif* of all plans for a world State, bourgeois scholars misrepresent as State sovereignty, whereas the very existence of sovereign States is a natural consequence of the economic structure of society, and both sovereignty and the State will disappear only when this structure is changed.

The deep roots of wars are found in the economic system and in the specific class structure of society which it determines. Moreover, bourgeois concepts of a world State originate, and by their class nature can not but originate, from the possibility of creating a world State and liquidating wars without affecting the economic system of capitalism.

In stressing the basic distinction between Marxism and bourgeois pacifism on the question of the causes of wars, V. I. Lenin wrote: "Socialists always have condemned wars among

[32] Lenin, "О лозунге соединенных штатов Европы" [On the Slogan United States of Europe], ibid., XXVI, 354.

peoples as a barbaric and brutal affair. But our attitude toward war differs in principle from that of bourgeois pacifists (proponents and advocates of peace) and anarchists. At the outset we distinguish ourselves by the fact that we understand the inevitable connection of wars with the class struggle within a country; we understand the impossibility of eliminating wars without eliminating classes and creating socialism".[33]

As already has been pointed above, contemporary international organizations by their very nature can not take as their purpose the struggle against these basic causes of wars, but they can do much in the struggle against the causes of the order "produced" from the basic causes.

Under contemporary conditions, the plans to create a world State not only are utopian, but reactionary. Attempts to implement them even partially would bring great harm to the cause of developing and strengthening the United Nations and other international organizations as instruments of peace, since they are directed against the very bases of contemporary international organizations, defined by the laws of societal development.

The plans for a world State conceal the reactionary character of imperialism, creating the illusion of a peaceful, progressive imperialism. In criticizing Kautsky's reactionary theory of "ultra- imperialism", V. I. Lenin pointed out that it suggests to workers "that imperialism is not bad, that it is close to inter- (or ultra-) imperialism, and is capable of ensuring permanent peace".[34]

Irrespective of the aspirations of their authors, bourgeois concepts of a world State objectively reflect the policy of imperialist monopolies which, having stretched their tentacles

[33] Lenin, "Социализм и война (Отношение РСДРП к войне)" [Socialism and War (Attitude of RSDPR to War], ibid., XXVI, 311 [First published at Geneva in August 1918 – *WEB*].

[34] Lenin, "Империализм, как высшая стадия империализма (популярный очерк)" []Imperialism as the Highest Stage of Imperialism (Popular Essay)[, ibid., XXVII, 416.

to many countries, would strengthen their position as world exploiters with the aid of any form of world government.

In belittling the significance of State sovereignty and calling for its liquidation, bourgeois concepts of a world State disarm peoples ideologically and facilitate interference by imperialist powers in the internal affairs of weaker States for the purpose of suppressing liberation movements, for the purpose of the economic and political enslavement of peoples".[35]

The plans to create a world State are linked in imperialist ideology with the struggle against social revolutions and the national liberation movement. As Jessup correctly points out, a world State "will enact law and will take steps to suppress armed rebellion against its authority ... The right of resistance would not be recognized ... The law of a world State would therefore deny the right of revolution".[36] "The international community", Jessup continues, "would have to take cognizance of and remedy situations within States which are provocative of rebellion. It would have to be prepared, as the federal government of the United States is prepared, to render armed assistance to any of its members whose local forces are inadequate to preserve domestic peace and tranquillity".[37]

Bourgeois concepts of a world State objectively mislead peoples both on the internal and international planes. On the internal plane, they parry the blow from the capitalist system, alleging that the roots of wars are not linked with the social system of an exploitative society. On the international plane, they are oriented in essence at undermining the basic

[35] See A. I. Denisov, "Империалистическая идея 'всемирного правительства' и 'европейской федерации' и ее реакционная роль" [Imperialist Idea of "World Government" and "European Federation" and Reactionary Role Thereof], Вестник Московского университета; серия общественных наук [Herald of Moscow University: Series Social Sciencs], no. 7 (1949), pp. 97-112; D. B. Levin, О современных буржуазных теориях международного права [On Contemporary Bourgeois Theories of International Law] (1959), pp. 54-58.

[36] Jessup, *Modern Law of Nations*, p. 185.

[37] Ibid., p. 186.

principles of contemporary international organization, as well as at diverting attention from the urgent problems of perfecting international organizations as instruments of ensuring peace and developing international cooperation. As a French professor, E. Giraud, has properly pointed out, "... in proposing today to realize the impossible, they impede useful efforts and in no way further the progress of mankind".[38]

The interstate character of contemporary international organization is dictated by the objective developmental laws of our epoch. And from the viewpoint of the interests of strengthening international peace and security, international organizations of the interstate type are the best form of international organization for our days.

3. *Ways of Strengthening the United Nations*

The question of ways to develop the United Nations is of particular significance because of the importance of the Organization itself and because of the trend toward departing from the basic provisions of the Charter under the slogan of strengthening, it has been manifested in the United Nations with special strength.

It follows from what has been said previously that the question of strengthening international organizations, and especially the United Nations, as instruments of peace and of the development of international cooperation must be approached by taking into account the laws of societal development which define the basic features of contemporary international organizations. Taking account of these laws means not only that any innovations having the purpose of improving the United Nations should not be divorced from the realities of today, but also, above all, that they should conform to the laws of societal development in our epoch – that is to say, should reflect the basic, protracted, profound processes of international relations and not be the product of a temporary

[38] E. Giraud, "La révision de la Charte des Nations Unies", *Recueil des cours*, XC (1956), 326.

co-relation of forces similar to the "Uniting for Peace" Resolution 377(V).

An analysis of the juridical nature of the United Nations as laid down in its Charter shows that as a whole it reflects the laws of societal development in our epoch. According to the Charter, the United Nations is an interstate organization of the peaceful coexistence of States of different social systems which should function on the basis of the sovereign equality of all its Members" (Article 2[1]). The principle of peaceful coexistence "to practice tolerance and live together in peace with one another as good neighbours" (Preamble) runs throughout the entire Charter. The Charter strengthens the inadmissibility of the Organization's interfering "in matters which are essentially within the domestic jurisdiction of any state" (Article 2[7]), which excludes questions of the socio-economic system of States from the sphere of activity of the United Nations. The Charter contains guarantees against transforming the Organization into the instrument of States of a single social system. The basic purposes of the Organization are to maintain international peace and security and to develop cooperation in various spheres. Only the provisions of the Charter relating to decolonization, which as a whole were a step forward but as a result of the opposition of imperialist powers inadequately reflected the corresponding law of societal development, were overtaken by the course of events.

If the Charter provisions fundamentally correspond to the laws of societal development of our epoch, then a basic condition for increasing the effectiveness of the United Nations as an instrument of peace is to purify its practice of those violations of the Charter which sometimes are presented, without any grounds, as a new constitution of the United Nations.

In its Memorandum of 10 July 1964 "Regarding Certain Measures to Strengthen the Effectiveness of the United Nations in the Safeguarding of International Peace and Security", the Soviet Government justly pointed out: "The United Nations Charter contains the essential principles for peaceful and good-neighbourly relations among States. Therefore, to enhance the effectiveness of the United Nations in keeping the peace means first of all putting an end to violations of the Charter, permanently ridding the Organization of all remnants of the `cold war' period, creating within the United Nations a situation favourable to the cooperation of all States as equals".[39]

Not breaking the fundamental principles of the Charter, not attempting to transform the United Nations into the likeness of a world State, which could lead only to the disintegration of the United Nations, but strengthening the fundamentals of the Charter by strictly complying with the Charter's provisions – this is the only means of increasing the effectiveness of the United Nations as an instrument of peace and international cooperation.

In this respect, restoring the relationship between the General Assembly and the Security Council provided by the Charter and refraining from attempts to circumvent the unanimity principle of permanent members of the Security Council have special significance.

The General Assembly Resolution of 3 November 1950, well- known under the name "Uniting for Peace", was the clearest manifestation of the policy of the United States and its allies, which had the purpose of transferring the center of gravity in deciding basic questions of maintaining peace and security from the Security Council to the General Assembly in order to use the then existing favorable co-relation of forces in the United Nations organ to ensure their complete domination in the Organization. After 1956, with the changed situation in the General Assembly in connection with the admission of a large number of new members, the United States had attempted already, as Professor Stoessinger correctly points out,[40] to give the greatest possible power to the Secretary

[39] Doc. No. S/5811 (XIX), 10 July 1964, p. 3.

[40] J. G. Stoessinger, *The United Nations and the Superpowers* (1965), pp. 170-171.

General, who at the time faithfully and loyally served the Western powers.

A change of situation in the Secretariat and the General Assembly undoubtedly was an important if not decisive factor in changing United States policy with respect to the Security Council. Since the Soviet Union always insisted that the Security Council fulfill its duties in conformity with the Charter, this change led to the Security Council beginning to work again and, as some observers remark, under these conditions "the problem of the veto in practice does not arise".[41]

These reassuring symptoms show that a return to the Charter provisions on the general question of maintaining peace and security, despite the pessimistic appraisals of certain writers,[42] is by no means impossible.

Imparting to the United Nations a truly universal character is of the greatest significance for strengthening the Charter. The fact, for example, that the Western powers have made the representation of the Chinese People's Republic impossible in the United Nations already has caused enormous harm to the United Nations and the cause of peace.

The requirement that the Charter be strictly complied with relates to a number of those provisions which arise out of the fundamental principles of this organization. This is not only a requirement of international law, but also a requirement of political wisdom and international morality. The United Nations, just as other international organizations, was created by an international treaty, a Charter in which the member States determined that the Organization would act in conformity with the provisions of the Charter. The cardinal principle of international law, *pacta sunt servanda*, is fully applicable to the United Nations Charter. Respect for this principle is a fundamental principle of international legality.

41 R.-J. Dupuy, "Des nations unanimes et désunies', *Comprendre*, nos. 31-32 (1968), p. 34.

42 See, for example, M. Virally, *L'O.N.U. d'hier à demain* (1961), p. 67.

The aforesaid does not mean that work should not be done to perfect existing mechanisms of the United Nations. However, here it is very important to eliminate as soon as possible such remnants of the "cold war" as the intersession committee, the collective measures committee, the United Nations Commission for Korea, and others.

In evaluating the existing United Nations system, it should not be forgotten that the United Nations is not a self-sufficient organization; the activity of the Organization depends upon the policy of member States and especially the policy of the great powers. Of course, the United Nations exerts influence upon the policy of States. It is necessary, however, to proceed from the real situation and the nature of the United Nations; the influence of the policies of States upon United Nations actions is primary and decisive.

Therefore, the principal factor in increasing the effectiveness of the United Nations as an instrument of peace and international cooperation is the forces which could exert pressure upon the ruling classes and the governments of States whose policy does not correspond to the interests of peace and consequently the requirements of the United Nations Charter. There are such forces in modern society; these are the forces of peace.

One could say that all this is not a full guarantee against an outbreak of war. This is certainly true. The many wars that have occurred since the Second World War, particularly the aggressive war of the United States in Vietnam which has aroused the deep indignation of world society, are evidence of this. But to reveal existing guarantees of peace, imperfect but real, is much better than to build castles in the sky, which are destroyed at their first confrontation with reality and which make the forces of peace disorganized and unprepared for that great struggle against the forces of aggression which they must wage constantly and with more energy and organization.[43]

[43] See G. I. Tunkin, "Une organisation internationale universelle: illusions et réalité", *Comprendre*, nos. 31-32 (1968), pp. 68-79.

PART VI.
THE GENERAL CHARACTER AND FORMS OF STATE RESPONSIBILITY UNDER INTERNATIONAL LAW

The historic changes that have taken place in international law since the Great October Socialist Revolution have necessarily also affected that branch of international law relating to State responsibility. We must dwell on these changes, for they still are far from adequately treated and worked out in international legal doctrine.

The sanction as an "... indication of those measures of State coercion which are applied to those violating a prohibition or those failing to execute the command of a norm of law" is inherent in norms of international law as legal norms.[1] Of course, in international law both the sanctions themselves and their realization have many peculiarities in comparison with sanctions in national law.

Responsibility in international law, in any event responsibility in a broad sense, embraces both the problem of sanctions and the question of their realization.[2] That is to say, international legal responsibility is the legal consequences of violating norms of international law.

The legal consequences of violating norms of international law take many forms and may affect not only the offending State, but also the injured State, other States, and international organizations. Such consequences may, for example, depending upon the character of the breach, include the duty of the offending State to compensate for the damage caused; the right of the injured State to apply enforcement measures permitted by international law against the offending State; the right of other States to render assistance to the injured State; and perhaps the duty of an international organization to undertake certain actions against the offending State.

The subjects of international legal responsibility are the subjects of international law; consequently, they are above all, and primarily, States. At the same time, responsibility of an

[1] A. I. Denisov (ed.), Теория государства и права [Theory of State and Law] (1967), p. 291.

[2] As applied to national law, O. E. Leist believes that "... responsibility is the application and realization of a sanction in the event of a breach of law". O. E. Leist, Санкции в советском праве [Sanctions in Soviet Law] (1962), p. 85.

international organization is not precluded, for example, in the event that it fails to fulfill a treaty which it has concluded with a State or with another international organization. In isolated instances there occurs responsibility of natural persons. Thus, the principle of individual responsibility (side by side with State responsibility) for crimes against peace, war crimes, and crimes against humanity is recognized in contemporary international law.[3]

In the present work we are not concerned with the responsibility of international organizations and natural persons, limiting ourselves only to State responsibility.

State responsibility may arise either as a result of an unlawful action of a State (for example, violations by State authorities of the immunity of a foreign diplomatic representative) or as a result of an unlawful failure to act, that is, the failure of a State to take measures which it must effectuate in order to fulfill its obligations under international law (for example, legislative measures necessary to fulfill an international treaty to which the said State is a party).

Since the actions of a State in practice are expressed in the actions of its agencies, the international legal responsibility of a State arises out of the actions of its agencies (State administration, legislative, and judicial).

In intending, as already has been indicated, to dwell primarily upon certain new phenomena in the field of international legal State responsibility, we leave to one side the "traditional" disputes over State responsibility for actions of its agencies and officials exceeding the limits of their authority (*ultra vires*), for actions of superior and inferior agencies, in questions of fault, in denial of justice, and other such areas.

International legal State responsibility arises in the event it violates its obligations under international law. One should

[3] See the charters and judgments of the Nuremberg and Tokyo international military tribunals and the United Nations General Assembly resolution of 11 December 1946 confirming the principles of international law recognized by the Charter of the Nuremberg tribunal.

point in this connection to one very widespread but mistaken view that the causing of damage by one State to the interests of another necessarily entails international legal responsibility. Causing damage is not necessarily a violation of international law and consequently does not necessarily entail international legal State responsibility.[4] A State's action may be wholly lawful and all the same cause damage to the interests of another State, especially if such interests are understood broadly.

Since treaty and customary norms have identical binding force, State responsibility arises in the event of a violation of either customary or treaty norms of international law.[5] What difference can there be in the question of responsibility when in one case a State has violated a particular customary principle or customary norm of international law, and in another case, a principle or norm fixed in an international treaty? Take, for example, the case of a violation of the principle of freedom of the high seas. As long as the 1958 Geneva Convention on the High Seas had not entered into force, this principle was a generally-recognized customary principle of international law; after the Geneva Convention had entered into force, this principle, in the form in which it was fixed in this Convention, became a treaty norm for its parties. Of course, there are no grounds for believing that responsibility for a violation of this principle changed once it had become a treaty [norm] for the respective States. A violation of either customary or a treaty norm of international law is an international delict.[6]

The legal consequences which ensue for a State as a result of its violation of international law are the content of international legal responsibility.

[4] This proposition can be regarded as generally recognized. See, for example, D. Anzilotti, *Corso di diritto internazionale* (4th ed.; 1955), I, 404; A. Ulloa, *Derecho internacional publico* (4th ed.; 1957), II, 251-252; A. Verdross, *Международное право*, transl. F. A. Kublitskii and R. L. Naryshkina, ed. G. I. Tunkin (1959), P. 353; P. Guggenheim, *Traité de droit international public* (1954), II, 2.

[5] P. Fauchille, *Traité de droit international public* (1922), I (Part 1), p. 517.

[6] One cannot, therefore, agree with the authors of the textbook Международное право [International Law] published in 1947, who distinguish between responsibility for a delict and responsibility for a violation of an international treaty (p. 148).

CHAPTER XVII. THE CHARACTER OF STATE RESPONSIBILITY UNDER INTERNATIONAL LAW BEFORE THE GREAT OCTOBER SOCIALIST REVOLUTION

Under the old international law State responsibility included the obligation of an offending State to compensate damage caused, as well as the application of enforcement measures, including measures utilizing armed force.

Under the influence of civilist concepts in the science of international law, the view was widespread that State responsibility amounted to the duty to compensate damage caused. According to this concept, the failure of a State to fulfill its obligations under international law entailed a new obligation: the obligation to compensate damage (financial and moral) caused to another State.

The concept was worked out in detail in the second half of the nineteenth and in the beginning of the twentieth centuries.

A. Heffter, in noting that international law does not know "crime" in the form in which it exists in national law, believed at the same time that the concept of "breach of law" does exist in international law. "Each such breach of law", he said, "obliges the one acting unlawfully to give satisfaction to the one who has suffered damage, since always when an arbitrary action results in a wrong (*Ungleichheit*), this violation must be eliminated; this is the law of justice (*Gerechtigkeit*).[1]

F. F. Martens, crediting Heffter with creating the concept that international legal obligations originate from delicts, points out that "Heffter's theory on this question suffers only from the defect that it mixes together civil law with international".[2]

1 A. Heffter, *Das europäische Völkerrecht der Gegenwart auf den bisherigen Grundlagen*, ed. F. H. Geffcken (8th ed.; 1888), p. 220

2 F. F. Martens, Современное международное право цивилизованных народов [Contemporary International Law of Civilized Peoples] (3d ed.; 1895), I, 429.

At the same time, Martens expresses essentially the same idea as Heffter. "A crime", says Martens, "gives the victim a right to compensation for financial damage and moral injury caused to him. Although one does not speak in international relations of crimes committed by a people, nevertheless it is possible here to violate a right establishing, just as in private relations, the obligation of the guilty party to make financial compensation, to restore property, or to give moral satisfaction to the injured State".[3]

In his monograph *Völkerrecht und Landesrecht,* H. Triepel devotes comparatively little attention to general questions of State responsibility, considering primarily the more specific problems of State responsibility for the actions of its agencies, of individuals located on the State's territory, and so forth. However, he also works out these questions on the basis of the said concept.[4]

We find a considerably expanded and better founded elaboration of this concept in Anzilotti's special monograph devoted to the problem of State responsibility in international law, published in 1902. "State responsibility", says Anzilotti, "is in the nature of reparation, and not of satisfaction; consequently, the right of the injured State is limited by the requirement of compensating damage and of possible guarantees for the future, but it can not acquire the character of punishing the guilty State".[5] In developing this notion, Anzilotti goes on to point out that "a juridical relationship which arises between States as a result of the violation of a right, and which reflects responsibility, has the essential features of a liability relationship".[6] In his treatise on international law Anzilotti says: "As a result of an unlawful action, that is, speaking generally, as a result of a breach of an international

[3] Ibid.

[4] H. Triepel, *Völkerrecht und Landesrecht* (1899), p. 323.

[5] D. Anzilotti, *Teoria generale della responsibilita dello stato nel diritto internazionale* (1902), p. 96.

[6] Ibid., p. 97.

obligation, there emerges a new juridical relationship between the State to which the said unlawful action is imputed and the State in respect of which this obligation was not fulfilled; the first is bound to effectuate compensation, and the second may demand such compensation. This constitutes the sole consequence which international norms, being an expression of the mutual promises of States, can link with the breach of law ...".[7]

The distinction between civil and criminal responsibility, Anzilotti goes on to point out, and between compensation of damage and punishment, which exists in national law, is completely unknown in international law, which also reflects in this respect a stage of social development long since passed by national law. "It was characteristic of an earlier stage in the development of law that compensation of damage was at the same time a punishment, which consisted of compensating the harm caused".[8]

In the last edition of his treatise on international law, however, published posthumously, Anzilotti withdraws somewhat from his earlier point of view. Previously, Anzilotti had denied the "satis- faction" character of responsibility and had maintained that it bears only the character of "reparation". Now, although he says that responsibility in international law remains generally "within the framework of civil responsibility", he recognizes two forms of responsibility: satisfaction and reparation. Responsibility is expressed as satisfaction when nonfinancial damage has been caused, although, he says, there are instances when satisfaction, arising out of the infliction of nonfinancial damage, is expressed in the payment of a specific amount of money. By reparations Anzilotti means responsibility which arose in consequence of the infliction of financial damage and which is

[7] Anzilotti, *Corso di diritto internazionale*, I, 385-386.

[8] Ibid., p. 386.

expressed either in restitution or in com- pensation of the harm.[9]

This concept was, in fact, also predominant in bourgeois international legal literature during the period of the League of Nations. It is true that the working out of the problem of State responsibility at that time was limited almost exclusively to the problem of State responsibility for damage caused on its territory to the person or property of aliens. The emphasis, therefore, was laid upon compensation of damage.

Fauchille, for example, formulated this point of view as follows: "When State responsibility occurs, the question is one of reparations, that is, of restoring the previously existing situation, of compensation for damage caused to interests, or of satisfaction, which is expressed in a disavowal or removal of an official from a post, initiating the prosecution of the guilty person, public declarations, apologies made by way of diplomacy, and so forth".[10]

In a monograph on the responsibility of States in international law, C. Eagleton has asserted that the failure of a State to meet obligations under international law "imposes upon the guilty state the further obligation to make reparation for the injury caused ...".[11] "Responsibility", says Eagleton, "is simply the principle which establishes an obligation to make good any violation of international law producing injury, committed by the respondent State".[12]

C. de Visscher defined States responsibility thus: "International responsibility is a basic idea which amounts

[9] Ibid., pp. 425-427.

[10] Fauchille, *Le droit international public*, I (Part 1), p. 535.

[11] C. Eagleton, *The Responsibility of States in International Law* (1928), p. 3.

[12] Ibid., p. 22.

to the duty of a State to eliminate the consequences of an unlawful act ...".[13]

The concept that State responsibility is expressed in an obligation to compensate financial and moral damage caused by an unlawful act also runs throughout the various draft codifications of norms of international law relating to State responsibility for damage caused on its territory to the person or property of aliens.

Thus, in the "Bases for Discussion" drawn up by the preparation committee of the Conference for the Codification of International Law in 1929, State responsibility is defined as follows: "Responsibility involves for the State concerned an obligation to make good the damage suffered insofar as it results from failure to comply with the international obligation. It may also, according to the circumstances, and when this consequence follows from the general principles of international law, involve the obligation to afford satisfaction to the State which has been injured in the person of its national, in the shape of an apology (given with the appropriate solemnity) and (in proper cases) the punishment of the guilty persons".[14]

An analogous formulation was given in a resolution of the Institute of International Law, adopted in 1927, on the international responsibility of States for damage caused on their territory to the person or property of aliens.[15]

The Harvard draft gave the following definition of State responsibility: "A state is responsible, as the term is used in this convention, when it has a duty to make reparation

[13] C. de Visscher, "Le déni de justice en droit international", *Recueil des cours,* LII (1935), 421; see also E. M. Borchard, *The Diplomatic Protection of Citizens Abroad* (1928), p. 178.

[14] United Nations, *Yearbook of the International Law Commission 1956*, II, 255.

[15] H. Wehberg, *Tableau général des résolutions de l'institut de droit international* (1957), p. 139.

to another state for the injury sustained by the latter state as a consequence of an injury to its national".[16]

The said concept also was reflected in the judgments of the Permanent Court of International Justice. Thus, the Court's decision of 26 July 1927 in the dispute between Germany and Poland over "the Chorzow factory", said: "It is a principle of international law that the breach of an engagement involves an obligation to make reparation in an adequate form. Reparation therefore is the indispensable complement of a failure to apply a convention and there is no necessity for this to be stated in the convention itself".[17]

The said concept artificially narrowed State responsibility, reducing it to the obligation of an offending State to compensate the damage caused. Furthermore, it was not logically coordinated: if a violation of an international obligation gave rise to a new obligation, the obligation to compensate the damage caused, then a violation of the latter should, according to this concept, give rise to a further new obligation, and *ad infinitum*.[18]

In fact, the proponents of this theory also have proceeded on the basis of the possibility of applying enforcement measures to the offending State. Much attention has been devoted in international legal literature to questions of intervention, reprisals, and, finally, to war as a reaction to a violation of international law. Actually, the said concept amounted to the obligation to compensate harm as though it were the first stage of effectuating responsibility. If the offending State did not fulfill this obligation, enforcement measures could be taken against it.

We find this interpretation, for example, in F. Liszt. He says that a guilty State should first restore, insofar as this is

[16] Harvard Law School, "Research in International Law", *American Journal of International Law*, XXIII (1929), 140.

[17] Permanent Court of International Justice, Collection of Judgments, Series A, No. 8, *Case Concerning the Factory at Chorzow* (1927), p. 21.

[18] Guggenheim, *Traité de droit international public*, ii, 64.

possible, the previously existing situation and pay monetary compensation. In serious cases, in addition to financial compensation, satisfaction is required which consists of an expression of condolences, a salute to the flag of the injured State, and so forth. If the threat of a recurrence of the illegal actions exists, it is possible to take security measures which might be expressed in particular in a pledge of part of the State's territory. If the offending State refuses to grant financial compensation or satisfaction, coercion is admissible. First, the question must be one of using arbitration or measures of self-help of a nonmilitary nature, and as a last resort, the injured State may resort to war.[19]

According to another concept, the international law of that time provided a number of consequences for a delict, beginning with the obligation to compensate the damage caused and ending with the use of armed force. This view was held, for example, by J. C. Bluntschli, who wrote: "In international law, the strength of the legal order also is ensured by the fact that new law emerges out of a breach of law. The illegality committed is transformed into a right of the victim to demand from the offender, in accordance with the circumstances, restoration of the previously existing situation, compensation of damage, satisfaction, retribution, or punishment. When a breach of law consists only of the failure to fulfill an obligation assumed, without injuring the prestige of the State and without breach of the peace, it can be equated to a civil breach of law, which gives the injured person the right to initiate a civil suit for the purpose of restoring the previously existing legal situation (for example, the return of

[19] F. Liszt, *Das Völkerrecht* (11th ed.; 1918), p. 182. In a number of doctoral dissertations defended not so long ago at the University of Geneva, the authors maintained that responsibility under international law amounts to the obligation to compensate damage caused and that only the failure to fulfill this obligation can entail sanctions. P. A. Bissonnete, for example, writes: "Since the injured State is obliged to demand compensation of damage before resorting to sanctions, one can conclude that the consequence in general international law of a breach of law is reparation". P. A. Bissonnete, *La satisfaction comme mode de réparation en droit international* (1952), p. 12. See also P. A. Zannas, *La responsabilité internationale des États pour les actes de négligence* (1952), p. 22; A. Suat Bilge, *La responsabilité internationale des États et son application en metiére d'actes législatifs* (1950), pp. 15, 36.

property, payment of a debt, or compensation of damage). In such instances international law also is satisfied only by elimination of the illegality and restoration of the right".[20]

If damage has been caused to the honor and dignity of a State, in Bluntschli's view the injured power has the right to demand appropriate satisfaction. Such satisfaction goes somewhat beyond simply restoring the situation as it existed. Depending on the circumstances, it may be expressed in punishment of the guilty persons, and so forth. If necessary, enforcement measures are applied to obtain satisfaction.

When a breach of law takes the form of an intrusion into the legal sphere of another State, the latter, says Bluntschli, has the right not only to secure elimination of the breach of law, restoration of the previous situation, as well as compensation of damage, but also satisfaction, a penalty, and sometimes, depending upon the circumstances, other guarantees against the renewal of unlawful actions. If there has been a breach of the peace, the injured State also has the right to punish the offender. The provision of the criminal law that juridical persons can not be subjected to criminal punishment does not apply in international law. "A State which permits a breach of the peace may thereby create a danger to its own existence, and a war to which it has given rise may lead to its destruction. This is punishment under international law, and world history is evidence of its reality".[21]

This point of view, which might be called the concept of the "proportionate reaction to a violation of international law", as well as the theory that a violation of international law entails the obligation to compensate damage caused, and that only in the event this obligation is not fulfilled can sanctions be applied to the offending State, have given to a certain degree a distorted idea of international legal reality of that time.

[20] J. C. Bluntschli, *Das moderne Völkerrecht der civilisirten Staten* (2d ed.; 1872), p. 259.

[21] Ibid., p. 260.

Even if one believes that under the old international law a State could lawfully resort to war only in the event its rights were violated (the "just war" doctrine), international law all the same did not oblige a State first to submit a claim concerning compensation of damage and to appeal to arms only in the event of a refusal to satisfy this claim. The Hague conventions of 1899 and 1907 do not contain such provisions.

As regards the "proportionate reaction" to a violation of international law, this principle could have been considered operative only with respect to compensation of damage and to reprisals; it did not, however, extend to war. If again one proceeds from the concept of "just war", under the old international law a State could resort to war in defence of any right which, in its opinion, had been violated.[22]

The Hague conventions of 1899 and 1907 do not contain any legal norms which would limit the right of a State to resort to war irrespective of the seriousness of the breach of law. It is true that the conventions of 1899 and 1907 concerning peaceful settlement of disputes distinguish between "serious disagreements or disputes" and international disputes "involving neither honour nor vital interests". In the first instance, the possibility of the recourse to arms is expressly mentioned in the conventions. Article 2 of these conventions says: "In case of serious disagreement or dispute, before an appeal to arms, the Contracting Powers agree to have recourse, as far as circumstances will allow, to the good offices or mediation of one or more friendly powers". In the second instance, the possibility of recourse to arms is not mentioned. Article 9 of the conventions says: "In disputes of an international nature involving neither honour nor vital interests, and arising from a difference of opinion on points of fact, the Contracting Powers deem it expedient and desirable that the parties who

[22] *De lege feranda,* Bluntschli suggested certain limitations of the right of a State to resort to war. Article 520 of the Code of International Law which he compiled provided: "A lawful *causus belli* justifies war only when restoration of the violated right and appropriate satisfaction and compensation are impossible to obtain without difficulty through peaceful means". Ibid., p. 291.

have not been able to come to an agreement by means of diplomacy, should, as far as circumstances allow, institute an International Commission of Inquiry, to facilitate a solution of these disputes by elucidating the facts by means of an impartial and conscientious investigation".[23]

In dividing conflicts between States into the two said categories, the conventions of 1899 and 1907 on the peaceful settlement of international disputes (the provisions of both conventions on this question are identical) contain no provisions as to the grounds upon which a State could resort to war.

For a war to be considered "just", it was required only that military actions were commenced with an advance and unambiguous warning, which must have taken the form of either a reasoned declaration of war or an ultimatum with a conditional declaration of war.[24] However, the nonfulfillment of even this requirement did not entail in practice any juridical consequences.

War was considered by many authors as one of the international legal methods of settling disputes among States, although, as is shown farther on, this was by no means so. The fact that they called war an "extreme measure" had no juridical but only practical significance, since naturally if a State could secure satisfaction of its claims without using force it would be common sense for it to prefer not to appeal to arms. "In any event", wrote Martens, "not arbitration but war remains up to the present time the usual means of deciding international disputes".[25] Another well-known Russian international lawyer, N. Korkunov, wrote: "A State which avoid the voluntary

[23] L. A. Modzhorian and V. K. Sobakin (comps.), Международное право в избранных документах [International Law in Selected Documents], ed. V. N. Durdenevskii (1957), II, 248-249.

[24] See the 1907 Convention on the Opening of Military Actions, ibid., III, 40.

[25] Martens, Современное международное право [Contemporary International Law], I, 13.

performance of duties falling upon it can be compelled to do so by military actions undertaken against it".[26]

We have mentioned the "just war" doctrine, according to which a State could resort to war only in defense of a violated right. To a certain extent, however, this doctrine idealized the actual situation in the old international law. The Hague conventions of 1899 and 1907, which may be in this domain, did not contain provisions that one State could resort to war against another only in the event its rights were violated. The actual situation was such that, although a State which had unleashed a war attempted, as a rule, to cite in justification of its actions any real or imagined claims resting on international law, States, especially strong ones, did not want to assume an obligation under which one could resort to war only on the basis of claims which could be justified legally. It is not surprising, therefore, that the majority of international lawyers of that time, taking the actual situation into account, rejected the "just war" doctrine.[27]

Bluntschli, who was a proponent of the "just war" doctrine, pointed out that war in reality was a factual state of affairs, but in the interests of peace, he said, it is important as far as possible to regard it as a lawful measure of self-help, that is, as a measure undertaken in defense of a violated right.[28]

In the old international law, at least in those instances when it was undertaken in defense of a violated right, war outwardly was represented as an enforcement measure with respect to the offending State. On this basis, some writers considered war to be a sanction. Korkunov wrote, for example, that in international law coercion "not only is not impossible, but even, on the contrary, nowhere does it take on such vast dimensions

[26] N. Korkunov, Международное право [International Law] (1886), p. 4.

[27] H. Kelsen, *Principles of International Law*, ed. R. W. Tucker (2d ed.; 1967), p. 33.

[28] Bluntschli, *Das moderne Völkerrecht*, p. 287.

as in international life, appearing here in the terrible form of war".[29]

One can name Kelsen and Guggenheim among the contemporary authors who adhere to the view that war was a sanction under the old international law. Moreover, they also believe that this position has been retained in contemporary international law. "If reprisals and war", Kelsen wrote, "– typical measures of self-help – are not considered as legal sanctions because a minimum of centralization is considered to be an essential element of the law, the social order we call general international law cannot be regarded as law in the true sense of the term".[30]

In P. Guggenheim's view, war is a "measure of legal protection", a "sanction" of international law.[31]

We already have spoken of the unfounded assertions of Kelsen and Guggenheim that war is inadmissible under contemporary international law. The question which interests us now is war in connection with the problem of sanctions in international law. In this respect one also can not agree with Kelsen and Guggenheim.

First of all, even if regarded only as a reaction to a violation of international law, war under the old international law was not dependent in any way upon the seriousness of the breach of law, which is an essential constituent element of a sanction. As already has been pointed out, a State could resort to war in the event of any violation of international law which affected its rights.

The consequences of war had absolutely no connection with responsibility for the breach of law committed. With the outbreak of war, a special international law – the law of war – came into effect. Absolutely nothing remained of the

[29] Korkunov, Международное право [International Law], p. 4.

[30] Kelsen, *Principles of International Law*, p. 31.

[31] Guggenheim, *Traité de droit international public*, II, 93.

relations which arose in consequence of the breach of law that led to war. According to the law of war, the parties were in an equal legal position. The former offender ceased to exist. The legal consequences of war also had no connection whatever with the initial breach of law.

The legal consequences of war did not depend upon whether a State began the war in defense of a violated right or without any legal grounds, as, for example, to seize parcels of land from a neighbouring State, but were determined by the results of the armed contest between the belligerents. International law sanctioned that which was gained by force. This was the "right of the victor".

This situation again testifies to the fact that the "just war" doctrine had no foundation in the old international law. The justness or unjustness of a war meant nothing in the old international law. The justness or unjustness of a war meant nothing, either for the conduct of the war or for its consequences.

Under the old international law, war created a new legal situation characterized by the unlimited right of the victor, that is to say, by the right of the victor limited only by his physical possibilities to force the defeated side to fulfill the demands submitted to it. These demands juridically did not depend upon whether they were submitted by the State which had unleashed the war or the State upon whom the attack was committed.

Also, they need not have been in accordance with the claims put forward before the war. Moreover, they could be submitted by the party which before the war had not put forward any claims at all against the defeated State.

The said claims had a special legal basis, the right of the victor, which thus was an inevitable corollary of the admissibility of war as a method of settling international disputes. Professor Lauterpacht, even in 1952, maintained that "international law sets no limits – other than that determined by compelling considerations of humanity – to the discretion of the victor...".[32]

This means that, contrary to the generally accepted view, war was regarded under the old international law not just as a legal method of settling disputes.

If this had been so, the victor could pretend to lay claims only to the satisfaction of claims which had led to the war, that is to say, could pretend to lay claim only to the settlement to this advantage of the dispute which actually had existed.

Thus, with its external resemblance to an enforcement measure, war was not a sanction under the old international law. It was a factual state of affairs whose origin virtually was unregulated by international law, but to which international law linked specific juridical consequences.

What has been said also means, and this was an important feature of the old international law, that the principles of international legal State responsibility in essence were not extended to war and its consequences.

International law contained certain principles of State responsibility relating to violations of the laws and customs of war. Thus, the Fourth Hague Convention of 1907 established that the belligerent party which violates the laws and customs of war "shall, if the case demands, be liable to pay compensation. It shall be responsible for all acts committed by persons forming part of its armed forces".[33] There was the well-known institute of military reprisals; however, the principles of responsibility did not extend as a whole to war and its consequences.

International law, having recognized the "right to wage war", did not contain principles and norms under which the unleashing of wars would be appraised as aggression. As regards

[32] L. Oppenheim, *International Law*, ed. H. Lauterpacht (7th ed.; 1952), II, 603.

[33] Article 3 of the 1907 Convention on the Laws and Customs of Land Warfare, Modzhorian and Sobakin (comps.), Международное право в избранных документах [International Law in Selected Documents], III, 42.

the consequences of war, international law recognized the "right of the victor". Naturally, therefore, the question of responsibility for war did not arise, and the juridical consequences of war were not linked with the circumstances which had led to war.

CHAPTER XVIII. STATE RESPONSIBILITY UNDER CONTEMPORARY INTERNATIONAL LAW

1. The Concept of the International Legal Criminal Responsibility of a State

In attempting to comprehend the changes which have occurred in the domain of international State responsibility, some bourgeois jurists have come to the conclusion that anew type of State responsibility – criminal responsibility – has emerged in international law. The proponents of this concept have maintained that whereas at an earlier stage of the development of international law State responsibility was restricted to the duty to compensate damage caused, then contemporary international law goes further, providing for the criminal responsibility of a State as a subject of international law.

The concept of the criminal responsibility of a State has been propagated to a certain extent in bourgeois international legal literature since the First and, especially, the Second World Wars. Proponents of this concept fell into two categories: some adhere to the view that only a State can be the subject of international criminal responsibility, and individual persons can bear criminal responsibility only under national law (Bustamante, Donnedieu de Vabres); others believed that both a State and individuals could be subjects of criminal responsibility under international law (Pella, Saldana, Levy).[1]

One of the most active propagandists of the criminal responsibility of States, a Romanian professor, V. V. Pella, maintained in his works, particularly in *La criminalité collective des États et le droit pénal de l'ávenir*, published in 1925,[2] that

[1] For greater detail, see D. B. Levin, "Проблемы ответственности в науке международного права" [Problems of Responsibility in the Science of International Law], Известия академии наук СССР; отделение экономики и права [News of the USSR Academy of Sciences, Division of Economics and Law], no. 2 (1946), pp. 99-115.

[2] V. V. Pella, *La criminalité collective des états et le droit pénal de l'ávenir* (1925).

criminal responsibility of a State already exists in international law and that full recognition of this new type of responsibility would have great significance in increasing the effectiveness of international law.

Proceeding from the premise that international law should develop along the same path as national law, Pella believed that criminal responsibility of a State must inevitably emerge in international law and that the domain of its application would expand. He maintained that a "State has its own will and, consequently, is capable of committing crimes ...".[3]

We should like to affirm as forcefully as possible", Pella wrote after the Second World War, "that *if* criminal law is to be called upon to protect international peace and civilization, one should not exclude the principle of criminal responsibility of a State therefrom".[4]

In his work *La guerre-crime et les criminels de guerre,* published in 1946, Pella appended "A Plan for an International Criminal Code" which he had prepared before the Second World War. Proposals for an international criminal code had been worked out by the author for the International Criminal Law Association, the Inter-Parliamentary Union, and the International Law Association. These proposals were discussed in committees of the said organizations, and thus the final "Plan for an International Criminal Code" reflects not only Pella's point of view but to a certain extent also the point of view of a number of other proponents of the concept of international criminal responsibility of a State.

The following classification of the crimes of States is given in the "Plan for an International Criminal Code":

(1) War crimes, reflected in the commission by a State first of one of the following actions: (a) declaration of war upon

[3] Pella, "La repression des crimes contre la personalité de l'état", *Recueil des cours,* XXXIII (1930), 821-822.

[4] Pella, *La guerre-crime et les criminels de guerre* (1946), p. 58.

another State; (b) intrusion of armed forces upon the territory of another State, with or without a declaration of war; (c) attack by land, naval, or air forces, with or without a declaration of war, upon the territory, vessels, or aircraft of another State; (d) sea blockade of coasts or ports of another State; (e) support of armed bands which, having been formed on its territory, intrude into the territory of another State, or a refusal, despite the demand of the State being subjected to the intrusion, to take on its own territory all measures in its power to deprive the said bands of any assistance or protection.[5]

(2) Production, sale, or use of prohibited means of waging war, and other violations of the laws and customs of war.

(3) Creation and training of armed forces exceeding the prescribed contingents.

(4) Extermination, enslavement, or persecution, in time of peace or war, of specific groups of the population for reasons of race, politics, or religion.

(5) Failure to take measures to prevent crimes against the independence and territorial integrity of another State which have been prepared on the territory of the State concerned.

(6) Admittance or the rendering of aid to persons and organizations which are preparing on the territory of the State crimes against the interests of another State, particularly an attempt against the life and liberty of the head of a foreign State, members of the Government, and so forth.

(7) Interference in the internal political struggle in another State.

(8) Indefinite threats to use force against another State.

[5] The author refers in this connection to the text of the definition of aggression worked out by the Committee on Security Questions of the General Commission of the 1933 Conference on Disarmament on the basis of the Soviet draft definition of aggression.

(9) Conducting manoeuvres or mobilization for the purpose of a military demonstration.

(10) Violation of the immunity of foreign diplomatic representatives.

(11) Counterfeiting of money and any other disloyal actions committed by one State for the purpose of causing injury to another, or against whose commission the State does not take the necessary measures.

(12) Any other actions which may violate normal international relations.[6]

Pella includes as criminal sanctions which should be applied to a State: diplomatic sanctions (warning, breaking off of diplomatic relations, recalling the exequatur from consuls, and so forth); legal sanctions (sequestration of the property of a State's nationals, and others); economic sanctions (economic blockade or boycott, embargo, and others); other sanctions (censure, penalty, deprivation for a certain time of representation in international organizations, deprivation of a mandate to administer a trust territory, complete or partial occupation of the territory of a State, deprivation of independence).[7]

In addition, the "Plan for an International Criminal Code" provides for security measures that might be undertaken with respect to a State which has committed a crime, namely: destruction of strategic railways and fortifications; prohibiting military production; confiscation of armaments; limitation of the size of armed forces; complete disarmament; the formation of demilitarized zones on the territory of the State and the establishment of control over them; distribution of military units at various points of a State's territory for the purposes of control.[8]

[6] Pella, *La guerre-crime et les criminels de guerre*, pp. 148-150.

[7] Ibid., pp. 153-154.

[8] Ibid., p. 155.

Pella proposed to create within the framework of the United Nations International Court a special criminal chamber to consider cases concerning the crimes of States.[9]

The draft code prepared by Pella has gone no further.

H. Lauterpacht, who also is a proponent of international criminal responsibility of a State, writes: "The comprehensive notion of an international delinquency ranges from ordinary breaches of treaty obligations, involving no more than pecuniary compensation, to violations of International Law amounting to a criminal act in the generally accepted meaning of the term".[10]

In Lauterpacht's view, the State and the persons acting on its behalf bear criminal responsibility for such violations of international law as by reason of their gravity, ruthlessness, and contempt for human life place them in the category of criminal acts as this is understood in the law of "civilized countries".[11] Lauterpacht includes as such crimes the wholesale massacre of aliens resident within a State's territory and the preparation and launching of an aggressive war. Lauterpacht suggests that universal recognition of the principles of international law relating to the punishment of war criminals is new evidence of the existence of the criminal responsibility of a State, since war criminals bear punishment for actions which they commit, as a rule, on behalf of agencies of the State.[12]

The theory of the unity of the paths of development of international and national law, according to which the development of law represents a unified process wherein national law and international law are only at different stages,

[9] Ibid., p. 129.

[10] L. Oppenheim, *International Law*, ed. H. Lauterpacht (8th ed.; 1955), I, 339.

[11] Ibid., p. 355.

[12] Ibid., p. 356; H. Donnedieu de Vabres, "Le procès de Nuremberg devant les principes modernes du droit penal international", *Recueil des cours*, LXX (1947), 562.

is a basic concept of the criminal responsibility of a State (see Chapter IX).

Proponents of the concept of the criminal responsibility of a State are prepared to acknowledge that until recently international law was unaware of the criminal responsibility of a State, but they explain this by the fact that international law supposedly was in a primitive state. They maintain, however, that recently international law has moved far forward, as a result whereof, by analogy with national law, the criminal responsibility of a State has emerged.

It is characteristic that objections to the concept of criminal responsibility of a State in bourgeois literature were based, as a rule, on this same theory of the unity of the paths of the development of law. Thus, Anzilotti writes in *Teoria generale della responsabilita dello stato* that in a sense compensation for damage in international law replaces punishment, but the analogy is not significant. In the early stages of the development of law, Anzilotti continues, punishment (*poena*) is not distinguished from compensation for losses because punishment "had a private, and not a public character"; punishment was compensation, and vice versa. The theory that punishment is distinct from compensation for damage was formulated at a time when a State found itself in a position to assume the function of defending an objective right, "consequently, at a stage of development which international law still has not reached and possibly will never reach".[13] In his treatise on international law Anzilotti again says that the difference between civil and criminal responsibility is unknown to international law because the latter is at an earlier stage of development than national law.[14]

J. Basdevant's objections to the concept of the criminal responsibility of a State follow along the same line. In his preface to J. Dumas's book, *De la responsabilité internationale des États*, in

13 D. Anzilotti, *Teoria generale della responsabilita dello stato nel diritto internazionale* (1902), pp. 96-97.

14 Anzilotti, *Corso di diritto internazionale* (4th ed.; 1955), I, 386.

which the author adheres to the concept of the international legal criminal responsibility of a State, Basdevant says with regard to the views of the book's author: "There is no doubt that these views, in comparison with existing law, are in advance of their time".[15]

Consequently, for both Anzilotti and Basdevant, there is no criminal responsibility in international law not because this law is of a special kind, but because it is at a lower stage of development in comparison with national law.

Other critics of the concept of criminal responsibility of a State proceed from the fact that criminal responsibility is inapplicable to corporations. Thus, even R. Phillimore wrote in his *Commentaries Upon International Law*: "To speak of inflicting punishment upon a State is to mistake both the principles of criminal jurisprudence and the nature of the legal personality of a corporation. Criminal law is concerned with a natural person; a being of thought, feeling, and will. A legal person is not, strictly speaking, a being of these attributes, though, through the mediums of representation and of government, the will of certain individuals is considered as the will of the corporation; but only for certain purposes. There must be *individual* will to found the jurisdiction of criminal law. Will by *representation* can not found that jurisdiction".[16]

In a two-volume monograph, *The Crime of State,* Professor P. N. Drost develops a concept fairly close to the views of Phillimore just quoted. Drost suggests that "acts of State" may be crimes of State under international law. But "crimes of State", according to Drost, are not "governmental crimes". A State can not be a criminal.[17]

Proceeding from the concept which regards the State as a fiction, Drost rejects the concept of criminal responsibility of a State under international law. "... the State as such", he says,

15 J. Dumas, *De la responsabilité internationale des États* (1930), p. xi.

16 R. Phillimore, *Commentaries Upon International Law* (3d ed.; 1879), I, 5.

17 P. N. Drost, *The Crime of State* (1959), I, 283-292.

"can not act or do anything at all. It can not defend its crimes for exactly the very same reason that it can not commit crime".[18]

At the same time, Drost recognizes a State's financial responsibility for an international delinquency. In his view, State responsibility is limited to "civil liability".[19]

As regards criminal responsibility for "crimes of State" under international law, it falls upon individual persons. In this connection Drost believes that if it is impossible to imagine a "criminal State", then a "criminal government" is impossible. "A criminal State", he writes, " is juridically speaking a nonsense; the criminal government, on the contrary, a juristic reality and challenge of the first order ... The punishability of the State is both a legal and a practical impossibility. Governments could and should be punished, if the international legal order were to provide the implementation of criminal justice".[20] However, even in the event of the criminality of a government under international law, in Drost's opinion the crimes always remain "individual crimes", and natural persons bear criminal responsibility for them.[21]

In lectures at the Hague Academy of International Law in 1927 on the topic "Crimes et délits contre la sureté des États étrangers", Professor M. Bourquin conceded that international law possibly is moving toward a "revival" of the idea of criminal responsibility of a State. At the same time, he believed that the concept of a "crime of State" was still far from having achieved the "necessary technical definiteness" in prevailing law.[22]

One must also note that the concept of the criminal responsibility of a State in international law was developed

[18] Ibid., p. 293 [Drost is quoting a remark of Justice R. Jackson at the Nuremberg Trial – *WEB*].

[19] Ibid., p. 294.

[20] Ibid., p. 304.

[21] Ibid., p. 305.

[22] M. Bourquin, "Crimes et délits contre la sureté des États étrangers", *Recueil de cours*, XVI (1927), p. 124

primarily by criminologists, who have been more inclined to transfer national law into international law than are specialists in international law, amongst whom this concept has found and finds comparatively few advocates.[23]

The concept of the international criminal responsibility of a State did not obtain support in the International Law Commission, which discussed this question in connection with the problem of State responsibility for damage caused on its territory to the person and property of aliens. The Commission's rapporteur on this question,

G. Amador, touched upon the question of criminal responsibility only with respect to natural persons in the draft articles contained in his first report.[24] In the commentary to this report, however, the rapporteur actually favored the criminal responsibility of a State.[25]

Almost all members of the Commission who expressed themselves on the question of the criminal responsibility of a State were agreed that such responsibility is unknown to contemporary international law and that the Commission should not put forward a detailed proposal (Francois, Amador, Krylov, Fitzmaurice, Žourek).[26]

A correct understanding of the changes which have taken place in the area of international legal State responsibility can not be achieved by mechanically transferring the categories of national law into international law. Obviously, it is necessary, taking into account the peculiarities of international law, to establish the basic features of the new phenomena in international law and not to attempt to squeeze them into the Procrustean bed of national law categories.

[23] A. N. Trainin was completely correct in noting this. See A. N. Trainin, Защита мира и борьба с преступлениями против человечества [Defense of Peace and Struggle with Crimes Against Humanity] (1956), p. 38.

[24] United Nations, *Yearbook of the International Law Commission 1956* (1957), II, 220.

[25] Ibid., p. 183.

[26] Ibid., I, 239-241.

The correct view already has been expressed in Soviet literature that the concept of criminal responsibility of a State is wholly unfounded, although the argumentation advanced against this concept is not sufficiently full and precise.

The late correspondent-member of the Academy of Sciences of the USSR, A. N. Trainin, who made a significant contribution to working out the question of the responsibility of war criminals, decisively rejected the concept of the criminal responsibility of a State in international law. In noting that as a subject of international law a State may be a subject of international legal responsibility, that sanctions may be applied to a State, Trainin pointed out that these sanctions are not criminal law sanctions. "Criminal sanctions, and this is a generally-recognized position, are determined by agencies of criminal justice", wrote Trainin.[27] However, he said, there was no organ of criminal justice in the League of Nations system and none exists now in the United Nations system.

On the plane of substantive criminal law, Trainin went on to say, the concept of the international criminal responsibility of a State also is unfounded. Criminal responsibility rests upon guilt, in the form of fault or negligence; the concepts and institutes of imputability, the stages of committing a crime, complicity, and punishment play a very essential role in criminal justice. Without such concepts and institutes criminal law and criminal responsibility are inconceivable. However, all the said institutes and concepts can not be applied to a State. Therefore, concluded Trainin, in the domain of substantive law, as in the domain of procedure, attempts to regard the sanctions applicable to a State as criminal sanctions prove to be "in profound incongruity with the basic principles of criminal justice".[28]

There is no exact indication that the concepts of guilt and complicity are inapplicable to a State as a subject of international

[27] Trainin, Защита мира и борьба с преступлениями против человечества [Defense of Peace and Struggle with Crimes Against Humanity], p. 41.

[28] Ibid., pp. 41-42.

law, although the international legal concept of guilt can not be identified with the concept of guilt in national legal systems. On the same basis, Trainin's argumentation against the concept of criminal responsibility of a State is completely correct. It proceeds from the fact that the criminal sanction as a category of national law is not applicable as a sanction of international law with respect to a State which is a specific subject of this distinctive legal system.

Proponents of the concept of criminal responsibility of a State suggest that if in international law there are sanctions which fall outside the limits of civil law responsibility in national law, these are criminal sanctions. But this conclusion is the result of transferring concepts of national law into international law without taking into account the specific features of the latter. If certain international legal sanctions fall outside the limits of civil law responsibility, this still does not mean that such sanctions are necessarily criminal sanctions.

The list of criminal sanctions for States cited by Pella in his "Plan for an International Criminal Code" shows clearly enough how artificial it is to equate these categories of State responsibility to criminal punishments under national law.

The noncomparability of international legal sanctions in respect of a State with criminal sanctions results from the incomparability of a State and individuals. International law, whose subjects are above all politically sovereign entities – States – has its own types of sanctions and means of effectuating them.

We find no mention whatever of the criminal responsibility of a State in the documents relating to the surrender of Germany and Japan, in the Statutes of the Nuremberg and Tokyo International Military Tribunals, nor in the peace treaties of 1947. Meanwhile, where, if not in these documents, should criminal responsibility for the gravest delinquencies committed by aggressors be mentioned if criminal responsibility of a State were in mind at all?

When aggressive war and certain other violations of international law are called crimes, one only wishes to emphasize thereby, with regard to the State, the especially dangerous character of the delinquency. On this plane, as Professor R. Ago has noted correctly, the question becomes purely terminological.[29] As regards natural persons, the specific executors of such actions, in contemporary international law the question is one in reality of an international crime and of the criminal responsibility arising therefrom.[30]

2. *Some New Aspects of State Responsibility*

(a) *Prohibition of the use of force and State responsibility*. As already has been pointed out, the principle of international legal State responsibility in the old international law essentially did not extend to war or its consequences in general.

The emergence of the principle of the prohibition of aggressive war, later transformed into the principle of the prohibition of the use or threat of force in international relations, signified a revolution in international law generally and also introduced fundamental changes into the institute of international legal State responsibility.

The elimination of the "right of a State to go to war" led to the disappearance of the "right of the victor" which arose directly out of the unlimited right of a State to resort to force. Eliminating the "right of the victor" in turn meant the elimination of such institutes of international law as "conquest" and "indemnities".

[29] See R. Ago, "Second Report on State Responsibility", in United Nations, *Yearbook of the International Law Commission 1971*, II, p. 184.

[30] See M. Iu. Raginskii and S. Ia. Rozenblit, Международный процесс главных японских военных преступников [International Trial of Main Japanese War Criminals] (1950); P. S. Romashkin, Военные преступления империализма [War Crimes of Imperialism] (1953); Romashkin, Преступления против мира и человечества [Crimes Against Peace and Humanity] (1967); Trainin, Защита мира и борьба с преступлениями против человечества [Defense of Peace and Struggle with Crimes Against Humanity]; A. I. Poltorak, Нюрнберкский процесс [Nuremberg Trial] (1966); N. S. Alekseev, Ответственность нацистских преступников [Responsibility of Nazi Criminals] (1968).

The institute of conquest, which was based directly on the "right of the victor", was clear evidence of the fact that war under the old international law represented a means not only of settling international disputes but also of changing a legal situation. According to the old international law, the victorious State had the right to annex the part of the defeated State's territory which it occupied, and if the enemy were completely defeated, to seize all of its territory, the defeated State being regarded as subjugated.

As regards the seizure of the occupied part of the defeated State's territory in those instances when the enemy had not been completely defeated, even though the view was widespread in international legal doctrine that such acquisition is legally justified in a peace treaty,[31] in reality the basis of annexing the territory was the "right of the victor". Only the victor, irrespective of the causes and character of the war, had the right to appropriate the enemy territory he had occupied during the war. The extent to which he succeeded in realizing this right depended upon the co-relation of forces.

F. F. Martens wrote with regard to conquest as a method of acquiring territory: "This most ancient method of acquisition remains up to the present the most frequently applied".[32]

"According to the correct point of view", says Oppenheim in his treatise on international law, "occupied territory may be annexed by a belligerent on the grounds that his enemy, having ceased military operations, has given up every right he had over this territory".[33]

[31] See, for example, F. von Liszt, Международное право [International Law], transl. from 2d ed. by M. Mebel', ed. V. E. Grabar (1902), pp. 313-325.

[32] F. F. Martens, Современное международное право цивилизованных народов [Contemporary International Law of Civilized Peoples] (2d ed.; 1887), I, 353.

[33] Oppenheim, Международное право [International Law], transl. from the 6th ed. by A. A. Santalov and V. I. Shiganskii; ed. S. A. Golunskii (1950), II(2), p. 137.

A second form of the institute of conquest was "subjugation", which was reflected in the elimination of the armed forces of a State, the occupation of its entire territory, and its annexation by the victorious State.

The well-known Swiss specialist on international affairs, Max Huber, wrote: "A subject of international law has the individual right, arising from international society, to annihilate other such subjects fully or partially; it thereupon acquires that in which their material existence is expressed, that is to say, it acquires their State territory".[34]

In Fauchille's treatise on international law, we read: "The complete defeat of one belligerent State by another (*debellatio*) puts an end to the war by eliminating the political existence of one of the adversaries. The State disappears, dies away as a legal entity".[35]

"Subjugation", and the "right of the victor" on which it was based, are regarded by some bourgeois writers as institutes of prevailing international law, which does not correspond to reality at all and objectively is a manifestation of reactionary trends in bourgeois international legal doctrine.

Kelsen, for example, writes: "The territory of a conquered state may be annexed by a victorious state with the intention of incor- porating it permanently or with the intention of disposing of it sooner or later, for instance, by ceding it to a third state or by establishing a new State on it. Whatever the intention of the conqueror may be, the annexed territory legally becomes its own territory, even if the war waged by the victor against the vanquished was an illegal war and the annexation of the vanquished state as international delict".[36]

C. C. Hyde says in his treatise on international law: "It may be in fact possible for a belligerent to occupy the entire domain of

[34] M. Huber, *Die Staatensuccession* (1898), p. 20.

[35] P. Fauchille, *Traité de droit international public* (1921), II, 1030.

[36] H. Kelsen, *Principles of International Law*, ed. R. W. Tucker (2d ed.; 1967), pp. 313-314.

its enemy, and after having overcome all resistance, to destroy its life as a State and to appropriate its territory as the fruits of victory".[37]

Professor C. Rousseau, of the University of Paris, also believes that a State may, by the total defeat of the adversary, annex its territory.[38]

In Oppenheim's well-known English treatise on international law, revised by Lauterpacht, it says: "Although complete conquest, accompanied by destruction of the enemy's armed forces, actually puts an end to armed combat, and thus to war, nevertheless the final ending does not come yet, since everything depends on what kind of decision the victor takes concerning the fate of the defeated State. If the victor wishes to restore to his post the captured or exiled head of the defeated State, he ends the war with the conclusion of the ensuing peace treaty. But if the victor wishes to take possession of the whole conquered territory, he annexes it and this formally ends the war by subjugation".[39]

Many statesmen of the Western powers are trying to rely upon the specter of the "right of conquest". Thus, the United States Department of State, in a memorandum on the Berlin question of 20 December 1958, maintained that the rights of the Western powers to occupy German territory "... derive from the total defeat of the Third Reich and the subsequent assumption of supreme authority in Germany".[40]

The well-known American pundit, Walter Lippman, in criticizing this position of the Department of State, wrote:

[37] C. C. Hyde, Международное право, его понимание и применение Соединенными Штатами Америки [International Law, Understanding and Application Thereof by the United States of America], ed. B. A. Dranov (1954), VI, 386.

[38] C. Rousseau, *Droit international public* (1953), p. 250; Rousseau, *Droit international public* (4th ed.; 1968), pp. 152-153.

[39] Oppenheim, Международное право [International Law], II(2), p. 139.

[40] "Legal Aspects of the Berlin Situation", *The Department of State Bulletin*, XL (1959), 9.

"For some strange reason we have decided to maintain that our rights in Berlin are based on the right of conquest. I would not say that this is the kind of reason that ought to be cited by the defenders of civilization". Lippman called the "right of conquest" a "primitive, stupid, and detestable principle".[41]

The elimination of the "institute of conquest" went hand in hand with the emergence and strengthening of the principles of the prohibition of aggressive war in international law.

Being a resolute opponent of reactionary institutes of international law from the first days of its existence, the Soviet State has opposed annexations and indemnities. The Dekret on Peace adopted by the Second All-Russian Congress of Soviets on 8 November 1917 said: "The Workers' and Peasants' Government, which was created by the Revolution of 24-25 October and which rests upon the Soviets of Workers', Soldiers', and Peasants' Deputies, proposes to all belligerent peoples and their governments to begin negotiations immediately for a just, democratic peace.

"The just and democratic peace for which the overwhelming majority of the workers and toiling classes, exhausted, worn out, and tormented by the war, yearn is the peace that the Russian workers and peasants have demanded definitely and steadfastly since the overthrow of the Tsarist monarchy; such a peace the Government considers to be an immediate peace without annexations (that is, without seizing foreign lands, without forcibly annexing foreign peoples) and without indemnities".[42]

In the League of Nations period, the small States, fearful for the fate of their territories, repeatedly introduced proposals concerning the nonrecognition of forcible seizures of territory. These proposals, however, went nowhere. A number of documents adopted at inter-American conferences after

[41] Правда [Pravda], 11 April 1959, p. 2.

[42] Ministerstvo inostrannykh del SSSR, Документы внешней политики СССР [Documents of Foreign Policy of the USSR] (1957-), I, 11-12.

the First World War also contain provisions relating to nonrecognition of conquest as a method of acquiring territory.[43]

One must agree with Professor H. Wehberg, who says: "It is necessary to emphasize as strongly as possible that the classical theory of acquisition of territory by subjugation (*debellatio*) assumed with regard to annexation, the admissibility of war. As long as war was considered a lawful means of settling disputes, it was completely logical that international law provided for the possibility of acquiring foreign territory by means of war. This was the time when in the final analysis the law of force was operative and the weak were at the mercy of the arbitrariness of the strong".[44]

With the emergence in international law of the principle of the prohibition of aggressive war, and later of the principle of the prohibition of the use of force in international relations, the "right of conquest" fell to the ground, since it had rested upon recognition of the State's right to wage war, upon recognition of war as a means of settling international disputes.

A second basic consequence of the "right of the victor" was the institute of indemnities.

In an exploitative society, war was a means of enriching the ruling classes. Complete pillage or destruction of property on the adversary's territory occupied by forces of the victor was a common practice in antiquity and in the Middle Ages. Grotius cited Livy's statement that: "when everything is placed under the command of the one who has the advantage in war, then any appropriation of property and the discretionary imposition of penalties depend upon the arbitrary action of the conqueror".[45] And Grotius himself considered this rule

[43] H. Wehberg, *Krieg und Eroberung im Wandel des Völkerrechts* (1953), pp. 90-97.

[44] Ibid., p. 102.

[45] H. Grotius, О праве войны и мира [On the Law of War and Peace], transl. A. Sakketti; ed. V. N. Durdenevskii (1956), p. 671.

to be a prevailing norm of international law. He wrote: "For, as the things which had belonged to individuals, do, by the laws of war, become the property of those who conqueror them, so also the property of the general body becomes the property of the victors, if these so choose". He cited Xenophon in this connection: "There is an ancient law among men that when an enemy town is taken the property and money come into the possession of the victor".[46]

Indemnities have been in especially wide use since the end of the eighteenth century, having replaced to a significant extent the unorganized plundering of the population by the victorious country with organized plundering.

The institute of indemnities was founded upon the "right of the victor". A characteristic feature of indemnities was the fact that the victor, irrespective of who began the war and how it was waged, had the right to compel the defeated State to pay it a sum whose amount usually was fixed by the peace treaty. The victor, and he only, irrespective of the circumstances of the origin of the war, had the right to demand payment of indemnities from the defeated State.

Although indemnities usually were called "compensation of war costs", which might include the expenses of the victorious State in waging the war and the damage caused to it and to its nationals as a result of the war, in fact it was tribute imposed by the victor upon the vanquished; the amount of such tribute was determined solely by the co-relation of their strength.

"The principle of an indemnity for war costs", wrote Fauchille, "imposed by the victor upon the vanquished, is admissible and understandable when the indemnity includes the expenses of the victor in carrying out military actions and the damage inflicted in consequence of the adversary's resistance. But in the nineteenth century indemnity of war costs in practice became for the victor a means of enrichment

[46] Ibid., p. 640.

at the expense of another, a means of satisfying an insatiable greed for enrichment".[47]

It should be noted that the practice condemned by Fauchille is characteristic not only of the nineteenth century; it was dominant both in the feudal period and in slave-owning society.

As already has been pointed out, the Soviet State proposed in the Dekret on Peace to renounce indemnities in concluding a peace treaty which would have put an end to the First World War.[48] There is no doubt that the Soviet State's opposition to indemnities as an institute of international law, in which the basis of international plunder and robbery clearly was reflected, the consistent policy of the Soviet State directed against the old international-legal concepts, and the growth of the democratic movement in all countries and the increase in its influence, dealt a decisive blow to the institute of indemnities.

In the Versailles Treaty the allies already had refrained from using the term "war costs" and spoke only of "reparations". Under the Versailles Treaty, Germany acknowledged responsibility for all losses and damage incurred by the Entente and its nations in consequence of the war unleashed upon them by Germany and its allies (Article 231). Germany was obliged to compensate all damage caused to the civilian population of the Allied and Associated Powers (Article 232).

In the documents relating to the termination of the Second World War, in the working out of which the Soviet Union took an active part, there is, of course, no allusion whatever to indemnities. The question is one of reparations as one form of responsibility for the unleashing and waging of an aggressive war by Germany, Japan, and their allies.

[47] Fauchille, *Traité de droit international public*, II, 1041.

[48] Документы внешней политики СССР [Documents of Foreign Policy of the USSR], I, 12.

The communique of the Crimea Conference of the leaders of the three allied powers – the Soviet Union, United States of America, and Great Britain – of 4-11 February 1945 pointed out: "We have considered the question of the damage caused by Germany to the Allied Nations in this war and recognized it as just that Germany be obliged to make compensation for this damage in kind to the greatest extent possible".[49]

It was pointed out in the decisions of the 1945 Berlin Conference of the three powers that "in accordance with the Crimea decision that Germany be compelled to compensate to the greatest extent possible for the loss and suffering that she has caused the United Nations and for which the German people can not escape res- ponsibility, the following agreement on reparations was reached ...".[50] Here, therefore, is emphasized the link between Germany's responsibility for aggressive war and its duty to compensate for the damage caused by this war.

The Protocol concerning the talks among the heads of the three governments at the Crimea Conference said with regard to the question of reparations in kind from Germany: "Germany must pay in kind for the losses caused by her to the Allied nations in the course of the war". It was further pointed out in this Protocol that the removal of equipment, machine tools, vessels, and so forth as reparations from Germany "should be carried out chiefly for the purpose of destroying the war potential of Germany".[51] Compensation for material damage is linked in this document with measures of a preventive character directed against a renewal of an aggressive policy on the part of Germany.

[49] Ministerstvo inostrannykh del SSSR, Сборник действующих договоров, соглашений и конвенций, заключенных СССР с иностранными государствами [Collection of Treaties, Agreements, and Conventions in Force Concluded by the USSR with Foreign States] (1925-), XI, 69.

[50] Ibid., p. 114.

[51] Ibid., p. 81.

The 1947 peace treaties, in pointing out that Germany's former allies bear "their share of the responsibility for this war", establish that these States must compensate the appropriate allied powers for losses caused by "military actions and occupation" of territories of those States, it being stipulated that compensation of these losses be made not in full, but in part.

Thus, as a result of the expansion of the principles of State responsibility for war and the elimination of the "right of the victor", the institute of indemnities was replaced by reparations.

The institute of reparations which superseded the institute of indemnities differs fundamentally from the latter. If indemnities were based upon the "right of the victor", then the institute of reparations is based, as is correctly pointed out in Soviet literature,[52] upon the principle of international legal State responsibility. This means that the institute of reparations, just as the principle of responsibility for aggressive war in general, is directed at the maintenance of international peace.

The emergence in international law of the principle of the prohibition of aggressive war and of the principle of the prohibition of the use of force in international relations (the principle of nonaggression) signified the end of the "right of the victor". Victory in and of itself can not give rights to either side.

In contrast to the old international law, the aggressor at the present time is not simply a party to an armed conflict; the aggressor is a lawbreaker; its actions, representing from the very beginning the gravest criminal violation of international law, can not create any rights whatsoever for him. Being a breach of the law which entails State responsibility, the actions of the aggressor remain such irrespective of the outcome of the armed conflict.

[52] See V. V. Evgen'ev, Международно-правовое регулирование репараций после второй мировой войны [International Legal Regulation of Reparations After the Second World War] (1950), p. 65.

War on the part of States opposing the aggression or enforcement measures undertaken by the United Nations against the aggressor by decision of the Security Council are a lawful use of force. States acting against the aggressor have specific rights which, however, do not arise from the fact of victory.[53] Indeed, if such rights arose from the fact of victory, as they did under the old international law, the victorious side would have them irrespective of which side committed the aggression and unleashed the war.

The major distinctive feature of the new international law in the field of State responsibility is responsibility for aggression. Such responsibility is derived from the principle of the prohibition of the use of force in international relations. Aggression is the gravest breach of the law, for its consequences at the present time could be the greatest calamity for all mankind. Hence the gravity of responsibility for such a breach of the law.

The application of the principle of international legal responsibility to war and its consequences was reflected and strengthened in international treaties and agreements relating to the Second World War.

The Declaration concerning the defeat of Germany and the assumption by the allies of supreme authority with respect to that country says that Germany bears responsibility for the war.[54] It is emphasized in the Potsdam Agreements that the "German people have begun to atone for the terrible crimes committed under the leader- ship of those whom in the hour of their success, they openly approved and blindly obeyed". In those same Potsdam Agreements it says further that the "German people can not escape responsibility" for the loss and suffering which Germany caused to the United Nations.[55]

53 See G. I. Tunkin, "Берлинский вопрос в свете международного права" [Berlin Question in the Light of International Law], Международная жизнь [International Life], no. 3 (1959), p. 48.

54 Сборник действующих договоров [Collection of Treaties in Force], XI, 84.

55 Ibid., pp. 109, 114.

The principles of responsibility for aggressive war also were reflected in the 1947 Peace Treaties. It says in the Peace Treaty with Italy: "Whereas Italy under the Fascist regime became a party to the Tripartite Pact with Germany and Japan, undertook a war of aggression and thereby provoked a state of war with all the Allied and Associated Powers and with other United Nations, and bears her share of responsibility for the war ...".[56]

The peace treaties with Finland, Romania, Bulgaria, and Hungary also say that, having become allies of Hitlerite Germany and having participated on her side in the war, these countries bear their "share of responsibility for this war".[57]

A clear expression of the application of the principle of responsibility with respect to Germany and Japan is the documents of the Nuremberg and Tokyo international military tribunals, which affirmed that aggressive war is the gravest criminal violation of international law that entails the international responsibility of the State and the criminal responsibility of natural persons who are guilty of committing crimes against peace, war crimes, and crimes against humanity.

Thus, instead of the "right of the victor", contemporary international law provides State responsibility for aggression. This means that the legal consequences of war are not determined by the outcome of the armed conflict, not by who is victorious. The Charter of the Organization of American States of 30 April 1948 correctly points out that "victory does not give rights".[58]

The legal consequences of an armed conflict are determined first of all by the fact of which State committed the aggression and, con- sequently, must bear responsibility for this gravest

[56] Preamble of the 1947 Peace Treaty with Italy, ibid., XIII, 88-89.

[57] Preamble of the 1947 Peace Treaty with Finland, Romania, Bulgaria, and Hungary, ibid., XIII, 26, 54, 203, 235.

[58] Article 5. L. A. Modzhorian and V. K. Sobakin (comps.), Международное право в избранных документах [International Law in Selected Documents], ed. V. N. Durdenevskii (1957), II, 202.

breach of law. Ad- ditional responsibility can be added to this for violating the laws and customs of war, as occurred with regard to Hitlerite Germany and Japan.

If, however, contemporary international law prohibits States from resorting to war in international relations and war is not a means of acquiring State territory, this does not mean that sanctions can not be applied to the aggressor in the form of taking away part of its territory. An aggressor State going unpunished corresponds least of all to contemporary international law, which provides severe responsibility for a breach of the peace.

We must dwell upon incorrect interpretations of this question.

H. Wehberg, for example, writes: "... The use of force in and of itself can not destroy the right of another, at least not such a far- reaching right as the right to territory. The unlawful use of force, as such, can not destroy an existing right. Not to accept this position is to acknowledge that might stands above right".[59]

There is, however, a material condition in this argument. First, Wehberg says that the use of force in and of itself can not destroy an existing right, and this is true. Second, he speaks of the unlawful use of force, but also makes the reservation that the use of force as such can not destroy a right. In this case the reservation not only is unnecessary, but is incorrect, since the unlawful use of force not only can not as such destroy a right but also is the gravest breach of the law. One can not place on the same level a just use of force, that is, a use of force permitted by international law, and an unjust use of force, that is, a use of force in violation of international law. This vagueness, as we shall see later, leads Wehberg to some wholly incorrect conclusions.

He has not avoided the confusion which often arose when this question was discussed between the First and Second World Wars. The fact is that, strange as it may seem at first glance,

[59] Wehberg, *Krieg und Eroberung im Wandel des Völkerrechts*, pp. 102-103.

the oft- encountered maxim "any change of State territory carried out with the aid of force is contrary to international law" is imprecise and essentially untrue.

The aggressor and the victim of aggression do not have equal status under contemporary international law, which is developing in the direction of applying ever more severe measures against an aggressor, since at the present time aggression threatens mankind with incalculable casualties. Wehberg is mistaken when he places an aggressor and the other States which have opposed him on the same level; in doing so he in essence pays tribute to the obsolete concepts which he himself so resolutely opposes.

Here is what Wehberg says: "The proposition that the unlawful use of force in and of itself can not eliminate a foreign right must also operate to the advantage of those States which waged an aggressive war and which suffered defeat from the States against whom the attack was committed. It is true that a State subjected to an attack has the right of self-defense, but only to repulse the attack. Self-defense does not permit, however, the use of armed force which goes beyond repulsing the attack. A State subjected to an attack can only defend itself and also take measures to obtain compensation for damage".[60]

A West German professor, W. Schätzel, expresses himself in the same vein. Calling any increment of territory an annexation, the author attempts to substantiate the proposition that no territorial changes whatever are admissible in consequence of war. "The question of the admissibility of annexation as a result of war", says Schätzel, "comes down to the question of the admissibility of war".[61] Confusing the distinction between an aggressive and a defensive war, the author in fact attempts to limit the international legal responsibility of the aggressor, asserting that responsibility for aggression can not lead to territorial changes.

60 Ibid., pp. 103-104.

61 W. Schätzel, "Die Annexion im Völkerrecht", *Archiv des Völkerrechts*, II (1950), 2.

There are both correct and incorrect propositions in the arguments. The "right of the victor" is rejected, and this is completely correct. But at the same time, the responsibility of the aggressor also is rejected. It turns out that no measures whatever can be taken with regard to the aggressor except measures for the purpose of compensating the damage caused.

However, the responsibility of the aggressor State under contemporary international law is not limited to compensation for damage caused. It also includes those measures with regard to an aggressor which may be expressed, in particular, by taking away part of its territory for the purpose of preventing aggression in the future.

The allies in the anti-Hitlerite coalition proceeded from these very propositions with respect to the aggressor States in the Second World War.

The taking of certain territories from Germany and Japan in consequence of the Second World War differs fundamentally from the previous seizures of territory which took place on the basis of the "right of the victor". The actions of the allies with regard to Germany and Japan were based above all on the principle of international legal State responsibility for the aggression which it committed. The juridical classification of the taking of certain territories from Germany and Japan which was done in connection with the Second World War, in those instances when this taking went beyond the limits of compensating the respective States for territories previously seized from them by Germany and Japan, is completely different from the seizure of territory on the basis of the "right of the victor". Here is found the application and confirmation of a new progressive principle directed toward the maintenance of international peace – the principle of responsibility for aggression.

(b) Subjects of legal relations in instances of international legal State responsibility. The violation of international law by a State gives

rise to specific legal relations. Who are the participants in such legal relations, or, in other words, for whom do international competences and duties arise in consequence of breaches of the law?

Under contemporary conditions, this question acquires especially important significance, particularly with regard to breaches of the law which endanger peace.

According to the old international law, in the event of a breach of international law, legal relations arose only between the offending State and the State whose subjective right was violated in consequence of the unlawful actions of the first State. Proceeding from the fact that international law regulates relations among sovereign entities, Anzilotti pointed out that no one State can consider itself a judge when a violation of international law is committed by another State unless its own rights are affected by this breach of the law. "States", he wrote, "have neither the right nor the duty to suppress violations of international law as such, but only the right to react against those violations which are aimed directly against them ...".[62] In the latter instance the injured State may, however, take action against the offender not for the purpose of compelling it to respect the violated international law, but only in order to realize its own illegally violated right.[63]

Anzilotti, it is true, recognized the interest that all States have in compliance with norms of international law and the possibility of collective actions against the offending State, but not on legal grounds.

This concept even now is adhered to mechanically by the majority of bourgeois international lawyers.

"According to the generally-accepted doctrine", writes Rousseau, "international responsibility is always a relationship between one State and another State". In explaining this proposition, he says that international responsibility

[62] Anzilotti, *Teoria generale della responsibilita della stato*, p. 88.

[63] Ibid., pp. 88-89.

"presupposes that one State complains of damage caused to it and demands compensation".[64]

Verdross also points out that the legal relations arising in connection with international legal responsibility are legal relations between the offending State and the State which directly suffered damage in consequence of this breach of the law. "International legal responsibility", he says, "arises in principle *only* with regard to *those States* which are the immediate victims of unlawful international actions. Accordingly, in the event of the violation of a norm of customary law or of a multilateral treaty, in principle only those States may act which have suffered damage from the breach of international law. The existence in other States of purely idealistic interests in preserving the international legal order is insufficient motive for submitting demands".[65] At the same time, Verdross admits the possibility of coming to the support of an injured State. But, he adds, "in this event independent action does not take place, but only support of the State which has suffered from the breach of the law".[66]

This theory also was reflected in the decisions of the Permanent Court of International Justice, particularly in its decision in the case of the *Phosphates in Morocco*.[67]

According to another theory, in the event of more serious violations of international law, any State, even though it has not suffered direct damage from the breach of the law, has the right to take measures against the offending State.

Thus, Heffter believed that there are those violations of international law which affect all States equally and which give

[64] Rousseau, *Droit international public* (1953), p. 357; G. Schwarzenberger, *International Law and Order* (19710, p. 35.

[65] A. Verdross, Международное право [International Law], transl. F. A. Kublitskii and R. L. Naryshkina; ed. G. I. Tunkin (1959), pp. 355-356.

[66] Ibid., p. 357.

[67] Permanent Court of International Justice, Series A/B, Judgments, Orders and Advisory Opinions, *Phosphates in Morocco* (1938), p. 28.

them all the right to take measures against the offender. Heffter includes among the said breaches of law, in particular: the organized striving for world domination or for domination over territory belonging to all nations (as, for example, the high seas), violation of the rights of diplomatic representatives, refusal to satisfy claims which have been widely recognized, and others.[68] Bluntschli[69] and L. Kamarovskii[70] have expressed analogous opinions.

The danger of this concept consisted not so much in the fact that it provided the possibility of collective State actions in the event of violations of international law, as in the fact that the occasions for such actions were chosen arbitrarily and were justified by references to those norms of international law which in reality did not exist. This theory, therefore, frequently was used to justify collective interventions (for example, interventions of the Holy Alliance).

This theory, which in fact was an exceedingly free or, more precisely, arbitrary interpretation of international law of that time, had comparatively few supporters. According to the then predominant theory, the general interest of a State was insufficient grounds for submitting any demands whatever to the offending State.

The rule that only the injured State has the right to submit claims against a delinquent State or to undertake enforcement measures against it permitted by international law remains valid even at the present time for a significant number of breaches of international law affecting only relations between two States: that which violated international law and that which suffered directly therefrom.

[68] A. Heffter, *Das europäische Völkerrecht der Gegenwart auf den bisherigen Grundlagen* (8th ed.; 1888), pp. 224-225.

[69] See J. C. Bluntschli, *Das moderne Völkerrecht der civilisirten Staten* (2d ed.; 1872), pp. 264-265.

[70] See L. A. Kamarovskii, О международном суде [On an International Court] (1881), p. 7.

Contemporary international law, however, does not stop at this. Very important new elements, which still have not been reflected in science, have emerged.

Thus, according to the old international law, war between two States was regarded as a matter concerning only them. Juridically, every State had the right to resort to war in order to effectuate its claims; consequently, it waged war on the basis of this right. Other States against whom no armed actions were directed had no right to object.

These provisions of international law were explained in the final analysis by the character of international relations existing then, and above all by the character of economic ties among States. War between two States could not affect or only slightly affected other States by virtue of the insufficiently broad international ties.

In this respect the situation has changed materially and continues to change. The intensification of international ties has led to the fact that any war to a greater or lesser extent directly affects the interests and even the rights of all States. An enormous danger has appeared of any armed conflict between States developing even into a world war which, with the existence of modern types of weapons, promises incalculable suffering and sacrifice for peoples. Peace has become virtually indivisible. "Whereas four centuries ago there was every reason to recognize that peace is indivisible", said the Minister of Foreign Affairs of the USSR, A. A. Gromyko, in a Statement, "then it is many times more correct in our day with the modern means of waging war, when only minutes are required to overcome the distance between the most remote countries of the world".[71]

These changes in the international situation have been reflected in international law. Such principles of international law have emerged as the principle of nonaggression and the

[71] Statement of the Minister of Foreign Affairs of the USSR, A. Gromyko, on the Occasion of the Speech of the Secretary of State C. Herter, Правда [Pravda], 31 August 1959, p. 2.

prohibition of the use of force in international relations and the still more far-reaching principle of peaceful coexistence.

A breach of the peace, or a threat to breach the peace, now affects not only the interests, but also the rights, of all States. From the aforesaid principle of international law arises the subjective right of a State to peace.

The maintenance of international peace in our time is the concern of all States.[72] Under contemporary international law every State has not only the right but to a certain extent also the duty to take measures within the limits permitted by international law for the purpose of ensuring international peace and security and, therefore, to demand that other States have complied with norms of international law relating to the securing of peace.

On these provisions of international law in particular are based the numerous statements of the Soviet Union against the policy of individual States aimed at knocking together aggressive blocs, against the entry therein of a particular State, against creating foreign military bases or launching sites for missiles on their territories, and against other actions leading to an aggravation of the international situation or directly creating a threat to the peace, to say nothing of actions which already are a breach of the peace or acts of aggression.

A Note of the Soviet Government sent in December 1957 to the governments of member States of the United Nations said: "The Soviet Government proceeds from the fact that in contemporary conditions every government bears responsibility not only for the fate of the people of its own country but also to a certain extent for the fact of world peace, and therefore can not be indifferent to the aggravation of the international situation which has occurred. If, unfortunately for mankind, the world plunges into a new war, no State can feel secure. In this event the conflagration of a nuclear and missile war undoubtedly would bring to all

[72] See, for example, H. Rolin, "Verso un concetto di ordine publico realmente internazionale", *Communicazioni e studi*, X (1960), 72.

peoples incalculable misfortune whose consequences would be experienced by many generations of people".[73]

In their replies to these ideas of the Soviet Union many States attempted to assert that such notions supposedly are an interference in internal affairs, since every State can freely enter into agreements with other States and carry out any military measures on its territory insofar as it is not bound by special agreements.

The reference to internal affairs in this case, however, is completely unfounded. The concept of "internal affairs" is not a terri- torial concept, and in no way signifies that any measures undertaken by a State on its territory relate to its "internal affairs". There is still less basis for classifying as "internal affairs" aggressive military agreements concluded by a State with other States. The actions of a State affecting international peace and security do not at the present time relate exclusively to the domestic jurisdiction of a State.

The right of a State which is not an immediate victim of damage as a result of a breach of the law to take specific measures in the event of such a breach does not arise only in connection with breaches of the law which affect or might affect the maintenance of international peace and security. It arises, for example, in the case of a violation of the principle of self-determination of peoples, the Nuremberg principles, the principles of freedom of the seas, of the principle of conserving living resources of the sea, and so forth.

Thus, in the aspect which we are examining, a peculiarity of the legal relations arising under contemporary international law as a result of a violation of international law is, first and foremost, the fact that the subjects of these legal relations can be not only the delinquent State and the State which has suffered directly, but in a number of instances other States as well.

[73] Правда [Pravda], 13 December 1957, p. 3.

A second peculiarity of the said legal relations is that international organizations also can be party to them. In a number of instances international organizations, in conformity with the provisions of their charters, not only have the right but also are obliged to take a particular measure in the event of a violation of international law. Thus, in the event of aggression, legal relations arise not only between the victim State of the aggression and the aggressor State, but also among all other States and the aggressors (the right to use force against an aggressor by way of collective self-defense) and among the United Nations and other States. The United Nations is obliged to take measures against an aggressor; States waging a struggle against an aggressor must notify the Security Council immediately of the measures they are taking, and so forth.

(c) Types and forms of State responsibility in contemporary international law. We intend to touch upon basically two questions here: the nature of sanctions in contemporary international law and the methods of effectuating them.

According to the theory predominant in bourgeois international legal doctrine before the First World War and frequently even at the present time (see above), sanctions are alien to international law, which knows no authority standing above States, and State res- ponsibility is reflected only when an obligation arises to compensate damage caused. This theory did not even reflect the true situation in the old international law, since, as already pointed out, the failure of a delinquent State to perform the obligation to compensate damage caused gave to the injured State the right to apply enforcement measures with regard to that State.

The character of sanctions in contemporary international law is materially different from sanctions in the old international law. This is linked above all with the emergence of new international delicts and the division, which has been established in international law, of all international delicts into two categories: especially dangerous violations of international law which in international documents and literature frequently are called international crimes; and other violations of international law.

In Soviet legal literature the notion of the need to distinguish "between simple violations of international law and international crimes undermining its very foundations and most important principles" already has been expressed.[74]

In his work on State responsibility in contemporary international law, D. B. Levin, making this generally correct notion more precise, writes: "In contemporary international law, insofar as the question is one of an international delict, there is being formed side by side with the previous concept of a breach of international law a new concept of an international crime, or crime against humanity, designating that conduct of a State which undermines the foundations of the international community".[75]

In our view, the division of international breaches of law into delicts and crimes already has taken shape in international law, but there is no doubt that the category of international crimes is tending to expand. This is the result of the struggle of the forces of peace and progress, reflected in the fact that international law is becoming ever more irreconcilable toward actions infringing the foundations of the peaceful coexistence of States, the freedom and independence of peoples, "the dignity and worth of the human person" (Preamble, United Nations Charter).

The category of international crimes[76] includes first and foremost crimes against peace, war crimes, and crimes

74 Levin,"Проблема ответственности в науке международного права" [Problem of Responsibility in the Science of International Law], p.105.

75 D. B. Levin, Ответственность государств в современном меж- дународном праве [Responsibility of States in Contemporary International Law] (1966), p. 22.

76 The use of criminal law terminology presents certain well-known inconveniences, but there still is no other appropriate terminology. In any event, the use of such terminology in international law does not necessarily mean, despite the opinion of some authors, and in this case does not signify, "the renaissance of a criminal law concept as regardes State responsibility". C. Čepelka, *Conséquences juridiques du délit en droit international contemporain* (1965), p. 63.

against humanity as they have been defined in the charters and judgments of the Nuremberg and Tokyo international military tribunals. The United Nations Charter, General Assembly resolutions, and other State practice strengthen these provisions.[77]

Also included in this category of international delicts are the practice of colonialism, the refusal to grant independence to colonial peoples, and racial discrimination, insofar as they already have not been covered by the international crimes just enumerated. Recognition of these actions as not only international delicts but also as especially dangerous delicts, that is, international crimes, has been reflected in United Nations General Assembly resolutions, in the Convention on the elimination of all forms of racial discrimination, in the covenants on human rights, and in many other international documents, as well as in the day-to-day practice of States.[78]

It is not our task to establish a more precise listing of violations of international law which enter into this category. We merely have attempted to show that this category of especially dangerous violations of international law, named international crimes, exists in contemporary international law.

Comparatively few changes have occurred in the domain of sanctions in the case of ordinary violations of international law. State responsibility remains reparational in character. Sanctions come down to compensation for the damage, being accompanied by possible enforcement measures if the delinquent State does not fulfill this duty. The legal relations arising in consequence

[77] On this question, see Trainin, Защита мира и борьба с преступлениями против человечества [Defense of Peace and Struggle with Crimes Against Humanity]; Romashkin, Преступления против мира и человечества [Crimes Against Peace and Humanity]; Poltorak, Нюрнбергский процесс [Nuremberg Trial]; Levin, Ответственность государств в современном международном праве [Responsibility of States in Contemporary International Law], pp. 22-29.

[78] See Romashkin, Преступления против мира и человечества [Crimes Against Peace and Humanity], pp. 321-350; D. I. Baratashvili, Новые государства Азии и Африки и международное право [New States of Asia and Africa and International Law] (1968), pp. 113-181; Levin, Ответственность государств в современном международном праве [Responsibility of States in Contemporary International Law], p. 21.

of the delict are limited as a rule to the injured State and the delinquent State. International organizations also frequently participate at the present time in such legal relations within the spheres of operation of international organizations.

As regards sanctions relating to the international crimes of a State, phenomena new in principle have emerged. And even the international delicts of this category are a new phenomenon in international law. In this case, sanctions are not limited to compensation for damage, but also include measures having the character of preventive punishment. It must be emphasized again in this connection that the question is one of an international legal category, as distinct from a category of national law.[79]

The measures provided for by the Potsdam agreement concerning Germany are an example of such sanctions. These measures, as is obvious, did not amount to compensation for damage. They included the occupation of the entire territory of Germany, the assumption of supreme power by the allies, and in general the effectuation of measures having

[79] The attempt of a Czechoslovak author, C. Čepelka, to disprove this proposition and to cram the situation existing in contemporary international law into the procrustean bed of the old "reparational theory" clearly failed. Čepelka maintains that the traditional doctrine of "compulsory reparations also is a suitable theoretical base for contemporary international law". He asserts that under contemporary international law an obligation arises first for the aggressor State to effectuate restitution and to compensate the injury committed as a result of its violation of international law, but he also permits in supplementation thereof satisfaction, which in his view also is the only obligation of the aggressor State. Among the forms of satisfaction, he says, "the obligation to give guarantees for the future against the recurrence of the delict which is in question" has special significance.
Čepelka, therefore, reduces the sanctions with regard to an aggressor State to the "obligations" of the aggressor State. As is clear from the propositions he develops, the effectuation of such sanctions necessarily presupposes the conducting of negotiations and the conclusion of an agreement with the aggressor State. Either thesis is obsolete and does not correspond to contemporary international law. Under contemporary international law the question is one in the case above all of the right of the United Nations or of the States fighting against aggression to impose sanctions on the aggressor State. The sanctions themselves are not limited to "obligations" of the aggressor State, but also include direct measures of coercion which can be imposed on the aggressor even without negotiations, and not just as a result of its failure to fulfill "reparational obligations" or "obligations to grant satisfaction". See Čepelka, *Consequences juridiques du delit en droit international con- temporain*, pp. 62, 73.

the purpose above all: (1) to eradicate German militarism and Nazism and to guarantee that Germany never again threatened her neighbors or the maintenance of peace; to prevent with this purpose any fascist or militarist activity and propaganda; to encourage the development of democracy in Germany; (2) to eliminate excessive concentration in the German economy, cartels, syndicates, trusts, and other monopolistic combinations which enabled fascism to come to power and the preparation and effectuation of Hitlerite aggression.

The application of sanctions against a delinquent State in the event of a threat to the peace, breach of the peace, or act of aggression relates, first and foremost, to the jurisdiction of the United Nations. One can say the same about sanctions regarding international delicts relating to this category such as the refusal to grant independence to colonial peoples, the practice of colonialism, racial discrimination, and so forth, since all these delicts are regarded as a violation of the principles of the United Nations Charter which create or might create a threat to international peace.

Individual States, of course, also have the right to react against this kind of violation of international law. Means of pressure on the offender which might be applied by individual States outside the limits of the United Nations are rather numerous, but they differ materially from the means applied by the United Nations.

The United Nations Charter does not limit the right of the Organization to take measures with or without the use of armed force either in the event of a threat to the peace or in the event that a breach of the peace of act of aggression already has been committed. Meanwhile, in the absence of an armed attack, individual States only can take measures of pressure which are not connected with the use of armed force against other States. Only in the event of an armed attack can a State use armed force against the attacking State, but in this event the question already is not one of sanctions but one of using the right of self-defense.

The aforesaid classification of international State responsibility has been based upon the degree of danger of the international delicts. It is not arbitrary, but reflects the actual situation existing in international law.

A classification of State responsibility based on the nature of sanctions also has a certain significance.

The view has been expressed in Soviet literature that on this plane State responsibility under international law may be political, material, or moral.[80]

It seems to us that one cannot speak of moral responsibility as a special type of responsibility for the following reasons. First, the expression "moral responsibility" can be understood as responsibility that is not legal, but arises from a violation of rules of international morality. For that reason it is in fact more correct to speak in this case of political responsibility, since the so-called moral satisfaction contemplated is political action.

The expression "political responsibility" also is not very apt since it too has a nuance of nonlegal responsibility.

There is no doubt that all types of the responsibility of a State as a political entity have to a certain extent a political character. Nonetheless, one can hardly object to isolating financial responsibility as an independent type of responsibility. At the same time, there are forms of responsibility not linked to financial compensation. It is more correct to treat all these forms of nonmaterial responsibility as political responsibility.

In this case we will have two types of responsibility – political and financial. All forms of State responsibility except financial responsibility, from so-called moral satisfaction to the various measures connected with limiting a State's sovereignty, and so forth, will be treated as political responsibility.

80 See F. I. Kozhevnikov (ed.), Международное право [International Law] (1957), p. 126; Trainin, Защита мира и борьба с преступлениями против человечества [Defense of Peace and Struggle with Crimes Against Humanity], p. 43.

And finally, the question arises of whether the duty of a delinquent State to bear these sanctions corresponds to the right of a State or international organization to apply the sanctions.

In the opinion of R. Ago, an Italian professor, the question in this case is not one of the subjective right to which the obligation of the State that has committed the delict to bear the sanction corresponds. Here one has in view the legal capacity to effectuate the sanction or, that is to say, the capacity granted by the right "to cause damage to another in the form of a sanction, to commit an action or omission which in another instance is prohibited, but which becomes legal precisely and exclusively as a sanction".[81]

This viewpoint, in our opinion, does not take into account the specific nature of international law sufficiently. Norms of international law, including norms relating to sanctions, are created on the basis of agreement between States which are subjects of this system of law. In principle there is no authority in international law standing above States and capable of effectuating sanctions. Sanctions in international law are applied by States individually or collectively or by an international organization on the basis of its charter, that is, an international treaty.

Therefore, in international law and in the case of effectuating sanctions, States or an international organization effectuate rights which correspond to the duties of the delinquent States to subordinate themselves to these sanctions.

If a State against whom sanctions were being undertaken had no duty to subordinate itself to them, it could regard the measures applied against it as actions with regard to which it had no legal obligations whatever and against which, therefore, it could lawfully act.

However, the action of a State which has committed a breach of law against sanctions applied to it would be a new

[81] Ago, "Le délit international", *Recueil des cours*, LXVIII (1938), 429-430.

breach of law. This is especially obvious in the example of the United Nations applying sanctions. The offending State can not oppose the application of sanctions undertaken on the basis of a legally adopted decision of the Security Council. If, for example, enforcement measures were undertaken against any State pursuant to such a Security Council decision, the said offending State would be bound to submit to them.

SEVERAL REFLECTIONS IN CONNECTION WITH THE DRAFT "CHARTER OF THE INTERNATIONAL TRIBUNAL FOR THE CONSIDERATION OF CASES CONCERNING CRIMES COMMITTED ON THE TERRITORY OF FORMER YUGOSLAVIA

G.I.Tunkin

The present document was the very last to come from the pen of the late Professor G. I. Tunkin. It was found on his desk at home after his death. Prepared for the Ministry of Foreign Affairs of the Russian Federation, the Ministry made the text available for inclusion in the revised Russian-language posthumous edition of Tunkin's Theory of International Law (2000). It appears in English for the first time in my translation – WEB.

1. The draft of the Legal Department has been prepared very skilfully and may be sent to the United Nations Secretary General in this form.

2. At the same time, being guided by the principle that there is nothing done which can not be done better, I consider it possible to propose for discussion the following reflections.

3. In the draft it is suggested that the Security Council create a committee of members of the Security Council plus States formed on the territory of the former Yugoslavia. In addition, any other State may become a participant of the Tribunal. This evidently was dictated by the aspiration to add to the resolution of the Security Council a certain treaty element.

It seems to me that this does not strengthen, but weakens, the legal base of the Tribunal. In fact, on what basis would these States be participants of the Tribunal? There is no treaty. To attempt to create a Tribunal on the basis of a treaty, as experts of the ECSE suggest, would truly derail the matter, and if successful would create a dangerous precedent. Dangerous because this opens the road for the arbitrary creation of such tribunals in the future. It is essential that this question be within the competence of the Security Council, and the United Nations Charter offers sufficient grounds for this.

4. It is advisable to determine the functions of the committee by a general but all-embracing formula, having said, for example, that the committee, being an auxiliary organ of the Security Council, deals with all questions connected with ensuring the activity of the Tribunal.

5. I think that 9 members of the court of first instance is sufficient.

6. The proposal concerning the election of members of the court of first instance by members of the International Court of Justice is appropriate. It furthers the greater "internationalization" of the Tribunal.

7. The term "Chancellery" is a narrow technical one; better to substitute the term "Procuracy".

8. As regards the question of applicable law, the provisions contained in the draft do not give rise to objections in substance. But for the purposes of granting to the Tribunal somewhat greater freedom of action, which would be justified in this instance evidently, and also to approximate this draft to the Statute of the International Court of Justice, it would be advisable to discuss this proposal: to devote a special article to this issue and to offer the following text of this article:

"When deciding cases the Court shall apply: the present Charter,

treaty and customary norms of international law,

the law of the State on whose territory the crime was committed to the extent to which it is not contrary to norms of international law,

general principles of law recognized by civilized nations".

It seems to me that such an article would advantageously distinguish our draft from other drafts.

31 March 1993

G. Tunkin

BIBLIOGRAPHY OF WORKS BY G. I. TUNKIN

W. E. Butler

References are provided only for the English-language editions of *International Affairs* and *New Times.*

Obituaries: *The Times*, 23 March 1993 [W. E. Butler]; Российский ежегодник международного права 1993-1994 [Russian Yearbook of International Law 1993-1994] (1995), pp. 9-12 (I. I. Lukashuk)

DISSERTATIONS

1. Парламентская реформа 1832 года в Англии [Parliamentary Reform of 1832 in England]. Moscow, 1938. 120 p. (Defended at the Moscow Juridical Institute, 1938; Candidate of Legal Sciences).

Contents: I. English Electoral Law Before the Reform (Historical Outline); II. The Reform Movement; III. The Reform Bill.

Abstract: Moskovskii iuridicheskii institut NKIu Soiuza SSR. Ученые записки [Learned Papers] (Moscow: Iuridicheskoe izd-vo NKIu SSSR, 1941), III, 16-17.

2. Корейский вопрос после второй мировой войны в свете международного права [Korean Question After the Second World War in the Light of International Law]. Moscow, 1954. 949 p. (Defended at the Moscow State Institute of International Relations; the degree of Doctor of Legal Sciences was confirmed 8 January 1955).

Contents: I. International Agreements Concerning Korea After the Second World War and the Principle of Self-Determination of Nations; II. The Liberation of Korea by the Soviet Army, the Democratic Transformation in

North Korea; III. The Occupation of South Korea by American Forces; IV. Negotiations in the Joint Soviet-American Commission for Korea; V. The Creation by American Occupation Authorities of a Separate Puppet Government in South Korea; VI. The Formation of the Korean People's Democratic Republic; VII. The Korea Question at the Third and Fourth Sessions of the United Nations General Assembly; VIII. Korea in the Plans of the Aggressive Policy of American Imperialists in Asia in Connection with the Victory of the People's Revolution in China; IX. Civil War and United States Aggression in Korea;

X. Violation of the Laws and Customs of War by United States Armed Forces in Korea; XI. United States Aggression Against China; XII. The Struggle to End the War in Korea and the Peaceful Settlement of the Korea Question.

Abstract: Корейский вопрос после второй мировой войны в свете международного права [Korean Question After the Second World War in the Light of International Law]. Moscow, 1954. 24 p. 60 ptd.

Translated: "The Korean Question After the Second World War in the Light of International Law", *Sudebnik*, XI (2006), pp. 391-429 (W. E. Butler).

"The Korean Question After the Second World War in the Light of International Law", in W. E. Butler (transl. & ed., *G. I. Tunkin: Selected Works*. Clark, New Jersey, Talbot Publishing, 2025, pp. 3-55.

BOOKS

3. (ed.), Конституция и основные законодательные акты Федеративной Народной Республики Югославии [Constitution and Basic Legislative Acts of the Federative

People's Republic of Yugoslavia], comp. A. M. Zubov and A. A. Khanov (Moscow, izd-vo Inostrannoi literatury, 1956).

4. Основы современного международного права; учебное пособие [Fundamental Principles of Contemporary International Law:

5. Instructional Manual] (Moscow, 1956). 48 p. (Высшая партийная школа при ЦК КПСС). 20,000 ptd.

Translated: *Hsien-tai kuo-chi-fa ti chi-pen wen-t'I* (Peking, Shih-chieh chih-shih ch'u-pan she, 1958).

"Grundlagen der modernen Völkerrechts", in E. Menzel, ed., *Drei sowjetische Beitrage zur Völkerrechtslehre* (Hamburg, Hansischer Gildenverlag, 1969), pp. 1-57.

"Fundamental Principles of Contemporary International Law", *Sudebnik,* XI (2006), pp. 793-841 (W. E. Butler).

"Fundamental Principles of Contemporary International Law", in W. E. Butler (transl. & ed., *G. I. Tunkin: Selected Works*. Clark, New Jersey, Talbot Publishing, 2024, pp. 56-118.

6. Вопросы теории международного права [Questions of the Theory of International Law] (Moscow: Gosiurizdat, 1962). 330 p. 3000 ptd.

Translated: *Das Völkerrecht der Gegenwart: Theories und Praxis,* transl. Klaus Wolf, ed. Herbert Standke (Berlin, Staatsverlag der DDR, 1963). 280 p.

A Nemzetközi jog elméletének kérdései, transl. P. Bela, ed. M. Ferenc (Budapest, Kozgazdasagi es jogi könyvkiado, 1963). 325 p.

Zagadnienia teorii prawa miedzynarodowego, transl. W. Morawiecki. Preface by M. Lachs (Warsaw, Panstwowe wyd- wo naukowe, 1964). 412 p.

Droit international public; problèmes theoriques, Preface by M. Virally (Paris, Editions A. Pedone, 1965). 250 p.

al-Qānūn al-duwalt al-'āmm, transl. from the French edition by Ahmed Rida, revised by E. Foda ([Cairo], al-Haiy' at al- Misriyat al-'Ammah li'-Kuttāb, 1972).

Reviews: Советское государство и право [Soviet State and Law], no. 5 (1963), p. 167 (R. L. Bobrov).

Правоведение [Jurisprudence], no. 1 (1963), pp. 141-144 (A. N. Talalaev).

Советский ежегодник международного права 1963 [Soviet Yearbook of International Law 1963] (1965), pp. 550-553 (D. B. Levin).

American Journal of International Law, LVII (1963), 673-676 (J. N. Hazard).

Canadian Yearbook of International Law, II (1964), 335-338 (E. McWhinney).

Hastings Law Journal, XVI (1964), 138 (D. Berger).

Revista Española de Derecho Internacional, XVII (1964), 169- 192 (M. Aguilar Navarro).

Staat und Recht, XIII (1964), 1451-1464.

Year Book of World Affairs, XIX (1965), 276 (G[eorg] S[chwarzenberger]).

Annuaire français de droit international, XI (1965), 1115-1118 (A. Ch. Kiss).

Archives de Philosophie de Droit, XII (1967), 384 (K. Stoyanovitch).

Communicazioni I studi, XII (1966), 921-922 (P. Ziccardi).

International and Comparative Law Quarterly, XIV (1965), 1427-1428 (I. Lapenna).

Revue international de droit international public, XXXVI (1965), 861-863 (Ch. Rousseau).

Year Book of World Affairs, XX (1966), 292-293 (G[eorg] S[chwarzenberger]).

7. Идеологическая борьба и международное право (Moscow, izd- vo Mezhdunarodnye otnosheniia, 1967). 176 p. 6000 ptd.

Translated: *Ideologický boj a mezinácrodní právo,* transl. M. Srnská (Prague: Statni pedagogické nakladatelství, 1968). 118 p. Mimeographed.

Ideorogī Toso to Kokusai-hō, transl. Setsuo Iwafuchi (Kyoto: Hōritsu Bunka Sha, 1969). 215 p.

"Der ideologische Kampf und das Völkerrecht", in E. Menzel, ed., *Drei sowjetische Beiträge zur Völkerrechtslehre* (Hamburg: Hansischer Gildenverlag, 1969), pp. 307-461.

Reviews: Советский ежегодник международного права 1968 (1969), pp. 433-436 (L. A. Aleksidze).

Советское государство и право, no. 4 (1968), pp. 140-143 (E. T. Usenko).

Časopis pro mezinárodní právo, XI (1967), 372 (J. Toman).

American Journal of International Law, LXII (1968), 209-211 (J. N. Hazard).

8. Теория международного права [Theory of International Law] (Moscow: izd-vo Mezhdunarodnye otnosheniia, 1970). 511 p. 9000 ptd.

Translated: *Völkerrechtstheorie,* transl. H. Müller and V. Rathfelder, ed. T. Schweisfurth (Berlin, Berlin Verlag, 1972). 492 p.

Theory of International Law, transl. with an introduction by William E. Butler (Cambridge, Mass., Harvard University Press/London, George Allen & Unwin, 1974. Xxv, 497 p.

Reviews: Советское государство и право [Soviet State and Law], no. 12 (1970), pp. 144-147 (I. I. Lukashuk)

Allam-és Jogtudomanyi, XIV (1971), 101 (A. Csillag)

Časopis pro Mezinarodní právo, XV (1971), 88-91 (B. Gotz)

Pravnik, CX (1971), 606 (M. Srnská)

Staat und Recht, XIX (1970), 2019 (F. Seidel)

Ruch prawniczy, ekonomiczny I socjologiczny, no. 1 (1972), pp. 10-13 (J. Symonides)

Правна мисъл, no. 1 (1971), pp. 104-106 (E. G. Kamenov)

American Journal of International Law, LXV (1971), 416- 418 (W. E. Butler)

Nederlands Juristenblad, December 1970, p. 1385

Osteuropa Recht, XVIII (1972), 208-210 (D. Frenzke)

Comment: "Renewed Emphasis upon a Socialist International Law", *American Journal of International Law*, LXV (1971), 142-148 (J. N. Hazard)

"`Socialist International Law' or `Socialist Principles of International Relations'", *American Journal of International Law*, LXV (1971), 796-800 (W. E. Butler)

"Socialist International Law Revisited", *American Journal of International Law*, LXVI (1972), 596-600 (C. Osakwe)

"Обсуждение проблем теории международного права" [Discussion of Problems of Theory of International Law],

Правоведение [Jurisprudence], no. 6 (1970), 132-134 (V. L. Iushchenko)

9. *В. И. Ленин и современное международное право* (Moscow, izd-vo Znanie, 1970). 63 p. Coauthor: V. F. Fedorov. 53,000 ptd.

10. *Comparabilité des diplômes en droit international; étude structurelle et fonctionelle* (Paris, UNESCO, 1972). 83 p. Coauthor: R.-J. Dupuy. (English language edition, 1973)

11. (ed.). Международное право [International Law]. Moscow, Iuridicheskaia literatura, 1974. 590 p.

Reviews: Правоведение, no. 2 (1975), pp. 154-157 (M. V. Ianovskii) Советский ежегодник международного права 1975 [Soviet Yearbook of International Law 1975] (1977), pp. 332-335 (P. M. Kuris).

Also transl. into English, French, and Spanish.

12. (ed.). Международное право: учебник для вузов [International Law: Textbook for Institutions of Higher Education] (Moscow, Iuridicheskaia _nternatio, 1982). 566 p.

Translated: *International Law* (Moscow, Progress Publishers, 1986). 547 p.

Reviews: Правоведение [Jurisprudence], no. 5 (1983), pp. 109-111 (O. I. Tiunov)

Советские ежегодник международного права 1983 [Soviet Yearbook of International Law 1983] (1984), pp. 262-264 (D. B. Levin).

13. *Право и сила в международной системе* [Law and Force in the International System] Moscow, Mezhdunarodnye otnosheniia, 1983. 199 p.

Reviews: Советское государство и право [Soviet State and Law], no. 11 (1984), pp. 147-149 (D. I. Fel'dman, V. N. Likhachev)

Советский ежегодник международного права 1984 [Soviet Yearbook of International Law 1984] (1986), pp. 301-302 (D. B. Levin).

Дипломатический вестник. Год 1984 [Diplomatic Herald. 1984] (Moscow, 1985), pp. 342-344 (E. I. Skakunov).

Translated: *Law and Force in the International System* (Moscow, Progress Publishers, 1985). 344 p.

Recht und Gewalt in internationalen System. Kiel, 1986.

El derecho y la Fuerza en el Sistema Internacional. Mexico, 1989.

Also: Kyoto, 1989; Seoul, 1989.

14. (ed.), *From Coexistence to Cooperation: International Law and Organization in the Post-Cold War Era* (Dordrecht/Boston/London,

Martinus Nijhoff, 1992). xiv, 297 p. Co- editors: E. McWhinney, D. Ross, V. Vereshchetin.

15. *Теория международного права*, ed. L. N. Shestakov (Moscow, Izdatel'stvo "Zertsalo", 2000; reprinted, 2006). 416 p. 3000 ptd.

Translation: *Theory of International Law*, ed. L. N. Shestakov, transl. & ed. W. E. Butler (London: Wildy, Simmonds & Hill Publishers, 2003).

"Theory of International Law", in W. E. Butler (ed.), *G. I. Tunkin: Selected Works*. Clark, New Jersey, Talbot Publishing, 2024, pp. 119-649.

ARTICLES AND REVIEWS

1940

16. "Парламентская реформа 1832 г. В Англии" [Parliamentary Reform of 1832 in England], Ученые записки московского юридического института [Learned Papers of Moscow Juridical Institute] (Moscow, izd-vo NKIu SSSR, 1940), Vyp. II, 103-182.

1946

17. "Проблемы государственного устройства Китая" [Problems of State Structure of China], Советское государство и право [Soviet State and Law], nos. 8-9 (1946), pp. 31-46. Pseud.: M. Eremeev.

18. "К вопросу о Гонконге и Коулуне" [On the Question of Hong Kong and Kowloon], Новое время [New Times], no. 19 (1946), pp. 8-11. Pseud: M. Eremeev.

Translated: "Hong Kong and Kowloon", *New Times*, no. 19 (1946), pp. 8-10.

1947

19. "Государство и право франции от буржуазной революции до 1871 г." [State and Law of France from the Bourgeois Revolution to 1871], in Vsesoiuznyi _nternati iuridicheskikh nauk

ministerstva iustitsii SSSR, Всеобщая история государства и права. Часть III. От английской революции до великой октябрьской социалистической революции [Universal History of State and Law. Part III. From the English Revolution to the Great October Socialist Revolution] (Moscow, Iuridicheskoe izd-vo Ministerstva iustitsii SSSR, 1947), pp. 57-88. Part I, section II, chapter 1.

20. "К итогам национального собрания в Китае" [On the Results of the National Assembly in China], Известия [News], 11 February 1947, pp. 3-4. Pseud. M. Eremeev.

1948

20, (responsible ed.), Программа по международному публичному праву (для юридических институтов и юридических факультетов, университетов) [Syllabus for Public International Law (for Legal Institutes and Law Faculties)] (Moscow, Tipo. Moskovskogo iuridicheskogo instituta, 1948). Compiled by F. I. Kozhevnikov.

21. "О международной защите прав человека" [On the International Defense of Human Rights], Советское государство и право [Soviet State and Law], no. 7 (1948), pp. 1-10. Pseud. G. Tavrov.

1950

22. "Корейский вопрос после второй мировой войны" [The Korean Question After the Second World War], Советское государство и право, no. 7 (1950), pp. 27-42. Pseud. G. Tavrov.

Review: *Pravnik,* no. 8-9 (1950), p. 415 (V. Paul).

1951

23. "Изобличающие документы" [Damning Documents], Советское государство и право [Soviet State and Law], no. 8 (1951), pp. 92- 95. Pseud. G. Tavrov.

Review of: *Documents and Materials Exposing the Instigators of the Civil War in Korea. Documents from the Archives of the Rhee Syngman Government* (Pyongyang: Ministry of

Foreign Affairs of the Democratic People's Republic of Korea, 1950).

24. "Беззастенчивое нарушение международных соглашений и норм международного права" [Shameless Violation of International Agreements and Norms of International Law], Советское государство и право [Soviet State and Law], no. 9 (1951), pp. 49-61.

25. "Преступная война американских империалистов против корейского народа" [Criminal War of American Imperialists Against Korean People], Труды института права Академии наук СССР [Proceedings of Institute of Law of USSR Academy of Sciences], I (1951), 85-111. Pseud. G. Tavrov.

1952

26. "Договор подготовки войны" [Treaty of Preparation of War], Советское государство и право [Soviet State and Law], no. 2 (1952), pp. 41- 51. Pseud. G. Tavrov.

27. (ed.), with introduction, Конституция и основные законодательные акты Корейской народно-демократической республики [Constitution and Basic Legislative Acts of Korean People's-Democratic Republic], transl. from the Korean by Iu. N. Mazur and Han Dik Pon (Moscow, izd-vo Inostrannoi literatury, 1952), pp. 5-52. Pseud. G. Tavrov.

1953

28. "Советское определение агрессии в Организации Объединённых Наций" [Soviet Definition of Aggression in the United Nations], Советское государство и право [Soviet State and Law], nos. 2- 3 (1953), pp. 89-101.

1954

29. "Общеевропейский договор и международное право" [General European Treaty and International Law], Правда [Pravda], 10 April 1954, p. 3. Pseud. G. Tavrov.

30. "Коллективная безопасность и государственный суверенитет" [Collective Security and State Sovereignty], Правда [Pravda], 8 May 1954, p. 3. Pseud. G. Tavrov.

31. "Европейская безопасность и Организация Объединенных Наций" [European Security and the United Nations], Правда [Pravda], 28 May 1954, p. 3. Pseud. G. Tavrov.

32. "Атлантический договор и возрождение германского империализма" [The Atlantic Treaty and Birth of German Imperialism], *Правда*, 20 September 1954, p. 3. Pseud. G. Tavrov.

33. "Что скрывается за разговорами о 'восстановлении суверенитета' Западной Германии" [What is Concealed Behind Negotiations on the "Restoration of Sovereignty" of Western Germany], Правда [Pravda], 27 September 1954, p. 4. Pseud. G. Tavrov.

34. "Старые планы под новой вывеской (Западноевропейский союз и Европейское Оборонительное сообщество)" [Old Plans Under New Pretext (Western European Union and European Defense Community], Правда [Pravda], 14 December 1954, p. 3. Pseud. G. Tavrov.

1955

35. "Парижские соглашения и международное право" [Paris Agreements and International Law], Советское государство и право [Soviet State and Law], no. 2 (1955), pp. 13-22.

36. "Вопрос о запрещении атомного оружия и международное право" [Question Concerning the Prohibition of Atomic Weapons and International Law], Правда [Pravda], 26 May 1955, p. 3. Pseud. G. Tavrov.

37. "Законные права Китая в ООН должны быть восстановлены" [Legal Rights of China in United Nations Must Be Restored], Новое время [New Times], no. 28 (1955), pp. 3-5.

Translated: "China's Lawful Rights in the United Nations", *New Times*, no. 28 (1955), pp. 3-5.

38. "Германская Демократическая Республика – полноправный субъект международного права" [German Democratic Republic – Fully-Fledged Subject of International Law], Известия [News], 9 October 1955, p. 3.

39. "Европейские проблемы и Парижские соглашения" [European Problems and the Paris Agreements], Новое время [New Times], no. 44 (1955), pp. 6-9. Pseud. G. Tavrov.

Translated: "The Paris Agreements and European Problems", *New Times*, no. 44 (1955), pp. 6-8.

40. "В защиту прав человека" [In Defense of Human Rights], Известия [News], 10 December 1955, p. 4.

1956

41. "О некоторых вопросах международного договора в связи с Варшавским договором" [On Certain Questions of the International Treaty in Connection with the Warsaw Treaty], Советское государство и право [Soviet State and Law], no. 1 (1956), pp. 98-104.

42. "Корейский вопрос" [The Korean Question], Международная жизнь [International Life], no. 2 (1956), pp. 81-96. Pseud. G. Tavrov.

Translated: "The Korean Question", *International Affairs*, no. 2 (1956), pp. 82-96.

43. "За коллективную безопасность в Европе" [For Collective Security in Europe], Международная жизнь [International Life], no. 3 (1956), pp. 117-121.

Review of: Проблема коллективной безопасности в Европе [Problem of Collective Security in Europe] (Warsaw: Panstwowe wyd-wo Naukowe, 1955).

Translated: "For Collective Security in Europe", *International Affairs*, no. 3 (1956), pp. 121-126.

44. "Мирное сотрудничество или 'промежуточное состояние'" [Peaceful Cooperation or "Interim State"], Новое время [New Times], no. 25 (1956), pp. 8-11.

Translated: "Peaceful Cooperation or 'Intermediate Status'", *New Times*, no. 25 (1956), pp. 8-10.

45. "Мирное сосуществование и международное право" [Peaceful Coexistence and International Law], Советское государство и право [Soviet State and Law], no. 7 (1956), pp. 3-13.

Translated: *Academia Republicii Populare Romine, Institutul de Studii romino-sovietice*, no. 7 (1956), pp. 3-19.

Review: *American Journal of International Law* (1957), 69.

46. "Спор о Панамском канале" [Dispute Concerning the Panama Canal], Международная жизнь [International Life], no. 9 (1956), pp. 132-134. Pseud. G. Tavrov.

Reprinted: Известия [News], 7 September 1956, p. 3.

Translated: "The Panama Canal Dispute", *International Affairs*, no. 9 (1956), pp. 134- 136.

47. "Угрозы применения силы запрещены международным правом" [Threats of the Use of Force Have Beren Prohibited by International Law], Правда [Pravda], 2 September 1956, p. 5.

48. "Пора восстановить представительство Китая в ООН" [Time to Restore the Representation of China in the United Nations], Международная жизнь [International Life], no. 10 (1956), pp. 25-34.

Translated: "Time to Restore China's Representation in the U.N.", *International Affairs*, no. 10 (1956), pp. 27-35.

49. "Вооруженная агрессия против Египта – грубейшее нарушение международного права" [Armed Aggression Against Egypt – Flagrant Violation of International Law], Советское государство и право [Soviet State and Law], no. 10 (1956), pp. 10-16. Unsigned.

1957

50. "Soužiti státu dvou soustav a mezinárodni _nter", *Mezinárodni politika,* I (1957), 330- 337.

51. Review of: R. Quadri, *Diritto internazionale publico* (2d ed.; Palermo: G. Pruilla, 1956), in Советское государство и право [Soviet State and Law], no. 9 (1957), pp. 152-155.

52. "Некоторые новые явления в посольском праве" [Certain New Phenomena in Ambassadorial Law], Международная жизнь [International Life], no. 12 (1957), PP. 63-71.

Translated: "Some Developments in International Law Concerning Diplomatic Privileges and Immunities", *International Affairs,* no. 12 (1957), pp. 64-71.

53. "Вопросы посольского права на IX сессии Комиссии международного права ООН" [Questions of Ambassadorial Law at the IX Session of the United Nations International Law Commission], Советское государство и право [Soviet State and Law], no. 12 (1957), pp. 73-83.

54. "Социалистический интернационализм и международное право" [Socialist Internationalism and International Law], Новое время [New Times], no. 51 (1957), pp. 10-11.

Translated: "Socialist Internationalism and International Law", *New Times,* no. 51 (1957), pp. 10-11.

1958

55. "Co-existence and International Law", *Recueil des cours,* XCV (1958), 1-81.

56. "Женевская конвенция по международному морскому праву" [Geneva Convention of the International Law of the Sea], [International Life], no. 7 (1958), pp. 63-70.

Translated: "The Geneva Conference on the Law of the Sea", *International Affairs,* no. 7 (1958), pp. 47-52.

57. “Действия США – вооруженная агрессия” [Actions of the United States – Armed Aggression], Литература и жизнь [Literature and Life], 20 July 1958, p. 3.

58. “Американская агрессия на Дальнем Востоке – грубое нарушение международного права” [American Aggression in the Far East – Flagrant Violation of International Law], Правда [Pravda], 7 September 1958, p. 5.

59. (ed.), with preface, A. P. Movchan, Международная защита прав человека [International Defense of Human Rights] (Moscow: Gosiurizdat, 1958), pp. 3-4.

60. “Два проекта Комиссии международного права ООН” [Two Drafts of the United Nations International Law Commission], Советское государство и право [Soviet State and Law], no. 12 (1958), pp. 66-74. Coauthor V. A. Romanov.

1959

61. “Новый тип международных отношений и международное право” [New Type of International Relations and International Law], Советское государство и право [Soviet State and Law], no. 1 (1959), pp. 81-94.

Translated: “Ein neuer Typ der internationalen Beziehungen und das Völkerrecht”, *Sowjetwissenschaft,* III (1959), 709-726.

Reviews: *International Political Science Abstracts,* IX (1959), no. 2, pp. 248-249

L'URSS et les pays de l'Est, no. 1 (1960), pp. 51-52 (M. Mouskhely).

62. “Берлинский вопрос в свете международного права” [The Berlin Question in the Light of International Law], Международная жизнь [International Life], no. 2 (1959), pp. 46-56.

Translated: “The Berlin Problem and International Law”, *International Affairs,* no. 2 (1959), pp. 46-56.

"Die Berlin-Frage und das Völkerrecht", *Sowjetwissenschaft,* III (1959), 357-367.

"La Question de Berlin et le droit international", *Études soviétiques,* no. 133 (April 1959), pp. 21-24.

63. "XXI съезд КПСС и международное право" [XXI Congress of the CPSU and International Law], Советское государство и право [Soviet State and Law], no. 6 (1959), pp. 40-49.

Translated: "Der XXI. Parteitag der KpdSU und das Völkerrecht", *Aussenwirtschaftsdienst des Betriebsrates mit Recht der europ. Gemeinschaften,* VI (1959), 438-448.

64. "Советский союз и международное право" [The Soviet Union and International Law], Международная Жизнь [International Life], no. 11 (1959), pp. 52-60.

Translated: "The Soviet Union and International Law", *International Affairs,* no. 11 (1959), pp. 40-45.

65. "XI сессия Комиссии международного права ООН" [XI Session of United Nations International Law Commission], Советское государство и право [Soviet State and Law], no. 11 (1959), pp. 69-78. Co- author V. A. Romanov

Abstract: *International Political Science Abstracts,* X (1960), no. 1, pp. 92-93.

66. "Сорок лет сосуществования и международного права" [Forty Years of Coexistence and International Law], Советский ежегодник международного права 1958 [Soviet Yearbook of International Law 1958] (Moscow, izd-vo AN SSSR, 1959), pp. 15-42. English summary pp. 42-49.

Summary: *International Affairs,* no. 3 (1958), p. 125.

Translated: "Vierzig Jahre Koexistenz und Völkerrecht", in R. Arzinger, ed., *Gegenwartsprobleme des Völkerrecht* (Berlin: VEB Deutscher Zentralverlag, 1962), pp. 7-39.

67. "Незадачливые коментаторы международного права" [Unlucky Commentators of International Law], Известия [News], 27 May 1959, p. 5.

68. (ed.), with introduction, A. Verdross, Международное право [International Law], transl. F. A. Kublitskii, and R. L. Naryshkina (Moscow, izd-vo Inostrannoi literatury, 1959), pp. 5-18.

69. (ed.), with introduction, I. S. Pereterskii, Толкование международных договоров [Interpretation of International Treaties] (Moscow, Gosiurizdat, 1959), pp. 3-4. Coeditor S. B. Krylov.

1960

70."Хороший пример международного сотрудничество (к итогам конференции по Антарктике)" [Good Example of International Cooperation (On the Results of the Antarctica Conference], Международная жизнь [International Life], no. 2 (1960), pp. 55-60.

Translated: "An Example of International Cooperation", *International Affairs*, no. 2 (1960), pp. 42-45.

71. "The Role of International Law in International Relations", in F. Frhr. V. d. Heydte and others (eds.), *Völkerrecht und rechtliches Weltbild; Festschrift für Alfred Verdross* (Vienna, Springer Verlag, 1960), pp. 293-305.

72. "Необоснованные притязания" [Unsubstantiated Claims], Известия [News],18 February1960, p. 3.

73. "Introduction", Советский ежегодник международного права 1959 [Soviet Yearbook of International Law] (Moscow, izd-vo AN SSSR, 1960), pp. 11-15.

74. (ed.), with introduction, S. B. Krylov, История создания Организации Объединенных Наций [History of Creation of the United Nations] (Moscow, izd-vo IMO, 1960), pp. 3-9.

75. "Дипломатические привилегии и иммунитеты" [Diplomatic Privileges and Immunnities], in A. A. Gromyko and others (eds.), Дипломатический словарь в трех томах [Diplomatic Dictionary in Three Volumes] (Moscow, Gospolitizdat, 1960), I, 448-454.

76. "Источники международного права" [Sources of International Law], ibid., I, 573-576.

77. "Разоблаченная легенда" [Unmasked Legend], Правда [Pravda], 24 July 1960, p. 5.

78. "О юридической природе обычных норм международного права" [On the Legal Nature of Customary Norms of International Law], Вопросы международного права [Questions of International Law] (Moscow, izd-vo IMO, 1960), Vyp. 2, pp. 3-17.

79. "Конференция Ассоциации международного права" [Conference of the International Law Association], Вестник академии наук СССР []Herald of the USSR Academy of Sciences], no. 11 (1960), pp. 105-107.

80. "За мир без оружия и независимость народов" [For Peace Without Weapons and the Independence of Peoples], Советское государство и право [Soviet State and Law], no. 11 (1960), pp. 3-13. Peredovaia [Leading Article]: unsigned.

1961

81. "Проект кодекса консульского права (К итогам XII сессии Комиссии международного права ООН)" [Draft Code of Consular Law (On the Results of the XII Session of the United Nations International Law Commission], Советское государство и право [Soviet State and Law], no. 1 (1961), pp. 56-66. Coauthor: D. V. Bykov.

Summary: *Staat und Recht*, X (1961), 930-932.

82. (ed.), with preface, C. Berezows1i, Некоторые проблемы территориального верховенства [Certain Problelms of Territorial Sovereignty], transl. V. L. Kon (Moscow, izd- vo Inostrannoi literatury, 1961), pp. 5-12.

83. "Венская конвенция о дипломатических сношениях" [Vienna Convention on Diplomatic Relations], Международная жизнь, [International Life], no. 6 (1961), pp. 72-80.

Translated: "Vienna Convention on Diplomatic Relations", *International Affairs*, no. 6 (1961), pp. 51-56.

84. "Peaceful Coexistence and International Law", *The Ceylon Law Society Journal,* VII (1961), xvi-xviii.

Translated: *Tan San Tu Fan* [Vietnam], no. 1 (1961).

85. "The Role of International Law in Strengthening Peace", *United Nations Review,* VIII, no. 8 (1961), pp. 18-20, 36.

86. "Diplomatie und Völkerrecht", *Osterreichische Zeitschrift für Aussenpolitik,* I (1961), 292-301.

87. "Remarks on the Juridical Nature of Customary Norms of International Law", *California Law Review,* XLIX (1961), 419-430.

Review: *Boletin del Instituto de derecho comparado de Mexico,* no. 43 (1962), p. 43.

88. "Международноправовые аспекты заключения германского мирного договора" [International Legal Aspects of the Conclusion of a German Peace Treaty], Советское государство и право [Soviet State and Law], no. 10 (1961), pp. 179-192.

Summary: *Staat und Recht,* XI (1962), 384-387.

89. "Международные организации" [International Organizations], in A. A. Gromyko and others (eds.), Дипломатический словарь в трех томах [Diplomatic Dictionary in Three Volumes] (Moscow, Gospolitizdat, 1961), II, 279-283. Unsigned.

90. "Международноправовая ответственность государства" [International Legal Responsibility of States], ibid., II, 277-279. Unsigned.

91. "Мирное сосуществование" [Peaceful Coexistence], ibid., II, 297-300. Unsigned.

92. "Introduction", Советский ежегодник международного права 1960 [Soviet Yearbook of International Law 1960] (Moscow, izd-vo AN SSSR, 1961), pp. 15-23. English summary, pp. 23-27.

93. "Проблема международноправовой ответственности государства в Комиссии международного права ООН" [Problem of International Legal Responsibility of State in United Nations International Law Commission], ibid., pp. 92-101. English summary pp. 101-104.

94. "Der rechtliche Standpunkt", *Die Sowjetunion heute* [Bonn], VI (10 September 1961), pp. 3-4.

Reprinted: *Sowjetunion heute* [Vienna], no. 39 (24 September 1961).

95. (ed.), Проблемы международного права: сборник статей юристов-международников стран народной демократии [Problems of International Law: Collection of Articles of International Lawyers of Countries of People's Democracy] (Moscow, izd-vo Inostrannoi literatury, 1961).

1962

96. "XXII съезд КПСС и задачи советской науки международного права" [XXII Congress of the CPSU and Tasks of the Soviet Science of International Law], Советское государство и право [Soviet State and Law], no. 5 (1962), pp. 3-17.

Translated: "The 22nd Congress of the CPSU and the Tasks of the Soviet Science of International Law", *Soviet Law and Government*, I, no. 3 (1962/63), pp. 18-28.

Summary: *Staat und Recht*, XI (1962), 2259-2260.

97. "XXII съезд КПСС и проблемы советской науки международного права. Тезисы доклада" [XXII Congress of the CPSU and Problems of the Soviet Science of International Law. Theses of Report»], in Советская ассоциация международного права, V ежегодное собрание. 29, 30 и 31 января 1962 г. [Soviet Association of International Law, V Annual Meeting. 29, 30, and 31 January]. (Moscow, 1962), pp. 1-18.

98. "Враги Кубы попирают международное право" [Enemies of Cuba Flout International Law], Правда [Pravda], 19 September 1962, p. 5.

99. "XXII съезд КПСС и международное право" [XXII Congress of the CPSU and International Law], Советский ежегодник международного права 1961 [Soviet Yearbook of International Law 1961] (Moscow, izd-vo AN SSSR, 1962), pp. 15-28. English summary pp. 28-35.

100. "La guerre froide et le droit international", *Comprendre,* XXV (1962), 25-37.

101. (ed.), Очерки международного морского права [Essays on the International Law of the Sea] (Moscow, Gosiurizdat, 1962). Co-editor V. M. Koretskii.

1963

102. "Alcuni nuovi _nterna della responsabilita dello stato nel diritto internazionale", *Communicazioni e studi,* XI (1963), 1-49.

103. "Coexistence" in International Law Association, *Report of the 50th Conference Held at Brussels, August 19th to August 26th 1962* (London, 1963), pp. 263-264, 294-295.

104. "Право договоров на XIV сессии Комиссии международного права ООН" [Law of Treaties at the XIV Session of the United Nations International Law Commission], Советское государство и право [Soviet State and Law], no. 2 (1962), pp. 97-103. Coauthor B. N. Nechaev.

Summary: *Staat und Recht,* XII (1963), 1311-1312.

105. "Coexistence of Opposites: Soviet Attitude to International Law", *The Times,* 25 February 1963, p. 14, cols. 3-4.

106. "Принцип мирного сосуществования – генеральная линия внешнеполитической деятельности КПСС и Советского го- сударства" [Principle of Coexistence – General Line of Foreign Policy Activity of the CPSU and Soviet State], Советское государство и право, no. 7 (1963), pp. 26-37.

Summary: *Staat und Recht*, XII (1963), 2081-2082.

107. "Границы государств и мирное сосуществование" [Boundaries of States and Peaceful Coexistence], Известия [News], 27 August 1963, p. 2.

Translated: "Staatgrenzen und friedliche Koexistenz", *Die Sowjetunion heute*, VIII, no. 19 (1963), pp. 25-26.

108. "Пакт о ненападении – важный шаг к разрядке" [Non-Aggressions Pact – Important Step Towards I], Международная жизнь [International Life], no. 10 (1963), pp. 11-19.

Translated: "Non-Aggression Pact: Important Step Towards I", *International Affairs*, no. 10 (1963), pp. 9-14.

109. "Der Nichtangriffspakt-ein wichtigerSchritt zur Entspannung",

Sowjetwissenschaft, VIII (1964), 1-11.

110. "International Law and Peace", in *International Law in a Changing World* (New York: Oceana Publications, Inc., 1963), pp. 72-79.

111. "Успехи политики мирного сосуществования" [Successes of Policy of Peaceful Coexistence], Советский ежегодник международного права 1962 [Soviet Yearbook of International Law 1962] (Moscow: izd-vo AN SSSR, 1963), pp. 17-20. English summary pp. 21-24.

1964

112. "Идеологическая борьба и международное право. Тезисы доклада" [Ideological Struggle and International Law. Theses of Report], in Советская ассоциация международного права. VII ежегодное собрание 30, 31 января и 1 февраля 1964 г. [Soviet Association of International Law. VII Annual Meeting, 30, 31 January and 1 February 1964] (Moscow, 1964), pp. 1-6.

113. "Международное право и государственные границы" [International Law and State Boundaries], *Известия*, 8 January 1964, p. 2.

114. "Право договоров на XV сессии Комиссии международного права ООН" [Law of Treaties at the XV Session of the Unnited Nations International Law Commission], Советское государство и право [Soviet State and Law], no. 2 (1964), pp. 84-92. Coauthor B. N. Nechaev.

115. "Le droit international de la co-existence pacifique", in *Mélanges offerts à Henri Rolin: Problèmes de droit des gens* (Paris: Editions A. Pedone, 1964), pp. 407-418.

116. "La codification des principes de co-existence pacifique", *Revue de droit contemporain*, XI, no. 1 (1964), pp. 79-89.

Translated: "Codification of the Principles of Peaceful Coexistence", *Review of Contemporary Law*, XI, no. 1 (1964), pp. 79-88.

117. "Новый тип международных отношений и международное право" [New Type of International Relations and International Law], in F. I. Kozhevnikov (ed.), Международное право [International Law] (Moscow, izd-vo Mezhdunarodnye otnosheniia, 1964), pp. 94-120 (Chapter 4).

1965

118. "Вопреки международному праву" [Contrary to International Law], Известия [News], 29 January 1965, p. 2.

119. "Военные преступники и реваншисты" [War Criminals and Revanchists], За рубежом [Abroad], no. 12 (1965), p. 5.

120. "Акт произвола" [Act of Arbitrariness], Известия [News], 13 February 1965, p. 2.

121. "Право договоров на XVI сессии Комиссии международного права ООН" [Law of Treaties at XVI Session of the United Nations International Law Commission], Советское государство и право [Soviet State and Law], no. 3 (1965), pp. 70-77. Coauthor B. N. Nechaev.

122. "Die rechtliche Natur der UNO und der Weg zur Festigung der internationalen Organisation", *Vereinte Nationen*, XIII (1965), 121- 126.

123. "Организация Объединенных Нации: 1945-1965 гг. (Международноправовые проблемы)" [United Nations: 1945-1965 (International Legal Problems], Советское государство и право [Soviet State and Law], no. 10 (1965), pp. 58-68.

Translated: "The United Nations: 1945-1965 (Problems of International Law), *Soviet Law and Government*, IV, no. 4 (1966), pp. 3-12.

1966

124. "The Legal Nature of the United Nations", *Recueil des cours*, CXIX (1966), 1-68.

125. "Право договоров на XVII сессии Комиссии международного права ООН" [Law of Treaties at the XVII Session of the United Nations International Law Commission], Советское государство и право, no. 4 (1966), pp. 56-62. Coauthor B. N. Nechaev.

126. "Законное право (ГДР должна быть принята в ООН)" [Legal Right (GDR Must Be Admitted to the United Nations)], Правда [Pravda], 15 September 1966, p. 3.

127. "Der Nürnberger Prozess und das Völkerrecht", *Blätter für deutsche und internationale Politik*, XI (1966), 790-797.

128. (co-ed.), Курс международного права (для юридических институтов и факультетов) [Course of International Law (For Legal Institutes and Faculties)] (2d ed; Moscow, Mezhdunarodnye otnosheniia, 1966). 648 p. (with F. I. Kozhevnikov, G. P. Zadorozhnyi, and others).

1967

129. "Air and Space Law. Charter of the United Nations", in International Law Association, *Report of the 52nd Conference Held at Helsinki, August 14-20, 1966* (London, 1967), pp. 172-173, 306, 321, 861.

130. "Конференция Ассоциации международного права" [Conference of the International Law Association], Советское государство и право [Soviet State and Law], no. 1 (1967), pp. 139-140. Coauthor O. V. Bogdanov.

131. "Необоснованные действия" [Unsubstantiated Actions], Водный транспорт [Water Transport], 7 January 1967, p. 122 [The *Zagorsk* at Port Dal'nyi].

132. "С точки зрения международного права" [From the Standpoint of International Law], Новое время [New Times], no. 8 (1967), pp. 7-8.

Translated: "From the Standpoint of International Law", *New Times*, no. 8 (1967), pp. 7-8.

133. "Великая Октябрьская социалистическая революция и становление нового международного права" [Great October Socialist Revolution and the Development of a New International Law], Правоведение [Jurisprudence], no. 1 (1967), pp. 19-28.

134. "Устарел ли Устав ООН?" [Is the United Nations Charter Obsolete?, Новое время [New Times], no. 20 (1967), pp. 10-12.

Translated: "Is the U.N. Charter Out of Date?" *New Times*, no. 20 (1967), pp. 10-12.

135. "Международно-правовые идеи Великой Октябрьской социалистической революции" [International Legal Ideas of the Great October Socialist Revolution], in Sovetskaia assotsiatsiia mezhdunarodnogo prava, X юбилейное ежегодное собрание, посвященное 50-летию Великой Октябрьской социалистической революции. 31 января, 1 и 2 февраля 1967 г. Тезисы докладов [X Jubilee Annual Meeting Devoted to the 50th Anniversary of the Great October Socialist Revolution, 31 January, 1 and 2 February 1967. Theses of Reports (Moscow, 1967), pp. 1-4.

136. "Новые принципы международного права" [New Principles of International Law], Новое время [New Times], no. 35 (1967), pp. 3-5.

Translated: "New Principles of International Law", *New Times*, no. 35 (1967), pp. 3-6.

137. "Понятие и сущность современного международного права" [Concept and Essence of Contemporary International Law], in V. M. Chkhikvadze and others (eds.), Курс международного права в шести томах [Course of International Law in Six Volumes] (Moscow, izd-vo Nauka, 1967), I, 9-38. Coauthor I. I. Lukashuk.

138. "Мирное сосуществование государств двух систем и международное право" [Peaceful Coexistence of States of Two Systems and International Law], ibid., I, 73-97 (Chapter 4).

139. "Принцип мирного сосуществования" [Principle of Peaceful Coexistence], ibid., II, 16-32 (Chapter 2).

140. "Борьба двух концепций в международном праве" [Struggle of Two Conceptions in International Law], Советское государство и право [Soviet State and Law], no. 11 (1967), pp. 140-149.

141. "Международноправовое значение Декрета о мире" [International Legal Significance of Decret on Peace], Вестник московского государственного университета: право [Herald of Moscow State University: Law], no. 5 (1967), pp. 3-12.

142. "The Union of Soviet Socialist Republics", in R.-J. Dupuy (ed.), *The University Teaching of Social Sciences: International Law* (Paris, UNESCO, 1967), pp. 93-98.

1968

143. "Le conflit ideologique et le droit international", in *Recueil d'Études de droit international en hommage à Paul Guggenheim* (Geneva, Imp. De la Tribune de Geneve, 1968), pp. 888-898.

144. "Сессия Института международного права" [Session of the Institute of International Law], Советское государство и право [Soviet State and Law], no. 2 (1968), pp. 112-113.

145. "ООН и права человека" [United Nations and Human Rights], Новое время [New Times], no. 9 (1968), pp. 4-6.

Translated: "The U.N. and Human Rights", *New Times*, no. 9 (1968), pp. 4-6.

146. "Агрессия против Вьетнама и международное право" [Aggression Against Vietnam and International Law], Новое Время [New Times], no. 33 (1968), pp. 14-15.

Translated: "International Lawyers Discuss Vietnam", *New Times*, no. 33 (1968), pp. 14- 15.

147. "Международно-правовые идеи Великой Октябрьской социалистической революции" [International Legal Ideas of the Great October Socialist Revolution], Советский ежегодник международного права 1966-1967 [Soviet Yearbook of International Law 1966-1967] (Moscow, izd-vo Nauka, 1968), pp. 15-24. English summary pp. 25-29.

148. Review of E. T. Usenko, Формы регулирования международного социалистического разделения труда [Forms of Regulation of International Socialist Division of Labor] (Moscow, izd- vo Mezhdunarodnye otnosheniia, 1965), ibid., pp. 316-317. Coauthor G.P.Kaliuzhnaia.

149. "Organisation internationale universelle: illusions et realité", *Comprendre*, nos. 31-32 (1968), pp. 69-79.

150. Review of R. Arzinger, *Das Selbstbestimmungsrecht im allgemeinen Völkerrecht der Gegenwart* (Berlin, Staatsverlag der DDR, 1966), in Советское государство и право [Soviet State and Law], no. 11 (1968), pp. 157-158.

151. "L'Agression américaine au Vietnam à la lumière du droit international", *Conference mondiale des juristes pour le Vietnam* (Brussels, Association internationale des jurists democrats, 1968), pp. 73-76.

152. "Remarks on the Normative Function of Specialized Agencies", in *Estudios de Derecho Internacional. Homenaje a D. Antonio de Luna* (Madrid, Instituto Francisco de Vitoria, 1968), pp. 282-291.

153. "The Principal Developments in International Law During the Course of the Last Half Century", *Revue egyptienne de droit international*, XXIV (1968), 1-3.

1969

154. "Menschenrechts und Völkerrecht", *Vereinte Nationen*, XVII (1969), 9-12.

155. "О материальной ответственности колонизаторов" [On the Material Responsibility of Colonizers], Новое Время [New Times], no. 9 (1969), pp. 8-10.

Translated: "Material Responsibility of the Colonial Powers", *New Times*, no. 9 (1969), pp. 8-10.

156. "Peaceful Coexistence and International Law", in G. I. Tunkin (ed.), *Contemporary International Law* (Moscow, Progress, 1969), pp. 5-35.

157. "Правовое положение Антарктики" [Legal Status of the Antarctic], in Sovetskaia antarkticheskaia ekspeditsiia, Атлас Антарктики [Atlas of the Antarctic] (Leningrad, Gidrometeorologicheskoe izd-vo, 1969), II, 97-104. Coauthor A. P. Movchan.

158. "Remarks on the Normative Function of Specialised Agencies", *Revista espanola de derecho internacional,* XXI (1969), 430-439.

1970

159. "Ленинский принцип мирного сосуществования и его практика" [Leninist Principle of Peaceful Coexistence and Practice Thereof], Правда [Pravda], 9 October 1970, pp. 3-4.

160. "Леинискиепринципыравноправияисамоопределения народов и современное международное право" [Leninist Principles of Equality and Self-Determination of Peoples in Contemporary International Law], Вестник московского государственного университета: право [Herald of Moscow State University: Law], no. 2 (1970), pp. 62-71.

161. "La coexistencia pacifica y las Naciones Unidas", *Foro Internacional,* XI (1970), 409- 420.

162. "В. И. Ленин и принципы отношений между социалистическими государствами" [V. I. Lenin and Principles

of Relations Between Socialist States] Советский ежегодник международного права 1969 [Soviet Yearbook of International Law 1969] (Moscow, izd-vo Nauka, 1970), pp. 16-29. English summary pp. 29-32.

163. "В. И. Ленин и принципы отношений между социалистическими государствами" [V. I. Lenin and Principles of Relations Between Socialist States], in Советская ассоциация международного права. XIII ежегодное собрание, посвященное 100-летию со дня рождения В. И. Ленина. 3-5 февраля 1970 г. Тезисы докладов [Soviet Association of International Law, XIII Annual Meeting Devoted to 100th Anniversary of Birthday of V. I. Lenin, 3-5 February 1970.Theses of Reports] (Moscow, 1970), pp. 3-9.

1971

164. "Два направления в мировой политике и мирное сосу- ществование" [Two Orientations in World Politics and Peaceful Coexistence], Мировая экономика и международные отношения [World Economy and International Relations], no. 2 (1971), pp. 3-13.

165. "`General Principles of Law' in International Law", in R. Marcic and others (eds.), *Internationale Festschrift für A. Verdross zum 80 Geburtstag* (Munich-Salzburg: Wilhelm Fink Verlag, 1971), pp. 525- 532.

166. "Международное право и идеологическая борьба" [International Law and Ideological Struggle], Международная жизнь [International Life], no. 10 (1971), pp. 34-43.

Translated: "International Law and Ideological Struggle", *International Affairs*, no. 11 (1971), pp. 25-31.

167. "Jus Cogens in Contemporary International Law", *University of Toledo Law Review*, nos. 1-2 (1971), pp. 107-118.

168. "Peaceful Coexistence", *Bulletin of Peace Proposals* [Oslo], no. 1 (1971), pp. 40-41.

1972

169. "Vertrag zwischen UdSSR und BRD", *Die Sowjetunion heute*, XVII, no. 8 (1972), p. 73.

170. "Мирное сосуществование и классовая борьба" [Peaceful Coexistence and Class Struggle], Вестник агенства речати "Новости" [Herald of "Novosti" Press Agency], no. 59 (1972), pp. 1-6.

171. "Задачи советской науки международного права в свете решений XXIV съезда КПСС" [Tasks of Soviet Science of International Law in Light of Decisions of XXIV Congress of CPSU], Советское государство и право [Soviet State and Law], no. 7 (1972), pp. 30-36.

172. "Zur Aufnahme der beiden deutschen Staaten in die UNO", *Vereinte Nationen*, XX (1972), 114-117.

173. "Новый тип международных отношений и международное право" [New Type of International Relations and International Law], in F. I. Kozhevnikov (co-ed.), Курс международного права [Course of International Law] (3d ed.; Moscow, izd-vo Mezhdunarodnye otnosheniia, 1972), pp. 52-65 (Chapter 4).

174. "XXIV съезд КПСС и проблемы советской науки международного права" [XXIV Congress of CPSU and Problems of Soviet Science of International Law], in Тезисы докладов XV ежегодного собрания Советской ассоциации международного права [Theses of Reports of XV Annual Meeting of Soviet Association of International Law] (Moscow, 1972), pp. 3-11.

1973

175. "Европа: исторический поворот" [Europe: Historical Turning-Point], Советская панорама [Soviet Panorama], no. 165 (1973).

176. "Принцип неприменения силы как закон международной жизни" [The Principle of Non-Use of

Force as a Law of International Life], Международная жизнь [International Life], no. 3 (1973), pp. 16-19.

Translated: "The Principle of Non-Use of Force as a Law of International Life", *International Affairs,* no. 4 (1973), pp. 13-15.

177. "Советская программа мира и некоторые проблемы международного права" [Soviet Program of Peace and Certain Problems of International Law], Советский ежегодник международного права 1971 [Soviet Yearbook of International Law 1971] (Moscow, izd-vo Nauka, 1973), pp. 13-25. English summary pp. 25-28.

178. "Vereinberkeit der Staatlichen souweranitet mit der Schaffung eines Systeme der kollektiwen Sicherheit in Europa", *Wissenschaft und Frieden* [Vienna], no. 3 (September 1973), pp. 30-39.

179. "Предисловие" [Preface], in P. Kuris, Международные право-нарушения и ответственность государств [International Law Violations and State Responsibility] (Vilnius, 1973).

1974

180. "Человек в современном мире: права и обязанности" [Man in the Contemporary World: Rights and Duties], Наука и жизнь [Science and Life], no. 1 (1974), pp. 102-106.

181. "Предисловие" [Preface], in R. L. Bobrov, Шаг, продиктованный историей (Международно- правовое признание Советского государства) [Step Dictated by History (International-Legal Recognition of the Soviet State] (Moscow, Mezhdunarodnye otnosheniia, 1974. 183 p.

182. "The Problem of Sovereignty and Organisation of European Security", *Revue belge de droit international,* X (1974), 1-10.

183 "Разрядка наприженности и международное право" [Détente and International Law], Коммунист [Communist], no. 11 (1974), pp. 107-117.

184. "Международно-правовые идеи Великой Октябрьской социалистической революции. Борьба Советского Союза и других социалистических государств за демократизацию международного права" [International Legal Ideas of Great October Socialist Revolution. Struggle of Soviet Union and Other Socialist States for Democratization of International Law], in Международное право [International Law] (1974), pp. 28-41.

185. "Сущность современного международного права" [Essence of Contemporary International Law], in Международное право [International Law] (1974), pp. 42-71 (with R.L. Bobrov and I. I. Lukashuk).

186. "Мирное сосуществование государств с различными социальным строем и международное право" [Peaceful Coexistence of States with Different Social System and International Law], in Международное право [International Law] (1974), pp. 72-85 (with R.L. Bobrov).

187. "Международное право в отношениях между социалистическими государствами" [International Law in Relations Between Socialist States], in Международное право [International Law] (1974), pp. 86-107 (with E.T. Usenko).

188. "Национально-освободительное движение и международное право" [National Liberation Movement and International Law], in Международное право [International Law] (1974), pp. 108-126 (with I. I. Lukashuk).

189. "Основные принципы международного права" [Basic Principles of International Law], in Международное право [International Law] (1974), pp.151-182 (with R.L. Bobrov).

190. "Международно-правовые вопросы гражданства" [International-Legal Questions of Citizenship], in Международное право [International Law] (1974), pp. 216-226.

191. "Защита прав человека в современном международном праве" [Defense of Human Rights in Contemporary International Law], in Международное право [International Law] (1974), pp. 232-238.

192. "Дипломатическое и консульское право" [Diplomatic and Consular Law], in Международное право [International Law] (1974), pp. 342-386.

193. "Международные конференции" [International Conferences], in Международное право [International Law] (1974), pp. 387-392.

194. "Юридическая природа современных международных огранизаций" [Legal Nature of Contemporary International Organizations], in Международное право [International Law] (1974), pp. 392-396.

195. "Ответственность в современном международном праве" [Responsibility in Contemporary International Law], in Международное право [International Law] (1974), pp. 554-573 (with D. B. Levin).

1975

196. "International Law: the Contemporary and Classic", in M. K. Nawaz (ed.), *Essays on International Law in Honour of Krishna Rao* (Faridabad, Thomson Press (India) Limited, 1975), pp. 48-57.

197. "Системный подход в науке международного права" [Systemic Approach in the Science of International Law], in Демократия и право развитого социалистического общества [Democracy and Law of Developed Socialist Society] (Moscow, 1975), pp. 482-486.

198. "Vereinbarkeit der Staatlichen Souveranität mit der Schaffung eines Systems der kollektiven Sicherheit in Europa", in *Probleme des Friedens, Der Sicherheit und der Zusammenarbeit* (Cologne, Paul Rugenstein Verlag, 1975), pp. 239-252.

1976

199. "Предисловие" [Preface], in A. I. Poltorak and L. I. Savinskii, Вооруженные конфликты и международное право: основные проблемы [Armed Conflicts and International Law: Basic Problems] (Moscow, Nauka, 1976). 416 p.

1977

200. "Первые внешнеполитические акты Советского государства и международное право" [First Foreign Policy Acts of Soviet State and International Law], Вестник Московского университета, серия 11, Право [Herald of Moscow University, series 11, Law], no. 5 (1977), pp. 50-59 (with E. A. Shibaeva and L. N. Shestakov).

201. "Вступительная статья" [Introductory Article], in Ian Brownlie, Международное право [International Law] (Moscow, izd-vo Mezhdunarodnye otnosheniia, 1977, I, pp. 5-20.

202. "Предисловие" [Preface], in Ian Brownlie, Международное право [International Law] (Moscow, izd-vo Mezhdunarodnye otnosheniia, 1977, II, pp. 5-8.

1978

203. "The Contemporary Soviet Theory of International Law", *Current Legal Problems*, XXXI (1978), 177-188.

204. "International Law and the Fight for I", *Review of Contemporary Law* (1978-79), pp. 11-28.

205. "Конституционные принципы внешней политики СССР" [Constitutional Principles of USSR Foreign Policy], Международная жизнь [International Life], no. 3 (1978), pp. 3-13.

206. "Функцирование международного права" [Functioning of International Law], in Тезисы докладов Всесоюзной конференции 3-6 октября 1978 г. [Theses of Reports of All-Union Conference of 3-6 October 1978] (Moscow, 1978).

207. "XXV съезд КПСС и основные проблемы советской науки международного права" [XXV Congress of the CPSU and Basic Problems of the Soviet Science of International Law], Советский ежегодник международного права 1976 [Soviet Yearbook of International Law 1976] (Moscow, izd-vo Nauka, 1978), pp. 11-29.

208. "International Law and the International System", *Recueil des cours*, CXLVII (1978), 1- 218.

1979

209. "Droit international et la _nte pour la paix", *Revue de Droit Contemporain*, no. 1 (1979).

210. "General Theory of Sources of International Law", *The Indian Journal of International Law*, XIX (1979), 474-482.

211. "Конституционные принципы внешней политики СССР и международное право" [Constitutional Principles of USSR Foreign Policy and International Law], in Конституция общенародного государства: вопросы теории [Constitution of All-People's State: Questions of Theory] (Moscow, 1979), pp. 318-338.

212. "The New System of International Law", in G. M. Wilner (ed.), *Jus et Societas: Essays in Tribute to Wolfgang Friedmann*. The Hague, Martinus Nijhoff, 1979, pp. 338-349.

213. "The New USSR Constitution and International Law", in *Estudios de derecho internacional. Homenaje al Professor Miaja de la Muela*. Madrid, Los Autires, 1979, I, pp. 505-517.

214. "Предисловие" [Preface], in *Derecho internacional* (Moscow, Progress Publishers, 1979).

215. "Закон о гражданстве СССР" [Law on Citizenship of the USSR], Советское государство и право [Soviet State and Law], no. 7 (1979), pp. 22- 30.

216. "Закон о международных договорах СССР" [Law on International Treaties of USSR], Советское государство и право [Soviet State and Law], no. 2 (1979), pp. 22-31 (with R. A. Müllerson).

217. Review of M. Lachs, *Space Law* (Leiden, 1977), in Советское государство и право [Soviet State and Law], no. 3 (1979), pp. 165-167 (with G. A. Osnitskaia).

218. Review of D. de Velasco, *Instituticiones de derecho internacional publico* (Madrid, 1978), in Советское государство

и право [Soviet State and Law], no. 8 (1979), pp. 153-155 (with O. L. Olteanu).

1980

219. "Soviet Theory of Sources of International Law", in *Völkerrecht und Rechtsphilosophie. Internationale Festschrift für Stephan Verosta zum 70 Geburstag*. Berlin, Duncker & Humblot, 1980, pp. 67-77.

220. "О международно-правовых принципах нового международного экономического порядка" [On the New International-Legal Principles of the New International Economic Order], Советское государство и право [Soviet State and Law], no. 9 (1980), pp. 88-96 (with V. M. Shishkin).

221. "Нюрнбергские принципы и современное международное право" [Nuremberg Principles and Contemporary International Law], Советский ежегодник международного права 1979 [Soviet Yearbook of International Law 1979] (Moscow, izd-vo Nauka, 1980), pp. 97-107.

1981

222. Review of: Nguyen Kok Din, P. Daie, and A. Pelle, *Droit international public* (Paris, 1980), in Советское государство и право [Soviet State and Law], no. 7 (1981), pp. 151-153 (with R. A. Müllerson).

223. "Основные направления науки и международного права в свете решений XXVI съезда КПСС" [Basic Orientations of Science and International Law in the Light of Decisions of the XXVI Congress of the CPSU", in Тезисы докладов Всесоюзного научно-координационного совещания [Theses of Reports of All-Union Scientific-Coordination Meeting] (Moscow, 1981).

224. "Против угрозы войны, за инициативы в пользу мира и разрядки" [Against Threats of War, for Initiatives in Favor

of Peace and I, Международные отношения [International Relations], no. 5 (1981).

1982

225. "Борьба СССР за международный правопорядок" [Struggle of USSR for International Legal Order], in XXVI съезд КПСС и развитие Советского государства и права [XXVI Congress of CPSU and Development of the Soviet State and Law] (Moscow, 1982), pp. 333-357.

226. *Contemporary International Law and New International Economic Order* (Moscow, Soviet Association of International Law, 1982).

227. "XXVI съезд КПСС и дальнейшее развитие советской науки международного права" [XXVI Congress of CPSU and Further Development of Soviet Science of International Law], in XXV ежегодное собрание Советской ассоциации международного права. Тезисы докладов [XXV Annual Meeting of Soviet Association of International Law. Theses of Reports] (Moscow, 1982).

228. "XXVI съезд КПСС и дальнейшее развитие советской науки международного права" [XXVI Congress of CPSU and Further Development of Soviet Science of International Law], Советский ежегодник международного права 1981 [Soviet Yearbook of International Law 1981] (Moscow, izd-vo Nauka, 1982), pp. 12-26.

229. "Понятие международного права" [Concept of International Law], in Международное право [International Law] (Moscow, 1982).

230. "Основные принципы международного права" [Basic Principles of International Law], in Международное право [International Law] (Moscow, 1982).

231. "Становление, сущность, источники и система современного международного права" [Development, Essence,, Sources, and System of Contemporary International Law], in Международное право [International Law] (Moscow, 1982).

232. "Международные конференции, международные организации и международное право" [International Conferences, International Organizations, and International Law], in Международное право [International Law] (Moscow, 1982).

233. "Ответственность в международном праве" [Responsibility in International Law], in Международное право [International Law] (Moscow, 1982).

234. "Дипломатическое и консульское право" [Diplomatic and Consular Law, in Международное право [International Law] (Moscow, 1982).

235. "Международное право и прогресс человечества" [International Law and the Progress of Mankind], in Международное право [International Law] (Moscow, 1982).

236. "Предисловие" [Preface], in R. L. Bobrov, Шаг, продиктованный историей (Международно-правовое признание Советского государства) [Step Dictated by History (International-Legal Recognition of the Soviet State] (Moscow, Mezhdunarodnye otnosheniia, 1982.) 174 p.

237. "Предисловие" [Preface], in D. B. Levin, Наука международного права в России в конце XIX и начале XX веков [Science of International Law in Russia at End of XIX and Beginning of XX Centuries] (Moscow, izd-vo Nauka, 1982).

238. "Modern International Law and New International Economic Order", *Report for the Conference of the International Law Association* (1982).

1983

239. "Observations des membres de la Septieme Commission sur le rapport provisoire. 4. Observations de M. Grigory Tunkin", *Annuaire de l'Institut de Droit International*, LX-1 (1983), pp. 365-366.

240. "Предисловие" [Preface], in J. de Arechaga, Современное международное право [Contemporary International Law] (Moscow, 1983).

241. "Comment" on Report of M. Virally, "The Distinction between Legal and Nonlegal International Texts", *Annuaire de l'Institut de droit international* (Paris, 1983).

1984

242. "Contemporary International Law – A New Historical Type of International Law", in J. Makarczyk (ed.), *Essays on International Law in Honour of Judge Manfred Lachs* (The Hague, Martinus Nijhoff, 1984), pp. 277-287.

243. "L'installation des missiles américains en Europe viole le droit international", in *Les consequences juridiques de l'installation eventuelle des missiles cruises en Europe* (Brussels, University of Brussels, 1984).

244. "Droit international et Modele généralement reconnu du systeme international", in *Le Droit des peuples à disposer d'eux-memes. Methodes d'analyse du droit international. Mélanges offerts a Charles Chaumont* (Paris, Editions A. Pedone, 1984), pp. 541-554.

245. *A New Dimension of International Law* (Moscow, Soviet Association of International Law, 1984). 23 p.

246. "Нормативная модель глобальной международной сис- темы" [Normative Model of Global International System], Вопросы философии [Questions of Philosophy], no. 11 (1984), pp. 91-102.

247. "Позивитизм в буржуазной науке международного права (на примере французской доктрины)" [Positivism in the Bourgeois Science of International Law (Example of French Doctrine)], Советское государство и право [Soviet State and Law], no. 2 (1984), pp. 102-110 (with R. A. Müllerson).

248. "Предисловие" [Preface], in Статус иностранцев в СССР [Status of Foreigners in the USSR] (Moscow, 1984), pp. 5-6.

Also published in the English, Arabic, Spanish, German, and French languages.

249. "Problems of Functioning of International Law as Part of International System", *The Indian Journal of International Law,* XXIV (1984), 18-24.

250. Review of Латинская Америка: Энциклопедический словарь [Latin America: Encyclopedic Dictionary] (Moscow, Sovetskaia entsiklopediia, 1979-82), in Советское государство и право [Soviet State and Law], no. 1 (1984), pp. 148-150 (with O. A. Zhidkov).

1985

251. "A New Dimension of International Law: Normative Model of Global International System", in B. Graefrath (ed.), *Probleme des Völkerrechts* (Berlin, Akademie-Verlag, 1985), pp. 267-283.

252. "Великая победа и современное международное право" [Great Victory and Contemporary International Law], Советское государство и право [Soviet State and Law], no. 5 (1985), pp. 24-32.

253. "Инструмент мира и безопасности в Европе (30-летие Вар- шавского Договора)" [Instrument of Peace and Security in Europe (30th Anniversary of Warsaw Treaty)], Вестник Московского университета: право [Herald of Moscow University: Law], no. 3 (1985).

254. "Международное право против угрозы ядерной войны" [International Law Against Threats of Nuclear War], *Panstwo I prawo,* no. 1 (1985).

255. "Победа советского народа в Великой Отечественной войне 1941-1945 годов и международное право" [Victory of Soviet People in Great Fatherland War of 1941-1945 and International Law], in XXVIII ежегодное собрание Советской ассоциации международного права. Тезисы докладов [XXVIII Annual Meeting of Soviet Association of International Law. Theses of Reports] (Moscow, 1985).

256. Review of: V. K. Sobakin, Равная безопасность: Принцип равенства и одинаковой безопасности в современных международных отношениях [Equal Security: Principle of Equality and Identical Security in Contemporary International

Relations] (Moscow, Mezhdunarodnye otnosheniia, 1984), in Советское государство и право [Soviet State and Law], no. 10 (1985), pp. 149-151 (with R. A. Müllerson).

1986

257. "Preface" in *International Law* (Moscow, Progress Publishers, 1986).

258. "Preface" in *Direito internacional* (Moscow, Progress Publishers, 1986) [Portuguese].

259. "40 лет Великой победы и международное право" [40 Years of Great Victory and International Law], Советский ежегодник международного права 1984 [Soviet Yearbook of International Law 1984] (Moscow, izd-vo Nauka, 1986), pp. 12-28.

260. "Империалистическая концептуальная модель глобальной международной системы и международное право" [Imperialist Conceptual Model of Global International System and International Law], in Методологические и теоретические проблемы юридической науки [Methodological and Theoretical Problems of Legal Science] (Moscow, 1986), pp. 172-186.

261. "Создание системы мирного сосуществования и международное право" [Creation of System of Peaceful Coexistence and International Law], Советское государство и право, no. 7 (1986), pp. 95-104.

262. "Nuclear Age and a Jurist in an Ivory Tower", in *Essays in Honor of Professor Roberto Ago* (Milano, 1987).

263. "О необходимости науки о межгосударственной системе" [On the Need for a Science on the Inter-State System], Вопросы философии [Questions of Philosophy], no. 1 (1987), pp. 85-93.

264. "Принцип неприменения силы в современную эпоху" [Principle of Non-Use of Force in Contemporary Era], Советское государство и право [Soviet State and Law], no. 9 (1987), pp. 98-106 (with R. A. Müllerson).

265. "The Role of Resolutions of International Organizations in Creating Norms of International Law", in W. E. Butler (ed.), *International Law and International System* (Dordrecht, Martinus Nijhoff Publishers, 1987), pp.5-20.

266. "Создание всеобъемлющей системы международной безопасности и международное право" [Creation of All-Embracing System of International Security and International Law], Советский ежегодник международного права 1986 [Soviet Yearbook of International Law] (Moscow, izd-vo Nauka, 1987), pp. 11-32.

267. "Предисловие" [Preface], in Всеобъемлющая система международной безопасности и международное право [All-Embracing System of International Security and International Law] (Moscow, IGPAN, 1987), pp. 3-4.

268. "The Role of Resolutions of International Organizations in Creating Norms of International Law", in W. E. Butler (ed.), International Law and International System (Dordrecht, 1987), pp. –.

269. "Создание всеобъемлющей системы международной безопасности и международное право", Советский ежегодник международного права 1986 (Moscow, izd-vo Nauka, 1987), pp. 11-32.

270. "Предисловие", in Всеобъемлющая система международной безопасности и международное право (Moscow, IGPAN, 1987), pp. 3-4.

1987

271. (ed.), L. V. Korbut and Iu. Ia. Baskin, Международно-правовой режим рек, история и современность [International-Legal Regime of Rivers, History and Modern Day] (Moscow, 1987).

272. (ed.), *International Law and Municipal Law. Proceedings of the German-Soviet Colloquium on International Law at the Institut für Internationales Recht an der Universitat Kiel*. 4-8 May 1987 (with R. Wolfrum).

1988

273. "International Law and Other Social Norms Functioning Within the International System", in B. Cheng and E. D. Brown (eds.), *Contemporary Problems of International Law: Essays in Honour of Georg Schwarzenberger on his Eightieth Birthday* (London, Stevens & Son Ltd., 1988), pp. 282-300.

274. "The Legal Bases of International Organization Action", in R.- J. Dupuy (ed.), *Manuel sur les organisations _nternationals* (Dordrecht, Martinus Nijhoff Publishers), 1988), pp. 261-276.

1989

275. "Понятие международного права" [Concept of International Law], Курс международного права [Course of International Law] (Moscow, 1989), I, pp. 9-29 (Chapter 1).

276. "Характер, сущность и функцинирование международного права" [Character, Essence, and Functioning of International Law], Курс международного права [Course of International Law] (Moscow, 1989), I, pp. 124- 158 (Chapter 4).

277. "Процесс создания норм и источники международного права" [Process of Creation of Norms and Sources of International Law], Курс международного права [Course of International Law] (Moscow, 1989), I, pp. 182- 219 (Chapter 6).

1990

278. "On the Primacy of International Law in Politics", in W. E. Butler (ed.), *Perestroika and International Law* (Dordrecht, Martinus Nihoff Publishers, 1990), pp. 5-12.

279. "International Politics and International Law in the Nuclear Age", in E. McWhinney, D. Ross, G. I. Tunkin, and V. Vereshchetin, eds., *From Coexistence to Cooperation: International Law and Organization in the Post-Cold War Era* (Dordrecht/Boston/London, Marinus Nijhoff, 1992), pp. 9-17.

280. "Remarks on the Primacy of International Law in Politics", in *Le Droit international au service de la paix, de la justice et du développement. Mélanges Michel Virally* (Paris, Editions A. Pedone, 1991), pp. 455-463.

1992

281. "Politics, Law and Force in the Interstate System", *Recueil des cours*, CCXIX (1992), 231-395.

282. "Речь Г. И. Тункина при вручении ему премии «Эн- циклопедия Британника» [Address of G. I. Tunkin at Awarding ot "Encyclopedia Britannica" Prize to Him], Советский ежегодник международного права 1989-90-91 [Soviet Yearbook of International Law 1989-90-91] (St. Petersburg, Sotsial'no-kommercheskaia firma "Rossiia-Neva", 1992), pp. 255-256.

1993

283. "Is General International Law Customary Law Only?", *European Journal of International Law*, IV (1993), 534-541.

1994

284. "Международное право: наследство XX века" [International Law: Legacy of the XX Century], Российский ежегодник международного права 1992 [Russian Yearbook of International Law 1992] (St. Petersburg, Sotsial'no-kommercheskaia firma "Rossiia-Neva", 1992), pp. 7-20. English summary, pp. 21-23.

285. "Несколько соображений в связи с проектом 'Устава между- народного трибунала для рассмотрения дел о преступлениях, совершенных на территории бывшей Югославии'," [Several Reflections in Connection with the Draft 'Charter of the International Tribunal for the Consideration of Cases Concerning Crimes Committed on the Territory of Former Yugoslavia'"], in *Теория международного права*, ed. L. N. Shestakov (Moscow, Izdatel'stvo "Zertsalo", 2000), pp. 383-384.

286. "Several Reflections in Connection with the Draft 'Charter of the International Tribunal for the Consideration of Cases

Concerning Crimes Committed on the Territory of Former Yugoslavia'", *Sudebnik,* V (2000), 629-630.

2003

287. "Several Reflections in Connection with the Draft "Charter of the International Tribunal for the Consideration of Cases Concerning Crimes Committed on the Territory of Former Yugoslavia", in G. I. Tunkin, *Theory of International Law,* ed. L. N. Shestakov; transl. W. E. Butler (London, Wildy, Simmonds & Hill, 2003), pp. 473-475.

2006

288. "Fundamental Principles of Contemporary International Law", *Sudebnik,* XI (2006), pp. 793-841 (W. E. Butler).

289. "The Korean Question After the Second World War in the Light of International Law", *Sudebnik,* XI (2006), pp. 391-429 (W. E. Butler).

2025

290. "The Korean Question After the Second World War in the Light of International Law", in W. E. Butler (transl. & ed.), *G. I. Tunkin: Selected Works*. Clark, New Jersey, Talbot Publishing, 2025, pp. 3-55.

291. "Fundamental Principles of Contemporary International Law", in W. E. Butler (transl. & ed., *G. I. Tunkin: Selected Works*. Clark, New Jersey, Talbot Publishing, 2025, pp. 56-117.

292. "Several Reflections in Connection with the Draft "Charter of the International Tribunal for the Consideration of Cases Concerning Crimes Committed on the Territory of Former Yugoslavia", in W. E. Butler (transl. & ed., *G. I. Tunkin: Selected Works*. Clark, New Jersey, Talbot Publishing, 2025, pp. 651-652.

INDEX OF NAMES

Abi-Saab, G. M., 162, 163, 278, 364, 365
Adenauer, Konrad, 172
Ago, R., 296, 298, 351, 365, 394, 566, 621, 648
Aguilar Navarro, M., 656
Aleksandrov, N. G., 410
Alekseev, N. S., 621
Aleksidze, L. A., 313, 316, 428, 657
Alvarez, A., 438, 439
Amador,, G., 618
Anand, R. P., 162, 163, 278, 548, 550
Anderson, S. V., 489
Antonowicz, L., 195, 511
Anzilotti, D., 79, 290, 355, 376, 378, 389, 390, 414, 417, 594, 596-598, 615, 636
Aquinas, Thomas, 398
Arechaga, E. Jimenez de, 234, 244, 267, 283, 308, 517, 519, 529, 690
Aristotle, 398
Aron, R., 442
Asbeck, F. M., 151, 156
Arzinger, D., 134, 195, 511, 668, 679
Avramov, S., 267

Baginian, K. A., 88, 91, 180
Baratashvili, D. I., 195, 397, 511, 644
Bartos, M., 173, 174, 209, 330, 363
Basak, A., 331
Basdevant, J., 261, 263, 275, 282, 283, 354, 615, 616
Baskin, Iu. Ia., 694
Bastid, S., 209, 326, 327, 386
Baxter, R. R., 262
Bela, P., 655
Beliakov, A. S. 495
Berber, F., 267, 446, 447
Berezowski, Cz., 108, 565
Bergbohm, C., 231, 232
Berger, D., 656
Bierzanek, R., 179
Bindschelder, R. L., 400
Bishota, M., 312
Bissonnete, P. A., 601
Blatova, N. T., 288, 346
Blix, Hans, 250, 541
Bloch, J., 407
Bluntschli, J. C., 302, 350, 602, 603, 605, 648
Bobrov, R. L., xix, 169, 170, 208-210, 313, 426, 430, 500, 501, 565, 656, 683, 684, 689
Bogdanov, O. V., 212, 216, 336, 676
Boiarshinov, V. G., 137
Bokor-Szego, H., 162, 163, 195, 203, 278, 330, 331
Borchard, E. M., 599
Borisov, S., 241
Bosc, R., 477
Bourquin, M., 418, 580, 617, 618
Bowett, D. W., 497, 529, 530, 567
Bratus, S. N., 430

Brierly, J, 255, 256, 259
Brownlie, Ian, 267, 280, 326, 345, 685
Buergenthal, T., 248
Bulganin, N. A., 80, 88
Bustamante y Sirven, A. S., 79, 610
Butler, W. E., xvii-xxix, 653-697
Bymkov, D. V., 670

Cahier, P., 300
Calvo, C., 458
Casanovas la Rosa, Oriol, 300
Castaneda, G., 326, 540
Cavaglieri, A., 262
Cavaré, L., 78
Čepelka, C., 643, 645
Chaumont, C., 209, 285, 386, 524, 525, 532, 569
Cheng, Bin, 261, 357, 358
Chernogolovkin, N. V., 195, 511
Chicherin, G. V., 134
Chistiakov, O. I., 130
Chiu, H., 252, 259, 563
Chizov, K. Ia., 507, 546
Chkhikvadze, V. M., 170, 171, 179, 180, 195, 220, 226, 256, 267, 288, 313, 330, 346, 353, 361, 410, 427, 565, 677
Clark, G., 549, 574-577, 579
Cobban, A., 200
Colliard, C. A., 545
Corbett, P., 482

Dahm, G., 234, 291, 307, 392, 393, 401
Daie, P., 688
Danevskii, V. P., 195
Darwin, H., 310, 311
Dehousse, F., 550
D'Estefano, M. A., 163, 267
Demisov, V., 112
Denisov, A. I., 410, 585, 592
Detter, Ingrid, 249, 250, 497, 541
Diez de Velasco, M., 369
Din, Nguyen Kok, 688
Dominguez-Campora, M., 142
Donnedieu de Vabres, H., 610, 614
Dranov, B. A., 624
Drost, H., 417
Drost, P. N., 616, 617
Duguit, Leon, 402, 403
Dulles, John Foster, 157, 453
Dumas, J., 615, 616
Dumitrescu, G., 195
Dupuy, R.-J., 461, 589, 658, 678, 694
Durante, F., 330
Durdenevskii, V. N., xviii, 67, 78, 181, 204, 236, 237, 241, 265, 266, 288, 290, 321, 361, 375, 379, 556, 604, 632
Dutoit, B., 407

Eagleton, C., 8, 200, 424, 598
Eden, Anthony, 510
Efimov, G. K., 330
Egor'ev, V. V., 212
Eichelberger, C. M., 324, 325
El-Erian, A., 566
Elias, T. E. O., 328, 329

Engels, F., xxxii, 406-408, 499, 500
Eremeev, M., 660, 661
Evgen'ev, V. V., 630

Fabrikova, E. M., 290
Falk, Richard, 325, 326, 490
Farbman, M., 143
Fauchille, F., 594, 598, 623, 627, 628
Fedorov, V. N., 556, 658
Fedoseev, P. N., 148
Feinberg, N., 550
Fel'dman, D. I., 226, 330, 336, 659
Feliciano, F., 486, 487
Fenwick, C., 78
Ferenc, M., 655
Filippov, S. V., 241
Fisher, R., 488
Fitzmaurice, G., 239, 240, 296, 342, 412, 618
Foda, E., 656
Francois, J. P. A., 618
Freeman, A. V., 154
Fremzke, D., 658
Friedmann, W., 249, 267, 289, 312, 329, 407, 439, 440, 490, 516, 517, 579, 580

Ganiushkin, B. V., 422
Garden, W., 458
Geamanu, G., 179, 307
Geffcken, F. H., 595
Gelberg, L., 267
Genovski, M., 267, 368, 565
Gianni, G., 264
Giraud, E., 249, 292, 441, 586
Giuliani, M., 379
Goodrich, L., 299, 519, 529, 537, 550, 555, 558
Golunskii, S. A., 622
Gorshenin, K. P., 222
Gotz, B., 657
Gouet, Y., 265
Gould, W. L., 165
Grabar, V. E., 622
Graefrath, B., 179, 691
Gromyko, A. A., 639, 669, 671
Gros, A., 566
Grotius, Hugo, 302, 375, 377, 424, 626, 627
Gubin, V. F., 241
Guggenheim, P., 12, 89, 188, 235, 236, 249, 265, 268-270, 277, 295, 302, 356, 357, 368, 392, 594, 600, 606

Hackworth, Green, 531, 532
Hajdu, G., 216
Hambro, E., 550
Haraszti, G., 289
Hazard, John N., 172, 173, 656-658
Heffter, A. W., 377, 595, 596, 637, 6t38
Heller, H., 377
Henkin, Louis, 312, 329, 441
Herter, Christian, 639
Heydte, F. A. Frhr. v. d., 392, 400, 401, 669
Higgins, Rosalyn, 334
Hildebrand, J. L., 704
Hotchkiss, H. G., 70
Huber, M., 623
Hull, Cordell, 509, 510

Hutchins, R., 572
Hyde, C. C., 13, 379, 624

Ianovskii, M. V., 330, 336
Iashchenko, A., 403
Ignatenko, G. V., 195
Iuranov, M., 348
Iushchenko, V. L., 658
Ivanov, S. A., 423
Iwafuchi, Setsuo, 657

Jackson, Robert, 617
Jenks, C. W., 343, 367, 439
Jessup, P., 156, 416, 447, 448, 472, 573, 585
Johnson, D. H. N., 327

Kalinkin, G. F., 237
Kaliuzhnaia, G. P., 346, 679
Kamenov, E. G., 658
Kaplan, M. A., 486
Kapustin, M. N., 426
Kamarovskii, L. A., 638
Kasme, B., 259
Katzenbach, N. B. de, 486
Kaufmann, E., 400
Kelsen, Hans, 8, 12, 42, 72, 79, 89, 165, 182, 187, 188, 235, 268, 276, 289, 290, 302, 319, 345, 356, 391, 392, 397, 401, 407, 414, 415, 417, 473, 547, 551, 567, 568, 573, 605, 606, 623
Kennan, George, 142, 471, 472, 476, 485
Kerimov, D. A., 410
Khaitsman, V. M., 212
Khanov, A. A., 655
Khrushchev, N. S., xviii, xx, xxi, 61, 93
Khvostov, V. M., 465
Kiss, Ch., 656
Klafkowski, A., 261, 267
Knowland, William, 172
Kon, V. L., 670
Kopelmanas, L., 283
Korbut, L. V., 694
Kordt, E., 150
Koretskii, V. M., 360, 361, 364, 525, 526, 673
Korkunov, N. M., 232, 237, 604-606
Korovin, E. A., xix, 4, 12, 65, 67, 71, 75, 78, 165, 204, 212, 226, 237, 265, 267, 288, 312, 321, 346, 361, 483
Kozhevnikov, F. I., xix, 12, 17, 67, 75, 218, 226, 236, 241, 254, 267, 288, 312, 321, 322, 330, 346, 361, 647, 661, 675, 676, 682
Krasil'shchikova, S., 511
Krasnokutskii, V., 403
Krylov, S. B., xix, 12, 17, 56, 67, 75, 78, 101, 197, 198, 204, 226, 236, 265, 266, 273, 288, 302, 320, 321, 348, 361, 364, 416, 510, 511, 550, 556, 618, 668, 669
Kublitskii, F. A., 154, 182, 234, 320, 351, 359, 394, 398, 594, 637, 668
Kulski, W., 165
Kunz, J., 151, 156, 261, 262, 283, 284, 290, 415, 472, 473
Kuris, P., 683

Kuznetsov, V., 541

La Pradelle, -, 358
Labeiri-Menachem, -, 117
Lachs, Manfred, 108, 184, 210, 236, 237, 244, 330, 451, 557, 655, 687
Lapenna, Ivo, 407, 656
Laun, R., 399, 442
Lauterpacht, H., 8, 78, 79, 101, 235, 256, 257, 259, 306, 328, 342, 344, 345, 348, 351, 354, 415, 416, 607, 608
Lazarev, M. I., 353
Le Fur, L., 360, 399
Leibholz, G., 60, 151
Leist, O. E., 592
Lenin, V. I., xxxii, 43, 92, 131, 134, 140-145, 148, 158, 385, 405, 499, 506, 507, 582-584, 680
Levin, D. B., xix, 187, 195, 267, 285, 290, 330, 346, 361, 362, 386, 395, 397, 402, 457, 460, 472, 483, 585, 610, 643, 644. 656, 659, 690
Likhachev, V. N., 659
Lippman, Walter, 624, 625
Lisovskii, V. I., 67, 266, 288
Lissitsyn, O. J., 270, 312, 329, 486
Liszt, F. von, 600, 601, 622
Livy, 626
Lukashuk, I. I., xix, xxviii, 255, 260, 267, 286, 288, 313, 330, 332, 346, 565, 653, 657, 677, 683, 684
Lukin, P. I., 313, 330, 362
Lunts, L. A., 56

McDougal M. S., xxiii, 270, 451, 452, 485-491
McNair, A., 307, 316, 533
McWhinney, E., 165, 176, 407, 656, 659, 695
Maiga, M., 311
Magarasevic, A., 267
Marcic, R., 680
Marek, K., 307
Makarczyk, J., 690
Malinin, S. A., 216, 324, 328, 330, 565
Malintoppi, A., 326
Martens, F. F., xx, 232, 233, 302, 315, 375, 376, 426, 595, 596, 604. 622
Marx, Karl, xxxii, 167, 405, 406, 408, 499, 500
Mazur, Iu. N., 662
Mebel', M., 622
Meissner, Boris, 142
Mendlovitz, Saul H., 572
Menzel, E., 655, 657
Mikoyan, A. I., 96
Minasian, N. M., xix, 267, 288, 312, 322, 361
Mints, I. I., 131
Mironov, N. V., 217, 349
Modzhorian, L. A., 78, 181, 190, 204, 226. 254, 288, 346, 421, 511, 604, 632
Molotov, V. M., 105
Monaco, R., 188, 305, 444
Moore, John Norton, 489, 490
Morawiecki, W., 655

Morelli, G., 262, 267, 283, 285, 305, 355, 391
Moreno Quintana, L. M., 189, 379, 445, 450
Morgenthau, Hans, 441, 442, 467, 469, 470, 476, 485
Morozov, G. I., 216, 224, 323, 495, 507, 511, 565
Mosler, H., 567, 569
Mouskhely, M., 667
Movchan, A. P., 160, 217, 218, 667, 680
Müller, H., 657
Müllerson, Rein, 687, 691-693

Nahlik, S., 267, 288, 289, 331, 368
Naryshkina, R. L., 154, 182, 234, 320, 351, 359, 394, 398, 594, 637, 668
Nawaz, M. K., 685
Nechaev, B. N., 673-676
Nehru, J., 452
Nicholson, H., 458, 459
Nisot, J., 304, 305
Novgorodtsev, P., 403

O'Connell, D. P., 267, 290, 326, 343
Oppenheim, L., 78, 79, 101, 235, 267, 291, 345, 351, 354, 415, 416, 608, 614, 622, 624
Oliver, Covey T., 472
Osakwe, C., 658
O'Shea, J. S. de Erice y, 400
Osnitskaia, G. A., 687
Ostrovskii, Ia. A., 217, 218
Outrata, V., 179, 288

Pal, R., 161
Pashukanis, E. B., xix, 165, 236, 423, 484
Paul, V., 661
Pavithran, A. K., 267
Pearson, L. B., 471
Pěchota, V., 288, 330
Pella, V. V., 610-614
Pelle, A., 688
Perassi, T., 295, 376, 378, 390, 391
Pereterskii, I. S., 56, 299, 668
Perkins, D., 467
Perrin, G., 403
Pescatore, P., 567
Plimpton, F., 172, 431
Phillimore, R. J., 358, 375, 616
Piontkovskii, A. A., 429, 430
Polianskii, N. N., 107
Poltorak, A. I., 183, 621, 644, 685
Pon, Han Dik, 662
Pope John XXIII, 578
Potter, Pitman, 42, 472

Quadri, R., 188, 270, 277-279, 284, 308, 386, 444
Quai, Lino di, 326
Quigley, John B. Jr., 407

Radoikovich, M., 174
Radoinov, P., 330
Raginskii, M. Iu., 621
Ramundo, B., 407
Rathfelder, V., 657
Redslob, R., 399

Reuter, P., 259, 267, 298, 308, 325, 444, 532, 561, 567
Rhee, Syngman, 33-35, 50
Rida, Ahmed, 656
Rolin, H., 640
Romano, S., 305
Romanov, V., 180, 667, 668
Romashkin, P. S., 4, 43, 183, 225, 410, 621, 644
Roosevelt, Franklin D., 555
Rosenne, S., 239, 343, 518, 519, 521
Ross, D., 659, 695
Rousseau, Ch., 78, 234, 235, 261, 267, 295, 307, 326, 354, 356, 358, 359, 368, 379, 624, 636, 637, 656
Router-Hamaray, B., 530
Rozenblit, S. Ia., 621
Rudenko, R. A., 222

Saba, H., 250, 340
Sahovic, M., 184, 278
Sakketti, A., 290, 302, 375, 626
Santalov, A. A., 622
Sauer, E., 399
Savinskii, L. I., 685
Scelle, G., xxii, 265, 283, 284, 403, 404, 417, 545, 573
Schätzel, W., 634
Scheuner, U., 307
Schirmer, G., 293, 386, 546
Schulz, J., 216
Schuman, F. M., 476
Schweisfurth, T., 657
Schwarzenberger, Georg, 267, 304, 326, 345, 401, 442, 448-450, 552, 569, 573, 574, 637, 656
Schwelb, E., 325
Seara Vasquez, M., 543
Séféraides, S., 377
Seidel, F., 658
Senin, M. V., 500
Sereni, A., 236, 262, 267, 277, 283, 305, 326, 444, 530, 531, 552, 564, 565, 570
Seyersted, F., 522, 523, 563, 570
Sharmazanashvili, G., 180, 184
Shebanov, A. F., 410
Shestakov, L. N., xviii, xxiii, xxiv, xxxi, 120-124, 660, 685, 696
Shibaeva, E. A., 251, 255, 550, 561, 565, 685
Shiganskii, V. I., 622
Shihata, I., 236
Shishkin, A. F., 127, 317, 687
Shokhor, I. S., 379
Shurshalov, V. M., 236, 288, 313, 315
Shvartsman, K. A., 127, 317
Sibert, M., 8, 42, 78, 200, 235, 400
Sierra, M. J., 379
Singh, N., 155, 550, 551
Skubiszewski, K., 249
Sloan, F. B., 327
Smith, H, A., 151, 417
Smyrmiadis, G., 399
Sobakin, V. K., 181, 190, 421, 604, 632, 692
Sohn, L., 549, 574-577

Sørenson, Max, 265, 267, 326, 570, 571
Sovetov, A., 468
Speranskaia, L. V., 195, 511
Sperduti, G., 417
Srnská, M., 657, 658
Standtke, Herbert, 655
Starke, J. G., 267
Starushenko, G. B., 194, 195, 511
Steiniger, P. A., 179, 565
Stoessinger, J. G., 558. 559, 588, 589
Stoianov, A. N., 302
Stone, J., 394, 488
Stoyanovitch, K., 656
Strupp, K., 42, 264, 280, 281, 349, 376, 379
Stuchka, P. I., xviii
Suat Bilge, A., 601
Suy, E., 301, 309
Syatauw, J. J. G., 154
Symonides, J., 658
Syromiatnikov, B., 403
Szabo, Imre, 218
Szaszy, I., 423

Tabata, K. S., 577
Tabio, Alvares, 312
Tai, Kim Din, 31
Talalaev, A. N., 137, 240, 255, 288, 313, 330, 565, 656
Tammes, A. J. P., 326
Tavrov, G., xvii, 661-664
Tiunov, O. I., 659
Tolchenov, M. P. 112
Toman, J., 657
Trainin, A. N., 183, 224, 618-620, 644, 647
Travers, -, 13
Triepel, 231, 233, 376-378, 596
Tucker, R. W., 182, 235, 356, 415
Tunkin, G. I., xvii-xxix, xxxi-xxxiv
Tunkin, V. G., xxxiv
Tuzmukhamedov, R. A., 195, 511

Ul'ianova, N., 353
Ulloa, A., 233, 265, 297, 379, 445, 446, 548, 550, 594
Underwood, J. L., 489
Usenko, E. T., 498, 500, 657, 679, 684
Ushakov, N. A., 204, 226, 556
Ustor, E., 309

Valki, L., 556, 565
Vallat, Sir Francis, 172, 311, 312, 327, 431
Vattel, Emer de, 290, 302, 375
Vecchio, G. del, 400
Velasco, D. de, 687
Vellas, P., 249, 340, 341
Verdross, A., 12, 78, 79, 134, 154, 155, 182, 233, 234, 235, 262, 266-268, 278, 283, 285, 291, 296, 306, 307, 320, 326, 327, 332, 345, 351, 359, 360, 386, 394, 398, 400, 401, 417, 443, 448, 566, 581, 594, 637, 668
Vereshchetin, V., 659, 695
Verosta, S., 134

Virally, M., 208, 267, 283, 316, 326, 340, 463, 550, 589, 655, 690
Visscher, C. de, 78, 153, 154, 189, 199, 235, 267, 283, 289, 312, 394, 401, 442, 443, 582, 598, 599
Vried, H. PM. De, 298
Vygodskii, S. Iu., 134
Vyshinskii, A. Ia., xix, 17, 21

Waldock, H., 250, 257, 267, 281, 296, 298, 308, 345, 351, 367, 444, 445
Wehberg, H., 599, 626, 633, 634
Wilner, G. M., 687
Wilson, Woodrow, 133
Wolf, Klaus, 655
Wolfke, K., 334
Wolfrum, R., 694
Wright, Quincy, 142, 440, 441, 580

Yasseen, M., 316, 566
Yemin, E., 536

Zacklin, R., 536, 542, 543
Zadorozhnyi, G. P., 323, 324, 676
Zakharova, N. V., 135
Zannas, P. A., 601
Zemanek, K., 134, 259, 260
Žhourek, J., 618
Zhukov, G. P., 398, 422
Ziccardi, P., 386, 656
Zlatopol'skii, D. L., 130
Zorin, V. A., 131, 134, 216

www.ingramcontent.com/pod-product-compliance
Lightning Source LLC
LaVergne TN
LVHW091521200926
848483LV00002B/267
* 9 7 8 1 6 1 6 1 9 6 9 5 0 *